D1584716

Time Out

Naples

timeout.com/naples

Time Out Guides Ltd
Universal House
251 Tottenham Court Road
London W1T 7AB
United Kingdom
Tel: +44 (0)20 7813 3000
Fax: +44 (0)20 7813 6001
Email: guides@timeout.com
www.timeout.com

Published by Time Out Guides Ltd, a wholly owned subsidiary of Time Out Group Ltd.
Time Out and the Time Out logo are trademarks of Time Out Group Ltd.

© **Time Out Group Ltd 2009**
Previous editions 2000, 2002, 2005, 2007.

10 9 8 7 6 5 4 3 2 1

This edition first published in Great Britain in 2009 by Ebury Publishing.
A Random House Group Company
20 Vauxhall Bridge Road, London SW1V 2SA

Random House Australia Pty Ltd 20 Alfred Street, Milsons Point, Sydney, New South Wales 2061, Australia

Random House New Zealand Ltd 18 Poland Road, Glenfield, Auckland 10, New Zealand

Random House South Africa (Pty) Ltd Isle of Houghton, Corner Boundary Road & Carse O'Gowrie, Houghton 2198,
South Africa

Random House UK Limited Reg. No. 954009

For further distribution details, see www.timeout.com.

ISBN: 978-1-84670-102-3

A CIP catalogue record for this book is available from the British Library.

Printed and bound by Firmengruppe APPL, aprinta druck, Wemding, Germany.

The Random House Group Limited supports The Forest Stewardship Council (FSC), the leading international forest
certification organisation. All our titles that are printed on Greenpeace approved FSC certified paper
carry the FSC logo. Our paper procurement policy can be found at http://www.rbooks.co.uk/environment.

Time Out carbon-offsets its flights with Trees for Cities (www.treesforcities.org).

Contents

In Context	15
History	16
Naples Today	30
Painting in Naples	36
Architecture	41

Sights	47
Royal Naples & Monte Echia	48
Centro Storico	54
The Port & University	64
Via Toledo & La Sanità	68
Capodimonte	76
Vomero	79
Chiaia to Posillipo	83
Campi Flegrei	88
Suburbs & Elsewhere	94

Consume	97
Hotels	98
Restaurants	111
Cafés, Bars & Gelaterie	131
Shops & Services	140

Arts & Entertainment	153
Calendar	154
Children	157
Film	160
Galleries	163

Gay & Lesbian	168
Music & Nightlife	170
Performing Arts	179
Sport & Fitness	185

Around Naples	191
Map & Introduction	192
Capri	196
Ischia	215
Procida	229
Pompeii & Vesuvius	233
Sorrento & Around	249
The Amalfi Coast	264
Further Afield	292

Directory	303
Getting Around	304
Resources A-Z	307
Further Reference	313
Vocabulary	314
Glossary	315
Index	316
Advertisers' Index	322

Maps	323
Naples by Area	324
Street Maps	325
Street Index	333
Naples Metro	336

Introduction

Stressful and chaotic it may be, but Naples remains a fascinating, compelling city. This three-millennia-old metropolis is eternally scrambling to keep its priceless patrimony from crumbling, while at the same time trying to play catch-up with modernity. Grand prix-style traffic, raucous squabbles, urchins' impromptu football games in dusty, litter-strewn *piazze*: the sheer, frenetic energy here is astonishing.

There's no denying that Naples can be unnerving. As Neapolitan wags are prone to tell new arrivals, welcome to the jungle. But they always say it with a broad smile, evoking a sense of what matters most in Neapolitan life: friends, family, good food and an inexhaustible sense of fun. Look beneath the city's entropic, squalid surface and you'll discover a dazzlingly rich cultural heritage, with a wealth of galleries and museums alongside architectural and archaeological treasures.

So raggle-taggle and helter-skelter is Naples that any guide to the area inevitably focuses as much, or more, on what lies outside the city. Certainly, as you venture further from the urban stew, the contrast couldn't be starker. While Naples languishes in the shadow of its reputation, celebrated destinations such as the Amalfi Coast and Capri exert a powerful allure and exude a consummate sense of serenity, drawing multimillionaires and lovers of beauty from around the world. The islands of Ischia and its tiny neighbour Procida are earthier yet equally charming havens, with a tranquility all of their own.

Then, of course, there are the outlying archaeological sites, at least a dozen of world-class stature. Take your pick, depending on your time constraints: Pompeii, Herculaneum, the Campi Flegrei or Paestum, to head the list. With extra time, you might try the little-visited enclaves to the north of Naples, such as Benevento, whose flawlessly beautiful ancient Roman arch is the most perfectly preserved of them all.

Whether you're taking an inaugural trip or visiting for the tenth time, staying in the city or exploring the region, there's plenty here to hold your attention. And don't be surprised if you fall under the spell of gritty, nefarious, magnetic Naples, as so many of even her most unforgiving detractors ultimately do. *Jeffrey Kennedy & Janice Fuscoe, Editors*

Naples in Brief

IN CONTEXT

A more dramatic history than that of Naples is hard to imagine, from the epicentre of classical culture to the terrors of Vesuvius and the brutality of today's Camorra. The city has been the pleasure-dome of emperors, the jewel in regal crowns and a political football of the unscrupulous, as well as Europe's most taboo backwater. The centuries have left their mark on Naples' architecture and art; although much has been lost, untold riches remain. *For more, see pp15-46.*

SIGHTS

World-class attractions include the unparalleled magnificence of Naples' setting (what other city can boast its very own volcano?) and the treasures on display in its stunning museums. Splendid churches and dignified palazzo vie for tourists' attention; below ground lie ancient, darkly atmospheric catacombs and burial grounds, and the remains of Greco-Roman Neapolis. *For more, see pp47-96.*

CONSUME

One taste of genuine Neapolitan pizza and you will know that, until now, you've been a pizza virgin. *La cucina napoletana* is justly celebrated, as are its caffè and gelato – to say nothing of such delicacies as *babà* and limoncello. Shopping mavens, meanwhile, will appreciate the city's unique artisanal goods and street markets. This section also details accommodation options to suit all pockets, from princely palazzi to budget B&Bs. *For more, see pp97-152.*

ARTS & ENTERTAINMENT

Most exciting of all, perhaps, is the city's dynamic contemporary art scene, with a wealth of private galleries and two ambitious public museums. Naples' rich opera, Baroque music and theatre traditions stretch back for centuries, although the language barrier can be tricky to negotiate. Nightlife of all kinds is mostly ad lib, and for most recreational activities – aside from a run in the park – you have to get out of town. *For more, see pp153-190.*

AROUND NAPLES

The second half of our guide covers the islands and resorts around the Bay of Naples and Campania. Indeed, many visitors bypass Naples altogether in favour of more scenic locales, such as the Sorrentine peninsula or Amalfi Coast; not necessarily a bad decision, especially if time is limited. In Around Naples, we highlight some of the most seductive – and blissful – spots this sunny corner of the world has to offer. *For more, see pp191-302.*

Naples in Profile

ROYAL NAPLES & MONTE ECHIA
This breezy coastal area shows off the grand public face of the city: a huge palace, two castles, a world-renowned opera house, smart cafés and even some greenery. Here, too, is the main port, with ferries to the islands. Like every district in Naples, it has a funky side – in this case the rather down-at-heel neighbourhood of **Monte Echia**. *For more, see pp48-53.*

CENTRO STORICO
Welcome to the nucleus of ancient Neapolis, founded by the Greeks and carried forward by the Romans. The streets seem run-down and dilapidated – but give the **Centro Storico** a chance, and you'll fall under its spell. The colourful merchandise, buzzing pizzerie and the sense of electrifying ferment make for a wonderful slice of Neopolitan vitality. *For more, see pp54-63.*

THE PORT & UNIVERSITY
The presence of the **University** has given rise to some of the city's most *simpatico* nightspots, and lively bars and clubs are one of the area's main attractions. Grand schemes are afoot here, too – namely an ambitious plan to refurbish the **port**, installing pedestrian-only zones and eliminating the shoreline highway. The area has seen attempts at urban renewal before – notably on **Corso Umberto**, filled with traffic and still awaiting the completion of the new metro line. *For more, see pp64-67.*

VIA TOLEDO & LA SANITÀ
This rambling swathe of cityscape is nothing if not varied, encompassing two notoriously grotty (albeit fascinating) enclaves of the Camorra, the **Quartieri Spagnoli** and **La Sanità**, the world's premier archaeological museum, and one of Europe's first and finest botanical gardens, rounded out by a seemingly endless shopping street. *For more, see pp68-75.*

CAPODIMONTE
The city's biggest park and a palace with one of the world's most superb art collections are perched atop a hill in a lavish display of wealth and power. The Bourbon king who commissioned the palace had planned a modest hunting lodge, but soon the project's scope – and costs – soared. *For more, see pp76-78.*

VOMERO
Ride one of the fêted funiculars up to this leafy residential district, topped off by a star-shaped fortress. The Parco della Floridiana provides more greenery and a villa, now home to a ceramics museum; and the Certosa di San Martino is a palace turned art museum. It's from this coveted eyrie and its terraced gardens that you can take in the most famous view of the bay, the city below, and Vesuvius beyond. *For more, see pp79-82.*

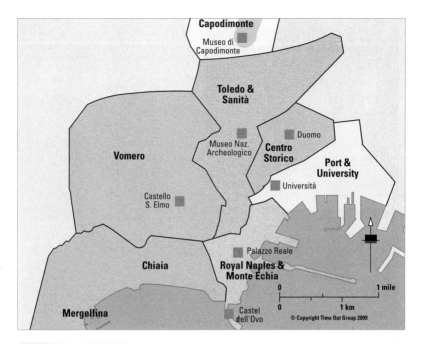

CHIAIA TO POSILLIPO

Stretched out along the shoreline, against a backdrop of pastel palazzi ascending the hills, this is Naples' most upmarket locale. It's the place where wealthy Romans and grand tourists chose to enjoy their sojourns; today, it's home to smart shops, galleries, beautiful parks and mansions. In the evening, the fashionable set flocks to its restaurants and bars. *For more, see pp83-87.*

CAMPI FLEGREI

This peninsula to the west of the city has some of the area's most significant archaeological remains and geothermal sights. In addition to its well-preserved Roman amphitheatre and ancient market, the port town of **Pozzuoli** boasts a fuming dormant volcano. The ruins of ancient **Cuma** and the grotto of Sibyl are essential sights; meanwhile, the areas around **Baia** and **Bacoli** are strewn with ancient palaces and temples. Near **Capo Miseno** you'll find the best beaches in the area, without having to head out to the islands. *For more, see pp88-93.*

THE ART CARD

Keen sightseers should consider investing in a **Campania Artecard**. Holders are entitled to free or reduced price entry to various major sights, including the Museo Archeologico Nazionale, the Città della Scienza and the Museo di Capodimonte; city transport to certain sites is also free. The card is widely available; if you buy it at the airport, you can use it to get the Alibus airport bus (*see p304*) into town. For more on the Artecard, *see p194.*

Regional Highlights

TAKE A HIKE

Well-kept, well-marked paths crisscross the **Sorrentine Peninsula** (*see p254* **Sorrento's heady heights**), scale the heights of the **Amalfi Coast** (*see pp264-291*) and offer unique perspectives on **Capri** (*see p212* **Scenic splendour**) and **Ischia** (*see pp215-228*). Fantastic views can be had from **Monte Faito** (*see p244*) and brooding **Vesuvius** (*see p245*), each a walker's paradise.

ARCHAEOLOGICAL & ARCHITECTURAL GEMS

No stay in Campania is complete without a day trip to **Pompeii** (*see p239*), but that's only part of the story. Nearby are the wonderful yet less familiar digs of **Herculaneum** (*see p234*), **Oplontis** (*see p239*) and **Stabiae** (*see p244*). Further south, there are dramatic Greek temples at **Paestum** (*see p295*), the last remaining complex of Magna Grecia.

Imposing reminders of the baroque grandeur of the region's past are everywhere. The *reggie* (royal palaces) in **Caserta** (*see p298*) and **Portici** (*see p234*) were the architectural wonders of their age, seriously challenging foreign competition from Versailles and Schönbrunn, and providing royals with their own oases away from the big smoke.

BEACH LIFE

Whether you're on the Amalfi Coast or heading off to one of the islands, the turquoise sea will always be beckoning. There are plenty of lidos on the Sorrentine peninsula (*see p260* **Call of the waves**); alternatively, you could immerse yourself in history at the **Bagni di Regina Giovanna** (*see p261*), a rock pool where Queen Joan was rumoured to bathe. Capri's fashionable bathing establishments include the famous **Canzone del Mare** lido (*see p201* **In the swim of things**), and the shingly **Bagno di Tiberio** beach lies at the foot of Palazzo a Mare, one of Tiberius's 12 villas on the island. Over on Ischia, close to the former fishing village of Sant'Angelo, the **spiaggia dei Maronti** (*see p227*) is a two-kilometre stretch of fine

sand; at **Cartaromana** (*see p218*) in the bay of Sant'Anna, you can swim in sight of the Castello Aragonese. Of Procida's beaches, those at **Chialollella** (*see p230*) are the most popular. Along the Amalfi Coast, every little town has a strip of beach. **Maiori** (*see p284*) is the largest. And if you're staying in one of the smarter hotels in **Positano** (*see p267*), you'll probably have the luxury of your own private beach.

SPAS & SPRINGS
Volcanic activity – in the form of spurting steam and boiling sulphurous springs – lurks close to the surface in **Ischia** (*see p220* **Taking the plunge**) and the **Campi Flegrei** (*see pp88-93*).

BACK TO NATURE
The gardens at Ravello's **Villa Rufolo** (*see pp288-289*) were the inspiration for Klingsor garden in Wagner's opera *Parsifal*, and when Greta Garbo wanted to be alone (with her lover Leopold Stokowski), she headed for **Villa Cimbrone** (*see p289*) and its spectacular grounds. On Ischia, the garden of composer William Walton, **La Mortella** (*see p225*), is a heady mix of tree ferns, magnolia and agaves – a magical backdrop to the classical concerts held amid the greenery. Capri's **Monte Solaro** (*see p199*) enjoys lovely views, and the terraced **Giardini di Augusto** (*see p201*) are also worth a visit. Experience breathtaking scenery and panoramic views at Sorrento's **Monti Lattari** and the nature reserve at **Punta della Campanella** (for both, *see p254* **Sorrento's heady heights**).

FINE DINING
It's easy to eat and drink well in the Campania region, but to experience high-end creativity in the kitchen, don't miss **Don Alfonso 1890** (*see p272*) in Sant'Agata sui due Golfi, **Rossellinis** (*see p290*) in Ravello, and Capri's **L'Olivo** (*see p210*).

The region has a long history of wine-making; these days, some excellent, energetic young wine-makers are taking advantage of the sunny slopes of Capri and the hanging vineyards of the Amalfi Coast. Head for Marisa Cuomo's winery in Furore (**the Gran Furor-Divina Costiera**, *see p276*) and take home a taste of the sun.

Time Out Naples

Editorial

Editors Jeffrey Kennedy (Naples), Janice Fuscoe (Around Naples)
Deputy Editor Elizabeth Winding
Listings Editor Marianna Raffaele
Proofreader Simon Cropper
Indexer Janice Fuscoe

Managing Director Peter Fiennes
Editorial Director Ruth Jarvis
Series Editor Will Fulford-Jones
Business Manager Dan Allen
Editorial Manager Holly Pick
Assistant Management Accountant Ija Krasnikova

Design

Art Director Scott Moore
Art Editor Pinelope Kourmouzoglou
Senior Designer Henry Elphick
Graphic Designers Kei Ishimaru, Nicola Wilson
Advertising Designer Jodi Sher

Picture Desk

Picture Editor Jael Marschner
Deputy Picture Editor Lynn Chambers
Picture Researcher Gemma Walters
Picture Desk Assistant Marzena Zoladz
Picture Librarian Christina Theisen

Advertising

Commercial Director Mark Phillips
International Advertising Manager Kasimir Berger
International Sales Executive Charlie Sokol

Marketing

Marketing Manager Yvonne Poon
Sales & Marketing Director, North America & Latin America Lisa Levinson
Senior Publishing Brand Manager Luthfa Begum
Art Director Anthony Huggins

Production

Group Production Director Mark Lamond
Production Manager Brendan McKeown
Production Controller Damian Bennett

Time Out Group

Chairman Tony Elliott
Chief Executive Officer David King
Group General Manager/Director Nichola Coulthard
Time Out Communications Ltd MD David Pepper
Time Out International Ltd MD Cathy Runciman
Time Out Magazine Ltd Publisher/MD Mark Elliott
Group IT Director Simon Chappell
Marketing & Circulation Director Catherine Demajo

Contributors

Introduction Jeffrey Kennedy & Janice Fuscoe. **History** Anne Hanley. **Naples Today** Cathryn Drake. **Architecture** Victoria Primhak. **Painting in Naples** Victoria Primhak. **Sights** all sections by Jeffrey Kennedy. **Hotels** Jeffrey Kennedy. **Restaurants** Nick Vivarelli. **Cafés, Bars & Gelaterie** Nick Vivarelli. **Shops & Services** Tui Cameron. **Calendar** Jeffrey Kennedy & Janice Fuscoe. **Children** Valentina Nesci. **Film** Antonio Tricomi. **Galleries** Cathryn Drake. **Gay & Lesbian** Jeffrey Kennedy. **Music & Nightlife** Amy Elford. **Performing Arts** Antonio Tricomi. **Sport & Fitness** Valentina Nesci. **Around Naples** all sections by Janice Fuscoe. **Directory** Jeffrey Kennedy & Janice Fuscoe.

Maps john@jsgraphics.co.uk, except: page 336, used by kind permission of MetroNapoli.

Photography Alys Tomlinson, except: pages 5, 6 (middle, right), 6 (bottom, left), 9, 15, 41, 43, 56, 60, 66, 82, 85, 90, 92, 96, 116, 121, 124, 126, 133, 150, 157, 180 (top right), 246, 249, 250, 253, 255, 256, 259, 260, 263, 264, 273, 274, 279, 292, 294 (bottom, right), 301, 302 Karl Blackwell; pages 6 (bottom, right), 77 courtesy of Museo di Capodimonte; page 16 AP/Press Association; page 19 Newfotosud / Rex Features; page 20, 37 Corbis; pages 27, 35, 181 Getty Images; page 39 The Bridgeman Art Library; page 73 Kyle Williams; page 87 Alfio Giannotti/Alamy; pages 94, 160, 179, 190, 209, 215, 216, 217, 219, 220, 223, 224, 227, 233, 237, 238, 245, 293, 294 (top, right), 294 (left), 297 Jonathan Perugia; page 95 Danilo Ascione/Shutterstock; page 128 Ed Marshall; page 137 Marzena Zoladz; page 168 Heloise Bergman; pages 62, 154, 155, 183 Alessandro Tortora; page 242 Sailorr / Shutterstock. The following images were provided by the featured establishments/artists: pages 5 (bottom, left) 33, 123, 158, 161, 162, 176, 177.

The editors would like to thank all contributors to previous editions of *Time Out Naples*, whose work forms the basis for parts of this book.

About the Guide

GETTING AROUND

The back of the book contains street maps of Naples. The maps start on page 323; on them are marked the locations of hotels (❶), restaurants (❶), and cafés, bars and *gelaterie* (❶). The majority of businesses listed in the Naples section of this guide are located in the areas mapped in this section; the grid-square references in the listings refer to these maps.

The Around Naples section of the book also contains a number of maps that relate to the destinations featured in that part of the book. The section begins on page 191.

THE ESSENTIALS

For practical information, including visas, customs and immigration, disabled access, emergency numbers, lost property and local transport, please see the Directory. It begins on page 303.

THE LISTINGS

Addresses, phone numbers, websites, transport information, hours and prices are all included in our listings, as are selected other facilities. All were checked and correct at press time. However, business owners can alter their arrangements at any time, and fluctuating economic conditions can cause prices to change rapidly.

The very best venues, the must-sees and must-dos in every category, have been marked with a red star (★). In the Naples Sights chapters, we've also marked venues with free admission with a FREE symbol.

PHONE NUMBERS

To reach a number in this book from within the city, dial the number as listed, complete with its area code (081). To reach a number from outside Italy, dial your country's international access code (00 from the UK, 011 from the US) or a plus symbol, followed by the Italian country code (39) and then the number, complete with its area code. For more on phones, including information on calling abroad and details of local mobile phone access, *see p311*.

FEEDBACK

We welcome feedback on this guide, both on the venues we've included and on any other locations that you'd like to see featured in future editions. Please email us at guides@timeout.com.

Time Out Guides

Founded in 1968, Time Out has grown from humble beginnings into the leading resource for anyone wanting to know what's happening in the world's greatest cities. Alongside our influential weeklies in London, New York and Chicago, we publish more than 20 magazines in cities as varied as Beijing and Beirut; a range of travel books, with the City Guides now joined by the newer Shortlist series; and an information-packed website. The company remains proudly independent, still owned by Tony Elliott four decades after he launched *Time Out London*.

Written by local experts and illustrated with original photography, our books also retain their independence. No business has been featured because it has advertised, and all restaurants and bars are visited and reviewed anonymously.

ABOUT THE EDITORS

Writer on all things Italian, as well as an editor and translator, **Jeffrey Kennedy** is a lifelong student of the city of Naples. **Janice Fuscoe** has edited two previous editions of *Time Out Naples*, and is also the editor of *Time Out Perfect Places Italy*.

A full list of the book's contributors can be found opposite. However, we've also included details of our writers in selected chapters through the guide.

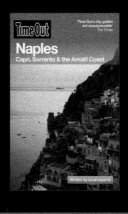

In Context

Galleria Umberto I. *See p49.*

History   **16**
Low life to high society   20
A rich cultural canvas   25
Key events   29

Naples Today   **30**
Heart of darkness   32

Painting in Naples   **36**
Profile The art of
backstabbing   39

Architecture   **41**
Profile Bombast bombed   44

Will the real Naples please stand up?
TEXT: ANNE HANLEY

N aples – who hasn't ruled the roost here? Greeks, Germans, Romans, Spaniards, French, Austrians and even Poles have all influenced, for better or (more often) worse, the beleaguered city.

Some suggest that the succession of invading rulers has contributed to the eccentric characteristics of its citizens, from the Neapolitan's sense of an eternal underdog status to a widely held mistrust of rulers, including the state, and even the emergence of and continued support for 'their own' in the form of the omnipresent Camorra. Indeed, the rise of the Camorra originally came about in order to 'protect' weak peasant farmers from greedy landowners... with a few conditions attached to make it worth the *camorrista*'s while.

Another telling influence in forming the Neapolitan character – besides an abortive revolt against taxation on food in the 17th century – was the plague in that same century, as well as numerous cholera outbreaks several centuries later. Add to that the perpetual threat that Vesuvius poses, and it's little wonder that life in this city has become singularly rough and ready, cheerfully wild and woolly, and decidedly helter-skelter.

*When she's not editing Time Out's Rome and Venice city guides, **Anne Hanley** runs garden design company La Verzura.*

IT'S ALL GREEK

In the eighth century BC, a small band of adventurers from the Greek island of Euboea set up a trading station near what is now Lacco Ameno (*see p222*), on the island they called Pithekoussai (Ischia). Ischia's volcanos were rumbling at the time, driving some of the less courageous newcomers across the bay to Cuma (*see p93*) on the mainland. There, they soon began to build trade links around the Mediterranean basin.

Infinitely more sophisticated than the tribes that had long populated the lush hinterland and sparser mountain region beyond, the Greeks made Cuma the area's most powerful city. The addition of a sibyl – a prophesying voice of the gods – in a local cave added to its clout. Confident in their control of the area, the Cuman Greeks spread down the coast, founding Parthenope (near Pizzofalcone, *see p52*) in c680 BC, Dikaiarchia (Pozzuoli, *see p89*) in c530 BC, and Neapolis ('New Town') in 470 BC; the Greek's grid pattern of the streets can still be seen in central Naples.

Yet as the Cuman Greeks were extending their sphere of influence, so too were the Etruscans. From their power base in Tuscany, these highly advanced people spread southwards from the ninth or eighth centuries BC, establishing their southern capital at Capua in about 600 BC. Conflict was inevitable between two such dynamic groups, and battles were fought at Cuma in 524 and 474 BC, both won by the Greeks. The clashes exhausted the strength of the two rivals, leaving them prey to the encroaching Samnites.

WHEN NOT IN ROME

Shepherds and fighters, the Samnite hill people took Capua in 424 BC and Cuma in 421 BC. Into this scenario stepped another tribe with a mounting lust for land and power: the Romans. Around 340 BC, the Romans began the job of bringing the Samnites to heel. By 328 BC they had turned on Neapolis, laying siege to the city; it held out for two years before grudgingly handing itself over to the conquerors. The city was forced to supply ships and men for Roman naval battles, and its assimilation into greater Rome sent its economy into a depression that was to last for centuries.

Neapolis continued to grow in population and cultural importance, while still clinging to its Greek identity and language. As all things Hellenic became fashionable in republican Rome, wealthy Roman offspring were often dispatched to the southern city for their education, while their parents soaked up the balmy climate in holiday villas along the coast from Cuma to Sorrento. To make communication and transport easier, the Appian Way (Via Appia), the first major Roman highway, was begun in 312 BC.

HANNIBAL & EMPIRE

The idyll suffered the occasional brutal interruption. In the Second Punic War (218-201 BC), the Romans battled Hannibal's Carthaginian forces back and forth across the plains of the Neapolis hinterland; during the Roman Civil War (88-82 BC), Sulla occupied Neapolis and massacred a large proportion of its inhabitants during his triumphal march on Rome, where he was to rule as dictator from 82 to 79 BC; and in 73 BC, runaway slave Spartacus established the headquarters of his slave army on the slopes of Mount Vesuvius, and set out on rampages up and down the Italian peninsula.

But by the time the Roman Empire was established in 27 BC, Neapolis was once again a centre of learning, attracting writers, teachers and holidaymakers. Virgil lived here for many years, composing the *Georgics*, and died here, so some believe; the sybaritic General Lucullus built a home where Castel dell'Ovo now stands (*see p52*).

Although the city flourished under the Empire, it wasn't so in the surrounding region, where agriculture was hit hard by imports of cheaper grain and oil from Rome's new possessions in Africa and Spain. In the largely abandoned areas around the Volturno estuary to the north of the city and Paestum to the south, malaria was rife. By the time Vesuvius erupted in AD 79, burying many surrounding towns beneath a layer of lava and ash, Pompeii was already little more than a ghost town, having suffered a devastating earthquake some years before.

IN CONTEXT

VANDALISED BY GOTHS

As the Empire declined, so did Naples and its environs, which from the early fifth century were prey to attacks by Goths and Vandals. The latter razed Capua in 456, and the former won and lost Naples itself several times during the fifth century, despite works to strengthen the walls in 440. It was in Naples that the Western Roman Empire truly came to an end, when the last emperor, Romulus Augustulus, imprisoned by the Goth King Odoacer, died in 476.

In Byzantium (Constantinople), the Eastern emperor Justinian was keen to assert his power over Italy. In the 530s he dispatched his prize general, Belisarius, to do the job. In 536, Naples' walls held Belisarius at bay for three weeks. Then one of the general's men spotted a water conduit leading into the city, and a handful of crack fighters crawled inside. Attacked from within and without, Naples fell.

The Byzantines continued to harry the increasingly demoralised Goths until 553, when the last Goth ruler was killed. The following year, Naples became a Byzantine-controlled duchy, with dukes, magistrates and military leaders appointed by the Eastern emperor's Italian representative, the Exarch of Ravenna. By 645, this tight rein had loosened, and a Neapolitan by the name of Basilio became the city's first native duke.

With a population of 40,000, Naples was flourishing once again, its importance growing in inverse proportion to that of declining Capua. Yet marauding invaders continued to threaten the area. In 568, the Germanic *longobardi* (Lombards) swept across the Alps, taking northern Italy without much of a struggle and moving swiftly down the peninsula. Their sieges of Naples – in 581, 592 and 599 – were largely unsuccessful, though much of the Campania region, including Capua and, in 625, Salerno, fell to them. At the same time, Naples was beset from the sea by Saracens. In the ninth century came the Franks, who were sworn enemies of the Neapolitans.

INDEPENDENCE DAY

Uninterested in territorial aggrandisement, the little duchy was content to ensure its own independence by playing off its conflicting allies (Byzantium and the Pope in Rome) and foes (Lombards, Franks and Saracens) against one another, sealing secret pacts, and balancing loyalty against distance, coherent policy against tactical advantage.

While Naples played Machiavellian games to keep the wolves from the door, the city was growing in beauty and wealth. Churches were built, schools were founded and artists and goldsmiths worked furiously to decorate the proud duchy. In the mid tenth century, with Saracens attacking from the sea and disgruntled Byzantines besieging from the landward side, Duke John III still found time to dispatch monks to libraries around Christendom to copy manuscripts sacred and profane to enrich his splendid collection. Industry and trade flourished, with Neapolitan textiles in great demand.

Beyond Naples and the lands directly under its control, things started to look up for the Lombard-dominated territories after the Germanic overlords converted to Roman-style Christianity in the seventh century. Firmly settled in their southern dominions, the Lombards embarked on a bout of building and learning, especially in their capital at Benevento (*see p297*). By the eighth century, however, divisions were appearing in the united Lombard front, as Salerno grew in importance and wealth. In 849, Benevento and Salerno split, weakening the Lombard position. Capua, too, became a separate principality in the tenth century.

Not far from Salerno, Amalfi had emerged as a law unto itself, resisting Lombard encroachment, slipping out of the control of the Duchy of Naples and continuing to swear fealty to Byzantium – an invaluable trading partner for this growing sea power.

THE CRAFTY NORMAN CONQUEST

This fragmented state of affairs was soon to come to an end. In a final show of strength in 1027, the Lombard Prince Pandolf IV of Capua seized power in Naples, helped by Neapolitan barons keen to oust the reigning Duke Sergio IV. Holed up in

Gaeta, Sergio turned to an unruly band of Normans who had strayed into southern Italy. He married his sister to their leader, Rainulf Drengot, then made him the Count of Aversa. The combined Neapolitan and Norman force soon drove the Lombards out of Naples.

With Aversa – a small town north of Naples – as a power base, the Normans grew in number as more compatriots arrived from France, grew wealthier through mercenary activities, and became increasingly power-hungry. In 1062 they took Capua; in 1073, Amalfi. In 1077, Lombard Salerno fell to Robert Guiscard ('the Crafty') – a member of the powerful Hauteville (Altavilla) family, who made the city his mainland capital.

The Normans besieged Naples for two years, to no avail. Robert set his sights on Byzantium, but died in his bid to oust the Eastern emperor. His brother Roger concentrated his efforts on southern Italy, most of which was firmly under Norman control by 1130, the year when his son was crowned Roger II, King of Sicily. The Norman monarch demanded that Duke Sergio VII of Naples recognise him as sovereign. Sergio obliged, then recanted, joining an anti-Norman League that scored numerous bloody victories against the French interlopers. Having identified Naples as the centre of opposition, Roger laid siege after siege to the city, but was driven back by inclement weather and disease.

Sergio, having made another of his temporary pledges to support Roger, died fighting for the Normans in October 1137. The Neapolitan people turned to the anti-Norman Pope Innocent II for help, holding out against the Norman king for a further two years. But when Innocent was taken prisoner by the Normans, Naples was left with little choice; in August 1139, a delegation vowed to support the Sicilian crown in Benevento.

Despite the lengthy struggle, the capitulation was not an unpopular one. When Roger visited Naples in autumn 1140, 30,000 joyous people turned out to greet him. Roger was impressed by the great houses and lavish churches; outside the city walls, trade flourished in two separate ports. With its incorporation into the Kingdom of Sicily, though, Naples was overshadowed by Palermo. A model of stability and efficiency, the Norman kingdom was highly centralised, leaving little scope for independent action by its constituent parts. The Neapolitan nobility – for centuries a thorn in the side of the ruling dukes – swore fealty to the Norman crown in exchange for land and privileges.

The Norman conquest coincided with a period of high agricultural production in the Campanian countryside, and explosive growth in the shipping trade; relative peace and prosperity also meant a livelier market for the city's artisans. This general well-being

IN CONTEXT

Vesuvius. *See p17.*

IN CONTEXT

Low life to high society

The scandalous rise of Lady Emma Hamilton.

Former army officer Sir William Hamilton (1730-1803) was British envoy to the Neapolitan court for 18 years. Hamilton built himself a solid reputation not only as a fine diplomat, but also as a learned volcanologist and avid collector of antiquities. Shortly after the death of his wife in 1782, however, his reputation took a turn for the worse, as a famous beauty with a dubious past entered his life.

In order to be free to marry well, Lord Hamilton's penniless nephew, Charles Francis Greville, sent his uncle his much-loved mistress, then known as Emma Hart. Born in 1761 and a blacksmith's daughter, Amy (some accounts record 'Emy') Lyon had worked as a maid and prostitute. By the age of about 20, though, she had conquered high society as the preferred model of such courtly painters as Sir Joshua Reynolds and George Romney. Greville had intended Emma as a pleasant, short-lived dalliance for his bereft uncle, but, to everyone's shock, Sir William kept her on, and she soon became the second Lady Hamilton.

The fashionable set was scandalised by the match; Casanova himself, the libertine nonpareil, observed, 'Mr Hamilton is a genius and yet he has ended by marrying a mere girl... he is bound to pay dearly for his folly; and if his wife is amorous of him, she will kill him.' As it turned out, though, Emma knew her business well. She became the bosom friend of Naples' Queen Maria Carolina (the sister of Marie Antoinette), and delighted crowned heads far and wide with her exquisite abilities as a dramatic dancer. When the hero of the Nile, Admiral Horatio Nelson, came to Naples in 1798, a spark was struck between the pair, and the rest is history – their affair has been the stuff of romance and legend ever since.

The only abiding mystery is what prompted Sir William to flaunt the glaring fact so openly (even to Emma's bearing a daughter and naming her Horatia). In Naples and later in London, the three of them set up in fine style together, in a notorious ménage à trois that dominated high society and the scandal sheets for nearly a decade.

may explain Naples' loyalty to Roger's vacillating grandson Tancred, when his throne was contested by the more dynamic Heinrich Hohenstaufen of Swabia, son of Holy Roman Emperor Friedrich Barbarossa and son-in-law of Roger.

THE GERMANS ARE COMING

After Tancred's death in 1194, Heinrich became king of Sicily and punished Naples by ripping down its walls. Three years later he died, leaving a three-year-old heir. Still smarting from its punishment, Naples entered into the dynastic struggles of the German emperors, wholeheartedly backing the claims of Otto IV of Brunswick over those of the baby king Friedrich II. The city decided to recognise Otto as sovereign, sticking by him through papal excommunications and various routs on the battlefield.

It was a wonder, then, that the victorious Friedrich, when he was safely on the thrones of the Holy Roman Empire and southern Italy in 1214, decided to invest so much in Naples and treat it with such munificence. Although his brilliant and artistically astonishing court remained in Palermo, he rebuilt Naples' fortifications and made the city an intellectual centre of his Italian kingdom, establishing a new university.

Nothing, however, could erase Naples' historic hatred of the Hohenstaufen family. In 1251, after the death of Friedrich II, the city rose up against attempts by his son Conrad to assert control. With the backing of Pope Innocent IV, it declared itself a free commune, resisting sieges until 1253, when the imperial forces broke through.

When the emperor died the following year, the commune was briefly re-established. In 1258, Conrad's illegitimate brother Manfred became king of Naples, but the Neapolitans seized the first possible opportunity to discard their Hohenstaufen sovereign. Charles of Anjou had hardly completed his invasion of Sicily in 1265 before the city rushed to pledge its loyalty to the newly arrived French dynasty.

ANJOU AND ARAGON

To set themselves apart from their predecessors, the Anjous moved the capital of their Italian kingdom from Palermo to Naples, though the realm continued to be called the Regno di Sicilia. New buildings went up, and merchants and craftsmen from across Mediterranean Europe flocked to the booming city. Charles I (who reigned over all southern Italy 1265-82) had the Castel Nuovo built, and a wealthy, well-planned quarter grew up around it.

In Sicily, things didn't go so smoothly for the Angevin kings. Resentful at the removal of the capital from their soil, as well as at harsh taxes imposed by the newcomers, Sicilian barons began plotting with Pedro III, king of Aragon, to overthrow Charles. The rebellion went into top gear on Easter Monday 1282, when French soldiers were killed after vespers outside a Palermo church; over the following night, in a riot that became known as the *vespri siciliani*, 2,000 French people were killed. The ensuing Vesper Wars dragged on until 1302, raging through Sicily and up and down the southern mainland, until Charles finally acknowledged that Sicily was lost and was reduced to ruling the southern Italian mainland.

Naples thrived as the Anjous sought to make the city a fitting capital for their dynasty. Under the third Angevin king, Robert (reigned 1309-43), the Castel Sant'Elmo (*see p81*) was built. However, the city's success caused lasting harm to the area around it. Naples' port expanded exponentially, sounding the death knell for former naval powers such as Amalfi, Gaeta and Salerno. While the primarily agricultural regions immediately surrounding the city capitalised on the food demands of the growing populace, the foothills of the Apennines became increasingly poor and depopulated, and diseases such as malaria flourished in the marshy districts around the mouth of the Volturno, and in the Sele valley south of Salerno.

Naples' relationship with its French rulers was loyal, though never unquestioningly so. When András of Hungary, husband of the beautiful and highly intelligent Queen Juana I (reigned 1343-81), was murdered in 1345, the Neapolitan people caught and wreaked vengeance on his suspected murderers. King Lajos I of Hungary suspected, however, that Juana might have had something to do with his brother's demise, and invaded Naples in 1348. Juana remedied the situation by fleeing to her county of Provence, and selling her city of Avignon to the Pope in return for absolution for any misdemeanours she might have committed. In 1352 she returned to Naples to a rapturous welcome. Thirty years later, when Juana backed the anti-Pope Clement VII, her own people rose up to overthrow her in favour of her cousin Charles III of Durres (reigned 1381-86), a champion of Pope Urban VI.

THE STRUGGLE FOR POWER

When Charles's son Ladislas (reigned 1386-1414) died, the Neapolitans defended his sister, Joan II (reigned 1414-35), against her second husband Jacques de Bourbon, who tried to wrest power away from her. They also backed Joan's chosen heir, her cousin René of Anjou (Good King René of Provence) against the claims of Alfonso 'the Magnanimous' of Aragon (King Alfonso V of Sicily), whom she had previously adopted, then disinherited.

But Alfonso was more than a match for René, whom he drove out of Naples shortly after Joan's death. Southern Italy was one kingdom again, and a long period of Spanish control had begun. With his leech-like crowd of Catalan followers, Alfonso (reigned 1442-58) failed to ingratiate himself with his Neapolitan subjects, despite his lenient treatment of a city that had fought tooth and nail to prevent him taking its crown. His illegitimate son Ferdinando (also known as Don Ferrante, reigned 1458-94) won some hearts when he ejected the overbearing freebooters and championed the arts and trades of the expanding city.

Naples' powerful barons, however, continued to oppose the Aragonese presence; some even persuaded France's King Charles VIII to occupy the city in 1494. But the Neapolitan people rose up against French domination, reinstating King Ferdinando's grandson, Ferdinando II (known as Ferrandino) to the throne.

On Ferrandino's premature death the following year, the people pressed for the crown to be given to his young widow Joanna, sister of Spain's King Ferdinando 'the Catholic'. The barons, on the other hand, conspired to place Ferrandino's uncle Federico (reigned 1496-1501) on the throne. This enraged France and Spain, which marched on Naples in 1501.

ENTER THE HABSBURGS

When the French arrived first, Federico hoped to salvage something for himself by agreeing to hand over Naples and part of his realm to the French King Charles VIII. But when the great Spanish General Consalvo di Cordoba appeared at the city walls in 1503, the people promptly let him in, and Spain's King Ferdinando added the Neapolitan crown to his already impressive list of titles, reigning from 1503-16.

Ferdinando visited his new acquisition during 1506, conferring privileges on the nobles and the *piazza* – the people – and leaving behind him the first of a long succession of viceroys who would be feared, hated and mistrusted for the next two centuries. With the arrival of the viceroys, the locals' say in the running of their own affairs greatly diminished. The parliament served almost exclusively to rubber-stamp cynically named *donativi* – not in fact donations, but crippling taxes. Even the barons were deprived of their near-omnipotence. During his term of office, Pedro di Toledo (viceroy 1532-53) had no qualms about imprisoning or even executing nobles who had previously enjoyed impunity.

REIGN FROM SPAIN

Although violent Neapolitan protests halted attempts to introduce the Spanish Inquisition, and the city reaped some benefit from the viceroys – especially Toledo, who was responsible for vast redevelopment to improve living standards in the city, building the now disreputable Quartieri spagnoli (*see p43*) – Spanish rule did little to improve Naples' lot. In the early days, the city did profit from the extraordinary economic boom resulting from the Spanish conquest of the New World. Still, the inflation-fuelled slump that ensued hit hard in a city with no strong trade infrastructure. The slump was accentuated by short-term administrators who had little interest in stamping out the endemic corruption in the realm's bureaucracy, and by chronic crime levels in the unpoliced countryside (which often failed to produce enough food to feed the population).

Yet it was on this depressed part of its dominions that Spain depended to finance its European wars. Taxes were levied on just about every commodity or transaction: on flour and bread, on tobacco, on rents, on hemp and on imported metals. Even ransoms paid to release Neapolitans from Turkish pirates were subject to tax. But the levy most certain to set the city aflame was the one on fruit and vegetables.

SAY YOU WANT A REVOLUTION

The tax sparked the worst uprising to hit Spanish-controlled Naples. In 1647, Neapolitans rallied behind a 27-year-old fisherman from Amalfi called Tommaso Aniello (known as Masaniello), who headed a bloody revolt until his assassination. Masaniello was pro-king but anti-levy. His task of leading the undisciplined mob was rendered all the more difficult by a vacillating viceroy, the Duke of Arcos. The Duke promised to suspend the tax but didn't, armed the people then sent his troops to gun them down, and pledged greater clout in parliament to the masses while stationing troops to cover the retreat of the barons' henchmen after they had murdered Masaniello. By April 1648, the Neapolitans had grown tired of the upheaval. Endlessly optimistic, they settled for a new viceroy – the Count of Oñate – and a promise of more reasonable taxes in future.

At the beginning of the 17th century, Naples was Europe's biggest city, with a population of over 300,000. The plague that ravaged the area for six months in 1656 left three-quarters of the population dead. But the rest of Europe, sinking deeper into dynastic struggles and other wars of succession, had little time to worry about the devastation caused by disease in this poverty-stricken outpost.

THE END OF THE LINE

When it became clear that the last of the Spanish Habsburgs, Carlos II (Carlo V of Naples, reigned 1665-1700), would die childless, various crowns needed to be reassigned. England, France and Holland agreed that Spain and the Spanish Netherlands should pass to the Austrian Habsburg Archduke Karl (younger son of the Holy Roman Emperor, Leopold I), with Naples and Sicily going to France. But Carlo rejected this arrangement: he had been persuaded by his Bourbon brother-in-law, King Louis XIV of France, that only a Bourbon would keep Spanish dominions intact.

On Carlo's death in 1700, Louis' grandson Philippe of Anjou became Felipe V of Spain, sparking a continental conflict that would last from 1701 to 1714. When France backed Felipe and invaded the Spanish Netherlands, Britain, Holland and Austria formed an anti-French alliance. But when Archduke Karl unexpectedly became Holy Roman Emperor Karl VI in 1711 after the death of his older brother, the allies baulked at fighting to extend his power and dominions still further.

Sick of the succession of Spanish viceroys, and hoping for their own independent monarch in the shape of a minor Habsburg, Neapolitan nobles sought Austrian victory in the War of Spanish Succession. The Neapolitan people, as much at loggerheads with their nobles as ever, were happy to support Spain's new Bourbon king, and Felipe V was given a tumultuous welcome when he visited the city in 1702. In 1707, however, Austrian forces occupied southern Italy, and Naples once again found itself with a series of Habsburg-appointed viceroys at its helm.

Succession in Poland caused the next major European shake-up (1733-35), pitting Russia and Habsburg-controlled Austria (in favour of Augustus III) against the Franco-Spanish Bourbon alliance (which backed Stanislav I, father-in-law of France's Louis XV).

IN CONTEXT

'THE MOST BEAUTIFUL CROWN IN ITALY'

When the War of Polish Succession broke out, the squat, ugly, but likeable Spanish Infante Don Carlos, younger son of Felipe V and the scheming Elisabetta Farnese, was in Florence, amusing himself (according to the British envoy of the time, Horace Mann) by shooting the eyes out of birds in the Gobelins tapestries in the Pitti Palace and whisking courtiers' wigs off with strategically placed hooks and lines. Elisabetta had sent her teenage son, with a 40,000-strong army, to occupy her family's dominions in Parma and Piacenza. He was also to take over Tuscany on the death of Gian Gastone Medici. But when the Bourbons entered hostilities with Austria, Elisabetta set her sights higher. Shortly after his 18th birthday, she ordered her son to mobilise his army, and to take 'the most beautiful crown in Italy'.

Don Carlos's procession south was largely good-natured and mostly unimpeded. Austria failed to reinforce its embittered, over-taxed city of Naples, and he entered the city in triumph in May 1734. In July 1735, having expelled the Austrians from the whole of southern Italy, he was crowned Carlo III of the Kingdom of Sicily. Although the Peace of Vienna (1738) obliged him to cede Parma, Piacenza and most of Tuscany to Austria, he was confirmed as king of an independent southern Italian realm. Finally, Naples was a capital again, with a king it could call its own.

THE AGE OF ENLIGHTENMENT

With the Age of Enlightenment in full swing, the king (supported, from 1737, by his wife Maria Amelia of Saxony, upon whom he doted) transformed his capital into a city worthy of the times. No opera lover, he built one of Europe's finest theatres, the San Carlo (*see p51*); although he was no scholar, he established the Biblioteca Nazionale. Under Carlo's rule, the excavation of Herculaneum and Pompeii got under way. The 16th-century Palazzo Reale was extended and refurbished (*see p51*). To pursue his passion for hunting, Carlo had magnificent palaces built at Portici, Capodimonte and Caserta. To house the city's poor, he built the enormous Albergo dei Poveri (*see p72*).

The death of the Austrian emperor in 1740 plunged Europe into war again. Unwillingly, Carlo was prevailed upon to back the Franco-Spanish-Prussian alliance contesting the accession of the late emperor's daughter Maria Teresa to the Austrian throne. Once the redoubtable empress had secured her crown (and Naples had been forced to capitulate in humiliation to her British allies, who threatened to bombard the city from the sea in 1742), Carlo could settle back down to the business of running his kingdom.

In 1759, he abdicated and returned to Spain, to succeed his father as King Carlos III. As he did, he left his eight-year-old son Ferdinando under the tutorship of his most trusted adviser, Tuscan lawyer Bernardo Tanucci. Tanucci had been instrumental in seeking to introduce bureaucratic and fiscal reforms into the shambolic state, though the continued power of the feudal barons limited his success. Even more resounding was his failure to provide Ferdinando with a monarchical education.

When the highly educated and strong-willed Maria Carolina, daughter of the Austrian empress, arrived in Naples to marry the young king in 1768, she was shocked. He played with toys, spoke coarse local dialect, enjoyed rough games with low-class youths and hated anything bookish. Ferdinando was, however, most impressed by his clever young wife, whose orders – especially in matters of state – he accepted unquestioningly.

BRITISH NAVAL HERO STEPS IN

With the birth of her first son in 1777, Maria Carolina entered the Council of State, as was stipulated in her marriage contract. From this position of strength, she was able to engineer the downfall of her arch-enemy Tanucci.

In 1778, she adopted as her favourite John Acton, a wandering British naval hero, who may have become her lover. Born in France, Acton had made vast improvements to the Tuscan navy before being summoned to modernise Naples' neglected fleet. In Spain, King Carlos was furious that a subject of his enemy Britain should be gaining

IN CONTEXT

A rich cultural canvas

Naples is no newcomer to the tourist trail.

Throughout the 17th, 18th and early 19th centuries, no young gentleman's education was complete without a 'grand tour' – a lengthy jaunt through the cultural capitals of contemporary and classical Europe, including, of course, Naples. Not only was Naples a magnetic stopover for resting (and playing) on the tourist's adventurous slide down the Italian peninsula, it was also one of the greatest epicentres of ancient culture: the place of myth, the Greeks, Roman emperors and their scandals and glories, sites of slave revolts and decisive battles.

The rich – and newly-discovered – archaeological heritage of Pompeii and Herculaneum combined powerfully with the awe-inspiring beauty of the bay and the smouldering backdrop of Vesuvius – the killer volcano that had, at the same time, ensured that so much of ancient culture would be preserved for future generations. Some attribute the famous phrase, 'See Naples and die,' to the brilliant German grand tourist Goethe. Could he have been referring to the city's perpetual sense of danger,

under the glowering Vesuvius? Or, more likely, to the sense of ultimate beauty the place evoked, whereby a kind of mystic sublimation of life itself seems to occur? Goethe had this to say about his reaction to the place: 'I can't begin to tell you of the glory of a night by full moon when we strolled through the streets and squares to the endless promenade of the Chiaia, and then walked up and down the seashore. I was quite overwhelmed by the feeling of infinite space. To be able to dream like this is certainly worth the trouble it took getting here.'

The light-suffused gouache paintings from the era reveal how the grand tourists perceived the city. They were merely the postcards of the age, brought home by the dozen by every visitor, but now the originals grow more precious every year. Reproductions decorate sweet boxes and hotel walls everywhere you look: day scenes with peasant folk doing an impromptu tarantella, say, or night scenes with fishing boats bobbing on a ruddy sea, reflecting erupting Vesuvius' flaming display.

influence in his former realm. Indeed, Acton was apt to pass classified information from the queen's lips to the British ambassador, Sir William Hamilton (*see p20* **Low life to high society**), and steered Naples into an iron-clad alliance with Britain. He served Naples faithfully, however, displaying rare honesty and organisational powers in the midst of ministers who were known for their inefficiency. He may also have attenuated the worst excesses of the queen's hysteria following the outbreak of the French Revolution. For Maria Carolina the revolution was shock enough, but the execution of her sister Marie Antoinette in 1793 was too much.

Naples entered enthusiastically into the anti-French alliance. A Neapolitan army of 60,000 troops occupied French-held Rome on 27 November 1798, with the triumphant King Ferdinando at its head. But Karl Mack, the Austrian general who led the Neapolitan forces, proved to be a bungler. When France's General Championnet marched back into Rome 11 days later, the Neapolitans fled, with the French at their heels.

A RIGHT ROYAL RETREAT

In Naples, news of the defeat was greeted by the fiercely royalist masses with ferocious attacks on those Neapolitan liberals who had championed French ideals of liberty and equality. The massacre ended only as the French entered the city, and the Repubblica Partenopea was declared in January 1799.

The royal family, with Acton, fled to Sicily on board Admiral Horatio Nelson's ship the *Vanguard*. In Naples, efforts – confused and botched – by Republican leaders to introduce pro-equality reforms failed to impress the poor, who took advantage of the early withdrawal of the French military to rise up and force liberals to take refuge in the city's forts.

Further south, the queen's envoy Cardinal Fabrizio Ruffo led his raggle-taggle Christian Army of the Holy Faith up the boot of Italy, in a bloody campaign to oust the French and their sympathisers. In June, the Republican leaders agreed to a capitulation, the terms of which were promptly ignored by Nelson and King Ferdinando. More than 200 executions – which included those of the royalist-turned-rebel Admiral Francesco Caracciolo – were carried out.

Naples was a minor player on the European chessboard, and easily sacrificed by allies in general disagreement over how to cope with the vast Revolutionary and then Napoleonic armies descending on them. When France beat Austria at Marengo in 1800, becoming the dominant European power on land and debilitating Naples' chief ally, the kingdom bartered its independence for those parts of Tuscany that still belonged to the Neapolitan crown. Only Britain stood by the little kingdom; but with French troops poised in Rome, this friendship was more a red flag to a bull than any guarantee that there would be no invasion.

FRENCH EMPEROR, KING OF NAPLES

In 1805, Austria suffered another crippling defeat on the battlefield at Austerlitz, and French forces under Joseph Bonaparte occupied Austria's ally Naples on 14 January 1806. The royals fled to Sicily, and Joseph was declared king of Naples, replaced on the throne by Napoleon's brother-in-law Joachim Murat in 1808 when Joseph was crowned king of Spain.

Try as they might, the Napoleonic rulers failed to win the hearts of the fiercely royalist southern Italians. The numerous reforms introduced under French rule were, on the face of it, to the advantage of the people: feudalism was abolished and land redistribution begun; absolute power was wrested from the hands of the Neapolitan aristocracy and the towns of Campania grew in status and importance. Murat gave the city its Orto Botanico (botanical garden, *see p75*) and made efforts to stamp out southern Italy's endemic banditry.

Though their weak-willed ex-monarch Ferdinando dithered in Palermo – under the thumb of British ambassador Lord William Bentinck, who first forced Ferdinando to

IN CONTEXT

promulgate a democratic constitution, and then to send his by now fanatically scheming wife Maria Carolina into exile in Austria in 1811 – the Neapolitan masses remained doggedly hostile to the French, rising up against them on innumerable occasions. They were also singularly unimpressed by Murat's efforts to create a united Italy when Napoleon's star waned.

During ten years of French rule, Naples' rightful monarch spent much of his time hunting in the Palermo hinterland, while the British – the only power that could have reinstated him in his capital – used Sicily as their Mediterranean power base.

KINGDOM OF THE TWO SICILIES

At the Council of Vienna in 1816, Europe's victorious conservative monarchies confirmed Ferdinando as Naples' ruler; he took the new title of King Ferdinando I of the Kingdom of the Two Sicilies. The old king received a rapturous welcome when he returned to Naples. But he and his successors misjudged the changing times, and the enthusiasm soon paled.

Ferdinando responded to the demands of the shadowy Carbonari liberal reform movement (a secret society seeking a unified Italy) by promulgating a parliamentary constitution in 1820. However, he then stood contentedly by as his reactionary ally Austria sent troops into his kingdom to quash these dangerous signs of anti-absolutism. Ferdinando died in 1825; his successor, Francesco I, had shown early signs of liberal leanings, but these soon disappeared when he took the throne.

Ferdinando II, who became king in 1830, managed to bring Naples' huge public debt under control. He also helped the poor at the behest of his first wife, the saintly Maria Cristina of Savoy, and initiated a series of important public works, including the completion of the Portici railway, Italy's first, which opened in 1839. But the king was as committed to absolutism as his predecessors had been. Liberal movements were watched by an efficient spy network, and all revolts were ruthlessly put down, sometimes before they even began.

IN CONTEXT

Liberation. *See p28.*

IN CONTEXT

GARIBALDI TAKES THE BISCUIT

In 1847-48, when the city of Naples joined the more openly rebellious Sicily in demanding a constitution, Ferdinando granted it, but then played moderate and extreme liberal camps off against each other until he could justify dissolving the bickering parliament in 1849.

Ferdinando II's son Francesco II (reigned 1859-60) came to the throne in mid-Risorgimento, as Piedmontese troops fought to oust the Austrians from northern Italy. Each victory for these Italian unification forces was greeted with joy in Naples, but the new king still couldn't see that his harsh repression of liberalism could not continue. It was becoming clearer – even to those who had backed the Bourbons so enthusiastically – that Italian unification could only bring change for the better.

With unification troops having taken Sicily and much of the southern mainland, Francesco agreed to the introduction of a constitution in June 1860. It was too little, too late. The city's residents turned out en masse to welcome unification general Giuseppe Garibaldi, with an enthusiasm boosted by the fact that he had established his credentials as a royalist, rather than a republican. When Garibaldi entered Naples on 7 September 1860, banners hanging from every window showed the cross of the Piedmontese royal family, the Savoys. On 21 October the city voted overwhelmingly in favour of joining a united Italy ruled by Vittorio Emanuele II of Savoy.

It was to be ten years before the Unification of Italy was complete – with the capture of Rome. For Naples, integration into the national fabric meant that any faint glory that still clung to the once-flourishing capital evaporated. It was Rome that the Unification leaders aspired to, and Rome was now to be designated capital of the newly united realm. Despite some housing reforms instituted after a devastating cholera epidemic in 1884, Naples languished in growing neglect and poverty.

DON'T MENTION THE WAR

Naples' strategic importance – as a port, and as the gateway from southern to northern Europe – was only fully recognised once again during World War II; this time it was to the city's detriment. Aerial bombardments tore through its historic centre and waterfront, while its incomparably rich state archive was destroyed by the city's German occupiers.

The Germans were ejected in an uprising known as *Le Quattro giornate napoletane* (the four days of Naples). Between 27 and 30 September 1943, residents of Naples paved the way for the arrival of the Anglo-American forces. When the Allies finally entered the city's blackened shell, they found Neapolitans eking out the most pitiful of livings. The injection of Allied food and funds – coupled with Allied reliance on underworld figures to get things done – served more to fuel the black market and crime than to put the city back on its feet.

Reconstruction was carried out in an unregulated, lawless fashion; in the early 1970s, an official enquiry found that almost none of the post-war buildings in the Naples area – a large majority of them horrendous eyesores – had acquired planning permission. Beset by local government corruption, high crime and unemployment rates, and decaying urban infrastructure, Naples had entered one of its darkest ages.

THE RETURN OF THE KING?

Although the monarchy was abolished in 1946, there is a pretender to the now-defunct throne. Vittorio Emanuele, Prince of Naples (Vittorio Emanuele Alberto Carlo Teodoro Umberto Bonifacio Amadeo Damiano Bernardino Gennaro Maria di Savoia, to give him his full title) claims to be the Prince of Naples, Duke of Savoy, and head of the House of Savoy. Having spent most of his life in exile, the Duke returned to Italy, only to become embroiled in charges of criminal association, corruption and exploitation of prostitution in 2006. He has denied all allegations, and in 2007 requested compensation from the State in return for the family's years of exile, and the restitution of the family's confiscated propertities. The city's turbulent history, it seems, refuses to stay buried.

Key Events

Campania in brief.

c1800 BC Vesuvius erupts, burying several Bronze Age settlements.
8th century BC Greeks arrive in Ischia, and develop Cuma as a trading centre.
470 BC Greeks found Neapolis as a further bulwark against the Etruscans.
326 BC Romans colonise Neapolis and the region, after a long siege.
73 BC Spartacus leads a slave revolt.
27-37 AD Emperor Tiberius reigns from his 12 villas on the island of Capri.
79 AD The eruption of Vesuvius buries Pompeii and Herculaneum.
476 Last Roman emperor Romulus Augustulus dies in Naples.
553 General Belisarius regains Naples for the Byzantine Empire.
568 Invading Lombards gain a strong foothold in Campania.
6th-8th centuries The coastal area is beset by Saracen corsair raids; Amalfi becomes an important maritime power.
1062-1140 Normans take the region, and establish the Kingdom of Sicily and Naples.
11th century Salerno becomes known as a centre of medical learning.
1194-1265 The Norman period gives way to Hohenstaufen rule.
1265-1435 Angevin (French) rule is establised for almost two centuries.
1442 Alfonso I establishes Spanish dominion.
1525-9 Italian noblewoman Vittoria Colonna establishes a brilliant salon of poets, philosophers and intellectuals on the island of Ischia.
1647 The Masaniello peasant revolt against Spanish rule is put down.
1656 Plague wipes out two thirds of Naples' 300,000 citizens.
1734 The Spanish Infante Carlo di Borbone ascends to the throne of Naples and makes the city his capital.
18th century Inexpert excavations begin at Pompeii and Herculaneum.
1752 The temples at Paestum are discovered during road-building.

1752-74 The Reggia at Caserta is built.
1759 King Carlo leaves Naples to assume the crown of Spain as Carlos III.
1768 Carlo's son, Ferdinand, marries the scheming Maria Carolina of Austria, who ousts reformers (1777), abetted by her English favourite Sir John Acton.
1799 Napoleon establishes the Parthenopean Republic, overseen by his brother Joseph.
1801-15 Joachim Murat, Napoleon's brother-in-law, rules as King of Naples.
1815 Spanish Bourbon rule returns in the shape of King Ferdinando I of the Kingdom of the Two Sicilies.
1860 Garibaldi enters Naples and the perennially royalist citizens vote in favour of the unification of Italy under a Savoy monarchy.
1884 A cholera epidemic sparks housing and infrastructure reform.
1897-1933 Capri becomes a magnet for an international array of writers, artists, aesthetes and libertines.
1940s World War II bombs ravage Naples' port and damage or destroy many of its architectural treasures and archives, along with most of the historic centre of Benevento.
1943 During the *Quattro giornate*, the local population rises up against German occupiers.
1944 Vesuvius's most recent eruption.
1949 Emilio Pucci invents 'Capri pants'.
1950s-70s Capri and the Amalfi coast attract the international jet set.
1970s Cholera breaks out in Naples.
1980 A severe earthquake in central Campania leaves some 3,000 dead.
1993-2000 Mayor Antonio Bassolino makes significant strides in improving the quality of life in Naples.
2008 A drawn-out rubbish disposal crisis is partially resolved by sending in the army.
Present Work continues on the new underground system; stations display international contemporary art.

IN CONTEXT

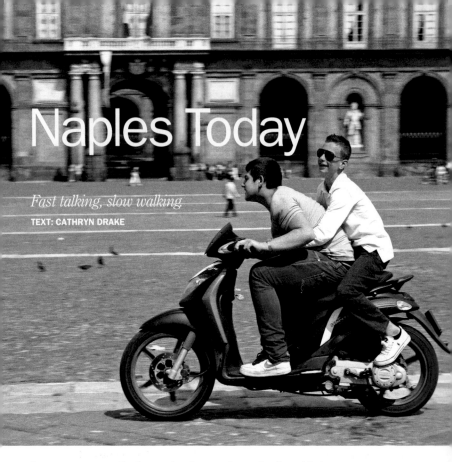

Naples Today

Fast talking, slow walking

TEXT: CATHRYN DRAKE

In contemporary Naples, splendour and squalor live side by side – both equally picturesque and exhilarating. Straddling dramatic hills overlooking the Mediterranean sea, with views to the craggy island of Capri and the dark outline of Mount Vesuvius inland, the city is characterised by grand Baroque churches and Pompeian red palazzi. Its patina of peeling elegance barely conceals a volatile, ritualistic underside.

Once the seat of a kingdom and the largest European capital after Paris, Naples has been a major centre of culture, high and low, since Greek times. Of late it has been known mostly for the seemingly unstoppable reign of the Camorra crime families, and the culmination of a rubbish disposal crisis – which caused a cholera epidemic in the city as recently as 1973. On the streets, these enduring undercurrents have manifested themselves in violent blood feuds and overflowing detritus, alongside visually florid religious processions and fetishistic altars adorning street corners.

A CONTEMPORARY RENAISSANCE

In 1993, Antonio Bassolino became mayor of Naples and, with a left-wing city council, ushered in a new political era, offering hope to the city's beleaguered citizens. The previous decade had seen Naples worn down by the worst misgovernment in its recent history, when political instability unworthy of even a banana republic meant administrations rarely lasted more than six months. These were the years of *Tangentopoli* (Bribesville), when public services were moribund across Italy and politicians didn't even begin to do what they were elected for. Nowhere was the fallout felt more keenly than in Naples: just 300 clapped-out buses served more than a million passengers, rubbish often lay uncollected on city streets for days on end, and few policemen were interested in taking control of the increasingly chaotic traffic.

A member of the post-Communist Democratic Left Party, Bassolino devoted his energies to changing Naples' abysmal reputation in Italy and abroad, largely through cultural and tourism initiatives. In this he was aided by the 1994 G7 meeting, held in Naples at the behest of Italian President Carlo Azeglio Ciampi. It was a brilliant coup: as the G7 leaders talked and strolled in the shadow of Vesuvius, the world was treated to stunning images of a freshly scrubbed city, every bit the magnificent old European capital. The following year the city was listed as a UNESCO World Heritage site, praised for its exceptional cultural value and outstanding setting on the Bay of Naples.

An extensive expansion of the transport system began in 1994, including new regional train lines and metro stations that incorporated striking contemporary art (*see p60* **Metro contextual**). While digging for a station in Piazza del Municipio, three Roman imperial ships and the port of the ancient city of Neapolis were discovered; exposed sections of the excavation will be a feature of the new underground station. In the meantime, an exhibition space in the metro walkway leading to the Museo Archeologico Nazionale displays the artefacts unearthed. In 2010, the Monte Sant'Angelo station, designed by Future Systems and artist Anish Kapoor, will open in Fuorigrotta, a largely modern quarter on the periphery of the city; meanwhile, architect Zaha Hadid has drawn up designs for the high-speed train station of Napoli Afragola, which will serve as a regional hub connecting the city to the south.

With the opening of two impressive contemporary art museums, the Palazzo delle Arti Napoli (PAN; *see p84*) and Museo d'Arte Contemporanea Donna Regina Napoli (MADre; *see p75*), and the increasing international presence of its commercial galleries, Naples has once again emerged as one of the cultural capitals of the world. Bassolino also cleaned up the city centre – notably the stately Piazza del Plebiscito, for years an ugly parking lot. His efforts attracted investors and tourists alike, and are still paying dividends: the number of visitors to Naples has leapt since his tenure, drawn to the region by its natural beauty, peerless archaeological remains and excellent cuisine.

TROUBLE IN MIND

Although Bassolino, now governor of Campania, improved the city's image and began to tackle the social issues that shape its darker side, he barely scraped the surface. In 2001 he was replaced by Rosa Russo Jervolino, Naples' first female mayor, who has carried on the struggle. However, the deeply-rooted social and political problems are not so easily remedied, and of late Naples has been like a city at war. Mafia gang wars came to a head in 2004, when the northern outskirts of Scampia and Secondigliano were littered with bodies, culminating in hundreds of arrests and a raid that involved more than 1,000 police officers. Citizens took to the streets in public demonstrations against the Camorra crime syndicate (*see p32* **Heart of darkness**).

By late 2007 Naples was submerged in an estimated 100,000 tons of refuse, after overflowing landfills were closed down. The city turned into a rat-infested, open-air rubbish dump, and residents again staged round-the-clock protests; newspapers reported that production of mozzarella, for which Naples is famous, had dropped due to dioxin in the Campanian soil. European Union officials criticised Italy for its poor

IN CONTEXT

Heart of darkness

Living in the shadow of organised crime.

American writer and academic Alexander Stille is the author of *Excellent Cadavers*, an investigation of the Sicilian Mafia and the execution of prosecutors Falcone and Borsellino, and *The Sack of Rome*, which examines the rise of Silvio Berlusconi.

Time Out (TO): How does the Mafia affect day-to-day life in Naples?
Alexander Stille (AS): In almost all of southern Italy, Naples included, in all kinds of ways. For example, around 90 per cent of buildings in southern Italy are built illegally. So who are the construction firms that build in an archaeological zone or on a protected coastline? Some might not be connected to organised crime, but plenty are. They are used to breaking the law and acting with impunity. So you have poorly constructed buildings in places where they shouldn't be; building on the side of Vesuvius, for example, doesn't happen without local Camorra groups allowing it to happen.

Why is the standard of living in southern Italy 30 per cent lower than in the rest of Italy? Even though it's a comparatively cheap labour market, nobody wants to invest there. Why? Because here's what happens: you decide to build a factory, and very quickly you'll have people telling you who to hire, which construction firm to use, where to buy cement, who is going haul away your trash… If you don't agree, suddenly you have all kinds of trouble: trucks blown up, tires slashed, intimidation. There is essentially a kind of Mafia or Camorra tax, which guarantees that doing business there will be expensive and unpleasant.

TO: Do unemployment levels have a lot to do with the phenomenen?
AS: It can be a help: it makes it easier to recruit inexpensive workers who are prepared to kill, steal or deal drugs for small amounts of money. But poverty alone doesn't guarantee organised crime; many parts of the world have high unemployment and no Mafia phenomenon. It's more to do with a demand or need for protection, and who can supply it. If you look at places like Afghanistan right now, where the state is very weak, local warlords are prepared to intimidate and use violence to dictate what happens; it's very much about the weakness of the state and an inability to apply the law in a thoroughgoing way.

TO: Do you think the Italian political system will ever be free from the hold of the Mafia?
AS: Giovanni Falcone, the great Mafia prosecutor from Sicily, said, 'The Mafia is a human phenomenon, and like all human phenomena has a beginning and an end.' Because the Mafia phenomenon was created by specific historical events, it is also kept going by specific political and socioeconomic structures. There will always be crime in some form or another, but the kind of crime that the Mafia and Camorra represent is something different, and is related to the conduct of the state. If the Italian state wants to do its job differently, it can get rid of the Mafia.

In recent history, there have been times when the Italian state got very serious about cracking down on the Mafia. In the early 1990s, they arrested thousands of Mafia people and had hundreds of witnesses working for the government. The Mafia was actually exploring ways to work out a kind of negotiated solution; they were practically ready to go out of business. And the political system came to their rescue: a bunch of people were elected to parliament and to heads of government who started systematically

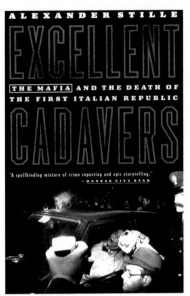

ALEXANDER STILLE

EXCELLENT

THE MAFIA AND THE DEATH OF
THE FIRST ITALIAN REPUBLIC

CADAVERS

"A spellbinding mixture of crime reporting and epic storytelling."
– KANSAS CITY STAR

drug smuggling; the Neapolitans have always been involved in smuggling operations and getting things in and out of customs. The Sicilians found that useful, and so they worked together – there was money to be made for everybody. These people are all in the same kind of business, so without stepping on each other's toes they can cooperate in international schemes that require investments: going in on a major drug shipment, say, and splitting the proceeds. That kind of cooperation has gone on for some time, but it's not integral to either organisation.

TO: Would you say that the Camorra is the most powerful of the Italian crime organisations?
AS: The Camorra may lead crime groups in terms of murders, but that's not necessarily a measure of that much; not having to kill people can be a sign that things are going very well for you and that you're very powerful.

What you can say, unfortunately, is that the Camorra in Campania, the 'Ndrangheta in Calabria, and the Sicilian Mafia are all incredibly powerful. They drag down a third of one of the great countries of Europe and the world. They represent a huge drain on the national economy – and, more tragically, a real stunting of the possibilities for people living in those regions. You cannot seriously entertain doing all kinds of things with your life, which is why you see many of the brightest people from these areas living in Rome, Milan, Paris, London or New York. Are you going to be a great architect operating out of Palermo? Or even a world-class doctor? There is a lot of evidence that the Mafia is deeply involved in hospitals because there is so much money in the healthcare system. It's a tragic situation, and one that has not been dealt with.

dismantling the Mafia legislation that had created all of this trouble for organised crime, and they [the Mafia] got out of the particular corner that they were in.

TO: Is the Camorra related to the Sicilian Mafia? What is the relationship between the two organisations?
AS: We know that they have worked together at certain moments, but most of these groups are very territorial. Mafia families have a certain territory, and you generally have Camorra groups that dominate a particular town or neighbourhood. They're highly localised, and derive their power from a rooted presence in a particular place.

They do have relationships with other groups, though. Back in the 1950s and '60s, the Camorristi and Mafiosi cooperated in cigarette and

IN CONTEXT

'In 2008, the Interior Minister announced that Camorra drug gangs had declared civil war on the state; 500 more soldiers were sent south.'

management of the long-coming disaster – also blamed on the Camorra, which has infiltrated the rubbish-collecting industry with its control of illegal dumps. Governor Bassolino and Mayor Jervolino, both from left-wing opposition parties, in turn accused Prime Minister Silvio Berlusconi's conservative government of skimping on proper law enforcement and neglecting the south financially.

Finally, in 2008, the newly re-elected Berlusconi fulfilled campaign promises by deploying army troops to stifle escalating mafia violence and clean up the mounds of trash. But by autumn, in response to the killing of several African immigrants, Interior Minister Roberto Maroni announced that the Camorra drug gangs had declared civil war on the state, and 500 more soldiers were sent south. Meanwhile, vigilantes torched Roma camps in the wake of a nationwide backlash against immigrants. The homicide rate in Naples was climbing once again, and mounting unemployment (less than half of the city's under-24s are employed) triggered a sense of insecurity and fear that undermined the recent civic improvements. To add insult to injury, in summer 2008 the Italian State declared the ancient ruins of Pompeii, Italy's most visited archaeological site, to be in a state of emergency due to deterioration resulting from vandalism, careless tourists and government budget cuts.

SUBLIME CHIAROSCURO

The Neapolitans (who live, after all, in the shadow of an active volcano) are accustomed to dramatic contretemps. The last time Mount Vesuvius erupted was in 1944, and although that's dangerously recent in geological terms, it doesn't stop people constructing illegal homes in its red zone.

Naples is decadent and Baroque in architecture and spirit. Unlike in the monumental showcase that is Rome, here the rich and poor live in close proximity, creating an intimate atmosphere of teeming humanity that seems more characteristic of North Africa than Europe – particularly in the warren of streets surrounding the city's central spine, referred to as Spaccanapoli. Passing through the narrow alleyways lined with ground-level apartments – strikingly reminiscent of Havana, in Cuba – you can see whole families at the dinner table, with the door thrown wide open.

It's a city that inspires, and even necessitates, ingenuity and a good sense of humour; Neapolitans are known for being inventive, feisty, and expressive. First-time visitors are invariably overwhelmed by the noise and motion, and dumbstruck when a motorcycle mounts the pavement to circumvent street traffic. Back alleys often feature Fellini-esque scenes – a drug addict losing consciousness against a wall but never quite falling, or a heavily painted prostitute in a polka-dot dress, straddling a motorcycle – which invoke a dreamlike sense of unreality rather than fear. You eventually learn to go native when, in a traffic jam, you ask the taxi driver if he wouldn't mind traversing into the oncoming lane, or heading down a one-way street the wrong way – and he complies without hesitation.

Although the drama and frisson of the Neapolitan streets is compelling, it unfortunately goes hand in hand with other, less charming realities, such as petty crime. Neapolitans are themselves not immune to the infamous *scippo* (scooter-propelled purse snatching), but tourists are especially easy targets, with their attention diverted on all sides by soaring church façades and frenetic traffic. The best protection is to use common sense: be attentive to what is going on around you and keep your

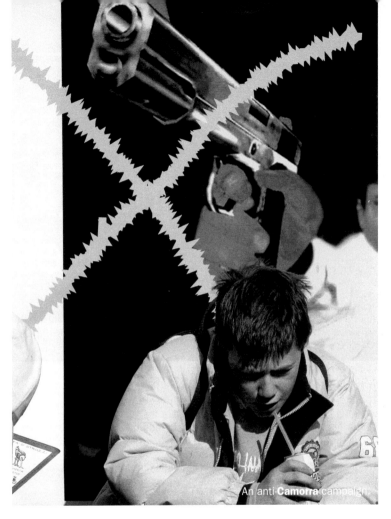
An anti-**Camorra** campaign.

bags close and away from the street. Visits to the lively, characteristic neighbourhoods of Sanità, Miracole and Vergini are best made in daylight; the fascinating and historic Quartieri Spagnoli, meanwhile, is home to some of the poorest of Naples' poor, with one of Europe's highest rates of unemployment. That said, it is extremely unlikely that visitors will be in any danger of serious violence, which is restricted largely to the high-rise apartment buildings of the northern suburbs.

The mass of contradictions that emerge from the meeting of Naples' auspicious beginnings with its troubled present are perhaps what make it such a fascinating place. Neapolitans are famous for their skilful sleight of hand in cheating you out of small change, yet a longstanding local tradition entails leaving enough money at the coffee bar to cover the next customer's espresso. You will rarely find so many willing or charming conversation partners on the streets of any other city, and Neapolitans in general, it seems, are always ready to help. The hope is that their resilient and endearing spirit will eventually bring more than just periodic interludes of peace to ancient Naples.

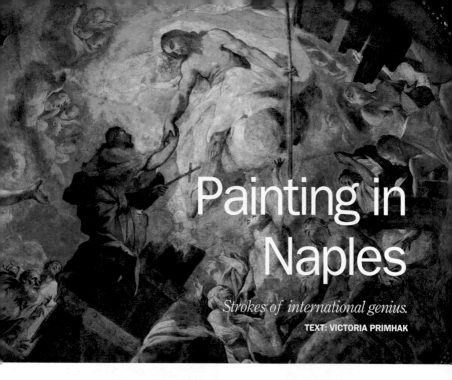

Painting in Naples

Strokes of international genius.

TEXT: VICTORIA PRIMHAK

If Naples' dramatic natural setting is a gift for landscape artists, the fluctuations in the city's fortunes have also left their mark on Neapolitan painting. Over the turbulent centuries, great artworks were commissioned and then lost – Giotto's frescoes in the Castel Nuovo, say, or some priceless Caravaggios – as tastes and rulers changed.

For centuries, the Church and ecclesiastical orders were the foremost patrons of art. Across the ages, though, the paintings in the city's churches have been neglected, stolen or damaged. In some cases, only what was hidden for centuries, underground or beneath layers of paint, survived; only in recent decades have serious restoration efforts begun.

The city's rulers also left their mark on Naples' artistic output. In the 17th century, the Spanish viceroys developed an insatiable appetite for local works; sadly, many of these left Naples with their owners. During his four-year term, Count Olivares amassed enough art to fill 40 ships; today, much of his collection graces the Prado in Madrid.

Naples' great families also put together private collections, many of which were broken up as noble fortunes declined in the 19th century. In a few cases, they were left to the state, and can now be found in the Museo di Capodimonte and the Certosa-Museo di San Martino, or religious institutions such as the Pinacoteca Girolamini and Pio Monte della Misericordia.

CLASSICAL ART

Naples and the Campania region are home to some of the world's greatest examples of classical art. Much of it – including mosaics from Pompeii and marble and bronze statues from Herculaneum – can be seen in the Museo Archeologico Nazionale (*see p70*). But there's plenty still in situ (or nearby). The frescoed slabs from the Tomba del Tuffatore (480 BC), now in the museum in Paestum (*see p296*), are the only surviving examples of classical Greek painting in Magna Grecia. The detail of two male lovers intent on their conversation in the banquet scene, and the image of the diver – perhaps symbolic of the sudden passage from life to death – have come to symbolise Greek culture in Italy.

The heights of Roman figurative art can be seen in the wall paintings in Pompeii (at Villa dei Misteri and Casa dei Vettii, *see p240*), with their warm, intense tones dominated by the russet-brown colour known as Pompeian red.

It is difficult, however, to spot a truly local tradition in these classical examples. Only with the coming of Christianity did Campanian art really take off, in the frescoes and mosaics decorating the catacombs of the city. The paintings in San Gennaro (*see p76*) date from the second century AD, when Christianity was a clandestine cult. The lack of a gold background, use of classical elements and figures collocated in space differentiate the local early Christian art from the Byzantine tradition, although the influences gradually mingled.

The domination of Naples by foreign powers was inevitably reflected in art. The arrival of the Angevins in the 13th century (*see p21*) led to an initial decline in local art, as painters and architects were imported first from France and then from other parts of Italy. **Pietro Cavallini** was brought from Rome; his refined use of colour and calm naturalism can be seen in the frescoes (1309) that decorate the Brancaccio chapel in San Domenico (*see p56*) and the church of Santa Maria Donnaregina (*see p63*).

Giotto arrived from Florence and worked as court painter from 1328 to 1334, decorating Castel Capuano (*see p58*), Castel Nuovo (*see p50*) and Santa Chiara (*see p56*). Though only traces of his own work remain, he influenced many local painters. His Neapolitan pupil **Roberto di Oderisio** (active 1340-70) continued Giotto's experimentation with space and perspective in the fresco cycle of Old Testament stories in Santa Maria Incoronata (*see p49*). In the same church, Oderisio offers an arresting glimpse of Angevin court life in *The Sacraments* and *The Triumph of the Church* (1352-54). But power struggles in the late 14th century halted the innovations

IN CONTEXT

San Domenico.

'Religious commissions were a counterpoint to a troubled period scourged by earthquake, volcanic eruption, epidemics, famine and riot.'

in Neapolitan art. Few examples remain from the period, in which the late Gothic style prevailed; the most notable are frescoes in San Giovanni a Carbonara (*see p75*) by **Leonardo da Besozzo** and **Perinetto da Benevento**.

The Renaissance touched Naples around 1450, with the advent of Alfonso of Aragon (*see p22*), who brought Aragonese and Catalan culture to the city. **Niccolò Antonio Colantonio** (active in Naples 1440-70), the most important Neapolitan painter of the 15th century, was to fuse the Flemish and Burgundian traditions left over from the last of the Anjous with the new Renaissance spirit. His extraordinary capacity for reproducing Flemish painting can be seen in *St Jerome in his Study* (1445) in Capodimonte (*see p78*); the tiny books on the shelves and the objects on the saint's desk need a magnifying glass to be appreciated properly.

In the early 16th century, Naples' Spanish viceroys were little more than transient bureaucrats, uninterested in commissioning art. The task of patronising the arts fell to the new monastic orders that arrived in the city from the 1530s. In the monasteries, emotional and tortured Mannerism dominated. The Mannerist style of the Sienese **Marco Pino** (c1525-c1587) can be seen in the brilliance of the twisted figure of Christ in San Domenico (1564, *see p56*); his later paintings for Santi Severino and Sossio (1571-77, *see p65*) were tempered by his knowledge of Spanish figurative painting.

A GOLDEN AGE

Counter-Reformation fervour and immense sums spent on building and decorating churches and monasteries provided a fertile climate for the golden century of Neapolitan art. Religious commissions were a counterpoint to a troubled period scourged by earthquake, volcanic eruption, epidemics, famine and riot, and the repressive regime of the Spanish viceroys.

Few of the founders of the so-called Neapolitan School were Neapolitan. **Michelangelo Merisi da Caravaggio** (*see p77* **Profile**), the most influential, fled to Naples in 1606. His theatrical intensity, stark naturalism and vivid contrasts struck a chord with the local passionate temperament. His super-realistic *Flagellation* (in Capodimonte) and *Seven Acts of Mercy* for the Pio Monte della Misericordia revolutionised the tired Mannerist tradition. He paved the way for the creation of a Neapolitan school of Caravaggisti. His follower **José de Ribera** (c1588-1652) was born near Valencia, but spent his working life in Naples (*see right* **Profile**). His sensational style and bold originality quickly caught on among the Spanish viceroys and religious orders, and his sadistic martyrdoms became the last word in religious taste. Ribera's taste for vivid narrative was sometimes grotesque, as in *Drunken Silenus* (Capodimonte), but he gradually developed an extreme pictorial elegance with refined colours, which can be seen in the *Pietà* (1637) in the Certosa-Museo di San Martino. In contrast, from the 1630s there was a move towards a neo-Venetian painterliness and Bolognese classicism, evident in the intimate works of **Massimo Stanzione** (c1585-1656), who was to decorate the most important Neapolitan churches, including the Certosa-Museo di San Martino, Gesù Nuovo (*see p55*) and San Paolo Maggiore (*see p63*).

Mattia Preti (1613-99) brought new life to the city in his four-year stay, by his use of light as the basis of composition. His extraordinary use of colour, light and shadow is best seen in the *Stories of the Lives of San Pietro Celestino and Santa Caterina di Alessandria*, painted for the nave of San Pietro a Maiella (*see p63*). Local boy **Luca**

Profile The art of backstabbing

Murderous machinations on the Neopolitan art scene.

Ribera's **Pietà**.

By all accounts, the immensely successful José de Ribera – also known as *Lo Spagnoletto*, the Little Spaniard – was also immensely ambitious and murderously ruthless. The story goes that he formed a tyrannical cabal with Greek-born Belisario Corenzio and Neapolitan Battistello Caracciolo, and that only with the group's consent could other artists work on religious commissions in the city. The plot thickened when it came down to securing the plum job of decorating the Cappella di San Gennaro in the Duomo.

The cabal's would-be competitors soon began suffering grievously. The commissioners first selected the noted Cavaliere d'Arpino, but he was assailed and forced to take refuge in the monastery of Monte Cassino. Then came Guido Reni; his assistant was

hurt in a mysterious attack, and told to pass the message on to his master. Nearly ready to give up after another choice simply disappeared with his two assistants, the commissioners had one more possibility in the person of Domenichino (a sensitive soul), winning him over with a handsome fee and a promise of protection.

Domenichino immediately became the target of an insidious assault, comprising threatening letters and slander; even the plasterers were bribed to ruin his frescoes by mixing ashes into the mortar. At one point Ribera convinced the viceroy to order some pictures from Domenichino, but Ribera had them carried off before they were finished, or, another tale relates, retouched and ruined them before the viceroy saw them. Finally, afraid for his life, Domenichino returned to Rome, until he was persuaded to return to Naples. He died there soon afterwards, having probably been poisoned.

In the end, however, the cabal failed to achieve its nefarious purpose. Caracciolo died the same year as Domenichino, the Greek two years later; and Ribera painted only one altarpiece for the chapel, *The Martyrdom of San Gennaro*. The decorations were ultimately completed by Giovanni Lanfranco, but Ribera reportedly indulged his malice in at least one other instance: he deliberately ruined Massimo Stanzione's *Dead Christ*, at the entrance of San Martino, under the pretext of cleaning it.

TO DIE FOR?
To see the talent that Ribera so envied, take a look at the frescoes in the Cappella di San Gennaro in the **Duomo** (*see p59*), painted by Domenichino before his untimely end.

Giordano (1634-1705), moving from airy, Baroque visions to iridescent rococo, dominated the scene for nearly 50 years. Known as *Luca fa presto* ('Luca does it quickly'), he was a prolific painter. He banged out thousands of paintings and, well into his 70s, completed the frescoes in the Certosa-Museo di San Martino in just a few days. **Francesco Solimena** (1657-1747) merged naturalism and the influence of Preti and Giovanni Lanfranco (1582-1647).

The **Certosa-Museo di San Martino** (*see p81*) is a magnificent compendium of Neapolitan Baroque. Artists vied for commissions from the fabulously rich but famously stingy Carthusian monks. With works by Caracciolo, Stanzione, Ribera, Lanfranco and Giordano, the chapel is a unique gallery of 17th-century Neapolitan painting.

Artemisia Gentileschi (1593-c1652), who lived in Naples from 1630 until her death, experimented with dramatic chiaroscuro effects. Her *Judith Beheading Holofernes* (Museo di Capodimonte) had a great impact on Neapolitan painting. (The victim of a well-publicised rape, Artemisia often dwelt on the theme of female vengeance.)

The flourishing, passionate atmosphere of the city affected its artists, most notably the larger-than-life **Salvatore Rosa** (1615-73), an artist, poet, actor and musician who painted romantic battle scenes, *banditi* and the poetic landscapes that were particularly popular in 18th-century England, creating a mythic view of the south of Italy, eagerly investigated by Gothic novelists and travellers on the grand tour.

CAMPANIA ON CANVAS

Landscape painting reached the height of its popularity in the 18th century, when the taste for the picturesque, the classical and the sublime made the spectacular scenery around Naples, the bay islands and the classical sites a must for the grand tourist (*see p24* **A rich cultural canvas**). The most popular image was the panoramic or bird's-eye view of Naples from the sea. Vibrant, lustrous portraits of the city painted in 1700 by **Gasper Van Wittel** (c1652-1736) – a few of which remain in the Certosa-Museo di San Martino – revolutionised landscape painting, with their synthesis of naturalism and the Dutch School. The warm Neapolitan light and local colour inspired him to combine reality and humanity in scenes like *Largo di Palazzo* and *Galleys in the Port.*

With the growth of Romanticism, foreign painters were drawn to lyrical, emotional Naples. Vesuvius fast became a favourite theme, embodying the heroic and diabolic in a blend of the picturesque and the sublime. Frenchman **Pierre-Jacques Volaire** (1729-1802) captured this spirit in his dramatic *Eruption of Vesuvius with the Bridge of the Maddalena*, now in Capodimonte. **Joseph Wright** of Derby (1734-97), known for his vivid experiments with light and shadow, also painted Vesuvius erupting.

Not all collectors wished to experience such strong emotions. A market grew for standardised, sentimental images of Naples in gouache. In the 19th century, artists expressed their individual, contemplative interpretations of the Bay of Naples. Dutchman **Antonio Pitloo** (1791-1837) infused his real-life landscapes (some now in the Certosa-Museo di San Martino) with natural colour and life, inspiring the Posillipo school. **Giacinto Gigante** (1806-76), many of whose works are in Capodimonte, was the leader of this school, where impressions of an idyllic landscape are depicted in delicate, romantic fashion. **Filippo Palizzi** (1818-99) continued to experiment, contrasting natural colours, light and contours (in the Certosa-Museo di San Martino).

Perhaps most interesting of all was the Welsh painter **Thomas Jones** (1742-1803). Having been a mediocre painter of British landscapes, Jones came to Naples in 1776 and stayed until 1783, during which time he painted a series of tiny pictures recording small, intimate details of the city. *A Wall in Naples* is nothing but that, with a hint of sky in the background some forgotten washing on a small line hanging from a tiny window. It's a scene that could have been painted yesterday. Almost anticipating later painters such as Edward Hopper in his evocation of daily life in almost deserted cityscapes, Jones is now considered to be one of the first modern painters; some of his paintings can be found in London's National Gallery.

Architecture

Every storey tells a story.

TEXT: VICTORIA PRIMHAK

The brooding silhouette of Vesuvius looms large over Naples and is visible for miles around. Look closer and you'll find its presence surrounds you in the stone of the buildings: the yellowish *tufo*, a soft eruptive stone, bombarded by volcanic gases, is the very fabric of the city; the grey-black *piperno* is fast-cooled lava, used in ornamental detail, and the darker *pietra lavica* is slow-cooled lava, slabs of which make up the roads. Besides the mighty volcano, countless settlers left their mark on Naples over the centuries, from the ancient Greeks to the Spanish; World War II bombs, unscrupulous property developers and earthquakes did their best to blow it all away in the 19th and 20th centuries.

Even before the modern age, Naples had major problems. By the 1500s, lack of space was one. Moving the city walls outwards failed to solve the problem, so Neapolitans built upwards instead. Within the crowded tenements, class stratifications governed the height that people lived at. The poor lived in tiny, street-level *bassi*, and the upper classes occupied the light, airy, first- and second-floor *piano nobile*.

Over the centuries, Naples' palazzi were subject to all sorts of tinkering, from the addition of low-ceilinged top storeys and jutting-out loos to the remodelling of ancient façades. As late as the 1960s, jerry-built extensions were crammed onto historic rooftops. The result is a fascinating hotchpotch. In this city of layers, every building tells the story of its people.

TRACES OF GREECE AND ROME

The temples in **Paestum** (*see p295*) and the sanctuary of the Sybil in **Cuma** (*see p93*) testify to the existence of thriving Greek communities in Campania. Nothing remains of the original settlement of Paleopolis, but the chequerboard plan of Neapolis (founded by the Greeks around the seventh century BC) can still be clearly seen from the belvedere of **San Martino** (*see p81*). The Roman *decumani* (main roads) – now Via Anticaglia, Via dei Tribunali and Spaccanapoli (*see p54*) – intersected from north to south by *cardines* (smaller roads), followed the original Greek layout. The Greek *agora* (marketplace, later the Roman forum) stood near today's Piazza San Gaetano; sections of the Greek walls can be seen just below street level in **Piazza Bellini** (*see p59*).

Centuries of construction have overlaid the remains of the Roman city, but they're still there: there's a fascinating glimpse of market life beneath **San Lorenzo Maggiore** (*see p61*) and the **Duomo** (*see p59*), and an area of Roman baths has been incorporated into the museum behind **Santa Chiara** (*see p58*). Other relics found their way into later buildings: two columns and marble bases from a temple to Castor and Pollux can be seen in the 16th-century façade of **San Paolo Maggiore** (*see p56*).

The kind of prosperous town-planning that passing centuries obscured in the city is very much in evidence at **Pompeii** (*see p239*) and **Herculaneum** (*see p234*). But the Campania Felix of the Romans is dotted with other, smaller reminders of the extent to which this region, with its mild climate and spectacular landscape, was prized in ancient times. There are sumptuous homes in **Castellammare di Stabia** (*see p244*), **Capri** (*see p196*) and near **Sorrento** (*see p249*), as well as temples at **Baia** (*see p92*) and vast amphitheatres in Pozzuoli and Capua Vetere.

CHRISTIAN BUILDERS

When Emperor Constantine embraced the cult of Christianity in AD 313, its followers came out of hiding and built places of worship near the burial sites of their early saints. Taking the Roman basilica (a meeting place with columned porticos outside) as their model, the Christians turned them sideways and inside out, putting the entrance at one end and the columns in the interior to form side aisles. Paleo-Christian basilicas can still be seen above the catacombs of **San Gennaro** (*see p76*) and in the fourth-century **Santa Restituta**, incorporated into the Duomo (*see p59*) in the 13th century.

During the early Middle Ages the real stratification of the city began, with new constructions going up above the Greek and Roman ones around the *agora* and forum in Piazza San Gaetano. These in turn made way for later buildings; nothing remains of the civic architecture of the period. Further south, the early Middle Ages are better represented: the religious architecture along the Amalfi coast, in **Ravello** (*see p286*) and **Salerno** (*see p292*), is a harmonious mix of Byzantine and Romanesque styles.

EARLY RENAISSANCE

In the 11th century, the Normans made Palermo the capital of their southern Italian kingdom, and Naples became a quiet political backwater. But the city expanded west towards **Castel dell'Ovo** (*see p52*) when Roger II made the castle his Neapolitan citadel, as well as inland when Roger's son William built **Castel Capuano** (*see p58*) to house his humanist court, peopled by artists and architects.

The new king chose **Castel Nuovo** (*see p50*) as his home, sending for the Mallorcan Guillermo Sagrera in 1449 to oversee alterations. Sagrera produced a trapezoid plan with five huge towers, inspired by similar buildings in Provence and Catalonia, and designed the Sala dei Baroni, with its magnificent, lofty vaulted ceiling. But the crowning glory of the early Renaissance in Naples was the **Arco di Trionfo**, a double arch flanked by Corinthian columns, celebrating the virtues and power of the Aragon dynasty, between the two high towers of the entrance to the Castel Nuovo. Its style is clearly Tuscan, showing just how quickly Sagrera's Catalan-Majorcan manner became interwoven with Italian influences.

The same Tuscan flavour was popular with Neapolitan nobles: **Palazzo Maddaloni** (Via Maddaloni 6), for example, has a Renaissance portal and a smooth, rusticated, yellow and grey *tufa* façade (contrasting with late Gothic elements such as the low arches in the courtyard, the vestibule and arch behind); the diamond-pointed rustication of the façade of the church of **Gesù Nuovo** (*see p55*) was originally the fortified front of a palace. The Tuscan influence reached its apex in the **Palazzo Gravina** and the Brunelleschi-style chapels in **Sant'Anna dei Lombardi** (*see p69*) next door.

SPANISH STYLE

The arrival of troops from the recently united Kingdom of Spain in 1503 changed the face of the city. The fortifications of Castel Nuovo were beefed up, a task that took 30 years, and a new city wall with polygonal bastions was built from Via Foria to Castel Sant'Elmo, and east along the seafront to protect Naples from attack from the sea.

In 1540, the most avid builder of all the Spanish viceroys, Pedro de Toledo, ordered an opulent new palace, more or less where today's Palazzo Reale stands. To cope with a chronic lack of housing (the population had almost doubled to 220,000 inhabitants in 50 years), he extended the walls to increase the city area by a third. Illegal shantytowns were razed to make way for new quarters, and an impressive thoroughfare, **Via Toledo** (*see p68*), was created to link the old and new parts of town. On the hillside to the west of Via Toledo, the **Quartieri spagnoli** (*see p68*) was built to house Spanish troops; as demand for housing grew, the single-storey dwellings rose to four or five floors.

THE BAROQUE

The extravagant flourishes of the Baroque appealed to the Neapolitan imagination, and few employed them more extensively than Cosimo Fanzago (1591-1678), the city's most prolific church architect, who spent 33 years revamping the **Certosa-Museo di San Martino** (*see p81*). The **Guglia di San Gennaro** (*see p58*) epitomises his decorative exuberance; the gruesome bronze skulls on the façade of the church of **Santa Maria del Purgatorio ad Arco** (*see p63*) show him in glummer Counter-Reformation mood.

The advent of the Bourbon dynasty in 1734 produced a rash of imposing civic buildings, which gave Naples a veneer of modernity without imposing any true order on its architectural chaos. Among the crop of ambitious architects was Fernando Fuga; only one-fifth of his design for the **Albergo dei Poveri** poorhouse (*see p72*) was ever completed, but even so it was Europe's largest civic construction. The restored central section provides a tantalising glimpse of his dream. Meanwhile, Giovanni Antonio Medrano designed the **San Carlo** opera house (*see p181*), which made Naples one of Europe's musical capitals, and the **Palazzo Reale** at Capodimonte (*see p78*). Luigi Vanvitelli gave the city the imposing Foro Carolino, today **Piazza Dante** (*see p69*), though his crowning glory – and perhaps the finest product of the Neapolitan Baroque – was the Reggia at **Caserta** (*see p301*) and its glorious gardens.

IN CONTEXT

Palazzo delle Poste e Telegrafi. *See p46.*

Profile Bombast bombed

Reduced to rubble by air strikes, the city's churches rose anew.

Art historians often lament the Baroque-ification of Romanesque, Gothic and Renaissance art and architecture – an overlay of over-the-top architectural flourishes that was the 16th-century product of Counter-Reformation zealotry, and an attempt to revive a Church that was losing its absolutist grip on the masses.

Santa Chiara.

Consequently, when the bombs of World War II blasted so many Neapolitan edifices to smithereens, some people may have seen it as an opportunity to undo the other, earlier sort of aesthetic damage. With realms of marble and stucco reduced to rubble, the complex elements of the Baroque vocabulary were beyond salvaging. There was little choice in some cases: it was either raze to the ground what was left of the structures, or restore them to their earlier, simpler style. The damage was significant; it was estimated at the time that some 40 important churches suffered a direct or indirect hit, resulting in near demolition. Yet within a year or so, projects to restore all 40 were already underway.

The most renowned of all the casualties, of course, was **Santa Chiara** (*see p56*). All that survived the blast were portions of its walls and a handful of its very earliest features, the rest consumed or irreparably charred by a fire that burned for days. Carefully restored according to the original plans, it now stands as one of the world's monumental

examples of Gothic architecture. A touch of Baroque remains; happily, Domenico Antonio Vaccaro's delicate and unique cloister of majolica tiles was spared, virtually untouched.

Other churches that suffered damage and have since been put right – albeit with significant nods to necessity – include **San Paolo Maggiore** (*see p56*), the **Gerolomini**, the **Santissima Annunziata** (*see p65*), which was built over an earlier foundation in 1760 by Vanvitelli, and **San Pietro Martire** (*see p67*), all of which were left with gaping wounds in their roofs or domes. The Renaissance church of **Mont'Oliveto** also suffered in the German aerial attack of March 15, 1944: the sculptured altarpiece by Benedetto da Maiano was a casualty, but a restorable one, as were Antonio Rossellino's relief of the Nativity and the monument to Maria of Aragon.

One of the greatest irreversible disasters, though, was the burning of the university: three works by Baroque artist Francesco Solimena were lost, and some 50,000 irreplaceable volumes were reduced to ashes.

A CITY IN CHAOS
For more on the war's devastating effects on the city, and the struggle to establish order in its aftermath, read *Naples '44*, written by British Intelligence Officer and writer Norman Lewis.

IN CONTEXT

Indeed, it was the Bourbon love of the countryside (and hunting) that gave the architects of the day their grandest canvas. Medrano began work on the Reggia at **Portici** (*see p234*), later to be replaced by Fuga and Vanvitelli; the royal palace sparked a building boom along the coast south of Naples, on the so-called **Miglio d'Oro** (*see p234*). The nobles' villas were built with two aspects – one up to the live volcano, the other down to the sea.

Two other 18th-century notables were Ferdinando Sanfelice and Domenico Antonio Vaccaro, who designed many of the city's private and religious buildings. Sanfelice's work was an organic but lively blend of decorative stucco and stonework that was imitated across the city. His staircases in **Palazzo Sanfelice** (*see p71*), **Palazzo Serra di Cassano** (*see p52*) and **Palazzo dello Spagnuolo** (*see p71*) are spectacular. Vaccaro's touch is best seen in the cloister of **Santa Chiara** (*see p58*), a splendid tiled affair in shades of blue and yellow.

SPECULATION AND 'RENEWAL'

In the early 19th century, the city's French rulers introduced neoclassical touches in **Piazza del Plebiscito** (*see p48*). This style was continued by Ferdinando I, on his restoration, in the church of **San Francesco di Paola** (*see p51*), which was designed by Pietro Bianchi. Nobles fled the crowded centre, building seafront palaces along the **Riviera di Chiaia** (*see p84*); up on the hill of Vomera, the simple, two-storey **Villa Floridiana** (*see p82*), with its English-style garden, was built for Lucia Migliaccio, the morganatic wife of King Ferdinando.

Urban renewal projects – designed to impose some order on Naples' haphazard development – degenerated into wholesale destruction of poorer but nonetheless historic areas of the old city centre. Set up with the best of intentions in 1839, the Consiglio Edilizio (building council) soon became a vehicle for rampant speculation. Clearance of the city's ancient slums started in Via Duomo, radiating out to the bay, and an entire nave of the basilica of **San Giorgio Maggiore** (*see p56*) was destroyed. Plans to hack a new road through the 15th-century **Palazzo Cuomo** sparked uproar; the philanthropist Prince Gaetano Filangieri financed the rebuilding of the façade 20 metres (66 feet) further back, at the same time designing the interior to accommodate his extensive art collection.

The eclectic, revivalist style of Anglo-Italian architect Lamont Young dictated the fashion in the late 19th century. His creations range from the neo-Gothic **Palazzina Grifeo** (Parco Grifeo 37) to the pseudo-Tudor **Castello Aselmeyer** (Corso Vittorio Emanuele 166). Young's sense of the weird and wonderful caught on. Neo-medieval and Chinese-style villas can still be seen along Via Posillipo, whereas art nouveau decoration flourished in buildings for the new, rich professional classes in **Vomero** (*see p79*) and Via dei Mille.

A cholera epidemic in 1884 gave unscrupulous speculators further scope. The Società per il Risanamento, owned by northern bankers, built straight, 'clean' streets by ruthlessly razing not only insalubrious slums, but 57 historic *fondaci* (merchants' yards, shops and lodgings) and medieval and Renaissance buildings. Before their destruction, the slums were recorded for posterity by painter Vincenzo Migliaro, whose works can be seen in the Certosa-Museo di San Martino (*see p81*).

Between the two world wars, the country's Fascist regime made its mark on Naples. The **Palazzo delle Poste e Telegrafi** (*see p68*), with its sleek black and white marble façade and rectangular steel windows, and other monumental public buildings in Piazza Matteoti, are prime examples of totalitarian art deco. The white Stazione Marittima was a paean to classicism, and the **Mostra d'Oltremare** (*see p96*), blending gardens, water features and exhibition spaces, extolled the regime's colonial pretensions. Rationalist architect Adalberto Libera built the groundbreaking **Villa Malaparte** (*see p198*) in 1939 on Capri, a brick-red house perched on a rocky promontory: a dramatic flight of steps led to a flat roof terrace, where its owner used to cycle.

IN CONTEXT

BOMBS, BUILDINGS AND... BOATS?

Allied bombs did immense damage to Naples' Centro Storico during World War II – as did the retreating German forces. Ironically, painstaking restoration work returned to the city such gems as the church of Santa Chiara, rebuilt to its original specifications and without its later Baroque trappings (see p44 **Bombast bombed**).

Elsewhere in the city, however, bomb sites gave way to a concrete jungle. Naples' sole skyscraper, the inappropriately named Jolly Hotel, which stands just off Piazza del Municipio, was permitted by Mayor Achille Lauro in the 1950s, as was the rebuilding of the railway station at Piazza Garibaldi. The havoc wreaked by construction magnate Mario Otieri inspired film director Francesco Rosi's searing indictment, *Le Mani sulla città* (*Hands Over the City*) of 1963. Not all postwar architecture was without charm, though. After the devastation of Santa Lucia, Giò Ponti, a pioneer of modernism, was hired to create the **Royal Continental** (see p108) in 1954 and, in 1962, the **Parco dei Principi** in Sorrento (see p257), now one of the world's hippest hotels. In **Vietri sul Mare** (see p284), the Ceramica Artistica Solimene, a ceramics factory designed by Paolo Soleri, a student of Frank Lloyd Wright, is an undulating wall of green and orange ceramic-covered columns.

Unregulated and unchecked, the concrete sprawl spread beyond the city limits, making the fortunes of ruthless property developers. In Portici, 18th-century villas were engulfed by modern apartment blocks, built in the shadow of the decidedly non-dormant Vesuvius. Huge council estates, built in the 1970s outside Naples to house the city centre's poor, became crime-ridden ghettos. Meanwhile, the coastline and islands were riddled by unlicensed villa development for holiday homes.

Gradually the tide turned, as local authorities started greening what was left or promoting ambitious renewal projects. Concrete carbuncles, such as some of Scampia's notorious tower blocks – named Le Vele ('the sails') after the shape of the buildings – have been knocked down, as has the incomplete Hotel Fuente on the cliffs of the Amalfi coast.

Sadly, Naples was wounded further by the 1980 earthquake – some historic buildings are still shored up with iron chains – and yet again the council turned a blind eye to building work in the rush to rehouse people, much of which remains in legal no-man's land.

HOPE FOR THE FUTURE

The 1980s brought an ambitious project to extend the city eastwards. However, the **Centro Direzionale** (see p95 **Centro Direzione**), designed by Japanese architect Kenzo Tange, was unappealingly isolated on marshy land near the city's prison and a derelict industrial area. Now home to offices, law courts and residential property, it was the intended site of the *municipio* and NATO's new Allied Forces Southern Europe HQ – but both ideas were summarily shelved, and many of the buildings remain underoccupied. By day it is still shiny and upbeat; after dusk it becomes dangerous.

Sustainable town planning is the buzzword for 21st-century Naples. Abandoned industrial buildings and warehouses on the seafront are being converted, and the central station is being given a serious makeover. The underground railway is being extended and embellished (see p60 **Metro contextual**), though progress has been partly impeded by the exciting – if problematic – discovery of Roman shipyards. In 2005, two museum developments brought a buzz to the city's art scene: **MADRe** (see p75), the museum of contemporary art, was created within the Donnaregina monastic complex, with Portuguese architect Alvaro Siza at the helm; and **PAN** (see p84) opened up in the 17th-century Palazzo Carafa di Roccella. A drive to rescue decrepit buildings and once-stately *piazze* has also changed the face of this long-suffering city, whose Centro Storico holds UNESCO heritage status for the unique beauty of its architecture. True to tradition, though, illegal building continues, and chronic air pollution threatens the fabric of Naples' buildings.

Sightseeing

Fontana dell'Immacolatella. *See p52*.

Royal Naples & Monte Echia **48**
  Monumental May 50
  Walk A right royal
    promenade 53

Centro Storico **54**
  Walk Passeggiata antica 57
  Metro contextual 60
  City of blood 62

The Port & University **64**
  Profile Santa Maria
    del Carmine 66

Via Toledo & La Sanità **68**
  Worshipful bones 73
  Green getaway 74

Capodimonte **76**
  Profile Caravaggio 77

Vomero **79**
  Funiculì, funiculà! 80

Chiaia to Posillipo **83**
  Sea Naples... 87

Campi Flegrei **88**
  Satyricon submerged 91

Suburbs & Elsewhere **94**
  Profile Centro Direzionale 95

Royal Naples & Monte Echia

Royal privilege and commanding sea views.

It was on the tiny island of Megaris, where the imposing **Castel dell'Ovo** now sits, that Naples was founded over 2,500 years ago. According to legend, that was where passing sailors found the body of the siren Parthenope, who drowned herself after being jilted by Ulysses. The mariners buried her on the rock, and the settlement of Parthenope or Paleopolis ('old town') was established. Megaris and Monte Echia were settled as a trading colony in 680 BC by Greeks from nearby Cuma; two centuries later, the settlers moved inland to found Neapolis ('new town').

For over a thousand years, this area was the centre of monarchic power. With the postwar demise of Italy's royal family and the relocation of many government offices to the Centro Direzionale, though, it has become a mishmash of historical sites, exclusive shops and low-rent housing. Still, it remains an important point of reference for making sense of the city.

Map p332	**Cafés, Bars &**
Hotels p99	**Gelaterie** p132
Restaurants p114	

ROYAL NAPLES

Start at the vast, neoclassical **Piazza del Plebiscito**. One of the most splendid *piazze* in Italy, if not Europe, until 1994 it was a grimy, oil-streaked expanse of tarmac used as a bus depot and car park. Restored to its former glory, complete with a new surface of local volcanic cobblestones, it's now traffic-free. This is a key site for major city events: concerts, political rallies, New Year's Eve parties, an annual Christmas art installation (*see p166*) and even a horse show in May.

The piazza is dominated by the church of **San Francesco di Paola** and the **Palazzo Reale** (for both, *see p51*). The semicircular colonnade with Doric columns that adorns this stately piazza was begun in 1809 under French ruler Joaquim Murat; San Francesco di Paola

was added later by the restored Bourbon monarchy in thanks for the end of the French occupation. The bronze equestrian statues of Bourbon kings Carlo III and Ferdinando I are by Antonio Canova.

Adjoining Piazza del Plebiscito to the north-east, Piazza Trieste e Trento is home to Naples' most elegant watering hole, the **Gambrinus** (*see p132*) – a favourite of Oscar Wilde. Guided tours to the underground 16th-century water system, the **Acquedotto Carmignano** (*see p50*), depart from here. Also in the square is the church of **San Ferdinando** (open 8am-noon, 5-7pm Mon-Sat; 9.30am-1pm Sun), which has scenes from the lives of illustrious Jesuits on its ceiling and some fine 19th-century marblework by Tito Angelini and the Vaccaros in the chapel in the left-hand transept.

Leading west out of the square, Via Chiaia is packed with clothes shops, which vary enormously in price and quality. Amorous athlete and supreme self-publicist Giacomo Casanova and the infinitely more serious German poet Johann Wolfgang von Goethe both stayed at the imposing **Palazzo Cellamare** (no.149; not open to the public) in the 18th century – though not at the same time.

Pedestrianised, shop-lined Via Toledo leads north from the square; on its right-hand side is the entrance to the magnificent **Galleria Umberto I**. This steel- and glass-covered cross-shaped arcade was completed in 1890, and generally compares favourably with its slightly older counterpart, the Galleria Vittorio Emanuele II in Milan; unlike its Milanese twin, the mosaic bull under the central dome has no testicles. The former sleazy air of the place has diminished, allowing visitors to better enjoy the elaborate neo-Renaissance decorations and fine engineering. During a World War II air raid, all the glass was blown out of the massive dome.

Heading east out of Piazza Trieste e Trento, Via San Carlo leads past the illustrious **Teatro San Carlo** royal opera house (*see p51* and *p180* **Profile**) and the gardens of the **Palazzo Reale** (*see p51*), and into the heavily congested **Piazza del Municipio**. On the southern side of the piazza rise the darkly majestic towers of the 13th-century **Castel Nuovo** (*see p50*). At its northern end, the early 19th-century **Palazzo San Giacomo** was built to house the massive bureaucracy of the Bourbon monarchs. Today, it's the headquarters of Naples city council, and a magnet for all kinds of protesters.

An easily missed door on the right of the palazzo leads to the charmingly royalist 16th-century church of **San Giacomo degli Spagnoli** (restoration currently in progress; open 10.30am-2pm Sun). Behind the altar, the tomb of Spanish viceroy Don Pedro di Toledo sits amid the crumbling remains of a very theatrical chapel. If you can find the sacristan, ask him for the keys.

The centre of Piazza del Municipio has long been a battleground of construction sites and archaeological digs. Work on the new metro

Piazza del Plebiscito.

line has been going for years; in 2004, workmen turned up the remains of the old Roman harbour and three ancient ships, which slowed things down even more. A massive urban renewal plan drawn up by Portuguese architect Alvaro Siza will eventually incorporate the metro platforms with subterranean restaurants, bars and shops; it also calls for a transparent, illuminated gallery that will cut a deep trench between Palazzo San Giacomo and the Stazione Marittima.

Via Medina is the original site of the impressive 15th-century **Fontana di Nettuno**; almost opposite the fountain stands the deconsecrated church of **Santa Maria Incoronata** (open 9am-5.30pm Mon-Sat). Adapted from a courthouse in the 14th century to commemorate the coronation of Angevin Queen Joan I, the church was reputedly a favourite with Petrarch, Boccaccio and Giotto. Inside, frescoes by Giotto's pupil Roberto Oderisi show scenes from the coronation.

On the opposite side of the street, the **Pietà dei Turchini** church (open 7-11am, 5-7pm Mon-Fri; 5-7pm Sat; 9.30am-1.30pm Sun) started life as a poorhouse, where children were dressed in turquoise shifts. The imposing police headquarters (*Questura*) at the end of the street on the left dates from the Fascist period, as does the post office beyond.

Fronting Castel Nuovo is the main port, Beverello, and the 1930s **Stazione Marittima**

INSIDE TRACK
HORSING AROUND

It is a tradition in Piazza del Plebiscito to close your eyes, with your back to the Palazzo Reale, and try to walk between the two bronze horses. It's not half as easy as it seems, due to the imperceptible slope of the piazza.

SIGHTS

SIGHTS

Monumental May

A sneaky peek behind closed doors.

Once a year, Naples' hidden historic gems open their doors to the public gaze. **Maggio dei Monumenti** (Monuments in May) is a glorious cultural beanfeast, still growing in stature, organisational finesse and international standing, despite the goofy-sounding 'themes' it has been saddled with in previous years.

It all began in 1994, when Naples' new mayor, Antonio Bassolino, started giving the city a much-needed shake-up, and the term 'Neapolitan Renaissance' was coined. Secondary schools were encouraged to 'adopt' abandoned monuments. There were plenty to choose from: palazzi, churches and miscellaneous sites galore were taken in hand by kids, who researched their history, cleaned them up, produced information sheets and showed guests around during open days, which were concentrated in May.

The idea took off, and was officially launched as Maggio dei Monumenti. Now even the most reluctant doors are prised open for rare chances to view the city's little-known treasures. From the last weekend in April until the first weekend in June, there are guided tours of monuments

Castel Nuovo.

and districts, open days, concerts and exhibitions in venues across the city.

The only problem is finding up-to-the-minute information on the programme (most events are at weekends) with sufficient notice to be able to plan your holiday. The city council's website, www.comune. napoli.it, is a good place at which to start. Alternatively, try the Osservatorio Turistico Culturale information office (Piazza del Plebiscito 14, 081 247 1123).

– the departure point for ferries for Sicily, Sardinia, North Africa and the islands. From the port, public transport heads west past the military and tourist harbour and run-down public gardens and through the smoggy Galleria della Vittoria tunnel; hop out at the end by the offices of *Il Mattino*, Naples' paper, and head into the Santa Lucia area (*see p52*).

Acquedotto Carmignano

Via Chiaia 1-2 (Bar Gambrinus) (081 400256/ www.lanapolisotterranea.it). Bus 24, C22, C82, R2. **Open** *Guided tours only* 9pm Thur; 10am, noon, 6pm Sat; 10am, 11am, noon, 6pm Sun. **Admission** €10; €5 reductions. **No credit cards. Map** p332 K12.
Naples' historic infrastructure extends for miles beneath the city centre, at a depth of 40m (130ft) and more. A maze of water ducts and cisterns dug into the rock during the 16th and 17th centuries, the Carmignano drainage system was developed under the Spanish viceroys; the volcanic *tufa* rock that was extracted was used to build the houses above. The tunnels were in use until the disastrous cholera epidemic of 1884, and also acted as air-raid shelters in World War II. Non-claustrophobes can take an hour-long tour; booking is not necessary.

★ Castel Nuovo (Maschio Angioino)

Piazza del Municipio (081 795 5877/081 420 1241). Bus C25, R2, R3. **Open** 9am-7pm Mon-Sat; 9am-2.30pm Sun. Last entry 1hr before closing. **Admission** €5; free under-18s, over-65s. **No credit cards. Map** p332 L12.
Called *nuovo* (new) to distinguish it from the older Castel dell'Ovo, this castle is better known locally as the Maschio Angioino (Angevin stronghold). It was built in 1279 by Charles of Anjou and used by subsequent Angevin monarchs as a royal residence and fortress. It also became a centre of arts and literature, attracting such illustrious characters as Petrarch, Boccaccio (some of the best tales of the *Decameron* are set in Naples) and Giotto who, in around 1330, frescoed the main hall and chapel.

Precious little of Giotto's work remains. The castle's current appearance is the result of radical alterations that were carried out by the Aragonese monarchs in the mid 15th century; the splendid triumphal arch was added for the entry into the city of Alfonso I 'the Magnanimous' of Aragon in 1443, a scene that is depicted in the relief above the portal. Subsequent changes to the interior decoration of the palace occurred during the reign of the Viceroy.

The castle has housed Naples' *museo civico* since 1992, with access via an internal courtyard after the ticket office. In the far left-hand corner of the enclosure, an area of glass flooring enables visitors to examine various ancient finds. These include the foundations and cemetery areas (replete with skeletons) of a convent that long pre-dates the castle itself. An adjacent staircase leads to the Sala dei Baroni, named after the mutinous barons arrested here while conspiring against King Ferrante in 1486 (*see p22*). Giotto's frescoes have disappeared; not so the unusual, umbrella-vaulted ceiling that now hovers dramatically over Naples City Council meetings.

The plain yet elegant Cappella Palatina, also shorn of its Giottos (bar tiny traces in the embrasure of the right-hand apsidal window), is the only section that remains from the Angevin period.

The *museo civico* is housed on two floors. The first contains paintings from the 15th through to the 18th century, with much local colour; the second 19th- and 20th-century works by Neopolitan artists. There's also a fine bronze door, commissioned in 1475 by the Aragonese to commemorate their victory over the Angevins (the embedded cannonball probably dates from a sea battle off Genoa in 1495, when the door was being shipped to France). Don't miss the views from the fortress towers, accessible by lifts.

★ Palazzo Reale

Piazza Trieste e Trento/Piazza del Plebiscito 1 (081 580 8111/081 400547/www.palazzoreale napoli.it). Bus 140, 152, C18, C19, C12, R3. **Open** 9am-7pm Mon, Tue, Thur-Sun (last entry 6pm). **Admission** €4; €2 reductions; free under-18s, over-65s. **No credit cards. Map** p332 K13.
Work on the Royal Palace started in 1600, under the rule of the Spanish viceroys, by Neapolitan architect Domenico Fontana. The bulk of the palazzo was completed in two years, although a number of features (such as the staircase) were added 50 years later. The Bourbon monarchs had the building extended eastwards in the mid 18th century, when niches were added to the façade. Under French rule in the early 19th century, the interior took on its current neoclassical appearance, and the hanging gardens and statues of Naples' kings were added later that century.

The ticket office is on the left-hand side of the portico that skirts Piazza del Plebiscito, with access to the 30 royal apartments through the well-appointed bookshop. The apartments, overwhelming in size and number, house a collection of paintings (interesting for their portrayal of Neapolitan rulers and customs), frescoes, tapestries, chandeliers and furniture from the 17th to the 19th centuries. The gilt-and-stucco ceilings are impressive, as is the gloriously ornate Teatrino di Corte (1768), a private theatre. The pleasant roof garden features flowerbeds, fountains and neoclassical benches.

The Palazzo Reale also houses the Biblioteca Nazionale (081 781 9111, www.bnnonline.it) national library, with its grand reading rooms and collections of manuscripts and musty books, some dating to the fifth century. There's also a tourist office just off the

Cortile d'Onore, open on weekdays only and stocked with excellent leaflets for a number of sites and events in Naples. The gardens within the palace complex, dotted with modern sculpture, offer a quieter alternative to the nearby Giardini Publici.

FREE San Francesco di Paola

Piazza del Plebiscito (081 764 5133). Bus 24, C22, C82, R2, R3. **Open** 8am-noon, 3-5pm daily. **Admission** free. **Map** p327 J13.
One of Naples' neoclassical rarities, San Francesco is surprisingly unpopular with the locals. Flanked by curving colonnades reminiscent of Saint Peter's square, the church itself is an imitation of Rome's Pantheon. It was erected in 1817 by King Ferdinando, in thanks for the repossession of his kingdom after the period of French rule. It takes its name from a saint who, conveniently, came from the town of Paola in Calabria, near to where Joaquim Murat – Napoleon's brother-in-law and Naples' king from 1808 to 1815 – had been shot by Ferdinando's police after an ill-fated attempt to lead an Italian uprising. The apex of the dome stands 53m (174ft) above the ground – ten metres higher than its Roman counterpart.

★ Teatro San Carlo

For listings, see p181.
The original San Carlo theatre was built in 1737 in just eight months, to a design by Giovanni Medrano; after it burned down in 1816, it was rebuilt in less than a year. Second in prestige only to Milan's La Scala, the San Carlo has lavish decor with acres of red velvet and intricate gilded stucco moulding, and an unusual revolving clock in the vault of the proscenium arch. A century and a half ago, foreign tourists complained of the noise during performances; in the boxes, the local aristocracy would chat, eat meals and play cards. Twenty-minute guided tours, organised by Itinera (www.itineranapoli.com), are available by reservation, subject to rehearsals and performances. Alternatively, put on your poshest togs and catch a performance (*see p181*).
► *For more on San Carlo's history, see p180.*

MONTE ECHIA & AROUND

Rising to the south-west behind Piazza del Plebiscito is **Monte Echia**, the remains of the crater rim of an extinct volcano and the site of ancient Paleopolis. It's a 20-minute walk from Piazza del Plebiscito up Via Egiziaca a Pizzofalcone and salita Echia to the scruffy public gardens on top of Monte Echia. From the terrace here, you can see the sinister observation posts of the modern police headquarters and bask in a rather cluttered but glorious view of one of the cradles of Western civilisation.

On the northern side of the hill, the Pizzofalcone district is home to more military and police establishments, including the **Nunziatella** military academy, with its

SIGHTS

INSIDE TRACK
COMING DOWN THE MOUNTAIN

The easiest way to ascend Monte Echia is by taking the free lift, tucked behind a newsstand towards the eastern end of Via Chiaia. If you go up for dinner, though, be warned that the service stops at 10.30pm – after which you'll have to walk down under your own steam.

Baroque church (*see below*), and the rather melancholy-looking Palazzo Serra di Cassano. Here, too, are the early 17th-century churches of **Santa Maria degli Angeli** (Largo Santa Maria degli Angeli, 081 440756, open 5-7pm daily) and **Santa Maria Egiziaca a Pizzofalcone** (Via Egiziaca, 081 764 5199, open 10am-1pm, 5.30-7.30pm Mon-Sat; 5.30-7.30pm Sun). The former has an enormous dome, not immediately visible from the road, a splendid barrel-vaulted ceiling and, in the first chapel on the right, two marble reliefs by Tito Angelini.

From Monte Echia, the rampa di Pizzofalcone zigzags down towards the Castel dell'Ovo. On the seafront, Via Partenope and Via Sauro skirt the Santa Lucia district (*see below*), then pass by Pietro Bernini and Michelangelo Naccherino's **Fontana dell'Immacolatella** (1601) and back to Piazza del Plebiscito (*see p48*). Savour Naples' briny side as you inhale seafood smells wafting from the extractor fans of the waterfront restaurants and admire the yachts packed into the marina on the island of Megaris.

FREE Castel dell'Ovo
Via Partenope (081 240 0055). Bus 140, C24, C25, C28, R3. **Open** 8.30am-7.30pm Mon-Sat; 8.30am-2pm Sun. **Admission** free. **Map** p332 K15/16.

The castle you see today is the result of 1,000 years of military occupation, beginning in Norman times. The Aragonese gave the fortress its present look in the 16th century: prior to that, a monastic community lived here. Earlier still, it was part of the estate of Roman general Lucullus. When the poet Virgil stayed here in the first century BC, local legend recounts he buried an egg (*uovo*), predicting that when the egg broke disaster would strike – hence the castle's name.

After crossing the bridge, pass through the main portal and either climb up to the right, or bear left along to the far end of the *mole* (breakwater), where the gun emplacements used to stand. It's a strangely deserted spot, with Naples almost completely hidden from view by the castle. The rooms leading off the long climb up the ramp inside the castle itself are a mix of offices and exhibition areas; some are still being excavated and restored, and for the moment are only visible through glass.

FREE La Nunziatella
Via Generale Parisi 16 (081 764 1520). Bus C22. **Open** 9-10am Sun for Mass; by appointment at other times. **Admission** free. **Map** p327 J14.

Also known as Santa Maria Annunziata a Pizzofalcone, this pocket-sized Baroque jewel belongs to the adjacent military academy, founded by the Bourbon royal family in 1787. Originally built in the 16th century, La Nunziatella was redesigned by Ferdinando Sanfelice in 1737, gaining a harmonious blend of painting, sculpture and inlaid marble embellishments. Note the 18th-century marble altar by Giuseppe Sammartino.
▶ *For more on architect and painter Ferdinando Sanfelice, see p45.*

FREE Palazzo Serra di Cassano
Via Monte di Dio 14 (081 245 2150). Bus C22. **Open** by appointment only. **Admission** free. **Map** p327 J13.

It's hard to get a proper view of the trim façade of this 18th-century palazzo, hemmed in as it is by other buildings. One of the high points in Ferdinando Sanfelice's architectural career, it has a no-nonsense double stairway in cool grey volcanic stone, with a beautifully cut marble-pillared balustrade. The apartments feature fine frescoes and original furniture. The main entrance in Via Egiziaca was closed in 1799 by the Prince of Cassano in mourning for the death of his son Gennaro, one of the leaders of the short-lived Parthenopean Republic (*see p17*). Gennaro was beheaded in Piazza del Plebiscito, and the entrance, which at the time enjoyed an unobstructed view of the Royal Palace, remained closed until bicentenary celebrations in 1999. The palazzo is now the headquarters of the Italian Institute for Philosophical Studies.

SANTA LUCIA

Via Santa Lucia and Via Chiatamone wind through Santa Lucia, where the backstreets of the old fishermen's quarter, the **Pallonetto**, rise up towards Pizzofalcone. Its pavement cafés and restaurants make the neighbourhood an appealing shortcut or pit-stop between the Castel dell'Ovo and Piazza del Plebiscito.

The church of **Santa Lucia a Mare** on Via Santa Lucia (open 7am-noon, 5-7pm Mon-Sat; 7am-1pm, 5-7pm Sun) was rebuilt after its 19th-century predecessor was bombed during World War II; a church has stood on this site since the ninth century. Further up the street on the right is the tiny **Santa Maria della Catena** (Via Santa Lucia 12, open 8-10.30am Mon-Sat; 8.30am-1pm Sun). To the left of the altar is the tomb of Francesco Caracciolo; one of the leaders of the Parthenopean Republic (*see p17*), he was hanged on the orders of Admiral Nelson.

SIGHTS

Walk A right royal promenade

Take a stately stroll though history.

Begin at the **Castel Nuovo** (see p50), peering through the fence down into the archaeological digs next to the castle for a glimpse of the ancient city's port. Leaving Piazza del Municipio behind you, head along Via Santa Brigida, ducking into the massive **Galleria Umberto I** (see p49) and on to the famous **Teatro San Carlo** (see p51).

On your way, check out the gardens of the **Palazzo Reale** (see p51) or visit the royal apartments. Swing around to the front of the palace, where you will feel dwarfed by the kingly effigies lined up along its façade, as well as by the sprawling Piazza del Plebescito. After a peek into the church of **San Francesco di Paola** (see p51), cross the square to Via Cesario Console. Here, a narrow park looks over the Giardini Pubblici and across the bay to Mount Vesuvius.

Follow the curving Via Nazario Sauro along the seafront, and you'll arrive at the scene of the classic Naples stroll: past luxury hotels, the **Castel dell'Ovo** (see p52) and **Megaris** (see p48), and into the gardens of the **Villa Comunale** (see p85), rife with classical statuary. Take your time and stop for refreshment in one of the bars along the way.

When you come to the **Acquario** (see p84), exit the Villa on the city side and follow Via San Pasquale a Chiaia into the upmarket district of Chiaia (see p83). Keep heading upwards until you get to picturesque Piazza Amedeo. From here, you can take the Funicolare up to the Vomero neighbourhood (see p79) or, alternatively, stroll back along the chic Via dei Mille to Piazza dei Martiri, and eventually back to Piazza del Plebescito and on into the Centro Storico.

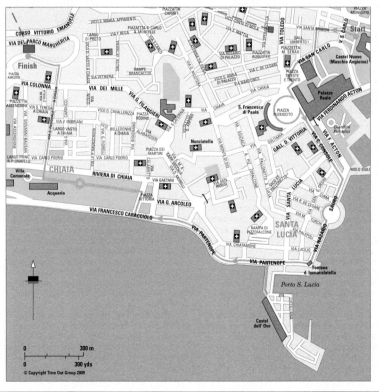

SIGHTS

Centro Storico

The ancient heart of an (almost) modern city.

The Centro Storico (historical centre) is
actually more of a *centro antico* (ancient
centre), thanks to the antiquity of the
orderly, grid-like plan on which this
part of the city was built. The three
decumani (main streets) that run
arrow-straight from east to west,
intersected from north to south by
cardines, faithfully follow the Greek
and Roman layout. The Spaccanapoli
is the ancient *decumanus inferior*, which
lay at the heart of Neapolis; where
tourists now tread, Romans once
walked, and Greeks before them.

The Angevins concentrated their
construction fervour here when Naples
became their capital in the 13th century,
and huge churches soared above lowly
houses. Today, the area is packed with
sightseers, necks craning to glimpse the
detail of decrepit palazzi, amid stalls selling second-hand books, joss sticks
and religious paraphernalia.

Map pp328-329
Hotels p101
Restaurants p116

Cafés, Bars &
Gelaterie p132

SPACCANAPOLI

Spaccanapoli is the central axis of old Naples,
changing its name as it flows along (on its
way, it incorporates vie Domenico Capitelli,
Benedetto Croce, San Biagio dei Librai and
Vicaria Vecchia). It divides the district in an
uninterrupted line – hence its collective name,
which means 'splits Naples'. Most of the street
is pedestrianised, and packed with tourists,
students and shops. The line-up ranges
from bookshops, bookbinders and musical
instrument stores (especially along Via
San Sebastiano, which runs towards the
Conservatorio di Musica, *see p183*) to
souvenir shops and fast food outlets.

Towards the western end of Spaccanapoli,
the Piazza del Gesù features a towering rococo
obelisk, the wonderfully ornate **Guglia
dell'Immacolata** (1747-50). The piazza is
surrounded by elegant palazzi (Degas was
a frequent visitor to the private Palazzo
Pignatelli di Monteleone at calata Trinità
Maggiore 53) and is overlooked by the unusual

façade of the church of **Gesù Nuovo** (*see right*)
and the apparently lopped-off bell tower of
Santa Chiara (*see p56*).

The short stretch of Spaccanapoli called Via
Benedetto Croce, named after the Neapolitan
philosopher and historian (1866-1952), is
crammed with prestigious palazzi. Croce's own
home, **Palazzo Filomarino** (no.12), has two
14th-century arches walled into the left-hand
staircase, and a courtyard portico that dates
from the 16th century. Look out for the late
16th-century doorway at the **Palazzo Carafa
della Spina** (no.45), guarded by a pair of
marble, lion-like creatures (their open mouths
were used to snuff out torches), with fauns
frolicking above the portal.

Work on the **Guglia di San Domenico**
in Piazza San Domenico began in 1658 in
thanks for the end of a plague epidemic, but
was only completed 99 years later. The piazza
is dominated by fine 16th- and 17th-century
palazzi (closed to the public), including the red-
ochre **Palazzo Corigliano** (no.12), **Palazzo
Casacalenda** (no.16) and **Palazzo Sangro**

Gesù Nuovo.

(No.9), in addition to the 13th-century church of **San Domenico Maggiore**. A short jaunt north past the Guglia to the Vico San Domenico leads to the funerary chapel of **Cappella Sansevero** (*see below*), home of sublime sculptures and creepy anatomical artefacts.

Before becoming Via San Biagio dei Librai, Spaccanapoli crosses piazzetta Nilo, site of the little church of **Sant'Angelo a Nilo** (*see p56*), which houses the only work by Donatello in Naples. In a small square by the church, a statue of the Nile god dates from Roman times, when Egyptians lived in this area.

Further down Via San Biagio dei Librai, at no.114, the **Monte di Pietà chapel** (open 9am-7pm Sat, 9am-2pm Sun) has statues of Safety and Charity by Pietro Bernini in its façade, and a 17th-century frescoed ceiling by Belisario Corenzio. At no.39 is the **Palazzo Marigliano**, with a carefully renovated façade from 1513 and a fine coat of arms; steps at the back of the courtyard lead to an 'invisible' garden (open 10am-2pm Mon-Fri).

The massive bulk of the church of **San Giorgio Maggiore** (*see p56*) stands where Spaccanapoli crosses Via Duomo. To the north on Via Duomo is the **Museo Civico Filangieri**, which has been closed for years for restoration. Its collections include applied art, armour, weapons and sculpture.

East of Via del Duomo, Spaccanapoli becomes Via Vicaria Vecchia, and passes the pretty church of **Sant'Agrippino** (no.86; still closed after flood damage in 2001). It was almost destroyed in World War II, but the delicate 13th-century arches in the apse have been salvaged, and furnishings from the now-derelict Santa Maria a Piazza (Via Forcella 12), which stands opposite, have been moved here.

★ Cappella Sansevero

Via Francesco de Sanctis 19 (081 551 8470/www. museosansevero.it). Metro Dante or Montesanto/ bus C57, R2, 24. **Open** 10am-5.40pm Mon, Wed-Sat; 10am-1pm Sun. **Admission** €6; €4-€5 reductions; free under-9s. **No credit cards. Map** p328 M8.

The funerary chapel of the Di Sangro family was built in 1590, but took on its current appearance in 1749-66, thanks to the eccentric prince of Sansevero, Raimondo di Sangro, who hired the leading sculptors of the day to decorate it. The high altar is carved in accordance with the then-fashionable 'picture hewn out of stone' criterion; the statues have titles like *Domination of Self-will*, *The Pleasures of Marriage* and *Shyness*. The *Veiled Christ* (1753), by Giuseppe Sammartino, is uncanny in its realism; so impressed was neoclassical sculptor Antonio Canova when he visited the chapel that he tried to buy it. The figures in the crypt, meanwhile, are downright macabre. Obsessed with embalming, the prince supposedly carried out experiments on defunct domestics, injecting their bodies with chemical substances to preserve them. Local lore has it that they were not always dead when the operations took place. By another account, the figures are only models – though no one can say exactly what they're made of.

FREE Gesù Nuovo

Piazza Gesù Nuovo (081 557 8111/081 557 8151). Metro Dante or Montesanto/bus E1, R1. **Open** 7am-12.30pm, 4-7.30pm daily. **Admission** free. **Map** p328 L9.

Embellished with diamond-shaped stonework, the façade of this extraordinary church was part of a 15th-century palazzo, before being transformed into a church for the Jesuit order at the end of the 16th century. The portals, windows and external decorations date from the conversion. Inside is a stupendous barrel-vaulted ceiling, and a dome that has been rebuilt several times. The inner façade has a large fresco (1725) by Francesco Solimena, and the ceilings and walls are a treasury of frescoes and paintings, with works by Giuseppe Ribera and Luca

---

INSIDE TRACK
DIVINE LANDMARKS

Look out for the city centre's three eye-catching *guglie* (spires), exuberant Baroque obelisks giving pious thanks for disasters averted through divine intervention. The first can be found on **Piazza del Gesù**, the second on **Piazza San Domenico** (for both, *see left*), and the third on **Piazza Cardinale Sisto Riario Sforza** (*see p58*).

San Domenico Maggiore

Giordano and marble statues by Cosimo Fanzago.
A large, busy room on the right-hand side of the
church is dedicated to Giuseppe Moscati (1880-1927),
who was canonised in 1987. The ex-votos covering
the chapel walls give an indication of local faith in
the miracle-working doctor, who treated the poor for
free and cured a man with terminal meningitis.

FREE San Domenico Maggiore
*Piazza San Domenico Maggiore 8A (081
459188/081 442 0039). Metro Dante/bus C57,
R2.* **Open** *Church 8.30am-noon, 4.30-7pm daily.
Treasury 4.30-7pm Fri; 9.30am-noon, 4.30-6pm
Sat; 10am-noon Sun.* **Admission** *Church free.
Treasury €3.* **Map** p328 L8.
This vast, castellated church has an extraordinary
rear entrance, with a curved double flight of marble
steps leading up from the piazza. However, it is best
entered from the side street, Vico San Domenico.
Here, the porticoed entrance dates from the late 13th
century, when the church was built, incorporating
the pre-existing church of Sant'Angelo a Morfisa.
The chapels include some fine works of art: 13th-
century marble tombstones (the first chapel on the
right); 14th-century frescoes by the great and
unjustly neglected Roman artist Pietro Cavallino
(second on the right); and a couple of paintings by
Mattia Preti (fourth on the right).

The Neapolitan headquarters of the Dominican
order, the monastery played host to the hermeticist
philosopher Giordano Bruno (burnt at the stake for
heresy in Rome in 1600), who studied here, and St
Thomas Aquinas, to whom the sixth chapel on the
right is dedicated. The figure of Jesus in the 13th-
century Crucifixion over the altar is said to have spoken to Thomas, offering him anything he wanted in
return for the nice things the saint had written about
Him. To this, Thomas replied, 'Nothing, if not You'.

The luminous sacristy has a fine ceiling fresco by
Francesco Solimena and a bizarre set of coffins; their
contents include the decapitated body of a victim of
the barons' conspiracy of 1486.

FREE San Giorgio Maggiore
Via del Duomo 237A (081 287932). Bus E1, R1.
Open 8am-noon, 5-7pm Mon-Sat; 8am-1pm Sun.
Admission free. **Map** p328 L8.
The original fourth-century basilica was built by St
Severus (364-410), when this area of Naples was
occupied by descendants of families driven out of
their homes by the AD 79 eruption of Vesuvius.
Severus's relics are behind the altar; his splendid
marble throne is to the right of the main aisle. The
vestibule, with its three Byzantine-Roman arches (at
the entrance in Piazzetta Crocelle ai Mannesi), was
the apse of the original basilica, and the only part
that survived an earthquake in 1640. Subsequently,
architect Cosimo Fanzago rotated the floorplan by
180°, placing the 17th-century apse and main altar
at the opposite end of the church.

★ FREE Sant'Angelo a Nilo
*Piazzetta Nilo (081 420 1222/081 551 6227).
Metro Dante or Montesanto/bus C57, R2.* **Open**
9am-1pm, 4.30-7pm Mon-Sat; 9am-1pm Sun.
Admission free. **Map** p328 M9.
Also known as the Cappella Brancaccio, on account
of its association with the family of that name, this
church contains the fine marble tomb of Cardinal
Rinaldo Brancaccio. Housed in a chapel to the right
of the altar, it was made in Pisa in 1426; Donatello
had a hand in its creation. The fine bas-relief portraying the Assumption on the front of the tomb,
the cardinal's head and the right-hand caryatid (a
column shaped like a person) are the only works by
the Tuscan artist in the whole of Naples. There's a
delicate bell tower, but it's quite difficult to see from
the narrow street.

FREE Santa Chiara
*Via Benedetto Croce (081 797 1235/museum
081 551 6673/www.monasterodisantachiara.eu).
Metro Dante or Montesanto/bus C57.* **Open**
*Church 7.30am-1pm, 4.30-8pm daily. Museum
& cloister 9.30am-5.30pm Mon-Sat; 10am-2.30pm*

SIGHTS

Walk Passeggiata antica

Treasures at every turn.

In a city so densely endowed with artistic treasures, the phrase 'so much to do, so little time' becomes a very real predicament. Our two city walks (for the other, *see p53*) attempt to provide a basic orientation as a context for further, in-depth exploration.

Piazza Dante is a good place from which to begin taking in Naples' historic centre. From here, head south along Via Roma and follow Via Sant'Anna dei Lombardi to Via Domenico Capitelli. This is the first stretch of **Spaccanapoli**, the age-old *decumanus* whose name seems to change every 50 metres. Pop into the churches of **Gesù Nuovo** (*see p55*) and **Santa Chiara** (*see left*), before making for **San Domenico Maggiore** (*see left*). Pause in the shadow of this medieval edifice for a *sfogliatella* and *caffè* at **Scaturchio** (*see p133*).

On weekends, head into the **Monte di Pietà Chapel** (*see p55*) in the Banca di Napoli, ready to be bowled over by its

Baroque opulence. Further along, at the intersection of Via San Biagio dei Librai and Via del Duomo, take a left and cross the street to explore the **Duomo** (*see p59*).

Back on Via del Duomo, take Spaccanapoli's parallel road, Via dei Tribunali, back towards Piazza Dante. The churches of **San Lorenzo Maggiore** (*see p61*) and **San Paolo Maggiore** (*see p63*), splendid in their own right, sit above subterranean archaeological sites worthy of exploration. Further along Tribunali is the intriguing church of **Santa Maria del Purgatorio ad Arco** (*see p63*), where a cult of the dead flourished for generations; indeed, aspects of it still linger on (*see p73* **Worshipful bones**). At the end of the street, follow Via Santa Maria di Costantinopoli, with a long pause in lovely Piazza Bellini, before ending your stroll in the wonderful **Museo Archeologico Nazionale** (*see p70*).

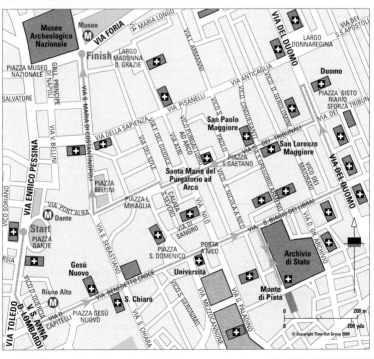

Sun. **Admission** *Church* free. *Museum & cloister* €5; €3.50 reductions. **Credit** AmEx, MC, V. **Map** p328 L9.

The church and convent of Santa Chiara was built for Robert of Anjou's wife Sancia in the early 14th century, and has always been a favourite with local aristocracy. Its Gothic features were hidden by Baroque restructuring in the mid 18th century, before a direct hit in an air raid in August 1943 (*see p44* **Bombast bombed**). In the 1950s, the rose window, portal, chapel arches, mullion windows, exterior flying buttresses and some altars and shrines were salvaged or faithfully copied, and the church was rebuilt along its original Gothic lines. To the left of the church, a door leads into the colourfully tiled, peaceful Baroque cloister; beyond, a museum has bits and pieces salvaged from the air raid, including some superb 14th-century friezes and busts, plus an archaeological area revealing a gymnasium and baths from the old Roman city.

THE CITY WALLS

Considering the sprawling chaos of modern Naples, it's hard to believe the city remained neatly confined within its walls from its Greek beginnings until the middle of the 17th century – yet remarkably, the city limits around the Centro Storico remained more or less unchanged for 2,000 years. In the early 15th century, King Ferdinando I had them extended by a few hundred metres, and 16th-century Spanish viceroy Don Pedro de Toledo beefed up defences by stringing walls or ditches between the city's five castles: Carmine (now gone), Capuano, Sant'Elmo, Nuovo and dell'Ovo.

A few minutes' walk from the eastern end of Spaccanapoli, the impressive **Porta Capuana** gate, with its carved marble triumphal arch and dark towers, dates from 1484. On nearby Via Muzy is **Castel Capuano**, the Hall of Justice (open 9am-6.30pm Mon-Fri). Built as a palace in the late 12th century, it owes its Renaissance appearance to 16th-century modifications. The façade is strikingly decorated with white plaster, contrasting with the ubiquitous black *piperno* stone. Between castle and gate is the

> **INSIDE TRACK**
> **ANCIENT REMAINS**
>
> Some have called Naples 'a Pompeii that was never buried': the only classical city that has survived with its essence intact, and with all its permutations and transformations continuously chronicled down to the present day. As one Neapolitan put it, 'We are Ancient Greeks first, not Romans, not Italians.'

early 16th-century **Santa Caterina a Formiello** (081 292316, open 9am-1pm Mon-Sat), considered one of the city's most beautiful Renaissance churches.

The street that heads north-east from the church, Via Carbonara, was once where the city's rubbish was burnt, hence its name; ten minutes up the street on the right is the lovely **San Giovanni a Carbonara** (*see p75*).

VIA DEI TRIBUNALI

Via dei Tribunali, the *decumanus maior* of Greek Neapolis, has maintained a commercial flavour since ancient times, and is lined with small shops and street markets. The flow of traffic is unbroken – and can be infuriating.

Beginning at the eastern end of Via dei Tribunali and heading west from the Castel Capuano, Piazza Cardinale Sisto Riario Sforza is home to another monumental Guglia, this one to **San Gennaro**. Residents erected it in thanks to the city's patron saint, after Naples escaped destruction by an eruption of Vesuvius in 1631. Opposite the monument, the 17th-century church of **Pio Monte della Misericordia** (*see p60*) contains Caravaggio's spellbinding *Seven Acts of Mercy*. In the church's *pinacoteca* (gallery) is a small collection that includes works by Giuseppe Ribera and Luca Giordano.

From here, you can't miss the **Duomo** (*see right*), Naples' cathedral. To reach the main entrance, turn down Via Duomo. Across the street is the **Quadreria dei Girolamini** (*see p60*), with a modest but lovely array of religious paintings.

Back on Via dei Tribunali, an incline leads up past the white façade of the early 17th-century church of the Girolamini (currently closed for restoration). Beyond it stands the medieval church of **San Lorenzo Maggiore** (*see p61*), and an extraordinary archaeological site where the streets of ancient Naples have been painstakingly unearthed.

A left turn off Via dei Tribunali, Via San Gregorio Armeno is home to the 16th-century church of **San Gregorio Armeno** (*see p60*). The street itself is famous for its Christmas nativity scenes; even in midsummer, crowds line up to buy this beloved Neapolitan art form.

Returning to Via dei Tribunali, look for the imposing church of **San Paolo Maggiore**. It stands on Piazza San Gaetano, the *agora* (marketplace) and later the forum of the ancient city. Beside the church is the entrance to a series of subterranean archaeological sites known as **Napoli Sotterranea** (*see right*).

The palazzo at no.339 (not open to the public) was built in the 13th century for Philip of Anjou; it has its original, sturdy four-span

The Duomo.

portico and a 13th-century portal. Opposite is the church of **Santa Maria del Purgatorio ad Arco** (*see p63*), famous for its skeletal proclivities. Not far away, the Baroque **Santa Maria Maggiore** (closed to the public) has a pretty Romanesque bell tower known as 'the Pietrasanta'. The adjacent **Cappella Pontano** (081 292316, open 9am-1pm Mon-Sat) is a Renaissance work from 1492, though the interior had a Baroque makeover.

Nearby is the small and bare 16th-century church of the **Croce di Lucca** (open 9am-1pm Mon-Sat), which was saved from demolition by the writer and philosopher Benedetto Croce. It still bears an unusual Fascist emblem on one external wall.

Continuing on Via dei Tribunali, the splendid church of **San Pietro a Maiella** stands next to the **Conservatorio di Musica** (*see p183*), illustrious alma mater of such musicians as Scarlatti and Pergolesi. Finally, the street reaches Piazza Bellini: with its abundant trees, beautiful architecture and sunny outdoor cafés, this is perhaps the most appealing square in the city.

★ FREE Duomo

Via del Duomo 147 (081 449097/www.duomodi napoli.com/www.museosangennaro.com). Bus E1, R2. **Open** *Church* 8.30am-12.30pm, 4.30-7pm Mon-Sat; 8.30am-1pm, 5-7pm Sun. *Archaeological area & baptistry* 9am-noon, 4.30-7pm Mon-Sat; 9am-noon Sun. *Museo del Tesoro* 9.30am-5pm Tue-Sat; 9.30am-2.30pm Sun. **Admission** *Church* free. *Archaeological area & baptistry* €3. *Museo del Tesoro* €5.50; €3.50 reductions. **No credit cards. Map** p328 N7.

Naples' cathedral dates from the fourth century, when the basilica of Santa Restituta was founded. In the late 600s the cathedral of Santa Stefania was constructed perpendicular to the original basilica, and at the end of the 13th century the current Duomo was built over Santa Stefania, incorporating Santa Restituta as a side chapel. The bland, 19th-century neo-Gothic façade is tucked away in an unprepossessing, heavily congested side street, so little prepares the visitor for the splendours within.

The gloom of the 100m (328ft) Latin-cross interior fails to obscure the fine gilt coffered ceiling (1621) and the paintings by Luca Giordano and his school. The large chapel on the right is the Cappella di San Gennaro, or Museo del Tesoro, which contains the relics of San Gennaro and a large number of bronze and silver statues of saints (many others are kept in the sacristy, and only put on public display in May and September).

The most famous remains of all are kept in a 14th-century French silver bust and two vials in a strongbox behind the altar. The bust contains Gennaro's skull; the vials his congealed blood. Three times a year the blood allegedly liquefies, most dramatically on Gennaro's feast day, 19 September (*see p62* City of blood). The chapel has a magnificent gilded bronze gate by Cosimo Fanzago (1668) and some fine frescoes by Domenichino (1631-43), depicting miraculous episodes from the saint's life. Above the right-hand altar, San Gennaro emerges unscathed from a fiery furnace in a painting by Giuseppe Ribera.

Back in the main church, to the right of the high altar, the chapel of Sant'Aspreno and the Minutolo family chapel have original Gothic decorations. Below the high altar, a magnificent late 16th-century *succorpo* or *confessio* (small chapel) by Tommaso Malvito houses a fine statue of a kneeling Cardinal Carafa and an urn containing more of San Gennaro's bones. The entrance to Santa Restituta is on the left side of the nave; inside, the ceiling painting is attributed to Luca Giordano. Carry on into the fourth-century baptistry – the oldest building of its kind in the West. Beneath the baptistry, the archaeological area showcases Greek and Roman walls, columns and roads, along with early Christian mosaics from the original Santa Stefania cathedral.

▶ *Naples' leading artists vied for the privilege of decorating the Cappella de San Gennaro – and not everyone played fair. For the full story, see p39.*

Napoli Sotterranea

Piazza San Gaetano 68 (081 296944/368 354 0585/www.napolisotterranea.org). Metro Dante or Montesanto/bus E1. **Open** *Guided tours* every 2hrs noon-4pm Mon-Fri; 10am-6pm Sat, Sun.* **Admission** €9.30. **No credit cards. Map** p328 M8.

Set 35m (123ft) below street level, these tunnels, aqueducts and chambers date from the dawn of the Greek city of Neapolis in the fourth century BC.

SIGHTS

Metro contextual

How the art scene went underground.

Piazza Dante.

Certain stations on the city's underground system act as a forum for rising artistic talents – yours to peruse for the price of a metro ticket. It's a scheme that has gone from strength to strength, and although some stops are in residential areas, and slightly off the beaten track for visitors, it's worth forking out €1.10 for a 90-minute ticket and taking a tour. For full details of participating stations on lines 1 and 6, see www.metro.na.it.

The best place to start is **Piazza Dante**, which features some big international names. As soon as you enter, you're hit by Joseph Kosuth's neon rendition of a

quotation from Dante's *Il Convivio*, entitled *Queste cose visibili* ('These visible things'). At 15 metres (49 feet) long, it's almost impossible to see all at once; the letters reflect to either side, and seem to wriggle as you pass them on the escalator.

Once the escalator ride is over, you're confronted by Jannis Kounellis's untitled piece. Train tracks bisect the wall, crushing toy trains and abandoned shoes as they go. Evoking travel, migration and flight, the piece has an undercurrent that's at once faintly comic and disturbing. Down the next escalator awaits one of Michelangelo Pistoletto's signature mirror pieces: an outline of the Mediterranean sea, *Intermediterraneo*. Finally, there are Nicola de Maria's gloriously vibrant mosaics.

The next stop is **Museo**, home to replica statues from the Museo Archeologico Nazionale (*see p70*) and works by various photographers. The highlight, though, is the 'Stazione Neapolis' exhibition, displaying Greek and Roman artefacts unearthed during the expansion of the metro system.

Also on line 1, **Materdei** station houses a colourful hotchpotch of pieces. Sol LeWitt's corridor, with its bright geometric murals and curvaceous plastic stalagmites,

---

Gradually incorporated into Naples' labyrinthine water supply system, they remained in use until the cholera epidemic of 1884. The tunnels stretch for almost 450km (270 miles); the guided tour covers a kilometre, and lasts about 90 minutes.

FREE Pinacoteca Girolamini

Via del Duomo 142 (081 294444). Bus E1, R2. **Open** 9.30am-12.30pm Mon-Sat. **Admission** free. **Map** p328 N7.

From the entrance, a flight of steps leads up to the right and into a splendid cloister planted with medlar and lemon trees. This small art gallery is one of Naples' most rewarding. The last two rooms (four and five) are the best, with Battista Caracciolo's superb chiaroscuro *Baptism of Christ* and other works, as well as Andrea Vaccaro's *Adoration of the Shepherds*, Luca Giordano's stirring *Mourning the Death of Christ*, and five paintings bearing the typical grotesque features of Giuseppe Ribera's school. Along the side walls are works by Neapolitan stalwarts Paolo de Matteis and Francesco Solimena. The 60,000-volume library is renowned, but closed to all but the most insistent.

▶ *For more on painting in Naples, see pp36-40.*

★ Pio Monte della Misericordia

Via dei Tribunali 253 (081 446944/www. piomontedellamisericordia.it). Metro Dante or Montesanto/bus C57, R2. **Open** *Church* 9am-2pm Mon, Tue, Thur-Sat. *Gallery* 9am-2pm Mon, Tue, Thur-Sun. **Admission** €5; €3-€4 reductions. **No credit cards. Map** p328 N8.

Pio Monte della Misericordia was established in 1601 by seven Neapolitan nobles, with the purpose of providing interest-free loans to the needy. Borrowers would leave items as security which could be auctioned if the loans were not repaid. The confraternity still exists today, and donates funds to schools, churches and hospitals. Above the chapel's high altar is Caravaggio's magnificent *Seven Acts of Mercy*, and the art gallery's collection includes delicate, satiny oils by Francesco de Mura, a St Anthony by Giuseppe Ribera, and a St Agnes by Massimo Stanzione in the Sala del Coretto.

FREE San Gregorio Armeno

Via San Gregorio Armeno 1 (081 552 0186). Metro Dante or Montesanto/bus C57, R2. **Open** 9am-noon Mon-Sat; 9am-1pm Sun. **Admission** free. **Map** p328 M8.

SIGHTS

is a delight. It's worth going up out of the station just to experience the full impact of Luigi Ontani's fantastic mosaic, which gives an impression of something between a grandiose Baroque theatre and an old Victorian swimming bath.

Next stop is **Salvator Rosa**, where the works include Perino & Vele's weird, life-sized, veiled Fiat 500s. The entrances are topped by steel-and-glass spires, and the surrounding gardens and buildings are adorned with bold mosaics and playful sculptures from the likes of Gianni Pisani, Mimmo Rotella and Ernesto Tatafiore.

Quattro Giornate showcases current Neapolitan artists, although some works are well hidden in this labyrinthine station. Look out for Sergio Fermariello's *Guerrieri* – a host of glyph-like figures who could be warriors from a cave painting, or fraught commuters. An image of artist Betty Bee peers out of a lightbox over one escalator, and works by Nino Longobardi and Umberto Manzo lurk round every corner.

At **Vanvitelli**, Vettor Pisani's line of prehistoric animals occupies the mezzanine, with two large-scale mosaics by Isabelle Ducroit on the platforms. Descending the escalator into the station,

you pass Mario Merz's final work before his death: a spiral neon light, representing the Fibonacci sequence.

Rione Alto, three stops away, is a bit of a trek, but its 120-metre (394-foot) corridor is an ideal space for lightbox installations by Bianco and Valente; polychrome panels by David Tremlett brighten up the mezzanine. Images by local artists cover the walls leading to the platforms; to complete the tour, leave the station to admire Antonio Tammaro's bronze statue and a fountain mosaic by Achille Cevoli.

Recent additions to the project include three more stations of the almost complete Alifano Line, which connects Naples with points north: **Giugliano**, **Aversa Ippodromo** and **Aversa Centro**. Some 20 international and local artists have contributed to the stations. Highlights include Jaume Plensa's tree-hugging bronze, entitled *where?*, and Eugenio Tibaldi's vast diptych of satellite views of suburban blight, *Economy Expressway*, both at Giugliano.

In 2010, the new **Monte Sant'Angelo** station, designed by architectural firm Future Systems with a monumental entrance by Anish Kapoor, will open in the long-neglected Fuorigrotta area.

SIGHTS

Built on the site of a Roman temple to the fertility goddess Ceres, the 16th-century church of San Gregorio owes its unflagging popularity to the cult of Santa Patrizia, whose relics are conserved here and whose blood allegedly liquefies not only on her feast day (25 August), when impressive celebrations are held, but also every Tuesday.

Patrizia might well have been Naples' patron saint, had the closed order of nuns that brought her relics from her native Constantinople in the eighth century not kept them secret. For many years only women were allowed to see them, but they are now on view to all in a chapel to the right of the altar. The church is preceded by a porticoed vestibule, and the interior is rich with Neapolitan Baroque. There are paintings and frescoes by Luca Giordano and Paolo de Matteis, and a fine 17th-century marble altar by Dionisio Lazzari.

To reach the adjacent convent and cloisters, continue up Via San Gregorio, under the arch, and turn left into Via Maffei; press the intercom at the first gate on the left. Still visible by the entrance are the bronze drums through which supplies were passed to the nuns. The cloisters, with their orange trees and pretty fountain, provide a tranquil refuge.

★ San Lorenzo Maggiore (archaeological site)

Via dei Tribunali 316 (081 211 0860/www. sanlorenzomaggiorenapoli.it). Metro Dante or Montesanto/bus C57, R2. Open 9.30am-5.30pm Mon-Sat; 9.30am-1.30pm Sun. Extended opening hours May, Dec. **Admission** €5. **No credit cards. Map** p328 M/N8.

At the heart of the most densely populated city in Europe, you can stand in silence and feel as if you've been whisked back to Graeco-Roman Neapolis. Excavations of this astonishing archaeological site are still under way, but have so far revealed sections of the city streets as they were 2,000 years ago, complete with a butcher's, a dyer's, a bakery and a porticoed arcade. Admission includes a visit to the Museo dell'Opera, a small museum with displays that span the site's long history.

★ FREE San Lorenzo Maggiore (church)

Via dei Tribunali 316 (081 211 0860/www. sanlorenzomaggiorenapoli.it). Metro Dante or Montesanto/bus C57, R2. **Open** 9am-noon, 5.30-7pm Mon-Sat; 9am-1pm Sun. **Admission** free. **Map** p328 M/N8.

City of blood

Superstitions are rife in Naples – along with a taste for the macabre.

San Gennaro.

To an outsider, everyday life in Naples seems to involve a tangled fabric of superstitions. Take the hand gesture for warding off the *malocchio* (evil eye): if a funeral procession should pass by, or if someone should be so foolhardy as to mention illness or misfortune, Neapolitans will inevitably make horns with their index and little fingers and point at the ground – in addition, most probably, to crossing themselves. Indeed, a central problem with trying to understand such practices is navigating the fuzzy line between charming custom and serious religious belief.

Not for nothing is Naples known as *urbs sanguinum* (city of blood). Consider the city's patron saint, San Gennaro. After he was beheaded in 305, his blood was brought to what became the catacombs of **San Gennaro** (*see p76*). About a century later, the first miraculous liquefaction of Gennaro's dried blood is said to have taken place, although the first official record of the miracle dates back only as far as 1389.

Gennaro's blood is said to bubble into action at the **Duomo** (*see p59*) three times a year: on the Saturday before the first Sunday in May, on 19 September (his feast day) and on 16 December, when crowds of devotees flock to witness the phenomenon. It usually takes between two minutes and an hour for the blood to liqueify, accompanied by the faithful's fervent prayers; in 1980, the miracle failed to occur – the very year that a devastating earthquake rocked southern Italy. Saintly blood is something of a Neopolitan theme; Santa Patrizia's also goes liquid, in the church of **San Gregorio Armeno** (*see p60*).

Neapolitans are also obsessed with death; just take a look at the bronze skulls at **Santa Maria del Purgatorio ad Arco** (*see right*), polished by the continual caresses of locals. Such things are taken very seriously, although few will admit it. Neapolitans generally assume an offhand attitude: 'It's not true,' they'll tell you, 'but I believe it anyway.'

There does seem to be a special concern with Purgatory, however. Along Via San Gregorio Armeno (*see p58*), in addition to the crib figures and omnipresent Pulcinella, you'll find painted figurines of various souls in flames: priests, gamblers, soccer players and even Berlusconi.

For other local fetishes, a quick look inside the chapel on the right in the **Gesù Nuovo** (*see p55*) will confirm that the tradition of ex-votos endures. Silver icons of bodies and body parts cover the walls from floor to ceiling; all sorts of designs are sold in some of the jewellery shops on Spaccanapoli. In the **Museo Archeologico Nazionale** (*see p70*), compare the ancient Roman terracotta breasts, penises and testicles to realise just how ancient and deeply held this belief is.

That brings us to another ever-present talisman: the *corno*. In its modern embodiment, it looks like a red pepper, but there seems little doubt that this popular amulet is a surrogate phallus, and derives from the ancient custom of men touching their genitals (testis is Latin for 'witness') when making an oath, seeking protection from evil, or calling on unseen powers for a stroke of luck. A *corno* must be given as a gift, rather than bought for yourself.

SIGHTS

More or less returned to its original 13th-century appearance thanks to post-war restoration work (*see p44* **Profile**), the vast, stern interior of this much-used church is in stark contrast to the tiny Baroque façade (1742), which was designed by Ferdinando Sanfelice. It was here that the *Decameron*'s Boccaccio fell in love with Fiammetta; Petrarch stayed in the adjoining convent, which served as the headquarters of the Parthenopean government in 1799.

Some traces of 17th- and 18th-century Baroque remain inside, notably in the third chapel on the right. On the high altar is an early 16th-century relief sculpture of Naples by Giovanni da Nola, and the left-hand transept chapel has two paintings by Caravaggio's disciple Mattia Preti. Sections of the original mosaic flooring are preserved under glass in the transept. Look out, too, for the splendid Gothic arch that leads into the delicate, cross-vaulted apse.

FREE San Paolo Maggiore

Via dei Tribunali (081 454048/www.sanpaolo maggiore.it). Metro Dante or Montesanto/bus C57, R2. **Open** *Church* 9am-1pm, 3-6pm Mon-Sat; 10am-12.30pm Sun. *Crypt* 8.30am-noon, 5-7.30pm daily. **Admission** free. **Map** p328 M8.
This lofty, majestic church, dating from the end of the 16th century, stands on the site of a Roman temple to Castor and Pollux. In front of the façade are two tall, white fluted pillars from the temple. The interior is notable for the colossal size of its Latin-cross interior, and the sacristy has fine frescoes by Francesco de Maria. The adjoining ex-convent at Via San Paolo 14 is an archive of legal documents from the 15th century onwards. The church's crypt, accessible from San Paolo's right aisle or directly from the piazza outside, is dedicated to San Gaetano.

FREE San Pietro a Maiella

Piazza Luigi Miraglia 393 (081 459008). Metro Dante or Montesanto/bus R1, R4. **Open** 7.30am-noon Mon-Sat; 10am-noon Sun. **Admission** free. **Map** p328 L8.
Approached from Via dei Tribunali, San Pietro looks for all the world like an English country church, with its cusp-shaped spire of *tufa* stone. Dating from the early 14th century, the interior has preserved many of its original Angevin features. The round and pointed arches contrast with the elaborate coffered ceiling, adorned with 17th-century paintings by Mattia Preti. Other lavish works of art include a fine *Madonna appearing to Celestinus V* by Massimo Stanzione in the fourth chapel on the right. Contrary to the official opening hours, the church is generally closed on August afternoons.

FREE Santa Maria del Purgatorio ad Arco

Via dei Tribunali 39 (081 551 0547/Hypogeum 081 446810). Metro Dante or Montesanto/ bus C57, R2. **Open** *Church* 9am-1pm Mon-Sat.

Hypogeum 10am-1pm Sat, or by appointment. **Admission** *Church* free. *Hypogeum* €2. **No credit cards. Map** p328 M8.
The three bronze skulls on the railings (a fourth was stolen in the 1950s), and its popular name, *cap'e morte* ('death's head'), are clues to why this 17th-century church has such a hold on Neapolitans. This was the centre of a death cult, in which people would adopt and look after the cache of skulls in the *hypogeum* (underground chamber). Inside, a winged skull and crossbones overlook the altar, and there are several Baroque paintings, including a circular *Madonna and Child* that some experts attribute to Giotto. Underneath the church, the *hypogeum* still contains a pile of venerated bones.
▶ *The Church has banned the practice of bone worship, although it's said to live on. See p73.*

THE DECUMANUS SUPERIOR

The third ancient *decumanus* runs parallel to, and north of, Via dei Tribunali, starting opposite the church of **San Giovanni a Carbonara** (*see p75*) at Via Santa Sofia. It passes the towering church of the **Santissimi Apostoli** (open 8-11.30am, 5.30-8pm Mon-Sat, 8.30am-1pm Sun), believed to have been built over a Roman temple to Mercury. The street then changes its name to Via dei Santissimi Apostoli, passing the 17th-century Baroque church of **Santa Maria Donnaregina**. Behind the church, on Vico Donnaregina, stands the original 14th-century church of the same name.

After the church, the street changes its name to Via dell'Anticaglia. A little further on, you'll reach two Roman brick archways that once joined a theatre on the south of the street to baths on the north.

Santa Maria Donnaregina

Vico Donnaregina 26/Via Settembrini 79 (081 1931 3016/www.museomadre.it). Bus E1. **Open** for exhibitions. **Admission** varies. **Map** p328 N7.
Step through the 17th-century portal and into a dainty porticoed cloister. On the left is the door to the deconsecrated 14th-century church, which is now incorporated into MADRe and has the same visiting hours (*see p75*). It was abandoned from the 1600s to the 1850s, eclipsed by the 17th-century church next door – which probably saved the building from a Baroque makeover.

Inside the older building, the bare interior has fan-vaults that, like the walls, bear traces of 14th-century Giotto-style frescoes. Tino da Camaino's magnificent marble tomb of Queen Mary of Hungary (1323) is against the left-hand wall. From the altar steps, looking up and back, the nuns' choir is visible, with its coffered ceiling and 14th-century frescoes by Pietro Cavallino. Depicting biblical scenes, saints and contemporary nobles, these are the most complete frescoes of their era in Naples.

SIGHTS

The Port & University

The crowded, chaotic waterfront scene.

It's ironic that Corso Umberto I, the arrow-straight boulevard built in 1884 to modernise Naples and isolate the city from the cholera-ridden port, should now threaten to engulf the rest of the city in its snarls of traffic. All day long, cars, buses and vans thrash for space along the four-lane highway, which runs from the 1960s Stazione Centrale railway station and its sprawling square, past the port area and ancient university.

The situation is unlikely to improve until the completion of the underground system – still years down the line – which will link the station area to the rest of the city and relieve much of the pressure on the overstretched road network. The waterfront, too, is set to undergo massive redevelopment over the coming years.

Map pp328-329	**Cafés, Bars &**
Hotels p103	**Gelaterie** p135
Restaurants p120	

Map pp328-329
Hotels p103
Restaurants p120

CORSO UMBERTO & THE UNIVERSITA

Corso Umberto I (known locally as il Rettifilo) runs from **Piazza Garibaldi** to **Piazza Bovio**. The former is a vast, rather unwelcoming car and bus interchange – also home to the Stazione Centrale train station – with an early 20th-century monument to Giuseppe Garibaldi (*see p28*) at one end. Meanwhile, work on the new underground line has turned Piazza Bovio into a building site; there's not much to see, and no end in sight.

At first glance, Corso Umberto seems little more than an array of tacky clothes shops and wall-to-wall street vendors. In fact, there's plenty to see, from the university area to the ill-famed Forcella district, and the colourful street market around Porta Nolana, by the station.

On the northern side of Corso Umberto, the **Università di Napoli Federico II** was founded in 1224. Although its faculties are dotted around the city, the area just east of Piazza Bovio remains the nucleus. West of the main building stand the headquarters of the 16th-century Università Orientale, so-called because its first students came from China for

religious training. Around the two universities cluster a host of churches – many perpetually closed for renovation – and splendid palazzi, some, alas, quite derelict.

On Via Monteoliveto, north-west of Piazza Bovio, **Palazzo Gravina** (no.3, open during university term-time, Sept-July) houses the architecture faculty; its 16th-century façade was restored after being destroyed by Swiss troops trying to flush out Italian patriots in 1848. North of the busy crossroads overlooked by the *Questura* (police station), Via Santa Maria la Nova leads to the church of the same name (Largo Santa Maria Nova 44, 081 552 3298, open 9am-1pm Mon-Sat), whose Renaissance façade matches that of Palazzo Gravina.

Via Santa Maria la Nova continues to Piazza Teodoro Monticelli, where the petite, early 15th-century **Palazzo Penne** (no.11, closed to the public) is one of Naples' last surviving houses from that era.

In Largo San Giovanni Maggiore, the small chapel of **San Giovanni Pappacoda** has a splendid early 15th-century ogival portal, a rare example of Gothic decoration in Naples. Now deconsecrated, the church is only opened for university graduation ceremonies. Opposite stands **Palazzo Giusso** (no.30, open during university term-time Sept-July), seat of the Università Orientale. The church of **San Giovanni Maggiore** (no.29, closed for restoration) was probably built on top of the ruins of a pagan temple in the fourth century, then rebuilt in the 17th and 18th centuries.

The main entrance to the Università di Napoli is on Corso Umberto, but an entrance further up Via Mezzocannone gives easier access to the **Centro Musei Scienze Naturali** (*see below*). Through the university buildings in Via Paladino, the church of **Gesù Vecchio** (no.38, 081 552 6639, open 7am-noon, 4-6pm Mon-Sat, 7am-noon Sun) dates from the late 16th century.

Further east, in Piazza Grande Archivio, the **Archivio di Stato** (no.5) was once the convent of the adjoining church of **Santi Severino e Sossio** (closed for restoration).

Near the station, the 13th-century church of **San Pietro ad Aram** stands guard over the notorious **Forcella** district. More than any other downtown area, Forcella lives up to the stereotype of lowlife Naples: racketeering, rip-off joints, gangland activity and petty crime. Above all, it has a long history of crushing poverty and neglect. Unwanted children, or children whose parents couldn't afford to care for them, ended up in the infamous foundling wheel beside the church of **Santissima Annunziata** (*see below*), and women were 'saved' in the convent of **Santa Maria Egiziaca** (now the Ascalesi Hospital, Via Egiziaca a Forcella 31). Even today, there's often an uneasy tension on the streets.

On the southern side of Corso Umberto, 50 metres from Piazza Garibaldi, pedestrianised Via Nolana leads to Porta Nolana. Just before this 15th-century city gate (the Circumvesuviana railway station is beyond), the scene explodes into a mass of colour and smells as you enter **Vicolo Sopramuro**, home to one of the most vibrant street markets in Europe. Open every morning, it has produce and fish spilling out of shops and stalls, as well as stores dealing in specialist merchandise such as leather or fabrics.

★ Centro Musei Scienze Naturali

Via Mezzocannone 8, Largo San Marcellino 10 (081 253 7516/www.musei.unina.it). Bus 14, CD, E1, R2. **Open** 9am-1.30pm, 3.30-5pm Mon, Thur; 9am-1.30pm Tue, Wed, Fri; 9am-1pm Sat, Sun. Closed Aug. **Admission** *All museums* €4.50; €3 reductions. *One museum* €2.50; €1.50 reductions. **No credit cards. Map** p328 M9.

These four delightful little museums – known collectively as the Centro Musei Scienze Naturali – are all located in and around the enormous Università di Napoli Federico II. Although the main entrance faces Corso Umberto, the easiest access to the museums is from Via Mezzocannone. The museums (in order of appearance) are: the mineralogy and geol-

ogy museum; the refurbished anthropology museum (on the first floor across the courtyard); the zoology museum (a favourite with kids); and the palaeontology museum, occupying the magnificent ex-Basilian convent and cloisters around the corner in Largo San Marcellino.

FREE San Pietro ad Aram

Corso Umberto I 292 (081 266055). Metro Garibaldi/bus R2. **Open** *Church* 8.15-11.30am, 5-7.30pm Mon-Fri; 7am-1pm Sun. *Crypt* closed for restoration. **Admission** free. **Map** p329 P8.

In the first century AD, the sea almost reached the current site of the Stazione Centrale, lapping against what would later become the estates of the convent of San Pietro ad Aram. It was here, according to local legend, that St Peter was driven ashore by a storm that stopped him from reaching Pozzuoli in AD 44. Undaunted, Peter seized the opportunity to convert Asprenus (who became the first bishop of Naples) and Candida, both of whom were eventually canonised. Although there is no evidence St Peter ever came to Naples, a cult celebrating his presence here was born and inspired centuries of restorations and expansions to his church. Inside the church is the altar where St Peter is said to have performed mass. The crypt (currently closed), possibly an ancient church itself, is a site of local worship of the souls of the dead (*see p73* **Worshipful Bones**). Today's complex is the product of 17th-century restorations and the demolition of two great cloisters to make way for the Rettifilo.

FREE Santissima Annunziata

Via dell'Annunziata 34 (081 283017/339 271 8901). Metro Garibaldi/bus R2/tram 1. **Open** *Church* 9.30am-noon, 5-6pm Mon-Sat; 9.15am-noon Sun. *Wheel* 9.30am-6pm Mon-Sat. **Admission** free. **Map** p329 O8.

The church owes its current appearance to Carlo Vanvitelli's mid 18th-century design. However, the whole Annunziata complex dates from the 14th century. It includes a courtyard and fountain, and a foundling wheel (*ruota*). Such wheels were once common throughout Italy and Spain. Women would place their unwanted newborn babies in them under the cover of darkness, and the babies would generally be reared by nuns; here, an adjoining orphanage (now a hospital) was set up for their care. Astonishingly, this

---

INSIDE TRACK
DODGY DEALINGS

It's estimated that some 50 per cent of the freight that comes into the **Port of Naples** is contraband, most of it Chinese and arriving under the cloak of night; from here, it is distributed all over Europe. The port area is unsavoury by day or night, but it is imperative not to stray here after dark.

Profile Santa Maria del Carmine

Miracles and murky goings-on in the church of Santa Maria.

The Carmine's history is as colourful as it is tragic. The original church was expanded and embellished in the 13th century, thanks to the mother of Conradin of Swabia, who was executed in 1268 in the adjacent Piazza Mercato, after an unsuccessful attempt to reclaim the kingdom of Sicily.

His mother provided a generous cash donation in exchange for the right to bury her 16-year-old son's remains here. They are believed to be underneath, or possibly in, the pedestal of the monument to Corradino erected in the transept. One thing is sure: they're not in the statue itself. SS agents sent by Hitler in 1943 searched in vain for the remains of that earlier German leader.

Opposite the monument is the pulpit where 27-year-old fisherman Tommaso Aniello (also known as Masaniello, *see p23*) delivered a fiery speech in 1647, calling on the people to rise up against the city's Spanish occupiers. He was later assassinated in the convent, and buried here in an unidentified tomb.

Legend has it that during a siege in 1439, a cannonball pierced the wall of the church and headed straight for the 14th-century wooden crucifix in a tabernacle under the transept arch. The statue's head miraculously ducked, the eyes closed and the brushed-back hair fell to one side; the crown of thorns fell off, and was never found again. Impressed, King Alfonso ordered a ceasefire – and on conquering the city, went to pay his respects to the image.

Popular devotion focuses, however, on the image of the Madonna Bruna behind the main altar, which has been associated with a number of miraculous events. The Madonna has her own fan site on Facebook, and on 16 July the faithful flock here to see the magnificent bell tower almost consumed in a blaze of fireworks, commemorating how La Bruna once saved the edifice from a conflagration. Sadly, her powers did not extend to saving the 18th-century frescoed ceiling, which was destroyed during World War II; the existing ceiling is a reproduction.

SAINTS AND SINNERS
The church is also thought to be secretly tied to the devotional activities of the Camorra. It's said to be one of the Black Hand churches, where the *Camorristi* reputedly offer candles and prayers before a big job, and request divine intercession on behalf of fallen cohorts. For more on the Camorra, *see p32*.

particular wheel remained in use right up until the 1970s. It's not a tourist attraction for Neapolitans, but a reminder of very recent, very harsh times; don't mistake the stoicism with which this symbol is borne for indifference. Anyone with the surname Esposito, from *expositus*, meaning 'laid before' the mercy of God, is a descendant of one of the foundlings.

Dominated by a large bell tower with a majolica clock, the entrance features a splendid carved marble portal (c1500) by Tommaso Malvito; in the apex, a Madonna gathers children under her cloak. The fine wooden doors (by Belverte and Da Nola) are also from the early 16th century. At 67m (220ft), the church's dome is one of the highest in the city.

▶ *For a truly splendid example of majolica tiling, don't miss the cloister at Santa Chiara; see p56.*

THE WATERFRONT

Via Nuova Marina (also known as La Marina) cuts along the port past **Piazza del Mercato**. Now a car park, the piazza lives up to its name (*mercato* means market), with shops selling a staggering array of toys, furniture, clothes and household items. The southern prospect over the sea is obstructed by a hideous modern construction. There is little to indicate that this was the site of the public burning, hanging and beheading of wrong-doers down the ages, including King Conradin of Swabia in 1268, and the leaders of the Parthenopean Republic (*see p29*) in 1799.

The executions took place beside the easternmost obelisk, and the names of the Parthenopean leaders are listed in sombre fashion just inside the church of **Santa Maria del Carmine** (*see left* **Profile**) in the adjacent piazza of the same name. Traffic streams to and from the motorway exit past the two remaining piers of the 14th-century **Porta del Carmine** gate (white with black piperno stone highlights) and the two towers from the same period – all that's left of the fifth castle in Naples' medieval defence system; the rest was demolished in 1906.

Naples' waterfront was subjected to heavy bombardment during World War II, and just two wonderful but little-known medieval churches – **Sant'Eligio Maggiore** and **San Giovanni a Mare** (for both, *see below*) – remain amid the semi-derelict old buildings and new office blocks.

The area south of Corso Umberto, between Piazza Bovio and Piazza Nicola Amore, is known as **I quattro palazzi**, after its four fine late 19th-century buildings. Within this area, the **Borgo degli orefici** (goldsmiths' district) still features an age-old community of silversmiths and goldsmiths, and *orefice* (goldsmith) often features in street names.

Further west, off Via Nuova Marina in Via Porta di Massa, the Faculty of Letters occupies the former convent of **San Pietro Martire**

(open during university term-time Sept-July), with its fine cloisters and church. Built in the late 13th century as a bulwark against portside vice, the church was remodelled in the 18th century. Portside vice, however, lives on – mainly in the form of clandestine goods from all over the world smuggled into the Port of Naples.

Via Marina continues past the notorious container port. Opposite the 16th-century church of **Santa Maria di Portosalvo** (closed for restoration), the Immacolatella quayside area – between the 18th-century **Capitaneria di Porto** (harbour master's office) and the fascist-era **Stazione Marittima** – has been earmarked for redevelopment. Until that happens, the area remains a hotchpotch of lorry and car parks, bollards and makeshift ticket offices.

The ferry port facilities on the western **Molo Beverello** dock – once a decidedly seedy place – have now been cleaned up and are fairly well organised. Sailing times are clearly indicated, and there are a couple of moderately priced bars to drink at while you wait for your boat.

FREE San Giovanni a Mare

Via San Giovanni Maggiore 8 (081 553 8429). Bus 14, CD, R2. **Open** 9am-noon daily; afternoons by appointment. **Admission** free. **Map** p328 L10.

So-called because the sea (*il mare*) used to lap against its walls, this 12th-century building is the only surviving Norman church in Naples. The foundations of the original apse can be viewed at the junction of the nave and the 13th-century transept. The first side altar on the left – with an unusual cambered arch – contains an exhibition of photos, documenting restoration work. If you can't find anyone to let you into the church, ask at Sant'Eligio Maggiore (*see below*).

FREE Sant'Eligio Maggiore

Via Sant'Eligio (081 553 8429). Bus 14, CD. **Open** 9am-2pm daily. **Admission** free. **Map** p329 O9.

This extraordinary 13th-century church was badly damaged in 1943; subsequent restoration work uncovered much of the original building. Sant'Eligio was the first church built in Naples by the Angevin monarchs. The leaping vertical height of the interior is accentuated by ribs and groin vaults. Outside, the fine Gothic archway and bell tower date from the 15th century; the clock is a 16th-century addition.

★ FREE Santa Maria del Carmine

Piazza del Carmine 2 (081 201196). Bus 14, CD, R2. **Open** 7am-noon, 4.45-7.30pm Mon-Sat; 7am-1pm, 4.30-7.30pm Sun. **Admission** free. **Map** p329 P9.

Boasting the city's tallest bell tower, at 75m (246ft), the church is part of an ancient complex. It includes a convent, which still provides succour for the needy and homeless. See *left* **Profile**).

Via Toledo & La Sanità

An enthralling mix of rags and cultural riches.

Bordering the Centro Storico and pedestrianised for much of its length, Via Toledo is generally considered to be the main street of a city that has no real centre. An astonishing assortment of characters, from bankers to beggars, stroll or struggle down the palazzo-lined route, while its flashy shops mask the harsh realities of life in the adjacent Quartieri Spagnoli.

Traffic-clogged Via Foria converges with Via Toledo at the wonderful Museo Archeologico Nazionale. Once complete, the ongoing restoration of the huge Albergo dei Poveri at the end of the street should boost the street's tourist appeal; in the meantime, the area's sights include the mighty archeological museum, weird catacombs and lush botanical gardens.

Map p332	Cafés, Bars &
Hotels p104	Gelaterie p135
Restaurants p122	

VIA TOLEDO & THE QUARTIERI SPAGNOLI

Created in the early 16th century by Spanish viceroy Don Pedro di Toledo (*see p22*), **Via Toledo** was rechristened Via Roma when Naples became part of the Italian republic in 1860. A recent return to its original name has led to confusion, so you may hear it called both.

Forming a link between the Quartieri Spagnoli and the old city to the east, the road was lined with elegant palazzi and lauded as one of Europe's most impressive streets. Where the homes of nobles and bankers once dazzled visitors, clothing retailers now hold sway. The palazzi are still there, though, visible above the shopfronts and from *cortili* (courtyards) behind impressive portals.

The street's pedestrianised area ends at the junction with Via Armando Diaz. East along Via Diaz, modern Piazza Matteotti is dominated by the vast, Fascist-era façade of the 1930s post

office, the **Palazzo delle Poste e Telegrafi**. Towering over the square from behind the modern Questura (police headquarters) is the 30-storey Jolly Hotel, one of the most unpopular eyesores to receive planning permission from the city council of the 1950s.

North of the post office in Piazza Monteoliveto, the 15th-century church of **Sant'Anna dei Lombardi** (*see p69*) was once part of a much larger convent. Some of the complex has been incorporated into the adjacent Carabinieri (police station) – scene of the *mani pulite* ('clean hands') anti-corruption enquiries of the 1990s.

Farther north, the grim 20th-century façade of the church of **Spirito Santo** (no.409, open 9-11.30am Mon-Sat, 10.30am-noon Sun) masks a lofty, cool, grey and white interior, above which looms one of the largest domes in the city.

The grid of streets on the slope west of Via Toledo constitutes the **Quartieri Spagnoli**, built to house Spanish troops during Don Pedro

Piazza Dante.

di Toledo's flourish of urban expansion in the 16th century (*see p43*). Cramped from the start, the Quartieri became home to some of the poorest of Naples' poor; buildings that were scarcely fit for Spanish horses 400 years ago became the damp, exhaust-filled dwellings of wretched human beings. Many still are, and the Quartieri holds some unenviable records: Europe's highest rates of unemployment and respiratory disease are just two of them.

Yet there's something fascinating – for the visitor – about this warren of streets. One attraction is the delightful **Via Pignasecca**, home to a chaotic street market. With the market in full swing, crowds of people streaming towards the city centre by funicular railway, and ambulances screaming around Pellegrini hospital, the swirling inferno is as loud as it is mesmerising.

INSIDE TRACK
WALK THIS WAY

Head to the southern stretch of Via Toledo to experience the *struscio*, that southern Italian phenomenon in which crowds of well-dressed people strut back and forth along the main drag. Neapolitans of all ages flock here to relax, chat, flirt, see and be seen; put your best clothes on and go with the flow.

FREE Sant'Anna dei Lombardi

Piazza Monteoliveto 44 (081 551 3333). Metro Montesanto/bus E1, R1, R4. **Open** 9am-noon Tue-Sat. **Admission** free. **Map** p328 K9.
Sant'Anna dates from the early 15th century, though it was refurbished in the 17th century and rebuilt after wartime bombing. Inside, its Renaissance sculptures include an extraordinary group of terracotta statues, *Mourning the Death of Christ*, by Guido Mazzoni (1492). The sacristy has a fine ceiling frescoed by Giorgio Vasari in 1544; the unusual inlaid wooden wall panels are from the same period. The church is currently undergoing restoration work, but visitors can still see the main sculptures.

PIAZZA DANTE

At the point where Via Toledo becomes Via Enrico Pessina, Piazza Dante – restored to undreamt-of elegance for the 2002 opening of its metro station – is defined by the crescent-shaped **Convitto Nazionale**, originally a state-funded boarding school for poor children from outside Naples. Designed in the mid 18th century by Luigi Vanvitelli, the Convitto has 26 statues representing the many virtues of Carlo III. At its northern end is the Port'Alba arch, built in the early 17th century and rebuilt 150 years later. A used book market rambles between the Porta and Via Santa Maria di Costantinopoli. The Piazza Dante metro station is also of interest, thanks to its impressive array of modern art (*see p60* **Metro contextual**).

Museo Archeologico Nazionale.

The **Museo Archeologico Nazionale**, home to some of Italy's greatest treasures, is further north on the smoggy, noisy Via Pessina. En route, in Via Bellini, stands the **Accademia delle Belle Arti** (081 444245, www.accademia napoli.it, open 10am-2pm Tue, 2-6pm Fri, €5), with its mid 19th-century façade in *tufa* stone and fine art collections. From the northern end of Via Bellini, the rather sleazy Galleria Principe di Napoli leads to Piazza Museo.

Beyond the museum on Via Santa Teresa degli Scalzi stands **Santa Teresa degli Scalzi** (no.43, open 10-12.30pm Sun), built in the 17th century and reworked in the 18th century. The church is largely neglected, its fickle congregation having decamped to the **Gesù Nuovo** (*see p55*). It is now run by a different order, who hope to establish regular opening hours.

Piazza Cavour, with its busy underground station (*see p60* **Metro contextual**) and public gardens, leads east out of Piazza Museo. The restored **Porta San Gennaro**, with a 17th-century fresco by Mattia Preti, formed part of the original 15th-century city walls.

★ Museo Archeologico Nazionale

Piazza Museo 19 (081 564 8941/081 440166/ www.archeona.arti.beniculturali.it). Metro Piazza Cavour or Museo/bus C57, R4, C63. **Open** *Museum* 9am-7.30pm Mon, Wed-Sun (last admission 1hr before closing). *Gabinetto segreto* 2.45-6.45pm Mon, Wed-Sun; guided tours 9.15am, 1.45pm. **Admission** €6.50; free under-18s & over-65s. **No credit cards. Map** p328 K7.

In 1777, King Ferdinando I selected this early 17th-century palazzo as the perfect home for the immense collection of ancient artefacts he inherited from his grandmother, Elisabetta Farnese. Discoveries from Pompeii, Stabiae and Herculaneum were later added, making this one of the finest archaeological museums in the world.

It should be noted, however, that restoration work means there are often gaps in the collection, and pieces may not where they should be. Due to reduced personnel, some rooms are unmanned or even closed, and queues are common. The best day to visit, for this reason, is Sunday.

The museum is distributed over four floors. The basement holds the Egyptian section, with objects imported into Italy during the Roman period and unearthed in excavations in Rome and the Campania region. There's a large collection of obelisks, busts, funerary statues, jewellery and sarcophagi from the Hellenic and Ptolemaic periods, and the obligatory mummy, once part of the Borgia collection.

The meandering ground floor houses the collection assembled by the powerful Farnese family (although the paintings are in the Museo di Capodimonte, *see p78*). Most of the pieces were filched from ancient sites in Rome during the 16th century, when Alessandro Farnese ruled as Pope Paul III (1534-49). In room 1, on the right of the entrance hall, are the *Tirannicidi* (tyrant-killers Armodios and Aristogitones, who did away with the cruel Athenian rulers Hippia and Hipparchos in 514 BC); it's a Roman copy of the fifth-century BC Greek original. In the same room is a Roman copy of Polycletus' *Doriforo*. Elsewhere on this floor is a series of busts and statues, some of which are simply enormous. There's the powerful *Ercole Farnese* (Farnese Hercules) between rooms 11 and 12, and the recently restored *Toro Farnese* (Farnese Bull) in room 16, a large marble group from the early third century AD. In room 8, the graceful Roman copy of a Greek Venus, *Venere Callipige*, glances backwards at her reflection in the water as she slips off her clothes.

Room 10 contains the delicate *Tazza Farnese*, a tiny dish made in Egypt during the Ptolemaic period. Consisting of four layers of sardonyx agate, it is renowned for its transparent beauty. The mezzanine floor houses mosaics, including a large-scale depiction of the battle between Alexander the Great and Darius from the House of the Faun in Pompeii in room 61.

Also here is the *Gabinetto segreto*, a collection of ancient pornography uncovered at Pompeii and Herculaneum. The explicit paintings and sculptures includes a vast range of phallus talismans – some winged, some jingling with bells, some with hats on. One item approaches the subject in pre-Freudian fashion, depicting a frantic struggle between the member and its owner. The high (or low) point is a sculpted Pan, caught in the act with a nanny-goat. Officially off-limits to under-11s, this collection has attracted controversy over the ages and was only reopened to the public in 2000.

The first floor contains artefacts from Pompeii, Herculaneum and other southern Italian sites. On the walls of the vast, echoing Sala Meridiana hang rare paintings on archaeological themes from the Farnese collection. On its floor, a line marks a zodiacal meridian; around noon, an oval bead of light snakes in through a hole high in the top right-hand corner of the room, striking the meridian in the appropriate zodiacal sign.

To the left as you enter the Sala, rooms 85 to 89 contain glassware, silver and pottery from Pompeii, and rooms 66 to 78 have friezes and frescoes from Herculaneum and Stabiae. To the right as you enter, the first entrance leads to rooms 114 to 117, with artefacts from the Villa dei Papiri in Herculaneum; note the lovely bronze Hermes in room 117. The second series of right-hand rooms (130 to 140) contains vases, bowls and funerary offerings from Greek and Roman Paestum, and other sites around Magna Graecia (ancient southern Italy).

The pre- and proto-historical sections are reached from the third corridor on the right. The upper mezzanine floor displays Palaeolithic, Neolithic and Early Bronze Age finds from the Campania region (rooms 148 and 149), and the lower mezzanine (rooms 145 and 146) houses finds from the Middle and Late Bronze Ages.

The main section (rooms 124 to 127) is arranged according to place, not time, and includes Palaeolithic bones and flints found on Capri (room 127); the Iron Age is best represented, with eighth- and ninth-century funerary relics from a number of necropolises from Capua to Ischia.

LA SANITA & BEYOND

Between Via Foria, Via Santa Teresa degli Scalzi and the hill of Capodimonte is an area made up of three districts: **La Sanità** ('healthy', because it was outside the city walls), **I Miracoli** (thanks to the miracles wrought around saintly inmates of the catacombs) and **Le Vergini** (named after a pre-Christian, no-sex-please, Greek religious group).

Now densely populated and *folkloristico* (a plaque marks the house where dearly loved Neapolitan comedian Totò was born at Via Antesaecula 109), the area is honeycombed with underground burial places: the early Christian **Catacombe di San Gaudioso** under **Santa Maria della Sanità** (for both, *see p72*), the **Catacombe di San Severo** (*see p73*), and the comparatively new **Cimitero delle Fontanelle** (*see p75*). The area was popular for burials as it remained outside the city walls until the 18th century; burial within the walls was forbidden for public health reasons.

Along with its incredible catacombs, the area contains two architectural gems (visible from the outside only) by 18th-century architect Ferdinando Sanfelice. **Palazzo Sanfelice** (Via Sanità 2 and 6), the architect's own home, is now sadly dilapidated, but the magnificent 'flying' staircase in **Palazzo dello Spagnuolo** (Via dei Vergini 19) has recently been restored to its former glory. Further east, pine-tree-lined Piazza Miracoli is home to the 17th-century **Santa Maria dei Miracoli** (Largo dei Miracoli 35, 081 440189, open 5-7.30pm Mon-Sat).

These districts are home to congested street markets, where locals clamour for fresh produce and household items. La Sanità, in particular, buzzes with activity. Note the number of scooter drivers without helmets; locals know that they must *fa' canosce* – make sure their faces are visible so they are recognised and won't be mistaken for an outsider threatening the neighbourhood turf. Needless to say, visits to La Sanità, I Miracole and Le Vergini are best made in daylight.

INSIDE TRACK
HOLD ON TIGHT

Exercise caution while navigating the Via Toledo and La Sanità, and surrounding side streets. Tourists are easy targets for petty criminals – especially the infamous *scippatori*, who drive by on scooters looking for bags to snatch. Keep your wits about you and your bags to the side facing away from the street, or carry valuables safely out of sight.

SIGHTS

Beyond Porta San Gennaro, just off Via del Duomo, is the **Museo d'Arte Contemporanea Donna Regina Napoli**, or MADRe (*see p75*), a relatively new modern art museum. Back on the Via Foria, the traffic crawls relentlessly along, past the lush **Orto botanico** (*see p74* **Green getaway**) to Piazza Carlo III, dominated by the fearsome bulk of the **Albergo dei Poveri**. Carlo III commissioned the poorhouse to shelter the homeless and destitute, keeping them out of sight and mind; rumour had it that once inside, you left only in a coffin.

Construction began in 1751 and was finally completed in 1829. Vast as it is – the façade measures 354 metres (1,239 feet) and the building covers 103,000 square metres (26 acres) – the Albergo is only one fifth of the size of Ferdinando Fuga's original design. In 2000, a project to repair serious damage from general decay and the effects of the earthquake of 1980 began – originally due for completion in 2006 – wishful thinking for so enormous an endeavour, especially in Naples. Work continues, although some sections host temporary exhibitions.

Via Santi Giovanni e Paolo runs north-east out of the eastern end of Piazza Carlo III. The great tenor Enrico Caruso (1873-1921) was born at no.6. A dingy plaque on the wall introduces this as the house 'where the world first heard his voice'. Naples itself heard little more of it; slated by Neapolitan critics early in his career, Caruso left the city and never came back.

★ Catacombe di San Gaudioso/ Santa Maria della Sanità

Via della Sanità 124 (081 544 1305/www.santa mariadellasanita.it). Metro Piazza Cavour or Museo/bus C51, C52, R4. **Open** *Church* 8.30am-12.30pm, 5-8pm Mon-Sat; 8.30am-1.30pm Sun. *Catacombs* 9.30am-12.30pm daily. *Guided tours* 9.30am, 10.15am, 11am, 11.45am, 12.30pm daily. **Admission** €5. **No credit cards**. **Map** p328 K5.

Tunnelled out of the Capodimonte hillside in Roman times for use as water cisterns, these labyrinthine catacombs were used as a burial site from the fifth century onwards. In 452, the burial of St Gaudiosus – a North African bishop and hermit – made the site an important shrine. The damp, musty caves have patches of fifth- and sixth-century mosaics, and frescoes from the fifth, 17th and 18th centuries. A fascinating range of burial techniques is in evidence. Note the method used from 1620 to 1650: the corpse was walled upright in a niche with its head cemented into the rear wall. After the bodily fluids had drained away (the malediction *puozza sculà*, 'may you drain away', is still in use), the headless body was buried and the skull removed, to be repositioned over a frescoed portrait of the illustrious deceased. The remains of St Gaudiosus and the skulls were all transferred to the nearby Cimitero delle Fontanelle (*see p75*) during the cholera epidemic of 1974.

In the 17th century, the Dominican friars that tended the chapel of San Gaudioso in the catacombs built the Greek-cross-plan basilica of Santa Maria della Sanità above it. There's a fine Madonna and

Santa Maria della Sanità.

child with St Hyacinth, St Rosa of Lima and St Agnes by Luca Giordano in the second chapel on the right.

From the transept, steps lead down to the fifth century Cappella di San Gaudioso, which was rebuilt in the tenth and 15th centuries. The church is home to a painting of Mary, found nearby. Rumour has it that after it was discovered, the plague ceased and Mary brought *sanità* (health) to the area. Another, less comforting, local story has it that Camorra blood *giuramenti* (blood oaths) took place in the catacombs

– a tale that won't be mentioned on the guided tour, although the Sanità is a Camorra stronghold. The hour-long tours leave from the basilica; call ahead to request an English-speaking guide.

FREE **Catacombe di San Severo**
Piazzetta San Severo a Capodimonte 81 (081 544 1305). Metro Piazza Cavour or Museo/bus R4. **Open** *Church* 9am-noon Sat-Sun. *Catacombs* closed for restoration. **Admission** free.

Worshipful bones

The cult of the dead that refuses to stay buried.

Neapolitans have unique traditions for dealing with their dead, the origins of which have been obscured by time. Although many of the ritual observances – of which the modern Church takes a dim view – are on the wane, some locals still practise rites that to outsiders can seem downright macabre.

The Neapolitan cult of the dead involves caring for the skulls – *capuzzelle*, in local dialect – and bones of the unknown dead. People 'adopt' skulls in the city's *hypogea* (underground tombs), bringing the bones gifts, clothes, pillows and flowers, or even building small wooden houses for them. In return, the souls belonging to the skulls are supposed to protect and grant favours to their caretakers.

With its cavern and side galleries, the **Cimitero delle Fontanelle** (*see p75*) was once an ancient quarry for *tufa* building stone. First used for modern burials in the 17th century, it acquired a new importance during the cholera epidemic of 1835, when city authorities deposited bodies from other city cemeteries here. During a similar outbreak in 1974, more bones were brought here from the catacombs of San Gaudioso (*see left*). About 40,000 skulls and bones were subsequently stacked up around the cavern, all in need of some tender loving care. After World War II, grieving parents took up the practice of adopting skulls in memory of sons missing or killed in action.

Such rituals were practised for centuries in the catacombs of **Santa Maria della Sanità** (*see left*); some still endure in **Santa Maria del Purgatorio ad Arco** (*see p63*) and **San Pietro ad Aram** (*see p65*). Although the Church forbade the worship of non-saintly human remains in 1969, a visit to the *hypogeum* of the Purgatorio church (open only on Saturday mornings)

reveals that such practices live on: a few skulls with their attendant bones are surrounded by flowers, jewellery and ex-votos, giving thanks for boons granted.

One of the bony tenants, known locally as Lucia, wears a crown. Some say she was a young girl who died on the eve of her wedding day; others maintain she was a princess in love with a commoner. Her father opposed the marriage and locked her up in a convent, where she died of a broken heart. Lucia is believed to protect newlyweds and brides-to-be, some of whom visit the 'Principessa' to seek her blessing.

Among traditionalist Neapolitan families, the most fascinating custom involves the exhumation of a loved ones' remains after several months' burial in a shallow grave, or after a year or more. What's left of the body, newly brought to the light of day, is then ritually cleansed by close relatives before being permanently reinterred. An earthy explanation for the procedure is that of simple confirmation of identity: Camorra bosses who want to 'die' when they go into hiding sometimes order the pilfered corpses of others to be buried in their stead.

SIGHTS

Green getaway

Exhausted by the pace of city life? Escape is at hand.

A steep double flight of stone steps, topped off by impressive balustrades adorned with Neoclassical urns, leads up and out of the smoggy chaos and into the **Orto botanico** (*see right*). Plane trees, palms and riotous vegetation tower above the broad, shady park, where hundreds of species flourish.

Despite the constant roar of traffic below, and the proximity of the vast, rat-infested remains of the Albergo dei Poveri (*see p72*), the garden provides a surprising – and welcome – haven of peace in an otherwise overwhelming city.

It was founded in 1807 by Joseph Bonaparte, when Naples was ruled by his brother, the Emperor. It was the fulfilment of an 18th-century plan by the Bourbon king Ferdinand IV – a royal project that had been cut short by the revolutionary climate and upheaval of the late 1700s.

Created for the purposes of scientific research, this is one of Europe's earliest true botanical gardens. Similar parks in previous centuries had been laid out as mere curiosities: showcases for the bizarre plant species carted back from colonies, designed purely for pleasure.

The Orto now boasts some 9,000 species: palms, aquatic plants, cacti, ferns and shrubs, carefully collected in the last two centuries from all over the world. Labelled and arranged according to type, the plantings include an extensive cactus section, a lush fern grove, and a veritable orchard of every type of citrus.

The charming *castello* at the centre of the park pre-dates the garden by some 150 years. Along with the grounds and greenhouses (not open to visitors), it now belong to Naples University's science department. Inside the castle is a well-organised museum of paleobotany and ethnobotany, displaying fossilised plants and leaves as well as tools, weapons, musical instruments and other artefacts from across the globe, all fashioned from plants and trees.

SIGHTS

Built in 1573, the church stands on the site of a monastery complex and much earlier church, founded by Naples' first bishop, Severus. When Severus's saintly body was moved to San Giorgio Maggiore (*see p56*) in the ninth century, the site lost its importance. On the left side of the nave, steps lead down to a tiny cubicle containing all that is left of the original catacombs. A wall fresco from the late fourth century depicts St Peter and St Paul, alongside the city's own San Gennaro and San Severo.

FREE Cimitero delle Fontanelle

Via delle Fontanelle 154 (081 296944/081 557 3913). Metro Piazza Cavour or Museo/bus C51. **Open** *May only* 10am-noon, 3-5pm Fri, Sat; 10am-noon Sun. **Admission** free. **Map** p331 J5. The Cimitero is closed for restoration, although it does open up during the Maggio dei Monumenti. *See also p73* **Worshipful bones**.
▶ *Venerable bones remain on display in the hypogeum at Santa Maria del Purgatorio ad Arco, open on Saturday mornings; see p63.*

★ Museo d'Arte Contemporanea Donna Regina Napoli (MADRe)

Via Settembrini 79 (081 1931 3016/www.museo madre.it). Metro Piazza Cavour or Museo/bus 47, CS, E1. **Open** 10am-9pm Mon, Wed-Fri; 10am-midnight Sat, Sun (last entry 1hr before closing). **Admission** €7; €3.50 reductions; free to all Mon. **No credit cards**. **Map** p328 N6.
For years, Naples lacked a proper contemporary art gallery – but 2005 saw the opening of two large-scale, publicly funded galleries, PAN (*see p84*) and MADRe. The palazzo that houses this pleasant, well-appointed museum was completely overhauled by Portuguese architect Alvaro Siza, who created a main display space on the ground floor and three upper floors of smaller connecting rooms.

Granted, it's not Guggenheim Bilbao or Tate Modern, but it is a highly functional space. The first floor hosts site-specific installations by international artists such as Jeff Koons and Richard Serra; highlights include a couple of Joseph Kosuth's cryptic neon signs, Anish Kapoor's marvellously illusory blue space and Rebecca Horn's mirrored skulls. Neapolitan in exile Francesco Clemente also returned to fresco two rooms in their entirety. The subject is Naples itself, and the superstitions that make the city tick. Staff are numerous and knowledgeable, though not all speak English.

The upper floors are given over to temporary exhibitions; artists have included Jannis Kounellis (featuring his notorious dozen live horses), Rachel Whiteread and Robert Rauschenberg. There's also a bar and restaurant, where a visit can be combined with a lively aperitif.

★ FREE Orto botanico

Via Foria 223 (081 449759/www.ortobotanico. unina.it). Metro Piazza Cavour or Museo/bus 14,

MADRe.

15, 47, CS, C51. **Open** 9am-2pm Mon-Fri, by appointment only. **Admission** free. **Map** p329 O5.
A stroll around the city's botanical gardens makes for a refreshing change of pace. The Orto botanico also hosts an array of performances, especially in the summer; check local listings for details.

Note that visits are by appointment only, and the garden closes at 2pm (last entrance is at 1.30pm). Calling to book on the same day is generally fine; leave your name when you phone, and on arrival your name will be crossed off the list. *See left* **Green Getaway**.

FREE San Giovanni a Carbonara

Via Carbonara 5 (081 295873). Metro Piazza Cavour or Museo/bus 110, E1. **Open** 9am-1pm daily. **Admission** free. **Map** p329 N6.
This 14th-century church stands at the top of a dramatic flight of steps (added in 1707 by Ferdinando Sanfelice) above the modern church of the same name. At the head of the staircase, the chapel of Santa Monica (closed to the public) has a marble Gothic portal. The church entrance is to the left of this portal; inside, magnificent sculptures abound. The monument and tomb of King Ladislas (1428) behind the main altar is 18m (63ft) high, and shows Renaissance touches in its mainly Gothic design.

The round chapel behind the altar has a complex, majolica-tiled floor, 15th-century frescoes portraying the lives of the hermits, and the tomb of Gianni Caracciolo (1433), the much-hated lover of Ladislas' sister and successor, Queen Joan II (*see p22*).

SIGHTS

Capodimonte

The dizzy heights of artistic achievement.

Split into its constituent parts, the name of this small and verdant enclave becomes *capo di monte* – literally, 'top of the hill'. Commanding the heights of a hill set to the north of the city centre, Capodimonte has long been considered an oasis of artistic, architectural and natural beauty.

For this it is indebted to King Carlo III, who saw the area's hunting potential in the 18th century and decided to construct a magnificent royal palace here, set in splendid grounds. His palace is now an immensely popular museum, home to a formidable art collection that attracts visitors from around the globe.

The atmospheric Catacombe di San Gennaro, with their ancient tombs, mosaic and frescoes, are another draw. Finally, there's the stately 19th-century observatory, open for guided tours.

Map p325   Hotels p105

INTRODUCING THE AREA

The **Museo di Capodimonte** (*see p78*) is the biggest tourist draw in these parts, and richly deserves its popularity. Although the area around the museum teems with visitors on sunny Sundays, the rest of the park is often strangely deserted. Laid out in the mid 18th century to a design drawn up by Ferdinando Sanfelice, five tree-lined avenues radiate from a hub near the palace. Smaller buildings are dotted about, including the **Reale Fabbrica delle Porcellane** (royal porcelain factory). Work in the factory came to a standstill in 1759, as Carlo shifted the whole operation to his native Spain when he returned to take the crown; the factory is now a craft school.

Nearby attractions include the fascinating yet unsung **Catacombe di San Gennaro** (*see right*). South-west of the park on Via Capodimonte, the pseudo-classical 20th-century church of the **Madre del Buon Consiglio** (open 8am-12.30pm, 4.30-7.30pm daily) is a bombastic imitation of St Peter's in Rome. The **Osservatorio Astronomico** (*see p78*), south-east of the park, bears witness to scientific progress made during the Bourbon Restoration.

On the road curving down from Capodimonte's Porta Grande are the **Ponti Rossi**, the well-preserved remains of an aqueduct built during the reign of Emperor Claudius (AD 41-54) to bring fresh water to Naples from the mountains near Avellino. Byzantine forces breached the city walls in 536 through this aqueduct, after some admirable military espionage.

The City Sightseeing tourist bus stops at the Catacombe di San Gennaro and Capodimonte before descending back into the city centre; Naples' public transport system also provides connections to the area. Although the Capodimonte Museum and its park are a haven of high culture and peace, a wave of robberies in the surrounding area means it's wise to stick to the tourist sites.

Catacombe di San Gennaro

Via Capodimonte 16 (081 741 1071/081 744 3714). Bus 24, 110, R4. **Open** *Guided tours only* 9am, 10am, 11am, noon, 2pm, 3pm Tue-Sat; 9am, 10am, 11am, noon Sun. Closed afternoons in Aug. **Admission** €5; €3 reductions. **No credit cards.** From a pleasant garden (its entrance is to the left of the church) overlooking Sanità, steps lead down into the two-level catacombs, with their fascinating – if

Profile Caravaggio

The extraordinary life and works of the other Michelangelo.

The **Flagellation**.

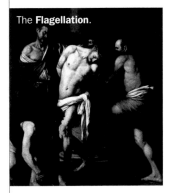

Although Michelangelo Merisi da Caravaggio spent less than four years in Naples, he left a rich artistic legacy. Having made his name in Rome in the late 1590s, Caravaggio was as famous for his innovative compositions and extraordinary ability to recreate lifelike detail as for his unconventional behaviour. He fled Rome in 1606 with a price on his head, having killed a thuggish playboy, Ranuccio Tomassoni, in a duel.

He ended up in Naples – at the time, the wealthiest city in Italy, and home to the powerful Colonna family, his longstanding patrons. Local artists and collectors flocked to meet the man who had caused such a stir in Rome, and Caravaggio held informal court at the Taverno del Cerriglio on Via Sanfelice, a haunt for gamblers, prostitutes, poets and artists on the make.

Although the last few years of Caravaggio's life, prior to his death in 1610 at the age of 39, are among the most mysterious, he did at least paint during this time. Of the works he painted in Naples, three remain in the city. *Seven Acts of Mercy* hangs in the Pio Monte della Misericordia (*see p60*). Depicting the acts of mercy described by St Matthew,

the painting is life-sized, dark and chaotic – like a snapshot of Neopolitain life down darkest Via Tribunali. A pair of angels look as if they're fighting and about to fall out of a window. Below them, an innkeeper offers hospitality, a rich man cuts his cloak in two and offers half of it to a naked beggar, a dead body is carried through the chaos, and a woman suckles an old man at her breast.

The *Flagellation*, painted for the church of San Domenico (a copy of it, by Luca Giordano, still hangs there), is now in the Capodimonte museum (*see p78*). Again, there's something very Neapolitan about the scene: a shaft of light illuminates Christ's extraordinarily lifelike form, tormented by a pair of dodgy-looking characters.

The *Martyrdom of St Ursula* can be seen in gallery of the main branch of Banca Intesa Sanpaolo on Via Toledo (no.185, www.palazzozevallos.com). It has a similarly photographic quality, despite a slightly smudgy finish: Marcantonio Doria, who commissioned it, put it out in the sun to dry when the paint was still wet, 'because Caravaggio puts it on thick', and the paint melted. Its figures loom almost three-dimensionally out of the dark background, while Saint Ursula looks at her wound with untheatrical surprise.

Several works now owned by galleries outside the city were also probably painted during the Neapolitan period, including the *Supper at Emmaus*. An earlier version hangs in London's National Gallery, and a second in Milan's Brera; long considered a poor copy, the Milan *Supper* is now thought to have greater vitality. It was painted by a man seemingly in a hurry yet at the height of his powers: the light is a single slash of paint, and a few daubs depict the diners' faces.

A LOST LEGACY?
Caravaggio's *Resurrection* (a subject he never painted again) was considered one of his finest works. It hung in the church of Sant'Anna dei Lombardi, until it was allegedly destroyed by an earthquake in 1792. Others insist it was merely moved for safekeeping, and never found. So that big, dark painting at a streetside *bancarella* might be worth a closer look...

SIGHTS

deteriorated – second-century frescoes. This was a burial place rather than a hideout; early Neapolitan Christians were persecuted in a far less systematic fashion than their counterparts in Rome. After the body of San Gennaro (St Januarius) was brought here from Pozzuoli in the fifth century, it became an important place of pilgrimage. Fine *arcosolia* (sarcophagi carved into *tufa* walls and topped with arched, frescoed niches) fill the upper levels in the main ambulatory, with fifth-century mosaics and frescoes from the second century in the vestibule, one possibly portraying Adam and Eve. The lower level has an eighth-century baptismal tub and a chapel dedicated to Sant'Agrippino. Catacomb tours take 40 minutes.

Regrettably, the early Christian basilica of San Gennaro has been closed to the public for years, and is currently used as a storeroom by the hospital.

★ Museo di Capodimonte

Porta Piccola Via Miano 2 (081 749 9111/www. museo-capodimonte.it). Bus 24, 110, C57, C63, R4. **Open** *Museum* 8.30am-7.30pm Mon, Tue, Thur-Sun (last entry 6.30pm). *Park* 8am-1hr before sunset daily. **Admission** *Museum* €7.50; €6.50 after 2pm; free under-18s, over-65s. *Park* free. **No credit cards.**

When construction began in 1738 on the palace that now houses one of Italy's largest and most artistically rich museums, King Carlo III envisaged no more than a hunting lodge. Seduced by plans for something far grander – and hard pushed to find space for the vast art collection he had inherited from his mother, Elisabetta Farnese – a monumental three-storey *palazzo reale* (royal palace) went up in the heart of a magnificent park covering seven sq km. Though it would be 100 years before the finishing touches were put to the building, the Farnese collection was installed by 1759; acquisitions by Carlo and later Bourbon monarchs enriched the gallery, and porcelain and weaponry were added in the late 19th century.

Over the years the palace acted as a repository for the royal collections, the main seat of the court, and a royal summer holiday home. Now an art museum with immense permanent collections, it's also the venue for internationally renowned exhibitions.

The main entrance is a regal affair. Cool, cavernous porticos on the ground floor hide bars and shops. The Farnese collection, along with the Bourbon collection, is upstairs, as are the smaller Borgia, porcelain and contemporary collections, and the armoury. There's information about the individual works of art (in English) in each room.

Italian art makes up the bulk of the Farnese collection. It starts in room 2 with groundbreaking portraits by Raphael and Titian. Umbrian and Tuscan schools are represented by Masaccio (the 15th century *Crucifixion* from a now-dismantled altarpiece in room 3 is one of the few additions to the collection since Unification in 1861). In room 5 you'll find

a copy by Marcello Venusti of Michelangelo's original (uncensored) *Last Judgment*, and an early work by Botticelli, the *Madonna with Child and Two Angels* in room 6. The prime representatives of the 15th-century Veneto tradition are Andrea Mantegna's *Portrait of Young Francesco Gonzaga* (room 8) and *St Euphemia* (room 7) and Giovanni Bellini's *Transfiguration* (room 8); note the blend of religious mysticism and realistic rural Veneto setting.

Titian's masterpiece, *Danaë*, is in room 11. In it, Danaë, daughter of King Argos, is seduced by Jupiter in the form of golden rain; the courtesan who modelled for the painting was probably the lover of a Farnese cardinal. El Greco's *El Soplon*, a version of a work mentioned by Pliny, is in the same room.

Sixteenth- and 17th-century works from the Farnese family's former duchy in the Emilia region are plentiful. Works by Correggio include the *Mystic Marriage of St Catherine* (1517) in room 12. Parmigianino's virginal *Antea* is also in room 12; Annibale Carracci's *Mystic Marriage of St Catherine* is in room 19, and his allegorical *Hercules at the Crossroads* is in room 20; Guido Reni's *Atlanta and Hippomenes* is in room 22. Not to be overlooked in this galaxy of Italian talent are Brueghel's two enigmatic pieces, *The Parable of the Blind* and *The Misanthrope*, both in room 17.

Also on the first floor are the royal apartments, including Queen Maria Amalia's boudoir (packed with Capodimonte porcelain), the magnificent ballroom, the dainty Pompeian drawing room, and a range of French furniture and paintings.

The second floor features works produced in Naples from the 13th to 19th centuries. All the greats are here, from Simone Martini's *St Ludovic of Toulouse* (room 65) to Caravaggio's *Flagellation* (room 78), which influenced generations of Neapolitan painters. Massimo Stanzione's *Moses' Sacrifice* is in room 89, his *Madonna and Child* in Room 93; Giuseppe Ribera's *St Jerome and the Angel* and the allegorical *Drunken Silenus* are in rooms 90 and 91; Pietro Cavallino's *St Cecilia in Ecstasy* is in room 94; Luca Giordano's *Madonna of the Canopy* is in room 103; and, in room 104, Francesco Solimena's *Aeneas and Dido* inspired his friend Alessandro Scarlatti to set the subject to music in 1696. A third-floor attic houses modern and contemporary paintings, including Warhol's *Vesuvius*. In rooms 106-111 there are three works by Artemesia Gentileschi, including *Judith Beheading Holofernes*.

FREE Osservatorio Astronomico

Salita Moiariello 16 (081 557 5111/081 557 5429/www.na.astro.it). Bus 24, 110, C63, R4. **Open** *Guided tours only* on reservation. **Admission** free.

This magnificent neoclassical building dates from 1819, and was commissioned by King Ferdinando I. The first observatory in Italy, it contains a fine collection of equipment, historical and modern, some of which may be used during the tour.

SIGHTS

Vomero

A leafy enclave with stunning views.

Look up from almost any vantage point in central Naples and you'll see two of the city's flagship monuments, Castel Sant'Elmo and the San Martino monastery, perched atop Vomero hill. Most of the area is now urbanised: gone are the days when families took the funicular up to what was a hilltop village for Sunday morning picnics in the country, surrounded by green fields and grazing sheep.

Road access improved in the 1970s when the *tangenziale* (city ring road) was built through the back of the hill, and Vomero now feels almost like a city in its own right. Its shops, schools and healthcare services attract custom from Naples and beyond, creating considerable congestion at times. Still, the air is a degree or two cooler up here, and the streets noticeably cleaner than in the city below.

Map p331	Cafés, Bars &
Hotels p105	Gelaterie p136
Restaurants p124	

INTRODUCING THE AREA

At the heart of the district is the diamond-shaped **Piazza Vanvitelli**. Here, the tree-lined, partly pedestrianised Via Scarlatti, whose *struscio* or *passeggiata* on summer evenings rivals that on Via Toledo, meets the traffic hell of Via Bernini. With elegant café tables spilling out on to pavements packed with well-heeled residents, Piazza Vanvitelli epitomises the district's pan-European, middle-class air. On summer evenings, the square fills with teenagers, who while away their time striking poses and chatting.

Three of Naples' four funicular railways lead up to Vomero (*see p80* **Funiculì, funiculà!**). The **Funicolare di Montesanto** brings you out closest to its star attractions, the **Certosa-Museo di San Martino** (*see p81*), a former Carthusian monastery turned museum, and the **Castel Sant'Elmo** (*see p81*). As you face the funicular, take the short cut to the left of it, passing the 1980s council administrative offices, and continue down Via Dalbono until it hits Via Angelini. Here, turn right and head down towards Largo San Martino, past the

castle on the right and some precariously perched late 19th-century villas on the left. It's ten minutes' walk in all.

The top station of the **Funicolare di Chiaia** on Via Cimarosa lies on the same road as the main entrance to Vomero's other crowd-puller, the green, almost wild **Parco della Floridiana** (*see p82*); the park also houses the **Museo Nazionale della Ceramica Duca di Martina** (*see p82*). A third funicular, **Funicolare Centrale**, provides a vital link with the port and the soul of Naples, Piazza Plebiscito and Via Toledo.

Before the funiculars were built in the late 19th and early 20th centuries, getting to Vomero involved scaling long flights of steps from the city centre. The steps are still there, looking a little forlorn, with weeds sprouting through the paving slabs and the odd scooter carcass. Poorly signposted, and decidedly strenuous if tackled from the bottom up, the steps enable you to make the journey down from Vomero in more panoramic fashion than the funicular, while avoiding its traffic-clogged roads (note that tackling the steps after dark is not advisable).

To reach the westernmost flight leading eventually down to Mergellina – the **Calata San Francesco** – cut through the Parco della Floridiana from its top gate on Via Cimarosa (with a detour to take in the magnificent views from its belvedere at the bottom end), then come out on to Via Aniello Falcone from the western gate, halfway down. Head west along Via Falcone and turn left down the steep *calata* (the road soon turns into steps), shortly after passing a splendid art nouveau palazzo on the right. Cut across Via Tasso and Corso Vittorio Emanuele, stopping to peek at Anglo-Italian engineer/architect/inventor Lamont Young's (*see p45*) **Castello Aselmeyer**. Incongruously perched at no.166, it marries the Tudor elements (bow windows, loggias) so dear to the English upper-middle class with Gothic picturesque. Carry on down Via Arco Mirelli until you get to Chiaia seafront and the western end of the Villa Comunale.

For a more panoramic but less genteel descent, take **Via Pedamentino San Martino**, which starts from Largo San Martino, in front of the Certosa-Museo di San Martino. On reaching traffic-choked Corso Vittorio Emanuele, turn left and you'll see a set of steps heading downwards, opposite the Funicolare di Montesanto station. These will bring you out in busy Montesanto, a major public transport hub. If, instead, you continue past the station on the *corso* and take the steps up Via Cupa Vecchia on the left, you'll discover one of the few patches of inner-city greenery open to the public: the small **Parco Viviani**, whose main entrance is on Via Santacroce 15.

Almost opposite, where the steps of Via Pedamentino San Martino meet the *corso*, is Vico Trinità delle Monache, which leads down to the **Parco dei Quartieri Spagnoli** (closed all Mon & Sun pm). It was created as part of an ongoing project to redevelop a one-time military hospital (which started life in the 17th century as the Trinità delle Monache convent); the buildings will eventually house a natural history museum, sports complex and concert areas. The first phase, a public park and play area, featureless save for a stand of magnificent umbrella pines, is now finished; in summer, the garden hosts some fine open-air concerts and film programmes (see www.sigbloom.it).

Funiculì, funiculà!

The train that climbed an active volcano.

'Jammo 'ncoppa, jammo ja', funiculì, funiculà!' ('Let's go, let's get on, the funiculi funicular') – thus runs the rousing chorus to an infectious Neapolitan song. Written in 1880, it was supposedly inspired by the glorious inauguration of a funicular railway that was designed to whisk devotees of the Grand Tour up the flank of Vesuvius, charging 20 shillings a ticket. A more cynical version of the story goes that the owner of the Vesuvian rail system, English tour operator Thomas Cook, commissioned the song as a promotional jingle in an attempt to popularise an otherwise daunting journey up a live volcano on an untested and frankly dubious mechanical contraption.

In any case, the ditty weathered rather better than the railway, which experienced severe cost overruns, violent insurrection from local tour guides and a series of eruptions; 1906, 1911, 1929 and finally the big one in 1943, which destroyed once and for all the jaunty dream of conquering the volcano.

Still, the idea of the funicular caught on marvelously in less forbidding areas: today, there are four funiculars in Naples, and another in Capri (*see p214*).

Castel Sant'Elmo

Via Tito Angelini 22 (081 578 4030/ 081 558 7708). Funicular Montesanto to via Morghen, Centrale to Piazzetta Fuga, or Chiaia to Via Cimarosa/bus V1. **Open** 9am-6.30pm Mon, Wed-Sun (last admission 1hr before closing). **Admission** €3; free with Certosa ticket. **No credit cards.** **Map** p331 G10.

Castel Sant'Elmo takes its name from the small church that stood here in the tenth century, St Erasmus – corrupted over the centuries to 'St Elmo'. A castle has stood here since 1329, when King Robert of Anjou modified a pre-existing Norman watchtower using the artists, architects and builders who were working on the adjacent monastery of San Martino. The castle acquired its massive six-pointed star shape in the mid 16th century, during an extensive reorganisation of city defences. In 1587 the ammunition dump was struck by lightning; the castle was badly damaged and 150 people died.

Over the years, the castle's dungeon has held many illustrious inmates, including heroes of the 1799 Parthenopean Republic, and it was a military prison until the mid 1970s. That might help to explain why the castle has never been a popular destination for Neapolitans. Its unmistakeable bulk has, however, long provided a focal point for pictorial cityscapes, including the extraordinary *Tavola Strozzi* in next door's Certosa-Museo di San Martino.

The ground floor of the castle is closed, although its gloomy interior can occasionally be glimpsed through the glass panels on the first floor – which is only opened during major exhibitions.

Piazza d'Armi, as the top floor is called, is in fact the castle's roof, and is best reached by lift; the 360° view over Naples is arguably the most breathtaking in the city. The walkway around the battlements is splendid, and a gently sloping path inside the castle leads you back down across the drawbridge, passing under the coat of arms of Carlo V.

▶ *If you're visiting the castle and the Certosa-Museo di San Martino, head to the Certoso first: your ticket will also get you into the castle.*

★ Certosa-Museo di San Martino

Piazzale San Martino 5 (081 229 4502/081 558 6408). Funicular Montesanto to Via Morghen, Centrale to Piazzetta Fuga or Chiaia to Via Cimarosa/bus V1. **Open** 8.30am-7.30pm Mon, Tue, Thur-Sun (last admission 1hr before closing). **Admission** (includes Castel Sant'Elmo) €6; €3 reductions. *Audioguide* €4. **No credit cards**. **Map** p331 H10.

This Carthusian monastery complex was founded in 1325, although its present appearance is the result of much 16th-century reworking. Renowned for its priceless architectural and artistic assets, San Martino was dissolved under French rule (1806-15); the monks returned only briefly before the *certosa* (charterhouse) was wrested from them again in the wake of Italian Unification in 1861. State of the art

Castel Sant'Elmo.

visitor facilities, airy rooms and terraced gardens with sweeping views over the Naples waterfront make the Certosa one of the city's must-sees.

The church's late 17th-century façade, opposite the ticket barrier, is by Cosimo Fanzago; it conceals remnants of the Gothic original, such as the pointed arches and cross-vaulted ceiling in the *pronaos* (projecting vestibule), which has 17th-century frescoes by Micco Spadaro depicting the persecution of Carthusians in England during Henry VIII's reign.

The church's interior contains as complete an array of Neapolitan art as you could hope for. Massimo Stanzione's *Deposition* (1638) dominates the inner façade, flanked by two fine portraits by Giuseppe Ribera, who is also responsible for the 12 paintings of prophets (1638-43) tucked into the spandrels of the arches. The delicate 18th-century marble altar balustrade is by Giuseppe Sammartino. The walls and side chapels feature paintings by the Vaccaros, Francesco Solimena and Stanzione. In the vaulted ceiling are frescoes (1637-40) by Giovanni Lanfranco: *Ascension with Angels*, *Apostles* and *Saints*. Bonaventura Presti used material already prepared by Fanzago for his intricate inlaid marble floor (1664).

The choir features Ribera's *Communion of the Apostles*, Guido Reni's *Adoration of the Shepherds* (1642), and Battista Caracciolo's *Washing of Feet* (1622), and the sacristy has some exquisite marquetry; on the cupboards, 56 panels depict biblical scenes. In the Cappella del Tesoro are Ribera's *Pietà* and frescoes by Luca Giordano; the *parlatorio* and chapter room (where there are several works by Battista Caracciolo) are also essential viewing.

A long passageway leads left out of the small *chiostro dei procuratori* into the *chiostro grande* (great cloister) – one of Italy's finest. This bright, sunny area was created in the 16th century by Giovanni Antonio Dosio; Cosimo Fanzago added the small monks' graveyard (note the skulls) and the busts and statues above the pillared portico, as well as the grotesque faces animating the well.

The Museo dell'Opera art gallery is beautifully laid out around the main cloister. The majority of the 17th- and 18th-century works, originally created for the monastery, is now housed in the prior's quarters in the southern wing (rooms 17 to 23). The collection includes works by Ribera (Sts Jerome and Sebastian), Lanfranco (*Our Lady of the Rosary*) and Stanzione (*Baptism of Christ*); Spadaro created the ceilings in rooms 14, 15 and 16. Room 8 contains a remarkable sculpture, the *Madonna and Child with the Infant John the Baptist,* by Pietro Bernini (father of the more famous Gianlorenzo).

The *certosa*, the Carthusian order and the history of Naples are constant themes in the works. There are splendid maps and landscape paintings, ranging from the anonymous *Tavola Strozzi*, with its detailed depiction of 15th-century Naples in room 32, and Didier Barra's bird's-eye view of Naples at the end of the 16th century, to a fine series of late 17th-century paintings by Gaspar Van Wittel in room 40. On the first floor are 19th-century paintings by local artists.

Another section is devoted to Nativity scenes, including a massive *presepe* (crib) with rare 18th-century pieces, named after its 19th-century creator, Cuciniello. It's a marvellous depiction of what life in Naples would have been like centuries ago, complete with lighting effects that simulate the diurnal cycle. You'll also find displays on theatre, shipping and, in the former pharmacy, glassware and porcelain.

Not all of the Certosa's treasures will be on display when you visit, due to the usual problems of understaffing and restoration. If you want to see a specific work, phone ahead.

★ Parco della Floridiana/Museo Nazionale della Ceramica Duca di Martina

Via Cimarosa 77 (081 578 8418). Funicular Montesanto to Via Morghen, Centrale to Piazzetta Fuga, or Chiaia to Via Cimarosa/bus E4, V1. **Open** *Park* 8.30am-1hr before sunset daily. *Museum* 8.30am-2pm Mon, Wed-Sun (last admission 1.15pm). **Admission** €2.50. **No credit cards. Map** p326 E11.

In 1815, King Ferdinando returned to Naples after ten years of French rule, accompanied by his second wife. Lucia Migliaccio, Duchess of Floridia, was given this splendid villa and garden. In the 1920s, it was purchased by the Italian government; the park was opened to the public, and the villa became a museum. The park is a favourite spot for walkers and joggers, and there's a memorable view from the terrace at the bottom of the garden.

The museum's basement showcases ceramics from China's Ming and Qing dynasties, along with a Tang drummer on horseback in room 24. The Meiping vase in the shape of a phoenix is particularly rare. The collection of Japanese porcelain includes pieces from the Edo period (1603-1867).

The ground floor has majolica pieces from the Middle Ages onwards. Room 21 has a walking stick with a glass top; inside it is a portrait of the King's second wife (wags joked that this was the only way he could get the unpopular lady into the court).

The first floor is dedicated to European ceramics. There's an early 18th-century picture frame from Sicily in room 2; some local biscuit pieces, two dishes from the royal dinner service, and the fine *Capodimonte Declaration* by Gricci in room 5; some splendid Meissen porcelain in room 6; pieces by Ginori (including *Three Putti with a Goat*) in room 9; china from Sèvres and Saint-Cloud in room 10; and an odd Meissen clock-cum-inkstand in room 14.

Parco della Floridiana.

Chiaia to Posillipo

Grand tour Naples, with a beach and nightlife to boot.

For many, Naples is synonymous with the characterful chaos of the Centro Storico – but for centuries, the main focus lay elsewhere. The Romantic poets and grand tourists steered clear of the crowded centre, exploring Chiaia and Posillipo instead.

Naples' topography is displayed to its best advantage here: the sweep of the bay, Capri on the horizon and Vesuvius slumbering to the south. The pine-clad hill of Posillipo, with the city fanning out to its side, recalls Goethe's romantic descriptions, although little remains of the German poet's idyll. Mergellina harbour still has a small fishing community among its sleek yachts, and some narrow, ancient *vicoli* (alleys) can be found between Piazza Amedeo and the Villa Comunale. This area remains wealthier and quieter than the old town, with its smart shops and elegant palazzi.

Map pp326-327	Restaurants p126
Hotels p108	Cafés, Bars &
	Gelaterie p136

CHIAIA

Piazza Amedeo is a transport hub, with a metro station, bus stop and funicular; as such, it's a good place from which to begin an exploration of Chiaia. A grubby traffic island is at the centre of the tree-lined, cobbled square (apparently uselessly, as cars continue to come from all directions), incongruously overlooked by splendid *stile liberty* (art nouveau) palazzi.

At no.14, **Palazzo Regina Margherita** (closed to the public) has a lovely, faded, majolica-tiled façade with mullioned windows. South from Piazza Amedeo, Via Ascensione – or the parallel Via Bausan – is where playwright Eduardo de Filippo was born; controversy still rages over the exact location. Via Bausan has several restaurants and bars, and is lively at weekends. In nearby Piazzetta Ascensione, the church of the **Ascensione** (081 141 1657, open 8-11am, 5-7.30pm Mon-Sat, 8am-1.30pm Sun) is a mid 17th-century Cosimo Fanzago creation.

Heading east out of the square, Via Colonna is home to the church of **Santa Teresa a Chiaia** (081 411208, open 8-10am, 6-7.30pm Mon-Sat, 9am-12.30pm, 6-8pm Sun), also designed by Fanzago (1650). It features a striking three-storey façade, a gracious double flight of curved steps, a handsome semicircular forecourt and several works by Luca Giordano.

Via Colonna, which becomes Via dei Mille and then Via Filangieri before turning right on to Piazza dei Martiri and Via Calabritto, is home to Naples' most exclusive clothes and jewellers' shops. Set amid the designer shops, in the 17th-century Palazzo Rocella, is the Palazzo delle Arti Napoli – better known as **PAN** (*see p84*). The zone just down from Via dei Mille is the place to see and be seen on weekend nights out, its streets teeming with the young and chic.

Piazza dei Martiri itself is dominated by four stone lions guarding an obelisk celebrating Victory, constructed in the mid 19th century in honour of the martyrs of the 1799 revolution. The piazza is flanked by two splendid palazzi (both closed to the public): the 19th-century, neoclassical **Palazzo Partanna** (no.58), with its original, mid 18th-century portal, and **Palazzo Calabritto** (no.30), with a fluted column portal by Luigi Vanvitelli.

Leading out of the piazza, the narrow Vico Santa Maria a Cappella Vecchia was once home to British Ambassador Sir William Hamilton, his wife Emma and her soulmate Admiral Horatio Nelson (*see p20* **Low Life to High Society**). A nearby archway, dated 1506, leads into the courtyard of what was a Benedictine abbey until 1788, after which it was rented out to a string of notables, including the Hamiltons. Under a second archway (no.31) is the house where Nelson was introduced to Emma in 1793.

Via Morelli leads into the cavernous Via Chiatamone, which was the road closest to the coast until the late 19th century, when the parallel Via Partenope, dotted with luxury hotels, was built. Via Chiatamone attracted the best and worst of Neapolitan tourism; in 1770, Giacomo Casanova visited a club in the 17th-century palazzo (now nos.26-30) to drum up business for a smart new brothel on Posillipo run by Irish madam Sarah Goudar.

To the west, tyres speed over cobbles along the once-picturesque **Riviera di Chiaia**, threatening life and limb of anyone rash enough to attempt the crossing to the sole park in this area, Villa Comunale, home to the tiny **Acquario** (*see below*).

Percy Shelley and his wife Mary stayed at no.250 (the original building was demolished in the 1950s) from 1818 to 1819. During this period they took a child to the church of **San Giuseppe a Chiaia** (081 681 898, open 5-8pm Mon-Sat; 8am-noon Sun) to be christened; the child's identity remains a mystery to this day. John Keats was less fortunate: around the same time, he spent three weeks stuck on a ship moored in the bay opposite. The sea was too rough to allow a landing, and Keats was left feeling feverish and violently seasick. **Villa Pignatelli** (no.200, *see below*) was built for Ferdinand Acton, the son of King Ferdinando I's prime minister, Sir John Acton.

A detour north from the Riviera di Chiaia along Via Santa Maria in Portico leads to the church of the same name (081 669294, open 8-1.30pm, 4.30-7.30pm daily), which has a life-size Nativity scene (1647) to the left of the altar.

★ Palazzo delle Arti Napoli (PAN)

Centro per le Arti Contemporanee, Palazzo Rocella, Via dei Mille 60 (081 795 8605/ www.palazzoartinapoli.net). Funicular Chiaia to Piazza Amedeo/bus C24, C25, C28, E6. **Open** 9.30am-7.30pm Mon, Wed-Sat; 9.30am-2.30pm Sun. **Admission** €5; €3 reductions. **Credit** *Bookshop only* AmEx, MC, V. **Map** p327 G12.

PAN has no permanent collection, but instead describes itself as a 'centre for arts and documentation'. A fourth-floor archive has catalogues and pictures of contemporary art activity in Naples stretching back over the last few decades. There are regular exhibitions (often drawn from the collections of other Neapolitan galleries), as well as film screenings, book presentations, lectures, discussions and theatre events. More off-the-wall shows have included a selection of Lou Reed's snapshots of his home town (the opening of the event was priceless, with the singer of 'Heroin' and 'Venus in Furs' politely greeting the somewhat traditional mayor). As a slightly labyrinthine collection of small rooms, it's not a great exhibition space – and with its mixture of activities, there's a sense that PAN is still trying to discover its true calling. It's worth keeping an eye on, though, as interesting shows often crop up.

► *Opened in the same year as PAN, the contemporary art museum MADRe is a very different proposition; see p75.*

Stazione Zoologica (Acquario)

Villa Comunale (081 583 3111/www.szn.it). Bus 140, 152, C10, C9, R3. **Open** *Mar-Oct* 9.30am-6pm Mon-Sat; 9.30am-7.30pm Sun. *Nov-Feb* 9am-5pm Tue-Sat; 9am-2pm Sun. **Admission** €1.50. **No credit cards. Map** p327 F14.

German naturalist Anton Dohrn founded this aquarium in 1872, making it one of Europe's oldest. The ground floor still contains the original 24 tanks, housing sea creatures from the Bay of Naples: coral, jellyfish, turtles, sea horses, an octopus or two, lobsters and starfish. Water for the tanks is brought in from 300m (1,050ft) out in the bay. Luckily for the inmates, it's filtered before being used. Legend has it that the entire contents of the aquarium were boiled up to make a massive fish soup during the famine that struck the city in 1944; the less than philanthropic truth is that its contents were cooked up for the British Allied Commander Field Marshal Henry Maitland Wilson, after the liberation of the city in the same year.

Villa Communale.

Mergellina.

MERGELLINA & PIEDIGROTTA

Further west, the Riviera forks: north of Largo Torretta lies the densely populated district of Torretta; towards the sea are the elegant palazzi of Viale Antonio Gramsci (renamed in the 1970s after the founder of the Italian Communist Party, but still sometimes referred to by its old name, Viale Elena). The huge, heavily fortified American consulate stands on its corner. Ahead, the traffic hell of Via Piedigrotta leads to the art nouveau Mergellina railway station.

Before the railway bridge is **Santa Maria di Piedigrotta** (081 669 761, open 7am-noon, 5-8pm daily). A church has stood on this spot, which is associated with apparitions of Mary of Piedigrotta, since the 13th century. This particular church is the fulcrum of the feast-day celebrations of Mary's nativity on 8 September (*see p155* **Music and movement**). The pavement beneath the bridge is unpleasant and rather isolated (when crossing it, watch for traffic and proceed with caution), but leads to the rewarding **Parco Vergiliano** (*see p86*).

Via Mergellina skirts the bay to the 'Chalets' – a ramshackle assortment of ice-cream parlours and late-night dives. In Largo Barbaia (from where Naples' shortest funicular ascends to the hillside suburbs above), Via Orazio climbs up Posillipo hill to Naples' most exclusive residential areas, which have little to offer but fine views and the self-satisfaction of wealth.

Back on the waterfront, the church of **Santa Maria del Parto** (Via Mergellina 21, 081 664627, open 5-8pm Mon-Sat, 8.30am-1pm, 5-8pm Sun) stands at the head of a long flight of steps (spare yourself the climb by taking the lift at no.9B). The church was built by 15th-century poet Iacopo Sannazzaro, whose tomb is behind the altar; its lights guided fishermen home. In the first side chapel on the right, the painting *St Michael Vanquishing the Devil* recalls a 16th-century episode in which an ambitious prelate, Diomede Carafa, was tempted by a local beauty, Vittoria d'Avalos. When she declared her love for him, he commissioned this work; the faces of the archangel and the serpent are those of

SIGHTS

★ FREE **Villa Comunale**
Riviera di Chiaia/Via Caracciolo (081 761 1131).
Bus 140, 152, C28, R3. **Open** *May-Oct* 7am-midnight daily. *Nov-Apr* 7am-10pm daily.
Admission free. **Map** p327 F14.
Swathes of historic buildings were demolished to make way for this royal park, designed by Luigi Vanvitelli. It was inaugurated in 1781 as the *giardini reali* (royal gardens) and originally only opened to the public once a year, on the feast of the Virgin Mary's nativity (8 Sept). The massive *Toro Farnese* – now in the Museo Archeologico Nazionale (*see p70*) – stood here until 1825, when it was replaced by a large bowl found in Paestum. Now surrounded by four lions, the bowl is the centrepiece of the Fontana delle Paparelle. The villa was restored for the 1994 G8 conference. There's a magnificent bandstand, built in 1887, and the small-is-beautiful Stazione Zoologica (*see left*).

★ **Villa Pignatelli**
Riviera di Chiaia 200 (081 669675). Bus 140, 152, C28, R3. **Open** 9am-2pm Mon, Wed, Thur, Sun; 9am-8pm Fri, Sat. **Admission** €6.
No credit cards. Map p327 F13.
Built in 1826 for Ferdinand Acton, the son of Naples' prime minister Sir John Acton, this villa is a mishmash of styles. The Rothschild family bought and enlarged the villa in 1841; it passed to the Pignatellis in 1867, and to the Italian state in 1952. Its magnificent ground floor rooms include the ballroom, dining room, library and a series of 'coloured rooms'; the green room contains a priceless collection of 17th- to 19th-century porcelain and majolica pieces. Room 1 displays works by 19th-century sculptor Vincenzo Gemito; room 2 has the collection's finest piece, Francesco Guarino's intense *St George* (c1650); and there are outstanding 18th- and 19th-century landscapes in room 6. The villa also hosts occasional, often excellent temporary shows.

INSIDE TRACK
LOVE ON THE LUNGOMARE

The long seafront stroll from Santa Lucia to Mergellina is a classic Sunday promenade. Keep an eye out along the **Lungomare** (seafront promenade) for clusters of padlocks attached to poles, painted with the names or initials of couples – the modern equivalent of true love knots.

SIGHTS

Diomede and Vittoria. What she thought of her portrayal as a snake is unrecorded.

Via Mergellina becomes Via Posillipo at Largo Sermoneta, where there is a fountain (1635) by Carlo Fanzago, Cosimo's son, named after the now-buried River Sebeto that flowed through Naples in ancient times.

★ FREE Parco Vergiliano

Salita della Grotta 20 (081 669 390). Metro Mergellina/bus C16, C24. **Open** 9am-1hr before sunset daily. **Admission** free. **Map** p326 B15.
To appreciate this splendidly peaceful spot, you'll need to climb a long flight of steps. For your pains, you'll get a view into the Crypta Neapolitana, a first-century AD road tunnel (now closed). Stories abound of the atrocious conditions in this primitive borehole, as cart-drivers fought to control their vehicles in the choking dust. (Conditions in the modern tunnel beneath it aren't much better.) At the top of the stairs stands what is controversially known as Virgil's Tomb, looking like a large dovecote. Although Virgil lived in Naples, he died in Brindisi; whether he was brought back here for burial is a question that has spawned no end of polemical volumes. The inscription on the tomb translates as 'Mantua bore me, Calabria took me, Naples holds me'.

POSILLIPO

The long, wide Via Orazio becomes Via Petrarca, and then, at the top of the hill, merges with Via Francesco Manzoni. It's lined by huge but discreet apartment buildings, some with guards on the gates: these are the homes of politicians, lawyers and business magnates. Turn left at the top of Via Manzoni and look westwards for wonderful views over the Bay of Pozzuoli and the site of the former steelworks at **Bagnoli**. As part of the area's redevelopment, the **North Pier** was opened in December 2005. Once the pier where ships unloaded ore and took away finished steel, it's now thronged with partygoers in summer. It extends out into the Bay of Pozzuoli, towards the isle of Nisida. Further down the hill, turn right up Viale

Virgilio for the **Parco Urbano Virgiliano** (open 9am-2pm Mon, Tue, Thur-Sun), a horseshoe-shaped park on top of Posillipo Hill with sumptuous views over the Campi Flegrei, and a busy clothes market on Friday mornings.

Back at the junction with Via Petrarca, a right turn (uphill) on to Via Francesco Manzoni leads to a Spanish watchtower, the **Torre Ranieri** (1530). One of a chain of towers along the coast, its signals could be seen from Baia.

From Largo Sermoneta down in Mergellina, cobbled Via Posillipo clatters gradually away from the bathing establishments set along the shoreline, passing the decrepit **Palazzo Donn'Anna** in the piazza of the same name. This rambling, partly derelict building has a long, sad history. The reputed site of Queen Joan II's cruel amorous pursuits in the 15th century, the original building was demolished in 1642 to make way for the present palazzo, designed by Cosimo Fanzago for an aristocratic couple. Alas, the young wife for whom it was built died within a few years of its completion. This is private property, although a polite word at the gatehouse may gain you admission to the porticoed terrace, with its wonderful view across the bay.

Shortly after the municipal bus depot on the right, the moody, grey, faux-Egyptian **Mausoleo** war memorial (Via Posillipo 155, open 9am-1pm daily) overlooks the road from a peaceful garden, shaded by massive pine trees. From Via Posillipo, three twisting lanes lead down to little beaches (*see right* **Sea Naples...**) – although they're definitely not for young children or poor swimmers. No buses service these routes, so it's a long haul back up again.

Via Russo passes the presidential summer residence **Villa Rosebery** (open during Maggio dei Monumenti; *see p50* **Monumental May**).

Via Marechiaro starts where Via Posillipo meets Via Boccaccio, and winds down to a tiny parking area surrounded by fish restaurants. The Calata del Ponticello a Marechiaro leads to a romantic spot overlooking a pebbly beach. A path to the sea on the left of the road, just before **Villa Pausilypon** (*see right*), descends to the pleasant cove of **La Gaiola**. There's a small shingle beach, and a long quay to swim from (*see right* **Sea Naples...**).

Via Posillipo continues on from the villa through a cutting in the headland, becoming Discesa Coroglio, then dropping sharply down towards the alternative entrance to the **Grotta di Seiano** (*see right*) and the sprawling, ex-industrial site of the Bagnoli steelworks, now occupied in part by the **Città della Scienza** (*see p159*) and a new pier. The island in the distance, Nisida, is home to a NATO naval support base and a juvenile reformatory, and is very much closed to the public, although the walk across the promontory that connects the island to the mainland is worth taking.

FREE Grotta di Seiano

Discesa Coroglio (081 230 1030/guided tours 081 795 2003). Bus 140 to Capo Posillipo, then F9. **Open** *Guided tours only* 9.30am, 10.30am, 11.15am Mon-Sat (jointly with Villa Pausilypon). Closed Aug. **Admission** free.

Once the private entrance to the ornate Villa Pausilypon, the tunnel was built by the architect Cocceius in the first century AD; he also designed the Grotta di Cocceio and the Crypta Neapolitana (*see p86*). Strengthened in 1840 by a series of load-bearing arches, the tunnel stretches for 770m (2,526ft) along the coast. En route, galleries provide magnificent views over the small Trentaremi Bay, named after the rowing boats used by the Romans. The fragile cliff into which the tunnel was bored is prone to landslides, and over the years access to the Grotta has been irregular; for the moment, though, it is open for guided tours.

FREE Villa Pausilypon

Discesa Coroglio 36 (081 230 1030). Bus 140 to Capo Posillipo, then F9. **Open** *Guided tours only* 9.30am, 10.30am, 11.15am Mon-Sat (jointly with Grotta di Seiano). **Admission** free.

Set in an area of stunning natural beauty on the Posillipo cliffs, this villa belonged to a Roman senator by the name of Publius Vedius Pollio. Access was, and still is, through the Grotta di Seiano. Apart from the remains of the villa itself, there's also an amphitheatre, which is used for occasional open-air concerts and has outstanding views over the small island of Gaiola. The island is the site of an ugly neo-classical villa, last owned by the Agnelli family; it is reputed to bring bad luck to all who possess it.

Sea Naples...

Posillipo's hidden bathing spots.

Visitors to Naples are often surprised to find that a city so famous for its climate doesn't have so much as a half-decent beach for swimming. As is the case with many other Mediterranean ports, the problem is the water quality. The sea here is certainly cleaner than it was some years back, following improvements in local sewage treatment. But the quantities of flotsam and jetsam, not to mention the discharge from hundreds of boats and ships in the bay, make swimming a potentially toxic business.

Since the prevailing north-westerly mistral wind tends to carry waterborne rubbish down towards the industrial coastal towns of Torre Annunziata and Castellammare di Stabia, the further north you go from Mergellina, the cleaner the water becomes. By the time you get to Via Posillipo, it's almost inviting – especially if you head around to the far side of the Campi Flegrei, where artificial coves add to the allure of the beach establishments (*see p190*).

In Posillipo, three charming, winding lanes lead down from Via Posillipo (and its continuations, Via San Strato and Discesa Coroglio) to the sea and *spiagge libere* (public beaches). The fact that none of the approach roads is served by public transport ensures a degree of peace and quiet, although the walk back up is a real challenge. Before motorboat fiends invade in July and August, though, this stretch of

coast can generally be relied upon for a relatively tranquil, uncrowded dip.

The first lane down, Via Russo, passes Villa Rosebery; at the end is a long rocky breakwater. The second, Via Marechiaro, starts where Via Posillipo meets Via Boccaccio; it winds downhill to a small car park and an overpowering smell of fried fish. The footpath passes assorted restaurants and bars around to the right to **Calata del Ponticello a Marechiaro**, where you can rent deckchairs and umbrellas in season.

Discesa la Gaiola drops down from Discesa Coroglio. Shortly before the road ends, a path on the left descends to the pleasant, shingly cove of **La Gaiola**; there are no restaurants here, so bring provisions for a picnic.

SIGHTS

Campi Flegrei

Ups and downs in the mythic Burning Fields.

The name Campi Flegrei (Phlegrean Fields) conjures up an area steeped in myth and history. Starting near Naples' western suburb, Fuorigrotta, and embracing the towns of Pozzuoli and Bacoli to the west, the Campi Flegrei are a geological marvel and an archaeological treasure trove. This is a land of bubbling, steaming volcanic activity, reputedly home to the Cumaean Sibyl, a Greek prophetess, and the entrance to the Underworld.

Roman emperors and aristocrats built fabulous summer palaces here; centuries later, 18th-century aesthetes such as Sir William Hamilton (*see p20*) found the landscape equally enchanting. Although modern development has stripped the area of some of its mystique, its classical legacy retains a powerful appeal.

Hotels p110   **Restaurants** p130

INTRODUCING THE AREA

Much of the aura of mystery that swathed the Campi Flegrei has been destroyed by the *abusivismo edilizio* – building without planning permission – that has covered swathes of the countryside with cement. The classical ring to the place names can be deceptive: **Arco Felice** (happy arch), named after the old Roman aqueduct spanning the road from Pozzuoli to Cuma, can be a traffic nightmare; **Quarto**, named after its distance from Pozzuoli (four Roman miles) has become an unlovely, 50,000-strong dormitory town for Naples; and **Lago Lucrino** (the Lucrine lake, famed for its oyster

INSIDE TRACK GREEN FIELDS

The latest park to be created here is the regional **Parco dei Campi Flegrei** (081 855 3225, www.parks.it/parco.campi. flegrei), which aims to restore some of the area to its pristine state. Cycle paths around the lakes are planned, along with hiking paths running from Lago Averna to Cuma and up to Monte Nuovo.

beds in antiquity) is now fringed by a disco, a supermarket and seafood restaurants.

Some areas, however, have been spared. Two volcanic craters (**Monte Nuovo** and **Astroni**) have been transformed into nature reserves, while **Pozzuoli** has been spruced up and gentrified, and its extensive underground Roman remains opened up to the public. **Baia** has a spectacular, state-of-the-art museum within its castle walls; at the end of the peninsula, **Capo Miseno** remains picturesque, and sports good beaches on its westward side.

ASTRONI

Astroni is one of the wonders of the Campi Flegrei: an entire volcanic crater carpeted with Mediterranean vegetation. Tapped by the Romans for its geothermal waters (the baths have never been discovered) and used by Naples' various dynasties as a hunting area from the 15th to 19th centuries, Astroni is now a World Wildlife Fund (WWF) reserve. A landslide after heavy rains in March 2005 blocked the road (near the site entrance) that winds down towards the lakes on the crater floor; visitors have since been channelled down a steeper path through holm oak woodland.

A shady picnic site has been laid out at the crater bottom, and screened observation walkways have been erected for birders by the lakeside, but much of the area is so dense in vegetation that birdwatching here requires a good pair of ears as well as binoculars. Although it sounds idyllic, be warned: access by public transport involves a two-kilometre walk through an isolated area and opening hours are subject to change, so phone ahead.

Riserva Naturale Cratere degli Astroni

Oasi WWF, Agnano (081 588 3720/www.wwf napolinord.it/oasiastroni.htm). **Open** 9.30am-2.30pm (last entry 1pm) Mon, Wed-Sun. **Admission** €5; €3 reductions; free WWF members. **No credit cards**.

POZZUOLI

Greeks from Cuma founded Dikaiarchia (ancient Pozzuoli) in c530 BC as a bulwark against encroaching Etruscans and Samnites, but few traces of the original settlement remain. The area regained strategic importance in the late third century BC during the Second Punic War, when the Romans were anxious to prevent Hannibal reaching the Tyrrhenian coast from nearby Capua. The hill overlooking the port, now known as **Rione Terra**, was colonised in 194 BC and the new settlement (Puteoli) rapidly expanded. In Imperial times, Puteoli was a thriving *entrepôt* port, several times larger than Pompeii. Extensive traces have survived, albeit often suffocated by the modern town.

The seafaring tradition is still strong. Pozzuoli is the closest mainland harbour to the islands of Procida and Ischia, and its ferry port does brisk business. Meanwhile, Neapolitans come here in droves to dine on fresh fish and *frutti di mare* at lower prices than in Naples.

Down near the port is the ancient fish and meat market, the *macellum*, commonly known as the **Serapeo** (Temple of Serapis). Its columns are visibly perforated by molluscs, showing that the *macellum* has spent much of its existence submerged in seawater. It's subject to a rising and sinking phenomenon called bradyseism, caused by geological shifts several kilometres below the earth's surface (*see p91* **Satyricon submerged**). Up on the hill above the port is the site of the original Roman colony, **Rione Terra**, a warren of ancient roads, shops and houses. Parts of the site can now be visited (*see p90*).

North-east of the port, the 40,000-seater **Anfiteatro Flavio** (Flavian amphitheatre) was the ancient world's third largest, after the Colosseum in Rome and Capua's amphitheatre. Rising above the congested roads, railways and ugly modern apartment blocks literally and figuratively, it was built mostly during Vespasian's rule (AD 70-79), though work may have started under Nero. The impressive *carceres* (cells) in the underground area below the arena indicate that the amphitheatre was used for *venationes* – contests involving exotic animals, shipped in through Puteoli's port from one of the Empire's distant provinces.

The large *fossa* (ditch) cutting across the arena may have contained the stage scenery, which was raised or lowered depending on the backdrop required. The underground cells are open to visitors, and the *cavea* (stalls) and the arena are back in use for rather more sedate musical entertainment from June to September;

Capo Miseno.

Pozzuoli.

information is available from the site ticket office or the Ufficio Informazioni dell'Azienda Cura Soggiorno Turismo (081 526 1481, www.infocampiflegrei.it). The area around the amphitheatre is scattered with beautifully carved marble fragments found in the Campi Flegrei, a wonderful open-air museum of sorts.

For a taste of just how 'burning' the Campi Flegrei still are, walk across the dormant volcanic crater of the foul-smelling Solfatara to the east of the town centre. The ancient Romans called the Solfatara the Forum Vulcani, and visited it with the same strange fascination as modern-day tourists. From an eerie lunar landscape, hissing wisps of sulphurous steam rise up; here and there are broad mud bubbles. According to locals, breathing deeply of the sulphur fumes does wonders for sinus and lung problems. On the north-eastern side of the crater, entrances to a *sudatorium* (built in the 19th century and now bricked up) form weird, intolerably hot saunas.

On Via San Gennaro, a few hundred metres south of the Solfatara, the 16th-century **Santuario di San Gennaro** church marks the spot where Naples' patron saint was decapitated. Legend has it that the deed was done beside the second column on the right; the congealed blood on a stone, kept in the first chapel on the right, turns a bright, healthy red on the days when a vial-full of what is said to be San Gennaro's blood liquefies in Naples' Duomo (*see p62* **City of blood**).

Rione Terra

Volcanic activity in the 1970s led to the mass evacuation of Rione Terra, Pozzuoli's densely inhabited and somewhat insalubrious 'acropolis' overlooking the modern port. As so often happens in these parts, a human tragedy was turned into an archaeological success story: with a massive injection of government funds, archaeologists excavated below the 17th-century palazzi and brought much of ancient Puteoli to light.

An underground visitors' walkway leads through the dense network of roads and passages that date, in some cases, from Puteoli's foundation in 194 BC. Much is revealed along the way: *tabernae* (simple restaurants), a *cryptoportico* (underground storeroom) and a *pistrinum* (bakery). On a lower level are some *ergastula* (cells for slaves), with surprisingly erudite graffiti that quotes from Catullus, and a frescoed *lararium* (household shrine). Beneath the *decumanus maximus* (the main road leading to the forum) is part of the impressive sewage system that channelled waste water into the sea. At the end of the walkway, visitors emerge just below a

SIGHTS

17th-century cathedral that was built around a major Roman temple, its columns revealed by a devastating fire in 1964.

The guided tour (English commentary is available on request for groups) lasts about an hour – but at the time of going to press, the entire site remained closed for restoration. Call 081 303 0380 or 081 855 1240 for an update.

★ Anfiteatro Flavio
Via Terracciano 75 (081 526 6007). **Open** *June-Sept* 9am-7.10pm Mon, Wed-Sun. *Oct-May* 9am-3pm Mon, Wed-Sun. **Admission** €4; €2

reductions (tickets valid 2 days, includes Cuma, Museo Archaeologico & Parco Archeologico e Monumentale di Baia). **No credit cards**.

FREE Santuario di San Gennaro
Via San Gennaro Agnano 10 (081 526 1114). **Open** 9am-noon, 4.30-6pm daily. **Admission** free.

★ Solfatara
Via Solfatara 161 (081 526 2341/www. solfatara.it). **Open** *Apr-Sept* 8.30am-7pm daily. *Oct-Mar* 8.30am-4.30pm daily. **Admission** €6; €5 reductions. **Credit** MC, V.

Satyricon submerged

The ups and downs of the Campi Flegrei.

The Campi Flegrei provides the most intriguing example in the world of the volcanic phenomenon known as bradyseism. Derived from the Greek words *bradus* (slow) and *sism* (movement), it's a kind of slow-motion ripple effect in the earth's crust. In the case of the Campi, magma chambers nearly five kilometres below the surface (under Pozzuoli harbour) experience emptying and refilling, which causes the surface directly above them to rise and fall – sometimes quite rapidly, as in the case of earthquakes and small gaseous eruptions within the Solfatara. The elevation can rise or fall by a metre or more in just a few years. Generally, though, the changes are slight, only becoming problematic over long passages of time.

In the Campi area, the phenomenon is of particular interest thanks to the proximity of the sea. One of the clearest examples is in the old *macellum* (indoor market) in Pozzuoli. The structure has fallen and risen back up again by at least ten metres since it was constructed in ancient times, and you can see marks on the columns where molluscs clung to the stone when it sank below sea level.

Equally famous is the submerged city of Baia. Once home to lavish palaces built by the wealthiest Romans, and the setting for the wild banquet scene in Petronius's *Satyricon*, its fabulous mosaics and statuary now sit on the sea floor. Yet as with Pompeii and Herculaneum (*see pp234-244*), the massive forces of volcanic and seismic activity not only destroyed the ancient world, but preserved its rich heritage for us to explore, study and appreciate.

INSIDE TRACK GOOD MIXER

We have Pozzuoli to thank for the existence of concrete. It was the source of *pozzolana*, a pink, sand-like volcanic ash that the Romans used to concoct the first cement, which soon became one of their chief building materials.

BAIA

From well before the Christian era until the 18th century, Baia (possibly named after Baios, a companion of Ulysses who, according to legend, was buried here) was one of Italy's prime holiday resorts, combining all the essential ingredients of sea air, health-giving mineral springs and glorious scenery. Modern Baia consists chiefly of unattractive strip development along the main coast road, with a plethora of bars, restaurants and gelaterie. In Roman times it was a different story, as wealthy aristocrats built splendid villas here. Although much of ancient Baiae now lies under the sea (the *città sommersa* can be seen from a glass-bottomed boat which operates from the port of Baia; *see right*), there's still a certain opulence about the site and its natural setting.

Emperor Caligula, who reigned from AD 37 to 41, built a causeway of boats and ships across the stretch of water from Baiae to Puteoli (now Pozzuoli). According to Roman historian Suetonius, this was intended to outdo Xerxes' celebrated bridging of the narrower Hellespont – or as a large-scale engineering feat to terrify the Germans and Britons into submission.

The **Parco Archeologico** is arranged in terraces overlooking the bay. At the top, the view from the Villa dell'Ambulatio gives a good idea of the layout. At the end of the *ambulatio* is the *balneum* (bathroom), a jewel of stuccoed artistry. The level below contains a *nymphaeum* (a grotto with a pool and fountain dedicated to the water-nymphs) or perhaps a miniature theatre; further down on the lowest terrace stands the Tempio di Mercurio (Temple of Mercury) and a large *natatio* (swimming pool) with an imposing dome (50-27 BC) that pre-dates the cupola of the Pantheon in Rome.

Housing some of the archaeological finds from the area is the **Museo Archeologico dei Campi Flegrei**. It's set in the atmospheric **Castello di Baia**, built late in the 15th century over the ruins of a Roman fort. The castle was given its present appearance between 1538 and 1550. There's a reconstructed *sacellum* (shrine) used for the cult of the emperors, represented here in flattering statues of Vespasian and Titus; the bronze equestrian statue of the unpopular Domitian was reworked to depict his successor Nerva after he had been deposed. On the upper level is a reconstruction of a *nymphaeum* that was excavated in the 1980s but lies, together with much of Baiae, under six metres of water. The statues, however, have been brought to the surface, and include a headless Odysseus plying Polyphemus (statue not found) with wine, a favourite theme of Roman sculptors. The rest of the castle is given over to a display of archaeological finds from across the Phlegrean Fields. Few of the explanatory panels are in English.

North of Baia, the **Lago di Averno** (Lake Avernus) was where Virgil led Dante down into the Underworld; the *sommo poeta* might think twice about getting his feet wet in its decidedly uninviting waters today. The sulphurous belching from beneath the surface of this crater lake was once said to be potent enough to stop passing birds dead, mid-flap. On the

Cumana Railway.

north-western shore, the **Grotta di Cocceio** (closed to the public) leads to a wide, perfectly straight tunnel that runs to the Sibyl's cave in Cuma. In antiquity, Averno was an inner harbour, connected by canals to the sea via the Lago di Lucrino, where stubs of Roman walls and arches can still be seen.

★ Museo Archeologico dei Campi Flegrei
Via Castello 39, Bacoli (081 523 3310/http://campiflegrei.napolibeniculturali.it). **Open** 9am-7pm Tue-Sun. **Admission** (includes Cuma, the Anfiteatro Flavio & Parco Archeologico e Monumentale di Baia) €4. **Credit** DC, MC, V.

Parco Archeologico e Monumentale di Baia
Via Sella di Baia 22, Baia (081 868 7592). **Open** 9am-6pm daily. **Admission** (includes Cuma, Museo Archeologico dei Campi Flegrei & Anfiteatro Flavio) €4; free under-18s, over-75s. **No credit cards**.

Parco Sommersa di Baia (Underwater City)
Piazza della Republica, Baia (boat trips 349 497 4183/www.baiasommersa.it). **Open** by appointment. Closed mid Nov-Mar. **Admission** €15; €9 reductions. **No credit cards**.
The Parco Sommersa di Baia can be visited through the cultural association of Baiasommersa. They will also arrange scuba-diving trips to various underwater sites. To arrange evening visits, contact the association in advance (prenotazioni@baiasommersa.it).

CUMA

The history of the Greek colony of Cumae is little known, but archaeological remains point to a flourishing settlement that was to have a considerable influence in Italy throughout the classical period. The settlement had extensive trading contacts with the Etruscans, and it was Cumaen Greeks who established further colonies at what would become Naples.

The Romans expanded the Greek site, building a forum to the east and a series of impressive tunnels that linked Cuma to the Lago di Averno, an important inland harbour for the Roman fleet.

In Book VI of the *Aeneid*, Virgil describes the fascination exerted by the cave of the Sibyl, a prophetess sacred to Apollo, as at Delphi. With its unearthly light shafts – the *centum ostia* (100 mouths), as the poet called them – in a long, echo-filled gallery, the cave is still an eerily atmospheric place. According to myth, it was here that the Trojan Aeneas received his instructions to descend to the Underworld beneath Lake Avernus (**Lago di Averno**, *see left*). Apollo, the god of light and divination, was worshipped here, as the temple on the lower level of the **Acropolis** reveals. On the highest level (it's worth trekking up to the top for the sweeping views through the oak woods) is the **Tempio di Giove** (Temple of Jupiter), built in the third century BC but manhandled by Roman refurbishers in Imperial times.

South of Cuma, the Acherusia Palus of old, now **Lago Fusaro**, has a *cascina* (lodge) designed in 1782 by Carlo Vanvitelli, joined by a causeway to terra firma. Beyond Lago Fusaro is Capo Miseno (Misenum), from where Pliny the Younger watched Vesuvius erupt in AD 79.

★ Parco Archaeologico di Cuma
Via Acropoli 1 (081 854 3060). **Open** May-Sept 9am-7.30pm daily. Oct-Apr 9am-5.30pm. **Admission** €2 (€4 includes the Parco Archeologico e Monumentale di Baia & the amphitheatre in Pozzuoli). **No credit cards**.

GETTING AROUND

The successful *artecard* museum and transport ticket (*see p194*) covers the area's major sights. There's the **Cumana** line rail service (*see below*), the **Metro del Mare** (boat shuttle service) that docks at Pozzuoli and Bacoli, and an improved bus services linking the area's major towns.

GETTING THERE

By bus
Buses M1 and 152 from Piazza Garibaldi by Naples' Stazione Centrale pass by the Solfatara and the church of San Gennaro, but you'll save time by taking the underground from Piazza Garibaldi to Pozzuoli, then taking buses or walking.

By car
Take the Tangenziale ring road westwards out of Naples (direction Pozzuoli) and veer off at the appropriate exit (for Astroni and Solfatara take exit 11 at Agnano). All sites listed are within a half-hour drive of the centre, traffic permitting.

By train
The **Cumana** railway (081 551 3328, www. sepsa.it) carries three or four trains every hour from the transport hub of Montesanto in Naples to coastal sites in the Campi Flegrei. For Baia, get off at Lucrino and take the bus to the old station in Baia, from which two bus lines depart to Cuma (CD or CS). For Pozzuoli (amphitheatre, Rione Terra and Solfatara), take the Metropolitana (Line 2) to Pozzuoli–Solfatara; there's a 1km walk up to the volcano. For Astroni, the most inaccessible of the sites, pick up bus C14 outside the station of Pianura on the Circumflegrea railway, which starts in Montesanto.

SIGHTS

Suburbs & Elsewhere

The sides of Naples that tourists rarely see.

The cheap cement blocks of postwar urban expansion have pushed the city limits far into the countryside around Naples. Today, most of its old bucolic charm has been replaced by a charmless suburban sprawl.

Nonetheless, there are still a few places that have been salvaged from the aesthetic devastation wrought in the 1950s and '60s. The 16th-century monastery of Eremo Santissimo still perches on its hilltop, as it has done for centuries, and parks and picturesque cemeteries offer welcome respite from the city. The suburbs are also home to large-scale sports and entertainment facilities – namely the gigantic Stadio San Paulo and the 5,000-seater Arena Flegrea.

SIGHTS

NORTH-WEST

The opening of the Collinare railway in the 1990s – a considerable feat of engineering – improved access to the city centre from the north-western suburbs, encouraging more construction in what was once Naples' green belt. What is left of the countryside has been preserved in the appealing **Parco urbano dei Camaldoli** and **Parco del Poggio di Capodimonte**.

FREE Eremo Santissimo
Via dell'Eremo 87 (081 587 2519/www.brigidine. org). Bus C44 from Piazza Medaglie d'Oro. **Open** *Church* 10am-noon daily. *Grounds* May-Oct 10am-8.30pm daily. Nov-Apr 10am-5pm daily. *Monastery* by appointment only. **Admission** free.
The chapel built here in 493 by St Gaudosius was replaced in 1585 by the current church and monastery. The monks' cells were little houses, each with its own garden, and the belvedere affords a high, hazy view over the Bay of Naples. Occupied by monks of the Camaldolese order until 1998 (by which time only three were left), the site was then taken over by the Sisters of St Bridget. A meticulous restoration of the buildings, kitchen gardens and walkways now allows the thriving religious community to cater for religious retreats, with prayer meetings and simple, serene accommodation. Visitors are very welcome, but groups are advised to make a courtesy call beforehand in order to avoid any disappointment.

FREE Parco del Poggio di Capodimonte
Viale del Poggio 60, Colli Aminei (081 795 4180/ 081 592 2699). Metro Colli Aminei/bus C38, R4. **Open** 9am-4pm daily. **Admission** free.
This unusual site opened in 2000, and swiftly became a local favourite. The park clings to an exposed hillside above the city ring road, offering little protection against sun or heavy rain (a notice at the entrance explains that the park may close during thunderstorms). There's a dramatic view over the palace at Capodimonte and out across the bay. The park has play facilities, smooth expanses of grass, a lake and lots of seating, making it an excellent place for energetic kids and frazzled parents.
▶ *For more tips on visiting the city with children, see pp157-159.*

FREE Parco Urbano dei Camaldoli
Via Sant'Ignazio da Loyola (081 7704 930/www. camaldoli.na.it). Bus C44 from Piazza Medaglie d'Oro. **Open** 7am-1hr before sunset daily. **Admission** free.
This inner-city park was founded in 1995 – in part to halt the uncontrolled expansion of urban development on the upper reaches of the Vomero hill. A number of paths on both sides of Via Rai wander across chestnut-wooded, orchid-strewn slopes, taking in breathtaking views over the Bay of Naples.

NORTH-EAST

When they die, most Naples residents will be laid to rest in a vast cemetery region north-east of the centre, towards Capodichino airport. On

Profile Centro Direzionale

Has the city's new business district lost its sense of direction?

For years, city planners eyed up the unlovely patch of land to the north of the tracks leading into Stazione Centrale. It would, they decided, make the perfect site for a fresh, upbeat civic centre, in an area with no ancient treasures to speak of. The shiny new development would be sign and symbol of the Naples Renaissance, with smart new business hotels and bold, soaring skyscrapers, housing the essential offices for the entire region; a model of sleek modernity.

Here was a site that could be razed unlamented and triumphantly reborn under a new name: Centro Direzionale. And so the gleaming new district, highly visible from trains to Naples, rose in the late 1980s from the ashes of a neglected industrial site.

The first fruits of a decades-long administrative battle over redevelopment of derelict eastern Naples, the Centro Direzionale is an incomplete version of a design by acclaimed Japanese architect Kenzo Tange. The district is dominated by the towering twin mirror-glass blocks of the Enel electricity board, and many state and corporate bodies are located here as well.

Unfortunately, as so often happens in Naples, the adage 'best laid plans' springs to mind. For one thing, the new Holiday Inn was built in a position where some rooms look down into the yard of the Poggioreale prison, the largest in Southern Italy.

Soon enough, intrigues and scams began to rear their ugly heads. In August 1990, for instance, an entire tower block went up in flames in mysterious circumstances, during the transfer of the Central Criminal Court and its archives.

Although the Centro functions adequately during office hours, the rest of the time it is a no man's land – a bleak cityscape reminiscent of a surrealistic Di Chirico painting, filled with dark corners, flitting shadows and very solid dangers.

It's a no-go zone after dark, yet even in the daytime it fails to take full advantage of its remarkable setting. The central avenue of the district could have been lined up with Vesuvius for a magnificent view, but instead the famous landmark is barely visible among the thicket of towers, leaving little to take your mind off the barren and debris-strewn expanse of windswept concrete.

BOUTIQUE CHIC
Kenzo Tange was also the architect behind the **Hotel Romeo** (*see p99*) – a sleek boutique addition to the city's hotel scene.

SIGHTS

INSIDE TRACK
GOING FOR A SONG

With inexpensive tickets and enticingly varied line-ups, the **Carpisa Neapolis Festival** (www.neapolis.it) is well worth checking out. In 2009, the Prodigy, the Virgins and actress-turned-rock-goddess Juliette Lewis were among the acts rocking the Arena Flegrea.

Via Santa Maria del Pianto, the **Cimitero Monumentale** (open 7am-5pm daily) houses more imposing, older graves (famous residents include celebrated tenor Enrico Caruso, and locally-adored comedian and actor Totò); the newer **Cimitero Nuovo** (Via Santa Maria del Pianto, 081 780 3236, open 8am-1pm daily) is nearby. On busy days, the area outside the graveyards hosts an animated cut-flower market, run under the watchful eye of the Polizia Mortuaria; flower traders have been known to gather flowers from graves and sell them the next day.

A quieter resting place can be found closer to the centre of town, by Piazza Santa Maria della Fede. Despite its name, the **Parco ex-cimitero degli inglesi** (Park of the former British Cemetery; open 9am-5pm Mon-Fri; 9am-1pm Sat, Sun) was an international and inter-denominational affair. It was closed in 1898, when the remains of the deceased were either repatriated or dumped in a common burial ground, and became a park. The larger tombs

are still there, however, and with its shady trees and friendly gardens, this is a corner of a foreign field that will be forever England.

FUORIGROTTA

So called because of its position outside (*fuori*) the two tunnels (*grotte*) into the Mergellina area, the eastern suburb of Fuorigrotta was developed under the Fascist government during the 1920s and '30s. The wide, regular streets of this downmarket residential district are rather soulless – but there are a few points of note.

Piazzale Tecchio lies at the heart of the district, which is best reached by taking the metro to Campi Flegrei or the Cumana railway to Mostra. The piazza was given a facelift for the soccer World Cup in 1990, and the gigantic 82,000-seater **Stadio San Paolo** (*see p185*) dominates the scene. On match days, it's a dazzling swirl of sky-blue shirts and scarves (*see also p186* **Azure passion**).

Beyond, the **Mostra d'Oltremare** was built in 1939-40 to show off 'achievements' in Italy's African colonies. Heavily bombed during World War II, it was rebuilt as a trade exhibition space in 1952. Concerts and festivals are held at the restored 5,000-seater **Arena Flegrea** (52 Piazzale Vincenzo Tecchio 49-50, 081 761 1221, 081 725 8000), open for shows from April until mid November. **Edenlandia** funfair (*see p157*), with its water rides and dodgems, is at the far end of the Mostra area.

Despite its gritty feel, the Fuorigrotta area is fast-becoming one of the city's focal points for art galleries (*see pp163-167*).

Edenlandia.

Consume

Hotels	**98**
Grand designs	107
Restaurants	**111**
The menu	112
Pizza perfection	117
Tutti foodie	118
Make mine a mozzarella	120
Profile Mario Avallone	123
Local flavour	124
Da bere?	128
Cafés, Bars & Gelaterie	**131**
Profile Caffè traditions	134
Caffè culture	137
Sugar & spice	138
Shops & Services	**140**
Only in Napoli	143
Marked-down markets	146
Made in Naples	150

Hotels

There's something to suit every budget – if you book ahead.

Any visit to Naples will involve its share of surprises, good and bad – and where you rest your weary head after a long day navigating around this confounding city can be one of the biggest. Try to make it a good one.

Accommodation options vary tremendously. At the upper end of the spectrum, grand, old-fashioned five-star affairs compete with luxurious new boutique establishments, set in gracious, antique-filled palazzi. Then there are the elegant, Liberty-style villas of the Centro Storico, with their fine period details and garden oases. A burgeoning selection of design hotels completes the picture, along with a good array of unpretentious, good-value options – set in decent locations, these days, rather than bunched depressingly round the train station.

STAYING IN NAPLES

Every *quartiere* in the city has its own distinctive flavour. For good restaurants, raw energy and true *napoletanità*, the **Centro Storico** (*see pp54-63*), **Via Toledo & La Sanità** (*see pp68-75*) and the **Port & University** (*see pp64-67*) are the best areas to explore.

For romantic views and a relaxed, exclusive feel, as well as a slew of art galleries, **Chiaia to Posillipo** (*see pp83-87*) and **Royal Naples** (*see pp48-53*) leave nothing to be desired. They're also handy for the ports of Mergellina and Beverello, for quick getaways to the islands. If you prefer leafy peace and quiet, retire to the less hectic, mostly residential **Vomero** (*see p79-82*) district, set on the hill above the centre.

Check exactly where a hotel is before you book: it may not have good transport links, or could be in too lonely a spot. A more expensive hotel in a central, safer area could save on taxis and tension in the long run.

For destinations outside Naples, refer to individual chapters in the **Around Naples** section of the book (*see pp191-302*).

> ❶ Red numbers given in this chapter correspond to the location of each hotel on the street maps. See *pp323-332*.

PRICES & CLASSIFICATION

Italian hotels are classified by the one to five star system; B&Bs, residences and *affittacamere* (rooms for rent) are not classified at all, and standards vary wildly. It's never a bad idea to ask to see your room before registering: if the desk clerk has your passport and credit card, it's much harder to negotiate.

In any case, it's always best to confirm prices and your reservation before you arrive, and to bring a print-out of the email with the agreed terms to avoid any problems when you come to check out.

In this book, we have listed hotels first by area, then according to their price bracket, based on the cost of a double room per night. We have classified hotels costing around €100 and under as budget; €100-€200 as moderate; €200-€350 as expensive; and €350 and above as deluxe. Prices include continental breakfast, unless otherwise stated. Some places give out vouchers for a nearby bar, where you can have the usual Italian breakfast of coffee and a *cornetto* (croissant). We have indicated hotels where internet access is available, and where it is free of charge.

If you're travelling with children, most hotels are happy to put another bed in the room – for which they should charge no more than 35 per cent extra. If you want a single room and are put in a double, you should be charged no more than the highest single rate, or 65 per cent of the price of a double.

CONSUME

ROYAL NAPLES

Note that seafront hotels along Via Partenope have been included in the **Chiaia to Posillipo** section; *see pp106-110.*

Deluxe

Romeo
Via Cristoforo Colombo 45 (081 017 5008/ www.romeohotel.it). Bus R2. **Rates** €330-€2,000 double. **Rooms** 83. **Credit** AmEx, DC, MC, V. **Map** p332 M11 **❶**

Here's hoping this brand-new design hotel is a harbinger of things to come in the Port area; the city fathers have big plans to spruce up and eventually even pedestrianise the zone. Meanwhile, this giant property has added a touch of upmarket appeal – though guests might prefer to hire a full-time car and driver in order to avoid the dingy and (at night) threatening streets outside. Designed by the late Kenzo Tange, the hotel is wonderfully lavish, and loaded with art and antiques. Rooms are luxuriously appointed with the sleekest of fittings, and the lovely rooftop spa and fitness centre features Hermès sunbeds. There's also a restaurant and a noteworthy sushi bar – worth a try even if you're not a guest.
Bar. Concierge. Disabled-adapted rooms. Gym. Internet (wireless; free). Parking (€22). Pool (1 outdoor). Restaurants (2). Room service. Spa. TV: pay movies.

Expensive

Miramare
Via Nazario Sauro 24 (081 764 7589/www. hotelmiramare.com). Bus 140, 152, C25. **Rates** €149-€299 double. **Rooms** 18. **Credit** AmEx, DC, MC, V. **Map** p332 L14 **❷**

This aristocratic Liberty villa, built in 1914, became the Hotel Miramare back in 1944. In the 1950s it sprang to fame when its restaurant and piano bar, the Shaker Club, drew top-name Italian and international singing stars for live performances. Small and family-run, it has a friendly, welcoming atmosphere. Breakfast is served on a roof-garden terrace with breathtaking views over the bay, and hammocks to relax in. Rooms vary in size – it's worth investing in those with sea views. Guests get a ten per cent discount at nearby restaurants La Cantinella (*see p115*) and Il Posto Accanto.
Bar. Concierge. Internet (high speed, free). Parking (€15-€20). Room service. TV.

Moderate

★ Chiaja Hotel de Charme
Via Chiaia 216, 1st floor (081 415 555/www. hotelchiaia.it). Bus R2, R3, R4. **Rates** €110-€165 double. **Rooms** 27. **Credit** AmEx, DC, MC, V. **Map** p327 J12 **❸**

Romeo.

CONSUME

Chiaja Hotel de Charme.

Tucked away off a courtyard, the former home of the Marchese Nicola Ledaldano (a portrait of the distinguished old gent hangs in the lobby) is now a friendly and elegant hotel. Despite the central location, a short stroll away from the Teatro San Carlo, it's pleasantly quiet. The conversion of a former brothel next door has added an additional eight rooms, each named after one of the women who worked there. Rooms are well appointed and dotted with antiques, staff helpful and very professional. *Disabled-adapted rooms. Internet (wireless, free). Parking (€18). TV.*

Hotel San Marco
Calata San Marco 26 (081 552 0338/www.san marcohotelnapoli.it). Bus C25, C55, C57, R1, R2, R3, R4. Rates €80-€140 double. **Rooms** 13. **Credit** AmEx, DC, MC, V. **Map** p332 L11 ❹
The San Marco is conveniently located in Piazza del Municipio, near the main port and a stone's throw from the city's sights, shops and restaurants. The rooms are comfortable, with double-glazing and air-conditioning.
Bar. Concierge. Internet (wireless, in the bar only, free). Parking (from €15). Restaurant. TV.

Mercure Napoli Angioino Centro
Via Agostino Depretis 123 (081 552 9500/ www.accorhotels.com). Bus C25, C55, C57, E3, R1, R2, R3, R4. Rates €160-€180 double. **Rooms** 89. **Credit** AmEx, DC, MC, V. **Map** p332 L11 ❺
Modern and comfortable, albeit somewhat anonymous, the Mercure is ideally located for forays into the Centro Storico, as well as quick getaways to the islands or the Amalfi Coast: it's just five minutes to the port at Beverello (and the airport bus). Rooms

are air-conditioned and soundproofed, business facilities are available, and there's a convenient, good-value underground parking lot nearby.
Bar. Business centre. Concierge. Disabled-adapted room (1). Internet (high speed & wireless). Parking (€15). Room service. TV: pay movies.

★ MH Design Hotel
Via Chiaia 245 (081 1957 1576/www.mhhotel.it). Bus R2. Rates €120-€180 double. **Rooms** 20. **Credit** AmEx, DC, MC, V. **Map** p332 K12 ❻
Run by two brothers, this handsome boutique hotel is decorated in calm neutral hues, and has an appealingly light and airy feel. The long entrance hall sets the tone, leading away from the bustling Via Chiaia and into a serene domain, punctuated by tasteful contemporary art. The guestrooms are understated yet plush, and the skylit breakfast room and bar on the top floor complete the sense of quiet comfort.
Bar. Concierge. Internet (high speed, free). Parking (free). Room service. TV.

Palazzo Turchini
Via Medina 21/22 (081 551 0606/www.palazzo turchini.it). Bus 201, C25, C55, C57, R1, R2, R3, R4. Rates €120-€150 double. **Credit** AmEx, DC, MC, V. **Map** p332 L11 ❼
This elegant 18th-century building was formerly a royal orphanage and famous music conservatory. Facing the Fountain of Neptune, the rooftop terrace has lovely views towards the Castel Nuovo. Bedrooms are beautifully fitted out, with elegant, contemporary styling, and are well insulated against the noise outside. Staff are friendly and discreet.
Bar. Concierge. Internet (high speed). Parking (€24). Restaurant. Room service. TV.

CONSUME

and a drink beside the charming pool. Bedrooms are stylish and individually decorated; some have private terraces. There is a complimentary supply of *limoncello* and *nocino* for guests.

Bar. Business centre. Concierge. Internet (wireless, high speed & shared terminal, free). Parking (€25). Pool (outdoor). Room service. TV.

Moderate

Caravaggio Hotel di Napoli
Piazza Cardinale Sisto Riario Sforza 157 (081 211 0066/www.caravaggiohotel.it). Metro Piazza Cavour/bus CS. **Rates** €120-€140 double. **Rooms** 18. **Credit** AmEx, DC, MC, V. **Map** p328 N7 ⑩
Occupying a restored 17th-century building, the Caravaggio's creamy colours and exposed stonework give it a pleasantly airy feel. Guest rooms are comfortable, albeit a little short of personality; some have a jacuzzi. It stands just behind the Duomo, opposite the Guglia di San Gennaro, so the view is charming; there's also a small roof garden. Staff can be a little prickly, but otherwise it's a good bet.
Bar. Business centre. Concierge. Disabled-adapted rooms. Internet (high speed, free). Parking (€20). TV.

★ Decumani Hotel de Charme
Via San Giovanni Maggiore Pignatelli 15, 2nd floor (081 551 8188/www.decumani.com). Metro Piazza Cavour/bus R2. **Rates** €99-€144 double. **Rooms** 23. **Credit** AmEx, DC, MC, V. **Map** p328 M9 ⑪
This newly-opened hotel is close to Santa Chiara and a mere stroll away from the lively University quarter. Rooms are elegantly appointed and decorated with tasteful antiques – as you'd expect in a historic palace, once home to the last bishop of the Bourbon Kingdom of Naples. The high point is the ballroom, decorated from floor to ceiling with lavish frescoes. In spite of the palatial surrounds, the atmosphere is convivial. *Photos p103.*
Concierge. Internet (wireless, free). Parking (€22). TV.

Budget

★ Bella Capri Hotel & Hostel
Via Melisurgo 4, Gate B, 6th floor (081 552 9265/www.bellacapri.it). Bus 1, R2. **Rates** €50-€80 double. **Rooms** 14. **Credit** MC, V, AmEx, DC. **Map** p332 M11 ⑧
Set half a block from the main port, with views of Capri and Vesuvius (ask for a room with a balcony), this modest establishment enjoys an ideal location for trips round the Bay and for exploring the city sights. Friendly staff bend over backwards to be helpful, and offer special deals for island trips and excursions. The unpretentious rooms are comfortable, if a trifle noisy. During business hours (Monday to Friday), the lifts only run with a five euro cent coin; once guests are checked in, the desk clerk can provide coins. *Photo p102.*
Bar. Internet (wireless, free).
▶ *Upstairs is a busy youth hostel with dorm beds for €20 per person; call the hotel for details.*

CENTRO STORICO
Expensive

★ Costantinopoli 104
Via Santa Maria di Costantinopoli 104 (081 557 1035/www.costantinopoli104.it). Metro Dante. **Rates** €220 double. **Rooms** 19. **Credit** AmEx, DC, MC, V. **Map** p328 L8 ⑨
A delightful discovery, this Liberty villa is a tranquil retreat in the heart of town, close to the social hub of Piazza Bellini. It was converted from an aristocratic palazzo, with glowing stained glass windows and wrought iron gates; there is a small, sun-filled garden where guests can enjoy breakfast

INSIDE TRACK
BAGGING A BARGAIN

Although Naples is seemingly full of hotels, there is a glut of business clients (it is, after all, the biggest city in southern Italy). At times, rolling up without a booking really doesn't pay – you'll find there's no room in any inn you like the look of. High season includes Easter, spring, autumn, Christmas and New Year. Bargains can be had in summer when the city gets too hot, and from January to March, when there's a general lull.

CONSUME

Donna Regina B&B

Via Luigi Settembrini 80 (081 446799/339 781 9225/www.discovernaples.net). Bus 47, 184, 201, CS. **Rates** €93-€120 double. **Rooms** 3. **Credit** AmEx, MC, V. **Map** p328 N6
Along the road from the new MADRe art museum, off the Via Duomo, this gracious apartment was formerly the Mother Superior's quarters in the 14th-century monastic complex of Donna Regina. Filled with family heirlooms, antiques and modern art, rooms are all ensuite and quite charming. Guests are welcome to relax in the elegant sitting room, and a traditional Neapolitan dinner is available on request.
Internet (wireless, free). Parking (€20). TV.

Palazzo Decumani

Piazza Giustino Fortunato 8 (081 420 1379/ www.palazzodecumani.com). Metro Dante or Montesanto. **Rates** €130-€220 double. **Rooms** 28. **Credit** AmEx, DC, MC, V. **Map** p328 N8
The latest designer addition to the area is housed in a meticulously restored belle époque edifice. Inside, rooms are deliciously sumptuous and scattered with contemporary art. Guest rooms are over the top (there are so many velvet pillows piled on the bed, you may wonder where you're supposed to sleep), but soothingly comfortable nonetheless. The staff are very helpful, and a superb breakfast buffet is another boon.
Concierge. Disabled-adapted rooms. Internet (wireless, free). Parking (free). TV.

Budget

Duomo

Via Duomo 228 (081 265988). Bus CS, R2. **Rates** €50-€65 double. **Rooms** 10. **Credit** MC, V. **Map** p328 N8
Run by three brothers, this quiet little hotel is an ideal base for sampling the action in the old quarter. Furnishings are plain but have a polished feel, and guestrooms are generally spacious and decorated in cheerful colours. There's no air-conditioning, though the ceiling fans help dispel summer stickiness. For breakfast, you'll have to head out to one of the many excellent bars in the area.
Internet (shared terminals, free). TV.

★ Hotel des Artistes

Via del Duomo 61 (081 446155/www.hoteldes artistesnaples.it). Metro Garibaldi or Piazza Cavour/bus CS, E1, R2. **Rates** €55-€100 double. **Rooms** 11. **Credit** AmEx, DC, MC, V. **Map** p328 M/N7
Housed on one floor of a noble residential building and opening out on to a peaceful courtyard, the old-fashioned Hotel des Artistes is a quietly comfortable option. Ideally located for exploring the old centre (the magnificent Duomo is just a few metres away), it's also nice and quiet.
Bar. Concierge. Disabled-adapted rooms. Internet (wireless, free). Parking (€15). TV.

Neapolis

Via Francesco del Giudice 13, off Via Tribunali (081 442 0815/www.hotelneapolis.com). Metro Piazza Cavour or Dante/bus 47, CS, E1. **Rates** €78-€115 double. **Rooms** 24. **Credit** AmEx, DC, MC, V. **Map** p328 L/M8
In the centre of the Centro Storico, close to the buzzing Piazza Bellini, the Neopolis is a decent and modestly priced choice. Little extras include a computer in every room with free internet access, and staff are particularly friendly. Windows are soundproofed, but the walls are a little thin; still, you'll wake up to an ample breakfast buffet.
Concierge. Disabled-adapted rooms. Internet (cable, free). Parking (€15). Restaurant. Room service. TV.
► *Guests here are given a discount at the adjoining La Locanda del Grifo, see p118.*

The view from **Bella Capri Hotel & Hostel**. See p101.

Decumani Hotel da Charme. See p101.

PORT & UNIVERSITY
Moderate

Hotel Una
Piazza Garibaldi 9/10 (081 563 6901/www.una hotels.it). Metro Garibaldi/bus CS, C30, C40, C55, C58, R2, R5. **Rates** €120-€150 double. **Rooms** 89. **Credit** AmEx, DC, MC, V. **Map** p329 P8 ⓱

Part of a Florentine chain, the Una occupies a renovated 19th-century building on the corner of Piazza Garibaldi and Corso Umberto I. An oasis of calm after the gritty chaos outside, its airy rooms feature *tufa* stone panels, pale green or Pompeiian red walls and understated Neapolitan motifs and prints. Service is polite and amenable, and the restaurant serves food all day. There's also a roof terrace, from which you can survey the city.
Bar. Concierge. Internet (wireless). Parking (€20). Restaurant. TV.

Budget

Donnalbina 7
Via Donnalbina 7, off Via Monteoliveto (081 1956 7817/www.donnalbina7.it). Bus 201, C57, R1, R2, R4. **Rates** €65-€90 double. **Rooms** 6. **Credit** MC, V. **Map** p328 L10 ⓲

Run by the charming Enrico Sanseverino, this popular B&B is set on a quiet street off a traffic-filled road, within easy reach of the Centro Storico and Via Toledo. Despite the low prices, bedrooms are spacious and unexpectedly swish, oozing minimalist chic. Each room is ensuite and has wireless internet, with original artwork on the walls. A stellar breakfast, brought to you in your room, includes a generous selection of fresh pastries, including *sfogliatelle*. There's a €10 discount per room if you pay in cash.
Internet (wireless, free).

Europeo & Europeo Flowers
Via Mezzocannone 109/c (081 551 7254/www. sea-hotels.com). Bus CS, C55, C57, E1, R1, R2, R4. **Rates** *Europeo* €50-€105 double. *Europeo Flowers* €65-€130 double. **Rooms** *Europeo* 17. *Europeo Flowers* 8. **Credit** AmEx, DC, MC, V. **Map** p328 M9 ⓳

Close to Spaccanapoli, the university district and the Centro Storico, the Europeo hotels are surprisingly cheap. Although they're somewhat basic, guest rooms are perfectly comfortable – those at Europeo Flowers have air-conditioning and modern frescoes, whereas the Europeo rooms are plainer. Neither hotel serves breakfast, but there are plenty of nearby eating options.
Concierge. Parking (€20). Internet (cable, free). TV.

Hotel Executive
Via del Cerriglio 10, off Via San Felice (081 552 0611/www.sea-hotels.com). Bus CS, C25, C57, R1, R2, R4. **Rates** €80-€100 double. **Rooms** 19. **Credit** AmEx, DC, MC, V. **Map** p328 L10 ⓴

Partly occupying a neighbouring monastery and hidden in a tiny side street off a busy thoroughfare, the Executive has cosy public rooms, furnished with antiques. Bedrooms are comfortable, though slightly lacklustre, and quiet – if the double-glazing is firmly shut. A good breakfast is served on the pretty, sunny roof terrace, and there's a gym.
Bar. Gym. Internet (high speed, free). Parking (€15). TV.

Suite Esedra
Via Cantani 12, off Corso Umberto I (081 553 7087/www.sea-hotels.com). Bus CS, C55, C58, E1, R2. **Rates** €70-€95 double. **Rooms** 17. **Credit** AmEx, DC, MC, V. **Map** p329 O8 ㉑

What it lacks in history (it opened in 1997), the Suite Esedra makes up for with its cosy atmosphere. Rooms are individually decorated with astronomy

CONSUME

motifs; the Venus suite, with its private rooftop plunge pool, is a delight. Handy for the Centro Storico, the port and the railway station, the hotel has only one drawback: it faces on to the thundering, traffic-jammed and somewhat insalubrious Corso Umberto I.

Bar. Gym. Internet (cable, free). Parking (from €15). Room service. TV.

TOLEDO & SANITA

Expensive

Mediterraneo
Via Ponte di Tappia 25 (081 797 0001/www. mediterraneonapoli.com). Metro Montesanto/ bus C25, C55, C57. **Rates** €140-€350 double. **Rooms** 228. **Credit** AmEx, DC, MC, V. **Map** p332 K11 ㉒

Now part of the Marriott chain, this centrally located hotel is stylish and very convenient for exploring the shops and the sights. Catering mainly for business people, its rooms are comfortable with contemporary decor; breakfast is served in the lovely roof terrace restaurant. There's also a cocktail and piano bar in the foyer.

Bar. Business centre. Concierge. Disabled-adapted rooms. Internet (web TV & wireless, free). Parking (€22). Restaurants (2). Room service. TV (pay movies).

Moderate

Il Convento
Via Speranzella 137A (081 403977/www.hotelil convento.com). Bus 24, C57, CS, R1, R3, R4. **Rates** €79-€139 double. **Rooms** 14. **Credit** AmEx, DC, MC, V. **Map** p332 K11 ㉓

Housed in a former convent dating from 1600, this hotel has been restored with an accent on the monastic, but ample comfort for its guests. Wood-beamed ceilings, plain, creamy white walls and grey stone floors dominate. The rooms (or 'cells', as they're known) are spacious, and some have a small terrace. The hotel, set just off the shopping street of Via Toledo, is handy for the port and all main sights; although it's in the Quartieri Spagnoli, it's safe enough. There are discounts for family groups.

Bar. Concierge. Disabled-adapted room. Internet (shared terminal, free). Parking (€18). TV.

INSIDE TRACK
SMOKE-FREE STAYS

Italy's anti-smoking legislation means that you cannot legally smoke in a public space. Although officially designated smoking bedrooms do exist, most hotels have simply banned smoking altogether.

Hotel del Real Orto Botanico
Via Foria 192 (081 442 1528/www.hotelrealorto botanico.it). Metro Piazza Cavour/bus 47, 147, 182, 201, C83, R5. **Rooms** 36. **Credit** AmEx, MC, V. **Map** p329 O5 ㉔

As its name suggests, this hotel overlooks the botanical gardens, which makes for a fine view as well as valuable peace and quiet. It's a ten-minute walk from the Duomo, the Sanità and the Museo Archeologico Nazionale, on a rather anarchic road. Inside there's a relaxed atmosphere, and rooms are well appointed.

Bar. Business centre. Concierge. Internet (high speed, free). Parking (€21). Restaurant. Room service. TV.

Budget

Hotel 241 Correra
Via Correra 241 (081 1956 2842/www.correra. it). Metro Dante/bus 24, 201, CS, C57, R1, R4. **Rates** €75-€120 double. **Rooms** 12. **Credit** MC, V. **Map** p328 K8 ㉕

This popular boutique hotel bills itself as the city's first 'art hotel', and it's certainly a colourful place. The entrance lies behind an iron gate, leading to a walkway facing a vast *tufa* wall. Inside, the walls are painted in reds, oranges and blues. Large, slickly modern rooms are painted in more pop art colours; service is equally warm. Decent breakfasts are served on the small, more conventionally decorated terrace.

Bar. Internet (cable, free). Parking (€18). Room service. TV.

Toledo
Via Montecalvario 15 (081 406800/www.hotel toledo.com). Bus 24, C57, CS, R1, R3, R4. **Rates** €60-€120 double. **Rooms** 22. **Credit** AmEx, MC, V. **Map** p327 J11 ㉖

Neapolitans may shudder at the thought of staying in the Quartieri Spagnoli, but the area's reputation for crime far outstrips reality. So long as you don't parade your diamond tiara about after dark, you're unlikely to encounter any problems. The three-floor, 17th-century palazzo that houses the Toledo has been nicely restructured, with a pretty roof garden and views over the Certosa-Museo di San Martino and Castel Sant'Elmo. The pedestrianised shopping area of Via Toledo is just a few steps away.

Bar. Concierge. Gym. Internet (wireless, free). Parking (€18-€25). Restaurant. TV.

CAPODIMONTE

Moderate

Hotel Villa Ranieri
Corso Amedeo di Savoia (081 741 6308/081 743 7977/www.hotelvillaranieri.com/it). Bus 24, 178, C64, R4. **Rates** €90-€189 double. **Rooms** 14. **Credit** AmEx, DC, MC, V.

Il Convento.

This beautiful 18th-century villa has become a charming four-star hotel, with mature gardens where a buffet breakfast is served in summer. It's nicely furnished in an antiquey style, but there's no lack of modern comforts. There are discounts for families with children, and it's especially good value in summer.
Bar. Disabled-adapted room. Internet (high speed & wireless). Parking (free). TV (pay movies).

Budget

Villa Bruna B&B
Via Santa Teresa degli Scalzi 154 (081 544 2079/www.bedandbreakfastvillabruna.com). Bus 178, 241, C64, R4. **Rates** €65-€70 double. **Rooms** 5. **Credit** AmEx. **Map** p328 K5 ㉗
This delightful little Liberty-style villa has a sunny garden, where breakfast is served and guests can relax with the family's cats and dog. It's located on the main road up the hill between Capodimonte and

the Museo Archeologico; there's an adjacent garage and good bus links. A nearby lift will also take you down to La Sanità. Each of the three rooms has very different decor; all are charming and cosy. The 'Romantic Room' has its own piano.
Internet (wireless, free). Parking (€10). Restaurant. TV.

VOMERO

Expensive

★ Hotel San Francesco al Monte
Corso Vittorio Emanuele 328 (081 423 9111/ www.hotelsanfrancesco.it). Funicular Centrale to corso Vittorio Emanuele/bus C16. **Rates** €180-€285 double. **Rooms** 45. **Credit** AmEx, DC, MC, V. **Map** p331 J10 ㉘
This hotel was converted from the Santa Lucia al Monte convent, founded in 1557 by the Minori Conventuali monks. All of its wonderfully furnished

Excelsior.

rooms – once severe monastic cells – have views over the bay. A sun roof and panoramic terrace with pool add to the charm, and the big back garden climbing up the Vomero hill offers breathtaking views and an open-air restaurant. A free hotel bus runs to and from the centre of town every half hour. *Bar. Disabled-adapted rooms. Internet (dataport). Parking (€25). Pool (outdoor). Restaurants (2). Room service. TV.*

Moderate

★ Grand Hotel Parker's
Corso Vittorio Emanuele 135 (081 761 2474/ www.grandhotelparkers.com). Funicular Chiaia to corso Vittorio Emanuele/bus C16, C27, C28. **Rates** €150-€190 double. **Rooms** 82. **Credit** AmEx, DC, MC, V. **Map** p326 E12
A favourite with 19th-century British travellers, Parker's has a long and august history. Despite some dark days (it was requisitioned by troops during World War II, and damaged by the 1980 earthquake), the building has now been restored to its original grandeur. Crystal chandeliers, antiques, paintings and statues abound, and there's a library of antique volumes. The rooms are lavishly furnished and comfortably equipped, and there's a plush spa. The two restaurants (one on the roof terrace) serve good international food. Specify when booking to ensure you get a room with the famous view. *Bar. Business centre. Gym. Internet (wireless & cable). Parking (€18-€30). Restaurants (2). Room service. Spa. TV.*

Budget

La Casa della Nonna
Piazza Medaglie d'Oro 27 (081 556 4843/www. lacasadellanonna.it). Metro Medaglie d'Oro/ funicular Centrale to Piazzetta Fuga or Chiaia to Cimarosa/bus C57, R1. **Rates** €60-€80 double. **Rooms** 3. **No credit cards. Map** p330 E8

'Grandma's House' is small B&B, located in a residential building on a large, central Vomero square. It's handy for sightseeing and transport links: the funicular, the metro and a lively bus that weaves down the hill to the Museo Archeologico Nazionale. You'll find three light and airy rooms (called Zio Attilio, Paula and Pina), each clean and charmingly furnished, a 1950s kitchen, and a sitting room with a piano. The balcony, where a good breakfast is served, has a great view of the bustling piazza and surrounding streets below. The owners are extremely friendly and helpful. *Internet (cable, free). Parking (€10-€20). TV.*

Hotel Cimarosa
Via Cimarosa 29 (081 556 7044/www.hotel cimarosa.it). Metro Vanvitelli/funicular Montesanto to Via Morghen, Centrale to Piazzetta Fuga or Chiaia to Via Cimarosa/bus C28, C31, C32, C36. **Rates** €70-€120 double. **Rooms** 19. **Credit** MC, V. **Map** p331 F10
Stylishly transformed from a simple *pensione* to a hotel by its architect owner, Sergio Arpaia, the Cimarosa is pleasantly located in the quiet (and safer) central Vomero. There are plenty of shops and restaurants nearby, not to mention the Certosa-Museo di San Martino (*see p81*), and it's just a short funicular ride from the centre. Ten of the 19 rooms have sea views; most are ensuite. All are spacious and individually decorated, with an airy, solidly contemporary feel. *Parking (€28). TV.*

CHIAIA TO POSILLIPO
Deluxe

Grand Hotel Vesuvio
Via Partenope 45 (081 764 0044/www. vesuvio.it). Bus 140, 152, C25. **Rates** €236-€490 double. **Rooms** 160. **Credit** AmEx, DC, MC, V. **Map** p332 K15

Grand designs

From turn of the century grandes dames to hip boutique hotels.

Naples' architecture is loved primarily for its Baroque extravaganzas. Inside and out, churches and palazzi writhe with multicoloured marbles and stuccos, swirling in florid arabesques. When it comes to hotels, however, the classic Neapolitan look is more neoclassical – the style favoured by the aristocratic early 19th-century cognoscenti who came here as part of their grand tour. The stately establishments that lined the Lungomare Partenope captured the era perfectly; the bombs of World War II devastated the strip, but the **Excelsior** (*see p108*) remains.

Perhaps an even better example is the **Grand Hotel Parker's** (*see left*), with Greco-Roman statuary and Empire antiques thronging its public rooms. The hotel's famous panoramic balcony, however, adorned with graceful, caryatid-like figures supporting clusters of lamps, betrays the style that came next: that of the belle époque. This light, bright, turn-of-the-century evocation of post-Unification and pre-World War I buoyancy spread throughout Italy, as well as the Western world. The exterior of the recently-restored **Palazzo Decumani** (*see p102*) provides a fine example.

Towards the end of the epoch, however, the style began to feel too cloyingly Victorian and overwrought. Influenced by Japanese art, a more mannered yet organic style evolved – that of art nouveau, with its emphasis on sinuous vegetation and floral motifs. In Italy the trend became established as 'Stile Liberty', named after the London shop that did so much to popularise the style.

Fine examples of Liberty style in Naples include **Constantinopoli 104** (*see p101*) and the entrance and foyer of the **Pinto-Storey** (*see p109*). Other buildings across the city feature Liberty architectural elements and details, such as curvaceous furnishings and stained glass. The celebrated **Gran Caffè Gambrinus** (*see p132*) provides an accessible example of the transition from belle époque to Liberty.

After the madness of World War I came the Bauhaus and other modernist creeds, and a desperate rejection of all cultural symbolism and motif. Decoration of any sort was banished as dangerously atavistic and confining: mankind needed clean, impersonal lines in open, uncluttered spaces in order to be liberated once and for all from the destructive habits and toxic residue of millennia past.

Fascist architecture firmly adhered to the new ideology – best exemplified in Naples by the **Palazzo delle Poste e Telegrafi** (*see p45*). The **Royal Continental** (*see p108*), created in the 1950s by architect Giò Ponti and restored over the last few years, is a less ponderous take on the concept. Ponti's work is typical of the modernist approach, emphasising stripped-down functionality and teaming primary colours with polished natural woods.

More recently, the austerity of modernism has given way to postmodernism, with its eclectic, omnivorous approach to architectural and decorative styles. Cutting-edge design, with references to the city's contemporary art scene, is integral to rising stars such as the **Romeo** (*see p99*).

Today, some of the city's most appealing accommodation options are actually the most ancient. Remodelled convents and monasteries such as **Il Convento** (*see p104*) and the delightful **San Francesco al Monte** (*see p105*) are artful reinventions of ancient buildings, injected with fresh energy and modern influences.

CONSUME

Grand Hotel Parker's.

Parteno.

Built in 1882, when the Santa Lucia seafront was created in a huge redevelopment, the Vesuvio was completely destroyed during World War II and rebuilt in 1950 with the addition of two extra floors. On the top floor is the roof-garden restaurant, named after Enrico Caruso, a favoured guest. Royalty, world leaders and top Italian footballers have all stayed in its stately rooms and opulent suites over the centuries – Queen Victoria, Grace Kelly and, more recently, Bill Clinton. The spa is wonderful.
Bars (2). Business centre. Disabled-adapted rooms. Gym (in spa). Internet (cable & wireless). Parking (€24). Restaurants (2). Room service. Spa. TV: pay movies.

Expensive

★ Excelsior
Via Partenope 48 (081 764 0111/www. excelsior.it). Bus 140, 152, C25. **Rates** €250-€360 double. **Rooms** 130. **Credit** AmEx, DC, MC, V. **Map** p332 K15 ❸

Royals, film stars and jet-setters of all ilks have walked the Excelsior's sumptuously decorated halls and corridors. A Neapolitan landmark, it exerts a heady glamour – helped by its enviable position overlooking the bay, with Vesuvius as the backdrop and the Borgo Marinaro right opposite. Every room is different, though all share a fin-de-siècle polish. The top-floor restaurant, La Terrazza, offers breathtaking views; for a pre-dinner tipple, there's a bar on the ground floor.
Bar. Disabled-adapted rooms. Internet (dataport). Parking (€23-€26). Restaurant. Room service. TV: pay movies.
▶ *For a taste of glamour at a fraction of the price, head to the hotel's ground-floor bar, which is open to non-residents.*

Paradiso
Via Catullo 11 (081 247 5111/www.hotel paradisonapoli.it). Funicular Mergellina to Sant'Antonio/bus C21. **Rates** €165-€230 double. **Rooms** 72. **Credit** AmEx, DC, MC, V.

Now owned by the Best Western hotel group, the Paradiso is situated high on the hill of Posillipo, away from the hustle and bustle of the city. From this idyllic perch, you can see all across the bay, then survey the traffic hell below and heave a sigh of relief that you're not in it. The rooms are airy and bright, and many have little private terraces. Views from the restaurant are lovely – especially when dusk falls, and lights twinkle around the curve of the bay.
Bar. Business centre. Concierge. Internet (wireless, free). Parking (€18). Restaurant. TV.

Royal Continental
Via Partenope 38-44 (081 245 2068/www.hotel royal.it). Bus 140, 152, C25. **Rates** €250-€400 double. **Rooms** 400. **Credit** AmEx, DC, MC, V. **Map** p327 J15 ❸

Built in the 1950s by modernist architect Giò Ponti, the Royal Continental may not grab everyone at first. However, it's functional and extremely comfortable, and staff are particularly helpful. It's favoured by business people, who probably don't have the time to appreciate its wonderful seafront location overlooking the Castel dell'Ovo. There's a delightful 1950s swimming pool on the roof, and a variety of smart room styles to choose from; the first floor rooms are perfectly restored time capsules of Giò Ponti's upbeat style.
Bar. Business centre. Concierge. Disabled-adapted rooms. Gym. Internet (high speed & wireless). Parking (from €20). Pool (outdoor). Restaurant. Room service. TV.

Santa Lucia

Via Partenope 46 (081 764 0666/www.santa lucia.it). Bus 140, 152, C25. **Rates** €285-€330 double. **Rooms** 96. **Credit** AmEx, DC, MC, V. **Map** p332 K15 ③⑤

Built in 1900, this long-established hotel enjoys marvellous views over the Bay. The furnishings are sober and traditional, the atmosphere quiet and relaxing, and the staff very professional. It's situated opposite the Castel dell'Ovo and the Borgo Marinaro, with its many bars and restaurants.
Bar. Disabled-adapted rooms. Internet (cable, free). Parking (€23-€26). Restaurant. Room service. TV: pay movies.

Moderate

Ausonia

Via Caracciolo 11 (081 682278/www.hotel ausonianapoli.com). Metro Mergellina/bus 140, C12, C16, C18. **Rates** €100-€108 double. **Rooms** 10. **Credit** MC, V. **Map** p326 C15 ③⑥

In a residential building on the seafront, this little hotel has a great location in Mergellina. There are no sea views, as the hotel faces an inner courtyard, but its hands-on owner has brought the sea to you: the rooms are cheerfully decorated with nautical motifs and paraphernalia. Old-fashioned and quirky, it's perfectly spick and span; equally importantly, it's quiet.
Bar. Internet (shared terminal). Parking (€15). TV.

Chiaia B&B

Via Palasciano 17 (081 240 4755/www.chiaia baiabb.it). Metro Piazza Amedeo/bus 140, C9, C10. **Rates** €80-€110 double. **Rooms** 3. **No credit cards. Map** p326 E13 ③⑦

Run by the charming Maria Luisa Giannini, this B&B has beautifully decorated rooms – each with a typically Neapolitan theme. It's on the second floor of a residential building, a short walk from the Riviera de Chiaia, and has a comfortable communal area with use of a kitchen and washing machine. Local and national phone calls are included in the room rate. Breakfast is served on the pretty roof terrace, or in your room if requested. The unique option of 'B&B and boat' is also offered, combining a stay on dry land with a three-day cruise on the family boat.
Internet (cable, free). Parking (€16-€18). TV.

★ Parteno

Lungomare Partenope 1 (081 245 2095/ www.parteno.it). Bus 140, 152, C25. **Rates** €99-€165 double. **Rooms** 6. **Credit** MC, V. **Map** p327 H14 ③⑧

Billing itself as Naples first B&B, this charming little property has recently been done up, and is now more like a boutique hotel. The location is truly exceptional, at the head of all the grand hotels on the picturesque seafront. The rather romantic rooms, each named after a flower, retain their high ceilings; some have French windows opening on to sea views. Staff are genuinely welcoming, and there are *cornetti* for breakfast.
Internet (wireless, free). Parking (€20). Room service. TV.

★ Pinto-Storey

Via Giuseppe Martucci 72 (081 681260/www. pintostorey.it). Metro Piazza Amedeo/bus C24, C25, C27, C28. **Rates** €83-€135 double. **Rooms** 16. **Credit** AmEx, MC, V. **Map** p327 F12/13 ③⑨

With its charming Liberty-style entrance and convenient location near the Via dei Mille shopping area, the Pinto-Storey is a good option in this price range, especially if you're seeking to avoid the hubbub of the Centro Storico. The rooms, although rather unimaginatively restored, are nonetheless very pleasant.
Bar. Internet (high speed & wireless). Parking (€25). TV.

Relais Posillipo

Via Posillipo 69/1 (081 248 3193/www.relais posillipo.com). Bus 140. **Rates** €100-€120 double. **Rooms** 12. **Credit** AmEx, MC, V.

Occupying a modern building with a glass façade, this four-star hotel offers fine views over the bay of Naples from its tranquil setting, high on Posillipo hill. A pleasant stroll brings you to the lovely Parco Virgiliano and Marechiaro, and there are good transport links down to Mergellina and across to Vomero. Rooms are decorated in crisp, calm blue

Pinto-Storey.

CONSUME

and white; many come with jacuzzis and private terraces, and there's a hotel boat available for excursions and hire.

Bar. Internet (cable). Parking (€10). Restaurant. TV.

Budget

Cappella Vecchia 11

Vico Santa Maria a Cappella Vecchia 11 (081 240 5117/www.cappellavecchia11.it). Bus C25, R3. **Rates** €80-€90 double. **Rooms** 6. **Credit** AmEx, MC, V. **Map** p327 H13 ⑩

There are six comfortable, air-conditioned rooms at this appealing B&B, with understated, colourful decor and modern art on the walls. The quiet, elegant Chiaia district makes an excellent holiday base: you're close to good nightlife and restaurants, as well as designer shops and antique dealers. There's a big car park right next door, too.

Internet (wireless, free). Parking (€18-€22). TV.

CAMPI FLEGREI

Moderate

Villa Giulia

Via Cuma Licola 178, Cumae (081 854 0163/ www.villagiulia.info). Accessible by car only. **Rates** €90-€150 double. **Rooms** 6. **Credit** AmEx, MC, V.

A kilometre from the sea and 20km (12 miles) from the centre of Naples, this beautiful farmhouse is a world apart. Set in lush gardens with an inviting pool and sunny terraces overlooking Ischia and nearby Cuma, it has rooms and apartments. The charming owners breed Siberian huskies nearby, and offer cookery courses to their guests. To reach the villa by car, take the Tangenziale Ovest in the Pozzuoli direction then exit at junction 13, signposted Cuma. See the website for detailed directions.

Parking (free). Pool (outdoor). Restaurant.

Villa Medici

Via Nuova Bagnoli 550 (081 762 3040/ www.hotel-villamedici.com). Metro Campi Flegrei then C9 bus or Cumana line to Agnano. **Rates** €65-€160 double. **Rooms** 15. **Credit** AmEx, DC, MC, V.

A charming three-star hotel in a converted Liberty-style villa, Villa Medici is well placed for forays into

the Campi Flegrei as well as the Centro Storico. Various well-equipped rooms and apartments are available, many with kitchenettes, and there's a pretty garden and pool. There are special seasonal offers and good discounts for family groups.

Bar. Concierge. Disabled-adapted room. Internet (high speed & wireless, free). Parking (free). Pool (outdoor). TV: DVD.

Budget

Agriturismo Il Casolare di Tobia

Contrada Coste Fondi di Baia, Via Pietra Fabris 12, Bacoli (081 523 5193/www.datobia.it). Bus SEPSA 1 from Piazza Garibaldi to Bacoli. Closed 2wks Dec-Jan & 2wks Aug. **Rates** €60-€70 double. **Rooms** 3. **Credit** AmEx, DC, MC, V.

This 19th-century farmhouse offers *agriturismo* accomodation in a volcanic crater – inactive, thankfully, for the last 10,000 years. Surrounded by gardens and vineyards, it's a wonderfully bucolic place in which to stay. Three rooms are available, each with two or four beds, and there are communal cooking facilities for breakfast and an open terrace with a jacuzzi. Under-twos stay free, and there are group discounts.

Parking (free). Restaurant.

▶ *For more on the restaurant, serving dishes made from garden-grown vegetables, see p130.*

Averno

Via Montenuovo Licola Patria 85, Arco Felice Lucrino, Pozzuoli (081 804 2666/www.averno.it). Bus M1 from Piazza Garibaldi. **Rates** €9 per person; €9 camper van or tent pitch; €3 car; €110-€140 bungalow. **Credit** AmEx, MC, V.

This large, well equipped campsite in the Campi Flegrei is a fair hike from Naples, but only two kilometres from the beach. There are one- or two-bedroom bungalows if you don't fancy sleeping under canvas, and facilities galore: a pool that's fed by thermal springs, a disco, tennis and go-karts, for starters (an extra charge applies to certain activities).

Bar. Gym. Internet (wireless). Parking. Pools (2, outdoor). Restaurant. TV.

★ Vulcano Solfatara

Via Solfatara 161, Pozzuoli (081 526 2341/ www.solfatara.it). Metro Pozzuoli/bus SEPSA 1 from Piazza Garibaldi. **Rates** €7.80-€9.60 per person; €5.80-€7.80 tent pitch; €8.50-€9.50 camper van; €45-€82 bungalow. **Credit** AmEx, V.

Half an hour from town on the metro and handy for the ferry port at Pozzuoli, this is the most convenient campsite for visiting Naples and around. It's also right on the leafy fringes of the bubbling, fuming Solfatara crater (*see p90*). The site has a handy bar/restaurant and shop, and bungalows for rent.

Bar. Disabled-adapted bathroom. Internet (high speed). Parking (from €4.60). Pool (outdoor). Restaurant. TV.

INSIDE TRACK
MONUMENTS IN MAY

If you're planning to visit Naples in May, book a hotel room well in advance: the **Maggio dei Monumenti** (see p50) invariably attracts hordes of visitors to the city.

Restaurants

Unforgettable food and time-tested recipes.

For Neapolitans, man was put on this earth to eat: sublime seafood, heavenly pasta, the original pizza and to-die-for desserts. Food is almost sacred, with details of dish preparations, meal compositions and mealtimes discussed – and often argued over – endlessly.

Unorthodox culinary methods can be viewed with horror, as something akin to a mortal sin. Although more inovative cuisine is emerging, the traditional still wins hands down among Neapolitans. It's difficult to eat badly here, though: mediocre establishments do exist, but they are few and far between, and the odds on eating gloriously well are in your favour. Just remember that 'smart' isn't always best: many of Naples' finest eating experiences can be had in spit-and-sawdust *trattorie* and *osterie*.

HOW TO ORDER

Ordering in a Neapolitan restaurant can be a palaver, but it can also be hugely entertaining. Although required by law to produce a menu, many places fail to do so. Instead, in smaller *trattorie*, the waiter may rattle off a list of dishes of the day – you'd be well advised to choose one of these, as the chefs, in their tiny, pristine kitchens, will be using the freshest ingredients available at the market that day. Menus may be in dialect (*see p112* **The menu**), or may list dishes named after a former chef or the owner's beloved mamma. You can sidestep difficulties by seeing what other diners are eating and simply pointing to what you fancy. There's no direct translation into English for a lot of Mediterranean fish and shellfish, so you may be none the wiser until the dish arrives.

The *menu del giorno* is generally excellent, and it's perfectly acceptable to order a *primo* (pasta course) but no *secondo* (main course). On the whole, portions are big. If you're not up to a full main course, replace it with a *contorno* (cooked vegetables such as peppers, aubergines, broccoli or courgettes), *antipasti misti di mare* (seafood hors d'oeuvres) or an *insalata verde* (fresh green salad).

About the author

Florentine by birth but an honorary Neapolitan by marriage, **Nick Vivarelli** *is the Italian Bureau Chief for* Variety.

TYPES OF RESTAURANT

Traditionally, an *osteria* is a tavern or inn – a humble establishment where wine is the main attraction, but food is also offered. The definition has blurred over the years, though; one of the priciest and most exclusive eateries in Rome is the venerable Osteria del'Orso.

A trattoria, meanwhile, was once defined as a small, family-run eaterie, with a simple menu and less formal service than you'd expect in a ristorante. Again, it has become a catch-all term; some self-proclaimed *trattorie* are little more than tiny soup kitchens, while others serve high-end cuisine with prices to match. As the differences between the categories has grown hazier, average prices (*see p114*) are often the best indicator of how smart a venue is.

A *tavola calda* is similar to a self-service cafeteria, while a *pizza al taglio* or *pizza rustica* joint dispenses large rectangles of pizza, sometimes reheated to order. A *rosticceria* sells a limited number of pre-prepared dishes, to take away or eat in; dishes usually include whole roasted chickens (also sold in half- or quarter-chicken portions). *Frigittorie* are snack stalls selling fried food (*see p113*).

> ❶ Blue numbers given in this chapter correspond to the location of each restaurant on the street maps. *See pp326-332.*

CONSUME

FISH & SEAFOOD

Naples is famous for its fish and seafood. To avoid an unpleasant surprise on the bill, ask your host to weigh the fish and quote you a price before it's popped into the oven.

The local clams known as *vongole veraci* are only available in summer. This is also the season for *cozze* (mussels); the most popular places to eat them are on Piazza Sannazzaro in Mergellina, or on Via Colletta near the law courts at Castel Capuano. It's best to eat *cozze* in high-end restaurants to avoid the risk of hepatitis.

If you see an asterisk on the menu, it means that the ingredient may have been frozen (*surgelato*); this is sometimes the case with calamari or *gamberi* (prawns).

VEGETARIANS

In the southern Italian culinary mind, 'meat' generally does not include ham or *pancetta* (bacon). Vegetarians should double check by asking '*c'è la pancetta/il prosciutto?*' ('is there bacon/ham in it?') when they are told that dishes such as *pasta e fagioli* (pasta and bean soup) or *pasta, patata e provola* (pasta with potatoes and smoked cheese) are valid vegetarian options.

PIZZA

Naples credits itself as the birthplace of the Italian pizza; certainly the city has developed pizza from the simplest food of the poor to a gourmet art form. *See p117* **Pizza perfection**.

Many of the best *pizze* are to be found in inexpensive places with huge queues where you simply cannot book. Don't be deterred: the turnover is often remarkably quick. Make sure, though, to single out the head waiter and establish your place in the queue: if you don't, you may be there all night. Listen out for your name carefully – the pronunciation may be barely recognisable.

The menu

Navigating your way around a Neapolitan menu.

CONSUME

ANTIPASTI

Alici marinate: anchovies marinated in lemon or vinegar with oil, garlic, chilli and parsley. **Antipasti di mare**: a selection of (usually) cold, cooked seafood such as octopus, squid, clams, smoked swordfish and marinated sardines, or *frittelle di cicinielli* – delicious fried patties of tiny, transparent fish. **Antipasti misti/di terra**: a selection of salamis, hams, cheeses and olives. **Bruschetta**: toast with chopped tomatoes, garlic, basil and oil, or, occasionally, aubergine or olive paste. **Fritto misto all'Italiana**: deep-fried breaded mozzarella bites, deep-fried pizza dough, potato balls (*crocchè*), rice balls (*arancini*) and courgette strips. **Funghi trifolati**: cooked, diced mushrooms with garlic, chilli and parsley. **Involtini di peperoni**: cooked peppers, rolled and filled with cheese and breadcrumbs. **Mozzarella e prosciutto**: mozzarella and parma ham. **Prosciutto e fichi**: parma ham and figs. **Prosciutto e melone**: parma ham and cantaloupe melon. **Soutè di vongole**: sautéed clams. **Impepata di cozze**: steamed mussels with black pepper, lemon and toast.

PASTA

Alla barese: with broccoli. **Alla bolognese**: tomato and ground beef sauce. **Alla genovese**: thick onion and meat (veal) sauce. **Al nero di seppia**: in squid ink. **Alla puttanesca**, **alla bella donna**: with tomato, capers, black olives and a touch of chilli. **Alla Santa Lucia**, **alla bella Napoli**, **alla pescatora**: with seafood and shellfish. **Alla siciliana**: with tomato, aubergine, basil and mozzarella. **Alla sorrentina**: with tomato and mozzarella, or provola. **Alle vongole**: with clams (specify *in bianco* if you don't want your clams cooked with tomato). **Al sugo**: simple tomato and basil sauce. **Con fagioli e cozze**: with beans and mussels. **E ceci**: with chickpeas, sometimes creamed. **E patate**, **con provola**: with potatoes and smoked mozzarella. **Ragù**: thick tomato and meat sauce.

OTHER FIRST COURSES

Gattò di patate: potato pie with mozzarella and ham or *salame*. **Sartù di riso**: baked rice with tomato sauce, mozzarella, peas and small meatballs.

PESCE & FRUTTI DI MARE (FISH & SEAFOOD)

Aragosta: lobster. **Astice**: crayfish. **Bianchetti**: whitebait. **Calamaro ripieno**: stuffed squid. **Frittura di paranza**: small, local deep-fried fishes. **Gamberi**: prawns. **Mazzancolle**: very large prawns. **Mussillo marinato**: marinated cod-like fish. **Orata**: a kind of bream. **Pezzogna**: locally caught type of sea bream (blue-speckled).

WINE BARS

Wine culture in southern Italy dates back to Roman times and beyond. Traditionally, both oil and wine were bought in *vini e olii* (wine and oil) outlets, but only the most hardened drinkers would actually spend time in these places.

You'll still find a couple of tiny tables squashed between barrels of oil and *vino sfuso* (wine from the barrel) in some shops; others have now become fully fledged restaurants.

Wine bars (*enoteche*) are comparative newcomers to Naples. Wine is generally accompanied by nibbles (*stuzzichini*) – but unlike northern Italy, where generous portions are often brought spontaneously, in Naples you might have to ask, and you may well be charged for them.

Wine lists often appear exhaustive, but to avoid disappointment and wasting time, it is worth asking '*Sono tutti disponibili?*' – 'Are they all in stock?'. *See also p124* **Local flavour.**

SNACKS

The food served in snack bars is incredibly cheap, with pizza slices (charged by weight) ranging from €1.50 to €2.50 each, and fried foods at 25¢ or 50¢ a piece. Some places have seats, for which there is rarely an extra charge. Most snack bars are fairly hygienic, and as long as the hot snacks haven't been sitting around for too long in a warm display cabinet, you should have no problems. It's worth going to the busier bars, where the turnover of food is brisk.

The pavement fried-food stalls (*friggitorie*), where bits and pieces are plunged into oil – sometimes smelling like engine oil – in a large wok-like pan on wheels, are almost a thing of the past. Those listed here are the classics.

Stalls selling *o per 'e o muss'e puorc* (pig's muzzle and trotters with salt and lemon, a Neapolitan speciality) in the Pignasecca area are generally clean. If that's not your idea of a tasty nibble, there are also huge, mobile,

Pignatiello: seafood soup served with fingers of toasted bread. **Polipo affucate/affogato**: literally 'drowned octopus', cooked in an earthenware dish with a little water and tomato. **Purpietielle/purpo/polpo/polipo**: octopus. **Scampi**: langoustine. **Seppie in umido**: similar to *polipo affucate*, but with cuttlefish. **Telline**: clams, sweeter than *vongole*. **Totano**: similar to squid. **Vongole veraci**: local clams, seasonal.

CARNE (MEAT)

Carne alla pizzaiola: meat served with a tomato and oregano sauce. **Carne al ragù**: slow-cooked beef in tomato. **Involtino**: a small roll of beef (or aubergine, *involtini di melanzane*) stuffed with ham and cheese. **Polpette**: meatballs, usually in tomato sauce.

CONTORNI (VEGETABLES)

Fagiolini all'agro: cooked green beans with garlic and lemon. **Friarielli**: broccoli rabe. **Melanzane a funghetto**: diced aubergine with tomato and basil. **Melanzane alla brace**: chargrilled aubergine dressed with garlic, chilli and parsley. **Peperoncini verdi**: long, sweet green peppers cooked in tomato and basil. **Peperoni in padella**: pan-fried peppers (often with capers and black olives). **Parmigiana di melanzane**: fried, sliced aubergines baked with tomato

sauce, mozzarella and basil; often ordered as a starter. **Pizza di scarole**: salty pie prepared with scarola. **Scarola 'mbuttit'/'mbuttonat'**: stuffed endive (usually with capers, pine nuts and olives). **Zucchine alla scapece**: deep-fried sliced courgette with vinegar and fresh mint.

FORMAGGI (CHEESE)

Caciovallo: ewe's milk cheese. **Caprese**: mozzarella, tomatoes and basil. **Fior di latte**: mozzarella made with cow's milk, as opposed to buffalo. **Mozzarella in carrozza**: deep-fried mozzarella, sandwiched between two squares of bread. **Mozzarella fritta**: deep fried, breaded mozzarella. **Provola**: smoked mozzarella. **Provola alla pizzaiola**: provola cooked in tomato and basil sauce. **Scamorza**: hard cow's milk cheese, usually grilled.

METHODS OF COOKING

All'acqua pazza (fish): simmered in water, flavoured with tomato, garlic and parsley. **Al gratin**: oven baked with topping of breadcrumbs, often in a béchamel sauce. **Al sale (fish)**: cooked encrusted in sea salt. **Con pomodoro al filetto**: cooked with fresh cherry tomatoes. **In bianco**: cooked without tomato. **Indorato e fritto**: deep-fried with flour and egg. **Macchiato**: 'stained' with a touch of tomato.

CONSUME

INSIDE TRACK
ANTIPASTI ALERT

If your host offers to bring 'a taste of everything' or to select some antipasti on your behalf, establish exactly what this will entail economically – smaller dishes can add up perilously quickly.

nocturnal sandwich stalls that sell a great range of doorstop sarnies; the hamburgers and hotdogs are often best avoided.

On the seafront along Via Caracciolo is a line of stalls selling hot, tasty *taralli* (crunchy pastry rings with black pepper and almonds) and *treccine* (the long, plaited version).

WHAT TO DRINK
The house wine served in most restaurants is local and good. The red is a surer bet than the white between April and November, when the current year's production arrives. Order *un bicchiere di rosso/bianco* (a glass of red/white) or *un quarto* (a quarter-litre carafe) to start, giving you the option of ordering more or opting for a bottled variety. *See also p124* **Local flavour**.

Many *osterie* and restaurants don't serve coffee, but may order it in from a nearby bar. They do, however, serve post prandial shots of traditional *digestivi* to help digestion (*see p128* **Da bere?**). These are often made on the premises and can be potent.

THE BILL & PRICES
Almost all restaurants charge a *coperto* (cover charge) – generally between €1 and €3 per person. When the bill arrives, check it carefully, and calmly query anything that is unclear or incorrect. In the past, tipping was almost

universally at your discretion – normally five per cent of the bill. However, it has become increasingly common for restaurants to try to charge an additional ten to 15 per cent *servizio*, on top of the *coperto*, which can up your bill considerably. Menus should clearly state both the *coperto* and service charges, where applied. In theory, restaurants are obliged to issue a receipt; in practice, this is often overlooked. Credit cards are generally accepted, but you may find the machine mysteriously ceases to function when it comes to payment time: cash in hand avoids paperwork and VAT payments.

Pizzas cost from €4 to €9, depending on the ingredients and location, meat dishes from €8 to €20. Seafood pasta ranges from €7 to €25, and fish costs from €40 to €60 per kilo. Simple *pasta al pomodoro* generally costs no more than €6. *Contorni* or *antipasti* can be pricey – from €2.50 to €5 each; desserts usually range from €3.50 to €8. The *vino della casa* will work out at approximately €3.50 per quarter. A bottle of reasonable local wine is usually around the €10 to €15 mark; serious wines are in the €30 range.

Average prices given below are for one person consuming a *primo*, *secondo* and a *contorno*, plus a dessert or antipasto, without wine. However, it is possible to eat for less if you opt for just a pasta dish with a *contorno*, which is often ample. For *pizzerie*, the price covers a pizza and one pre-pizza snack.

Budget establishments have been marked with a € symbol.

ROYAL NAPLES

Amici Miei
Via Monte di Dio 78 (081 764 4981/081 764 6063/www.ristoranteamicimiei.com). Bus C22, C25, R2. **Open** 1-3pm, 8-11.30pm Tue-Sat; 1-3pm Sun. Closed July, Aug. **Average** €35. **Credit** AmEx, DC, MC, V. **Map** p327 J13 **❶** Ristorante

La Bersagliera.

An old-fashioned, family-run restaurant with excellent cuisine. It's the perfect antidote to all that fish (there's none on the menu): come instead for the likes of mind-blowing *paccheri Amici Miei* (pasta with an aubergine and gorgonzola sauce), excellent char-grilled meat (the lamb and the steak in Barolo wine with radicchio are particularly tasty), vegetables and cheeses. Delicious home-made *dolci* include *crema pasticciera* served with brandied chestnuts, and chocolate mousse. The wine list is extremely impressive, as well as good value.

La Bersagliera
Borgo Marinaro 10-11 (081 764 6016). Bus C25. **Open** noon-3.30pm, 7.30pm-midnight Mon, Wed-Sun. Closed 1wk Jan. **Average** €50. **Credit** AmEx, DC, MC, V. **Map** p332 K15 ❷ **Ristorante**
A little jewel of the belle époque, La Bersagliera is filled with sepia photos and has a fine view of the harbour. Attracting a sophisticated clientele, it serves predominantly fish-based cuisine: try the house speciality of mussel and clam soup, the *taglierini alla Bersagliera* (fine ribbon pasta with baby octopus, tomato and olives) or the *orata* (gilt-head bream) baked in a salt crust.

La Cantinella
Via Nazario Sauro 23, Lungomare Santa Lucia (081 764 8684/www.lacantinella.it). Bus C25. **Open** 11.30am-3.30pm, 7.30pm-midnight Mon-Sat. Closed 2wks Aug. **Average** €50. **Credit** AmEx, DC, MC, V. **Map** p332 K14 ❸ **Ristorante**
As one of Naples' most renowned restaurants, this is the place for a sumptuous feast. Dishes such as *risotto alla zucca, champagne e provola* (risotto with pumpkin, champagne and provola) or *pappardelle zucchini e scampi* (home-made pasta with a sauce of courgette and langoustines) feature, alongside caviar, T-bone steaks and lobster; the set menus are worth investigating. The decor is slightly dated, and there's a cigar and piano bar alongside that stays open into the wee small hours. A perfect place for a little networking with Naples' elite.
▶ *On a budget? Try the €25 set menu at La Piazzetta (Via Nazario Sauro 22, 081 764 6195), a newly-opened annexe just round the corner.*

€ La Chiacchierata
Piazzetta Matilde Serao 37, Piazza Trieste e Trento (081 411 465). Funicular Centrale to Augusteo/bus 24, C22, C25, C57, R2, R3. **Open** 11am-3.30pm Mon-Wed; 11am-3.30pm, 7.30-11pm Thur-Sat. Closed 3wks Aug. **Average** €15. **Credit** MC, V. **Map** p327 J12 ❹ **Trattoria**
Classic dishes and homespun charm are the forte at this family-run trattoria. The clientele of local professionals comes as much for the atmosphere created by the family's bubbly matriarch as for the food. Try simple staples like *pesci del golfo* (fish from the bay) or *polpetti affogati* (baby octopus in tomato sauce). Seasonal daily specials are always available.

La Mattonella.

€ Ettore
Via Santa Lucia 56 (081 764 0498/www.ristoranteettore.it). Bus C25, R2. **Open** 12.30-3pm, 7.30pm-midnight Mon-Sat. Closed Aug. **Average** *Pizzeria* €15. *Trattoria* €30. **No credit cards. Map** p332 K14 ❺ **Trattoria & pizzeria**
Ever-popular Ettore pairs simple decor with a wide-ranging, traditional menu. Order a dish of *spaghetti alla puttanesca* (tomato sauce with capers, olives and fresh parsley), or sample one of the renowned pizzas. Another speciality is *pagnottielli* – rolled pizza dough stuffed with tasty fillings such as sausage and *friarielli* greens (*see p118* **Tutti foodie**) or *parmigiana di melanzane*.

€ Fratelli La Bufala
Via Medina 18 (081 551 0470/www.fratellilabufala.com). Bus 24, C25, C55, C57, R1, R2, R3, R4. **Open** noon-4pm, 7pm-midnight daily. **Average** €15. **Credit** MC, V. **Map** p332 L11 ❻ **Pizzeria**
A Neapolitan pizza franchise, Fratelli La Bufala has global aspirations, with outposts in London, Miami and Rio. As the name suggests, buffalo is central to the menu. Exquisite *mozzarella di bufala* is served atop pizzas, and there are juicy buffalo steaks and meatballs – plus buffalo ricotta desserts. Colourful, buffalo-themed artworks line the walls.

€ La Mattonella
Via Nicotera 13 (081 416541). Bus C25, R2. **Open** 12.30-4pm, 7.30-11.30pm Mon-Sat; 12.30-3.30pm Sun. Closed 2wks Aug. **Average** €20. **Credit** DC, MC, V. **Map** p327 J13 ❼ **Osteria**
This tiny *osteria* takes its name from the quirky collection of tiles (*mattonelle*) that decorate the walls. The antipasti are very moreish, as is the spaghetti with *calamaretti* (baby squid). Excellent

CONSUME

Trattoria San Ferdinando.

CONSUME

In a prime location by the yachts, this upmarket restaurant enjoys a fine view of Vesuvius. Although the fish and meat dishes are of a high standard, you can also enjoy a decent, inexpensive pizza: the seafood, tomato and mozzarella pizza is a good option. Service is slick, and there's a smart bar next door for diners wanting to linger.

★ € Trattoria Castel dell'Ovo
Via Luculliana 28, Castel dell'Ovo (081 764 6352). Bus 140, 152, C25. **Open** 1-3pm, 7.30pm-midnight Mon-Wed, Fri-Sun. **Average** €20. **No credit cards. Map** p332 K15 **⓫ Trattoria**
A simple choice right in the Borgo Marinaro, this trattoria charges half the price of its upmarket neighbours. It's a lovely spot in which to sit and savour tasty seafood, such as *spaghetti alle vongole* or *alle cozze*. The *Alici fritte* (fried fresh anchovies) are delicious, as are the bread and *taralli* (baked dough snacks).

Trattoria San Ferdinando
Via Nardones 117, Piazza Trieste e Trento (081 421964). Bus C22, C25, R2. **Open** 12.30-3.30pm, 7.30-11.30pm Wed-Fri; 12.30-3.30pm Mon, Tue, Sat. Closed 3wks Aug. **Average** €30. **Credit** AmEx, DC, MC, V. **Map** p332 K12 **⓬ Trattoria**
This lively local trattoria has a handwritten menu that might include *risotto asparagi e gamberetti* (prepared fresh, so it takes time), *pasta patate e provola* or *penne melanzane e mozzarella*. Most diners choose a couple of dishes, then add some of the *contorni* of the day. The atmosphere is always friendly, and the tables usually packed out with families and couples.

CENTRO STORICO

€ Antica Osteria Pisano
Piazzetta Crocelle ai Mannesi 1 (corner of Via Duomo & Spaccanapoli, 081 554 8325). Metro Dante or Museo/bus R2. **Open** noon-4pm, 7.30-11pm Mon-Sat. Closed Aug. **Average** €18. **No credit cards. Map** p328 N8 **⓭ Trattoria**
This excellent trattoria on the fringes of Forcella has a limited lunchtime menu and a more elaborate selection in the evening. Traditional favourites such as *pasta al sugo* or *alla genovese* are a particular forte, and the *contorni* are abundant and fresh – a fine substitute for a main course. The kitchen opens on to the restaurant, and staff are more than happy for you to have a gander. This place is popular but tiny, so be prepared to wait.

€ Antica Trattoria da Carmine
Via dei Tribunali 330 (081 294383). Metro Dante/bus R1, R2. **Open** noon-4pm Tue, Sun; noon-4pm, 7-11pm Wed-Sat. **Average** €18. **Credit** MC, V. **Map** p328 M8 **⓮ Trattoria**
This serviceable trattoria's strong suit is that it is open on Sunday. Located near San Lorenzo Maggiore, one of the most ancient churches in Naples, it serves

soups incluude *lenticchie e broccoli* (lentils and broccoli), *ceci* (chick peas) and *fagioli* (beans). Good *vino locale* is served in ceramic jugs from Vietri on the Amalfi Coast. It's not easy to get to – come from Via Monte di Dio or take the lift (*ascensore*) on Via Chiaia.

Pizzeria Marino
Via Santa Lucia 118 (081 764 0280). Bus 140, C25. **Open** 12.30-4.30pm, 7.30pm-midnight Tue-Sun. Closed 2wks Aug. **Average** €30. **Credit** AmEx, DC, MC, V. **Map** p332 K14 **❽ Pizzeria**
Set midway between Piazza Plebescito and the Castel dell'Ovo, this reliable pizzeria has a large dining room inside and plenty of outside tables in summer. Pizzas are classic – try the tasty Anastasia (cherry tomatoes, *mozzarella di bufala*) – and there's good antipasti and fried seafood.

★ La Terrazza
Hotel Excelsior, Via Partenope 48, Santa Lucia (081 764 0111/www.excelsior.it). Metro Mergellina/bus 140, C25, R2, R4. **Open** noon-3pm, 7-10.30pm Mon-Sat. **Average** €75. **Credit** AmEx, DC, MC, V. **Map** p332 K15 **❾ Ristorante**
Belle époque opulence and glorious bay views make the terrace here jaw-droppingly splendid; dress up and come for a special occasion. Service in the elegant dining room is formal and grand, and the fine food is classic Mediterranean, with a wide range of meat and fish and a delicious buffet of antipasti. There's also a privileged seating area (diners only) where you can sip pre- and post-dinner drinks.

Transatlantico
Borgo Marinaro, Santa Lucia (081 764 9201/ www.ristorante-transatlantico.com). Bus 1, 140. **Open** 12.30-3.30pm, 7pm-midnight Mon, Wed-Sun. **Average** €35. **Credit** AmEx, DC, MC, V. **Map** p332 K15 **❿ Ristorante & pizzeria**

up traditional staples like *pasta, patate e provola*. The beef fillet (*filetto a modo nostro*) comes on a bread bed with rocket, cherry tomatoes and parmesan; of the seafood dishes, try *spigola* (sea bass) baked with potatoes and balsamic vinegar.

€ Berevino
Via San Sebastiano 62 (081 060 5688/347 102 6865/www.berevino.org). Metro Dante or Montesanto/bus C57, R1, R4. Open 10am-3am Mon-Sat. Closed Aug. **Average** €18. **Credit** MC, V. **Map** p328 L8 ⓮ **Wine bar**

This wine bar and shop serves a delicious selection of nibbles to accompany your choice of wine from the extensive (though not international) wine list. It's particularly strong on Campanian wines.

★ € Cantina della Sapienza
Via della Sapienza 40 (081 459078). Metro Piazza Cavour/bus C57, R4. **Open** noon-3.30pm Mon-Sat. Closed 3wks Aug. **Average** €13. **No credit cards**. **Map** p328 L7 ⓰ **Osteria**

This is the closest thing to Neapolitan home-cooking you'll find. There are six menu combinations, none

Pizza perfection

Sample a slice of culinary genius.

Naples is the home of pizza. Wherever you are in the city, you're never far from an oven, crackling wood and the delicious aroma of freshly baked pizza.

Pizza has existed for thousands of years. It's said that at the height of the Persian Empire, the soldiers of Darius the Great (521-486 BC) baked a kind of flatbread on their shields, then added cheese and dates. Virgil (70-19 BC) describes how 'we devour the plates on which we fed' and there's evidence that an early form of pizza was baked in ancient Pompeii. Opinions on the etymology differ: it comes either from the Latin *pinsere*, meaning to pound or press, or the Greek *pitta*; as it happens, Neapolitans often fold pizza in one hand, eating it as you would a pitta.

By the 18th century, pizza was a staple food of the poorer classes. Pizza-makers stood on street corners with large vats of boiling fat, frying pizza for passers-by – with tomatoes for the richer folk. Today, such street-side stalls have all but disappeared, replaced by *pizzerie*. These, too, have a rich history; the oldest pizzeria in the city, and indeed the world, is Pizzeria Port'Alba, dating from 1830.

The margherita was created by Raffaele Esposito in 1889. Working for Pizzeria Brandi (still in business today), he was summoned to the Royal Palace to prepare pizza for King Umberto I and Queen Margherita. The Queen's favourite was based on the Italian tricolore flag – red tomatoes, white mozzarella and green basil – and afterwards named in her honour.

Pizza is a simple dish, but extremely difficult to produce well. The *pizzaiolo*, is justly proud of his position – a good pizza chef can command a high wage, as he encourages return business. *Pizzaioli* are

exclusively men; legend has it that only they can make the dough rise properly. Dough is freshly made each morning: after being kneaded for around 20 minutes until it has the desired non-sticky, elastic consistency, it is worked into balls, placed in wooden trays and left to rest for six to eight hours.

In 2004, the ministry for agriculture issued regulations outlining how a real Neapolitan pizza, *pizza verace napoletana*, should be made. The pizza must be round, no more than 35cm in diameter, and no thicker than 0.3cm in the middle with a crust of 1-2cm. The dough is shaped by hand on a flour-covered marble work surface, then the topping added. A large metal spatula is used to place the pizza in the wood-fired oven (*forno a legna*), at a temperature of 485°C, for 60 to 90 seconds. It should be served without delay.

Look for the sign outside *pizzerie* to sample one of the three authentic types: *pizza napoletana marinara* (San Marzano tomatoes from Vesuvius' slopes, garlic, oregano and olive oil), *pizza napoletana margherita* and *pizza napoletana margherita DOC* (the latter distinguished by its use of buffalo mozzarella).

CONSUME

CONSUME

Tutti foodie

Our pick of the local specialities.

Neapolitan cuisine is renowned throughout Italy and beyond, in part thanks to the superb seasonal range of ingredients grown in this volcanic region. The vegetables and fruit here are far tastier and juicier than further north – you'll probably never eat a more succulent peach, orange, or tomato. Local olive oil, although less subtle than that of Tuscany or Liguria, has a very smooth finish and is steadily improving.

Italy's Slow Food movement has prompted local authorities to promote independent, localised food production. Products are now being classified with the DOC and DOP (Denominazione di Origine Controllata/Protetta) quality control system: to qualify for DOC status, the entire production process must take place within the traditional area for that particular product, using tried and tested methods. Look out, too, for the Slow Food snail sign in approved shops and restaurants, and keep an eye out for ads for village *sagre* (food festivals) in outlying areas.

FRIARIELLI
Also known as broccoli rabe, this is a type of greens unique to the region. Sautéed with garlic and chilli, it has a slightly bitter, spicy taste. It's an ideal match for the local sausage, which is often laced with fennel.

OLIVE OIL
The finest olives in Campania are grown on the Sorrentine peninsula and the hills around the Cilento and Salerno. The Sorrento ogliarola olive benefits from a mild climate, scarce rainfall and sandy-volcanic soil; it tastes sweet with a subtle piquancy. Extra-virgin DOP Penisola Sorrentina is made of three varieties, whereas DOP Cilento and DOP Colline Salernitane use four or more; both are fairly fruity.

Making olive oil is an age-old business – this area was once part of Magna Grecia, and many ancient olive trees remain near Paestum. Two good producers are **Le Tore** (Via Pontone 43, Massa Lubrense, 081 808 0637, 333 986 6691, www.letore. com, open 8am-1pm, 5-8pm Mon-Sat, 8am-1pm Sun), which also has a lovely *agriturismo*, and **Olivicoltori Le Contrade** (Contrada Gaudo 9, Giungano, 339 229 4763, www.lecontrade.com, open by appointment only).

PASTA DI GRAGNANO
Produced using *grano duro* (durum wheat), this pasta is dried naturally to maintain its fragrance, nutritional value and consistency during cooking. Originally served as a sweet, pasta became a main dish in the 1700s. The Naples plains were

---

of which costs over €10, with different specials every day. Regular favourites include *pasta alla siciliana* (with aubergines, tomato and mozzarella) and *pasta al ragù*; the *parmigiana di melanzane* is outstanding. Expect friendly family service, fine desserts and good *vino locale* (red). It's also handy after a visit to the Museo Archeologico Nazionale.

€ Ciao Pizza
Via Benedetto Croce 42 (081 551 0109). Metro Dante/bus R1, R4. Open 9am-2am daily. Closed 2wks Aug. Average €4. No credit cards. Map p328 L9 ⑰ Pizzeria
Head here for tasty, traditional pizza triangles.
Other location Via San Carlo 3.

€ Di Matteo
Via dei Tribunali 94 (081 455262). Metro Dante/bus R1, R2. Open 9am-midnight Mon-Sat (open daily Dec). Closed 2wks Aug. Average €7. No credit cards. Map p328 M8 ⑱ Pizzeria
The decor may be unimpressive, but the pizzas are fabulous at this highly popular establishment. Di

Matteo is one of the few places where *ripieno fritto* (fried calzone pizza) is to be recommended. Delicious deep-fried bits and pieces (*frittura*) can be nibbled to keep hunger at bay while you wait; takeaways are also available.

€ Friggitoria-Pizzeria Giuliano
Calata Trinità Maggiore 33 (081 551 0986). Cumana Montesanto/bus R1, R4. Open 7am-10.30pm Mon-Sat. Closed Aug. Average €4.50. No credit cards. Map p328 L9 ⑲ Friggitoria & pizzeria
Probably the best *pizzette* (snack-sized pizza) in town: the *ripieno* and the *margherita* are exceptional. Potato croquettes and *zeppole* (deep-fried dough balls) are crisp and fresh.

€ La Locanda del Grifo
Via Francesco del Giudice 14 (081 442 0815). Metro Dante or Piazza Cavour/bus R1, R4. Open 12.30-3.30pm, 7pm-midnight daily. Average €25. Credit AmEx, DC, MC, V. Map p328 L8 ⑳ Trattoria

cylinders (*paccheri* – the word means 'big slap') and long tubes (*zitoni* – traditionally broken by unmarried women, known as *zitelle*). Pick some up at **Pastai Gragnanesi** (Via Giovanni della Rocca 20, Gragnano, 081 801 2975, www.pastaigragnanesi.it, closed Sun) or the **Pastificio Fratelli Setaro** (Via Mazzini 47, Torre Annunziata, 081 861 1464, 081 862 6913, www.setaro.it, closed Sat afternoon & Sun).

TOMATOES

Naples' red gold, tomatoes have shaped the regional cuisine. The tiny, slightly pear-shaped hillock variety, grown in the fertile volcanic soils of Vesuvius, is known as *piénnolo*. Whole stems are hung in doorways from August to mature and sweeten; these half-dried and sun-concentrated tomatoes are then used all year to 'colour' dishes. The better known DOP San Marzano plum tomato (*pummarola*), excellent for salads, is classically used for canning. It grows in a valley south of the Vesuvius; once at risk of disappearing, the real thing is still rare. Soorento has its own tomato too; large, pinkish and sweet. A good supplier is **Azienda Sabato Abagnale** (Via de Luca 23, Sant'Antonio Abate, 081 873 5300, closed Sun in July & Aug, Sat & Sun Sept-June).

once full of watermills grinding wheat, with pasta hung out to dry in the open air. Indeed, Gragnano's main street, Via Roma, was designed for drying pasta: bathed in sunlight all day long, it is cooled by gentle breezes. The finest producers still use the centuries-old *uomo di bronzo*, bronze threaders, to cut the pasta to shape. Traditional Neapolitan shapes are large

Attached to the Hotel Neapolis, this place offers old favourites as well as more original dishes, such as *paccheri di Gragnano* pasta with pecorino and squid, or fettuccine with walnuts and porcini. Outdoor tables face on to a pretty square, home to the church of Santa Maria Maggiore and a fine Romanesque campanile, complete with griffin – hence the name.

Palazzo Petrucci

Piazza San Domenico Maggiore 4 (081 552 4068). Metro Dante/bus C57, R2. **Open** *June-Sept* 1-2.30pm, 8-10.30pm Tue-Sat; 8-10.30pm Mon, Sun. *Oct-May* 8-10.30pm Mon; 1-2.30pm, 8-10.30pm Tue-Sat; 1-2.30pm Sun. **Average** €45. **Credit** AmEx, MC, V. **Map** p328 L9 ㉑ Ristorante

Located in the former stables of an ancient palazzo, this relative newcomer to the city's high-end restaurant scene serves Neapolitan nouvelle cuisine. The menu often changes, but may feature the superb *lasagnetta di mozzarella di bufala e crudo di gamberi su zuppetta di cavolo broccolo* – a bold liaison of mozzarella and raw prawns.

★ € Sorbillo

Via dei Tribunali 32 (081 446 643). Metro Dante/bus R1, R2. **Open** noon-3.30pm, 7-11.30pm Mon-Sat. Closed 3wks Aug. **Average** €5. **Credit** AmEx, V. **Map** p328 M8 ㉒ Pizzeria

This is the original and, without a doubt, best Sorbillo outpost. Run by a third generation family of *pizzaioli*, this miniscule, neon-lit space has three or four tables and a quick turnover. There are no nibbles, and a limited choice of pizza toppings, but the dough is truly excellent and only the finest ingredients are used. It's low-key and very friendly; there's a trendier, larger version on the same street (with higher prices), but foodies rate the pizza at this one higher.

★ La Stanza del Gusto

Via Santa Maria di Costantinopoli 100 (081 401578/www.lastanzadelgusto.com) Metro Dante or Museo. **Open** noon-11.30pm Tue-Sat; noon-3pm Sun. Closed 3wks Aug. **Average** *Cheese bar* €25. *Restaurant* €65. **Credit** AmEx, DC, MC, V. **Map** p328 L8 ㉓ Ristorante

CONSUME

This unique double locale is dedicated to innovative culinary riffs on Campanian cuisine, conceived by flamboyant chef Mario Avallone (*see p123* **Profile**). A move to new multilevel digs has resulted in a new ground-floor cheese bar, which serves soups, salads, *sformati* (quiches) and a paprika-laced burger, along with a fine array of cheeses. In the titular 'tasting room' upstairs (booking is essential), the menu changes almost daily depending on Avallone's whims. Reinterpreted classics such as *sartù di riso* (baked rice), lamb with ginger, Casertano pig in Aglianico wine or herb-basted grouper fish are served as *assaggi* – small tasting portions. Avallone is also an accomplished pastry chef, so leave room for dessert. The tasting menu makes good sense.

€ Trattoria La Campagnola

Piazzetta Nilo 22 (081 551 4930). Cumana Montesanto/Metro Piazza Cavour. **Open** 1-4pm, 7.30pm-midnight Tue-Sat; 1-4pm Sun. Closed 2wks Aug. **Average** €20. **Credit** AmEx, MC, V. **Map** p328 M8 ❷ **Trattoria**

With tables on the square and inside, past a TV room-cum-bar populated by local ancients, this unpretentious place attracts a wide spectrum of customers. Students, families and business people all come to enjoy the same thing – genuine Neapolitan cuisine at honest prices. There's a full menu, but the daily specials are a good bet, washed down with the fine house red. Portions are generous and the waiters are endearing.

Make mine a mozzarella

Sink your teeth into the city's cheese of choice.

There is something almost Freudian about Neapolitans and mozzarella. For them, the famous cheese is the softest, milkiest thing on earth after their mamma's breast. A dish with a white ball soaking in its brine is found in every true Neapolitan household – and never in the fridge.

Mozzarella is produced by hand, using buffalo milk, rennet and salt. The name comes from *mozzare* (to cut), and refers to how the fresh, shiny paste is lopped off and shaped into different-sized balls.

Mozzarella should be tender but not mushy, elastic but not rubbery. When poked, it must spring back into its original shape; when cut, it should ooze droplets of milk – and of course, it must melt in the mouth.

The best mozzarella dairies are around Caserta or Battipaglia, with the good stuff certified as Mozzarella DOC or Mozzarella DOP. These labels assure local origin and

proper production standards, and dispel any doubts that your mozzarella could be contaminated by the toxic substances that seeped into the soil in certain areas in recent years, prompting a brief scare.

Mozzarella is sold in a variety of shapes: small balls called *bocconcini* (little bites); plump spheres; and braids, called *treccie*. It also comes in a smoked form, provola. Provola is often used in Neapolitan cuisine, most notably melted over gnocchi in a rich dish known as *gnocchi alla sorrentina*. A variety of mozzarella made from cow's milk is called *fior di latte* and typically comes from Agerola; aside from being a bit leaner, *fior di latte* has a slightly more acidic bite.

In Naples, mozzarella is sold everywhere. The best bet is to buy it in a *salumeria* (deli); ask for *mozzarella di bufala*, and look at what the locals are buying.

If you want to see the buffalos grazing and learn how the cheese is made, visit a mozzarella farm for an overnight stay. A lovely place where you can combine a culinary whim with the gravitas of the ruins at Paestum is **La Tenuta Seliano** (Via Seliano, Paestum, 082 872 4544, www.agriturismoseliano.it, €75-€115 double). Its restaurant is open from April to October (average €28); call ahead, as opening hours are restricted.

Also near Paestum is the organic buffalo farm **Vannulo** (Via Galileo Galilei, Contrada Vannulo, Capaccio Scalo, 082 872 4765, www.vannulo.it). Besides great mozzarella, it also makes ultra-creamy buffalo milk yoghurt and gelato; there's a mozzarella shop (open 8am-5pm daily) and a separate yogurt shop (open 7am-7.30pm daily).

CONSUME

€ Un Sorriso Integrale

Vico San Pietro a Majella, Piazza Bellini 6 (081 455026/www.sorrisointegrale.com). Metro Dante or Piazza Cavour. **Open** noon-4.30pm, 7pm-midnight Mon-Sat. Closed 2wks Aug. **Average** €15. **Credit** MC, V. **Map** p328 L8  **Vegetarian**

This longstanding bastion of macrobiotic cuisine with a Mediterranean bent is tucked away in a quiet courtyard just off Piazza Bellini. Modestly priced, it's popular with students and has a friendly vibe at its communal tables. The daily mixed platter special is fresh and wholesome; after lunch, stock up on organic produce and healthy goods from the shop.

PORT & UNIVERSITY

€ Antica Pizzeria del Borgo Orefeci

Via Luigi Palmieri 13 (081 552 0996). Bus R2/tram 1. **Open** noon-3.30pm, 7-10.30pm Mon-Sat. Closed Aug. **Average** €10. **No credit cards**. **Map** p328 N10 **Pizzeria**

This simple pizzeria is tucked away on a side street in the old goldsmiths' zone (now pedestrianised and gentrified), opposite the imposing university building on the corner with Via Mezzacannone. Excellent pizzas – try the *friarielli e salsiccia* (local greens and sausage) – and a wide range of fresh fish dishes are served to tables outside and in.

★ € Da Michele

Via Sersale 1 (081 553 9204). Metro Piazza Garibaldi/bus R2. **Open** 10.30am-11pm Mon-Sat. Closed 2wks Aug. **Average** €10. **No credit cards**. **Map** p329 O8 **Pizzeria**

A seriously minimalist traditional pizzeria, Da Michele serves two types of pizza (margherita or marinara), beer, Coca-Cola and water. Service is friendly and fast, and the *pizze* are enormous, delicious and unbelievably cheap. Take a number at the door before joining the queue, and marvel at the theatrical *pizzaiolo*, staff and punters while you wait.

Europeo Mattozzi

Via Campodisola Marchese 4, Zona Porto (081 552 1323/www.europeomattozzi.it). Bus R2. **Open** noon-4pm, 8-11.30pm Mon-Sat. Closed 2wks Aug. **Average** €40. **Credit** AmEx, MC, V. **Map** p328 M10 **Ristorante**

A stroll away from Piazza Borsa, this old-fashioned restaurant serves delicious local staples such as clam and mussel soup or squid and peas, and fresh pasta dishes – *alla genovese* (mince and onions), say, or *con ceci* (with chickpeas). The fish is excellent: try the *fragaglie* (tiny, fried newborn fish). Sepia photographs compete with copperware for wallspace.

Mattozzi Giardino di Napoli

Via Pietro Colletta 25 (081 287884). Bus R2. **Open** noon-4.30pm, 7-11pm Mon-Sat. Closed Aug. **Average** €30. **Credit** AmEx, MC, V. **Map** p329 O8 **Trattoria**

Da Michele.

Fine homecooking is the order of the day in this friendly, intimate trattoria, where red wooden doors and wine barrels dominate the decor. Try the homemade *pappardelle* with peppers and calamari, or the delicately spicy pumpkin and shrimp risotto. The wine list is solid; the *pastiera* cake, baked by owner Salvatore d'Antonio, is top notch. Current president of Italy Giorgio Napolitano used to be a regular.

Mimì alla Ferrovia

Via Alfonso d'Aragona 19/21 (081 289 004). Metro Piazza Garibaldi/bus C30, C40, R2. **Open** noon-3.30pm, 7-11.30pm Mon-Sat. Closed 1wk Aug. **Average** €35. **Credit** AmEx, MC, V. **Map** p329 P7 **Ristorante**

A location by the law courts means plenty of celebrities and bigwigs have eaten at this restaurant; it's also the perfect foil to the chaos of nearby Piazza Garibaldi. Feast on platter after platter of tempting seafood, or eat a simple bowl of pasta or a good steak for only €9. The wine list is impressive, and the portion sizes for antipasti and *contorni* are generous. Service and decor are elegantly old-fashioned.

CONSUME

€ Il Piccolo Ristoro
Calata Porto di Massa int Porto (349 192 9074).
Bus C2. **Open** noon-3pm Mon-Fri, Sun; noon-
3pm, 7.30-midnight Sat. Closed 2wks Aug.
Average €20. **No credit cards**. **Map** p329 O10
❸❶ Trattoria
To find one of Naples' best kept secrets, enter the
port through Varco Pisacane, or head east for about
200m from the main port. Il Piccolo is housed in little more than a shack, with no sign outside (look for
the green and white canopy), but serves delicious fish
that's freshly caught each day. Family-run, it's probably the least expensive fish restaurant in the city.

€ Pizzeria Pellone al Vasto
Via Nazionale 93 (081 553 8614). Metro Piazza
Garibaldi. **Open** noon-3.30pm, 7pm-midnight
Mon-Sat. Closed 1wk Aug. **Average** €10.
No credit cards. **Map** p329 R6 **❸❷ Pizzeria**
A short walk from the station, the fiercely popular
Pellone is very much a neighbourhood pizzeria:
queues are immense in the evenings, although a
recent extension on Via Bari has improved matters
slightly. A vast oil painting of the Bay of Naples
dominates the entrance to the dining room. The
award-winning pizzas are immense, so either deny
yourself the delicious fried starters altogether or be
careful not to overindulge.

€ Taverna dell'Arte
Rampa San Giovanni Maggiore 1A (081 552
7558/www.tavernadellarte.it). Bus C25, R1, R2.
Open noon-3.30pm, 7-10pm Mon-Sat. Closed
2wks Aug. **Average** €25. **Credit** MC, V. **Map**
p328 M9 **❸❸ Trattoria**
Perched beside stairs leading up to a church,
dell'Arte has a pretty pergola and the perfect combination of homely atmosphere, good food and wine,
and attentive service. The menu is limited but ever
changing, combining imaginative flair with consis-
tently high quality. Typical dishes are *paccheri ai
carciofi* (classic Neapolitan large tube pasta with an
artichoke, pine nut and black olive sauce) or *calamaro con patate* (squid cooked with potatoes and a
little tomato). It's unsurprisingly popular, so booking is usually essential.

€ Trianon
Via Colletta Pietro, 46 (081 553 9426). Metro
Piazza Garibaldi/bus R1, R2. **Open** 11am-3.30pm,
6.30-midnight daily. **Average** €10. **Credit** MC,
V. **Map** p329 O8 **❸❹ Pizzeria**
This palatial pizzeria is a Neapolitan institution
dating from 1923, with marble tabletops, faded
frescoes, and fantastic pizza for next to nothing. It's
practically across the street from Da Michele: one
big difference is that there is never a queue here,
since it accommodates 450; the other is that there's
a wide choice of pizzas. Service is snappy, and the
old-world atmosphere quite unique. Don't ask for
Diet Coke.

VIA TOLEDO & LA SANITA

Ciro a Santa Brigida
Via Santa Brigida 71/73 (081 552 4072/www.
ciroasantabrigida.com). Funicular Centrale to
Augusteo/bus C25, R2. **Open** 12.30-3.30pm,
7.30pm-1am Mon-Sat. Closed 1wk Aug. **Average**
Pizzeria €25. *Ristorante* €50. **Credit** AmEx, DC,
MC, V. **Map** p332 K12 **❸❺ Ristorante & pizzeria**
Set on two floors (head upstairs for a seat overlooking the street; if you strain you can see Vesuvius),
Ciro has a huge list of *contorni* to choose from. The
choice depends on the season: *carciofi* (artichokes),
scarola (lettuce) or aubergine, perhaps; note that you
may be charged for a scoop of each, rather than for
a mixed plate. The fish – *pesce spada* (swordfish)
and prawns in particular – is good, too.

Il Garum
Piazza Monteoliveto 2A (081 542 3228/www.
ristoranteilgarum.com). **Open** 10.30am-3.30pm,
7-11.30pm daily. Closed 2wks Aug. **Average**
€25. **Credit** AmEx, MC, V. **Map** p328 K/L10
❸❻ Ristorante
This well-regarded *osteria* has tables outside on the
lovely Piazza Monteoliveto. The chef creates
Neapolitan cuisine with innovative touches, sometimes adding the namesake garum – a spice made
from fish to an ancient Roman recipe. The lunch
menu is great value for money, and staff are cheery.

Hosteria Toledo
Vico Giardinetto a Toledo 78, off Via Toledo
(081 421257). Funicular Centrale to Via Roma/
bus C25, R2. **Open** noon-3pm, 7pm-midnight
Mon, Wed-Sun; noon-3pm Tue. Closed 2wks Aug.
Average €30. **Credit** DC, MC, V. **Map** p332 K11
❸❼ Trattoria & pizzeria
Quality cuisine in the Quartieri Spagnoli, with traditional fare and generous portions. The courgette
'gazpacho' (*alla scapece*) is delicious, as is the *ziti al
ragù* (pasta with meat and tomato sauce). There's
good fish, too. Leave space for home-made *dolci*.

€ Mandara
Via Ponte di Tappia 90-92 (081 551 2964).
Metro Montesanto/funicular to Via Roma. **Open**
8am-8pm Mon-Sat. **Average** €10. **Credit** AmEx,
MC, V. **Map** p332 K11 **❸❽ Tavola calda**
A classic snack bar, with two small dining rooms, a
large choice of hot and cold dishes, a changing daily
menu, and home-made desserts (if it's in season, try
the fig tart). If you fancy some fresh *mozzarella di
bufala*, you're in the right place – Mandara is a
famous mozzarella maker from Mondragone.

€ La Taverna del Buongustaio
Via Basilio Puoti 8 (081 551 2626). Metro
Montesanto/bus 201, R1, R4. **Open** 1-2.30pm, 8-
11pm Mon-Sat. Closed 2wks Aug. **Average** €15.
No credit cards. **Map** p328 K9 **❸❾ Trattoria**

CONSUME

Profile Mario Avallone

Testing the boundaries on the fine dining scene.

Chef Mario Avallone is the man behind the pioneering La Stanza del Gusto – famous for its creative menu, and founded in one of Naples' edgier neighbourhoods. A homeboy of the much maligned Quartieri Spagnoli, Avallone began adulthood working in a bank, before moving to Sicily. There he grew increasingly interested in food – although the desire to cook, Avallone insists, was only born when he finally grew tired of eating out. He calls himself a lazy sleepwalker who eventually woke up in the kitchen.

After ten years in Sicily, Avallone returned to his native city, where his kitchen soon became the workshop of the Officine Gastronomiche Partenopee, the cultural association he founded in 1991. At first, it was just friends – a sort of sect for gluttons, he says – but the coterie soon began to expand.

The story goes that it all began with just one table, for which Avallone accepted reservations each evening. Soon it escalated on to stairway terraces around the Quartieri, as his unique recipes began to gain a following: cream of baccalà served in a cup, say, or orange cherry tomato soup with smoked ricotta; for dessert, a cup of coarse yet smooth chocolate and ricotta, or a pungent tart, lit with the subtle fire of peperoncino.

In 2007, the operation moved to a new site on Piazza Bellini, in the heart of the Centro Storico. The new home of La Stanza del Gusto is a large, three-level affair, comprising three separate enterprises: a tasting bar, a gourmet dining room and a cooking school.

Avallone has always been against playing it safe by serving

up Neapolitan classics – even though in this city, the mere suggestion of reinterpretation is seen by many as sacrilege. Instead, he is open to new influences, giving rise to an inventive style that is entirely his own.

Simplification, he says, is the way forward, allowing the ingredients 'to stand out in as elegant a way as possible'. Fresh, local produce, he insists, is key. 'There's nothing quite like the friarielli greens called "dogs' tongues", or mulberries or courgettes hand-picked by a farmer.'

Just don't go expecting pizza, or any other tried and tested Neapolitan stawarts. As Avallone proudly proclaims, 'My job is not to feed people, but to entice them to taste what I have prepared.'

SUPER MARIO
For more on **La Stanza del Gusto**, *see p119.*

CONSUME

Local flavour

A rich array of native grape varieties makes for superb local wines.

Vines were first brought to the rich Campanian soil by the Greeks in 800 BC, and have thrived here ever since. Now there's a clutch of energetic young winemakers really doing justice to grapes like aglianico – a red that can hold its own with Tuscany's sangiovese or Piedmont's nebbiolo – and rediscovering interesting local varieties such as piedirosso and gragnano. Worthwhile new wines are also emerging from the Cilento and Amalfi Coast.

Less scrupulous producers of rotten wines have jumped on the falanghina and aglianico bandwagon, though. Matters are further complicated by some producers bottling their finest wines as humble *vino da tavola* to bypass ploddingly restrictive DOC, DOCG or IGT regulations. As a result, the names of wineries and individual crus can be a more reliable indicator of quality than the official classifications.

REDS

Aglianico del Taburno
This full-bodied red ranges from ordinary to fabulous. Cantina del Taburno and Ocone are the best known producers, but La Rivolta in the Cilento also does a tasty version. Best with pasta with tomato or meat *sugo* sauce.

Costa d'Amalfi Furore Rosso
A piedirosso and aglianico blend, this delicious, full-bodied red from the Amalfi Coast matures well. The Gran Furor (Marisa Cuomo) label is by far the best.

Falerno del Massico
This wine – and its white equivalent – were known to the Romans, and were drunk on special occasions in ancient Pompeii. The best producers are Villa Matilde and Moio. It works very well with lamb.

Gragnano
A slightly fizzy, dry wine that should be drunk young, with vegetable soups or sausage dishes. Grotta del Sole is the best producer.

Montevetrano
In the hinterland of Salerno, Silvia Imparato makes one of Campania's most impressive reds. It's a blend of cabernet sauvignon and merlot, with a little aglianico thrown in.

Per'e Palummo
The 'foot of the dove' is a red grape native to Ischia, and makes a surprisingly complex wine. Look for D'Ambra and Pietratorcia (which uses the grape in its Ischia Rosso blend).

CONSUME

It's easy to miss this excellent trattoria, which is hidden down a side street that's crisscrossed with washing lines. The white tiled walls give the impression of being in somebody's kitchen, and the food is akin to homecooking. Don't expect a written menu; instead, the waiter rattles off a list of fish and meat dishes at quick-fire pace. If you don't catch it all, play safe and order the *orechietti con salsiccia e friarielli*.

€ Timpani e Tempure
Vico della Quercia 17 (081 551 2280/www. timpanietempura.it). Metro Dante/bus C57, R1, R4. **Open** 9.30am-3.30pm Sun, Mon; 9.30am-8.30pm Tue-Sat. Closed Aug. **Average** €15. **No credit cards. Map** p328 K9 ⑩ **Rosticceria**
This place mainly does takeaways, and specialises in delicious, traditional dishes sold by the kilo such as *timballi* and *sartù di riso* (baked pasta and rice dishes); a generous portion costs around €3.50. It also serves good wine by the glass.

€ La Vecchia Cantina
Via San Nicola alla Carità 13-14 (081 552 0226). Metro Dante or Montesanto/bus C57, R1, R4. **Open** noon-3.30pm, 7-11pm Mon-Sat; noon-3.30pm Sun. **Average** €20. **Credit** AmEx, DC, MC, V. **Map** p328 K9 ⑪ **Osteria**
Conveniently set next door to the fish market, this little *osteria* serves tasty renditions of the classics, at unbeatable prices. The grilled squid and swordfish are good, as is the *linguine con polpetti* (pasta with baby octopus). Try the *baccalà fritto* (fried salt cod) if you want to copy the locals.

VOMERO

€ L'Arte della Pizza
Via Santa Maria della Libera 5 (081 241 1907). Funicolare Augusteo. **Open** noon-4pm, 7pm-2am Tue-Sun. **Average** €25. **Credit** AmEx, MC, V. **Map** p330 C10 ⑫ **Pizzeria**

Piedirosso
Drink this light and very pleasant wine while it's young – two years old at most. Ocone and Grotta del Sole are solid producers.

Taurasi
Produced around Taurasi village near Avellino, this aglianico is serious competition for the Brunello of the north. Look out for the Feudi di San Gregorio, Mastroberardino, Terredora and Caggiano labels. It's a great match for steaks and roasted meats.

Vigna Camarato
Produced by Villa Matilde, this single cru aglianico has been attracting serious praise from Italy's wine critics.

WHITES

Asprinio d'Aversa
A crisp, light white from the Mazzoni area of Aversa; also a good *vino spumante*. Grotta del Sole and I Borboni are reliable.

Biancolella
The D'Ambra winery does great things with this Ischian grape – look out for its Tenuta Frassitelli cru. Pietratorcia blends it with fiano to produce the superb Scheria Bianco cru. It's good with fish, cheese or rabbit.

Coda di Volpe
A light, easy-quaffing white – best from the Sannio. Serve with *aperitivi* or bruschette.

Costa d'Amalfi Furore Bianco
This blend of biancolella and falanghina from the Amalfi Coast really works. Try the Apicella label, or the Fior d'Uva cru by Gran Furor (Marisa Cuomo). Drink with seafood antipasti.

Falanghina
The name means 'little stick'; in ancient times it was the first vine to be trained over a support. Fresh and fruity, it's the most popular white around. Try Villa Matilde, Mustilli, Ocone, Feudi di San Gregorio or Moio. It works wonderfully well with fish.

Fiano di Avellino
Another ancient, full-bodied white that is perfect with seafood and crustaceans. Feudi di San Gregorio is one of the best producers, closely followed by Terredora and Mastroberardino. The fragrant Kratos is produced in the Cilento by one-man band Luigi Maffini.

Greco di Tufo
One of the few whites that can be drunk more than a year after bottling, but still best young. Seek out the Feudi di San Gregorio or Mastroberardino labels. It works well with spicier foods.

Lacryma Christi
One of the most famous Campania wines. Its name derives from an old legend that Christ cried over Lucifer's fall from heaven, and his fallen tears on the land gave divine inspiration to the vines that grew there. The white is crisp and dry, the red remarkably full-bodied. Look for Mastroberardino, Feudi di San Gregorio, and Terredora.

Pizzaiolo Vincenzo Esposito is a master of his craft, and a bit of a showman. Not only are his creations decorated with pizza crust swans, they're also likely to arrive at your table with small Roman candles flaring festively. It isn't all for show, however; the flavours and textures are memorable, and it's well worth tracking down this slightly out of the way spot for an evening of fun and gustatory indulgence.

€ La Cantina di Donna'Elena
Via Tito d'Angelini 16 (081 578 6033). Funicular San Martino/Metro Vanvitelli. **Open** 12.30-3pm, 7.30-11.30pm Tue-Sun. Closed 3wks Aug. **Average** €20. **No credit cards. Map** p331 G10 **49 Trattoria**
On a residential street along from the Castel Sant' Elmo and Museo San Martino, this is a simple place. Solid cooking and bargain prices appeal to locals and tourists alike: steak, pasta and *m'peppata di cozze* (black peppered mussel soup) all cost around €10.

€ La Cantina di Sica
Via Bernini 17 (081 556 7520). Funicular Chiaia to Via Cimarosa or Centrale to Piazza Fuga/Metro Vanvitelli/bus C28, C31, C32, V1. **Open** 12.30-3.30pm, 7.30pm-midnight Tue-Sat; 12.30-3.30pm Sun. Closed 2wks Aug. **Average** €25. **Credit** AmEx, MC, V. **Map** p330 E10 **49 Trattoria**
You can't go far wrong with time-honoured dishes such as *ziti alla genovese* (pasta with very oniony mince sauce) or *tubettoni con gamberi e zucchine* (pasta with prawns and courgettes), albeit at slightly higher prices than the average trattoria. There's an interesting choice of fresh fish and meat, and truly delicious *contorni*; try the *parmigiana di melanzane* (layers of mozzarella and aubergine in tomato sauce). There's an excellent wine list, and the bar downstairs often hosts jazz or Neapolitan folk music performers. The tourist menu, available Tuesday to Friday, costs €15.

CONSUME

Dora.

Il Gallo Nero

Via Torquato Tasso 466 (081 643 012/www.
ilgalloneronapoli.it). Bus C24, 128. **Open** 8pm-
midnight Tue-Sat; 1-4pm Sun. Closed Aug.
Average €60. **Credit** AmEx, MC, V. **Ristorante**
A beautiful old Liberty villa owned by a Neapolitan
marchese, high on Vomero hill, Il Gallo Nero has a
pretty garden for alfresco summer feasts and a piano
bar. Paintings and antiques dominate the dining
room, and the service is charmingly old-fashioned.
The limited menu is classically Neapolitan, and
dishes feature outstanding produce – the freshest
fish and the best meat in Campania.

€ Osteria Donna Teresa

Via Kerbaker 58 (081 556 7070). Funicular
Chiaia to Via Cimarosa or Centrale to Piazza
Fuga/bus C28, C31, C32, V1. **Open** 1-3pm, 8-
11pm Mon-Sat. Closed 3wks Aug. **Average** €12.
No credit cards. Map p331 F10 ⑮ **Osteria**
Donna Teresa's small menu offers exemplary homecooking; the daily specials are as good a place to
start as any, and the fixed lunch is a bargain. Try
polpette (meatballs) in tomato sauce or *salsicce al*
sugo (sausages with tomato sauce) washed down
with a *quartino* of good house red.

CHIAIA TO POSILLIPO

★ Al Faretto

Via Marechiaro 127 (081 5750407/www.al
faretto.it). Bus 140. **Open** 12.30-4pm, 7.30-
midnight Tue-Sun. Closed 2wks Aug & 1wk
Jan. **Average** €35. **Credit** AmEx, MC, V.
Ristorante & pizzeria
Away from the hustle and bustle, with a terrific terrace overlooking the bay, this understatedly posh
establishment is perfect for a romantic candlelit
dinner. It also delivers in terms of what's on the
plate, thanks to its upmarket, classic cuisine. The
mozzarella is mouth-watering, the seafood pastas
and fish first-rate. Try the delicate *trancio di ricci-*
ola (amberjack fillets) or *crudo di gamberoni e*

scampi (raw Sicilian jumbo prawns and langoustines).
It also serves pizza, and has a solid wine list.
▶ *After dinner on the terrace, stroll down the*
steps to the moonlit Marechiaro, which inspired
a famous Neapolitan love song; see p86.

Al Poeta

Piazza Salvatore di Giacomo 134-135 (081 575
6936). Bus 140. **Open** 1-3.30pm, 8pm-midnight
Tue-Sun. Closed 2wks Aug. **Average** €40.
Credit AmEx, MC, V. **Ristorante**
This lovely little restaurant high on Posillipo hill
has won a loyal local following. Housed in a Liberty
villetta set back from Via Posillipo, its sunny terrace
faces a verdant residential square; inside, it's all
wood, white walls and copper pots. The food is traditional: deliciously fresh fish, accompanied by a
fine range of wines. Try the *linguine del mare di*
Posillipo, fresh *scialatielli* pasta with aubergine and
provola, fish of the day, or a flavoursome steak.

L'Amico Gamberone

Via Crispi 93 (081 665344). Metro Piazza
Amedeo/bus C24, C25, C26, C27. **Open**
noon-3.30pm, 7.30-10.30pm Mon-Sat; 1-4pm
Sun. Closed 3wks Aug. **Average** €30. **Credit**
AmEx, DC, MC, V. **Map** p326 E13 ⑯ **Trattoria**
A short walk from Piazza Amedeo, this trattoria has
low ceilings, a rustic feel and a tiny patio garden.
The seasonal menu is strong on seafood – start with
oysters or *taratufi* (giant red clams), delicious fried
fish (*cuoppo fritto del mare di Procida*), grilled *pesce*
azzurro in balsamic vinegar or octopus (*a ranfa e*
purp') seasoned with spicy oil and pepper. Pasta is
freshly made, the risotto is exquisite, and the *contorni*
are superb. The wine list is small but excellent.

Barrique

Piazzetta Ascensione 9 (081 662721). Metro
Piazza Amedeo/bus C24, C25, C26, C27, C28.
Open 7.30pm-1am daily. Closed Aug. **Average**
€35. **Credit** AmEx, MC, V. **Map** p327 F13 ⑰
Ristorante & wine bar

Expect an interesting variety of Italian wines from around Naples and other areas, served with a choice of well-flavoured salami, olives, cheeses and ham. There's also a handful of daily-changing pasta dishes. The interior is pleasantly done out in terracotta, with low lighting and a soundtrack of relaxed jazz.

Coco Loco
Piazza Rodinò 31 (081 415482). Metro Piazza Amedeo/Funicular Centrale to Via Roma. **Open** *July, Sept* 8-11.30pm Mon-Sat. *Oct-June* 8-11.30pm Mon-Fri; 1-3pm, 8-11.30pm Sat. Closed Aug. **Average** €60. **Credit** AmEx, DC, MC, V. **Map** p327 H13 ❹ **Ristorante**
With candlelit outdoor tables in a small pedestrianised square off Via Filangieri, and more convivial indoor seating, Coco Loco serves as an evening *ritrovo* for discerning locals, who roll up any time after 9.30pm. The *cucina* is subtle and innovative, including dishes such as *aragosta e gamberi alla catalana* (lobster and prawn salad with a hint of citrus fruit), designed by master chef Diego Nuzzo to get the tastebuds tingling. Service is courteous and efficient without being oppressive.

Da Pasqualino
Piazza Sannazzaro 77-79 (081 681524). Metro Mergellina/bus 140, C16, C24, R3. **Open** *Aug* noon-1am daily. *Sept-July* noon-1am Mon, Wed-Sun. **Average** €36. **Credit** AmEx, MC, V. **Map** p326 B15 ❹ **Pizzeria**
As one of the best *pizzerie* in the piazza, offering incredible value for money, this place tends to have long queues. The *frittura* is excellent: deep-fried mozzarella, potato croquettes and aubergines. The restaurant menu is reasonable, too; in summer, the square seethes with locals for as long as the *cozze* (mussels) are in season.

Donnanna
Via Posillipo 16B (081 769 0920/www.villa caracciolo.it). Bus 140 or walk from Mergellina. **Open** 1-3.30pm Sun; 8-11pm Tue-Sat. Closed 2wks Aug. **Average** €50. **Credit** AmEx, DC, MC, V. **Ristorante**
This stylish white and mirrored restaurant stands by the Bagni Elena, opposite Vesuvius and beside the ghostly Palazzo Sant'Anna, where it's rumoured Queen Joanna seduced muscle-bound fishermen before drowning them to ensure their discretion. Local art students created the Tiepolo-inspired Pulcinella frescoes. The owners, event organisers Sire, are responsible for state banquets and suchlike, so everything is hushed and polished; the organic ingredients are the finest money can buy. Typical fare is *tonarelli* pasta with *cicala di mare* (a crustacean), tomatoes and basil-scented oil or langoustines in saracen grain tempura. Desserts are exciting: Schweppes tonic and red wine sorbet, and orange tart with chocolate mousse. Call ahead, as it's often closed for private functions.

Don Salvatore
Via Mergellina 5 (081 681 817/www.don salvatore.it). Metro Mergellina/Bus 140, C16, C24, R3. **Open** noon-3.30pm, 7.30pm-midnight Mon, Tue, Thur-Sun. **Average** €45. **Credit** AmEx, DC, MC, V. **Map** p326 B16 ❺⓪ **Ristorante**
Delicious antipasti are a highlight here: order *cecinielle* (tiny, transparent fish fried in patties with batter), *polpo ai carciofi* (octopus with artichokes) or *calamaretti con uva passa* (baby squid with sultanas and pine nuts). Fish and meat dishes are excellent too: try the ancient recipe of *cuoccio* (parrot fish) with parmesan and fresh tomato or more recent creations such as scorpion fish in orange. The hospitable owner, Tonino Aversano, is passionate about wine.

Dora
Via Ferdinando Palasciano 30 (081 680519). Bus 140, C9, C18, C24, C25, C28. **Open** 1-2.30pm, 8pm-midnight Mon-Sat. Closed 3wks Aug & 2wks Dec. **Average** €70. **Credit** DC, MC, V. **Map** p326 E13 ❺❶ **Ristorante**
Exceptionally fresh fish, simply prepared, is key to the success of this much loved establishment, one of the city's tiniest restaurants. It serves excellent versions of standard *primi*, such as *spaghetti alle vongole*, as well as delicious oysters, giant prawns and fish soup; Dora's seafood linguine is almost a meal in itself. Fish, such as *pezzogna* (sea bream) or *sogliola* (sole), is cooked to perfection. Added delights are the tiled nautical decor and the moments when Dora and the waiters burst into song as they clear dishes. Prices are high for Naples, and booking essential.

€ La Focaccia
Vico Belledonne a Chiaia 31 (081 412277). Bus C22, C25. **Open** 11.30am-2am daily. Closed Aug. **Average** €10. **No credit cards**. **Map** p327 G13 ❺❷ **Pizza al taglio**
Choose from a delicious selection of pizza slices and focaccia. Try the *peperoni e patata* (peppers and potato) or *margherita al filetto* (cherry tomatoes and mozzarella). To be sure of a really fresh slice, watch the oven and buy what has just emerged. There's a huge range of beers, and wine by the glass and bottle. The TV is usually on; if you're a football fan, it's a good place at which to get involved in a match.

INSIDE TRACK
FOR RICHER, FOR POORER

Neapolitans tend to classify pizzas as being either *ricca* (rich) or *povera* (poor), depending on how thick the base is and on the quantity of its toppings. When it comes to pizza, however, rich isn't in the least bit better than poor. For 'rich', try **Mattozzi** (*see p129*); for 'poor', head for **Da Pasqualino** (*see above*).

CONSUME

Da bere?

Quaff a canarino or cool down with a granita.

To take your drinks order, a waiter will ask *Da bere?*. When your cue comes, simply say *Vorrei un/una...* ('I'd like a...') or *Mi può/potrebbe portare un/una...* ('Can/could you bring me a...'). For more on wines, *see p124* **Local flavour**; for coffee, *see p137* **Caffè culture**.

Aperitivo: a *calice di prosecco* (a glass of sparkling white wine) is typical. A bellini is prosecco with peach juice; typical bar drinks are a *negroni* (campari, martini rosso and gin), campari-soda, aperol or martini bianco or rosso. A classic Italian *aperitivo*, Campari is made from bitter orange peel. Very low or non-alcoholic versions are Crodino, Sanbitter or Aperolsoda (the latter is stronger tasting).

Ammazzacaffè, digestivo: digestif or 'coffee killer'. Typically Neapolitan options are *nocillo* (walnut liqueur) and, of course, limoncello, often home-made and served ice-cold. Others, not necessarily from the region, are *finochietto* (wild fennel liqueur) and *mirto* (myrtle). Brandy is also ubiquitous: you may be asked if you want a brandy *nazionale* or *estero* (local or foreign). Foreign usually means French, and the local version will be much cheaper – Vecchia Romagna is a classic Italian brand. *Strega* (meaning witch) liqueur is produced in nearby Benevento, once notorious for its witch population; made from 70 different herbs, the drink's yellow hue comes from saffron.

Grappa: Italy's firewater is a clear liquid distilled from grapes: the best are from single grape varieties and can be very expensive. Some of the Campania winemakers produce excellent grappas.

Amaro: bitter digestifs, made all over Italy. Famous brands are Amaro Lucano, the sweeter Averna and the rather strong Fernet Branca. Cynar is another popular bitter with an artichoke base.

Soft drinks: generally *una bibita*. Children love *sciroppi*, fruit cordials mixed with water; flavours include *orzata* (almond), *menta* (mint) and *amarena* (black cherry). *Cedrata* and *chinotto* are soft drinks made with citrus fruits (*cedrata* is from a giant lemon, *chinotto* is similar to bergamot). The latter is Italy's version of Coca-Cola, a refreshing, dark-coloured soft drink. *Lemonsoda* is like bitter lemon.

For fresh fruit juice, ask for a *spremuta di limone* or *arancia*. Street sellers offer a delicious mix of both, with a touch of *granita di limone* to sweeten and cool it. A *granita* is a wonderfully refreshing sorbet drink; besides fruit flavours, you can also get a *granita di caffè* (coffee ice) with *panna* (whipped cream).

If you've overindulged, ask for a *canarino* (little canary): boiling water with lemon juice, lemon zest and a touch of sugar.

Tisana: herbal tea – normally only *menta* (peppermint) or *camomilla* (chamomile) are available; ask for the latter and you'll be assumed to have an upset stomach.

Te: black tea, usually served with *limone* slices on the side. Ask for *al latte* if you want milk.

Caffè: a black espresso is the usual post-prandial drink, though in Naples it is consumed from dawn to well past dusk.

Water: tap water (*acqua del rubinetto*) is fine to drink, but it's not really the done thing to order it in a restaurant. Sparkling water is *acqua frizzante* (Ferrarelle, which is naturally carbonated, is the most famous local brand); *acqua naturale* or *liscia* is still water. Neapolitans prefer sparkling, so you may find that they'll bring you Ferrarelle unless you specify. Ask for *piccola* or *grande*, depending on what size of bottle you prefer.

Beer: *birra alla spina* is draught beer; *in bottiglia* is bottled. Italian beers are Peroni or Nastro Azzurro. Pizzerias often serve draught Tuborg beer (Danish, but also brewed in Italy). If you want a small, medium or large draught beer, ask for '*una birra piccola/media/grande alla spina*'. Bottled beers come in small or large versions.

Ice: *con ghiaccio, per favore* means 'with ice, please'.

Lemon: a slice of lemon is *una fetta di limone*.

Cold: *fresco/a: una bibita fresca*, a cold soft drink; *freddo/a: un caffè freddo, un te freddo*, an iced coffee, an iced tea.

Glass: *bicchiere* (for water, beer, soft drink) or *calice* (for wine; stress the first syllable). Many places don't bring you separate wine and water glasses, so you'll need to ask.

€ Mattozzi

Via Filangieri 16 (081 416378). Metro Piazza Amedeo/bus C25. **Open** 1-4pm, 7pm-midnight Mon-Sat. Closed 2wks Aug. **Average** €20. **Credit** AmEx, MC, V. **Map** p327 H13
Ristorante & pizzeria

This Neapolitan institution is always crowded, but the queues move swiftly. Pizzas here have more topping than at most places, and its fans say the dough is chewier. Try the *pizza cornicione* (with ricotta cheese stuffed in the outer crust) and *bomba fritta* (fried pizza dough filled with ricotta, parmesan and mozzarella, topped with tomato and basil sauce). Jumbo servings of pasta are another option.

€ Osteria da Tonino

Via Santa Teresa a Chiaia 47 (081 421533). Funicular Chiaia to Parco Margherita/Metro Piazza Amedeo/bus C24, C25, C26, C27, C28. **Open** 12.30-4pm Mon-Thur, Sun; 12.30-4pm, 7pm-1am Fri, Sat. Closed 2wks Aug. **Average** *Lunch* €15. *Dinner* €25. **No credit cards**. **Map** p327 F13 ⬤ **Osteria**

In business since 1880, Tonino is one of the busiest *osterie* in town. Dinner here is an experience worth queuing for: classic pasta dishes with chickpeas or lentils followed by *seppie in umido* (cuttlefish stewed in tomato) or *provola alla pizzaiola* (cheese with tomato and basil sauce). The fish dishes focus on local *pesce azzurro* such as sardines, salt cod or stockfish.

Il Paguro

Via Piscicelli 1 (081 761 8557/www.ilpaguro.org). Metro Amedeo/bus C24, C25, C26. **Open** noon-3.30pm, 7pm-midnight daily. Closed Aug. **Average** €30. **Credit** MC, V. **Map** p327 F13 ⬤ **Trattoria**

Run by chef-owner Sergio Cacciapuoti, this trattoria is named after the hermit crab, which you can sample cooked with almonds, prawns and squid ink. Other specialities include the *canastrella di bianchetti* ('basket' of whitebait), *linguine al nero di seppia* (pasta in squid ink) and rigatoni with scampi and almonds. The seafood antipasto Paguro is popular, as is the *pezzogna al sale* or sea bass cooked in truffle or gorgonzola. There's a delicious pear and ricotta tart to finish. It's good value for money, especially at lunch.

★ Poseidone

Via Partenope 1 (081 248 1324/www.ristorante poseidone.it). Bus 1, C25. **Open** noon-midnight Mon-Sat; noon-5pm Sun. **Average** €35. **Credit** AmEx, MC, V. **Map** p327 H14 ⬤ **Ristorante & pizzeria**

Poseidone has ample seating right on the promenade. The fish is memorable, the recipes interesting, the setting lovely and the service genuinely charming. The dish that combines mussels (when in season) and aubergine is a highlight; mixed fried fish served up in a full-size edible cornucopia is another. Don't miss the baked white chocolate dessert.

Féfé. *See p130.*

Rosiello

Via Santo Strato 10 (081 769 1288). Bus 140, C31. **Open** 12.30-4pm, 7.30pm-midnight Mon, Tue, Thur-Sun. Closed 1wk Aug. **Average** €70. **Credit** AmEx, DC, MC, V. **Ristorante**
Tables are set in a terraced, wisteria-draped garden, high above the restaurant's own lemon grove and vines, from which it makes wine and limoncello. Views over the Bay of Naples are wonderful; the food, although expensive, is generally high quality. There is a fine repertoire of pasta and fish, as well as wood-fired pizzas served on pretty ceramic plates. Popular with prosperous Posillipini and easily accessible by bus (it's right by the road going down to Marechiaro), this place has a lot going for it.

Umberto

Via Alabardieri 30/31 (081 418555/www. umberto.it). Bus 140, C22, C25, C28. **Open** 12.30-4pm, 7.15pm -midnight Tue-Sun. Closed 3wks Aug. **Average** €35. **Credit** AmEx, MC, V. **Map** p327 H13 **⑤⑦ Ristorante & pizzeria**
With a nod to Umberto's connection with the Napoli Film Festival, the menus here are decorated with the signatures of director Francesco Rosi and other luminaries. The walls are covered in black and white photos from the 1950s – mostly of couples smoking – and the clientele is a mixture of couples, business folk and groups of youngsters. Pasta parcels with spinach, ricotta and gorgonzola are a safe bet, as is the fresh and tasty *spaghetti alla vongole*. The carafes of house wine are eminently quaffable.

€ Vinarium

Vico Santa Maria Cappella Vecchia 7 (081 764 4114). Tram 1/bus C9, C18, C24, C25, C28, R3. **Open** varies; call for details. Closed Aug. **Average** €20. **Credit** AmEx, DC, MC, V. **Map** p327 H13 **⑤⑧ Wine bar**
With a fair range of reasonably priced wines to sample, Vinarium is noisy and very busy at weekends; be prepared to queue. Rather run of the mill platters of hams and cheeses, as well as *bruschette* and salads, are available.

CAMPI FLEGREI

€ Capo Blu

Via Sacello degli Augustali 11, Capo Miseno (081 523 6122/mobile 348 243 7550). Torregaveta rail & SEPSA bus. **Open** *July, Sept* 8pm-midnight Tue-Sun. *Oct-June* 12.30-3pm, 8pm-midnight Tue-Sun. Closed Aug. **Average** €25. **Credit** AmEx, MC, V. **Ristorante**
This hip beachside newcomer has won acclaim for its ability to veer off the traditional track without loosing its bearings. You'll find tasty tapas as starters, and fusilli in a merlot-infused radicchio fondue as a *primo*. *Secondi* include juicy pork chops with apple sauce, and there's a decent wine list to wash it all down. Reserve at lunchtime.

Il Casolare da Tobia

Contrada Coste Fondi di Baia, Via Pietro Fabris 12-14 (081 523 5193/www.datobia.it). Cumana rail to Lucrino, then Torregáveta bus to first stop/bus SEPSA 1 from Piazza Garibaldi to Bacoli. **Open** noon-3.30pm, 8-midnight Tue-Sat; 1-3.30pm Sun. Closed 1wk Aug. **Average** €30. **Credit** V. **Trattoria**
Using organic produce from their vegetable garden, owners Tobia and Elisabetta create seasonal banquets based on traditional recipes, with their own excellent *vino locale*; there's also impeccably fresh fish. Vegetarians should take care, though, as ham or animal fat lurks in many of the recipes. Il Casolare is set in a 10,000-year-old extinct volcano, and in summer Tobia organises barbecues around the hot tub; bring your swimming togs. Lunchtime booking here is obligatory, given the popularity of the €30 set menu.
▶ *There's accommodation here, too; see p110.*

★ Féfé

Via della Shoah 15, Case Vecchie, Bacoli (081 523 3011/www.fefeabacoli.it). Monte di Procida bus from Piazza Garibaldi or Piazza Municipio, get off at last stop. **Open** *June-Sept* 8.30-11pm Mon-Fri; 1-5pm, 8.30-11pm Sat, Sun. *Oct-Apr* 8-11.30pm Tue-Fri; 1-5pm, 8-11.30pm Sat; 1-5pm Sun. *May* 8.30-11pm Tue-Fri; 1-5pm, 8.30-11pm Sat, Sun. Closed 2wks Jan. **Average** €40. **Credit** AmEx, MC, V. **Ristorante**
On the picturesque port where Roman fleets once moored, this tiny restaurant serves delicious but relatively pricey dishes made from fresh ingredients. *Pasta zucchini e cozze* (pasta with courgettes and mussels) and *pezzogna al forno con patate* (blue spotted bream baked with potatoes) are popular choices. Féfé attracts the alternative bourgeoisie of Naples, and has a lot of regulars. The best tables are outside – book ahead or be prepared to queue. *Photos p129.*

La Prua

Via Napoli 2/4 (081 526 3616/www.laprua.it). Metro to Pozzuoli then coastal walk towards Bagnoli/bus C9, C10 from Piazza Vittoria to Bagnoli depot then walk towards Pozzuoli. **Open** *June-Sept* ; 7.30pm-midnight Mon; noon-3.30pm, 7.30pm-midnight Tue-Sun. *Oct-May* noon-3.30pm, 7.30pm-midnight Mon, Wed-Sat; noon-3.30pm Sun. Closed 2wks Aug. **Average** €35. **Credit** AmEx, MC, V. **Ristorante**
With wonderful views over the Bay of Pozzuoli – especially as the sun sets – this stylish restaurant lies on the coastal road between Bagnoli and Pozzuoli; it makes a lovely walk on a sunny day. Sit outside the restaurant on the eponymous prow-shaped rooftop or in the elegantly tiled dining room. Fish, unsurprisingly, dominates the menu. Try the *alici del golfo* (local sardines) or another *pesce azzurro*, such as *sauro* (mackerel) with one of the fine Campi Flegrei wines.

Cafés, Bars & Gelaterie

A populace powered by strong coffee and sublime sweets.

Any gourmand with even a passing knowledge of Italy's food culture will know that Naples is famous for more than pizza: there's coffee, too. How the city became the epicentre of coffee culture is disputed, although its status as a major port with strong links to South America and the Middle East must play a part. Nonetheless, the Neapolitans alone were responsible for creating a new way of brewing coffee, in the topsy-turvy stove-top coffeemaker still known as a *napoletana*; once a fixture in every Italian kitchen, it's now seen only in souvenir shops.

In addition to regular caffeine hits, Neapolitans enjoy a heady sugar rush – courtesy of delicious ice-creams, sold in a dazzling variety of flavours, and equally enticing pastries and cakes.

BARS

Here, a 'bar' can range from a tiny, standing-room-only coffee joint to a chic sit-down address, but all will sell hot and cold drinks, alcohol and sweet snacks.

Some offer more: a *bar-tabaccheria* sells cigarettes, bus tickets and phonecards, whereas a *bar-pasticceria* offers cakes, pastries and often ice-cream – also found in a *bar-gelateria*. The *bar-lotteria* is for playing Italy's lotteries and football pools; most have a copy of *La Smorfia*, a manual for converting dreams into winning numbers. Look for the sign saying 'Totocalcio' and ask for a *schedina* (coupon) for a flutter on the football.

CAFFE COMPLEXITIES

Neapolitan coffee is short and very, very strong. News articles have told of unfortunates who drank ten *espressi* in one day and keeled over dead as a result. Three or four over the course

> ❶ Green numbers given in this chapter correspond to the location of each venue on the street maps. *See pp326-332.*

of a busy day is an advisable maximum for people who wish to avoid caffeine-induced palpitations. The edge is taken off its bitter strength with sugar; if you don't want your coffee to come already sugared, ask for it *amaro* – although pre-sugared coffee is no longer the rule in many bars.

To retain your dignity, don't even think of asking for a 'moccacino' or any of the other concoctions served in Anglo-Saxon coffee houses. Instead, stick to the more classic variations on offer (*see p137* **Caffè culture**).

GELATERIE

Neapolitans are passionate about ice-cream, so you can expect the best. Ice-cream marked as 'produzione propria' (our own production) may be fresh but could contain commercial mixes. 'Produzione artigianale' means the ice-cream was handmade, not mass-produced, and is generally the highest quality.

Before you order, decide whether you want a *coppetta* (tub), *cono* (cone) or *brioches* (sweet buns). Prices usually begin at €1.50, going up for larger sizes. A basic €1.50 cone generally allows you to select two flavours; *panna* (whipped cream) may cost extra. When it comes to flavours, most gelaterie offer a bewildering array, broken down into *crema* (creamy) and *frutta* (fruit) varieties. Some of the most popular among the former include *fior di latte* (cream), *nocciola* (hazelnut), *stracciatella* (plain ice-cream with fragments of crunchy chocolate), *gianduia* (hazelnut and chocolate) and the super-sweet *zabaglione*, made with eggs and Marsala wine.

The classic *frutta* combination is *fragola e limone* (strawberry and lemon); more exotic flavours include *fichi d'india* (prickly pear), *limoncello* (lemon liqueur) or liquorice. Most gelaterie also offer *sorbetti* (sorbets) and *semifreddi* (a mousse/ice-cream combo), served with or without *panna*.

Then there's *granita di limone*, a rough-cut sorbet found at stalls around the city. An even rougher sorbet is *la grattata*, with ice scraped on demand off a large chunk and doused with flavoured syrup or lemon juice. While they may not always look very salubrious, the streetside stalls are generally perfectly clean. If in doubt, follow the locals: Neapolitans are as fussy about food hygiene as they are about flavour.

PASTICCERIE

Dolci are a serious business in Naples, and Neapolitans will happily cross the city for the perfect cakes, particularly on special occasions. Should you be invited for Sunday lunch, don't bring a bottle, but instead some finely wrapped pastries. (The popularity of this ritual means that large queues can form at top *pasticcerie* on Sunday mornings.) If you decide to eat your pastries seated at a table in a *bar-pasticceria*, feel free to avoid any misunderstanding by accompanying the waiter to the counter and pointing out the pastry you want. As for what to order, *see p138* **Sugar and spice**.

ROYAL NAPLES & MONTE ECHIA

Cafés & bars

Caffè del Professore
*Piazza Trieste e Trento 46 (081 403041).
Funicular Centrale to Augusteo/bus 24, C22, C25, C57.* **Open** 6.30am-2am Mon-Fri, Sun; 6.30am-3.30am Sat. **No credit cards. Map** p332 K12 ❶

INSIDE TRACK CHILL OUT

Although coffee cups are served scalding hot, it is quite acceptable (indeed, a sign that you are something of a connoisseur) to politely request a *tazza fredda* to avoid burning your fingers and lips.

A cheap-and-cheerful neighbour to Gambrinus (*see below*), this place has a few somewhat cramped tables outside at which to consume one of 60 types of coffee, including the house specialites *caffè alla nocciola* (hazelnut coffee) and *caffè al cioccolato* (chocolate coffee). If you're not put off by the traffic and mass of humanity passing by, this is a good, centrally located address.

Gran Caffè Gambrinus
Via Chiaia 1-2 (081 417582/www.caffe gambrinus.it). Funicular Centrale to Augusteo/ bus 24, C22, C25, C57. **Open** 7am-1am Mon-Thur; 7am-2.30am Fri-Sun. **Credit** AmEx, MC, V. **Map** p332 K13 ❷

Gambrinus owes its fame to its central location, the impressiveness of its flouncy art nouveau interior and its distinguished history; established over a century ago, its famous former clients include Oscar Wilde. In truth, it's quite expensive and service can be far from friendly. Its rather racy past is far behind it, too: in the 1930s the government closed down certain rooms that were the haunt of left-wing intellectuals, but these days you'll find more fur coats than anti-fascists. Still, it's a very convenient meeting place for an *aperitivo* (especially if you're going to San Carlo, just over the road).

▶ *Another blast from the past is the dignified La Caffettiera, see p137.*

Pasticcerie

Pintauro
Via Toledo 275 (no phone/www.pintauro.it). Funicular Centrale to Augusteo/bus 24, C22, C25, C57. **Open** 9am-8pm Mon-Sat; 9am-2pm Sun. Closed Aug. **No credit cards. Map** p332 K12 ❸

This hole-in-the-wall *pasticceria* is a local institution, famed for its *sfogliatelle*. Legend has it Mr Pasquale Pintauro stole the recipe of a richer version of *sfogliatelle* called Santarosa from a convent in Amalfi circa 1818, then concocted this simpler version for his clients. Service is basic; surliness is included.

CENTRO STORICO

Cafés & bars

★ Gran Caffè Aragonese
Piazza San Domenico Maggiore 5/8 (081 552 8740/www.grancaffearagonese.it). Metro Museo or Piazza Cavour/bus CS, E1, R2. **Open** 7am-midnight daily. **Credit** AmEx, DC, MC, V. **Map** p328 M9 ❹

A large selection of sweet and savoury food, tables outside, comfortable divans inside (a rarity), friendly service and daily newspapers make this bar a pleasant place in which to relax. Regulars include everyone from the buskers and beggars who hang out on the piazza to students and local arty types.

Mexico. See p135.

CONSUME

★ Intramoenia Caffè Letterario
Piazza Bellini 70 (081 290720). Metro Dante.
Open 10am-2am daily. **Credit** AmEx, MC, V.
Map p328 L8 ❺
This handsome, welcoming spot adorning Naples'
most beautiful piazza is a cultural club and café all
in one. It's great for meeting friends, or just passing
time with a good book and eyeing up Naples' hip
intellectual coterie.
▶ *This place is also popular with the gay crowd*
in the evening; see p168.

Gelaterie

★ Gay-Odin
Via Benedetto Croce, 61 (081 551 0794/www.
gay-odin.it). Metro Museo or Piazza Cavour/bus
CS, E1, R2. **Open** 9.30am-8pm Mon-Sat; 10am-
1.30pm Sun. Closed Aug. **Credit** DC, MC, V.
Map p328 L9 ❻
This small temple of top-notch *gelato* in the heart of
the Centro Storico is a heavenly outpost of the

revered, old-world Gay Odin chocolate factory (*see*
p136 **Inside track**). *Gelato* here achieves a perfect
balance between creamy and light, with the best
chocolate flavours in town; try the white chocolate
and hazelnut or *cioccolato al rhum*.

Pasticcerie

Scaturchio
Piazza San Domenico Maggiore 19 (081 551
6944/www.scaturchio.it). Metro Museo or Piazza
Cavour/bus CS, E1, R2. **Open** 7.20am-8.40pm
daily. Closed 1wk Aug. **Credit** AmEx, DC, MC,
V. **Map** p328 M9 ❼
Set right on bustling Piazza San Domenico
Maggiore, historic Scaturchio has a reputation for
making the best cakes in the city. It's resting on its
laurels a bit these days, but the speciality *ministeri-*
ale (rich, dark chocolate cake filled with rum-infused
cream) is a superb concoction, only produced from
September to May.
▶ *For the lowdown on other sweet treats, see p138.*

Profile Caffè traditions

The art – and etiquette – of coffee-drinking.

Coffee is an almost sacred ritual in Naples. Bets are settled and friendship acknowledged by the phrase '*ti offro un caffè*', and after eating out, Neapolitans often make a beeline to the nearest bar where superior coffee is served.

Amid the numerous varieties on offer (*see p137* **Caffè culture**), the one that really counts is the espresso, served piping hot in a lip-scalding cup (the cups are kept in a shallow tray of boiling water). Ground coffee is pressed down in a coffee machine, which heats purified water to 90-95°C. This then filters slowly to fill less than half of the tiny cup.

Coffee in Naples is often served *zuccherato*, with sugar heaped into the cup to create a thick paste at the bottom; if you don't want your coffee too sweet, ask for *amaro* or *non-zuccherato*, or don't stir. You'll also be given a glass of water, to clear your palate of foreign tastes prior to the coffee experience.

Most coffee is 'taken' standing at the bar, in a quick in-and-out process, but the phrase '*prendiamo un caffè insieme*' ('let's have a coffee together') is more than just a simple polite offer. It is rather an invitation to chat, to do business or to forge a closer relationship – the local equivalent of 'let's do lunch' – so all but the smallest cafés or bars have at least a few tables. (Beware: you can be charged up to three times more for your coffee at these.)

If you take the standing option, pay at the cash register first, elbow your way to the counter, and slap down your receipt with a 10¢ or 20¢ coin, an almost compulsory tip here. Don't expect bar staff to ask what you'd like: you'll wait all day. Instead, summon up all the assertiveness (not rudeness) you can muster, and ask for *due cappuccini* or *due caffè* (variations on 'please' or 'may I have' are unnecessary). Another tradition, peculiar to Naples, although dying out, is '*pago un caffè*', where you pay for two coffees: one is drunk, and the other is 'offered' to the next down-and-out to pass through the door.

If you are invited to a Neapolitan's house, you will immediately be offered a coffee, which in the old days would have been prepared in a *caffettiera napoletana*. The story goes that a Neapolitan gentleman was preparing a coffee for Milanese engineer Luigi Bezzera, and complained about the slowness of his coffeemaker. In response, Bezzera invented the *caffettiera napoletana* in 1901 – although it has now been replaced by the more efficient Moka. When it comes to good coffee, there's no room for sentimentality.

WHERE TO TAKE A TAZZINA
Gran Caffè Aragonese (*see p132*). Friendlier than your average café, with good grub, too.
Gran Caffè Gambrinus (*see p132*). Pop in for a quick coffee, and ponder Gambrinus' glory days.
Mexico (*see right*). Superb espressos, sumptuous iced coffees.

CONSUME

PORT & UNIVERSITY
Cafés & bars

Il... Caffè
Piazza Garibaldi 134 (081 204905). Metro Piazza Garibaldi/bus R2. **Open** 6am-7.30pm Mon-Fri; 6am-1pm Sat, Sun. **No credit cards. Map** p329 P8 ⑧
One of many Illy concept stores cropping up in Italian cities, this place is a tiny haven off the busy Piazza Garibaldi. Courteous staff serve a consummate espresso and quite a good cappuccino.

Pasticcerie

Attanasio Sfogliate Calde
Vico Ferrovia 2/4 (081 285675). Metro Piazza Garibaldi/bus R2. **Open** 6.30am-7.30pm Tue-Sun. Closed 2wks July. **Credit** DC, MC, V. **Map** p329 P7 ⑨
Hidden in the backstreets near the station, Attanasio is worth hunting out if you have a sweet tooth. The reason: *sfogliatelle*. They are the finest in the city, thus the best in the world. Fluffy, sweet and spicy ricotta cheese wrapped in flaky pastry, hot out of the oven – heaven. The only dilemma is which type: triangular, millefeuille-style *riccia* or oval, pie-like *frolla*.

Dolcezze Siciliane
Piazzale Immacolatella Vecchia (no phone). Bus 24, C25, R3. **Open** 7am-7pm Tue-Sat; 7.30am-2pm Sun. Closed June-Sept. **No credit cards. Map** p332 M11 ⑩
Fresh Sicilian *dolci* come here from Palermo by boat every morning. The shop is actually inside the port; enter from Piazza Municipio, turn left and keep walking – it's worth it. The *cannolo* (a crisp horn with sweet filling) has reduced grown men to tears.

VIA TOLEDO & LA SANITA
Cafés & bars

Caffè dell'Epoca
Via Costantinopoli 82 (338 314 8231). Metro Dante or Museo/bus 24, R1, R4. **Open** 7am-10pm Mon-Sat; 7am-2pm Sun. Closed 2wks Aug. **No credit cards. Map** p328 L8 ⑪
The Epoca serves a serious espresso, plus delicious *cornetti* (croissants) and pastries. Located near the school of fine art, it often exhibits students' work. There are a few tables outside during the summer.

★ Mexico
Piazza Dante 86 (081 549 9330). Metro Dante/bus 24, R1, R4. **Open** 7am-8.30pm Mon-Sat. Closed 2wks Aug. **No credit cards. Map** p328 K9 ⑫
Along with what is arguably the best espresso in Naples, Mexico also sells a wide range of excellent,

freshly roasted coffee in gorgeous '50s-style packaging; try the Harem or Moana blends. The *frappe di caffè* (iced coffee whisked up to pure froth) is a real treat. Mexico has other locations – on Via Scarlatti in Vomero, on Via Chiaia, and in Piazza Garibaldi near the station. *Photos p133.*

Gelaterie

Fantasia Gelati
Via Toledo 381 (081 551 1212). Funicular Centrale to Augusteo/metro Montesanto/bus R1, E3. **Open** 7am-1am daily. **No credit cards. Map** p328 K10 ⑬
A bright and crowded spot, Fantasia serves up an amazing array of creamy gelati, ranging from the classic *cioccolato* to the creative Benevento (nougat and chocolate chunks). The cakes are to die for, and there's also a tempting assortment of fruits and nuts filled with gelato, a southern Italian speciality.

Gelateria della Scimmia
Piazza Carità 4 (081 552 0272). Funicular Centrale to Augusteo/Metro Montesanto/bus R1, E3. **Open** *June-Sept* 11am-midnight daily. *Apr, May, Oct, Dec* 11am-10pm Mon,Tue-Thur, Fri; 11am-midnight Sat, Sun. *Jan-Mar, Nov* 11am-9pm Mon,Tue-Thur, Fri; 11am-midnight Sat, Sun. **No credit cards. Map** p328 K10 ⑭
One of the city's oldest and most renowned gelaterie, this place is sparsely furnished and often very busy. Go for the basic flavours and you won't be sorry (strawberry and lemon are an excellent combo). Look out for the intensely sweet house speciality – a chocolate-coated banana gelato on a stick. Bonbons and ice-cream sandwiches are equally tempting.

Pasticcerie

Pastisseria Capriccio di Salvatore Capparelli
Via dei Tribunali 325 (081 454310). Metro Dante. **Open** 7am-8.30pm Tue-Sun. Closed 2wks Aug. **No credit cards. Map** p328 N8 ⑮

> ### INSIDE TRACK
> ### JUST-A ONE CORNETTO
>
> Looking for a snack to eat with your caffè? A *cornetto* is a soft croissant which comes plain (*vuoto*) or filled with custard and black cherry (*alla crema*). Two alternatives are *briosce* and *graffa* – the former a plain, sticky bun of French descent, the latter a deep-fried, sugar-coated doughnut. Another version comes without a hole, and is stuffed with custard; this is called a *bomba*. **Moccia** (*see p139*) has the best, even in dainty sizes.

CONSUME

CONSUME

A few tables on the Via dei Tribunali make for a
prime people-watching spot. The gelato is of the traditional *produzione artigianale* (home-made) variety, and fresh, piping-hot *babà* (cake in rum syrup)
and *sfogliatelle* are delivered regularly from the
bakery next door.

VOMERO

Cafés & bars

FNAC
*Via Luca Giordano 59 (081 220 1000/www.
fnac.it). Funicular Chiaia to Cimarosa or Centrale
to Vomero/Metro Vanvitelli/bus V1.* **Open** 10am-
9pm daily. **No credit cards. Map** p330 E10 ⑯
Primarily a music, books and electrical goods shop
(*see p141*), FNAC also has a handsome – albeit
small – café, with stylish furniture and clean toilets (not always a given in this town). It hosts regular author talks and readings, along with varied
photography exhibitions.

Frigittoria Vomero
*Via Cimarosa 44 (081 578 3130). Funicular
Chiaia to via Cimarosa or Centrale to Piazza
Fuga/bus C28, C31, C32, V1.* **Open** 9.30am-
2.30pm, 5-9.30pm Mon-Fri; 9.30am-2.30pm,
5-11pm Sat. Closed Aug. **Average** €7.
No credit cards. Map p331 F10 ⑰
This is great place to pop into for breakfast: the
wonderful *graffe* (light doughnuts) are available
from 9.30am. A host of other fried delights are
ready from 10am, including mini-potato croquettes,
zeppole (deep-fried dough balls), courgettes, courgette flowers and aubergines fried in batter. It's
also a good place for a stop-off on the way to Castel
Sant'Elmo.

Gelaterie

Otranto
*Via Scarlatti 78 (081 558 7498). Metro
Vanvitelli/bus V1.* **Open** *June-Sept* 10am-11.30pm
daily. *Oct-May* 10am-11.30pm Mon, Tue, Thur-
Sun. **No credit cards. Map** p331 F10 ⑱

Don't let the minimal furnishings and lack of atmosphere put you off: ice-cream connoisseurs consider
Otranto one of the finest suppliers in the city. It's
well worth trying, even in the depths of winter.

Soave Prodotti Freschi Del Latte
Via Scarlatti 130 (081 556 7411). **Open**
8.30am-1.45pm, 4.30-8.30pm Mon-Sat; 10am-
1.30pm, 5.30-8.30pm Sun. **No credit cards.
Map** p330 E10 ⑲
It's not stylish, but this rock-solid traditional gelateria produces the goods: using only the freshest
fruit in season, it serves the best *fragolina di bosco*
(tiny wild strawberries) gelato in Naples.

Pasticcerie

Bellavia
*Piazza Muzil 27 (081 558 4475/www.pasticceria
bellavia.it). Metro Collana/bus V1.* **Open** 7.30am-
2pm, 4-9.30pm Mon-Fri; 7.30am-10pm Sat, Sun.
Credit AmEx, DC, MC, V. **Map** p330 E7 ⑳
Look for the trail of people carrying large, impres-
sively wrapped packages, and you'll soon find
Bellavia. Vomero's best-known cake shop is particularly renowned for its birthday cakes. If you're
around at Easter, don't miss the *pastiera* – a traditional cake made from ricotta cheese and rice-like
grano (wheat grain).

CHIAIA TO POSILLIPO

Cafés & bars

Bar Guida
*Via dei Mille 46, Chiaia (081 426570). Metro
Piazza Amedeo/bus C24, C25.* **Open** 7am-9pm
Mon-Sat. Closed 2wks Aug. **No credit cards.
Map** p327 G12 ㉑
Located slap in the middle of this swish part of town,
Guida has a good range of drinks and light lunches
(choose your sandwich contents from what's in the
food cabinet). Alternatively, opt for the not-so-light
house speciality – a grilled sarnie with prosciutto
crudo and cotto, mozzarella and provola di Sorrento.
There are a few seats where you can rest your weary
feet after touring the shops.

★ Caffè Amadeus
*Piazza Amedeo 5, Chiaia (081 761 3023). Metro
Piazza Amedeo/bus C24, C25.* **Open** 7am-1.30am
Mon-Wed; 7am-3am Thur-Sun. **No credit cards.
Map** p327 F12 ㉒
There's no seating inside Caffè Amadeus, but plenty
of tables set out on busy Piazza Amedeo make this
a good place at which to observe the youth of Naples
as they indulge in their customary evening pastimes
of posing on scooters, chatting and insouciantly
causing major traffic congestion. The art of the cappuccino is deftly demonstrated by Lorenzo, who will
inscribe the foam with any message you like.

La Caffettiera

Piazza dei Martiri 30, Chiaia (081 764 4243).
Bus C25. **Open** 7am-11pm Mon-Fri; 7am-midnight
Sat; 7.30am-11pm Sun. **Credit** AmEx, DC, MC, V.
Map p327 H13 ㉓

A classier bar than its rival Gambrinus, La
Caffettiera has the service, decor and well-heeled
clientele of the coffee houses of the past. The canopy-
shaded tables arranged outside are surrounded by
designer shops, and customers look as if they've
either just jumped off a yacht or are about to clinch
a major deal. The blue-rinse contingent lurks inside.

Caffetteria Colonna

Via Vittoria Colonna 13, Chiaia (081 404735).
Open 7.30am-9.30pm Mon-Sat. **No credit
cards.** **Map** p327 F12 ㉔

This tastefully wood-panelled café is popular among
local business types. There are large glasses of
whipped cream on the bar – help yourself to a dol-
lop for your coffee. It also has miniature cakes for
people unable to manage a whole one.

★ Chalet Ciro

*Via Francesco Caracciolo, Mergellina (081
669928/www.chaletciro.it). Metro Mergellina/bus
140, C24, R3.* **Open** 7am-3am Mon, Tue, Thur-
Sun. **Credit** AmEx, MC, V. **Map** p326 C15 ㉕

Chalet Ciro is one of the greats of the Neapolitan ice-
cream scene, and locals travel all the way across
town to eat here; expect a queue for pastries on
Sunday mornings too. After choosing from a vast
array of gelati and pastries, claim a seat outside and
watch the boats sailing into the port. *Photos p139.*

Caffè culture

Keep the caffeine flowing.

Brasiliano: espresso topped with frothy
milk and cocoa, sometimes with a dash
of alcohol. Varies from bar to bar.

Caffè: a short, very strong espresso;
known as a *ristretto*
('concentrated') further
north, this tooth
enamel-removing
strength is the
norm for the south.

Caffè alla nocciola:
an espresso with
sweet hazelnut
froth added.

Caffè americano:
something
approaching the
coffee you might
drink in Europe or
the United States – lots
of added hot water. Usually
served black.

Caffè corretto ('corrected'): espresso with
a dash of alcohol, usually grappa, but there
are other options (whisky, rum, Bailey's
or the sickly Vov liqueur).

Caffè d'orzo: a barley-based coffee
substitute prepared espresso-style.

Caffè freddo: iced coffee, usually very
sweet; only sold in the warmer months.

Caffè Hag or **decaffeinato**: decaf espresso
(this one's not always available).

Caffè latte: a milkier version of the
cappuccino, without cocoa.

Caffè lungo: a slightly less
concentrated version of the
standard caffè.

Caffè macchiato: an espresso with
just a touch of milk.

Cappuccino or **cappuccio**: usually more
coffee than milk; specify without
sugar (*amaro* or *senza zucchero*),
without cocoa (*senza cacao*) or
very hot (*molto caldo*); there
is a tendency to serve
it lukewarm to
enable customers
to drink up quickly
and get to work.
Forget your bad
habits from
home if you
want to do
as the locals
do: no self-respecting
Neapolitan would be seen
dead drinking one of these
any time after noon.

Cappuccino freddo: a cold cappuccino
without froth, which is often made with
sweet iced coffee.

Granita di caffè: a soothing, cooling
concoction of crushed ice, whipped
cream and potent coffee, eaten with
a spoon. Perfect when the temperature
starts rising.

Latte macchiato: hot milk served
with a dash of coffee.

Scekerato: hot espresso coffee,
sugar and ice, blended (once upon a
time in a cocktail shaker) for a sweet,
creamy, 'cake-mix' texture, with chocolate
on top. Naples is the only place in which
to have it.

CONSUME

CONSUME

Sugar and spice

Our pick of the local cakes and pastries.

Neapolitan pastries reflect the spirit of the city: colourful, creative, unrestrained and highly refined. Many have their origins in recipes brought by the French royals who once ruled the city.

CAKES AND TORTES

The pièce de résistance is **babà**, a spongy yeast cake doused in a light, rum-laced liquid. This mother of all alcoholic cakes comes in various shapes and sizes, and is served with or without whipped cream or custard and fresh fruit.

Pastiera napoletana is another speciality. Every true Neapolitan family has its own closely-guarded recipe for this traditional Easter pie, served year-round and stuffed with a mix of ricotta cheese, wheat kernels, candied fruit and orange flower water. As with *babà*, moisture and fragrance are essential, though this is a heavier affair. Finally, there's **torta caprese**. Deliciously dense and rich, it's a flourless chocolate cake with finely ground almonds in the mix.

PERFECT PASTRIES

Although some Neopolitan pastries are similar to those found in the rest of Italy, there's one key difference: they are usually bigger and more generously filled. **Sfogliatella** is a local standout; shell- or cone-shaped delights with an orange-flavoured ricotta filling. An integral part of everyday Neapolitan life, it comes in two varieties – *riccia*, a flaky puff-pastry pocket, and *frolla*, a smoother but less refined affair made from shortcrust dough. Try a warm one in the morning with your caffè. **Zuppetta** comprises puff pastry stuffed with custard and layered with liqueur-laced sponge cake, and **testa di Moro** is a creamy chocolate concoction, layered with sponge cake.

Cassatina napoletana is a round, super-sweet ricotta and sponge-cake affair with chocolate chips in the filling – not to be confused with the Sicilian *cassata*, which has a fruitier aftertaste. **Zeppola di San Giuseppe** is a deep-fried fritter that oozes custard, topped with black cherries. There's also a lighter baked version (*al forno*). Traditionally served on San Giuseppe's day (19 March 19), it has become a year-round treat.

Chalet Primavera

Largo Barbaia 1, Mergellina (no phone). Metro Mergellina/bus 140, C24, R3. **Open** *July-Sept* 8.30am-1am daily. *Oct-June* 8.30am-1am Tue-Sun. **Credit** AmEx, MC, V. **Map** p326 B16 ㉖
This is one of several 'chalets' along the stretch of the seafront near the Mergellina port. Twenty years ago these places were the height of Neapolitan chic; now they're deliciously retro, but still draw a fashionable crowd, especially at weekends. Admire the stunning views across the bay, incongruously interrupted by chattering families, courting teens, kids hanging out of cars and the roar of traffic.

Pinterré

Via Partenope 12, Chiaia (081 764 9822). Bus C25. **Open** 12.30-4pm, 7.30pm-1am daily. **Credit** MC, V. **Map** p327 J14 ㉗
Packed full of Naples' idle rich (and those with aspirations to join them), this large pavement café is an ideal spot for people-watching and for scrutinising the latest in designer gear and affectations. Its excellent sea view is marred only by the busy road between customers and the seafront. Snacks are fresh, and include pizza and good *dolci*.

Gelaterie

Bilancione

Via Posillipo 238B, Posillipo (081 769 1923). Bus 140. **Open** 7am-midnight Tue-Fri, Sun; 7am-1.30am Sat. **No credit cards**.
Staunchly old-fashioned in its ways, this is one of the city's most traditional gelaterie. The fantastic flavours of the ice-cream and mouthwatering sorbets attract a loyal following, and the benches afford spectacular views across Naples.

Chocolate

Piazza Giulio Rodinò 33, Chiaia (081 423 8415). Bus C25. **Open** 10am-11pm Mon-Sat; 10am-2pm, 6-11pm Sun. **No credit cards. Map** p327 H13 ㉘
The interior here is ultra modern, and flavours are equally fresh and appealing: *cannella* (cinnamon), say, or *cioccolato al peperoncino* (chocolate infused with hot peppers). The *semifreddi al bicchiere* (filled with a cross between mousse and ice-cream) and gelato cakes are transcendent.

Remy Gelo

Via Galiani 29, Mergellina (081 667304). Metro Mergellina/bus R3. **Open** 7am-midnight Mon-Fri; 7am-2.30am Sat, Sun. **No credit cards. Map** p326 C14 ㉙
Aficionados reckon this widely renowned gelaterie has lost ground to Bilancione and Chalet Ciro (for both, *see above*), but Remy Gelo still offers a huge range of ice-creams, sorbets and *semifreddi*. Each is made on the premises, and served up in all manner of different-sized tubs, pots and cones. There's also a delicious *babà*, filled with ice-cream.

La Torteria

Via Filangieri 75, Chiaia (081 405221).
Bus C25. **Open** 7am-9pm Mon; 7am-10pm
Tue-Fri; 7am-midnight Sat; 7am-11pm Sun.
Closed 1wk Aug. **Credit** AmEx, MC, V.
Map p327 H13 ③⓪
Sit at the tables across the road, but make sure you
go inside to look at La Torteria's cakes and ice-cream
cakes, produced in limited quantities by a family-
run company. One of the specialities is fruit
flavoured ice-creams packed into the peel or shell of
the fruit. Like the artistic cakes, the ice-cream walnuts, apples and mandarins look beautiful and
taste even better.

Pasticcerie

Gran Caffè Cimmino

*Via Filangieri 12-13, Chiaia (081 418303). Bus
C25.* **Open** 6.30am-10.30pm daily. Closed 1wk
Aug. **No credit cards. Map** p327 H13 ③①

Crowded with lawyers and yuppies, who descend
en masse for post-work *aperitivi*, this is an excellent café for delicious cakes and pastries (try the
torta al cioccolato bianco). Getting a seat, however,
can prove tricky.
▶ *Cimmino's second outpost is on Via Petrarca
in Posillipo (no.147, 081 575 7697). Set on the
promenade overlooking the bay, it's packed with
posh Napoletani buying cakes on Sundays.*

★ Moccia

*Via San Pasquale a Chiaia 21-22, Chiaia
(081 411348). Bus C25.* **Open** 7am-8.30pm
Mon, Wed-Sun. Closed Aug. **No credit cards.**
Map p327 F13 ③②
This is one of the most famous cake shops in the city,
with prices to match. Try the *fungo al cioccolato* (a
mushroom-shaped choux pastry filled with chocolate), a slice of the excellent pastiera, or, if you're here
around Carnevale time in late February, order the
delicate *chiacchiere* with chocolate sauce.

Chalet Ciro. *See p137.*

Shops & Services

See Naples and buy.

Shopping in Naples affords an insight into local culture. Its exuberant street markets and idiosyncratic shops are a breath of fresh air for visitors more accustomed to bland, big-name chains, and much of the eye-catching merchandise is unique to the city.

Neapolitans tend to trawl the shops in packs, at an enjoyably leisurely pace. Dressed in their finest designer gear (knock-offs or not), they meander from shop to shop, lingering to down an espresso or order a gelato, and to gossip with friends. Prepare to be distracted, fascinated and amused as you step into the lively street theatre that is Naples.

SHOPPING ETIQUETTE

Shopkeepers are attentive, and may follow you around the store; don't be afraid to say, 'No, grazie'. It's also perfectly acceptable to ask for a discount ('me fa lo sconto?') if you find something you like. Neapolitans are known for their directness and will appreciate yours.

If something you're trying on is particularly flattering, they will tell you so – emphatically. Women shouldn't feel harassed if shopkeepers exclaim how pretty they look: it's simply part of a culture where beauty is celebrated and compliments expected.

OPENING HOURS

It can take a while for visitors to adjust to the syncopated rhythm of Neapolitan shopping hours. Merchants generally open at 9.30am, then close for lunch at 1.30pm – at which time many a grown man heads to his mamma's house for pasta and a nap, married or not. Shops reopen at around 4.30pm, generally closing at 7.30pm.

Bear in mind that shops often deviate from their official opening hours. Many opt for an easy start to the week by not opening on Monday mornings in winter, while others end the week early in summer, closing at lunchtime on Saturdays. Hairdressers close on Mondays, and most food stores are closed on Thursday

afternoons. Few businesses are open on Sundays, and nearly every Neapolitan takes a holiday in August. You'll find the streets virtually empty and most businesses closed, with signs reading *Chiuso per ferragosto* (closed for summer holidays).

The big sales in Naples run twice a year, from mid January until mid March, and again in summer, from mid July to mid September. Great deals can be found, with prices slashed by 50 to 70 per cent.

WHERE TO SHOP

For designer brands such as Gucci, Versace and Prada, check out Via dei Mille, Via Filangieri, and the Piazza dei Martiri, in the Chiaia district.

For more moderately priced purchases, stroll along Via Chiaia, Via Toledo, Corso Umberto and through the Centro Storico. The Galleria Umberto is always worth a peek for everything from electronic items and cameras to designer clothes and cosmetics.

Brides-to-be should check out Via del Duomo, while Via dell'Annunziata is known for baby apparel. Jewellery stores still abound in the tangled web of alleys between Via Marin and Corso Umberto known as the Borgo degli Orefici, Naples' Gold Quarter. Via San Sebastiano is often called 'music alley', as it's lined with instrument stores; for booksellers, head for Via San Biagio de Librai.

Naples has plenty of markets (*see p146* **Marked-down markets**). Antique lovers should visit Fiera Antiquaria Napoletana; La Forcella is full-throttle fleamarket fun.

About the author
*Naples resident **Tui Cameron** covers the city for easyJet and Wizz Magazine.*

General

DEPARTMENT STORES

Coin
Via Scarlatti 90/98, Vomero (081 578 0111/
www.coin.it). Funicular Centrale to Piazzetta
Fuga or Chiaia to Via Cimarosa/bus C36. **Open**
10am-8pm Mon-Sat; 10am-2pm, 4.30-8.30pm Sun.
Credit AmEx, DC, MC, V. **Map** p331 F10.
This pleasant branch of Coin is useful for everyday
clothing and accessories.

Upim
Via Nisco 11, Chiaia (081 417520/www.upim.it).
Funicular Chiaia to Parco Margherita/Metro
Piazza Amedeo/bus C25. **Open** 9.30am-8pm Mon-
Sat; 10am-1.30pm, 4.30-8pm Sun. Closed Sun in
Aug. **Credit** AmEx, DC, MC, V. **Map** p327 G13.
Established in 1928, Upim offers good value for
money on a wide range of household wares and
clothes, as well as beauty products.

MARKETS

For food markets, *see p147*.

La Forcella
Nr train station, between Corso Umberto
& Piazza Garibaldi. **Open** 9am-noon daily.
Map p329 O8.
A veritable treasure trove of shoes, leather goods,
booze, perfume, crafts, knick-knacks and knock-offs.

Mercatino di Antignano (Vomero Market)
Piazza Antignano, Vomero. Metro Medaglie
d'Oro/bus R1. **Open** 8am-2pm Mon-Sat.
Snap up bargain-priced kitchenware, bags, clothes,
jewellery, shoes, towels, linen and lots more.

Mercatino di Poggioreale
Via Michelangelo di Caramanico, off Via Nuova
Poggioreale. Bus C61, C62. **Open** 7am-2pm Mon,
Fri-Sun. Closed Aug.
You'll find everything here, from top-of-the-range
brands to tat. The market is renowned for its range
of shoes; there are also rich pickings among the adult
and children's clothes, household goods and fabrics.

Mercatino di Posillipo
Viale Virgilio, via della Rimembranza, Posillipo.
Bus C27. **Open** 8am-1pm Thur. Closed Aug.
This is one of Naples' trendier markets, with stalls
piled high with cheap clothes, shoes and bags. Get
there early or you'll miss the best deals.

Mercato dei Fiori
Castell Nuovo, near Piazza Municipio, Royal
Naples. **Open** dawn-9am daily. **Map** p332 L12.

Tucked beside the Castel Nuovo, this early morning
market features verdant displays of flowers and
plants. Florists shop here, and bargains abound.

Specialist

BOOKS & MAGAZINES
English language

FNAC
Via Luca Giordano 59, Vomero (081 220 1000/
www.fnac.it). Funicular Centrale to Piazzetta
Fuga or Chiaia to Via Cimarosa/Metro Vanitelli/
bus C36. **Open** 10am-9pm daily. **Credit** AmEx,
DC, MC, V. **Map** p330 D9.
This multimedia store stocks English-language
books, CDs, DVDs, electronic items and digital cameras, and also sells concert and cinema tickets. It
stays open during the Italian lunch hour, when
everywhere else is closed.

Libreria Feltrinelli
Piazza dei Martiri, Via Santa Caterina a Chiaia
23, Chiaia (081 240 5411). Bus C25, C28. **Open**
10am-9pm Mon-Fri; 10am-11pm Sat; 10am-2pm,
4-10pm Sun. **Credit** AmEx, MC, V. **Map** p327
H13.
Recharge your batteries at this cool, three-storey
book and music shop. Magazines are on sale next to
the basement café, near a small selection of English
fiction, and theatre and concert tickets can be bought
at the in-store Concerteria outpost.
Other locations Via San Tommaso d'Aquino
70, Toledo (081 764 2111).

Universal Books
Corso Umberto I 22, Port & University (081 252
0069). Bus 105, C55, R2. **Open** 9am-1pm, 4-7pm
Mon-Fri. Closed 2wks Aug. **Credit** DC, MC, V.
Map p328 M10.
Universal is a haven of tranquility after the traffic-
filled streets outside. You'll find a good selection of
fiction and non-fiction English-language books.

INSIDE TRACK
BUYING A BRICK

Keep an eye on the goods when
purchasing from *bancarelle* (sidewalk
stalls). Although it is common for
storekeepers to wrap even the most
mundane purchases in colourful paper
(deodorant, for instance), unscrupulous
street vendors have been known to
substitute the DVD player you think you
are purchasing with an equally-weighted
piece of wood or brick.

CONSUME

Used & antiquarian

Antica Libreria Regina
Via Santa Maria di Costantinopoli 51/103,
Centro Storico (081 290925/081 459983/
www.libreriaregina.it). Metro Dante or Piazza
Cavour/bus R1, R2, R3. **Open** 9am-8pm Mon-
Sat. Closed Sat in July & 3wks Aug. **Credit**
AmEx, MC, V. **Map** p328 L8.
This specialist bookshop stocks a good selection of
19th-century gouache paintings of the Bay of Naples,
as well as books on Neapolitan culture and history.
▶ *For more on the gouache paintings collected*
by the grand tourists of yesteryear, see p24.

Bowinkel
Piazza dei Martiri 24, Chiaia (081 764 4344).
Bus C24, C28. **Open** 10am-1.30pm, 4.30-7.30pm
Mon-Fri; 10am-1.30pm Sat. Closed Aug. **Credit**
AmEx, DC, MC, V. **Map** p327 H13.
Bowinkel is Naples' most respected dealer in period
watercolours, prints and photographs; have a look
in the window even if you can't afford to buy.
Overseas shipping can be arranged on request.

Colonnese
Via San Pietro a Maiella 33, Centro Storico
(081 459858/www.colonnese.it). Metro Dante or
Montesanto/bus R1, R2, R3. **Open** 9am-1.30pm,
4-7.30pm Mon-Fri; 9am-1.30pm Sat. Closed 2wks
Aug. **Credit** AmEx, DC, MC, V. **Map** p328 L8.
A publishing house, cultural gathering place and
bookshop, Colonnese is a hotspot for the local
literati. Tomes tackle Neapolitan history in the 19th
and early 20th centuries, and there are old postcards,
prints and rare books to browse. Look out for book
readings and literary events.

CHILDREN
Fashion

Siola
Via Chiaia 111-15, Royal Naples (081 412580/
081 415036). Bus C25. **Open** 10am-1.30pm,
4.30-8pm Mon-Sat. Closed 2wks Aug. **Credit**
AmEx, DC, MC, V. **Map** p327 J13.
Expect upmarket children's clothes, with price tags
to match. The shelves are lined with top Italian
brands such as Blumarine and I Pinco Pallino, as
well as charming Japanese label Miki House.

Toys

Disney Store
Via Toledo 129, Toledo (081 790 1377).
Funicular Centrale to Augusteo/bus C25, R2.
Open 10am-8pm Mon-Sat; 10am-2pm, 4.30-8pm
Sun. **Credit** AmEx, DC, MC, V. **Map** p328 K10.
Familiar characters abound at the Naples outpost of
the Disney empire.

Leonetti
Via Roma 350, Toledo (081 412765). Funicular
Centrale to Augusteo/Metro Diaz/bus R1, R2, R4.
Open 10am-2pm, 3.30pm-8.30pm Mon-Sat.
Credit AmEx, DC, MC, V. **Map** p328 K9.
A monthly visit to Leonetti is a long-established
tradition for Neapolitan children. It stocks a vast
selection of classic and modern toys and games.

Toys Centre
Via Terracina 467, Mostra (081 239 9625/www.
giochipreziosi.it). Cumana rail to Mostra, then
bus 180, C3, C6, C7, C8, C15, C19. **Open** 10am-
7.30pm Mon-Sat. **Credit** AmEx, DC, MC, V.
Italy's version of Toys"R"Us sells all manner of
games, toys and dolls.

ELECTRONICS & PHOTOGRAPHY
Luxor Radio Euronics
Galleria Umberto 1, Royal Naples (081 418872).
Metro Dante or Montesanto/bus R2. **Open** 10am-
2pm, 4-8pm Mon-Sat. **Credit** AmEx, MC, V. **Map**
p332 K12.
This *elettrodomestico* store carries everything from
computer accessories to blowdryers and stove-top
espresso makers. Staff are generally very helpful.
Other location Via San Pasquale a Chiaia 2
(081 422313)

Maurizio di Cesare
Via Domenico Capitelli 19, off Piazza Gesù
Nuovo, Toledo (081 551 3114/www.maurizio
dicesare.com). Bus 24, 149, E1, R1. **Open** 9am-
1.30pm, 4-7.30pm Mon-Fri; 9am-1.30pm Sat.
Closed 1wk Aug. **Credit** MC, V. **Map** p328 K9.
A well-organised and friendly photo service.

Print Sprint
Via Cimarosa 166, Vomero (081 556 4506).
Funicular Chiaia to Via Cimarosa, Centrale to
Piazza Fuga/Metro Vanvitelli/bus C36. **Open**
9.30am-1.30pm, 4.30-8pm Mon-Fri; 9.30am-2pm
Sat. Closed 2wks Aug. **Credit** MC, V. **Map** p330
E10.
The ever-obliging Roberta and Sergio will help with
all your photographic needs.

FASHION
Designer

Anna Matuozzo
Viale Gramsci 26, Chiaia (081 663874/www.
annamatuozzo.it). Metro Mergellina/funicular
Mergellina/bus 152, C12, C19, R3. **Open** 9am-
7pm Mon-Sat. Closed Aug. **Credit** AmEx, DC,
MC, V. **Map** p326 C15.
Matuozzo's handmade shirts are the finest money
can buy; *see p150* **Made in Naples**.

CONSUME

Eddy Monetti

Menswear *Via dei Mille 45, Chiaia (081 407064/www.eddymonetti.it). Funicular Chiaia to Parco Margherita/Metro Piazza Amedeo/bus C25.* **Map** p327 G12.

Womenswear *Piazzetta Santa Caterina 8, Chiaia (081 403229). Bus C25.* **Map** p327 H13. **Both Open** 10am-1.45pm, 4.30-8.15pm Mon-Fri, 10am-1.45pm Sat. Closed 2wks Aug. **Credit** AmEx, DC, MC, V.

A byword for classic Neapolitan fashion for decades, Monetti is famous for its timeless style. Alongside the own-label collection are carefully-chosen pieces from other upmarket Italian designers.

Garlic

Via Toledo 111, Toledo (081 5524 4966). Metro Montesanto/bus 24, 105, R1. **Open** 10am-2pm, 4-8pm Mon-Sat. Closed 2wks Aug. **Credit** AmEx, DC, MC, V. **Map** p328 K10.

Only in Napoli

Souvenirs with an unmistakably local flavour.

The fact that Naples doesn't overtly cater to tourists makes up much of its charm. The city is rich in traditions, though, and certain items are distinctly Neapolitan.

CAMEOS

Made from shell, these dainty, Victorian-style carvings are sold at jewellery shops all over town. Their origins lie in the ancient Roman art of carving sardonyx and layered glass.

CAPODIMONTE PORCELAIN

An 18th-century Spanish king commissioned the first of the world-renowned Neapolitan ceramics, which continue to be produced, reproduced and sought after to this day.

CORNO

It may look like a red chilli, but *corno* means horn. This classically Neapolitan good luck charm is the direct descendant of the more anatomically correct ancient Roman version, as any visitor to the *Gabinetto segreto* (*see p71*) can attest. Jewellery shops carry fancy versions made from red coral, silver or gold, and plastic, glass and clay versions are sold by street vendors and knick-knack shops.

EX-VOTOS

Visit the side chapel in Gesù Nuovo (*see p55*) and you'll see little metal replicas of body parts covering the walls from floor to ceiling. Each ex-voto represents a part of the body that devotees believe was healed through divine intervention; the ex-votos are a way of offering thanks. Ex-votos are also collector's items, and can be purchased in jewellery stores and antique shops.

GOUACHE PAINTINGS

The most enduring images of Naples were painted in the 19th century (*see p24* **A rich cultural canvas**). Nowadays, you'll find these panoramic views in bookshops and antique stores. Most are reproductions, but there are still originals to be had.

LIMONCELLO

Local pastries such as *babà* and *sfogliatelle* won't survive a trip in your luggage, but a bottle of locally-brewed lemon liqueur will.

NEAPOLITAN CARD DECK

When business is slow, shopkeepers often play cards with their cronies. Befriend a local and you could soon be playing a hand of *scopa*, too, with a deck that has smaller dimensions than most, and different suits and figures.

PRESEPI

Naples is known for its tremendous array of nativity crèches, called *presepi*. You'll find plenty on Via San Gregorio Armeno (*see p58*), where it's Christmas all year round.

PULCINELLA

This mandolin-playing prankster (*see p184* **Punch drunk**) wears baggy white clothes and a black mask, and is often depicted holding a tambourine with the number 13, which is considered lucky in Naples. Masks and figurines are sold across the city.

CONSUME

Marinella.

CONSUME

Head here for an offbeat range of clothes, shoes and accessories by up-and-coming designers. The clothes tend to appeal to the young and trendy, rather than more mature shoppers.

Maxi Ho
Via Nisco 20, Chiaia (081 414 721). Funicular Chiaia to Parco Margherita/Metro Piazza Amedeo/ bus C25. **Open** 10am-1.30pm, 4.30-8pm Mon-Sat. **Credit** AmEx, DC, MC, V. **Map** p327 G13.
Stocking menwear and womenswear, this is the boutique of choice for fashionable Neapolitans. Designer brands include Marni, Fendi, D&G and Balenciaga.

Melinoi
Via Benedetto Croce 34, Centro Storico (081 552 1204). Metro Dante/bus 137, E1, R1, R3. **Open** *July-mid Aug* 10am-2pm, 4.30pm-7.30pm Mon-Sat. *Sept-June* 10am-2pm, 4.30-7.30pm Mon-Sat; 10am-2pm Sun. Closed 2wks Aug. **Credit** AmEx, DC, MC, V. **Map** p328 L9.
Labels at this boutique are sourced from as far afield as Iceland; European designers are also well represented. The designs are elegant but unusual, the service knowledgeable and charming.

Discount

Chi Cerca Trova
Via Fiorelli 3, Chiaia (081 764 7592). Funicular Chiaia to Parco Margherita/Metro Piazza Amedeo/ bus C25. **Open** *May-Oct* 10am-2pm, 4-8pm Mon-Fri; 10am-2pm Sat. *Nov-Apr* 4-8pm Mon; 10am-2pm, 4-8pm Tue-Sat. Closed 3wks Aug. **Credit** AmEx, DC, MC, V. **Map** p327 G13.

This Neapolitan institution is still going strong after two decades. The name means 'seek and you'll find', which is what this place is all about; the racks seem to go on for miles, and you can rummage for hours. Prices start at €5; eccentric owner Guiseppe Violante sometimes offers his clients coffee and rum babà.

General

Aspesi
Piazza San Pasquale 23-24, Chiaia (081 764 5399). Metro Piazza Amedeo. **Open** 9am-1.30pm, 4pm-8.30pm Mon-Sat. Closed 1wk Aug. **Credit** AmEx, DC, MC, V. **Map** p327 F13.
Aspesi stocks a good mix of mid-range designer clothing, as well as fabulous shantung silk pants.

Bistrot Mare
Via Alabardieri 24, Chiaia (081 418319). Metro Piazza Amedeo/funicular Amedeo/bus C28. **Open** 10am-1.30pm, 4.30-8pm Mon-Fri; 10am-1.30pm Sat. Closed 2wks Aug. **Credit** AmEx, DC, MC, V. **Map** p327 H13.
This little shop is usually full of shoppers checking out the beach and leisurewear. You'll find teens trying on tiny bikinis alongside well-upholstered mammas choosing holiday kaftans and matching sandals.

Capua
Via Carlo Poerio 48, Chiaia (081 248 1147). Bus C25, C28. **Open** 10am-1.30pm, 4.30-8pm Mon-Sat. Closed 2wks Aug. **Credit** AmEx, DC, MC, V. **Map** p327 G13.
Capua's cashmere sweaters, priced from €100, are available in a range of fabulous colours.

Cruising

Via dei Mille 54, Chiaia (081 419378). Funicular Chiaia to Parco Margherita/Metro Piazza Amedeo/ bus C25. **Open** 10.30am-1.30pm, 4.30-8pm Mon-Sat. Closed 2wks Aug. **Credit** AmEx, DC, MC, V. **Map** p327 G12.

Unimpeachably stylish attire that attracts young and fashionable male shoppers.

Paolo Fiorillo

Via Carducci 49-51 & 53, Chiaia (081 416252). Bus C25. **Open** 10am-1.30pm, 4-8pm Mon-Sat. Closed 2wks Aug & Sat pm summer, Mon am winter. **Credit** AmEx, DC, MC, V. **Map** p327 G13.

Floaty summer dresses, sporty clothes and a good range of shoes and sandals are crammed into this split-level boutique.

Phard

Via Toledo 155, Toledo (081 542 3116/www. phard.it). Funicular Centrale to Augusteo/bus C25, R2. **Open** 10am-8pm Sat. **Credit** AmEx, DC, MC, V. **Map** p328 K10.

Drop by for a quick fashion pick-me-up: with its inexpensive, ever-changing stock, Phard has been dubbed the Neapolitan version of Top Shop. **Other location** Via Chiaia 178 (081 410002).

FASHION ACCESSORIES & SERVICES

Accessories

Fratelli Tramontano

Via Chiaia 142-143, Royal Naples (081 414837/ www.aldotramontano.it). Bus C25, R2. **Open** *July, Aug* 10am-1.30pm, 4-8pm Mon-Fri. *Sept-June* 10am-1.30pm, 4-8pm Mon-Sat, 10am-1.30pm Sun. Closed 2wks Aug. **Credit** AmEx, DC, MC, V. **Map** p327 J13.

This is the place to come to for quality, handmade leather goods: handbags and luggage, shoes, wallets, belts and other accessories.

▶ *For more on the company's history, see p150.*

★ Marinella

Riviera di Chiaia 287A, Chiaia (081 245 1182/ www.marinellanapoli.it). Bus C28. **Open** 6.30am-1.30pm, 4-8pm Mon-Sat. Closed 2wks Aug. **Credit** AmEx, DC, MC, V. **Map** p327 H14.

Exquisite, traditional silk ties, as worn by the great and good. *See p150* **Made in Naples**.

Talarico Mario & C Snc

Vico Due Porte a Toledo 4B, Toledo (081 407 723/www.mariotalarico.it). Funicular Centrale to Augusteo/bus C25, R2. **Open** 6.30am-8pm Mon-Sat. **Credit** AmEx, DC, V, MC. **Map** p332 K11.

This is the place to purchase the finest umbrellas in the city; s*ee p150* **Made in Naples**.

Cleaning & repairs

Lavanderia

Largo Donnaregina 5, Centro Storico (328 619 6341). Metro Piazza Cavour/bus R2. **Open** 8am-7.20pm Mon-Fri; 8am-1.30pm Sat. Closed 3wks Aug. **No credit cards**. **Map** p328 N7.

Set in the Centro Storico, Lavanderia offers an efficient service and next-day collection.

Lavanderia Santa Chiara

Via San Giovanni Maggiore Pignatelli 36-37, Centro Storico (081 551 8460). Metro Dante/bus R1, R2, R3. **Open** 9am-1.30pm, 3-8pm Mon-Fri; 9am-2pm Sat. Closed 2wks Aug. **No credit cards**. **Map** p328 M9.

This reliable establishment offers washing, ironing and dry cleaning services.

MrCucito

Via Chiaia 49, Chiaia (081 408762/www.mr cucito.net/site/azienda.html). Bus R2/tram 1, 4. **Open** 9.30am-1.30pm, 4-8pm Mon-Fri; 9.30am-1.30pm Sat. Closed 3wks Aug. **No credit cards**. **Map** p327 J12/13.

Staff are happy to take on tailoring jobs large or small. They can even turn an old pair of jeans into a cute purse, if you so desire.

Jewellery

Angelo Fusco

Traversa II, 2-4, Borgo degli Orefici (081 204447). Bus CS, C55, E1, R2. **Open** 8.30am-6.30pm Mon-Fri; 8.30am-1pm Sat. Closed Aug. **Credit** AmEx, DC, MC, V. **Map** p328 M10.

Choose from a large assortment of watches, necklaces and bracelets, or have a piece made to order.

Arte in Oro

Via Benedetto Croce 20, Centro Storico (081 551 6980). Metro Dante/bus E1, R1, R2, R3, R4. **Open** 10am-7pm Mon-Fri; 10am-2pm Sat. Closed 3wks Aug. **No credit cards**. **Map** p328 L9.

Led by the Marciano brothers, the team of craftsmen at this Centro Storico jewellers produces beautiful replicas of classical Roman jewellery, as well as modern designs. Prices are reasonable.

Ascione

Piazzetta Matilde Serao 19, Galleria Umberto I, Royal Naples (081 421 1111/www.ascione.it). Funicular Centrale to Augusteo/Metro Municipio/ bus R1, R2, R4, C25. **Open** 10.30am-2pm, 4-7.30pm Mon-Sat. Closed 3wks Aug. **Credit** AmEx, MC, V. **Map** p332 K12.

Since 1855, the Ascione family has been one of the region's pre-eminent makers of coral jewellery. Some of the finest examples are showcased at this exclusive shop. Call ahead for an appointment to view the store's private collection, a veritable museum.

CONSUME

Marked-down markets

Fresh fish, designer frocks and more, all going for a song.

From très chic to tongue in cheek, Naples' markets have it all. A rich history of skilled craftsmanship and exquisite custom-made items is matched by a mischievous delight in designer knock-offs, bootlegged CDs and tat. Neapolitans shop the markets for the sheer adventure, and visitors to the city are advised to do the same.

Naples' best-known food markets are **Pignasecca** and **Porta Nolana Fish Market**, but the **Bancarelle a San Pasquale** and **Borgo S'Antonio Abate** (for all, *see p147*) are also good choices for fish, vegetables, fruit, cheeses and smoked meats. Other markets have a much wider remit: take **Fuorigrotta**, with its semi-permanent stalls selling food, kitchen gadgets and a hotch-potch of household goods.

Tucked beside the Castel Nuovo, the **Mercato dei Fiori** (*see p141*) adds a splash of colour to the early morning with its exotic flowers and houseplants. For antiques, try the **Fiera Antiquaria Napoletana** (*see p151*). One-of-a-kind treasures also crop up at **La Forcella** (*see p141*), which traces its origins to the sale of black market goods in World War II. Set near the train station, it's sometimes referred to as 'kasbah Forcella' by locals. **Poggioreale** (*see p141*), named after the nearby jail, has everything from luggage and booze to knick-knacks to knock-offs, and is very popular with locals.

For great deals on the latest styles, head to **Mercatino di Posillipo** (*see p141*), where bags, shoes and clothing are sold along a tree-lined boulevard, or Vomero's **Mercatino Antignano** (*see p141*). Suit yourself from head to toe at **Mercatino Via Imbriani** (*see p147*), where you'll find unlabeled designer togs, swimsuits and shoes. With any of the markets, arrive early to find the best deals, and don't be afraid to barter.

De Nobili

Via Filangieri 16B, Chiaia (081 421 685/www. denobili.com). Bus C25. **Open** 10am-1.30pm, 4.30-8pm Mon-Sat. Closed Aug. **Credit** AmEx, DC, MC, V. **Map** p327 H13.

De Nobili specialises in traditional, limited edition pieces in gold, precious stones and coral, including a line inspired by Neapolitan good luck charms.

Knight

Piazza dei Martiri 52, Chiaia (081 764 3837). Bus C25, C28. **Open** 9.30am-1.20pm, 4-7.30pm Mon-Sat. Closed 3wks Aug. **Credit** AmEx, DC, MC, V. **Map** p327 H13.

Established by an Englishman in 1868, this tiny jewellery shop sits on the corner of the famous square. Inside, the salon is dominated by an enormous safe; the charming Guiseppe Ferrara (who speaks English) will sit you down and show you items ranging from affordable photo frames to glittering, showstopping diamonds.

Light

Via Chiaia 225, Royal Naples (081 400325). Bus C25, R2, R4. **Open** 10am-1.30pm, 4-8pm Mon-Sat. Closed 1wk Aug. **Credit** AmEx, MC, V. **Map** p327 J12.

The window displays at Light sparkle with jewellery, beads and semiprecious stones. Choose from a selection of ready-made necklaces and bracelets, or order something according to your specifications. Prices are very reasonable, with items starting at around €20.

Lingerie & underwear

Intimissimi

393 Corso Umberto I, Port & University (081 202259/www.intimissimi.com). Bus R1, R2, R4. **Open** 10am-8pm Mon-Sat. Closed 2wks Aug. **Credit** AmEx, MC, V. **Map** p329 P8.

Intimissimi carries basic undergarments and pyjamas for men and women, as well as more frilly, flouncy lingerie.

Shoes

Deliberti

Via dei Mille 65, Chiaia (081 658 4363/www. deliberti.it). Funicular Chiaia to Parco Margherita/ Metro Piazza Amedeo/bus C25. **Open** 4-8pm Mon; 10am-1.30pm, 4-8pm Tue-Sat. Closed 2wks Aug. **Credit** AmEx, MC, V. **Map** p327 G12.

This Neapolitan shoe shop is part of a mini chain, with five outposts in the city. Service is friendly, and it's very popular with local shoppers.

Other locations throughout the city.

Ernesto Esposito

Via Santa Caterina a Chiaia 20, Chiaia (081 423 8325). Metro Piazza Amedeo/bus C25. **Open** 10am-1.30pm, 4.30-8pm Mon-Sat. **Credit** AmEx, MC, V. **Map** p327 H13.

A native of the city, Esposito designs women's shoes for such big names as Marc Jacobs, Louis Vuitton and Sonia Rykiel. This outlet is a smart showcase for his considerable talents.

FOOD & DRINK

For our pick of the city's heavenly *pasticcerie* (cake shops), *see pp131-139*.

Drinks

Limoné
Piazza San Gaetano 72, Centro Storico (081 299429). Metro Piazza Cavour/bus 202, R1. **Open** 11am-8.30pm Mon-Fri; 10.30am-8.30pm Sat, Sun. **Credit** MC, V. **Map** p328 M8.
Free tastes and tours are offered at this friendly limoncello shop, where organic lemon liqueur is made on site.

General

Antiche Delizie
Via Pasquale Scura 14, Toledo (081 551 3088). Metro Montesanto/bus 24, 105, R1. **Open** *July, Aug* 8am-2.30pm, 3-8pm Mon-Wed, Fri, Sat; 8am-3pm Thur. *Sept-June* 8am-2.30pm, 3-8pm Mon-Wed, Fri, Sat; 8am-3pm Thur; 9am-2pm Sun. Closed 1wk Aug. **Credit** AmEx, DC, MC, V. **Map** p329 O5.
Along with superb mozzarella and cheeses, Antiche Delizie stocks a mouthwatering selection of meats and preserves. Try the *caprignetti* (soft goat's cheese in herbs) and cheese with *tartufo* (truffles). There are local wines and home-made pasta dishes too.

Di per Di
Via Mezzocannone 99, Centro Storico (081 552 7438). Bus E1, R2. **Open** 8.15am-8.15pm Mon-Sat; 8.30am-1.30pm Sun. **Credit** AmEx, MC, V. **Map** p328 M9.
A cheaper version of GS (*see below*), this Italian supermarket chain has four branches in Naples.

Eder
Via Benedetto Croce 44, Spaccanapoli (081 551 7081). Metro Museo or Piazza Cavour/bus CS, E1, R2. **Open** 9am-8pm Mon-Sat; 9am-3pm Sun. **Credit** AmEx, MC, V. **Map** p328 L9.
This tiny shop sells local pastas and artisanal treats, luring in passers-by with enticing window displays.

GS
Via Morghen 28, Vomero (081 556 3282). Funicular Chiaia to via Cimarosa, Centrale to Piazza Fuga/Metro Vanvitelli. **Open** 8am-8.30pm Mon-Sat; 8am-1.30pm Sun. **Credit** AmEx, MC, V. **Map** p331 F10.
GS sells a pretty good selection of Italian staples.

Mandara
Via Chiaia 149C, Chiaia (081 417348). Metro Piazza Amedeo/bus R2. **Open** 8.30am-8.30pm Mon-Sat. Closed 1wk Aug. **No credit cards.** **Map** p327 J13.

Temptations abound at one of Naples' finest food shops: mozzarella that's as soft as clouds, beautifully creamy ricotta and excellent cured meats.

Markets

For fleamarkets and more, *see p151*. For an overview of the city's markets, *see left* **Marked-down markets**.

Bancarelle a San Pasquale/ Mercatino Via Imbriani
Via San Pasquale, Via Carducci & Via Imbriani, Chiaia. Bus C25. **Open** 8am-2pm Mon-Wed, Fri, Sat. Closed Aug. **Map** p327 F13.
Fruit, vegetables, spices and fish are sold in this noisy, colourful market between Via San Pasquale and Via Carducci. Clothes, underwear and jewellery stalls can be found in nearby Via Imbriani.

Mercato Sant'Antonio Abate (Buvero)
North of the train station on Borgo Sant'Antonio Abate. **Open** 9am-7.30pm Mon-Sat. **Map** p329 O5/6.
This open-air market is known also as Buvero, so keep this in mind when asking for directions. Stalls display seafood, local cheeses, smoked meats, fresh fruits and vegetables.

Pignasecca
Via Pignasecca & surrounding streets, Toledo. Metro Montesanto/bus 24, 105, R1. **Open** 8am-1pm daily. **Map** p328 K9/10.
One of the city's oldest markets, the bustling Pignasecca sells all manner of goods: fish, vegetables, deli goods, cut-price perfume, fashion and linen, and cheap and cheerful kitchenware.

Porta Nolana Fish Market
Nr Piazza Garibaldi. Metro Garibaldi/bus 14, 110, 125, R2. **Open** 7am-1.30pm daily. **Map** p329 P7.
Everyone shops here for the catch of the day, so come early for the best selection.

Specialist

Gay-Odin
Via Toledo 214, Toledo (081 551 3491/www. gay-odin.it). Funicular Centrale to Augusteo/ bus C25, R2. **Open** 9.30am-8.30pm Mon-Sat. Closed 2wks Aug. **Credit** AmEx, DC, MC, V. **Map** p328 K9.
Luscious piles of pralines and deliciously flaky *foresta* chocolate bars are among the delicacies at this venerable chocolate shop. The gelati are equally delicious (*see p133*).
Other locations throughout the city.
▶ *Visit the small, charming factory in Chiaia (Via Vetriera 12, 081 417843) to see the Willy Wonka-style production line in action.*

CONSUME

★ Tarallificio da Poppella
Via Sanità 148, Cavour, Via Toledo & La Sanità (081 291305). Metro Piazza Cavour/bus 51, 52. **Open** 7am-midnight daily. **No credit cards. Map** p328 L5.

Devour *taralli* in one of Naples' most authentic quarters. The spicy, almond-encrusted twists are highly addictive, so invest in a bagful.

GIFTS & SOUVENIRS

L'Antico
Vico Graziella 14, Piazza Municipio, Royal Naples (081 551 0582). Bus C25, R2, R3. **Open** 7.30am-4pm Mon-Fri. Closed Aug. **No credit cards. Map** p332 L11.

On a dingy alley lined with metal-working ateliers, L'Antico's cavernous premises are stuffed with repro antiques of every description, from Greco-Roman bronzes to Capodimonte porcelains. The quality is high and the prices low. Prowl around the stony passageways and you'll be surprised at what you'll find.

Eboli
Via Benedetto Croce 35-37, Centro Storico (081 551 6363). Metro Dante/bus 137, E1, R1, R3. **Open** 10am-7.30pm Mon-Fri; 10am-2pm Sat. Closed 3wks Aug. **Credit** AmEx, MC, V. **Map** p328 L9.

This street is crammed with jewellery shops specialising in silver ex-votos, offered to saints as thanks for 'divine' healings. The silver arms, legs, tummies, breasts, heads and bodies make intriguing gifts; Eboli also carries silver animals, so you can give thanks on behalf of your pet. Items start at around €10.

► *For other unusual souvenir ideas, see p143.*

Il Mondo dei Pastori
Via San Gregorio Armeno 46, Centro Storico (081 551 6205/www.ilmondodeipastori.it). Metro Dante/bus 137, E1, R1, R3. **Open** 9am-7.30pm Mon-Sat. Closed 1wk Aug. **Credit** MC, V. **Map** p328 M8.

Neapolitans take their Christmas nativity displays very seriously; it's a tradition that goes back centuries. This street is where they come to buy new heads and limbs, or to undertake major expansions. Ugo Esposito is a master of the art. He also produces hand-painted terracotta Pulcinellas, as well as various souls burning in the flames of Purgatory – a uniquely Neapolitan folk art (*see p62* **City of blood**).

Museum Shop
Via Benedetto Croce 12, Centro Storico (081 360 4228). Metro Dante/bus 137, E1, R1, R3. **Open** 9am-7pm Mon-Sat. Closed 2wks Aug. **Credit** MC, V. **Map** p328 L9.

Housed on the ground floor of philosopher Croce's family palazzo, this new shop offers a good range of museum repros (custom orders taken) and souvenirs, all very nicely done and therefore pretty pricy.

Napoli Mania
Via Toledo 312-313, Toledo (081 414120/ www.napolimania.com). Funicular Centrale to Augusteo/bus C25, R2. **Open** 10am-1.45pm, 4.30-8pm Mon-Sat. **Credit** AmEx, DC, MC, V. **Map** p328 K9.

There's generally a crowd of locals laughing at Napoli Mania's window display; inside you'll find gag gifts, T-shirts in dialect and other quirky items.

★ Ospedale delle Bambole
Via San Biagio dei Librai 81, Centro Storico (081 203067/www.ospedaledellebambole.it). Metro Piazza Cavour/bus E1, R1, R2, R3. **Open** call for details. **No credit cards. Map** p328 N8.

Naples' famous 'doll hospital' is a tiny shop and museum, filled with dolls, figurines, and traditional toys. Ask about visiting hours at the hospital where the 'operations' take place, in a nearby palazzo.

Scriptura
Via San Sebastiano 22, Centro Storico (081 299226). Metro Dante or Piazza Cavour. **Open** 10am-8pm Mon-Sat. Closed 2wks Aug. **Credit** AmEx, MC, V. **Map** p328 L8/9.

Quality writing implements and calligraphy supplies are sold here; many are beautifully packaged and make lovely gifts. There's a wide array of handmade leather purses, planners and journals as well.

Studio Artistico Lello Esposito
Vico San Domenico Maggiore 9, Centro Storico (081 551 4171/www.lelloesposito.com). Bus E1, R1, R3. **Open** call for appointment. **No credit cards. Map** p328 L8.

Best known for his Pulcinella masks, Lello Esposito also sells *corno* jewellery (*see p150* **Made in Naples**), models of Vesuvius and more from this little workshop in the ancient city centre.

Ceramics

Decumanus
Via Benedetto Croce 30/31, Centro Storico (081 551 8095/www.decumanus.net). Metro Dante/bus E1, R1, R3, R4. **Open** 9.30am-1.30pm, 4-7.30pm Mon-Sat. Closed 1wk Aug. **Credit** AmEx, DC, MC, V. **Map** p328 L9.

Decumanus sells reproductions of Capodimonte porcelain and period ceramics, as well as the kinds of souvenir that grand tourists might have triumphantly borne home.

Espace
Piazza Monteoliveto 11, Centro Storico (081 1956 9414/www.espacemonteoliveto11.it). Metro Dante/bus E1, R1, R3, R4. **Open** 10am-1.30pm, 4-7.30pm Mon-Fri. **Credit** MC, V. **Map** p328 L10.

A treasure trove of vibrant, colourful, contemporary ceramics, glass and plastics, designed by some of Naples' leading young artists.

Ospedale delle Bambole.

Spagnuolo
Via Benedetto Croce 55, Centro Storico (081 552 1102). Metro Dante/bus E1, R1. **Open** 10am-7pm Mon-Sat. Closed 3wks Aug. **No credit cards. Map** p328 L9.
Spagnuolo is ideal for stocking up on Neapolitan souvenirs, such as good luck charms and discounted Capodimonte porcelain figurines.

HEALTH & BEAUTY
Hairdressers & barbers

You generally don't need an appointment, but be prepared to spend a lot of time waiting.

Aveda
Via Giuseppe Fiorelli 12A, Chiaia (081 764 5599/ www.aveda.com). Metro Piazza Amedeo/funicular Amedeo/bus C25, C28. **Open** 9am-7pm Mon-Sat. Closed 2wks Aug. **Credit** AmEx, DC, MC, V. **Map** p327 G13.
Visitors in search of a reassuringly international name should head for Aveda's appealing day spa.

M Rubinacci
Via Francesco Crispi 34, Chiaia (081 680997). Metro Amedeo/bus C24. **Open** 9am-7pm Tue-Sat. Closed 3wks Aug. **Credit** AmEx, DC, MC, V. **Map** p326 E12.
This miniscule salon is always packed with women waiting to get their hair done. Cuts start from €13, colour €25. Manicures and pedicures are offered too.

Oasis Il Barbiere
Via Carlo Poerio 28, Chiaia (081 764 2434). Metro Piazza Amedeo/bus C24. **Open** 8.30am-8pm Tue-Sat. Closed 2wks Aug. **No credit cards. Map** p327 G13.
Gents in need of a cheap cut and a shave should head to this old-fashioned barber's shop.

Team Leo
Via Michelangelo da Caravaggio 288, Fuorigrotta (081 624641). Bus 181, C12. **Open** 9am-7pm daily. Closed 3wks Aug. **Credit** MC, V.
According to fashionistas, this is the place to go for a stylish cut. You enter through a tiny entrance cut into a huge wooden door; mind your head.

Opticians

Apetino Ottica
Via Giovanni Paisiello 41, Vomero (081 578 6933/www.apetino.it). Metro Cilea. **Open** *July-Sept* 9am-1.30pm, 4.30-8pm Mon-Fri. *Oct-June* 9am-1.30pm, 4.30-8pm Mon-Sat. Closed 2wks Aug. **Credit** AmEx, MC, V. **Map** p330 D9.
Helpful staff offer free eye tests, and a quick spectacles replacement service.

Capri People
Via Alabardieri 16, Chiaia (081 407343). Metro Piazza Amedeo/funicular Amedeo/bus C28. **Open** 10am-1.30pm 4.30-8pm Mon-Sat. Closed 2wks Aug. **Credit** AmEx, MC, V. **Map** p327 H13.
Capri People stocks sunglasses and spectacles galore, with the emphasis on fashion.

Ottica Sacco
Via Domenico Capitelli 35-37, off Piazza Gesù Nuovo, Centro Storico (081 552 2631/www. otticasacco.it). Bus 24, 149, E1, R1. **Open** 9am-1.30pm, 4.30-8pm Mon-Sat. Closed 2wks Aug. **Credit** AmEx, MC, V. **Map** p328 K9.
Prescriptions can be made up in an hour.

Pharmacies

Farmacia are indicated by a red or green cross; staff will make up prescriptions and give informal medical advice for simple ailments. The pharmacies listed below open on alternate Saturdays. Pharmacies often carry homeopathic

CONSUME

INSIDE TRACK
PROOF OF PURCHASE

Keep receipts handy after making any purchases. The Guardia di Finanza (finance police) occasionally ask to see shoppers' receipts (*ricevuta fiscale*). If you don't have them, you could be fined.

Made in Naples

Forget fleeting trends; these fashion stalwarts are here to stay.

Family counts for just about everything here – and that translates into traditions and skills that have been passed down through the generations. Few cities can compare with Naples' consummately talented seamstresses, tailors and leather-workers, and several small enterprises have made their mark on the international fashion scene through their unswerving dedication to quality and impeccable workmanship.

Most famous of all, perhaps, is **Marinella** (*see p145*). This tiny, elegant boutique, always thronged with customers, has been making ties since 1914. The likes of Prince Charles, Bill Clinton and Aristotle Onassis have all sported the shop's designs, and Marinella was commissioned to stitch ties for the world leaders attending the 1994 G7 Summit in Naples.

Oddly enough, the silks are made to order in England, as the original Signor Marinella was an avowed anglophile. Prices start at just under €100, and custom orders are welcome. You can visit the showrooms in a nearby palazzo to get the full flavour of the establishment, and to catch a glimpse of the seamstresses at work amid neat stacks of gorgeous silks.

Another Neapolitan institution that nods to English tastes is **Talarico** (*see p145*), famous for its silk umbrellas. This may be the 'land of the sun' according to the celebrated Neapolitan song, but when it rains it pours. A sumptuous Talarico umbrella, with its lifelong guarantee, will see you through any storm. Founded in

Talarico.

1860 and still family-run, the business also produces wonderfully elegant, old-fashioned walking sticks.

Shirts from **Anna Matuozzo** (*see p142*) bear price tags of around €1,000. The style is staunchly conservative, and adheres to the strictest standards of haute couture. Elegant, made-to-measure shirts in soft cottons are stitched by an all-female tailoring team, led by Signora Matuozzo. The striped designs are particularly sought after, as are the luxurious silk numbers.

Another Neopolitan classic is **Fratelli Tramontano** (*see p145*), which has been plying its trade for well over a century. The craftsmanship that goes into its handmade leather goods is remarkable: pieces include bags, shoes, wallets and belts. David Bowie, Neil Jordan and Bono are among its clients. Tramontano isn't afraid to add a modern edge to its designs: singer Patti Smith chose one of its contemporary handbags in purple suede – with studs, naturally.

medicines (*omeopatico*); for herbal remedies, natural beauty products, teas and essential oils, look for signs saying *erboristerie*.

Farmacia d'Arti
Piazza Municipio 15, Royal Naples (081 552 4237). Bus C25, R2, R3, V10. **Open** 8.30am-2pm, 3-8pm Mon-Fri & alternate Sat. Closed 2wks Aug. **Credit** MC, V. **Map** p332 L11.
Homeopathic products are a speciality at this well-stocked pharmacy, and the staff speak English.

Farmacia Greco
Piazza dei Martiri 65 (081 418027). Bus C25, C28. **Open** 9am-1.30pm, 4-8pm Mon-Fri & alternate Sat. Closed 2wks Aug. **Credit** AmEx, MC, V. **Map** p327 H13.

The head of this friendly, old-fashioned pharmacy, Dott Alessandro Iuliano, speaks English.

Shops

Il Chiostro Erboristeria
Via Santa Chiara 5, Centro Storico (081 552 7938). Bus E1, R1. **Open** 10am-6.30pm Mon, Wed; 10am-1.30pm, 4.30-7.30pm Tue, Thur, Fri; 10am-1.30pm Sat. Closed 3wks Aug. **No credit cards. Map** p328 L9.
This tiny Centro Storico establishment sells all sorts of herbal remedies and health food.

Fusco Profumeria
Corso Novara 1B, Port & University (081 283 421). Metro Garibaldi/bus 14, 110, 125, R2.

CONSUME

Open 9am-8pm Mon-Sat. Closed 1wk Aug.
No credit cards. **Map** p329 Q7.
Fusco Profumeria stocks a good range of perfumes
and cosmetics, at prices that are hard to beat.
Other location Corso Luci Arnaldo 110 (081
267618).

Helianthus
*Via Solimena 41, Vomero (081 578 2953).
Funicular Chiaia to via Cimarosa or Centrale to
Piazza Fuga/Metro Vanvitelli/bus C21, C28, C36.*
Open 9.30am-1.30pm, 4.30-8pm Mon-Sat. Closed
Aug. **Credit** AmEx, MC, V. **Map** p330 E10.
This welcoming shop has a large selection of nat-
ural remedies, health food and beauty products.

Sephora
*Galleria Umberto I 31-33, Royal Naples (081
420 2165/081 552 6677/www.sephora.com).
Funicular Centrale to Augusteo/Metro Municipio/
bus R1, R2, R4, C25.* **Open** 9.30am-8pm Mon-
Sat. **Credit** AmEx, MC, V. **Map** p332 K12.
Try out perfume, eyeshadow and powders to your
heart's content at Naples' branch of Sephora.

Spas & Salons

Culti SpaCafè
*Via Carlo Poerio 47, Chiaia (081 764 4619).
Metro Piazza Amedeo/bus C25.* **Open** 10am-
1.30pm, 4.30-8pm Mon-Sat. **Credit** AmEx, MC, V.
Map p327 G13.
Book in for a relaxing massage or mineral and mud
treatment at this tranquil retreat from the city.

Mirage Day SPA
*Via Porta Posillipo 135D (081 769 1436/
www.miragespa.eu). Funicolare Manzoni.*
Open 8.30am-10.30pm Mon-Sat. **Credit** MC, V.
The spa's facilities include a pool, Turkish baths and
a restaurant; various treatments are offered.

HOUSE & HOME
Antiques & art

★ Affaitati
*Via Benedetto Croce 21, Centro Storico (081
444427). Metro Dante/bus E1, R1.* **Open** 10am-
1.30pm, 4.30-7.30pm Mon-Sat; 10am-1.30pm Sun.
Closed Aug. **Credit** AmEx, MC, V. **Map** TK.
Family-run since 1885, this museum-like shop offers
a compendium of the best Neapolitan furnishings,
reflecting the Baroque period, Empire style, and
much more. Prices are fair, considering the quality.

★ Arte Antica
*Via Domenico Morelli 45, Chiaia (081 764 6897).
Metro Piazza Amedeo/bus R2, C25.* **Open** 10am-
1.30pm, 4-8pm Mon-Sat. **Credit** MC, V. **Map**
p327 H14.

This shop has an unrivalled array of prints, gouaches
and watercolours, ranging from 17th-century pieces
to early 20th-century works. Pride of place goes to
watercolours by such masters as Della Gatta, Ducros
and Lusieri. Prices run from €100 to over €150,000.

Campobasso
*Via Carlo Poerio 17, Chiaia (081 764 0770).
Bus C25, C28.* **Open** *July* 10am-1.30pm, 4.30-8pm
Mon-Fri. *Sept-June* 10am-1.30pm, 4.30-8pm Mon-
Sat. Closed Aug. **Credit** AmEx, MC, V. **Map**
p327 G13.
One of Naples' leading specialists in antique nativ-
ity scenes, this is a treasure trove of 17th-century
religious artefacts.

★ Fiera Antiquaria Napoletana
*Villa Communale, Via Caracciolo, Viale Dorhn,
Chiaia (081 761 2541/335 621 2723). Bus 25.*
Open *Sept-May* 3rd & 4th weekends (Sat & Sun)
of mth. Closed June-Aug. **Map** p326 C14/15-
E14/15.
Set along the gracious Riviera di Chiaia, the stalls
here offer a colourful clutter of furniture, paintings,
prints (usually fakes), jewellery and junk.

Iermano Antiquities
*Via Domenico Morelli 30, Chiaia (081 764 3913).
Bus C25, C28.* **Open** 10am-1.30pm, 4-8pm Mon-
Sat. Closed Aug. **No credit cards**. **Map** p327 H14.
Browse Iermano's local and European antiques;
18th- and 19th-century pieces are the mainstay.

Il Rigattiere
*Via dei Tribunali 281 at Piazza Gerolomini,
Centro Storico (081 299155). Metro Dante or
Piazza Cavour.* **Open** 9.30am-2pm, 5-9pm Mon-
Sat. **No credit cards**. **Map** p328 N8.
Besides selling bric-a-brac and antiques, the shop's
colourful proprietor also provides props for film
sets. It's paradise for magpie-eyed bargain hunters.

General

Ciccolella
*Via Bernini 57, Vomero (081 1956 9157/www.
ciccolella.it). Metro Vanvitelli/funicular Vomero/
bus C31, C28.* **Open** 10am-1.30pm, 4.30-8pm
Mon-Sat. Closed 2wks Aug. **Credit** AmEx, DC,
MC, V. **Map** p330 E9.
Marvel at Ciccolella's huge range of glass, crystal,
porcelain and silverware from names such as
Baccarat, Christofle, Lenox and Venini.

Frette
*Via dei Mille 2, Chiaia (081 418728). Funicular
Chiaia/Metro Piazza Amedeo/bus C25.* **Open**
10am-1.30pm, 4.30-8pm Mon-Sat. **Credit** AmEx,
DC, MC, V. **Map** p327 G12.
This Italian chain is known for its luxurious sheets,
towels and linen. Prices are correspondingly high.

CONSUME

MUSIC & ENTERTAINMENT
CDs and records

See also **FNAC**, *p141*.

Fonoteca
Via Morghen 31C-E, Vomero (081 556 0338/ www.fonoteca.net). Funicular Chiaia to Via Cimarosa or Centrale to Piazza Fuga/Metro Vanvitelli. **Open** noon-2am Mon-Sat; 6pm-2am Sun. Closed 2wks Aug. **Credit** AmEx, MC, V. **Map** p331 F10.
The stock here is brilliantly eclectic; staff will let you listen before buying, and there's a decent bar.

Music Romano
Piazzetta Pignasecca 18, Toledo (081 552 2343). Metro Montesanto/bus 24, 105, R1. **Open** 8am-8pm Mon-Sat. Closed 2wks Aug. **Credit** AmEx, DC, MC, V. **Map** p328 K9.
The Romanos specialise in Neapolitan music, from folk and classical to the latest contemporary artists.

DVDs

Blockbuster Italia S.P.A.
Via Piedigrotta 34, Mergellina (081 661774/ www.blockbuster.it). Metro Mergellina. **Open** 11am-11pm daily. **Credit** MC, V. **Map** p326 B14.
New and used films and DVDs to rent or buy.

Bulldog Store Napoli
Via Cimarosa 22, Vomero (081 344 1524/www. bulldogstorenapoli.it). Metro Vanvitelli. **Open** 10am-2pm, 4-9pm Mon-Sat; 11am-2pm, 5-9pm Sun. **Credit** MC, V. **Map** p331 F10.
This specialist shop sells movies and memorabilia.

Musical instruments

Loveri Strumenti Musicali
Via San Sebastiano, 74/75/72/66/10/8, Centro Storico (081 296755/www.loveri.com). Metro Dante/bus R2. **Open** 10am-1.30pm, 4-8pm Mon-Fri; 10am-1.30pm Sat. **Credit** AmEx, MC, V. **Map** p328 L8.

INSIDE TRACK POST-HASTE

Instead of looking for a post office when you need stamps, head to any tobacco shop (*tabacchi*) and purchase as many *francobolli* as you need. Let staff know which country your post is destined for, and whether you're buying stamps for a postcard (*cartolina postale*) or a letter (*lettera*). The city's small, red postboxes are found by most newsstands.

Loveri carries everything from traditional Neapolitan mandolins to modern synths and guitars. Its premises are on San Sebastiano, Naples' celebrated 'music alley'.

SPORTS & FITNESS
Synergy Fitness & Wellness Center
Via Nuova San Rocco 7, Capodimonte (081 744 4777). Bus 178. **Open** 7am-11pm Mon-Fri; 9am-6pm, 10am-2am Sun. **Credit** MC, V.
Choose from various hydrotherapy options (Turkish bath, sauna, whirlpool) as well as massages at this air-conditioned gym. There are classes in aerobics, martial arts, body building, gymnastics, boxing and Pilates, and a snack bar for post-workout refuelling.

TICKETS

Tickets are also sold at **FNAC** (*see p141*).

Box Office
Galleria Umberto I 17, Royal Naples (081 551 9188/www.boxofficenapoli.it). Funicular Centrale to Augusteo/Metro Municipio/bus C25, R1, R2, R4. **Open** 9.30am-1pm, 3.30-6.30pm Mon-Fri; 9.30am-1.30pm Sat. **No credit cards**. **Map** p332 K12.
A convenient place at which to pick up tickets for just about everything that happens in Naples.

Concerteria at Feltrinelli
Via Schipa 23, Chiaia (081 761 1221/www. concerteria.it). Bus C28/Cumana rail to Corso Vittorio Emanuele. **Open** 10am-1.30pm, 4.30-7.30pm Mon-Fri; 10am-1.30pm Sat. Closed Aug. **Credit** MC, V. **Map** p326 C13.
You can buy tickets for all sorts of events and concerts at this Chiaia-based agency.

TRAVELLERS' NEEDS
Dedalus Centroviaggi
Piazza Monteoliveto 2, Centro Storico (081 551 0643/www.dedaluscentroviaggi.it). Metro Dante/ bus R1, R3. **Open** 9.30am-1pm, 3.30-7pm Mon-Fri; 9.30am-1pm Sat. **Credit** AmEx, DC, MC, V. **Map** p328 L10.
Paride and his English-speaking team can make train, ferry, hotel and flight bookings, and recommend inexpensive accommodation.

Planet Travel
Via Aniello Falcone 352, Vomero (081 644 583). Bus C28. **Open** 10am-1.30pm, 4-7.30pm Mon-Fri; 10am-1.30pm Sat. **No credit cards**. **Map** p326 D11.
The efficient staff at Planet Travel are particularly good at making last-minute arrangements on behalf of weary tourists.

Arts & Entertainment

Calendar	154	Music & Nightlife	170
Music and movement	155	**Profile** Alex Colle	171
		Wailing in Old Napule	172
Children	**157**	A shore thing	176
There's a Pulcinella in			
everyone	158	**Performing Arts**	**179**
		Profile San Carlo	180
Film	**160**	Dance 'til you drop	182
Portrait of a politician	162	Punch drunk	184
Galleries	**163**	**Sport & Fitness**	**185**
Art on the outskirts	164	Azure passion	186
		The transatlantic marathon	188
Gay & Lesbian	**168**		

Calendar

Parades, processions and… liquefying blood?

Naples loves to party – and it's festivals with religious roots that blossom most extravagantly in this ancient, deeply faith-driven city. Easter and the period between Christmas and Epiphany are hugely important events, as are the thrice-yearly ritual involving what is said to be the liquefaction of the blood of San Gennaro, the city's patron saint, and the commemoration of the miracle of Santa Maria del Carmine.

Secular events range from the annual Pizzafest to more highbrow gatherings, such as the Napoli Teatro Festival Italia and Galassia Gutenberg Book Fair. The Maggio dei Monumenti, held each May, has gone from strength to strength, opening the city's secrets to curious visitors.

Events of all types tend to come and go in this anarchic city, so confirm as close as possible to the scheduled dates.

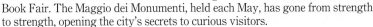

SPRING

Settimana Santa
Various locations (081 557 4111/081 449711/ www.chiesadinapoli.it). **Date** late Mar-Apr.
Easter week means processions and passion plays in the streets and piazzas.

Settimana della Cultura
Museums across Italy (800 991199/www. beniculturali.it). **Date** 1wk in Apr.
Italy's publicly owned museums offer free entry (and many stay open late) for this week of culture.

Napoli Marathon
www.napolimarathon.it. **Date** mid Apr.
Runners take to the streets for a full marathon, half-marathon, 4km fun run or leisurely walk.

Festa della Liberazione (Liberation Day)
Various locations. **Date** 25 Apr.
Concerts and gatherings celebrate the date when the Italian Resistance chased the Nazis out of Italy.

Festa di San Gennaro
Duomo, Via del Duomo 147 (081 542 2090/081 557 4111/www.chiesadinapoli.it). Bus E1, R2. **Date** 1st Sat in May. **Map** p328 N7.
The first of three dates each year when the patron saint's preserved blood is said to liquefy. Vast crowds gather to witness the phenomenon. *See p62* **City of blood**.

Maggio dei Monumenti
Various locations (081 542 2090/www.comune. napoli.it). **Date** May.
An impressive calendar of free events kicks off in late April, with concerts, exhibitions and access to monuments in the city that are normally closed to the public.
► *For more, see p50.*

Galassia Gutenberg
Stazione Marittima, Molo Angioino, Piazza Municipio (081 554 8911/www.galassia.org). Bus C25, R2, R3. **Date** late May-June. **Map** p332 L11.
The largest book fair in southern Italy is a four-day event, held at the end of May.

SUMMER

Napoli Film Festival
Various locations (081 588 5688/www.napoli filmfestival.it). **Date** mid June.
The film festival's venue and duration varies from year to year; check online for the latest information. Tickets are modestly priced, ranging from €4 for a single film to €20 for a festival pass.

Napoli Teatro Festival Italia
Various locations (081 1956 0383/www.napoli teatrofestival.it). **Date** June-July.
Theatrical and musical events starring local and international performers take place in venues across town; tickets cost €15.

Music and movement

Naples celebrates the Madonna of Piedigrotta.

September 7 each year is the feast day of the Madonna of Piedigrotta. The festival was born in the Middle Ages from the ashes of pagan fertility rites that took place at the foot (*piedi*) of Posillipo Hill, which was pierced as early as the first century AD by a tunnel (*grotta*), connecting Naples with points west. The spot now has a much expanded modern tunnel, as well as the Basilica of Piedigrotta.

Always celebrated with song and dance, the festival entered its golden age from the late 1800s to the 1960s. In 1853, a singing contest was introduced to the programme, and became hugely popular, spawning internationally acclaimed songs such as 'Te Voglio Bene Assaje' and 'O Sole Mio' (reinvented for Elvis Presley as 'It's Now or Never'). Tens of thousands of Neapolitans thronged the streets to listen to the singers and gawp at the elaborate allegorical floats.

After a lengthy hiatus, the tradition was reintroduced in 2007, featuring a concert in Piazza Plebiscito by Bryan Ferry, along with exponents of traditional Neapolitan song. Singer Nino d'Angelo became the artistic director in 2008, scoring a coup by persuading Pozzuoli native Sophia Loren to act as the festival's patron that year.

The festival will now comprise three parts: a huge concert in Piazza Plebiscito, featuring international stars; a grand parade of allegorical floats going from the Palazzo Reale to the basilica; and the Audizioni competition, showcasing new songs, which will go on for a week in piazze around the city.

ARTS & ENTERTAINMENT

ARTS & ENTERTAINMENT

Open Estate a Napoli
Various locations (081 542 2090/www.comune. napoli.it). **Date** June-Sept.
Open-air films, theatre and music are on the agenda for the 'Summer in Naples' season; around 100 free events are staged throughout greater Naples.

Brividi d'Estate
Orto Botanico, Via Foria 223 (081 542 2088/ www.ilpozzoeilpendolo.it). Metro Piazza Cavour or Museo/bus 14, 15, 47, CS, C51. **Date** July. **Map** p329 O5.
Outdoor musical theatre performances, usually on a mystery or thriller theme, are held in the Botanical Gardens most nights at 9pm. Tickets are €12-€16.

Carpisa Neapolis Festival
Mostra d'Oltremare, Fuorigrotta (081 725 8025/ www.neapolis.it). Metro Campi Flegrei/Cumana rail to Mostra. **Date** mid July.
An international line-up of rock groups appears at the largest musical event in southern Italy; in 2009, the Prodigy and the Virgins performed here. It's generally a two-day event. For more, *see p96*.

Santa Maria del Carmine
Piazza del Carmine 2 (081 557 4111/www. chiesadinapoli.it). Bus 14, CD, R2. **Date** 16 July. **Map** p329 P9.
Santa Maria del Carmine's well-attended feast day is celebrated with fireworks festooning the belltower of her church (*see p66* **Profile**).

Ferragosto
Various locations (081 557 4111/www.chiesa dinapoli.it). **Date** 15 Aug.
The Feast of the Assumption is celebrated across the region; in Pozzuoli there's a slippery pole contest, followed by fireworks.

AUTUMN

Festa di Piedigrotta
Various locations in the Piedigrotta area (081 214 0813/www.festadipiedigrotta.it). **Date** 10 days, early-mid Sept.
Parades, floats, music, dancing, street festivals and performances celebrate the feast day of the Madonna of Piedigrotta (7 Sept). *See p155.*

Festa di San Gennaro
For listings, *see p154.* **Date** 19 Sept.
The blood of Naples' patron saint is said to liquefy once again, amid frantic praying in the Duomo.

Pizzafest
Mostra d'Oltremare, Fuorigrotta (081 420 1205/ www.pizzafest.info). Metro Campi Flegrei/ Cumana rail to Mostra. **Date** 10 days mid Sept.
Naples celebrates its most famous dish with visiting chefs, pizza-making workshops and shows.

Independent Film Show
Fondazione Morra, Palazzo Ruffo di Bagnara, Piazza Dante 89 (081 414306/www.em-arts.org). Metro Dante/bus R1, R4. **Date** 5 days mid Nov. **Map** p328 K8.
This international avant-garde event showcases some three dozen films and videos.

WINTER

Festa di San Gennaro
For listings, *see p154.* **Date** 16 December
The blood of Naples' patron saint allegedly liquefies a third time on 16 December, this time within the heightened cultural context brought on by the annual Christmas fervour and festivities.

Natale a Napoli
Various locations (081 557 4111/www.chiesadi napoli.it). **Date** Nov-Dec.
Christmas is celebrated with a vast programme of free events, ranging from concerts and exhibitions to plays and parades. Few churches are without a crib; the 18th-century examples in the Certosa-Museo di San Martino (*see p81*) and the Palazzo Reale (*see p51*) are particularly fine.
▶ *Expect a seasonal shopping frenzy in the streets around San Gregorio Armeno (see p60) as everyone stocks up on traditional nativity figures.*

Capodanno (New Year's Eve)
Piazza del Plebiscito (081 542 2090/www. comune.napoli.it). Bus C25, R2, R3. **Date** 31 Dec. **Map** p332 K13.
A concert of classical, traditional and rock music welcomes in the New Year, lasting well into the morning. There are fireworks over Castel dell'Ovo.

La Befana (Epiphany)
Piazza del Plebiscito (081 542 2090/www. comune.napoli.it). Bus C25, R2, R3. **Date** 6 Jan. **Map** p332 K13.
The old hag who brings gifts to good children and leaves charcoal in the shoes of bad ones descends from the sky to distribute her presents in Piazza del Plebiscito. There's also a free concert, held in a different venue each year.

'O Cippo di Sant'Antonio
Various locations. **Date** 17 Jan.
In many quarters, Neapolitans clear out all their unwanted belongings, pile them in the streets and piazzas and set them on fire (a *cippo* is a bonfire).

Carnevale
Various locations (081 542 2090/www.comune. napoli.it). **Date** Feb.
This masked celebration before the start of Lent is a mere shadow of its formerly riotous self, although children still don fancy dress and proudly parade around town.

Children

Puppets and pizza keep the bambini content.

Living in a maelstrom of traffic and noise, Neapolitan children are fussed over and cosseted – and the old adage that they should be seen and not heard is enthusiastically ignored. This makes the city an extremely child-friendly place. Visiting *bambini* are given a warm welcome by locals, whose smiles and friendly overtures soon break down the language barriers.

Although an overload of churches and more serious-minded museums may not appeal, much of Greater Naples provides a perfect playground for children. Parks and green spaces are plentiful, and Pompeii and Napoli Sotterranea make for adventurous family outings; small fry will also appreciate the city's famed gelaterie and plethora of pizza joints.

ARTS & ENTERTAINMENT

SIGHTSEEING

If you've always thought that museums and children don't mix, Naples is a city that can change your mind. The **Città della Scienza** (*see p159*) in Bagnoli should be top of the agenda. Aimed at children, it takes a hands-on approach to science, with all sorts of wacky experiments for kids to try.

For a more traditional take on science, the four university museums housed in the **Centro Musei delle Scienze Naturali** (*see p65*) are packed with rocks, fossils and stuffed animals. To peep at turtles, seahorses, octopus and other marine life from the Bay of Naples, visit the **Stazione Zoologica** (*see p84*), a grand old 19th-century aquarium in Chiaia.

Children also enjoy exploring Naples' castles, and dreaming of being sword-wielding defenders of the **Castel dell'Ovo** (*see p52*) or **Castel Sant'Elmo** (*see p81*). The succession of billowy brides posing for wedding pictures by the entrance to Castel dell'Ovo will impress little girls, whereas those of a more macabre bent will relish dark tales of the dungeons at Castel Nuovo. Finally, there are the dodgems and rollercoaster thrills of **Edenlandia** (*see below*) and **Liberty City Fun** (*see p159*), both set on the outskirts of town.

About the author
Valentina Nesci writes about Italy for www.italiannotebook.com, *and publications such as* Edios *and* Comunicare.

Further afield, Portici is home to the **Museo Ferroviario di Pietrarsa** (*see p134*) – an enormous railway museum with plenty of gleaming locomotives to admire.

The volcanic activity of the area is also guaranteed to thrill children. In Pozzuoli, you can walk on the crater of a real but dormant volcano, the **Solfatara** (*see p91*). Boiling sulphurous gases rise continuously from underfoot, as do occasional eruptions of mud. Another exciting place to visit is **Lago Averno** (*see p92*), also located in the Campi Flegrei. The volcanic lake gets its name from a dark abyss that the ancient Greeks believed to be the entrance to the Underworld. Close by are the remains of the so-called Temple of Apollo and the cave of the Cumaean Sibyl (*see p93*), where the renowned prophetess received messages from the gods.

Vesuvius (*see p245*) is another must for kids; alternatively, you could take a trip to **Ischia** to see steam gushing from between the rocks on the beach at Sant'Angelo (*see p227*).

Archaeological sites such as **Pompeii** (*see p239*) can be brought alive with a spot of imaginative role play – not to mention a **Pompei Virtual Tour** (*see p159*), courtesy of the site's educational entertainment centre.

Attractions

Edenlandia
Viale Kennedy, Fuorigrotta (081 239 4090/ www.edenlandia.it). Metro Campi Flegrei/ Cumana rail to Edenlandia/bus 152, C2, C3.

There's a Pulcinella in everyone

Meet Pulcinella – a not-so-distant cousin of Mister Punch.

Bruno Leone is a *guarattellaro*, the puppet-master who brings the age-old character of Pulcinella to life in performances in theatres and on the streets. Taught by Nunzio Zampella, the last of the great Neopolitan puppeteers, Leone has breathed new life into the tradition.

Time Out (TO): You learnt from the last great interpreter of Pulcinella. How has the art of the guarattellaro evolved since then?
Bruno Leone (BL): From Nunzio Zampella, I learned the traditional repertoire of Pulcinella, which to me is a blueprint that can be used to recount any story, transcending space and time. Pulcinella is not only a character. He is the archetype of humanity, the symbol of people's desire to live. His girlfriend represents life itself, and there are three evil characters that try to divide them: the dog, the Guappo and the policeman – representing the fear of nature, the fear of others and the fear of authority. With these characters it's possible to recreate any tale, as well as to comment on current problems, from 9/11 to the problem of trash in Naples.

TO: Is there a risk that the stories may be too disturbing for a child?
BL: It's interesting that you mention that, because it is true that a few people are worried about Pulcinella. But Pulcinella doesn't deny fear, he battles it – and in doing so, he teaches us that confronting our fears is the only way to defeat them.

TO: Do you often perform outside Italy?
BL: Yes indeed! Travelling with Pulcinella, I was astonished to discover that he had relatives wherever I went. Puppeteers as far away as Brazil, Africa and even a remote village in China have a puppet that looks like Pulcinella, acts like Pulcinella and even speaks like him, thanks to the *pivetta* – a metal instrument that creates his characteristic clucking sound. By helping us to fight our fears through laughter, the character is a valuable friend of all the children in the world.
For details of shows, visit www.guarattelle.it.

Open *Mid Mar-mid June* 2-9pm Tue-Fri; 10.30am-midnight Sat, Sun. *Mid June-mid Sept* 5pm-midnight Tue-Fri; 10.30am-midnight Sat, Sun. *Mid Sept-mid Mar* 10.30am-midnight Sat, Sun. **Admission** €2.50. **No credit cards**.
Set in the suburb of Fuorigrotta, Edenlandia was the first theme park in Europe. It's a giddy whirl of dodgems, carousels, mini trains and water rides.

Liberty City Fun
Via Monteoliveto 48, Volla (081 774 0186/www. libertycityfun.com). Circumvesuviana train, stop at Volla. **Open** 9am-2pm, 4-10pm Tue-Fri; 9am-2pm, 4pm-midnight Sat; 9am-midnight Sun. **Admission** free; activity prices vary. **No credit cards**.
This giant complex has trampolines, carousels, pirate boats and rides, a quad track, a pizzeria and a pool; an area for grown-ups has bowling lanes, billiards and a restaurant. There's live music every Thursday night, and jugglers and magicians at the weekends.

Sights & museums

★ Città della Scienza
Via Coroglio 104, Posillipo (081 735 2111/www. cittadellascienza.it). Metro Campi Flegrei, then C9, C10 to Città della Scienza/bus 140 to Capo Posillipo, then F9. **Open** 9am-5pm Tue-Sat; 10am-7pm Sun. *Planetarium* every hr from 10am (last show 3.30pm) Tue-Sat. **Admission** €7; €5 under-18s; free under-4s. *Planetarium* €1.50. **Credit** AmEx, DC, MC, V.
Housed in a converted 18th-century factory, this modern science museum keeps children busy with interactive exhibitions, games and scientific curiosities. The Planetarium guides kids on a galactic voyage of discovery, while the Science Gym tackles the mysteries of evolution. Suitable for threes and over, it's a brilliant hands-on day out. There's also a popular programme of workshops, which need to be booked in advance. Families can easily spend the best part of a day here, lunching at one of the on-site restaurants.

★ Napoli Sotterranea
For listings, *see p59*.
Beneath the city lies Napoli Sotterranea – a thrilling network of tunnels and chambers, built by the ancient Greeks, which can be explored on special tours. The channels and cisterns were integrated into Naples' water supply system, and remained in use until the cholera epidemic of 1884; during World War II, parts of the tunnels were converted into air-raid shelters.

Pompei Virtual Tour
Via Plinio, 105, Pompei (081 578 3593/www. virtualpompei.it). Circumvesuviana train, stop in Pompei. **Open** groups only, by reservation. **Admission** €4.90. **No credit cards**.
The Educational Entertainment Centre shows a 3-D film of the ancient town in 79 AD, giving visitors the chance to witness the eruption of the Vesuvius.

OUTDOORS
Beaches

When it gets too hot to enjoy the city, the beach is the obvious alternative. Naples' authorities have been cleaning up the sea near the city, so you don't need to go far. To the west, **Posillipo** (*see p87* **Sea Naples...**) has a few rocky beaches; the walk back into town is quite tough. On the road to Cuma, Torre Gavetta has good sandy beaches, but its proximity to the (albeit processed) main Naples sewage outlet may put many off. Another option on the mainland is the **Campi Flegrei** area (*see p88*), with beaches around Capo di Miseno: **Milliscola** has full facilities and man-made coves.

For the best beaches, though, you need to put some distance between you and the city. Some of the cleanest water can be found around the islands of **Ischia** (*see pp215-228*), **Procida** (*see pp229-232*) and **Capri** (*see pp196-214*), and the boat rides out to them are fun for kids. Or, try the beaches around **Sorrento** (*see pp249-263*) or the **Amalfi Coast** (*see pp264-291*).

A more adventurous alternative to the beach is **Magic World** (Uscita Tangenziale Licola, Via San Nullo, Localita' Masseria Vecchia, Licola, 081 854 6792, www.magicworldacqua park.it, closed Oct-May), a vast water park with slides galore, in the town of Licola.

Parks

The city's green spaces offer a compendium of lovely views, play areas, colourful gardens and extravagant villas. Of particular note is the **Villa Comunale** (*see p85*), which runs along the bay of Chiaia for almost a mile, and was built to resemble the Jardin des Tuileries in Paris. The park is also home to the Stazione Zoologica, Europe's oldest aquarium (*see p84*). At the weekends and during the holidays, there are falabella horses to ride, and family tandem bikes on which to scoot up and down the pavement parallel to the park and seafront.

The calm, green **Parco della Floridiana** (*see p82*) up in Vomero is also an ideal place for families to take a Sunday stroll. Another option is the **Bosco di Capodimonte**, home to some 400 species of plant, and dotted with stately trees. Set to the north of the historic centre, the park is the largest in Naples, and home to the royal palace (now the art-filled **Museo di Capodimonte**, *see p78*) of Carlos III de Bourbon. Closer to the centre, don't overlook the lush **Orto Botanico** (*see p74* **Green getaway**) – though be sure to call ahead to reserve. The best option for sporty children, however, is **Parco Vergiliano** (*see p86*), with an outside gym and running track.

Film

A city with a role in cinematic history.

Naples holds a key place in the history of cinema. In the early 19th century, it was, along with Turin, the Italian capital of the seventh art; Rome only caught up later. Italy's pioneering female director Elvira Notari (1875-1946) lived and worked here, and the first purpose-built projection hall was constructed here. In fact, the Sala Iride still exists; alas, it now screens only porn.

More recently, directors have focused on the city's criminal underworld in films such as *Gomorra* and *Fortapàsc,* and also *Il Divo*. These tough, semi-documentaries are seen by many as long overdue coming-of-age works, not only for Naples but for Italy as a whole.

ARTS & ENTERTAINMENT

NAPLES ON SCREEN

Neapolitan actors, their craft rooted in the deep theatrical traditions of the city, have made monumental contributions to cinema. Every Italian recognises the inimitable Totó (1898-1967), and Sophia Loren became a symbol of Mediterranean beauty. Loren grew up in Pozzuoli, a few kilometres outside Naples; the town now has a cinema named after its homegrown Hollywood legend. Over the course of her long career, 'La Loren' has won two Oscars and worked with cinema's finest, from director Vittorio de Sica to Charlie Chaplin, Marlon Brando and Walter Matthau.

The cinematic careers of actor-playwright Eduardo de Filippo (1900-1984) and his brother Peppino (1903-1980) also reached brilliant heights, often in collaboration with Totó in some of his most exhilarating turns.

Directors here have always tried to capture the essence of this unique, elusive city and its complex social fabric. Francesco Rosi (b.1922) made his name tackling gritty, controversial issues, from political corruption to bullfighting; two of his most famous films, *La Sfida* and *Le Mani Sulla Città* (*see p46*) were shot in Naples.

The great Vittorio de Sica (1901-1974) figures prominently among the most important directors with Neapolitan credentials; he grew up in the city, although he was born in Lazio.

De Sica won four Oscars; his masterpieces include *Ladri di Biciclette* – known to English-speakers as *Bicycle Thieves* – and *La Ciociara* (*Two Women*). Additional highlights of his oeuvre include *Ieri, Oggi, Domani* (*Yesterday, Today and Tomorrow*) and *L'Oro di Napoli* (*The Gold of Naples*), both shot in the city. In 1960 he also played in the romantic comedy *It Started in Naples*, acting alongside Sophia Loren and Clark Gable.

The 1980s, with their climate of disenchantment and bitterness, belonged to beloved actor-director Massimo Troisi (1953-1994), whose work blended tough irony and sweetly disarming comedy in films such as *Ricomincio da Tre* and *Scusate il Ritardo*. His final – and most famous – film was the heartwarming *Il Postino*.

The 1990s brought a rich seam of works, thanks to the emergence of a number of young independent filmmakers. Antonio Capuano, Mario Martone, Pappi Corsicato, Antonietta de Lillo and Stefano Incerti depict a Naples that may be hard and pitiless, but is squarely in the international cinematic mainstream. Together

---

About the author

Native Neapolitan **Antonio Tricomi** *is the city's music, film and theatre editor for* La Repubblica.

INSIDE TRACK
THE LANGUAGE OF FILM

Unfortunately, Neapolitans share the Italian national distaste for subtitles, and virtually all British and American films are dubbed into Italian.

they also created a group film, *I Vesuviani*. Horror film director, Mariano Baino, born and raised in Naples, later transferred to London and then New York. He won a cult following with the masterful *Dark Waters*.

CURRENT TRENDS

For Neapolitan cinema, 2008 proved to be a pivotal year. Three significant films appeared, two of which were selected for Cannes: *Il Divo*, by Paolo Sorrentino (*see p32* **Heart of darkness**), and *Gomorra*, directed by Matteo Garrone. All three films confront powerful themes pertaining to the social and political fabric of the city, and have had a remarkable impact on public opinion.

Il Divo was shot partly in Naples by its Neapolitan director. It evokes the doings of kingpin Italian politician Giulio Andreotti, played by Toni Servillo. In his directing, Sorrentino taps into a visionary vein, displaying an incisive style and a formidable mastery of rhythm and language. *Gomorra*, based on the bestseller by Roberto Saviano, has an episodic structure, like that of the novel on which it is based. Set in the squalid suburbs of Naples, its tone is of brutal realism, as actors intermingle with non-professionals taken from the street, some of whom are genuine denizens of Naples' nightmarish underworld. Both films won accolades at Cannes.

The third film, *Fortapàsc*, is the work of Milanese director Marco Risi. Its name is the Italian transliteration of Fort Apache – which is what the Neapolitan suburb of Torre Annunziata was called in the 1980s. It tells the story of Giancarlo Siani, a 26-year-old journalist who was murdered in Naples after writing an article on the Camorra's links with politicians.

CINEMAS

The average price of admission is €7, with discounts for students and seniors at certain times – usually on Wednesdays. Midweek nights may be cheaper than weekends.

Astra

Via Mezzocannone 109, Port & University (www.astra.unina.it). Bus CS, R2. **No credit cards. Map** p328 M9.
In the heart of the university quarter, this historic art house is frequented by young cinephiles. It's not open every day, and mornings are devoted to university classes. Its façade comprises part of the ancient Greco-Roman wall.

Filangeri

Via Filangieri 43/47, Chiaia (081 251 2408). Metro Piazza Amedeo. **No credit cards. Map** p327 H13.

Gomorra.

The Filangeri's three screening rooms bear the names of the greats of Italian cinema: Rossellini, Magnani and Mastroianni. The programme is devoted to independent – and mainly European – film.

FREE Istituto Cervantes

Via Nazario Sauro 23, Lungomare Chiaia (081 1956 3311). Funicolare Mergellina/bus 152. **Map** p332 K14.
From September to June, this prestigious Spanish and Latin American cultural institute hosts free screenings of Spanish-language films, showcasing stars such as Penélope Cruz and Pedro Almodóvar.

Med Maxicinema

Viale Giochi del Mediterraneo, Agnano (081 242 0111). Cumana rail to Agnano/bus 152. **No credit cards.**
Eleven screens make this the largest multiplex in the Naples area. Its varied programme ranges from blockbusters to kids' flicks. Although the younger set loves it, it's not particularly popular with Neapolitans in general, as films are shown without an intermission.

Modernissimo

Via Cisterna dell'Olio 59, Centro Storico (081 580 0254/www.modernissimo.it). Metro Dante/bus 24, R1, R4. Closed 2wks Aug. **No credit cards. Map** p328 K9.

ARTS & ENTERTAINMENT

This former theatre was remodelled as a multiplex in 1994, with four screening rooms and a fifth room for videos. The usual fare is blockbusters, but some independents make it on to the bill. A stately old mirror is part of the original theatre's decor, and the seats in the main room bear lines from famous films.

Sala Iride
Vico X Duchesca 11, nr Via Alessandro Poerio (081 201269), corner of Piazza Garibaldi. Metro Piazza Garibaldi/bus 1, 152. **No credit cards.** **Map** p329 O7.
The first purpose-built cinema constructed in Italy, this historic movie-house now screens porn flicks.

FESTIVALS

Napoli Film Festival
Warner Village, Via Chiaia 149 (081 558 5688/ www.napolifilmfestival.com). **Map** p327 H13.
This ten-day festival takes place in June, with screenings at the Filangeri (*see p161*) and in the auditorium of the Castel Sant'Elmo (*see p81*). Launched in 1995, when it was called Modfest, the event has gradually evolved, building up a strong rapport with Hollywood. Stars such as Harvey Keitel, Sigourney Weaver, Cate Blanchett and Milos Forman have attended, and every year the festival programme is duplicated in New York.

Giffoni Film Festival
Various locations in Giffoni Valle Piana (089 802 3001/www.giffonifilmfestival.it).
The second most important film festival in Italy after Venice was founded in 1971 by Claudio Gubitosi, who is still its director. The festival takes place between July and August in Giffoni Valle Piana, a tiny town near Salerno with streets named after directors and actors. What makes the festival unique is that it concerns itself with children's cinema; even the jury is composed of kids. The festival has a US branch in Los Angeles, run by actor Jon Voight, and an Australian counterpart. French director François Truffaut declared it 'the most necessary of all festivals'. Numerous directors and actors have participated over the years, including Robert de Niro, Oliver Stone, Meryl Streep, Anthony Quinn, Roman Polanski and Meg Ryan.

Portrait of a politician

Rising talent Paolo Sorrentino discusses his controversial new film.

Director and screenwriter Paolo Sorrentino was born in Naples. His latest film, *Il Divo*, is a biopic based on the life of former Italian prime minister Giulio Andreotti; acclaimed by critics, it won the Prix du Jury at Cannes.

Time Out (TO): How did Il Divo come about?
Paolo Sorrentino (PS): The film was only possible thanks to the formation of a collective, which included the Film Commission of the Campania Region. At first, few were willing to touch the subject: they thought it too audacious, or too dangerous. But my film isn't about some 'message'. The only point is that the central Italian political leader, Giulio Andreotti, is an enigmatic, indecipherable figure. But that was also his game, right up until the accusations from turncoats that he was part of the Mafia. Only then did he realise the game of cat and mouse no longer worked. The film focuses on that transformation.

TO: How much of the film was shot in Naples?
PS: Quite a bit. Pecorelli's murder took place in Rome, but it was shot at the Mostra d'Oltremare in Fuorigrotta. The massacre of Capaci, which happened in

Sicily, we shot at the abandoned Italsider factory. Other scenes were filmed at the racetrack in Agnano, and at the central post office in Piazza Matteotti.

TO: How would you respond to the accusations by politicians and intellectuals that your film essentially makes Italy look bad in the eyes of the world?
PS: You can't create a work of power and quality without playing on tensions, and without bringing out some dissension. A film's role is not to provide PR for a country – that's what tourist boards are for. What a film does is simply to tell a story.

Galleries

An ever-changing scene that's resolutely cutting-edge.

Once the seat of kings and the largest European capital after Paris, Naples has, since Greek times, been a remarkable centre of cosmopolitan culture, both high and low. The city's current art scene, meanwhile, had its beginnings in the picturesque seafront district of Chiaia, whose mouldering antiquities and sweeping views of the Gulf of Naples, from the misty profile of Capri to looming Mount Vesuvius, proved a rich source of artistic inspiration.

The painterly backdrop of the volcano provides a constant reminder of impending obsolescence – a *memento mori* that conveys a frisson of urgency. The jarring beauty of the city's natural setting, added to its contagious urban energy, stimulate an appreciation for the here-and-now that sits uneasily with its many formidable bastions of historical tradition. It is from this irreconcilable disjunction that a keenly cutting-edge art scene has emerged.

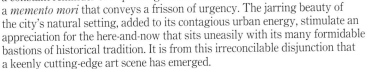

MOVERS & SHAKERS

It was in the late 1960s that Naples began to attract experimental artists from abroad – Cy Twombly, Joseph Beuys, Andy Warhol, Sol Lewitt – under the patronage of collectors Lucio Amelio and Pasquale Trisorio. Trisorio turned his Capri villa into an artists' residence, and Amelio's Modern Art Agency, opened in 1965, began to show the likes of Robert Rauschenberg and Gilbert & George, as well as artists of the Italian Transavanguardia movement.

After the disastrous 1980 earthquake, Amelio invited 65 artists, including Keith Haring, Jean-Michel Basquiat and Robert Mapplethorpe, to create the seminal 'Terrae Motus' exhibition to commemorate the catastrophe; it's now housed permanently in the Reggia at Caserta (*see p298*). In 1985, Amelio commissioned the wonderfully vivid *Vesuvius by Warhol* series for an exhibition at the Museo di Capodimonte, signaling the beginning of fruitful collaborations between private galleries and public museums.

About the author
Cathryn Drake is a freelance writer based in Italy, who reports on art, architecture and travel for publications such as Artforum, Metropolis *and the* Wall Street Journal.

More recently, Naples experienced something of a cultural renaissance after Antonio Bassolino (*see p31*) became mayor in 1993. The enterprising Bassolino initiated numerous projects promoting contemporary art – not least the groundbreaking project that brought striking art to the city's metro system (*see p60* **Metro contextual**).

In this fertile civic environment, a new generation of art galleries has sprung up, introducing an international roster of artists into a milieu previously defined by long-established venues such as **Galleria Lia Rumma** and **Studio Trisorio** (for both, *see p167*), which defined the city's avant-garde heyday. Among the young upstarts are **T293** (*see p166*), **Annarumma 404** (*see p165*), **Giangi Fonti** (*see p165*) and **Blindarte** (*see p167*) – the latter boldly venturing into the outlying suburb of Fuorigrotta (*see p163* **Art on the outskirts**). It's a far cry from well-heeled Chiaia, the city's traditional gallery district.

The launch of two publicly-funded contemporary art venues has also had a real impact on the art scene. The Palazzo delle Arti Napoli, better known as **PAN** (*see p84*), opened in Chiaia in 2005 with an eclectic, freewheeling line-up of exhibitions. That same summer, the Museo d'Arte Contemporanea Donna Regina Napoli, or **MADRe** (*see p75*), was inaugurated in a 17th-century palazzo, designed to spur gentrification and draw tourism to a run-down area near the Duomo. Retrofitted elegantly by Portuguese architect Alvaro Siza, the museum provides a cool, contemporary counterpoint to the chaotic ancient streets outside, and the nearby Museo Archeologico Nazionale (*see p70*).

MADRe's incursion into the historic centre paved the way for an increasingly vibrant city scene. The **Fondazione Morra Greco** (*see right*) began hosting exhibitions in the abandoned Palazzo Caracciolo d'Avellino. For their first space, T293's Paola Guadagnino and Marco Altavilla chose a decaying palazzo nearby, joining Umberto Raucci and Carlo Santamaria – who were well ahead of the game, having opened a gallery in the Centro Storico in 1992. **Galleria Raucci/Santamaria**

(*see p166*) has since moved into a new space behind the archaeological museum.

Naples has always managed to stay at the artistic cutting edge, while holding firmly on to the reins of its rich traditions. The **Museo di Capodimonte** (*see p78*), a former Bourbon royal palace with a commanding perspective of the entire Bay of Naples, continues its contemporary art programme – most recently with a survey of Louise Bourgeois's visceral sculptures and metaphorical cages. New works are juxtaposed with the historic paintings and furnishings of the National Gallery's permanent collection – a fantastic conflation of the historical and contemporary that epitomises the Neapolitan approach.

Art on the outskirts

Gallery director Memmo Grilli discusses the city's vibrant art scene.

In 2004, Memmo Grilli, the young director of modern and contemporary art at the Blindarte auction house (*see p167*), opened a storefront art gallery in the Fuorigrotta neighbourhood, which last saw glory in the Fascist era and is slated for urban renewal. He has gained critical success by scouring international art fairs in search of new talent, and showing innovative young artists who work in a wide array of media.

Time Out (TO): What makes Naples a good setting for a contemporary art gallery – and what problems does it pose?
Memmo Grilli (MG): Naples is, without a doubt, one of the capitals of contemporary art. The city has always seduced young artists, as well as more established names, and the artists we showcase often build strong bonds with the city and are very eager to return. In spite of the current absence of a major cultural event to bring Naples into the international spotlight, the city offers a series of initiatives throughout the year that increase the public's critical awareness and encourage collectors. The problems are those typical of the city in general: Naples has always been a difficult place, characterised by strong contrasts, which are an endless source of artistic inspiration as well as a school of life.

TO: What are the challenges of being located in a city suburb like Fuorigrotta?
MG: Just a two-minute drive from Mergellina station, on the other side of the tunnel,

Fuorigrotta is a vast, densely populated area that lost its green character after the unlawful concrete development of the 1960s. It's the only district of Naples where the majority of buildings are less than 50 years old.

Its young population is relatively uneducated, but attentive to innovation. The main attractions – including the Mostra d'Oltremare, the stadium and the university – are awaiting changes that will transform the area, which has great potential.

In any case, we are well positioned near the wealthy residential neighbourhoods of Chiaia and Posillipo, on a major traffic route that offers great visibility.

That said, location is really not that important for the gallery; our clients are from all over Italy and abroad, mostly the US, France, Germany, Britain, Spain and Switzerland. Many collectors become clients without having visited the gallery, or even Naples – but then they usually try to come at the first possible opportunity, as an excuse to visit the city.

TO: Tell us about the gallery's expansion.
MG: In October 2009 we will open new spaces that will complement the street-level gallery, adding three new rooms and an inner garden, designed by Neapolitan architects Sila Barracco and Mauro Smith. An elevator will connect the new gallery with the underground auction house offices and the other exhibition spaces.

The inaugural exhibition, 'Undefined Borders for Unlimited Perceptions', will

ROYAL NAPLES & MONTE ECHIA

One name to look out for is the **Annarumma 404 Gallery**. Francesco Annarumma exhibits international artists such as young American photographers Jen DeNike and Rashid Johnson, and has an eye for emerging talents. At the time of writing, the gallery was planning to move from its premises on Via Santa Brigida; for the latest information, see www.annarumma.404.com.

Galleria Fonti

Via Chiaia 229 (081 411409/www.galleria fonti.it). Bus C25, R2. **Open** 4.30-7.30pm Tue-Fri. Closed Aug. **No credit cards.** **Map** p332 K12.

Giangi Fonti's small upstairs space, located on a bustling pedestrian street full of clothing boutiques, exhibits young international artists, including conceptual artist Piero Golia, a Neapolitan who lives in Los Angeles.

CENTRO STORICO

Fondazione Morra Greco

Largo Avellino 17, off Via Anticaglia (081 210690/www.fondazionemorragreco.it). Metro Piazza Cavour or Museo. **Open** 10am-2pm daily. Closed Aug. **No credit cards.** **Map** p328 M7. Dental surgeon and art collector Maurizio Morra Greco began using the gutted Palazzo Caracciolo d'Avellino in 2006 to exhibit artists such as German artist Gregor Schneider, whose work deals with the

feature all of the gallery's artists – Julien Berthier, Simon Boudvin, Davide Cantoni, Sarah Ciracì, Adam Cvijanovic, Angela Detanico-Rafael Lain, Benny Droscher, Simon Keenleyside, Gian Paolo Striano and Berend Strik – as well as some new ones.

TO: Why do you think Naples has such a solid art market for a city of its size?
MG: Naples is the second-largest city in Italy, after Milan, with six million inhabitants. Many still consider it a major capital; after all, only 150 years ago, it was the ruling seat of a kingdom.

Investing in art is not a novelty here, as throughout history, important Neapolitan

families have always taken art investments seriously; promoting artistic research brought prestige to their name, and was a point of pride. It is enough to walk around the streets of Naples or enter a historic palazzo to understand the city's longstanding tradition of art patronage.

In any case, I think that geographical location is less important for the art market today than quality and professionalism – although it's nice if that encounter happens in a city as beautiful as Naples.

TO: What does the future hold for the city's contemporary art scene?
MG: I believe that its importance will continue to grow, in Italy and abroad. The city's potential is enormous, and there are so many important figures working here.

Unfortunately, there is still a lack of farsightedness and understanding that cooperation within the profession is indispensable for maintaining international competitiveness and developing the sector, thus benefiting the whole city.

TO: Who are your favourite historic artists?
MG: I am fascinated by art that remains relevant over time. From Caravaggio to Lucio Fontana, Italy has had the honour of providing a showcase to artists who have defined the history of art, and influenced everything that came after them. I feel a connection to these great masters, and I love to rediscover again and again in each of them their fundamental contributions to the history of art.

T293.

reconstruction of spaces. Another show was devoted to intimate video portraits by Estonian artist Mark Raidpere, with an installation about sea navigation by Sven Johne upstairs.

Galleria Overfoto
Viccolo San Pietro a Majella 6 (081 1957 8345/ www.overfoto.it). Metro Dante, Cumana or Montesanto. **Open** 11am-1pm, 4.30-7pm Tue-Fri; 11am-2pm Sat. **No credit cards.** **Map** p328 L8.
Located in a quiet courtyard off the charming Piazza Bellini, this gallery shows photography, painting, and video works. Most of the artists are Italian.

★ T293
Via Tribunali 293 (081 295882/www.t293.it). Metro Dante or Piazza Cavour. **Open** *Oct-mid July* noon-7pm Tue-Sat. *Sept* by appointment only. Closed mid July-Aug. **No credit cards.** **Map** p328 N8.

INSIDE TRACK ART PIAZZA

Every Christmas, the pedestrianised **Piazza Plebiscito** (*see p48*) hosts a temporary art installation. Interactive, innovative works are the order of the day: in 1995, the project's inaugural year, came Mimmo Paladino's *Salt Mountain* – quite literally a mighty heap of salt, on which local kids scampered. In 2008, five shiny, life-size bronze self-portraits by multidisciplinary Belgian artist Jan Fabre mingled with the crowds in the square.

T293 inhabits a cool, tranquil space in a decaying palazzo on the buzzing Via Tribunali, in the heart of the Centro Storico. Run by young curators Paola Guadagnino and Marco Altavilla, it shows thought-provoking conceptual work by young European and American artists.

VIA TOLEDO & SANITA

Fondazione Morra
Palazzo Ruffo di Bagnara, Piazza Dante 89 (081 564 1655/www.fondazionemorra.org). Metro Dante. **Open** during exhibitions only; admission by invitation. **Map** p328 K8.
This exhibition space, owned by longtime Neapolitan collector Peppe Morra, shows avant-garde stalwarts such as Julian Beck, Allan Kaprow, Shozo Shimamoto and Vettor Pisani. The foundation also organises a film festival and other cultural events.

Galleria Raucci/Santamaria
Corso Amedeo di Savoia 190 (081 744 3645/ www.raucciesantamaria.com). Metro Museo. **Open** 11am-1.30pm, 3-6.30pm Mon-Fri. Closed Aug. **No credit cards.**
Since 1992, Umberto Raucci and Carlo Santamaria have travelled constantly to discover and nurture new talent for their international stable of artists. The current line-up includes Brit Mat Collishaw, Irish émigré Padraig Timoney, American Tim Rollins and Swiss artist Ugo Rondinone.

★ Hermann Nitsch Museum
Vico Lungo Pontecorvo 29/d (081 564 1655/ www.museonitsch.org). Metro Dante. **Open** *Oct-June* 10am-7pm Mon, Wed-Sun. *July*

10am-7pm Mon, Wed-Fri. Closed Aug. **No credit cards. Map** p328 K8.
Set in a former electricity plant, with magnificent views that stretch as far as Mount Vesuvius and Capri, this museum and archive was opened in 2008 by the Fondazione Morra. It's dedicated to Viennese 'actionist' artist Hermann Nitsch's splatter paintings, and the relics of his orgiastic, bloody, theatrical mock crucifixions (by now more than 100). His work is strangely in keeping with the religious rites and iconography of the teeming Neapolitan streets, such as the 'miraculous' flowing of San Gennaro's blood in the Duomo three times a year (*see p62* **City of Blood**). Collector Peppe Morra has sponsored Nitsch's performances since the 1970s; one, *Lehraktion*, took place in 1996 within view of the museum, at a hilltop vineyard owned by Morra.

CHIAIA TO POSILLIPO

Alfonso Artiaco
Piazza dei Martiri 58 (081 497 6072/www. alfonsoartiaco.com). Metro Piazza Amedeo/bus C24. **Open** *Sept-May* 10am-1.30pm, 4-8pm Mon-Sat. *June-July* 10am-1.30pm, 4-8pm Mon-Fri. Closed Aug. **No credit cards. Map** p327 H13.
This well-regarded gallery shows a mix of high-profile and emerging artists including Giuseppe Penone, David Tremlett, Carl Andre and Wolfgang Laib, as well as young locals Bianco Valente.

★ Blindarte
Via Caio Duilio 10/4d, Fuorigrotta (081 239 4642/www.blindarte.it). Metro Campi Flegrei/ Cumana rail to Fuorigrotta. **Open** 10am-1pm, 4-7pm Mon-Fri. **No credit cards**.
Founded in 1999 as the first auction house in southern Italy, Blindarte opened a storefront contemporary art gallery above its subterranean offices five years later, soon to be expanded with a series of upper-level exhibition spaces. The young director, Memmo Grilli, is dedicated to exposing international emerging artists who work in a wide array of media, such as Brazilian conceptual artists Angela Detanico and Rafael Lain, American painter Adam Cvijanovic, and Italian artist Davide Cantoni, who burns his pictures on to paper. *See p164* **Art on the outskirts**.

Lia Rumma
Via Vannella Gaetani 12 (081 764 3619/www. gallerialiarumma.it). Metro Piazza Amedeo/bus C25. **Open** 11am-1.30pm, 4-7.30pm Tue-Fri; by appointment only Sat, Sun. **No credit cards. Map** p327 H14.
Opened in 1971, this blue-chip gallery has brought big international names such as Anselm Kiefer, Marina Abramovic, and Andreas Gursky to Naples, as well as nurturing Italian artists like Vanessa Beecroft and Franco Scognamiglio – although much of the buzz these days seems to be coming out of its newer Milan space.

Mimmo Scognamiglio
Via Mariano d'Ayala 6 (081 400871/www. mimmoscognamiglio.com). Metro Piazza Amedeo/ bus C24. **Open** *Sept-June* 10am-6.30pm Mon-Fri. *July* by appointment only. Closed Aug. **No credit cards. Map** p327 F13.
Since 1995, this gallery has exhibited homegrown and foreign talents, including British sculptor Anthony Gormley, Italian Mimmo Paladino, Israeli Nuri David, and American painter Christian Breed.

Studio Trisorio
Riviera di Chiaia 215 (081 414306/www. studiotrisorio.com). Metro Piazza Amedeo/ bus R3. **Open** 10.15am-1.30pm, 4-7.30pm Mon-Fri; 10.15am-1.30pm Sat. Closed Aug. **No credit cards. Map** p327 G14.
Inaugurated by Pasquale Trisorio in 1974 with a show of Dan Flavin's work, this well-established gallery is now run by Trisorio's daughter Laura, who shows international stars such as Daniel Buren, Rebecca Horn, Martin Parr and Enzo Cucchi.

Umberto di Marino Arte Contemporanea
Via Alabardieri 1 (081 060 9318/www.umberto dimarino.com). Metro Piazza Amedeo. **Open** *June-Sept* 4-8pm Mon-Fri. *Oct-May* 3-8pm Mon-Sat. **No credit cards. Map** p327 H13.
Recently relocated from the suburb of Giugliano to give its stable of young artists more exposure, this reputable gallery shows emerging conceptual practitioners such as Vedovamazzei and Mark Hosking, as well as painter Alberto di Fabio.

Alfonso Artiaco.

ARTS & ENTERTAINMENT

Gay & Lesbian

A small but firmly-established scene.

There is a long tradition regarding transvestites and transsexuals in Naples; the former have been an integral part of traditional Neopolitan theatre culture since the 17th century. Nonetheless, the gay and lesbian scene here remains pretty much a non-starter.

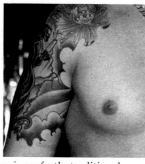

It's not that the ultra-Catholic Neapolitans are particularly homophobic; somehow, though, there seems to be little momentum to give rise to a decent bar and clubbing scene. Although locals are generally tolerant, adopting a live-and-let-live attitude, it still isn't a good idea to walk around hand in hand. Having said that, strolling arm in arm is perfectly traditional for all Southern Italians, male or female.

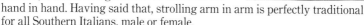

BARS & CLUBS

There are very few exclusively gay or lesbian establishments in the city; instead, most places are straight venues that function as gay meeting places or run gay nights one evening a week. There's usually no cover charge, but you're expected to have at least one drink. Your *consumazione* is marked on a slip of paper you receive at the entrance, and you pay on leaving. Gay men and lesbians mix in many of the same places.

Antica Birreria
Viale Kennedy 18, Fuorigrotta (337 865 856/ www.edenlandia.it). Metro Campi Flegrei/bus C14. **Open** 9pm-3am Thur. **Admission** €10. **No credit cards**.
This disco bar and pub, popular with gays and straights, has an American 'country' flavour, but the music is pure retro pop. Pints of beer are served at wooden tables, and there's a terrace in summer.

Depot
Via della Veterinaria 72, La Sanità (081 780 9578/www.depotnapoli.com). Metro Piazza Cavour or Museo/bus 14, 15, 47, CS, C51. **Open** 10pm-3am Tue-Thur; 10pm-5am Fri, Sat; 9pm-3am Sun. **Admission** €10. **Credit** AmEx, MC, V.
This is the kind of gay club you'd expect to find in any major European city, with a darkroom, labyrinth, cubicles, sling, gloryholes, naked parties with masks and more. There's plenty of information on the website.

★ Fiorillo
Via Santa Maria di Costantinopoli 99, Centro Storico (081 459 905). Metro Dante/bus 24, R1, R4. **Open** 6am-2am daily. **No credit cards**. **Map** p328 L8.
Fiorello is the fashionable meeting place du jour, facing the equally gay-friendly and very pretty Piazza Bellini. The gathering of the clan begins after dinner, when the pavement tables and chairs soon get packed out.

Intramoenia Caffè Letterario
For listings, *see p133*.
A straight meeting place for Naples' intellectuals, the Intramoenia – and Piazza Bellini in general – becomes a catwalk on summer evenings for self-confident gays to compare their tans and show off their designer togs.

Events & one-nighters

★ Free Lovers
Various venues (328 307 1105/328 944 6753/www.freelovers.it). **Admission** €10. **No credit cards**.
Currently the main source in town for what's going on in an organised way, Free Lovers usually stages events on a Thursday or a Saturday night.

i Ken
Via Toledo 210, Centro Storico (081 564 3108/392 388 7147/www.i-ken.org). Metro Montesanto, bus R2. **Admission** varies. **Map** p332 K12.

A fresh newcomer full of great ideas, such as a Gay Pride celebration in Piazza Bellini; admission is generally free. Check out the site for their latest efforts.

Macho Lato
Via Abate Minichini, 62, Corso Malta (081 780 3062/320 199 4834/www.macholato.it). Bus 548. **Open** *May-July* 10pm-2am Fri, Sun; 11pm-5am Sat. *Sept-Apr* 10pm-2am Thur, Fri, Sun; 11pm-5am Sat. **Admission** €10. **No credit cards**.
This group organises regular events for muscle-bound, leather-loving bears and the men who appreciate them, from Thursday to Sunday nights.

Velenika
Various venues (349 674 8557/www.velenika.it). **Admission** varies. **No credit cards**.
Velenika organises gay and lesbian parties in different locations across town.

BOOKSHOPS

Colonnese
Via San Pietro a Maiella 32-33, Centro Storico (081 459858/www.colonnese.it). Metro Dante, bus R1. **Open** 9am-1.30pm, 4-7.30pm Mon-Fri; 9am-1.30pm Sat. Closed 2wks Aug. **Credit** AmEx, MC, V. **Map** p328 L8.
This wood-panelled bookshop is full of treasures. Here you might uncover antiquarian books, modern editions (new and used), prints, postcards, books on Naples and Campania, and gay and erotic literature – along with tomes on witchcraft, featuring potions for impotence, love and jealousy.

Eva Luna
Piazza Bellini 72, Centro Storico (081 292372/ www.evaluna.it). Metro Dante/bus 24, R1, R4. **Open** 5.30pm-midnight Mon-Sat. Closed Aug. **Credit** AmEx, DC, MC, V. **Map** p328 L8.
An appealing little bookshop set in the Centro Storico, Eva Luna carries all manner of women's literature, along with an extensive choice of prints and postcards. The shop also hosts regular talks, music and poetry events; check the website to find out what's coming up.

Libreria Feltrinelli
Piazza dei Martiri, Via Santa Caterina a Chiaia 23, Chiaia (081 240 5411). Bus C25, C28. **Open** 10am-9pm Mon-Fri; 10am-11pm Sat; 10am-2pm, 4-10pm Sun. **Credit** AmEx, MC, V. **Map** p327 H13.
This cool bookshop, music store and café *(see p141)* stocks a limited selection of gay and lesbian publications in English. It's also a choice site for discretely eyeing up talent.

CINEMAS

No, these are not art-house cinemas with erudite gay programming. Venues such as **Argo** (Via Alessandro Poerio 4, Centro Storico, 081 554 4764), **Agorà** (Via Guantai Nuovi 6, Royal Naples, 081 552 4893) and **Casanova** (Corso Garibaldi 330, Port & University, 081 200441) show heterosexual porn flicks, but also attract gay men. Few tend to see much of the film, though.

Be careful in the vicinity of the railway station by the Casanova and Argo, as it can be quite unsavoury.

CRUISING

Centro Direzionale
Map off p329 R6.
After midnight and only by car. Very dangerous.

Ippodromo di Agnano
After midnight, only by car. Fairly safe.

Via Brin
Map off p329 R9.
After midnight – and again, only by car. Dangerous.

GAY ASSOCIATIONS

Arcigay-Circolo Antinoo
Vico San Geronimo alle Monache 17-20, Mezzocannone (081 552 8815/www.arcigay napoli.org). Bus C25, R1. **Open** 5-11pm Fri; 6.30-9.30pm Sun. Closed Aug. **Map** p328 M9.
Based in Bologna, the Arcigay organisation (www.gay.it) is Italy's most serious and highly regarded gay lobbying group. Its Naples offshoot organises films and events such as poetry readings, often in collaboration with other cultural associations in the city. Induction sessions are held for new members on a Friday. These premises house a small bar; up-to-the-minute information on bars, clubs and events is provided.

Arcilesbica-Circolo Le Maree
Vico Giuseppe dai Nudi 80, Centro Storico (081 549 6956/www.arcilesbica.it/napoli). Metro Dante or Piazza Cavour/bus R2, R4. **Open** 5.30-9pm Sat. Closed Aug. **Map** p328 K7.
An information point for lesbian events, bars and clubs in Naples and the surrounding area. There's also a gay and lesbian library, a magazine collection, and a small bar.

INSIDE TRACK
THE PINK PRESS

The **Naples Gay Press** website (www. napoligaypress.it) provides up-to-date information on the Greater Naples gay and lesbian scene, including cruising, clubs and special events.

ARTS & ENTERTAINMENT

Music & Nightlife

Take to the streets, then follow the beat.

The nightlife scene in Naples varies considerably, depending on where you choose to pass your *serata*. From the alternative, student-frequented bars and squares of the Centro Storico to the trendy *locali* of well-heeled Chiaia, there's something to suit everyone's style. Things tend to start a little later in Naples, with places filling up around the midnight hour.

Much of the action takes place in the open squares and alleys, with large groups gathering in the Centro Storico's Piazza Santa Maria la Nova, Piazza Bellini and Via Cisterna dell'Olio to enjoy a beer and a cigarette: although Italy's ban on smoking in public areas took effect in 2005, it's still widely flouted.

NIGHTLIFE, NAPLES-STYLE

Don't be surprised when what feels like the entire population of Naples takes to its cars in the suburbs of **Chiaia** (*see p83*) and **Mergellina** (*see p85*) for a few hours of horn-blowing, scooter-dodging (an essential skill in Naples) and furious gesticulating. This transit chaos is usually followed by a half-hour gelato break, drink or *passeggiata* (stroll), then it's back into the cars. The trendier clubs are to be found here, too, with the narrow streets transformed into crowded catwalks where the youth of Naples flirt and strut.

Most of the city's discos and clubs charge an entrance fee, which may or may not include one drink. In some places you'll be given a card that is stamped for every drink you purchase, and requires you to spend a certain amount on drinks before leaving the venue. Hold on tight to these cards; you'll be charged a fee should you lose them.

Some bars also have small dance floors where you're welcome to get up and shake your stuff should you feel like it. Sometimes, a membership card (*tessera*) is required for admission; there may be a small fee for the card, but once you carry one, entry is generally free on subsequent visits.

About the author

Amy Elford has worked as a translator in Naples since 2004, and also writes about the city's entertainment scene for the expat community

If techno and trance are your thing, you'll have to trek out to Ischitella, about half an hour north of the city, for events organized by the **Angels of Love** crew (www.angelsoflove.it) that take place in huge discos. Be warned: you'll never get there and back without a car.

Unless otherwise stated, admission to the venues listed in this chapter is free.

SOUNDS OF THE CITY

For such a vibrant city with a famously rich musical heritage, Naples' contemporary music scene is oddly dispirited. *Il canzone napoletano*, with songs such as 'Turna a Surriento', 'Funiculi, Funiculà' and 'O Surdato Annamurato' still defines Italian music for some people, but the sentimental traditional songs have had little positive influence on today's music scene.

It's surprisingly difficult to find a good live music venue in Naples, although some bars in

INSIDE TRACK
A FINGER ON THE PULSE

The website www.arealive.it lists up-and-coming gigs in and around the city, but the best source of information is the pocket-sized, monthly guide *Zero*. It's free, and you can pick up a copy in most bars and record shops

Profile Alex Colle

How DJ and producer Alex Colle took the city by storm.

Alex Colle, one of Naples' most popular DJs, has had Neapolitans shaking their stuff to some of the best music around for over ten years. He started out manning the decks at small parties for friends, but soon made a name for himself and graduated to large-scale events and clubs. In 2000, Colle gained an even wider audience when he became a DJ on Radio Ibiza, Southern Italy's most popular radio station. Despite being a fixture on the international circuit, appearing at clubs from San Francisco to Ibiza, his heart has remained in Naples, where, he says, the audiences are 'just unparalleled'.

Born in Naples, Colle learnt the basics by watching a friend at work on the turntables. 'I was passionate about observing him – watching every move he made, and learning all of his techniques.' Soon afterwards, he bought his own equipment, and began creating his own sound and style.

Colle's enthusiasm and passion for music is infectious. His musical creations are difficult to categorise, but are probably best described as deep minimal and tech house. It's the kind of music that can pack a dance floor in minutes,

and persuade even the most reluctant of dancers to get on their feet; for a taster, visit www.myspace.com/alexcolle.

In 2008 Alex joined forces with one of his close friends, vocalist Christian Key; the results of their collaboration can be found on MySpace under the stage names Future Phunk and Colle 'N' Key. As Future Phunk, the two scored a hit with *Let Me See You Move It* in 2008; more recently, they've found success as Colle 'N' Key with tracks like *Into the Night* and *Feel the Music*.

ARTS & ENTERTAINMENT

HIT THE DANCE FLOOR

Arenile (*see p176*). Dance on the sand, under the stars.

Mouse Club (*see p174*). Keep late hours with the city's student crowd.

Velvet Zone (*see p174*). An eclectic playlist keeps the dance floor buzzing.

the Centro Storico may squeeze a band or singer into a corner. In the summer months, though, the scene comes alive, with piazze and parks hosting local and international musical acts. Events tend to take place outside the city confines, requiring a taxi ride; keep an eye on posters in the Centro Storico and listings in local newspapers.

Just outside the city, **Duel Beat** (Via Antiniana 2A, 329 864 8804, www.duelbeat. com), is a cinema turned 'multiclub' with a rich line-up of bands and DJs, an exhibition area and a restaurant.

Any big names who make it this far south will probably end up in the **Palapartenope** (Via Barbagallo 115, Fuorigrotta, 081 570 0008, www.palapartenope.it); it has a cheap bar, but is utterly devoid of atmosphere. The outdoor **Arena Flegrea** (*see p96*) tends to be a better bet. Built by Mussolini and restored in 2001, it now hosts summer concerts on its pleasant

marble terraces. Performers have included Bob Dylan, Massive Attack, Iggy Pop, Santana, REM and Nick Cave, and the **Neapolis Festival** (*see p156*) is held here every July.

For smaller and local groups, check out the nightly club scene: **Velvet Zone** (*see p174*) and **Rising South** (*see p174*) for rock and dance; **Bourbon Street** (*see p175*) and **Around Midnight** (*see p177*) for jazz.

FESTIVALS & EVENTS

As well as the **Neapolis Festival** (*see p156*), keep an eye on the programme for the **Parco dei Quartieri Spagnoli** on Corso Vittorio Emanuele, which hosts various events from July through to September.

Other festivals to look out for include the **Ethnos Festival** (081 882 3978, www.festival ethnos.it), with its great line-up of world music acts, and the **Sguardo di Ulisse** (www.sig

Wailing in Old Napule

International influences and home-grown talents.

From whirling *tarantella* to avant-garde jazz, world music and modern folk, Naples has something for everyone. Being a port city, it has always been open to outside influences, with sailors bringing songs and music from Africa and the Middle East; other musical traditions, notably the *canzone napoletana*, were born here.

CANZONE NAPOLETANA

The origins of the *canzone napoletana* (Neapolitan song) can be traced back to 7 September 1837, the date of the first official **Piedigrotta Festival** and its signature tune 'Te Voglio Bene Assaje'. Performances at the festival were in the form of *audizioni*, where the audience chose the winning piece; music publishers would be inundated with new compositions from aspiring and established poets and musicians, and sheet music of the featured songs sold prodigiously.

The festival lost its relevance with the invention of radio and the jukebox, finally fizzling out in the 1970s – but not before producing 'Funiculì, Funiculà' (winner of the 1880 festival; *see p80*) and ''O Sole Mio' (second place in 1896), and making Naples the capital of Italian music. After a lengthly hiatus, the festival made a triumphant comeback in 2007 (*see p156* **Music and movement**).

Many credit poet Salvatore di Giacomo with inventing *canzone napoletana* as a genre. He hit upon the idea of fusing classical arias, chamber music and the voices of celebrated tenors with popular, working-class *tarantella* music and clipped dialect to create a distinctively Neapolitan sound.

This was the beginning of the end for the street musicians, or *posteggiatori*, who had played their mandolins and performed in cafés and *trattorie* throughout the city for at least six centuries. Tenor Enrico Caruso started out as a humble street musician in 1891, aged 17, before finding international success as an opera singer.

THE FOLK REVIVAL

The 1970s brought a revival of interest in more traditional folk music, with musicians exploring the traditional *tarantella* and *tammurriata* (*see p182* **Dance 'til you drop**). **Nuova Compagnia di Canto Popolare** (www.nccp.it) was one of the most successful and prolific groups to emerge, scoring its biggest hit in 1977 with 'Tammurriata Nera', a reworking of a 1944 tune about a girl's encounter with a US officer. Over 30 years later, the group still plays together; founder member Eugenio Bennato produced the very successful *Taranta Power* album and tour in 2001.

bloom.it), which organises double bills of a film and a band). The venues for both festivals change from year to year, but are generally in the city centre.

From July to September, the city holds a number of music and film events as part of the **Mezzonotte nei Parchi** festival (www.comune.napoli.it). Another biggie is the **Cornetto** (www.cornettoalgida.com), which is held in Piazza Plebiscito in June or July and has seen performances by the likes of Sting and Santana.

Jazz festivals take place in the **Parco Urbano Virgiliano** (*see p86*) on Posillipo Hill, at the **Mostra d'Oltremare** (*see p96*), and in the nearby towns of **Pomigliano d'Arco** (081 803 2810, www.pomiglianojazz.com) and **Nocera Inferiore** (www.jazzinparco.it).

The **Notte Bianca** (www.nottebiancanapoli.com), or 'white night', is an all-night festival of music, shows and performances in every

available space in the city, held in autumn. Streets and squares are packed with revelers, and mobility between events is nearly impossible (the 2006 event attracted two million people). Although it's great fun for punters, city officials invariably grumble about the cost; for a start, the clean-up operation afterwards doesn't come cheap. Check ahead if you're planning to go, in case the event is cancelled.

CENTRO STORICO
DJ bars & clubs

Kinky Jam Bar
Via Cisterna dell'Olio 21 (335 547 7299/www.kinkyjam.com). Metro Dante/bus 24, R1, R4. **Open** 9pm-3am Tue-Sun. Closed mid June-mid Sept. **No credit cards. Map** p328 K9.
From its name, you might be expecting a rather different sort of entertainment, but this little place is

The vibrant '70s scene also produced **Napoli Centrale**, led by saxophonist James Senese (son of a North Carolina military officer), who created a fusion of jazz, soul and roots. Edoardo Bennato (Eugenio's brother) became Naples' resident singer-songwriter, experimenting with American rock and his own city's traditions. One of Italy's biggest names, Pino Daniele, also began writing and recording at this time – his 1977 album *Terra Mia* was an instant success, and his rhythm and blues defined the city musically for over two decades. His signature tune, which expresses his disillusionment with the city government, is 'Napule è' (*Napul'è tutt nu suonn e a sap tut'o munn, ma nun sann a verità*: Naples is a dream and everyone knows it, but nobody knows the truth).

MIXING IT UP
Over the last few decades, the scene in Naples has been all about musical fusion. Formed in 1987, **Almamegretta** mixes dub, reggae, world music and techno, Neapolitan-style. The group's 1995 album *Sanacore* won widespead acclaim, and its fans include Massive Attack; its star has waned, though, since charismatic vocalist Raiz left to pursue solo projects in 2003. Raiz now regularly guests on other projects; he and former Police drummer Stuart Copeland have

recorded and regularly tour **La Notte della Taranta**, a celebration of the traditional *tarantella*.

Whether it's dance with **Planet Funk** or reggae-influenced **Jovine**; gangland rap from **Co'Sang**; songs about the Camorra and the harshness of growing up in Naples from local band **A67**; saxophonist **Daniele Sepe** and his eclectic mix of styles, from *tarantella* to avant-garde jazz; world music virtuoso **Enzo Avitabile** and chill-out violinist **Lino Cannavaciuolo**; or modern folk musicians **E Zezi** and international offshoot **Spaccanapoli** – Neapolitan influences are alive and well.

On a more local scale, from *quartiere* to *quartiere*, the *neo-melodici* are a strange phenomenon: dodgy-looking singers belting their hearts and lungs out in Neapolitan dialect accompanied by cheesy electronic keyboards and pumped-up bass. The resulting sound is part Arabic pop, part cut-price Tom Jones. Stars appear and disappear with amazing alacrity (though **Gigi d'Alessio** and **Nino d'Angelo** are leaders of the genre), and sing about the reality of life in the poorer parts of the city. Arguments abound as to whether the *neo-melodici* are contemporary bearers of an old musical tradition, cheesy rip-off artists, or an authentic sub-cultural expression of life in the Neapolitan ghetto; have a listen and decide for yourself.

actually a reggae bar. Neapolitans like their rock-steady and dub, and this is the best place in town in which to hear it. A DJ-bartender spins the tunes, and it stays open until the early hours. In summer, the crowd takes over the alleyway outside, much to the disdain of the few drivers crazy enough to attempt to pass.

Mouse Club
Via San Giovanni Maggiore Pignatelli 45 (349 674 8557). Metro Dante/bus 24, R1, R4. **Open** 9pm-4am daily. Closed June-Aug. **No credit cards. Map** p328 L9.
Mouse Club plays great dance music, keeping the small dance floor packed all night long. It's popular with local students, and has a fun, casual feel. Regardless of what time you leave, the music will be pumping, people will be dancing, and drinks will be poured until the early hours.

★ Rising South
Via San Sebastiano 19 (335 879 0428/www. risingrepublic.com). Metro Dante/bus 24, E1, R1, R4. **Open** *Oct-Apr* 10pm-2amTue-Sun. **No credit cards. Map** p328 L9/10.
This is one of the best-designed clubs in the city – a long, tunnel-like space with stone walls, dotted with comfy sofas and armchairs. Music sticks to a down-beat/nu-jazz/lounge vibe. Midweek, this tends to be a student haunt; at the weekend, you'll find one of the most diverse crowds in the city here. Note that in summer, the club moves to Pozzuoli (Via Napoli 35); check online or call for details.

Superfly
Via Cisterna dell'Olio 12 (347 127 2178/ www.superflynapoli.it). Metro Dante/bus 24, R1, R4. **Open** 7pm-3am Mon, Wed-Sun. Closed mid June-mid Sept. **No credit cards. Map** p328 K9.
This diminutive bar barely has room for the two bar-tenders and the DJ, never mind customers. It can get jam-packed within minutes; undeterred, the good-natured crowd spills out into the street. With trance music in the background, it's a great place to go to with friends for a chat and a good cocktail. Don't hesitate to ask for your favourite drink; staff are more than happy to mix up bespoke requests.

INSIDE TRACK LIGHTING UP

Although Italy's ban on smoking went into effect nationwide in 2005, it hasn't been observed – not in anarchic Naples, at least. Most smokers blithely ignore 'no smoking' signs, and when it comes to lighting up, the locals' rule of thumb is simply to smoke wherever they see other people smoking.

Velvet Zone
Via Cisterna dell'Olio 11 (339 670 0234/ 328 957 7115/www.velvetzone.it). Metro Dante/bus 24, E1, R1, R4. **Open** 11pm-2am Wed, Thur, Sun; 11pm-3am Fri, Sat. Closed mid May-Sept. **Admission** €5-€10. **No credit cards. Map** p328 K9.
Known to one and all as Velvet, this warren-like space is dark, claustrophobic and atmospheric. It's also your best bet for a night of dancing in the Centro Storico. DJs spin eclectic sounds (from minimal techno to '80s revival to downbeat to rock) every night; occasion-ally there's live music (usually local or Italian dance-oriented groups). Sit in one of the smaller rooms and chat, or get sweaty on the crowded dance floor. The *tessera* (membership card) is sometimes waived for out-of-town visitors, but you'll be expected to have a few *consumazioni* (drinks).

PORT & UNIVERSITY
DJ bars & clubs

Aret' a' Palm
Piazza Santa Maria la Nova 14 (339 848 6949). Metro Montesanto/bus R1, R3. **Open** 6pm-2.30am daily. **No credit cards. Map** p328 L10.
In Neapolitan, Aret' a' Palm means 'behind the palm', and sure enough, this small but stylish bar is located near an incredibly tall palm tree on a quiet square in the centre of town. The only live music is when the staff feel inspired to strum on a guitar; oth-erwise, DJs spin a soundtrack of jazz and world music so loud that it's audible even if you sit at one of the tables out in the piazza.

Live music

★ Kestè
Largo San Giovanni Maggiore 26-27 (081 551 3984/www.keste.it). Bus CS, R2. **Open** 10pm-2am Mon-Thur; 10pm-3am Fri-Sun. Closed Aug. **No credit cards. Map** p328 L9.
Situated opposite the Oriental university, Kestè is a bar, café, live music venue and restaurant all rolled into one. The attractive interior is on the small side, and tables tend to spill out on to the square. This is an enjoyable place for a lunchtime drink, or an evening *aperitivo* before going on to eat elsewhere. On Friday and Saturday evenings, however, it's worth hanging around later into the night for live music.

★ Mamamu
Via Sedile di Porto 46 (320 669 5222). Metro Dante/bus R2. **Open** 9.30pm-4am Wed-Sun. Closed June-Sept. **No credit cards. Map** 328 M10.
Tiny, and usually packed to beyond the rafters, Mamamu has been a live music venue for over ten years. Bands are usually local, and can be heard

from an upstairs seating area if the space in front of the stage becomes too congested – this place is exceedingly popular with the local student population. Admission is free, and Sundays are devoted to film screenings.

VIA TOLEDO
Live music

Bourbon Street
*Via Vincenzo Bellini 52/53 (338 825 3756/
338 590 1403/www.bourbonstreetjazzclub.com).*
Metro Dante/bus 24, R1, R4. **Open** 9pm-3am Tue-Sun. Closed May-mid Sept. **No credit cards. Map** p328 K8.
Bourbon Street is a large, centrally located space that's dedicated to jazz, with shows every night except Monday. It usually gets quite crowded and attracts a cheery mix of bright young things and slightly older jazz buffs. There's a decent range of beers to complement the varied bunch of bands that take to the stage.

Galleria Toledo
For listings, *see p179.*

Mamamu.

ARTS & ENTERTAINMENT

A shore thing

It's never too late to hit the beach.

For Neapolitan clubbers, summer means the sound of the surf mixed with top quality DJs in one of the many nightclubs along the coast. Inspired by the success of similar ventures in Ibiza, many a lido has realised that the big business starts after the sun goes down.

Although Naples may not rival the Isla Blanca for the quality of its beaches, it can match it for the sheer length of its coastline. Clubs such as **Music on the Rocks** (*see p269*) in Positano have been capitalising on their spectacular locations for years, and canny Neapolitan venues are keen to follow suit.

The best example of the evolution from the city streets to the beach is **Arenile** (Via Coroglio 14B, Bagnoli, 338 881 7715, www.arenilereload.com, open June-Sept 10pm-4am daily, Oct-May 10pm-4am Fri, Sat), the closest beach club to the city centre. Once a fairly scummy beach in the shadow of the decommissioned steelworks at Bagnoli, Arenile was cleaned up as part of a neighbourhood renovation. It experienced

modest success as a beach, until the owners realised that most people were turning up in the evenings to hang around the bar and catch the great sunsets. These days it draws the crowds with live music (BB King and Suzanne Vega have played here, although the focus is generally indie and dance), followed by a disco on the sand.

Vibes on the Beach (Via Miseno 52, Capo Miseno, 081 523 2828, open June-Sept 9am-2am daily, Oct-May 9am-2am Fri, Sat) was originally an offshoot of the city centre Vibes bar. The management soon decided they were having more fun on the beach, and moved there permanently. Attracting a slightly older crowd than Arenile, Vibes on the Beach is more about chilling than raving. The bartenders mix superb frozen cocktails, accompanied by a downbeat/ nu-jazz soundtrack.

The nearby **Lido Turistico** (Via Lido Miliscola 21, Bacoli, 081 523 5228, www.lidoturistico.com, open May-Sept 8am-1.30am Mon-Wed, 8am-4am Thur-Sun)

Nabilah.

This hip theatre (*see p179*) screens films and, during the cooler months, hosts an eclectic programme of alternative Italian and international bands, in collaboration with local promoters Wake Up and Dream (www.wakeupandream.net).

VOMERO
DJ bars & clubs

B Side
Via Aniello Falcone 275 (333 596 8162). Bus C28. **Open** 8pm-4am Tue-Sun. Closed Aug. **Credit** AmEx, DC, MC, V. **Map** p326 D11.
One of the many bars on this strip, B Side has fine views over the city. The outside seating area is ideal for enjoying an evening *aperitivo*, or dinner. Thursday evenings are dedicated to experimental techno and electronica music. If you're not up for grooving on the small dance floor, ask the friendly barman for the backgammon set and while away the evening with a delicious cocktail or two.

Fonoteca
Via Rafaele Morghen 31 (081 556 0338/www. fonoteca.net). Metro Vanvitelli/funicular Centrale to Piazza Fuga. **Open** 10am-1am Mon-Wed; 10am-2am Thur-Sat; 6.30pm-1am Sun. Closed 2wks Aug. **Credit** AmEx, DC, MC, V. **Map** p331 F10.
Fonoteca made its name as the best record shop in Naples; it now includes a bar/café, and stays open until late. Browse through the large collection of new and used CDs, then grab a beer or a cocktail in the trendy bar area. Often heaving with the Vomero cognoscenti, this is an essential stop for music fans.

Live music

Around Midnight
Via Bonito 32A (333 700 5230/www. aroundmidnight.it). Metro Vanvitelli/funicular Montesanto to San Martino/bus V1. **Open** 10pm-2am Wed-Sun. Closed July, Aug. **No credit cards**. **Map** p331 F9.
Local jazz musicians, along with combos from across Italy, play the standards here on most nights. The premises are small, and can become uncomfortably crowded, but the atmosphere is unpretentious and friendly.

CHIAIA TO POSILLIPO
DJ bars & clubs

Bluestone
Via Alabardieri 10 (081 423 8455/339 830 8523/www.bluestonenapoli.it). Metro Piazza Amedeo/bus C25, R3. **Open** Sept-July 7pm-3am Tue-Sun. Closed Aug. **Admission** €10 Thur; other nights vary. **Credit** AmEx, MC, V. **Map** p327 H13.

feels more like a glorified beach bar, where the sea comes almost right up to the row of tables and chairs.

Upping the style ante, **Nabilah** (Via Spiaggia Romana 15, Fusaro, 081 868 9433, www.nabilah.it, open May-Sept 9pm-3am Fri-Sun) is the summer version of **S'Move** (*see p178*). Inviting sofas are arranged around low, white tables with designer candles, surrounding the DJ console. Sitting on a sofa with a chilled drink in your hand and your bare feet on the sand is a wonderfully decadent experience, and worth the steep bar prices.

Alternatively, enjoy an *aperitivo* under the white canopied gazebos at the **Sohal Beach Club** (Via Spiaggia Romana, Fusaro, 081 868 9355, 338 102 0968, www.sohal.it, open June-Sept, times vary), a little further along the beach, before dancing the night away.

A tip for all beach locations: remember that high heels may get buried in the sand. If you're feeling daring, bring your swimming togs and go for a dip later – though be sure to stay in the shallows if you've had a few too many drinks.

The major drawback of the beach scene is its relative inaccessibility. That said, Bagnoli is accessible by metro, and the clubs in Fusaro are within walking distance of Torre Gaveta at the end of the Cumana railway line. As for getting home… well, be prepared to stay late!

ARTS & ENTERTAINMENT

INSIDE TRACK
THE ART OF APERITIVO

If you find yourself slowing down in the early evening, recharge as the locals do with an *aperitivo* – a glass of prosecco, perhaps, or a Campari soda. Accompanying snacks range from bar staples such as peanuts and olives to mini pizza platters, small sandwiches and, in more generous establishments, even pasta and rice dishes. If you're on a budget, you can definitely make a meal of an *aperitivo* – just don't be shy about helping yourself.

The latest place to see and be seen, Bluestone offers live music in a cool atmosphere. It's worth arriving early if you plan to sit at one of the tables in front of the stage; they soon fill up. If you want to make a night of it, go for dinner there too.

Enoteca Belledonne
Vico Belledonne a Chiaia 18 (081 403162/www. enotecabelledonne.com). Metro Piazza Amedeo/ bus C25, R3. **Open** *10am-2pm, 5pm-1am Mon-Sat. 7pm-midnight Sun. Closed 2wks Aug.* **Credit** DC, V. **Map** p327 G13.
Granted, it's not a DJ bar, but this upmarket bar is a local institution, and an essential port of call if you're in the area. Wriggle through to the back room to find a seat, or stand at the bar with Chiaia's lawyers and moneymakers, enjoying an after-work aperitivo. Despite its clientele, this old-style *enoteca*

is wonderfully relaxed, and has excellent, reasonably priced wines by the glass. It's packed between 7pm and 9pm.

★ S'move
Vico dei Sospiri 10A (081 764 5813/www. smove-lab.net). Metro Piazza Amedeo/bus C25, R3. **Open** *7pm-2am daily. Closed Aug.* **Credit** MC, V. **Map** p327 H13.
The smartest venue in this part of town, S'move boasts upmarket decor and a lively vibe. The area's beautiful people make up most of the clientele, but it's refreshingly welcoming. There's no dance floor per se, but the music, ranging from Latin to house and techno, encourages even the glacially cool to shake a limb or two.
► *S'move's management also manages the Nabilah beach venue in summer; see p177.*

OTHER AREAS

CSOA Officina 99
Via Gianturco 101 (081 734 0853/www.officina 99.org). Metro Gianturco/bus 81, CS. **Open** *Oct-June 8.30pm-3am Tue, Fri, Sat. Closed July-Sept.* **Admission** varies. **No credit cards**.
Naples' most famous *centro sociale* (a semi-legally occupied space), the Officina is located in an abandoned factory in the mean streets south-east of Stazione Centrale. It hasn't spruced itself up like its sibling set-ups the Brancaleone in Rome or the Leonkavallo in Milan, and remains cold, cavernous and edgy. But there's fun to be had here for anyone who's ever gone in for unusual piercings or walked around with a dog on a bit of a string. Payment is voluntary; around €3 for live music is typical.

Bluestone *See p177.*

Performing Arts

A rich cultural scene that's rooted in tradition.

The origins of Neapolitan theatrical tradition lie deep in the city's Greco-Roman past. The famous *commedia dell'arte* evolved from ancient farces, especially the quintessential Neapolitan figure of Pulcinella. Combined with French influences, that tradition gave birth to what has become recognised as mainstream Neapolitan theatre.

Music and dance, although in some ways enjoying equally ancient local roots, have evolved along their own uniquely Neapolitan lines; the whirling tarantella, say, or the more widespead, joyful *tammuriata*.

Then there is, of course, the opera. A vision of gilded opulence, the stately San Carlo remains one of Italy's finest opera houses.

THEATRE

Neapolitan theatre is, for many, synonymous with playwright Eduardo de Filippo (1900-1984), whose most famous works include *Questi fantasmi* (*These Ghosts*) – brought to the New York stage as *Souls of Naples* in 2005 by actor and director John Turturro. Other key 20th-century Neapolitan playwrights include Viviani, Santanelli, Ruccello and Moscato – the latter three influenced by Pinter and Genet, though not forgetting their ancient roots.

More recent experimental works have been penned by Neiwiller, Martone, Servillo and Salemme – and in 2008, the city launched the **Napoli Teatro Festival Italia** (*see p184*). Yet despite its many rich offerings, the theatre scene in Naples remains an essentially closed world, unless visitors can manage fluent Italian – and in many cases, Neapolitan dialect.

For traditional Neapolitan theatre, see also the **Teatro Trianon Viviani** (*see p184*).

Galleria Toledo

Via Concezione a Montecalvario 34, Toledo (081 425037/081 425834/www.galleriatoledo.org). Metro Montesanto/bus E2. **Open** *Box office Sept-May 10.30am-1.30pm, 5.30-7pm Mon-Sat. Performances Oct-May 9pm Mon-Sat; 6pm Sun.* **Tickets** €14-€45. **No credit cards**. **Map** p328 K10.

The focus at this small, modern theatre is on new experimental theatre, in Italian. There's also a good cinema programme.

Mercadante

Piazza Municipio 1, Royal (081 551 3396/www.teatrostabilenapoli.it). Bus 24, C22, C25, C57, R2. **Open** *Box office 10.30am-1pm, 5.30-7.30pm Mon-Sat. Performances 9pm Mon-Wed, Fri, Sat; 5.30pm Thur; 6pm Sun. Closed Aug.* **Tickets** €11.50-€30. **Credit** AmEx, DC. **Map** p332 K11.

Dating from 1779 and recently given a major facelift, this beautiful theatre is divided into two performance spaces. It's known for its high-profile productions: actors and directors who have worked here include Mario Martone, Luca Ronconi and Roberto de Simone, as well as Peter Brook and John Turturro.

Teatro Nuovo

Via Montecalvario 16, Toledo (081 497 6267/ 081 425958/www.nuovoteatronuovo.it). Metro Montesanto/bus E2. **Open** *Box office 5.30-9pm Tue, Wed; 11am-12.30pm, 6-9pm Thur-Sat; 4.30pm until performance. Performances mid Oct-May 9pm Tue-Sat; 6pm Sun.* **Tickets** €14-€18. **Credit** AmEx, MC, V. **Map** p328 K10.

INSIDE TRACK TOUGH CROWD

Warm in their appreciation when a performance merits it, audiences at **San Carlo** can be devastatingly cool when it doesn't. However big a name you are, you risk being whistled (the Italian equivalent of booing) off the stage if you don't come up with the goods.

Profile Teatro San Carlo

The city's indomitable opera house.

The opera scene in Naples is all about the magnificent Royal Theatre of San Carlo (*see right*) – designed in 1737 by Giovanni Maria Medrano, at the behest of King Carlos I de Bourbon. Celebrated composers such as Rossini, Donizetti and Bellini have all served as its director, and many of the world's greatest operas have seen their debuts here – among them *La Donna del Lago*, *Lucia di Lammermoor* and *Luisa Miller*.

It's the oldest active opera house in Europe, and performances have never been suspended save between May 1874 and December 1876, due to the economic crisis following the Unification of Italy. Not even the devastating fire of 1816 – after which the present-day structure was completed in just ten months – or the tragic events of World War II succeeded in closing the theatre down.

Dedicated to the sainted namesake of the king who commissioned it, San Carlo is a place of pilgrimage for opera devotees. Behind its austere façade, the regal grandeur of its design, lighting and decoration

have enchanted visitors for centuries. The French writer Stendhal reports having had his eyes dazzled and soul ravished at the sight of this 'sultan's palace', and famous Grand Tourist Samuel Sharp found it 'as remarkable an object as any man sees in his travels'.

Inside, it seems as if anything that couldn't be lined in velvet has been gilded. But there was a method to the madness: the soft fabric enhances the superb acoustics, and it's said that the sound of a piece of paper being crumpled on the stage can easily be heard up in the very last row of the gods.

Other luxurious touches include mirrors in every box, oriented in such a way so that occupants could see the Royal Box without craning their necks – which would have been considered very bad form. By way of a glance in the mirror, no one would upstage the royals, who, of course, had always to begin the applause. The Royal Box itself is constructed entirely from humble papier-mâché, the material of marionettes – and its extreme fragility has given restorers here headaches for centuries.

WHAT TO WEAR

There are no dinner jackets to be seen in a San Carlo audience, but 'casual' here means stylish and elegant; jeans and T-shirts are acceptable in the low-profile top-floor seats, but may provoke hostile stares in the stalls.

New, experimental theatre is the rule here, at the rapid clip of about one production per week. The programme sometimes includes international works, but performances are always in Italian.

Cabaret & musicals

A few theatres, such as the **Bellini**, offer mainstream musicals – mainly retreads of US and British warhorses, in Italian. The programme at the **Mercadante** (*see p179*) also features the odd musical.

More important in terms of Neapolitan tradition is cabaret. On a small, dimly-lit stage, with perhaps a chair for a set and minimal make-up and costumes, one or two actors will riff – sometimes crudely – on society's foibles and ills. Neapolitan cabaret reached its peak in the 1970s with an enormously successful trio known as La Smorfia, which gained wide popularity thanks to TV exposure and whose work still enjoys a cult following. The three members, Lello Arena, Enzo Decaro and Massimo Troisi, played on the intolerance of the poor, uncultured youth from the suburbs against the suffocating rhetoric of everything traditional: theatre, culture, religion and politics. The group broke up in 1981 to allow its members to pursue solo careers; most successful was the much-loved actor and director, Troisi, who died at 41 just after finishing work on *Il Postino*.

Today, virtually all cabaret in Naples draws on the group for inspiration, although admittedly without their brilliance. Notable performers include I Ditelo Voi, Ardone-Peluso-Massa, Alessandro Siani, Paolo Caiazzo, Rosalia Porcaro and Rosaria de Cicco.

Bellini
Via Conte di Ruvo 14-19, Toledo (081 549 9688/www.teatrobellini.it). Metro Piazza Cavour or Museo/bus 24, R1, R4. **Open** *Box office* 10.30am-1.30pm, 4-7pm Tue-Sat; 10.30am-1pm, 4.30-5.30pm Sun. *Performances* 9pm Mon-Sat; 5.30pm Sun. Closed Aug. **Tickets** €10-€30. **Credit** MC, V. **Map** p328 L8.
This recently remodelled theatre has an eclectic programme, but the focus is mainstream musicals (in Italian) and concerts of Neopolitan music.

Portalba
Via Port'Alba, Piazza Dante (081 549 9953/ 348 380 5762/www.cabaretportalba.it). Metro Dante or Montesanto/bus R1, R4. **Open** *Box office* 10am-1pm; 4-7pm Mon-Sat. *Performances* Sept-May 9pm Thur-Sun. **Tickets** €20-€30. **No credit cards. Map** p328 K8.
This tiny space showcases Neapolitan cabaret and also hosts musical events, including evenings of traditional Neapolitan song.

★ Tam
Gradini Nobile 1, corner of Via Martucci, Chiaia (081 682 814/www.tamteatro.it). Metro Piazza Amedeo. **Open** *Box office* 10.30am-1pm, 4.30-8pm Tue, Thur-Sat; 4.30-8pm Sun. *Performances* 10.30pm Thur-Sat; 10pm Sun. Closed Aug. **Tickets** €10-€23. **Credit** MC, V.
Cosy, colourful and lots of fun, it's cabaret here at full-force every weekend, with dinner or bar service as an option.

Totò
Via Frediano Cavara 12e, corner of Via Foria, Piazza Cavour (081 564 7525/www.teatrototo.it). Metro Piazza Cavour. **Open** *Box office* 4.30-7pm Tue-Sun. *Performances* 9pm Tue-Sat; 6pm Sun. Closed July-Sept. **Tickets** €15-€20. **No credit cards. Map** p328 L7.
Named after the great Neapolitan comic actor, this small theatre specialises in comedy (often with music) and cabaret.

OPERA

Teatro San Carlo
Via San Carlo 98F, Royal Naples (081 797 2331/081 797 2412/www.teatrosancarlo.it). Bus 24, C22, C25, C57. **Open** *Box office* 10am-7pm Tue-Sun. *Performances* times vary. Closed Aug. **Tickets** €20-€250. **Credit** AmEx, DC, MC, V. **Map** p332 K12.

Massimo Ranieri. See p183.

Dance 'til you drop

The mysterious art of the tarantella.

Although the tarantella is often seen as a Neapolitan dance, it has its roots further south. Some say its name came from the city of Taranto in Puglia, and others believe the dance was linked to the bite of the tarantula, and the moves imitated the effects of a tarantula bite – or were intended to cure it. *Essere morsi dalla taranta* (to be bitten by the tarantula) does indeed mean to lose self-control, as if possessed, and to dance in a frenzy to the point of collapse. In any case, the dance's roots have been traced back as far as the Dionysian cults brought over by the Greek colonists who settled in Italy's boot heel and toe.

Wherever its origins lie, it is certain that the tarantella is a kind of healing dance, originally danced only by women (called *tarantata*). The dance was brought to Naples and formalised in the 17th or 18th century, becoming a dance for couples or groups at the Bourbon court. Although traditional versions of the dance continued to flourish throughout the south, the tarantella came to be identified with Naples.

The accompanying music is as celebrated as the dance itself, and the two are inseparable. Always in six-eight and four-four time and usually in a minor key, pieces bring to mind flamenco, Arabic and gypsy music. Sung pieces for the tarantella are invariably sad tales of lost or thwarted love, and endless longing for lovers far away over distant seas.

The only essential instruments are the *tamburo* (a large drum) and the *nacchere* castanets, used by the dancers and accompanying musicians. Other than that, anything that comes to hand can be used: acoustic guitars (sometimes in the *battente* style, where the body of the guitar is struck), *zampogna* bagpipes, flutes, whistles, and even accordions.

The steps for the dance look simple, but are difficult to perform well. Dancers take alternate steps, moving ever closer – though never quite touching – in time with the ever-increasing speed of the music. There is a sinuous twisting of the arms; forearms seem to weave shapes around one another while the dancers' wrists dart back and forth, fingers snap and castanets clack.

Women (and the occasional man) wind long scarves and handkerchiefs suggestively around their partners, or swirl them in time with the melancholy crescendos of the music. Long skirts are obligatory for women – though thankfully, the traditional knickerbockers are no longer de rigueur for men.

Although solidly traditional programming gives San Carlo a rather staid image, the standard is often exceptional, and its reputation as being second only to Milan's La Scala is deserved. Openings here are Neapolitan high-society events (complete with the obligatory anti-fur protesters). Although many go to the opera *per farsi vedere* (to be seen), chunks of the audience are diehard opera buffs. Traditionalists at heart, San Carlo-goers can give innovative works a rough ride: if it's not a classic, it has to be very good to escape being rubbished. Still, an increasing number of 20th-century works in recent symphonic seasons hasn't driven the public away.

The opera season runs from January to December, but is suspended in late July and August due to the heat. The *abbonamenti* (subscription) system allows opera-goers to reserve their seats for the whole season, so much of the theatre is often booked up. What is left over tends to be the dregs: high up, or far off to the left of the stage. Don't despair, though, as good stall seats can be found (but bear in mind that sightlines from many parts of the theatre aren't great, so try to secure central places).

The San Carlo also has a ballet and an orchestral season. In summer, performances take place outside – you might watch a ballet in the courtyard at Castel Nuovo, or opera in the Arena Flavio in Pozzuoli. The theatre has its own ballet troupe, school, choir and orchestra. It often has wonderful international soloists and famous visiting conductors and orchestras, although tickets frequently sell out way in advance.

► *For more on San Carlo's history, see p180.*

CLASSICAL MUSIC

Composers such as Alessandro and Domenico Scarlatti, Niccolò Iommelli and Leonardo Leo are among the most prestigious exponents of the Neapolitan Baroque. Musicians in the city continue to pay homage to those traditions – in particular, the ensembles connected to the **Pietà dei Turchini** and **Associazione Scarlatti**. Naturally, **Teatro San Carlo** (*see p181*) hosts performances of a wide range of classical works.

Around Naples, it's likely you'll see one of the variations of the dance – the *tammuriata* or the *pizzica*. The latter is supposedly a ritualised version of sword-fighting, in which scarves take the place of weapons. One couple dances at a time, while others stand by and watch. Couples are often formed of two women, or occasionally two men; there are no sexual connotations.

More common, however, is the *tammuriata*. Here, sexual connotation runs rife, and the words to songs (often improvised) range from the merely naughty to the outrageously obscene. The dance's roots lie in harvest festivals in the agricultural areas behind Mount Vesuvius; it was – and still is – a dance of merrymaking and joy, best performed or observed with a flagon of rough, local red wine beside a blazing bonfire.

There is something so indelibly ancient about the tarantella that it resists almost every form of modernisation. Although George Balanchine worked out a pas de deux version, few other choreographers have touched it. Musically, it has moved on (Eugenio Bennato's Taranta Power project, Daniele Sepe's jazz, Almamegretta's dub and the Nuova Compagnia di Canzone Popolare have each found different

ways to reinvent the sounds), but the form of the dance remains the same.

The tarantella and its cousins are still best witnessed in the many small *feste di paesi*, or local saints' days, in the small towns that run between the Vesuvius as far north as Caserta and up into the hills around Benevento and Avellino. Don't forget your hanky.

At the time of writing, Naples' famous music school, the **Conservatorio di Musica** (Via San Pietro a Majella 34, 081 564 4411, www.san pietroamajella.it) was closed to the public for refurbishment. Call to find out if student performances in the recital hall have resumed. The music school is also home to a well-stocked library, holding a museum of manuscripts and rare prints, as well as other music memorabilia.

★ Associazione Scarlatti
Piazza dei Martiri 58, Chiaia (081 406011/ www.associazionescarlatti.it). Metro Amedeo/ bus 1, 4, 152, C24, C25. **Open** *Box office* 10am-1pm, 3.30-6pm Mon-Fri. *Performances* 9pm, days vary. Closed June-Sept. **Tickets** €15-€25. **Credit** MC, V. **Map** p327 H13.
This is one of the main venues and conservatories for Baroque music, and renowned worldwide.

Pietà dei Turchini
Via Santa Caterina da Siena, Chiaia (081 402395/www.turchini.it). Metro Mergellina, C16.

Open *Box office* 30mins before performance. *Performances* 6.30pm Mon-Fri. Closed Aug. **Tickets** €10. **No credit cards. Map** p327 J12. This is the premier conservatory for Neapolitan Baroque music, though the performance schedule can include departures from orthodoxy and venture into popular traditions from Naples and elsewhere.

NEAPOLITAN SONG

The songs of Naples had their heyday in the late 19th and early 20th centuries, when artists such as Enrico Caruso and Gilda Mignonette conquered the world. It was a golden age of song, with poets writing passionate lyrics and talented composers setting them to soaring melodies. Nowadays, the consummate interpreter of these traditional songs is Massimo Ranieri (*photo p181*), whereas Peppino Di Capri gets the credit for linking the tradition to rhythms derived from 1950s rock. More recent standout voices include Pino Daniele, Nino d'Angelo, Edoardo Bennato and

ARTS & ENTERTAINMENT

Enzo Gragnaniello, while Roberto de Simone is an important Neapolitan musicologist, composer and director.

The **Nuova Compagnia di Canto Popolare** was formed in 1967, with the remit of preserving the traditional musical patrimony of Naples and the south, from the medieval period to the 20th century. It continues its work today, giving rise to performers such as Peppe Barra, Eugenio Bennato and Patrizio Trampetti, as well as the folk groups Musicanova and Zezi.

Teatro Trianon Viviani

Piazza Calenda 9 (081 225 8285/www.teatro trianon.it). Metro Garibaldi. **Open** *Box office* 10am-1.30pm, 4-7.30pm Mon, Tue, Thur-Sat; 10am-1.30pm, 5-8pm Sun. *Performances* 9pm Mon, Thur-Sat; 5.30pm Tue; 6pm Sun. Closed June-Sept. **Tickets** €10-€32. **Credit** AmEx, MC, V. **Map** p329 O8.

The Trianon re-opened not long ago, with a new focus on traditional Neapolitan theatre and song. Singer Nino d'Angelo directs the enterprise with aplomb, managing to please the deeply traditionalist Neapolitans who populate the Forcella quarter. Inside the theatre, you can see some of the remains of ancient Greek Neapolis.

DANCE

Naples is the land of the tarantella, a sprightly, carefree dance known worldwide – at least in its softer, folkier version (*see p182* **Dance 'til you drop**). You are likely to see the dance performed in squares in the Centro Storico during warmer months; today's most famous musician-dancer-singer is Marcello Colasurdo.

Naples also has an important school of classical ballet, directed by Anna Razzi and based at the **Teatro San Carlo** (*see p181*).

FESTIVALS

In July and August, the lack of air-conditioning in the city's theatres generally makes them too hot to bear. Instead, performances are held out of doors (and out of town) in spectacular alternative venues. The most spectacular of all the region's outdoor summer events is Ravello's **Festival Musicale di Villa Rufolo** (*see p288*) which runs from June to August. The **Concerti al Tramonto** on Anacapri (*see p195*) are another chance to hear music in a sublime setting.

FREE Emozioni Pasqua

Various venues (081 410 7211). **Admission** free. Easter week brings a series of free concerts in central venues, some by famous performers.

Napoli Teatro Festival Italia

For listings, *see p154*.

Napoli's theatre festival, held in June and July, features quality Italian and international works in venues all over the city: Teatro San Carlo, Real Albergo dei Poveri and Piazza Carlo III, along with theatres, museums and archaeological sites.

★ Piedigrotta

For listings, *see p155*.

For a week in early September, this lively festival animates the city with colourful floats, dancing and music: the annual song competition is a major draw. For details, *see p155* **Music and movement**.

Punch drunk

How Naples fell in love with Pulcinella.

Now renowned throughout the world, the stock character of Pulcinella was ostensibly invented in the 1500s by the actor Silvio Fiorillo, of the famed *commedia dell'arte*. Its true origins, however, lie much further back – not least in the fourth-century Roman farces popular in the area around ancient Capua, at the time one of the Empire's main cities. The direct ancestor of Pulcinella is the character Maccus, who covered his face with the same signature black half-mask, sported an enormous pot belly, and was endowed with an inimitably raspy voice.

For centuries now, Pulcinella has symbolised the insatiable plebeian, always hungry and always in conflict with the established order: a character noted

for his over-the-top vivacity, slyness, and rebelliousness. He embodies the generally dire circumstances of the life of the lower classes in Naples and Campania, along with the many opportunities therein for dramatic slapstick. Within memory, the greatest interpreters of the rascally icon of Naples have been Eduardo de Filippo, Massimo Troisi (in the Ettore Scola film *Il viaggo di Capitan Fracassa*) and Massimo Ranieri (in film and on stage).

Pulcinella is also the main character of Neapolitan puppet shows, known as *guarattelle*, the grand maestro of which is Bruno Leone, who incarnates Pulcinella in his own matchless way (*see p158* **There's a Pulcinella in everyone**).

Sport & Fitness

Have a flutter at the races, or sample more active pursuits.

For sports fiends (and those who have overindulged in the local cuisine), Naples offers a wide spectrum of sporting activities. Its heady array of spectator and participatory sports ranges from the national game, football, to Roman-style horse racing at the Ippodromo di Adnano, and the Gulf Marathon (in which athletes swim from Capri to Naples).

For walking, cycling or jogging, the *lungomare* of Via Caracciolo is the ideal location; skates and rollerblades can be hired on Sunday mornings, when the road is closed to traffic. A full list of the city's local sport clubs and athletics facilities can be found at www.inaples.it. Other sport facilities – particularly for water sports – can be found on the islands of Ischia, Capri and along the coasts of Amalfi and Sorrento.

SPECTATOR SPORTS
Football

The football (*calcio*) season runs from September to June. Serie B matches are usually played on alternate Saturday afternoons, and Serie A games are on Sundays (check the local press to be sure), at the impressive 80,000-seater **Stadio San Paolo** in Fuorigrotta. Tickets must be bought in advance at the Azzurro Service ticket office or at certain Lotto sales points in *tabbacheria*; they're also sold online on the Calcio Napoli website, www.sscnapoli.it.

In an attempt to curb the problem of stadium violence, Italian law demands that each individual produce government-issued ID; bags and bottles are generally prohibited. Ticket prices vary, but usually range between €50 for the curve (where you'll be in the thick of the most passionate supporters) to €100 for a numbered grandstand seat. Attending a match is an intense experience – especially if Naples manages to win a goal or even a game.

Azzurro Service
Via Francesco Galeoata 17, Fuorigrotta (081 593 4001/www.azzurroservice.net). Cumana rail to Mostra or Leopardi/Metro Campi Flegrei/bus 180, 181, C2, C6, C7, C8, C9, C10, C15. **Open** 9am-12.30pm, 4-6.30pm Mon-Fri. **Credit** MC, V.

★ **Stadio San Paolo**
Piazzale Teccio, Fuorigrotta (081 593 3223/www.sscnapoli.it). Cumana rail to Mostra/Metro Campi Flegrei/bus 180, 181, C2, C6, C7, C8, C9, C10, C15. **Open** for matches.

HORSE RACING
★ **Ippodromo di Agnano**
Via Raffaele Ruggiero 1 (081 735 7111/www.ippocity.info). Metro Campi Flegrei, then bus C2, C6. **Admission** €3; women & children free. Closed 2wks Aug. **No credit cards**.
The racing here is trotting or horse-and-buggy racing – akin to ancient Roman carriage racing, but decidedly less dangerous. On summer evenings, races begin at 8.30pm daily, except Monday and Friday; the weekend meetings are particularly colourful. In the winter, races are organised three times a week, starting at 2.30pm. Look out for the Gran Premio Lotteria, an internationally acclaimed event that takes place every spring and showcases some of the best horse riders in the world. The programme changes month by month, so check the website for up-to-date information.

ACTIVE SPORTS
Archery

★ **Archery Partenopea**
Terme di Agnano (081 570 9736/081 618 9111/348 383 1777/www.arcieriapartenopea.com).

Azure passion

Recent seasons have seen a return to form for the boys in blue.

In 2007, crowds of exultant Neapolitans filled the streets. Teenagers zoomed by, several clinging precariously upon a single motorcycle, waving Neapolitan flags and shouting '*Forza Napoli!*' The city's football team, the **Società Sportiva Calcio Napoli**, had finally regained its place in Serie A (the Italian equivalent of the Premier League) after a tumultuous few years that had left morale at an all-time low.

The Neapolitan team was born in 1904, thanks to the efforts of English shipping agency employee James Poths and Italian architect Emilio Anatra. Its glorious past is closely tied to that of Argentinian player Diego Armando Maradona, who made history wearing the sky-blue jersey and became a living legend during the 1980s. With Maradona on side, the team claimed two domestic championships, the UEFA Cup and two Coppe Italia. The Neapolitans felt unbeatable, and festooned apartments and buildings everywhere with banners and flags.

Unfortunately, the 1986-1987 season proved them wrong, when AC Milan trounced them at home. Nonetheless, the team rebounded the following year, winning the UEFA cup and the Italian *scudetto* (the national league) in quick succession, much to their fans' delight.

By the 1990s, though, it seemed the glory days were over. In 1991, Maradona's personal problems began to interfere with the team's performance. He turned up late to training sessions or missed them altogether, and fell into dubious company. The fans held their breath as Maradona

played his last game for Naples on 17 March 1991; he was found guilty of drug use and disqualified shortly afterwards.

The Neapolitans, however, have never forgotten their idol, and even withdrew the number 10 shirt as a tribute to their much-loved captain. Walls across the city still bear graffitti tributes to the mighty Argentinian, while the shrine at Bar Nilo in Spaccanapoli features one of Maradona's hairs, carefully preserved and worshipped like a saint's.

In the mid 1990s, the team tried to regain some credibility by appointing prestigious coaches such as Claudio Ranieri and Marcello Lippi (who trained the victorious Italian World Cup Team in 2006). Unfortunately, economic problems soon put paid to the team's dreams of glory. Corrado Ferlaino, the owner of the club for over 30 years, was forced to sell up, and two subsequent owners were unable to reverse the club's decline.

Already languishing in Serie B and having changed hands three times in as many years, the club was declared bankrupt in 2004 and pushed back to Serie C1, where it would remain for over two years.

Since then, Naples' team has risen from the ashes, meritoriously regaining its place in Serie A. In the 2008-2009 season, it ended up in a very respectable eleventh place, just two positions below Lazio, and five from Roma. Although the team will have to intensify their efforts to be in with a chance of winning the next *scudetto*, it has come a long way from the ignominious doldrums of Series C1. *Forza Napoli* indeed!

Metro Campi Flegrei/bus C2, C6, C14, C15.
Open Summer 9am-8.30pm daily. Winter
10am-5pm daily. **Credit** MC, V.
Play Robin Hood for the day, and let the arrows fly.
Targets are available at distances ranging from 10m
(35ft) all the way to 90m (295ft). Although a membership fee is normally required, staff will give one-
off lessons by appointment for €12. If you drive
there, ask for detailed directions and be prepared to
tackle a one-lane dirt road – the setting is decidedly
pastoral, and well off the beaten track. If you plan
to take public transport, call ahead to arrange a lift.

Boating

The Gulf of Naples is ideal for sailing
enthusiasts, and boat hire is readily available
to those in possession of a license. **Jordan
& Jordan** (Via Chiatamone 63, 081 240 5228,
www.jordanandjordan.it, closed Sat, Sun) is a
charter service with boats that cost from €1,600
to €7,600 per week. It also offers an on-board
bed and breakfast service from October to
May, allowing landlubbers to sleep on the
boat without leaving the port.

In Pozzuoli, **Cataboat** (Via Sacchini 29, 081
853 0500, www.cataboat.com, closed Sat, Sun)
has boats from €1,400-€7,000 per week, and
charters catamarans and boats. If you'd prefer
a humble rowing boat, you can to hire one on
the stairs by the Castel dell'Ovo bridge.

Bowling

Bowling Oltremare
Viale Kennedy 12, Fuorigrotta (081 624444/www.
bowlingoltremare.it). Cumana rail to Edenlandia/
bus C2, C3, C5. **Open** 9am-2am Mon-Thur,
Sun; 9am-4am Fri, Sat. **Credit** AmEx, MC, V.
This traditional 20-lane bowling alley is next to
Edenlandia (see p157). There are also ping-pong and
pool tables for hire.

Cycling

Although initial impressions may suggest that
anyone who mounts a bicycle in Naples must
be mad, there are some wonderful off-road
cycling areas scattered around the city. The
Bosco di Capodimonte (see p159) is an oasis
far from smog and traffic, although the steep
hill to reach the park can be a slight deterrent.

The ride along the seafront from the Centro
Storico to Mergellina is a far easier option. The
hills around Monte di Procida beyond Pozzuoli
(see p89) offer spectacular views over the
islands of Ischia and Procida.

Fishing

You can fish almost everywhere in and around
Naples without a permit. The only prerequisite
is a yearly membership card that can be
purchased from the **Federazione Italiana
della Pesca Sportiva** (www.fipsas.it), which
has an office in every province.

Golf

Fans of crazy golf can try to sink a ball into a
model of Vesuvius that can be found at Via
Terracina 228, Fuorigrotta. Opening times are
erratic, and there's no phone, but it's generally
open at the weekend. Admission costs €5.

ARTS & ENTERTAINMENT

Archery Partneopea.

Setting the pace

Whether it's in the sea or on the streets, Neapolitans love a marathon.

There's nothing like the adrenaline rush, the sweat pouring down your temples, legs made of incandescent heat and pain, feet bouncing rhythmically off the ground and salt in your lungs from the Neapolitan seaside. But the **Napoli Marathon** (*see p154*), held every year in mid April, isn't the only marathon the city has to offer.

An international array of long-distance swimmers gather to compete in the **Gulf Marathon** (www.caprinapoli.com) – an epic, 36km (22.4 mile) swim from the Marina Grande in Capri to the seafront in Naples, finishing at the Rotonda Diaz beach. It's a slog of seven hours or so, depending on conditions out in the bay. To date, the fastest time is six hours, 35 minutes and three seconds, set by US swimmer Paul Asmuth in 1982; German athlete Angela Maurer holds the women's record, after swimming the course in seven hours and eight seconds in 2003. The swimmers generally take the plunge in June; check online for details.

For those who prefer to stick to dry land, another unusual option is the **Park to Park** (www.parktopark.com). The race starts in Naples' Parco Vergiliano in late May, and finishes in New York's Central Park in mid June or July. Although some competitors only tackle the first half of the course, others fly to New York to reach the finish line; the male and female race winners can win their flights across the Atlantic.

Most of the runners gathered at the start of the track in Naples are Italian, exchanging greetings of *Uè guagliò* (hey dude) and standing so close to one another that the few tourists present find themselves surrounded, as if in a warm hug. Italian songs waft through the air, and feet are stomping on the ground. It's 7.58am, and the atmosphere is one of collective anticipation. Runners check their watches, and a man with the typical 'pizza belly' is pulling on his shoelaces, checking whether or not they are tight enough.

At 7.59, the runners move closer to the starting line. Then comes the motorcycle, with two men astride. One wave of the arm, and a horde of colourful sports clothes, sunglasses and number tags floods into the streets.

The run started in 2007, inaugurated by singer Pino di Maio (also a runner in the race), who mesmerised the crowds with the Hymn of Mameli, the Italian national anthem, in chorus with thousands of voices. It didn't matter whether you knew the lyrics, or if you sang out of tune. All you needed was the determination to sing, and to tackle a ten-kilometre run afterwards. Then, for the truly dedicated, fly thousands of miles to cross the finish line in New York.

Volturnogolf
Via Domitiana km 35+300, Pinetamare Castelvolturno (081 509 5150/www.volturno golf.com). Bus M2. **Open** *June-Sept* 8am-8pm daily. *Oct-May* 8am-5pm daily. **Admission** *Daily green fees* €45 Mon-Fri; €55 Sat, Sun. *Club hire* €20. *Cart* €5. *Car* €45. **Credit** AmEx, DC, MC, V.
Golf is still very much a minority sport in Italy, and this 60-hectare course is some distance from the city, in the grounds of the Holiday Inn Resort. It's the only fully equipped course in Campania: par 71, 5,972m (19,600ft) in length, and with its own driving range. The hotel also has two tennis courts, a swimming pool, table tennis, mountain bikes for hire, a gym and a spa.

Gyms

★ Athenae
Via dei Mille 16, Chiaia (081 407334/www. athenae.it). Metro Piazza Amedeo/bus C22, C25, C28. **Open** *Oct-June* 8am-10.30pm Mon-Fri; 9am-6pm Sat; 9am-12.30pm Sun. *July-Aug* 8am-10.30pm Mon-Fri. **Admission** *Non-members* €10 daily. **Credit** DC, MC, V. **Map** p327 12G.
The Athenae offers a wide range of facilities and activities, such as bodybuilding, spinning, aerobics, weights, step and some martial arts. Other facilities include Turkish baths, a bar and a squash court (there's a €12 per half hour charge for non-members; the gym hires out rackets).

Bodyguard
Via Torrione San Martino 45, Vomero (081 558 4551). Funicular Montesanto to Via Morghen, Centrale to Piazzetta Fuga, Chiaia to Via Cimarosa/Metro Vanvitelli/bus E4, V1. **Open** *Oct-June* 8.30am-11pm Mon-Fri; 10am-7pm Sat. *July-Sept* 8.30am-11pm Mon-Fri. Closed 2wks Aug. **Admission** €10. **Credit** AmEx, DC, MC, V. **Map** p331 9F.
As well as weights, bicycles, a sauna, walking and running machines – along with aerobics and dance classes – you'll also find a bar here.

The **Napoli Marathon**.

Horse riding

Dressage was originally developed as a method of training horses for war, by teaching them precise movements; there is some evidence that such manoeuvres were developed by the ancient Greeks, who founded Naples. Modern dressage began during the Renaissance, when Neapolitan noble Federico Grisone founded a riding academy in Naples in 1532.

Complesso le Caselle

Via Montagna Spaccata 519, Pianura (081 588 6748). Cumana rail to Pianura, then bus P8. **Open** *May-Sept* 9am-8.30pm Tue-Sun. *Oct-Apr* 10am-1pm, 3-7pm Tue-Sat; 10am-2pm Sun. **Admission** from €10/15min outing; €30/lesson. **Credit** AmEx, MC, V.

Groups of up to three riders can follow a scenic 50-minute trail through the nearby woods. It's particularly popular during the summer months, so call ahead to check availability.

Jogging

Known in these parts as *footing*, jogging is popular with fitness enthusiasts of all ages. The lungomare (*photo p190*) of Via Caracciolo, from Castel dell'Ovo to Mergellina is ideal for a short run, especially on Sunday mornings when the road is closed to traffic.

For cleaner, fresher air, **Parco Vergiliano** (*see p86*) in Posillipo, with its spectacular views of the bay, and **Bosco di Capodimonte** (*see p159*), are extremely popular. The Bosco's green acres are also ideal for cycling or a quick game of frisbee or football (keep the ball in your bag until you're well inside, as ball games on the grounds are theoretically banned).

SCUBA DIVING

Centro Sub Campi Flegrei

Via Napoli 1, Pozzuoli (081 853 1563/www. centrosubcampiflegrei.it). Cumana rail to

Gerolomini/Metro Pozzuoli. **Open** 10.30am-1pm, 4.30-8.30pm Mon, Wed-Sun. **No credit cards**.
The gulf of Naples is great for diving enthusiasts, and the *città sommersa* of Baia (*see pp92-93*) is as good as it gets. A half-day excursion (8.30am-1pm) with one dive costs €30, and a full day (8.30am-5pm) with two dives and lunch on board is €60. Equipment can also be rented at €15. Dives can also be arranged along the Neapolitan coast or on the islands, and courses are run at all levels via PADI-accredited instructors. Friendly, careful tuition is also available in English.
▶ *There's also good diving to be had around the island of Procida (see p230) and Sorrento's protected Marine Park of Punta della Campanella (see p260).*

SKIING

In the winter months, the south of Italy offers a handful of half-decent ski resorts, none of them more than a couple of hours' drive from the city, and all of them popular weekend destinations with the locals. The roads to the slopes are often clogged on winter Sundays, so travel mid-week if you can.
The two main resorts are **Roccaraso** (086 460 2148, 086 462210, www.roccaraso.net, day pass €33), 153km (95 miles) from Naples, and the less demanding **Campitello Matese** (087 478 4137, www.campitello.com, day passes from €19, weekend passes from €45), 145km (90 miles) from the city.

SWIMMING

The cleanest water close to Naples can be found in the **Posillipo** area (*see p87*), and at the sandy beaches of **Capo di Miseno** (*see p88*) on the tip of the Campi Flegrei – which also provide a wonderful panorama of the islands of Ischia and Procida. **Milliscola** beach, one of the most popular spots with the locals, is located here. The only potential drawback of Posillipo and Capo di Miseno is that the beaches are commercially run and can be quite crowded in high season. If possible, it's better to go in June or early September. **La Gaiola**, a small but charming beach in Posillipo, attracts swimmers and scuba divers alike, as its clear waters contain relics from the Roman era.
To use the city's many swimming pools, you need a special membership card, but **Collana** is open to everyone.

Collana

Via Rossini, Vomero (081 560 0907). Metro Quattro Giornate/bus C30, C32. **Open** *July, Aug* 10am-3pm, 4-8pm Mon-Sat; 9am-4pm Sun. **Admission** €4 Mon-Sat; €5 Sun. **No credit cards**. **Map** p330 9C.
You'll find this popular city-owned indoor pool inside the same sprawling complex that housed Calcio Napoli football club's sacred former home ground. The pool measures a decent 25m (82ft) in length. The basic admission price includes access to a glorious sundeck with deckchairs for lounging.

TENNIS

Tennis San Domenico

Via San Domenico 64, Vomero Alto (081 645660). Bus C36 from Piazza Vanvitelli. **Open** 8am-10pm Mon-Fri; 8am-6pm Sat; 8am-2pm Sun. **Court hire** €12/hr. **No credit cards**.
The five floodlit clay courts of the San Domenico tennis club are located beneath a busy flyover, which confers a strangely apocalyptic atmosphere to every game. Rackets can be provided free of charge. Separate gym facilities are available after an informal medical examination and equipment induction for €6 per day.

YOGA

Siddharta

Via Santa Maria della Neve 18, Chiaia (081 668426/www.siddhartascuola.org). Metro Mergellina/bus 140, C12, C18, C19, C24, R3. **Open** *Lessons* 3-7pm Mon, Wed-Fri; 10am-2pm Tue. Closed Aug. **Admission** €40. **No credit cards**. **Map** p326 13C.
This yoga centre offers single lessons and, for the very dedicated, a comprehensive 12-month programme. Check the website for details.

Jogging on the **lungomare**. *See p189.*

Map Around Naples   192

Introduction   **194**
 Festivals & events   195

Capri   **196**
 Maps Anacapri & Capri   197
 In the swim of things   201
 Walk Scenic splendour   212

Ischia   **215**
 Profile Castello Aragonese   219
 Taking the plunge   220
 Nature's cure?   226

Procida   22⁹

Pompeii & Vesuvius   **23³**
 Map Herculaneum   23⁵
 Map Pompeii   24³

Sorrento & Around   **24⁹**
 Map Sorrento   25²
 Walk Sorrento's
  heady heights
 Call of the waves   254
                                      26⁰

The Amalfi Coast   **264**
 Map The Amalfi Coast   26⁵

Further Afield   **29²**
 Profile Reggia di Casserta   30⁰

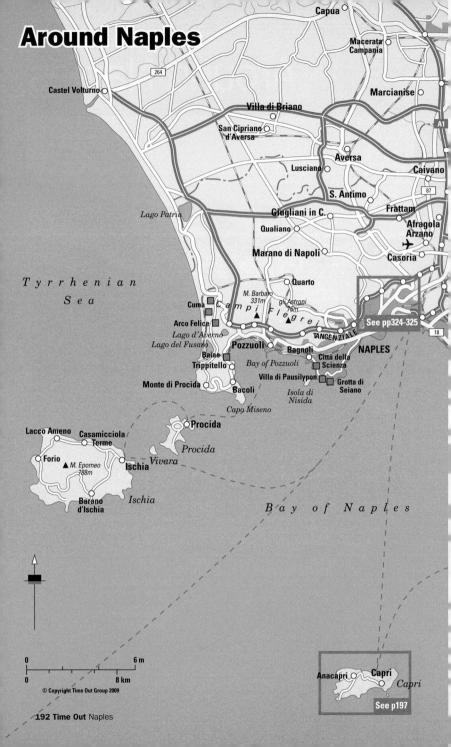

Around Naples

Capua

Macerata
Campania

Marcianise

Castel Volturno

264

A1

Villa di Briano

San Cipriano
d'Aversa

Aversa

Caivano

Lusciano

87

S. Antimo

Frattami

Lago Patria

Giugliani in C.

Afragola
Arzano

Qualiano

Marano di Napoli

Casoria

*T y r r h e n i a n
S e a*

Quarto

M. Barbaro
331m

*gli Astroni
76m*

Campi Flegrei

See pp324-325

18

Cuma

TANGENZIALE

NAPLES

Arco Felice

Lago d'Averno
Lago del Fusano

Pozzuoli

Bagnoli

Bay of Pozzuoli

Città della
Scienza

Baiae

Trippitello

Villa di Pausilypon

Grotta di
Seiano

Monte di Procida

Bacoli

*Isola di
Nisida*

Capo Miseno

Procida

Lacco Ameno

Casamicciola
Terme

Procida

Forio

▲ *M. Epomeo
788m*

Ischia

Vivara

Barano
d'Ischia

Ischia

B a y o f N a p l e s

0   6 m

0   8 km

© Copyright Time Out Group 2009

Anacapri

Capri

Capri

See p197

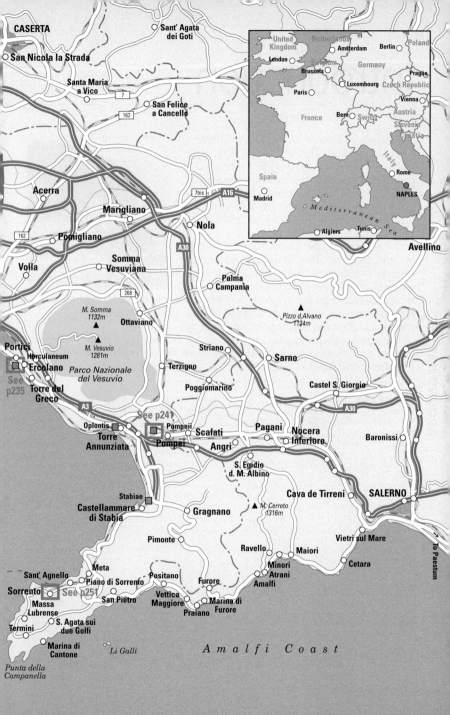

Introduction

Idyllic escapes from the city.

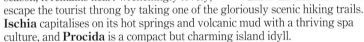

The islands and resorts around Naples afford countless opportunities for day trips, short stays and longer breaks, if you feel like a change of pace. The dramatic vistas, twisting coastal road and clifftop towns of the **Amalfi Coast** exert a heady glamour; on the other side of the peninsula lies **Sorrento**, with its lidos, lemon groves and rugged, mountainous hinterland.

Out in the azure bay, the three beautiful islands of Capri, Ischia and Procida feel a world away from the city. Crowded as **Capri** may be in high season, it remains heart-wrenchingly lovely; escape the tourist throng by taking one of the gloriously scenic hiking trails. **Ischia** capitalises on its hot springs and volcanic mud with a thriving spa culture, and **Procida** is a compact but charming island idyll.

The region is also known for its extraordinary archaeological sites. Everyone may have heard of **Pompeii**, but **Herculaneum**, **Oplontis**, **Stabaie** and **Paestum** boast riches of their own.

SMART ART

To make life easier for visitors as they explore the art and museums of Naples and Campania, the local authority has introduced the Campania Artecard. Offering free and reduced admission to various sights, and free public transport with selected cards, it's good value if you're planning to do a fair amount of sightseeing.

It's easiest to buy the card once you arrive in Naples. It's available from the port, stations, major sights and some travel agencies; if you buy one at the airport, you can use it to take the Alibus airport bus (*see p304*) into town.

The three-day card comes in various versions, offering a range of itineraries. Some include sights in central Naples, whereas others extend to the Campi Flegrei and entire Campagnia region; prices vary accordingly. With certain cards, entry to all the sights covered is free. Others entitle holders to free entry to the first few sights visited, then half-price entry to the rest.

Prices start at €12 for the Centro Antico card (which includes the Museo Archeologico Nazionale and other sights in the Centro Storico, transport not included) or the Castello di Napoli card (which, as its name suggests, covers the city's castles). If you're planning to visit the Campi Flegrei, there's a €16 card that includes

public transport and gives you free entry to the first three sites, with half-price entry thereafter.

For those who want to venture further afield, the three-day Tutta la Regione card (€27) offers access to museums, galleries and archaeological sites across Campania. It includes free access to two sights and half-price admission to the rest – so it makes sense to visit the most expensive places first (Pompeii, Herculaneum, Paestum, or the Museo Archeologico in Naples, say). Free transport is also part of the deal: the train from Naples to Paestum makes the card good value if you don't stop for breath. A trip on the Alibus airport bus is also included, as well as a return trip on the MM1 Metro del Mare in summer.

A seven-day card covering the entire region and offering free entry to the first five sights costs €30, but doesn't include transport. Meanwhile, the Artecard 365 allows two free entries to all sites within 365 days; transport is not included.

Artecard holders are also eligible for a range of discounts on private museums, cultural events and other attractions in the region.

For more information on the various packages offered, and to enquire about discounts for 18-25s, check online at www.campaniartecard.it, or phone 800 600 601 or (from mobile phones) 06 399 67 650.

Festivals & events

Feast days and classical concerts fill the cultural calendar.

THE AMALFI COAST

On the first Sunday in June, the **Regata Storica delle Antiche Repubbliche Marinare** (www.amalfinet.it/regatta) is a spectacular boat race hosted annually, in turn, by the original four Italian Maritime Republics: Amalfi, Genoa, Pisa and Venice.

On 25-27 June, processions and fireworks mark the **Festa di Sant'Andrea**; the fishing fleet is blessed by local priests.

Celebrations for **Byzantine New Year** start at around 11pm on 31 August with drums and trumpets for the Byzantine Palio; medieval tournaments take place in Amalfi's port.

Just east of Amalfi, Atrani (*see p278*) celebrates the **Feast of Maria Maddalena** on 22 July with fireworks and a procession. In the last week in August, stalls selling seafood and local wine are set up around the main square and on the beach for the **Sagra del Pesce Azzurro** festival.

In Positano (*see p267*), a procession and fireworks on 15 August mark the **Feast of the Assumption**. Two days later (17-19 Aug), there are sunset re-enactments of the Saracen landing of 15 August 1558.

Ravello Concert Society (089 858149, www.ravelloarts.org) holds classical concerts from March to early November at the Villa Rufolo and venues along the coast. Look out for the *concerti all'alba*, in which an orchestra welcomes the sunrise in a breathtaking spectacle that begins at 4am.

Held from June to September, **Ravello Festival** (www.ravellofestival.com) is Italy's oldest music festival, with classical concerts inspired by the artists who stayed in Ravello.

CAPRI

A statue of the town's patron saint, **San Costanzo**, is carried to the sea on 14 May, and participants are blessed. At the end of May, the **Three Gulfs Regatta** (www.tre golfi.it) starts in Naples at midnight, and ends in Capri the following day.

Summer in Anacapri brings the **Concerti al tramonto** ('concerts at dusk'), with performances from June to August in the Villa San Michele (*see p209*). On 13 June, a statue of the town's patron saint, **Antonio di Padova**, is carried around the town.

Mid June brings the three-day **Capri Tango Festival** (www.capritangofestival.com).

ISCHIA

In Lacco Ameno (*see p222*), a procession and fireworks honour the town's patron saint, **Santa Restituta**, on 16-18 May. The **Easter Procession** in Forio (*see p223*) is even more dramatic, sometimes halting traffic for miles around. On 26 July, fireworks mark the **Festa di Sant'Anna** (www.festadi santanna.it), and torchlit boats sail around Ischia Ponte (*see p215*).

Secular celebrations include the **Ischia Film Festival** (www.ischiafilmfestival.it), in early July; summer classical concerts and chamber recitals at **La Mortella** (*see p225*) are another cultural draw.

August's **Expo Ischia** (www.expo-ischia. blogspot.com) summer fair is a far brasher affair, with appearances by 'sexy bombas' and the winner of Italy's *Big Brother*.

In early September, **Ischia Jazz Festival** (www.ischiajazz.com) attracts big names such as Archie Shepp and Billy Cobham.

POMPEII & VESUVIUS

For July's **Festival delle Ville Vesuviane** (081 732 2134, www.villevesuviane.net), classical concerts are held in stately neoclassical villas in Ercolano (*see p234*).

In Torre Annunziata (*see p239*), 22 October brings a procession for the feast of the town's patron saint, the **Madonna della Neve** (Our Lady of the Snow).

SORRENTO

On **Holy Thursday** in Easter Week, white-hooded penitents carry a veiled Madonna through town. On **Good Friday**, black-hooded penitents file through town. The 16 July is the **Festa di Madonna del Carmine**, and the **Festa di Sant'Anna** (26 July-3 Aug), is a week-long celebration with music, food and wine, taking place at the Marina Grande.

In early July, the **Lemon Festival** in Massa Lubrense (*see p262*) is a celebration of Sorrento's most important fruit, with ice-cream, lemon *babà* and limoncello.

On 26-29 July, the **Sea Festival** is held on the seafront at Sant'Agnello (*see p258*). Expect food stalls, music, walking tours and trips to Punta Campanella Marine Reserve.

The **Incontri Musicali Sorrentini** (081 807 4033, www.sorrentotourism.com) music festival takes place in late summer in the Chiostro della Chiesa di San Francesco. *For more, visit www.in-campania.com.*

AROUND NAPLES

Capri

Villas, vistas and VIPs.

From pastoral idyll to imperial hideaway, intellectuals' retreat and millionaires' playground, Capri has worked her magic for centuries, luring millions to her shores. Thousands of visitors pour in each day, most of them on day trips from Naples or Sorrento. The invading hordes spend untold sums in cafés, chichi boutiques and souvenir stores, before making the obligatory visit to the famous Blue Grotto.

But it's easy to forgive Capri for being so popular. Glinting waves, merging into an azure sky, lemon groves, bougainvillea-draped terraces and rocky, heather-strewn slopes exude a wild natural beauty, sending even hardened city dwellers into reveries. It's hard to imagine how such a small island could bewitch so many – until you get here and experience it for yourself.

INTRODUCING THE ISLAND

Traditionally, Capri town has been regarded as chic and urbane, whereas Anacapri, on the high ground of Monte Solaro, is more rugged, rural and down-to-earth. Although less pronounced than in the past, the contrast still holds true; luxury hotels and villas cluster around Capri town, while Anacapri is home to a working population of smallholder-farmers.

To fully appreciate the island's fascination, stay overnight; by day, the Piazzetta, Capri's heart and home to the world's most famous *passeggiata*, is jammed with pedestrians. In the evening, though, as the sky darkens to cobalt and the last of the day-trippers drifts down to the port, the island reveals herself to be one of the Med's most elegant open-air living rooms.

The best time to visit is out of season (May or October), when the weather is cool enough to

INSIDE TRACK
WHAT'S IN A NAME?

It's thanks to long-time resident Gracie Fields that most people wrongly pronounce the island's name Ca-*pree*, rather than *Ca*-pri, with the emphasis on the first syllable. In Gracie's worldwide hit 'Isle of Capri', 'walnut tree' was erroneously rhymed with Capri – and it stuck.

really explore but warm enough to get a suntan. From November to March, Capri practically closes down; only a fraction of the island's hotels and restaurants stay open. For some, this is the perfect time to savour the island at its simple best.

GOAT ISLAND

The origin of the island's name is much debated, deriving either from *capreae* (a Romano-Italic word meaning 'island of goats') or *kaprie* (Greek for the 'place of the wild boar'). There are no boars these days, but you might see the odd goat. Capri has been inhabited since prehistory, by Neolithic tribes and later by the Greeks of Cumae and Neapolis (Naples); Virgil associated it with the Teleboans, a legendary race of Greek pirates. For centuries, it was more a strategic outpost than a settled community.

In 29 BC, Octavian – soon to become Emperor Augustus – landed here. Charmed by its beauty, he persuaded the Greeks of Neapolis to take back the already Romanised and much larger island of Ischia and give him Capri instead, for use as a private estate. Although he never lived here, Augustus set about building villas and water cisterns, and took an active interest in the island's traditions.

TIBERIUS'S CAPRI

Augustus's successor, Tiberius, ignored the island for years, before finally visiting in AD 27. He never returned to Rome, spending the

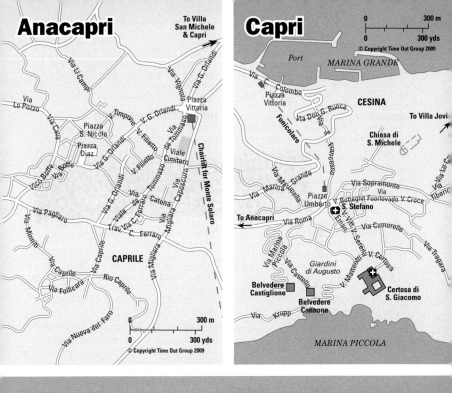

Anacapri

To Villa San Michele & Capri

Via Li Campi
Via G-Orlandi
Via Vignola
Via G-Orlandi
Via Lo Pozzo
Via Cava
Via Timpone
V.G. Orlandi
Piazza Vittoria
Via de Tommaso
Piazza S. Nicola
V. Filietto
Piazza Diaz
Via G-Orlandi
Via Boffe
Urco Boffe
Via Boffe
Viale Cimitero
V. Filietto
Viale
Via Capuscio
Chairlift for Monte Solaro
Via Miniera
Via G-Orlandi
Via Je. Ferraro
Via de. Ferraro
Via Migliara
Via Capuscio
Via Pagliaro
Trav. C. Ferraro
C. Ferraro
Via Caprile
Via Migliara
CAPRILE
Rio Caprile
Via Follicara
Via Nuova del Faro

0   300 m
0   300 yds
© Copyright Time Out Group 2009

Capri

0   300 m
0   300 yds
© Copyright Time Out Group 2009

Port
MARINA GRANDE
Via C. Colombo
Piazza Vittoria
Via Don G. Ruoca
CESINA
Funicolare
Via S. Francesco
To Villa Jovi
Chiesa di S. Michele
Via Madotella
Via Marina Grande
Via Sopramonte
Via Croce
V. Botteghe Fuorlovado
V. Croce
Via Tiberio
To Anacapri
Piazza Umberto
S. Stefano
Via Emani
V. Le Botteghe
V. Serena
V. Camerelle
Via Roma
Via Camerelle
Via Tragara
Via Marina Piccola
Via Matteotti
V. Certosa
Giardini di Augusto
V. Castello
Belvedere Castiglione
Certosa di S. Giacomo
Belvedere Cannone
Via Krupp
MARINA PICCOLA

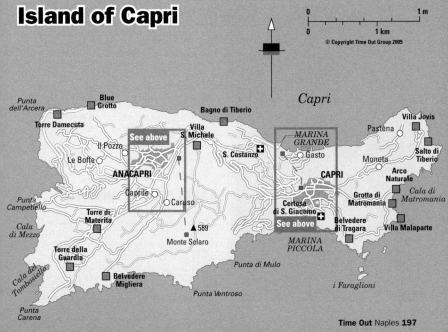

Island of Capri

0   1 m
0   1 km
© Copyright Time Out Group 2009

Capri

Punta dell'Arcera
Blue Grotto
Torre Damecuta
See above
Bagno di Tiberio
Villa S. Michele
MARINA GRANDE
Villa Jovis
Pastena
Il Pozzo
S. Costanzo
Gasto
Moneta
Salto di Tiberio
Le Boffe
ANACAPRI
CAPRI
Arco Naturale
Punta Campetiello
Caprile
Caruso
Certosa di S. Giacomo
See above
Grotta di Matromania
Cala di Matromania
Cala di Mezzo
Torre di Materita
▲ 589
Monte Solaro
MARINA PICCOLA
Belvedere di Tragara
Villa Malaparte
Torre della Guardia
i Faraglioni
Cala del Tombosiello
Belvedere Migliera
Punta di Mulo
Punta Carena
Punta Ventroso

last ten years of his life on Capri. His reign on the island – absolutist to the point of derangement – has been the subject of much historical embroidery. Suetonius, the scandalmongering author of *De Vita Caesarum* (Lives of the Caesars), depicted Tiberius as a misanthropic reprobate with a predilection for orgies and debauched erotica. Evidence of prisons, torture and execution chambers in Tiberius's villas testify to his other preferred form of entertainment. Suetonius is, however, almost the sole literary source for the final years of the emperor's life, and some believe his account to be vindictive and one-sided.

After Tiberius' death in AD 37, his 12 villas crumbled into ruin and the island was forgotten by the outside world, save as a place of exile for Roman undesirables. Later it came under the sway of the Abbey of Montecassino, then of the Republic of Amalfi. Thereafter it followed the fortunes of Naples, passing meekly from Anjou then Aragon to Spanish rule. Never entirely self-sufficient, the islanders faced starvation many times, enduring repeated Saracen pirate attacks as well as the plague. In the 18th century the Bourbons hunted here; while the king went looking for quails, warships circled the island checking for pirates.

During the Napoleonic Wars, the British occupied Capri as a bastion against the French Kingdom of Naples, but some brilliant decoy tactics by a French invasion force led to its speedy recapture in 1808. This period saw Austrian envoy Norbert Hadrawa run off with marbles, mosaics and valuables from the villas; their ruins were then plundered to build forts.

INTELLECTUAL INVASION

With its balmy climate and classical past, Capri soon became less of a military prize and more of a magnet for artists and intellectuals. The first hotel, the Hotel Pagano (now La Palma), was opened in 1822; after the Blue Grotto was rediscovered in 1826 by German poet August Kopisch and local fisherman Angelo Ferraro, tourists started to roll in. With a reputation as a haven for Greek and Sapphic lovers, an aura of licentiousness hung around the island where Tiberius had supposedly swung both ways with such abandon.

Gay Capri's finest years were the first two decades of the 20th century, when British writer Norman Douglas (whose *South Wind* is still the definitive Capri novel) and perfumed French aesthete Jacques Fersen helped keep island boys in pocket money.

Foreigners, including Fersen and Scandinavian doctor Axel Munthe (*see p208*), began building villas. Writer Curzio Malaparte, a sort of Italian Ernest Hemingway, famous in the 1940s and '50s, also built here. Designed by Adalberto Libera, his brutalist red house on Punta Massullo, **Villa Malaparte**, which he called *Casa Come Me* (house like me), is one of the island's more unusual landmarks. It played host to famous figures such as Jean Cocteau and Albert Camus, and appeared in Jean-Luc Godard's *Le Mépris*; these days, it's open for the occasional art exhibition.

The funicular was built in 1907, and the port opened in the '30s; until then, visitors arrived in rowing boats, among bags of mail and provisions, and were carried ashore to stop their feet getting wet. It was only after World War II, when it was used as an American base, that Capri began to attract billionaires, heiresses, Hollywood stars and jetsetters. Thereafter, a tidal wave of hotel construction destroyed most of Capri's farmland, making it forever dependent on tourism.

CAPRI TOWN & AROUND

Landing in **Marina Grande** in high season can be a stressful undertaking. Day-trippers and touts swarm around the harbour, and the tacky souvenir stores and touristy bars are a far cry from the Capri of yore. To make your escape, join the queue at the ticket desk for bus or funicular tickets; once you've got these, you can squeeze on to a tiny orange bus up to Capri or Anacapri, or take the funicular to Capri town.

Capri.

The **Piazzetta**.

Alternatively, take a motor launch to Capri's most famous sight, the **Blue Grotto** (*see p202*). It's worth experiencing, despite the expensive palaver a visit entails; the iridescent quality of the blue light inside is mesmerising.

Midway up the road linking the Marina to Capri town, the bus passes the island's non-Catholic **cemetery** (open 7am-7pm Mon-Wed, Fri-Sun). Created in 1878 for the growing community of foreign residents, it's the final resting place of Norman Douglas and Gracie Fields, among others. Far from the tourist trail, it's a good starting point for visitors wishing to explore Capri's free-thinking and artistic past.

The funicular, which offers splendid views as it crawls up the hill, emerges on the piazza at the end of Via Roma, Capri town's access road. Above the funicular station is a terrace with a bar, from which to drink in the view over the Marina and **Monte Solaro**. A picturesque bell tower separates this antechamber from the Piazzetta (officially Piazza Umberto I): core of the Capri experience, archetype of the perfect Mediterranean island square, and the town's main pedestrian traffic chicane.

In Capri, all roads seem to lead to the **Piazzetta**. With its four rival bars (distinguished by colour-coded tables) it's one of the best places at which to see and be seen. Grab a table, order a drink (you only live once), sit back and enjoy the show. Once the religious and administrative centre of the island, it's now pleasingly decadent. Around it run the narrow alleys of the old town, whose vaulted streets,

low arches, loggias and courtyards were built as a means of hampering marauding pirates.

On the south side of the square, the main parish church of **Santo Stefano** (open 8am-1pm, 4.30-7pm daily) sits pretty at the top of a flight of steps. The present Baroque structure was built on the site of an earlier church; inside, the *intarsia* marble flooring in front of the main altar comes from the **Villa Jovis** (*see p202*). Legend has it that the painting of the Madonna in the first chapel on the left was thrown down a cliff by invading Turks, but remained intact. In front of the church, the **Museo del Centro Caprense Ignazio Cerio** (*see p202*) houses relics of Capri's pre-history.

Take Via Madre Serafina from the top of the church steps (keep to the right) and enjoy a wander through medieval Capri. This lane eventually becomes the steep Via Castello, at the end of which is the **Belvedere Cannone**. Named after a French cannon placed here, it used to be known as *Malerplatte* – painters' square – due to its popularity with German artists, and affords magnificent views over the **Faraglioni** (*see p201*) and **Marina Piccola**.

From the Piazzetta, Via Vittorio Emanuele (the closest Capri comes to a main street) descends past boutiques and limoncello outlets to the **Grand Hotel Quisisana** (*see p205*), doyen of the island's luxury hotels. Continue down Via Federico Serena to Via Matteotti, a curving lane that opens on to an unexpectedly rural scene of olive groves, a medieval monastery and the sea.

Marina Piccola.

The monastery – the **Certosa di San Giacomo** (*see p202*) – can be reached via a walled avenue at the eastern end of Via Matteotti. It was established in 1371 by Count Giacomo Arcucci, powerful secretary to Queen Juana I, who became a monk when he fell from favour in 1386. The Carthusian brotherhood of San Giacomo owned land, grazing and hunting rights to most of the island – bringing it into frequent conflict with islanders. When plague broke out in 1656, the monks sealed themselves off to avoid infection instead of tending to the sick; the *capresi* responded by dumping the corpses of plague victims over the monastery wall. Dissolved by Napoleon in 1808, the *certosa* became a prison and military hospital.

At the other end of Via Matteotti are the **Giardini di Augusto** (open dawn-dusk daily), a panoramic series of terraced gardens that once formed part of the estate of German arms manufacturer Alfred Krupp. Beyond the gardens stands a monument to Lenin, who stayed in the villa above with Maxim Gorky. Opposite, the Via Krupp is a wonderful hairpin path built in 1902, which winds down the cliff linking the Certosa to the Marina Piccola.

Back up at the Quisisana, Via Camerelle heads east past elegant boutiques and bars to Via Tragara, lined with upmarket hotels. This is the route of the evening *passeggiata* (stroll) – just long enough to work up an appetite for dinner, and with a wonderful view at the end from the Belvedere di Tragara, which overlooks the three rock stacks known as the **Faraglioni**. The outermost stack is home to a species of blue lizard found nowhere else in the world. Freeclimbers are allowed to scale the rocks, but must seek prior permission through the tourist office.

The paved path that descends from here is one of the best walks on the island (*see p212* **Scenic splendour**), via the mysterious **Grotta di Matermania** and photogenic **Arco Naturale**. The classic excursion from Capri town, though, is the easy hike up to Tiberius' **Villa Jovis** (*see p202*). From the Piazzetta, Via Le Botteghe leads to a crossroads just below the island's prettiest church; the tiny chapel of **San Michele** (open Apr-Oct 9am-7pm daily; Nov-Mar 10am-5pm daily). Beyond here, the path dawdles past imposing villas and more humble *capresi* dwellings until the houses thin out and the going gets steep. Just before the remains of the villa, **Parco Astarita** is an unassuming but scenic patch of grass under the pines.

Within the Villa Jovis complex is the tiny medieval church of **Santa Maria del Soccorso**, occasionally open for exhibitions.

In the swim of things

The best spots at which to pitch your beach towel.

The sea around Capri is so incredibly beautiful – and tantalisingly close – that you'll long to dip at least a toe into it. It can be frustratingly difficult to get to, though: here are the best places at which to take the plunge.

Most beaches are rocks or platforms with steps into the sea; if you yearn for sand between your toes, there's always **Marina Grande**. Too close to the port for comfort? Far nicer is the **Bagno di Tiberio** (Via Palazzo a Mare, 081 837 0703). A ten- to 15-minute walk from the port, it's a lovely spot for lunch.

Lido da Luigi (Via Faraglioni 5, 081 837 0591, www.hotelcertosella.com) has one of the best addresses on the island – perched on a stone platform on Stella, the first of the Faraglioni Islands. The views are spectacular, and the area is perfect for diving. Get a boat from Marina Piccola, or walk from Punta Tragara.

For small children, **Marina Piccola** is your best bet. Arrive early and you won't pay a penny for your postage stamp place on its pebbly beach, which has a fine view of the Faraglioni. Otherwise, pay for a lido. **La Canzone al Mare** (Via Marina Piccola 93, €16- €27), co-founded by singer Gracie Fields in 1933, is sandy, and popular for lunch and with families; the low, rocky outcrop of the Scoglio delle Sirene has a mellow feel and a great bar.

Punta Carena is more popularly known as Faro, as the biggest lido here is the **Lido del Faro** (*see p210*). The rocks face the island's lighthouse, and the stretch includes free beaches as well as lidos, with bars overlooking the bay. It seems a world away from the Piazzetta, and is as popular with *anacapresi* grandparents as their grandchildren. A ten-minute bus ride from Anacapri, it's also the starting (or finishing) point for the **Sentiero dei Fortini** fortress walk (*see p212* **Scenic splendour**).

By the Blue Grotto, the **Lido Nettuno** (081 837 1362, www.clubnettunocapri.com) is hugely popular in summer; it has a pool, direct sea access, a restaurant, a bar and a fitness area.

AROUND NAPLES

Certosa di San Giacomo.

Fersen's neoclassical **Villa Lysis** (closed Sun), built in 1905, is further along as the crow flies on Via Lo Capo, but you'll need to take a different path at an earlier fork to get there.

Blue Grotto

(081 837 0973). **Open** 9am-2.30pm daily. **Admission** €10.50 plus €11 rowing boat fee from Marina Grande. **No credit cards**.
Discovered in Roman times, the Blue Grotto and its famously iridescent light subsequently became associated with evil spirits, and was given a wide berth by locals. That all changed with its rediscovery in 1826, when it re-emerged as a fêted tourist attraction. If the sea is even slightly rough, trips are cancelled; allow plenty of time for your visit, as there may be a long wait to get inside.

FREE Certosa di San Giacomo

Viale Certosa (081 837 6218). **Open** 9am-2pm Tue-Sun. **Admission** free.
Recently restored, the Certosa is an atmospheric place. It's partly abandoned, partly given over to municipal uses – including a school, a library, temporary exhibitions and a museum dedicated to the lugubrious canvases of German painter and Capri resident Karl Wilhelm Diefenbach. The simple church has a fine 14th-century fresco above the door; among the three praying women to the left of the Virgin is Queen Juana, the monastery's co-founder.

Museo del Centro Caprense Ignazio Cerio

Piazzetta Cerio 5 (081 837 6681/www.centro caprense.org). **Open** 10am-1pm Tue-Sat. **Admission** €2.50. **No credit cards**.

The archaelogical museum's collections include the fossilised skeletons of long-extinct mammals, unearthed below the Grand Hotel Quisisana.

★ Villa Jovis

Viale Amadeo Maiuri, Via Tiberio (081 837 0381). **Open** 9am-1hr before sunset daily. **Admission** €2. **No credit cards**.
The best time to visit Villa Jovis is as soon as it opens, at 9am, before the bulk of the day-trippers make their way up. Not much is left of the Roman complex, yet it is still imposing in all its splendid, solitary glory. The most impressive remains are those of the huge cisterns in the centre and the long, straight loggia to the north, which ends in the 330m (1,155ft) Salto di Tiberio – the precipice from which the emperor reportedly hurled people who annoyed him. The story may be mere fabrication, but the stunning view across to Punta della Campanella on the mainland is real enough.

Where to eat

Although Capri has proud culinary traditions (faithfully recorded by Elizabeth David), the stream of day-trippers gives restaurants little incentive to strive for higher standards, and encourages high prices. Most menus tend to be quite similar – and however delicious ricotta and herb-filled *ravioli capresi*, seafood pasta and baked *pezzogna* (bream) may be, they can become monotonous. Often, the only alternative is pizza.

The smarter hotels have some impressive restaurants: **Quisisana**'s Rendez Vous (*see p205*) or **L'Olivo** at Capri Palace (*see p212*).

Restaurants frequently charge a *coperto* (cover charge) as well as 15 per cent service; menus should clearly state this. It's best to avoid restaurants that serve all-day meals, and always ask to see a menu with prices. If you are ordering fish, ask to see it and get an estimated price. Most restaurants close for the winter, but many reopen for Christmas and New Year.

★ Aurora

Via Fuorlovado 18/22 (081 837 0181/www. auroracapri.com). **Open** noon-3pm, 7pm-midnight daily. Closed Nov-Mar. **Average** €60. **Credit** AmEx, DC, MC, V.

Spot the stars at one of Capri's oldest and most popular restaurants; even if you're not sitting next to one, you can check out the photos of celebrities who've eaten at this charmingly unsnooty place. The chef creates beautifully presented dishes from a Neapolitan and *caprese* repertoire, such as spaghetti with clams or bream in a crust of potato with spinach. Thin-crust pizzas are a treat, and desserts delicious; a particularly fine wine list means you might be served a lovely Amarone by the glass. Outdoor tables give a prime view of the *passeggiata*.

★ La Capannina

Via Le Botteghe 14 (081 837 0732/www. capannina-capri.com). **Open** *May-Sept* noon-3pm, 7.15pm-midnight daily. *Mid Mar, Apr, Oct* noon-3pm, 7.15-11.30pm Mon, Tue, Thur-Sun. Closed Nov-mid Mar. **Average** €55. **Credit** AmEx, DC, MC, V.

This old-fashioned, family-run place is one of the best known – and most consistent – restaurants on Capri. Opened in the 1930s, it's a top celebrity haunt (come in the evening), delivering textbook renditions of the classics. Expect perfect *ravioli capresi, totani* (stuffed squid) and *linguine allo scorfano* (linguine with scorpion fish), the house speciality.

Da Gemma

Via Madre Serafina 6 (081 837 0461/www. dagemma.it). **Open** *Aug* noon-3pm, 7pm-midnight daily. *Apr-July, Sept-Oct* noon-3pm, 7pm-midnight Tue-Sun. Closed Nov-Mar. **Average** €35. **Credit** AmEx, DC, MC, V.

This island institution was Graham Greene's favourite restaurant; it's still run by the same family. Fish is baked in an old bread oven, and good pasta and pizza are served: try the sausage and *friarelli* (pepper) pizza, which is popular with regulars. The premises nestle under the arches of the old town above Via Roma, with lovely views outside and old black and white photos of famous punters inside.

Da Paolino

Via Palazzo a Mare 11 (081 837 5611). **Open** 7.30-11.30pm daily. Closed Nov-Mar. **Average** €60. **Credit** AmEx, MC, V.

At the end of Marina Grande, set in a wonderful lemon grove, Da Paolino is one of Capri's most popular restaurants – and rightly so. The enormous antipasti selection is renowned, but take care not to overload; you'll need to save room for *primi* such as pasta with courgette flowers and wonderful *secondi*, featuring the freshest seafood. Book ahead.

Il Geranio

Via Matteotti 8 (081 837 0616/www.geranio capri.com). **Open** 12.30-3pm, 7.15-11.30pm daily. Closed Nov-Mar. **Average** €50. **Credit** AmEx, DC, MC, V.

Make the most of Il Geranio's charming location by asking for a table on the veranda, with its views over the Giardini di Augusto and beyond to the sea and I Faraglioni. 'The Geranium' serves a mix of modern Mediterranean and classic Neapolitan dishes, with an emphasis on the freshness of the produce: expect succulent prawns in garlic and chilli or fat tubes of pasta doused in fresh tomato and seafood sauce. Wine is from the region, and desserts can be walked off with an after-dinner stroll along the charming Via Krupp.

★ Le Grottelle

Via Arco Naturale (081 837 5719). **Open** *July, Aug* noon-3pm, 7pm-midnight daily. *Apr-June, Sept-Oct* noon-3pm, 7-11pm Mon, Wed-Sun. Closed Nov-Mar. **Average** €60. **Credit** MC, V.

On the path leading to the Arco Naturale, half inside a cavern and half perched on a terrace overlooking a verdant slope and the sea, Le Grottelle is hard to beat – especially on a clear, moonlit night. The food is earthy and reliable, with *primi* such as *ravioli capresi* followed by *gallinella* (gurnard), chicken or rabbit; finish with the best *torta caprese* (chocolate cake) you're ever likely to taste. Its local wines are especially good.

★ € La Savardina da Edoardo

Via Lo Capo 8 (081 837 6300/www.caprila savardina.com). **Open** *June-Aug* noon-3pm, 7-11pm daily. *Mid Mar-May, Sept, Oct* noon-3pm, 7-11pm Mon, Wed-Sun. Closed Nov-mid Mar. **Average** €25. **Credit** AmEx, MC, V.

Head to this rustic restaurant, an appetite-building 20-minute walk from the Piazzetta up towards Villa Jovis (*see left*), for proper homecooking and to see

---

**INSIDE TRACK
A TASTE OF TARALLI**

Sfizi di Capri on Via Parroco Canale (081 837 4105) is Capri's best bakery. It sells delicious slabs of pizza and *torte rustiche* (savoury flans) to take away, and no fewer than 12 types of *taralli* – crunchy little dough rings, eaten as snacks.

---

where real *capresi* live. In warm weather, tables are arranged in an orange grove with views over country villas and smallholdings. Ingredients are almost all home-grown, including the courgette flowers that make such a delicious starter. The ravioli are good, as is rabbit and *parmigiana di melanzane* (aubergines baked with parmesan).

Verginiello

Via Lo Palazzo 25 (081 837 0944). **Open** noon-3pm, 7.30pm-midnight daily. Closed Nov-mid Dec. **Average** €35. **Credit** AmEx, DC, MC, V.
On a little side road off tourist-jammed Via Roma, Verginiello is a decent budget option serving a vast menu of *caprese* classics and wood-fired pizza. The kitchen works with whatever the catch of the day brings, but expect mussels, clams and bream. Although this large trattoria sees its fair share of day-trippers, it's also popular with locals, and remains open most of the year. Service is friendly, and the view over the Bay of Naples very pretty.
▶ *Verginiello's owners also have some rooms for rent nearby; call for details.*

Cafés, bars & gelaterie

The island's social hub is the glamorous Piazzetta (Piazza Umberto I), its four bars staffed by elegant waiters in cream-coloured jackets. Although Capri isn't as exclusive as it used to be, almost everyone who's anyone has sat and sipped a drink here.

The oldest of the four bars is the **Piccolo Bar** in the corner (081 837 0325), open until 2am in high season. The locals' choice, this place is good for people who like to watch rather than be watched, especially if you grab one of the tables by the window upstairs. Below the church, **Bar Tiberio** (081 837 0268, closed Nov & Wed from Dec-Feb) attracts a young crowd and visiting Neapolitans; it has the best cakes and cocktail nibbles. The **Gran Caffè** (081 837 0388, closed Nov-Feb), the most elegant, is favoured by tourists, while **Bar Caso** (no.4, 081 837 0600, closed Tue from Oct-June) serves good *granite* (crushed ice drinks) and is a popular gay haunt. Any one of them affords a perfect vantage point from which to watch the show unfold in what Norman Douglas called 'the world's little theatre'.

Look up and you'll see **Pulalli** (Piazza Umberto I, 081 837 4108, closed Nov-Mar, Tue in Oct, Apr-June). Once a simple *locanda*, it's now a wine bar inside the clock tower that overlooks the Piazzetta, serving excellent food. The locals have their morning coffee at **Bar Funicolare** (Piazza Diaz, 081 837 0363, closed Jan-Feb & Thur from Oct-Dec, Mar-June) next to the cable car entrance.

The rich and the beautiful who think the Piazzetta has lost its edge now congregate at the **Quisi Bar** (closed mid Oct-mid May), the terrace bar of the Grand Hotel Quisisana (*see p205*), especially at *aperitivo* time.

For ice-cream and *granite*, try **Trattoria Scialapopolo** (Via Le Botteghe/corner Gradoni Sopramonte 5, 081 837 9054, closed Wed & Feb). Costanzo Spataro used to sell his ices and drinks from a barrow, then set up a little bar in 1952, selling delicious, freshly made hot and cold food to eat in or take away, at bargain prices. His nickname 'Scialapopolo', is a contraction of *scialare il popolo* – 'to make everyone eat and drink to their hearts' content'.

At **Buonocore** (Via Vittorio Emanuele 35, 081 837 7826, closed Nov-Mar & Tue in Oct, Apr-June), sample the famed *caprilù* lemon and almond cakes or *torta caprese*. The cool, tiled interior is perfect for coffee and cake, and the *rosticceria* counter has hot, ready-made dishes.

Away from the centre, **Bar Lindos** (Via Matermania 2, 081 837 6493, closed Jan-Feb & Sun in Oct-Dec, Mar-Apr) is a pleasant resting place en route to Villa Jovis. It's also opposite a supermarket – handy for picnic provisions.

Nightlife

Capri nightlife revolves around hotels, bars and restaurants. The Piazzetta stays open late and has a lively buzz; there's also a handful of discos and smooth nightclub-cum-bars where there might be some dancing on the tables.

The most famous is the charismatic Guido Lembo's **Taverna Anema e Core** (Via Sella Orta 39E, 081 837 6461, www.anemaecore.com, closed Tue, Wed in Easter-June, Sept, Oct & Nov-Mar). Opened in 2005, **Pantarei** (Via Lo Palazzo 1, 081 837 8898, www.pantareicapri.it, closed Nov-Mar & Tue in Apr-June, Sept-Oct) is a seemingly ever-expanding club-cum-lounge bar, restaurant and spa, with plenty of space inside and out for mixing with the beautiful people. Admission is free except on Saturdays, when you'll pay €20.

Capri's cultural scene has quietened down considerably since the days when it was a hub for European intellectuals. Cinephiles rely on two cinemas: the **Auditorium** in Capri town and the **Apollo** in Anacapri, both largely

INSIDE TRACK HOT PANTS

In 1949, Emile Pucci opened a boutique here and launched his daringly-cropped Capri pants. For a pair of made to measure Capris, go to **La Parisienne** (Piazza Umberto I 7, 081 837 0283, www.laparisiennecapri.it, closed Oct-Mar): they only take a day to make.

Via Camerelle.

The other Capri speciality is food and drink. Limoncello, a potent lemon liqueur, has become the statutory Italian restaurant *digestivo* in the past decade or so. For authenticity and high standards, buy at **Limoncello di Capri** (Via Roma 85, 081 837 5561, www.limoncello.com, closed Jan, Feb). Capri also has a handful of very old and increasingly good wines; go to **Vinicola Tiberio** (Via Trieste e Trento 28, 081 837 1261, www.tiberiocapri.it, closed Sun & Nov-Feb). There's also an *enoteca* and gourmet food shop, **Capannina Più Gourmet** (Via le Botteghe 39/41, 081 837 8899, www.capannina-capri.com, closed Feb & Sun from Oct-Apr).

Other shops specialise in antiques, ceramics and gifts. The wonderful **Sud Capri Gallery** (Via le Botteghe 4/6, 081 837 0165, closed Jan-Easter) sells glass, ceramics and presents, all made in Italy. Perfume is another big seller; limited-production **Carthusia** perfumes – made locally according to old convent recipes – are lovely gifts to take home. Men's products are made with a base of rosemary from Monte Solaro, women's with wild carnation. Of the three shops on the island, the biggest is on Via Camerelle (no.10, 081 837 0529, www.carthusia. com, closed Jan, Feb).

Visitors hankering after the older, loftier Capri of philosophers, poets and artists should visit **La Conchiglia**, a local publisher with 70 or so titles in its catalogue (a few of which are in English translation), all dealing with the island's history or its literary denizens. Its main outpost (Via Camerelle 18, 081 837 8199, www.laconchigliacapri.com) has a wide array of second-hand books on Capri – many in English – and a good range of antique prints.

showing dubbed foreign films. Modest exhibitions or performances are occasionally held in the **Certosa di San Giacomo**, the **Cerio Museum** (for both, *see p202*) or in upmarket hotels, mainly featuring local artists.

Shopping

Capri town is label-lovers' heaven, with its concentrated cluster of designer boutiques. The big hitters – Ferragamo, Gucci, Fendi, Alberta Ferretti, Cavalli, Prada – are crammed into tiny, prestigious outlets along Via Vittorio Emanuele and Via Camerelle.

You'll also find several stores selling the famous Capri sandals so beloved of jetsetting icon Jackie O. Handmade ones can be found at **Canfora** (Via Camerelle 3, 081 837 0487) and **Giuseppe Faiella** (Via Le Botteghe 21, closed Jan, Feb & Sun in Mar-May, Oct-Dec), whose family has been making them since 1917. Over in Anacapri, head to **Antonio Viva** (Via Orlandi 75, 081 837 3583, www.sandalo caprese.it, closed Dec-Feb).

For cashmere jumpers and wraps, made on the island, try **Le Farella** (Via Fuorlovado 21C, 081 837 5243, www.farella.it, closed Jan-Feb & Sun in Oct-Dec, Mar). On the same street, handbags and luggage made from famous Santacroce leather are sold by Neapolitan masters **Tramontano** (no.1, 081 837 4401, www.tramontano.it, closed Nov-Mar); **Intimo Anna** (no.23) has lovely undies and pyjamas.

Where to stay

In keeping with its image, Capri teems with chic (and often wildly expensive) hotels, such as the **Diva Suites** (081 837 0104, www.lacanzone delmare.com, €400 double) at the lido where Emilio Pucci and Noel Coward used to bask, **Le Canzone del Mare** (see *p201* **In the swim of things**). Equally, there are small, old-fashioned *pensione* for a taste of old Capri.

Booking well in advance is always a good idea; check websites too, as hotels often have cut-price offers, especially in low season. Most close from November-mid March, though some reopen for a week or two over Christmas.

Grand Hotel Quisisana

Via Camerelle 2 (081 837 0788/www.quisisana. com). Closed Nov-mid Mar. **Rates** €320-€690 double. **Credit** AmEx, DC, MC, V.
Set in five acres of gardens, this Capri institution began life in 1845 as a sanatorium (the name trans-lates as 'Here one heals'), but soon transformed itself

AROUND NAPLES

Via Krupp. *See p201.*

into the island's top hotel. Behind the cream and white neoclassical façade are two swimming pools (one inside, one outside) a shady garden, a gym and a spa. Service is impeccable, but the decor can feel a little anonymous, and the sheer size of the place may leave you cold. Many rooms have magnificent views over the Giardini di Augusto (*see p201*), and there's a good array of restaurants and bars on site.

▶ *Whether you're staying at the hotel or not, aperitivi on the terrace of the Quisi Bar are de rigueur (see p204).*

Hotel Quattro Stagioni Capri
Via Marina Piccola 1 (081 837 0041/www.hotel 4stagionicapri.com). **Rates** €70-€130 double. **Credit** AmEx, MC, V.
This charming, family-run hotel sits on the bend of the road leading down from Capri to Marina Piccola, and offers the best of both worlds: guests can wander downhill to the beach or meander uphill towards the Piazzetta. There's also a bus stop nearby. Rooms are simple but comfortable, and there are sunny terraces to relax on. Book ahead.

Hotel Weber Ambassador
Via Marina Piccola 118 (081 837 0141/toll-free 800 842 623/www.hotelweber.com). Closed Nov-Mar. **Rates** €130-€220 double. **Credit** AmEx, DC, MC, V.
With some of the finest views on the island – over to the Faraglioni islands with Marina Piccola below – this hotel also offers good value accommodation. Rooms with no sea view cost considerably less; you can enjoy the view from the roof terrace, and the beach is just two minutes away. The sea view rooms

and suites are lovely, though, opening out on to geranium-filled terraces. Breakfast, air-conditioning and a shuttle bus to Capri are expensive extras.

★ JK Place
Via Provinciale Marina Grande 225 (081 838 4001/www.jkcapri.com). Closed Nov-Mar. **Rates** €700-€900 double. **Credit** AmEx, MC, V.
Opened in 2007, JK Place is wonderfully stylish, and the backdrop for many a fashion photoshoot. The white clifftop villa was designed by guru Michele Bönan, who has created a luxurious yet fun feel: think seaside elegance with fur-trimmed curtains and zebra skin footstools. The lounge area, with a palette of cool greys and vases of lilies, has a library of arty books to peruse. Most bedrooms have views of Vesuvius and Naples, and the relaxing spa area overlooks a lovely infinity pool. Breakfasts can be enjoyed on the terrace overlooking the sea and Marina Grande, and the restaurant (though not the pool) is open to the public. It's terribly glamorous, but the vibe is one of a home from home. Staff are friendly and exceptionally helpful.

Luna
Via Matteotti 3 (081 837 0433/www.lunahotel. com). Closed Nov-mid Apr. **Rates** €210-€460 double. **Credit** AmEx, DC, MC, V.
The view is the thing here. Although the Luna is soberly furnished in a slightly old-fashioned style, the cheerful colours of the common areas, peaceful setting and spectacular position overlooking the Certosa and the sea make up for any design shortcomings. The hotel is approached via a pretty walk, shaded by bougainvillea and surrounded by gardens,

with an Olympic-size swimming pool and a restaurant (open for dinner only) perched on a rocky balcony above the sea.

La Minerva
Via Occhio Marino 8 (081 837 0374/www.la minervacapri.com). Closed mid Nov-mid Mar. **Rates** €140-€420 double. **Credit** AmEx, MC, V.
Away from the crowds, in a prime spot overlooking the sea, the Minerva is a delightfully traditional place with a loyal clientele. With five storeys of flower-filled terraces, charming original architectural detail and better views than its three-star peers, it's easy to see why. The superior rooms have terraces, and deluxe rooms have whirlpool bathtubs and private sea-facing terraces. There's no pool, unfortunately, but you can pay to use facilities at one of the neighbouring hotels.

La Prora
Via Castello 6 (081 837 0281/www.albergo laprora.it). Closed Nov-Mar. **Rates** €160-€180 double. **Credit** AmEx, DC.
Tucked away in the maze of streets above Via Roma, this charming little hotel is reached via the portico beside Santo Stefano on the Piazzetta. Built by a retired sea captain (*prora* means prow), the hotel sits proud on a bluff; some of the rooms have lovely sea views. All in all it's a quiet, central option, away from the crowds in old Capri.

Punta Tragara
Via Tragara 57 (081 837 0844/www.hotel tragara.it). Closed Nov-Mar. **Rates** €300-€780 double. **Credit** AmEx, DC, MC, V.
Designed by Le Corbusier in the 1920s as a private villa, this pink hotel also served as US headquarters during World War II. It has one of the best views and most impressive exteriors of any hotel on the island. The rooms, each with its own balcony overlooking the Faraglioni, are stylish and grand; the views are breathtaking; and the terrace bar, with its heated seawater pool, is a wonderful spot from which to watch the sun setting. Under-12s are not admitted.

Relais Maresca
Via Provinciale Marina Grande 284 (081 837 9619/www.relaismaresca.it). Closed Nov-Apr. **Rates** €150-€400 double. **Credit** AmEx, MC, V.
The location, down on Marina Grande, isn't great; on the plus side, the hotel is handy for the ferry and its bright, luxurious Mediterranean decor and lovely roof terrace compensate for a great deal. Perfect for boat-spotters, it offers a fine view of the ferry traffic and hustle of port life, and is a short stroll away from the popular Da Paolino (*see p203*).

La Scalinatella
Via Tragara 8 (081 837 0633/www.scalinatella. com). Closed Nov-Mar. **Rates** €300-€560 double. **Credit** AmEx, DC, MC, V.

La Scalinatella is a lovely boutique hotel with a magnificent, Moorish-style façade and country-house feel – perfect for a romantic weekend. Most of the rooms and suites have private terraces overlooking the Faraglioni rocks, and are tastefully decorated with Mediterranean-inspired interiors.
▶ *Next door is the slightly cheaper Casa Morgano (081 837 0158, www.casamorgano. com), run by the same owners. It has spa facilities, a pool and a series of bougainvillea-filled terraces.*

La Tosca
Via Birago 5 (081 837 0989/www.latoscahotel. com). Closed mid Nov-mid Mar. **Rates** €70-€140 double. **Credit** MC, V.
It may only have one star, but La Tosca is a wonderful option for visitors on a budget. It's spotlessly clean, decorated in a spare but elegant style, and is centrally located, in a quiet lane leading down to the Certosa. There are only 12 rooms, so book ahead. Rooms (many of which have balconies) are large, and continental breakfasts are served on a terrace overlooking the sea. Staff are friendly, attentive and very helpful when it comes to making arrangements and offering advice.

Villa Igea
Via Fuorlovado 36 (081 838 0111). Closed Nov-Mar. **Rates** €315-€1,550 apartment. **No credit cards.**
Anyone looking to rent an apartment could do worse than the lovely residences in this huge, yellow and white Liberty-style villa in central Capri. Sleeping two to four people, the apartments are a real bargain, especially in low season. The minimum booking is one week.

★ Villa Marina Hotel & Spa
Via Provinciale, Marina Grande 191 (081 837 6630/www.villamarinacapri.com). Closed Nov-Mar. **Rates** €500-€1,250 double. **Credit** AmEx, MC, V.
On the way from Marina Grande to the Piazzetta, the five-star Villa Marina has 27 luxury rooms, named after famous former visitors to Capri (Douglas, Malaparte, Marinetti, Munthe, Neruda et al). Each room is individually and extremely tastefully styled, perhaps with a mini library or stylish stone 'sharing' baths. Facilities include the on-site Stai spa, an infinity pool and a roof terrace with spectacular sea views. The charming staff couldn't be more helpful, and a shuttle bus transports guests to and from the port.

Resources

First aid
Guardia Medica *Piazza Umberto I (081 838 1239).* **Open** 24hrs daily.
In a medical emergency, the Guardia Medica will arrange transport to the mainland.

Internet
Capri Tech Internet Corner *Bar GabBiano, Via Cristoforo Colombo 76 (081 837 6531).*

Police
Carabinieri *Via Provinciale Marina Grande 42 (081 837 0000).*

Post office
Via Roma 50 (081 978 5211).
Via Provinciale Marina Grande 152 (081 837 7229).

Tourist information
Azienda Autonoma di Cura, Soggiorno e Turismo *Piazzetta Cerio 11, Marina Grande (081 837 0634/www.capritourism.com).* **Open** *Apr-Sept* 8.30am-8.30pm Mon-Sat. *Oct-Mar* 9am-3pm Mon-Sat.
Azienda Autonoma di Cura, Soggiorno e Turismo *Piazza Umberto I (081 837 0686).* **Open** *Apr-Oct* 8.30am-8.30pm Mon-Sat. *Nov-Mar* 9am-1pm, 3.30-6.45pm Mon-Sat.

ANACAPRI & AROUND

Incredibly for such a small island, the first road linking Capri town and Anacapri was only built in 1872. Until then, the two villages led different lives on the opposite sides of the seismic fracture and wall of cliffs that split the island in two.

Set on the cliff's western side at the base of Monte Solaro, the loose-knit cluster of houses that forms Anacapri is interspersed by olive groves and vineyards. A community of farmers and artisans began to form here in Greek times, but only really condensed into a proper village in the late Middle Ages. Anacapri's rural way of life and centuries of physical isolation are reflected in the proud, feisty character of the *anacapresi*, who preferred to work as ships' caulkers for the navy of Naples than have anything to do with the *capresi* down below.

The only means of communication between the two villages was the **Scala Fenicia**, a steep flight of around 900 steps built by Capri's first Greek settlers. Still in existence, it leads up from Marina Grande (the island's only proper port, which the *anacapresi* were forced to use even though it was in 'enemy territory') to the tiny chapel of **Sant'Antonio**, just below Villa San Michele.

When Swedish doctor Axel Munthe first walked up here in the late 19th century, overtaking the village postwoman (who couldn't read), the hostess of Anacapri's one and only inn told him that she had 'once been down to Capri', but it hadn't impressed her much. If rural Anacapri today receives as many visitors as swish Capri town, it is largely thanks to Munthe. His book, *The Story of San Michele,*

filled chilly northerners with longing for the 'warm South', bringing the rustic characters of Anacapri vividly to life. Translated into over 30 languages, Munthe's memoir continues to sell steadily around the world, more than seven decades after its publication in 1929.

Munthe first set foot on Anacapri in 1874 as a young medical student. It wasn't until 15 years later, when he had become the youngest and most sought-after society doctor in Paris, that he was able to realise his dream of building the clifftop **Villa San Michele** (*see right*), on the site of one of Tiberius's villas and a medieval chapel. Designed in an eclectic style that mixes Romanesque and Renaissance influences with Moorish trills, the villa and its trim gardens are studded with fragments of classical statuary.

The ruined **Castello di Barbarossa** on the crest above, named after the Greek pirate who destroyed it, is part of the same property; it can be visited on a free guided tour on Thursdays at 4pm (Apr-Oct; places are limited, book a day ahead). The hillside also has a resident population of peregrine falcons; weekend guided tours are organised in spring and autumn (call 081 837 1401 for details).

Munthe was the first of a steady trickle of foreign residents who preferred Anacapri's quiet charm to the more glitzy delights of Capri town: writers Compton Mackenzie and Graham Greene had houses here, and Queen Victoria of Sweden had a summer villa at Caprile, just south of the town. Today, the peace and quiet that attracted these escapees is challenged by the busloads of tourists that come to visit Villa San Michele and offload their euros in a slough of tacky souvenir shops. Away from this thankfully limited outbreak of bad taste, and out of season, Anacapri is an idyllic place in which to see the island's more rural side.

Gateway to the town, and the setting-down point for the buses that connect Anacapri with Marina Grande and Capri town, is little **Piazza Vittoria**. Most visitors head straight along the souvenir-lined Via Capodimonte to Villa San Michele. From the square, the pedestrianised Via Giuseppe Orlandi leads west past the tourist office into the centre of the old town. Halfway down on the right is the **Casa Rossa** (*see right*), an antiquity-encrusted folly built in 1876 by a former Confederate soldier, JC MacKowen, who wrote one of the first travel guides to the island.

On the left, Via San Nicola leads to Piazza San Nicola, dominated by the church of **San Michele Arcangelo** (*see right*). Continuing down Via Giuseppe Orlandi past the quaint church of **Santa Sofia**, constructed in 1510 (look out for carved *Pietà*) you reach the pretty district of **Le Boffe**; with its pavilion-like, round-roofed arches, it's the oldest part of town.

Also worth a visit is the **Parco Filosofico** (*see right*), on the way to Migliera. Meander through this 'Philosopher's Park', set up in 2000 by Swedish intellectual Gunnar Adler-Karlsson and his wife, and peruse some 60 quotations by Western philosophers, written in English and Italian on little ceramic tiles.

From Anacapri, two bus routes run west (*see p213*). One goes to the **Blue Grotto** (*see p202*), via the remains of **Villa Damecuta** (ask the bus driver to drop you off by the side road to the villa). One of Tiberius's 12 imperial villas, it was devastated first by the volcanic rain of Vesuvius, then by pillaging troops. Today, little remains, but it's a pretty spot for a picnic, covered in wild flowers in spring. The second bus goes to the lighthouse at **Punta Carena**, on Capri's south-western tip. Just before the lighthouse is one of the island's less crowded rocky beaches (to be avoided when the wind is blowing in from the west).

For walks from Anacapri, *see p212* **Scenic splendour**. An easy alternative to hiking up Monte Solaro is to take the *funivia* (funicular) from the station on Via Caposcuro (081 837 1428, www.seggioviamontesolaro.it, open Mar-Oct 9.30am-4.30pm daily, Nov-Feb 9.30am-3pm daily). The journey takes 12 minutes and costs €6 for a single, €8 return.

Casa Rossa
Via Giuseppe Orlandi 78 (081 838 2193). **Open** *May-Sept* 10.30am-1.30pm, 5.30-9pm Tue-Sun. *Oct-Apr* 10.30am-5pm Tue-Sun. **Admission** €2. **No credit cards**.

Anacapri.

Painted a striking shade of red, the crenellated former home of 19th-century American expat John MacKowen houses a permanent exhibition of landscapes, painted by various artists.

FREE Parco Filosofico
Via Migliera (081 837 1499/www.philosophical park.org). **Open** 9am-1hr before sunset daily. **Admission** free. **No credit cards**.
Inside the Philosophical Park, meandering paths lead past quotations from great thinkers, inscribed on majolica tiles. It's a peaceful, meditative place for a stroll.
▶ *The superb Da Gelsomina alla Migliera (see p210) is just opposite the park.*

San Michele Arcangelo
Piazza San Nicola (081 837 2396). **Open** *May-Sept* 9am-7pm daily. *Oct-Apr* 9am-2pm daily. **Admission** €2. **No credit cards**.
Beyond a standard Baroque façade lies an unusual Greek cross nave, enlivened by a delightful octagonal majolica floor dating from 1761. The theme is Eden, complete with Adam and Eve frolicking among ostriches, camels and crocodiles, as well as a few mythical creatures.

Villa San Michele
Viale Axel Munthe 34 (081 837 1401/www.villa sanmichele.eu). **Open** *May-Sept* 9am-6pm daily. *Apr, Oct* 9am-5pm daily. *Nov-Feb* 9am-3.30pm daily. *Mar* 9am-4.30pm daily. **Admission** €5. **No credit cards**.
There might be the odd visitor who tends to agree with writer Bruce Chatwin, who wrote in his Munthe-debunking essay 'Self-love among the Ruins' (reprinted in *Anatomy of Restlessness*) that in Pasadena or Beverly Hills, Munthe's creation wouldn't get more than a passing glance. Still, the views are spectacular, and the villa and gardens are preserved with Nordic tidiness by a foundation whose members are nominated by the Swedish state. Look out for the small Egyptian sphinx that gazes out to sea, which dates from the 11th century BC. It appears on countless postcards and posters, embodying the elusive, mystical spirit of Capri.
▶ *The gardens also host delightful concerts; ask at the tourist office (see p213) for information.*

Where to eat

Unsurprisingly, you're best off avoiding any establishment offering a €10 menu for a plate of pasta with salad and a drink.

€ Al Nido d'Oro
Viale de Tommaso 32 (081 837 2148). **Open** *May-Oct* noon-3.30pm, 7.30pm-midnight daily. *Nov-Apr* noon-3.30pm, 7.30pm-midnight Mon, Tue, Thur-Sun. **Average** €12. **Credit** AmEx, MC, V.

The Golden Nest is a simple, old-fashioned option just off Piazza Vittoria in central Anacapri, serving wood-fired pizzas and solid trattoria fare. There are pretty murals on the white walls, and jaunty gingham tablecloths. The menu offers excellent value for money. Many of the pizzas have been named after occupations – try the 'builder' or the 'upholsterer'.

★ Da Gelsomina alla Migliera

Via Migliera 72 (081 837 1499/www.da gelsomina.com). **Open** *May-Sept* 11.30-3.30pm, 7-11pm daily. *Oct-Dec, Mar, Apr* 11.30am-3.30pm Mon, Wed-Sun. Closed Jan, Feb. **Average** €35. **Credit** AmEx, MC, V.

Far from the madding crowd, this little oasis nestles in a vined hilltop in the *anacaprese* countryside. It boasts a stunning sea view and excellent food to match its scenic location. The menu revolves around fish- and meat-based local classics, cooked to perfection; the wine is delicious and the tiramisù superb. It's perfect for a day out with the kids, as it also has a swimming pool (open 10am-7pm); there are seven rooms for rent. Anacapri is half an hour's walk away; transfers can be arranged if you call ahead.

L'Olivo

Capri Palace Hotel, Via Capodimonte 2B (081 978 0111/www.capri-palace.com). **Open** 12.30-2.30pm, 7.30-10.30pm daily. Closed Nov-Mar. **Average** €150. **Credit** AmEx, MC, V.

Set within one of the island's most prestigious hotels, L'Olivo features impeccable decor, service and cuisine, best consumed on the delightful terrace. Chef Oliver Glowig's restaurant is the only establishment in Capri to have won two Michelin stars, thanks to his exquisite use of local produce and blending of humble *cucina povera* with haute cuisine. Typical fare includes squid stuffed with provola cheese and bay, or sea bass with oysters, seaweed and aniseed jelly. The wine list is one of the island's best.

Nightlife, arts & entertainment

Holidaymakers like to have a sundowner at the scenic **Lido del Faro** (Via Punta Carena, 081 837 1798, www.lidofaro.com, closed Nov-Mar; *see p201* **In the swim of things**), which also does decent food. Visitors who want to feel like royalty try the elegant (and expensive) **Bar degli Artisti** in the Capri Palace (*see right*). There's a handful of seasonal clubs; **Calambè** (081 837 2336) is at nearby Cala di Limmo.

In summer, Anacapri hosts a free music festival, with international performers (from Cuban to Kenyan), dodgy Italian pop, classical music, jazz and cinema, shown outside. Ask at the tourist office (*see right*) for the programme. The open-air **Teatro La Porta** (Via Axel Munthe 11, 081 837 2748, closed mid Oct-Apr) and nearby **Villa San Michele** (*see p208*) also host classical recitals, although the Teatro is closed for the 2009 season. Club **La Lanterna Verde** (Via Giuseppe Orlandi 1, 081 837 1427) hosts live music all year round.

Where to stay

Da Gelsomina alla Migliera (*see left*) also has rooms for rent.

Caesar Augustus

Via Giuseppe Orlandi 4 (081 837 3395/ www.caesar-augustus.com). Closed Nov-Mar. **Rates** €430-€550 double. **Credit** AmEx, MC, V.

Transformed into a hotel over 60 years ago, this luxury villa is set 1,000 feet above the sea, on a cliff looking out to the Bay of Naples and Marina Piccola. It capitalises on its magnificent setting with a two-tiered infinity swimming pool, which seems to extend into the sparkling blue sea below. The fragrant garden and terraces and many of the bedrooms have the same stupendous view. The modern rooms have antique furniture, king-size beds, tiled floors, marble bathrooms and balconies; some have jacuzzis and terraces, high above the sea.

Cala di Limmo

Via Nuova del Faro 122 (081 837 2488). Closed Jan-Feb. **Rates** €70 double. **No credit cards**.

This is a very simple place, with just three rooms. It's set in a large garden overlooking the Punta Carena and its lovely lighthouse, where you'll see the island's best sunsets. Set on the bus route into town, it's in a quiet spot without being isolated. The friendly owner also allows visitors to pitch camp in the grounds.

Capri Palace Hotel & Spa

Via Capodimonte 2B (081 978 0111/www.capri-palace.com). Closed Nov-Mar. **Rates** €330-€2,400 double. **Credit** AmEx, DC, MC, V.

Perched 300m (984ft) above the sea, the elegant Capri Palace has tailored every detail to perfection. White- and cream-hued decor, tastefully decorated rooms and a lovely pool and spa are glamorous yet understated. The catering is equally impressive: there's an unforgettable breakfast buffet, the superb L'Olivo (*see left*), and a cool cocktail bar, Bar degli Artisti. Owner Tonino Cacace has filled the hotel with modern art, including paintings by De Chirico, and has created three 'art suites'. Four rooms and two suites have their own private pools; the top suite, the Megaron (beloved of shy Hollywood stars), has a private roof garden with an olive tree and a panoramic swimming pool. The hotel also has three boats for private use.

Hotel San Michele

Via Giuseppe Orlandi 1/3/5 (081 837 1427/www.sanmichele-capri.com). Closed Nov-Mar. **Rates** €150-€400 double. **Credit** AmEx, DC, MC, V.

This large, rose-coloured hotel on the main road to Capri has the island's biggest swimming pool, and is a popular choice for families (it even offers swimming lessons). The decor is comfortable and old-fashioned, and service is friendly. Rooms have views over to Monte Solaro or of the sea, and some have sizeable sun terraces. If you're staying here in August, you can help to celebrate Ferragosto (August 14), when the hotel hosts a lively gala evening around the pool.

Villa Eva
Via Grotta Azzurra, trav. Via La Fabbrica 8, Anacapri (081 837 1549/www.villaeva.com). Closed Nov-Feb. **Rates** €70-€140 double. **Credit** AmEx, MC, V.
One of the cheapest options in Anacapri, Villa Eva is also, happily, one of the loveliest. Located en route from Anacapri to the Blue Grotto, the villa is set in a forest, with fantasy architecture, a stunning garden and a lovely pool. The rooms are spacious, and have appealing little patios overlooking the garden. It has a deal with a nearby restaurant, where guests are given special rates, and is within walking distance of the swimming platforms near the grotto, and Villa Damecuta (*see p209*).

Villa le Scale
Via Capodimonte 64 (081 838 2190/www.villale scale.com). Closed Nov-Mar. **Rates** €450 double. **Credit** AmEx, DC, MC, V.
This historic house has been transformed into an intimate, secluded retreat, open to residents only. There is an enchanted feel to the place: a jewel of a pool is set in lush gardens, filled with pomegranates, hydrangeas, palms and hibiscus. Built by a local baron in the 1800s, the house is furnished with art and antiques. Every room or suite – there are eight in total – is quite different, with antique pieces from the Far East or North Africa, and, depending on the theme of the room, a jacuzzi, Turkish bath, plunge pool or duplex shower. There's a lovely bar and restaurant, and guests can play tennis; those with buoyant bank accounts can rent out the whole villa. Children under 12 are not allowed.

Resources

First aid
Guardia Medica *Via Caprile 30 (081 838 1240).*

Internet
Capri Tech Internet Corner *Bar Due Pini, Piazza Vittoria 3 (081 837 1404).*

Police
Carabinieri *Via Caprile (081 837 1011).*

Post office
Viale de Tommaso 8 (081 837 1015).

Tourist information
Azienda Autonoma di Cura, Soggiorno e Turismo *Via Giuseppe Orlandi 59 (081 837 1524/www.capritourism.com).* **Open** *Apr-Sept* 9am-7pm Mon-Sat. *Oct-Mar* 9am-3pm Mon-Sat.

GETTING AROUND

Capri town is closed to all forms of motorised traffic beyond the bus terminus on Via Roma (bar little luggage-bearing electric trolleys, which are also licensed to carry people with disabilities). If you're staying in an upmarket hotel, you should be met at the quay by a porter, who'll have your luggage sent up to the hotel. Most of the swankier hotels in Anacapri, and some mid-range ones, have their own minibus.
Otherwise, the funicular, buses and taxis are at the end of the quay; the funicular to the left, taxis and buses to the right.
All public transport on the island – including the funicular from Marina Grande to Capri town, but not the Monte Solaro cable car – is covered by the **Unico Capri** ticket, which comes in three versions: €1.40 for a single trip, €2.20 for an hour on the whole network (allowing you to change at Anacapri for the Blue Grotto, for example) or €6.90 for a day pass. Tickets should be bought from the terminus and shown to the driver on boarding. If you get on at an intermediate stop, tickets can be bought from the driver. You can obtain a rechargeable Unico Capri prepaid card by leaving a deposit of €2.

By boat
For the **Blue Grotto** (*see p202*), take a speedboat from Marina Grande. A complete circuit of the island (*giro dell'isola*) is also offered by a number of operators, including **Lasercapri** (081 837 5208, www.lasercapri.com, €13) and **Gruppo Motoscafisti** (081 837 5646, www.motoscafisti capri.com, €14) in Marina Grande.
You can also rent small motorboats from Marina Grande or Marina Piccola (a licence is not required). Try **Capritime** (329 214 9811, www.capritime.com) for boat hire or trips in a typical Capri boat (*gozzo*) or a luxury speedboat, sail boat or yacht. Prices start at €175 for an afternoon on a boat (including captain, fuel and light snacks) accommodating up to six people.

By bus
In high season, be prepared to queue – especially if you get on at the Piazza Roma bus terminus or in Anacapri. The three main services are Marina Grande–Capri (6am-midnight, 6am-2am July-Sept), Marina Grande–Anacapri (6am-7pm, and until 10pm to connect with Caremar boats) and Capri–Anacapri (6am-2am). Other routes, with less frequent services, are Capri–Marina Piccola, Capri–Damecuta; Anacapri–Grotta Azzurra

Walk Scenic splendour

The Med's most glamorous island is also a walker's paradise.

Il Faraglioni

The Arco Naturale

There's some fine rambling to be had on Capri – and thanks to Monte Solaro, some trails are almost alpine in character. The following walks, at their best in spring and autumn, are old favourites; note that the fourth walk is for more experienced walkers. Suitable footwear, suncream, a decent hat and plenty of water are essentials – along with a jersey on cooler days.

ANACAPRI TO THE BLUE GROTTO
Time 1hr. **Grade** easy.
In the cooler season, one of the best ways to visit the **Blue Grotto** (*see p202*) from Anacapri is to walk down and take the bus back. From Piazza Armando Diaz in Anacapri, Via Cava and Via Lo Pozzo lead down to a path that continues past orchards and smallholdings to the parking lot above the Blue Grotto, which is also the bus terminus. Stop for a picnic en route at the **Villa Damecuta** (*see p209*).

ANACAPRI TO MIGLIERA
Time 45mins. **Grade** easy.
Another good walk from Anacapri is the flat, contour-hugging stroll to **Migliera**. Take Via Caposcuro, to the left of the Monte Solaro chairlift (*see p209*), and continue along it for a couple of kilometres (it soon changes its name to Via Migliera), in a landscape

that's about as rural as you get on Capri. Stop for lunch and a swim at **Da Gelsomina** (*see p210*). At the end of the path, the Belvedere di Migliera affords spectacular views over the cliffs below Monte Solaro.

I FARAGLIONI, GROTTA MATROMANIA & THE ARCO NATURALE
Time 1hr. **Grade** easy, but a stiff climb; the opposite way round is easier.
After the stroll up to **Villa Jovis** (*see p202*), this classic round trip is easily the best of the paved walks that depart from Capri town. From the **Belvedere di Tragara** (*see p200*), take either of the sets of steps that head downwards. After a steep turn-off down to the right to the Faraglioni (where there's a small, rocky beach platform), the path continues east around the wooded slopes of Monte Tuoro, with views over the rocky coast and **Villa Malaparte** (*see p198*).

Soon after the villa, the path becomes a flight of steps that leads up to the **Grotta Matromania**; some believe the huge cavern was sacred to the cult of Cybele (the Great Mother). The steps continue up to a junction by bar-restaurant **Le Grottelle** (*see p203*). Turn right here, and in a few minutes you'll see the steps leading to **Arco Naturale**, a limestone arch that was a favourite with Romantic travellers. To head back to Capri town, carry on straight past Le Grottelle along Via Matermania. Before you know it, you're back in the Piazzetta.

MONTE SOLARO VIA THE PASSETIELLO

Time *Up* 2hrs. *Down* 1hr 15mins. **Grade** *Up* a tough scramble. *Down* moderate.

From the terrace above Capri town's funicular station, the sheer mountain wall that divides Capri town from Anacapri looks impenetrable, aside from the road, with its beetling orange buses, and the zigzag **Scala Fenicia** staircase (*see p208*). But there is a third way up, all but invisible from below: the **Passetiello**. Although it's nowhere near as difficult as it looks, it's rather more than a Sunday stroll: the total ascent is 350 metres (1,149 feet), and it's only for hale and hearty walkers with no fear of heights.

From the Piazzetta, walk down Via Roma to the four-way junction known as Due Golfi. Take the road down to Marina Piccola, turning right almost immediately on to the paved lane that leads up past the side of the island's hospital. A little further on, a wooden map indicates the beginning of the path proper, marked with red and white flashes (though the colour scheme has changed at least once in recent years).

Villas and allotments give way to a forest of holm oak, and the going becomes steep.

Above the tree line, a tumble of rocks leads to a narrow gully – the Passetiello, a secret pass in the wall of rock that separates Capri from Anacapri. French soldiers used this route to surprise English troops quartered down below in 1808. Once over the pass, you emerge on the ridge of **Monte Santa Maria**, with magnificent views. Follow the marked path that heads left (due south), just below the ridge, to the hermitage of **Santa Maria a Cetrella** (open 2-5pm Thur), founded by Dominicans in the 14th century.

From here, the summit of **Monte Solaro** can be reached by taking the wide path that leads north-west to the pass of La Crocetta, where it joins the path up from Anacapri.

THE FORTRESS WALK

Time 3hrs each way. **Grade** easy.

A marked footpath, dubbed *Il Sentiero dei Fortini,* has been laid out along the lovely, little-visited west coast of the island: it connects **Punta Carena** and its impressive lighthouse with **Punta dell'Arcera**, not far from the Blue Grotto. You walk past five ruined Napoleonic forts and towers. Bring your swimming gear, as some of the coves along the way are hard to resist. The path tends to be too high to allow easy access, but there's a small set of steps into the water near the **Punta Campetiello**.

The **Belvedere di Tragara**.

(Blue Grotto) and Anacapri–Punta Carena (Faro).
Call **ATC** (081 837 0420) for information, or
Staiano Autotrasporti (081 837 2422,
www.staiano-capri.com) for the Blue Grotto
and Punta Carena lines.

By funicular railway

Departures from the station at Marina Grande to
Capri town (and vice versa) run every 15 minutes
(6.30am-10.10pm Apr-June; 6.30am-11pm
July-Sept; 6.30am-9pm Oct-Mar), and are run by
SIPPIC (081 837 0420); a return trip costs €2.80.

It can get crowded in high season, especially
in the early evening when the day-trippers leave;
if you need to get to Marina Grande quickly, take
the bus or walk (it takes 15-20 mins, via the path
that starts next to the entrance to the funicular).

By scooter

Given the motor traffic restrictions and
considering the congestion on Capri's narrow
roads, scooters are not necessarily the best way
to get around in high season. Out of season, it's
a different story. For this all-Italian experience,
try **Noleggio Motorino** (Via Marina Grande
280, 081 837 7941, €50/day, €15/hr) by the port,
or on Piazza Barile in Anacapri (no.26, 081 837
3888, €55/day, €15/hr).

By taxi

Capri's seven-seat, open-top taxis are unique to
the island. Allow €15 from the port to Capri town
(they can go no further than the taxi rank by the
bus terminus in Via Roma) and a few euros more
to Anacapri. There are only a couple of vintage
cars left on the island, but they can be booked
(Capri 081 837 0543; Anacapri 081 837 1175).
Short distances are charged according to a meter
reading; tour prices are negotiated, depending
on the season, duration and route chosen. You
can hail a cab, call or go to the ranks.

GETTING THERE

Naples newspaper, *Il Mattino*, publishes daily
updated timetables of all bus, train, sea and air
connections to and from Naples. On Capri, the
tourist offices give out a free timetable, updated
fortnightly, with sea crossings; these are also
posted on the Capri tourist board website (www.
capritourism.com). The services mentioned below
run daily. *See also p304* **Ferries & hydrofoils**.

By helicopter

Hollywood stars and anyone really pressed for
time can take a helicopter from Capodichino
airport in Naples to the heliport at Anacapri;
prices start from €1,500 per one-way flight for up
to four people. The flight takes about 17 minutes.
Contact **Sam Helicopters** (082 835 4155, 800
915012, www.flywithsam.it).

By sea from the Amalfi Coast

Consorzio Linee Marittime (089 873301,
081 871483, www.amalficoastlines.com) runs
hydrofoils Apr-Oct between Salerno, Amalfi,
Positano and Capri. From Positano, the journey
time is 30 minutes; fares range from €13-€14.50.

By sea from Ischia

Services run all year round, but are most frequent
from mid Apr-mid Oct. There are four hydrofoils
daily (three in the morning, one in the afternoon).
Two are run by **Alilauro** (081 991888, 081 497
2238, www.alilauro.it); the others are run by local
companies **Rumore Marittima** (www.rumore
marittima.it) and **Capitan Morgan** (081 985080).
From mid June-mid Sept, **Consorzio Linee
Marittime** also runs connections from Ischia.
Fares start at €15.50.

By sea from Naples

NLG Linea Jet (081 837 0819, 081 552 7209,
www.navlib.it) and **SNAV** (081 428 5555,
081 837 7577, www.snav.it) run hydrofoils
(hourly in summer) from the central quay of
Molo Beverello. SNAV also runs hydrofoils
from Naples' Mergellina dock at the western
end of the bay (every 2hrs in summer; handy
for the mainline train station and metro at
Napoli Mergellina). Crossing time by hydrofoil
is around 40 minutes.

Caremar (081 837 0700, www.caremar.it) also
runs six daily ferries from Beverello, all year
round. Three are high-speed *traghetti veloci*
(50mins); the others take 80 mins. Ferries are
cheaper, and the only option when the sea is too
choppy for the hydrofoils. The last boats leave
around 8.30pm (winter), 10pm (summer). Ferries
cost €9.60, hydrofoils and fast ferries €12.50-€16.

By sea from Sorrento

Caremar (*see above*) and **LMP Alilauro** (081
837 6995, www.consorziolmp.it) hydrofoils leave
from Sorrento's Marina Piccola for the 20-minute
crossing to Capri (at least half-hourly in summer).
There are also less frequent conventional ferries.
Ferries cost €9.80, hydrofoils €14.

By sea metro

The **Metro del Mare** (199 600700, www.metro
delmare.com) runs mid June-early Sept, linking
the main coastal towns of the Campania region.
It has six lines; Capri is on the MM4 connecting
Naples's Beverello quay to Sapri via Capri or
Acciarola, Casal Velino, Palinuro and Camerota.
There are only two boats a day, but it saves time
if you're coming from or heading to the Cilento.

By water taxi

Water taxis are operated by **Sercomar** (081 837
8781). A taxi (six people maximum) from Naples
to Capri costs €600; Sorrento to Capri is €400.

Ischia

A green and pleasant land.

Visitors to the 'green island' can be thankful for its proximity to neighbouring Capri, which siphons off some of the tourist hordes. Still, Ischia has no shortage of admirers: even a brief visit will reveal how wonderfully green and lush the island is, thanks to its volcanic soil.

A day trip isn't enough to fully appreciate Ischia's delights, though; at least a day or two is needed to discover its secrets. There are excellent restaurants (if you know where to look); great hotels, tucked away in hidden corners; exotic gardens and verdant forests. The island's bubbling thermal springs and potent volcanic mud have also drawn visitors for centuries, and its long-established spa scene continues to thrive.

INTRODUCING THE ISLAND

Although the Greeks were the first to arrive on the island, in the eighth century BC, it was under the Romans that Ischia became famous for its thermal cure treatments. Under Neapolitan rule in the Middle Ages, it suffered badly from attacks by North African Saracens. Throughout its history, various parts of the island (which is really a complex volcano) have opened up, unleashing devastating lava flows. In 1301, lava inundated the area between what is now Ischia Porto and Ischia Ponte, forcing its inhabitants to leave the island for Baia on the mainland. When they returned, they crowded on to the **Castello Aragonese** (*see p219*), a fortified rocky outcrop off Ischia Ponte.

The Castello was hotly fought over by the Angevins and Aragonese throughout the 14th century, and remained a place of refuge from marauding Saracens, who continued to menace the island until as late as 1796.

When Ischia supported the Parthenopean Republic in 1799, King Ferdinando's British allies soon overran the place. The British had more trouble ousting the French, who occupied Ischia in 1806; the devastation that the British, under Nelson, wreaked in their bombardment of the Castello Aragonese can still be seen.

These days, the island that was so desperately coveted by the Saracens is once more being overrun, this time with luggage-toting visitors and island-hopping yachters, here for its relaxing spas or a chance to spend a night or two in the Castello's cloister (*see p221*).

Note that Ischia's churches tend to open to the public at the discretion of their priests. In general, most can be visited from around 7am to 11am or noon, and from 5pm or 6pm to 7pm or 8pm. To be sure of getting in, go immediately before or after Mass (times are posted on the door). Bear in mind that many churches are known by several different names.

BOOKING A HOTEL

Most visitors tend to stay in the generally unattractive (though mercifully low-rise) accommodation in Ischia's main port towns and villages, and it's easy to miss the better, more hidden options.

Many hotels offer only half board (meaning breakfast and dinner are included), especially during the summer. Ask firmly for *camera con*

INSIDE TRACK
MONSTROUS STIRRINGS

According to Greek mythology, after Typhon rose up against the gods, hurling mountains at them, a vengeful Zeus imprisoned him below Ischia. There the unfortunate monster remains for all eternity. He hasn't tried to shrug the weight off his back since an earthquake in 1883, but his sighs of fiery vapour and hot rivers of tears give away his presence.

colazione (bed and breakfast), though, and most will reluctantly quote you a price. Single supplements, and steep ones at that, are almost always applied if you're travelling alone.

Most hotels close from mid October to Easter, though this is not a hard and fast rule; many will open earlier or close later if the weather permits. A number of hotels now also open around Christmas and New Year.

ISCHIA PORTO & ISCHIA PONTE

Once two separate towns, **Ischia Porto** and **Ischia Ponte** (formerly called Villa dei Bagni and Borgo Celsa, respectively) stretch from the ferry port to Castello Aragonese, linked by a busy, tree-lined road. Colourful Porto is one long hotel- and shop-filled agglomeration, whereas Ponte maintains some of its sleepy fishing village charm.

The swift and complex manoeuvring of ferries and hydrofoils in the little port can distract you from the uniqueness of the harbour itself. Until 1854, this was an inland lake in an extinct volcanic crater, but when the island fell under Spanish control, King Ferdinando II was sickened by the smell of its brackish waters, and demanded that an opening be made to the sea. Be prepared for traffic jams blocking access to the ferries on busy Sunday evenings, and throughout the whole of August.

Overlooking the port, the church of **Santa Maria di Portosalvo**, also built in 1854, was another of Ferdinando's good works. East of the church, the former royal palace is now a military spa, of all things, its gateposts guarded by imposing lions. Across the road, another

old spa, the **Antiche Terme Comunali**, now houses government offices and hosts occasional (often mediocre) art exhibitions.

Over on the eastern shore of the port, via Porto leads past restaurants and bars out to the point at **Punta San Pietro**, dominated by a dark-red underwater research station (closed to the public).

Ischia's (theoretically) pedestrianised main drag, Via Roma, which becomes Corso Vittoria Colonna, is usually packed. Lanes running north of via Roma lead to the town's main beach, **spiaggia del Lido**. Where corso Colonna meets via Gigante, you'll find the church of **San Pietro** (also known as the Madonna delle Grazie in San Pietro), a Baroque extravaganza with a curving façade.

Just beyond the junction with Via d'Avalos, a gate off the main road leads to the slightly unkempt but beautifully shady gardens of the **Villa Nenzi Bozzi** (open 7am-1hr before sunset daily). Looking uphill from here, the stone pines – those that haven't been sacrificed to creeping construction – are all that remain of the woods planted in the mid 19th century on the great lava flow from Monte Arso; beneath them is an entire village, Geronda, that was buried in the devastating eruption of 1301. The little chapel of **San Girolamo** (venerated for its splendid painting of the Madonna della Pace) commemorates the disaster.

The eastern end of Corso Colonna, and Via Pontano, run along the dark sands of **spiaggia dei Pescatori**, where fishing boats pull up among the sunbathers; from here, there's an unimpeded view across to the Castello. At the top of the steps off corso Colonna, the church of **Sant'Antonio in Santa Maria delle Grazie**

Spiaggia dei Pescatori.

Ischia Porto.

(or Sant'Antonio a Mandra) was built in the 18th century to replace the 14th-century original cut down by Arso's lava flow. Inside are the remains of San Giovanni Giuseppe della Croce, the island's patron saint.

Via Seminario is home to the **Palazzo del Vescovado** (Bishop's Palace, currently closed for restoration), where early Christian relics and historic objects are on display. Opposite, Vicolo Marina leads to the 16th-century **Palazzo Malcoviti**; stark and forbidding as you approach, the palazzo hides a pretty flower-filled courtyard behind.

On via Mazzella, the 17th-century church of **Santo Spirito** (also known as San Giovanni Giuseppe) has a fine 18th-century marble altar. Across the road from here, the **Cattedrale dell'Assunta** (or Santa Maria della Scala) became Ischia's cathedral after its predecessor in the Castello Aragonese was bombarded by the Royal Navy in 1809. The original 12th-century church was replaced in the 17th and 18th centuries, but the 14th-century baptismal font survived, as did the Romanesque wooden crucifix, and a 14th-century painting of the Madonna in the right-hand end of the nave.

The building facing the cathedral, Palazzo dell'Orologio, is home to the engaging **Museo del Mare** (*see p218*), where nets, tackle, photos, stamps and a few posters of films shot on the island chart Ischia's relationship with the sea. Via Mazzella continues to the lovely 1432 **Ponte Aragonese** bridge, and

then on to the Castello Aragonese. The colourful victim of an Italy-wide craze following on from the success of a film called *Ho Voglia di Te* (I want you), the bridge's lampposts are covered in padlocks or 'locks of love', secured by lovers who throw the key into the water as a symbol of their enduring devotion.

The rocky outcrop on which the **Castello Aragonese** sits was fortified in the fifth century BC by Greeks from Syracuse in Sicily. Since then it has been used as a stronghold by Romans, Goths, Arabs and just about every other group that ruled, or tried to rule, Naples. When Monte Arso erupted in 1301, it was within the thick walls of the castle that the locals sought protection.

Alfonso of Aragon fortified the crumbling rock in the mid 15th century, adding the bridge and making the Castello into an impregnable fortress where the island's inhabitants could

---

INSIDE TRACK
AS SEEN ON SCREEN

The fictional Mongibello of Anthony Minghella's *The Talented Mr Ripley* was filmed in Ischia and Procida, with **Palazzo Malcoviti** (*see left*) serving as the palatial apartment where the glamorous Dickie Greenleaf (Jude Law) and Marge (Gwynneth Paltrow) lived.

AROUND NAPLES

take refuge during Saracen attacks. Over the centuries, its influnce waxed and waned (*see right* **Profile**), leaving a rich historial legacy for visitors to explore.

There's a lift up to the castle's higher levels, but if you're feeling energetic, take the magnificent tunnel hewn through the solid rock by King Alfonso. Paths to the Castello's various churches, exhibition spaces and viewpoints are clearly signposted. Although it's now a tourist draw, the Castello is privately owned, and the former ruler's residence at the top of the building is closed to the public.

Ischia's own private Atlantis, the Roman town of Aenaria, may lie immediately to the east of the Castello Aragonese. According to contemporary records, this thriving settlement sank beneath the waves some time during the second century AD. Underwater explorers have come up with a number of ancient artefacts from the zone, lending credence to the legend.

Around the Bay of Cartaromana, the 16th-century chapel of **Sant'Anna** overlooks rocks thrusting out of the sea. The annual Feast of Sant'Anna (26 July) sees brightly decorated fishing boats and rafts from Ischia, Procida and Capri competing for a trophy in the bay, and a spectacular firework display. Nearby, the square **Torre Michelangelo** (open for the odd concert in summer) may or may not be where the Renaissance genius stayed when attending Vittoria Colonna's court (*see right* **Profile**).

★ Castello Aragonese
Via Pontile Aragonese (081 992834/www. castelloaragonese.it). **Open** 9am-1hr before sunset daily. **Admission** €10; €6 reductions. **No credit cards**.

Museo del Mare
Via Giovanni da Procida 2 (081 902319/081 907277/www.museodelmareischia.it). **Open**

July, Aug 10.30am-12.30pm, 6.30-10pm daily. *Apr-June, Sept, Oct* 10.30am-12.30pm, 3-7pm daily. *Nov-Jan, Mar* 10.30am-12.30pm daily. Closed Feb. **Admission** €3. **No credit cards**.

Where to eat & drink

Alberto Ischia
Via Cristoforo Colombo 8 (081 981259/mobile 349 655 3963/www.albertoischia.it). **Open** noon-3pm, 7-11pm daily. Closed Nov-mid Mar. **Average** €60. **Credit** AmEx, DC, MC, V.
Boasting a starry clientele (Gwyneth Paltrow, Kate Moss and the late Anthony Minghella among them), Alberto's sits on a platform jutting out over the blue sea. It serves imaginative versions of local favourites; the marinated fish carpaccio is famous and the pasta with *spigola* (sea bass), almonds and tomato is excellent.

★ € Un Attimo DiVino
Via Porto 103 (081 1936 8069). **Open** *Apr-Oct* 11am-2am daily. *Nov-Mar* 11am-2am Mon, Tue, Thur-Sun. Closed 1wk Jan. **Average** €30. **Credit** AmEx, MC, V.
'A moment of wine' is an *enoteca gastronomica* owned by chef Raimondo Triolo – and what an experience it is. Over 700 wines are available, many of them lining the walls, and the simple and seasonal food is exceptionally good: a raviolo of mozzarella steamed in a fish sauce, say, followed by sea bass cooked in potato batter and drizzled with basil oil, with unbelievably good tiramisù to finish.

★ Bar Calise
Via Sogliuzzo Antonio 69 (081 991270). **Open** *Apr-Oct* 7am-2am daily. *Nov-Mar* 7am-midnight Mon, Wed-Sun. **Credit** MC, V.
Partially hidden in a pine-filled park and one of the oldest bars in Ischia, Bar Calise has been a hit with locals and tourists for almost a century. Customers flock here for morning coffee, a pastry-based sugar rush in the late afternoon, or a chance to dance or listen to local music on summer evenings. A second Bar Calise can be found near the ticket offices at the Port, and the owners also run a disco-pub/pizzeria in Casamicciola Terme.

★ € Da Ciccio
Via Luigi Mazella 32 (081 991686). **Open** *May-Sept* noon-3.30pm, 7.30pm-midnight daily. *Oct-Apr* 11.30am-3.30pm, 7.30pm-midnight Mon, Wed-Sun. **Average** €30. **Credit** AmEx, DC, MC, V.
Not to be confused with the bar of the same name found at Ischia Porto, Da Ciccio is a family-run fish restaurant in Ponte. Expect excellent local dishes like *calamari ripieni* (stuffed squid), *polipetti affogati* (baby squid 'drowned' in tomato sauce) and *frittata di paranza* (fish omelette), enhanced by friendly service and reasonable prices.

Profile Castello Aragonese

The rise and fall of a mighty fortress.

First fortified in the fifth century BC, the rocky outcrop that accomodates the **Castello Aragonese** (*see left*) has been used as a stronghold for centuries. Beleagured locals have long found refuge here, sheltering within the castle's sturdy walls when Monte Arso erupted in 1301, and during the Saracen pirate attacks that plagued the island for centuries.

In the 16th century, the castle was home to a brilliant court that centred around the beautiful and devout Vittoria Colonna, wife of Ischia's feudal chief, Ferdinando Francesco d'Avalos. Her verses were praised by the poet Ludovico Ariosto, her learning by the humanist philosopher Pietro Bembo. But it was Vittoria's profound and touchingly platonic relationship with Michelangelo that ensured her lasting fame. 'Nature, that never made so fair a face, remained ashamed, and tears were in all eyes', wrote the artist in 1574, after watching over the dying Vittoria.

By the 18th century, the Castello was home to 2,000 families, 13 churches and a few Poor Clare (Clarisse) nuns. A hundred years later, with the Saracens no longer a threat, the families had moved out and the castle was falling into ruin. What time hadn't destroyed, the British finished off when they bombarded the island in 1809 in a bid to oust its French occupiers. The crippled fortress later became a prison.

Inside the castle, the 18th-century church of the **Immacolata** has a stark white interior built to a Greek cross plan, and holds temporary exhibitions. The convent of **Santa Maria della Consolazione**, founded in 1575, proved a convenient place for families with more titles than funds to park their dowry-less younger

daughters. The girls were consigned to a life of prayer until they died, at which point their corpses were placed sitting upright on macabre thrones in the *cimitero* beneath the convent. The living nuns visited their decomposing sisters daily as a stark reminder of mortality. The nuns remained immured in their convent until 1809.

Built after the 1301 eruption, the **ex-Cattedrale dell'Assunta** was given a heavy Baroque reworking in the early 18th century; the stucco decorations that survived the British shelling are eerily lovely. Restoration of the crypt revealed frescoes dating from the 13th to 16th centuries, some by the School of Giotto; in 2001, another, much older, fresco was found behind one of the walls. The elegant, grey and white hexagonal church of **San Pietro a Pantaniello** dates from the mid 16th century.

I'M KING OF THE CASTELLO
Book in to **Il Monastero** (*see p221*) and you can spend the night inside the ancient castle walls.

Taking the plunge

Where to sample Ischia's centuries-old spa culture.

Negombo.

GIARDINI POSEIDON
Via Mazzella, Spiaggia di Citara (081 908 7111/www.giardiniposeidon.it). **Open** 9am-7pm daily. Closed Nov-Mar. **Admission** €28 all day; €23 after 1pm. **Credit** (treatments only) AmEx, MC, V.
This grand old spa complex comprises saunas, 21 pools, jacuzzis and a long private beach – all run with firm Teutonic efficiency. Terraced pools and a bar on the volcanic cliff-side offer fine sea views.

NEGOMBO
Via Baia di San Montano, Lacco Ameno (081 986152/www.negombo.it). **Open** 8.30am-7pm daily. Closed mid Oct-mid Apr. **Admission** €32 all day; €29 after 1pm. **Credit** AmEx, DC, MC, V.
In a beautiful garden with more than 500 exotic plant species, the Negombo has various thermal and sports facilities, including a number of inviting pools. Guests also have access to the pretty San Montano beach.

PARCO TERMALE APHRODITE APOLLON
Via Petrelle, Sant'Angelo (081 999219/ www.aphrodite.it). **Open** 8am-6pm daily. Closed Nov-Feb. **Admission** €25 all day; €18 after 1pm. **Credit** AmEx, DC, MC, V.
Rambling over the headland east of Sant'Angelo, the Aphrodite has 12 pools, as well as saunas and gyms; a boat-taxi from Sant'Angelo port is included in its admission fee. Massages (from €30) and fitness and medical treatments are extra.

TERME BELLIAZZI
Piazza Bagni 134, Casamicciola (081 994580/www.termebelliazzi.it). **Open** 8am-1pm, 5-7pm Mon-Fri; 8am-1pm Sat. Closed Nov-mid Apr. **Admission** free. **Credit** AmEx, MC, V.
This slightly dreary shrine to the healthy body is built over ancient Roman pools, and offers massages (€16-€45), a dip in the heated pool and whirlpool bath (€25) and mud treatments (€30). The waters here are said to help alleviate respiratory disorders.

TERME DI CAVA SCURA
Via Cava Scura, Spiaggia dei Maronti, Serrara Fontana (081 905564/081 999242/www.cavascura.it). **Open** 8.30am-8pm daily. Closed mid Oct-mid Apr. **Admission** free. **No credit cards**.
Hewn out of tall cliffs at the end of a long coastal walk, this is a spa for devotees. There's a natural sauna in a dingy cave, grave-like baths with steaming sulphurous water (€10), massages (€20) and thermal and beauty treatments (from €20).

TERME DELLA REGINA ISABELLA
Piazza San Restituta, Lacco Ameno (081 994322/www.reginaisabella.it). **Open** 8am-1pm, 4-7pm Mon-Sat; 8am-1pm Sun. Closed Jan-Mar. **Admission** free. **Credit** AmEx, DC, MC, V.
This spa is decidedly in the grand style, with massages ranging from €37-€93, a whole host of skin treatments and personal gym programmes.

Ice Da Luciano
Via Luigi Mazzella 140 (333 238 3056). **Open**
Mar-Apr 9.30am-9pm daily. *May-Sept* 7.30am-
2am daily. Closed Oct-Feb. **No credit cards**.
Popular with locals and an obligatory stop during a
passeggiata along the Via Mazzella – Ischia Ponte's
main drag – is relative newcomer Ice Da Luciano.
Owner Luciano sticks to traditional flavours, and is
particularly proud of his mint with chocolate chip.
▶ *For more on Italian ices, see p131.*

€ Oh! X Bacco
Via Luigi Mazzella 20 (081 991354). **Open**
Mar-Dec 11am-3pm, 6.30pm-midnight Mon,
Wed-Sun. Closed Jan, Feb. **No credit cards**.
A shrine to Bacchus, this wine bar serves hearty
bruschette (from €3), salads, *salumeria* (charcuterie)
and cheeses. There's an excellent *menu di degus-
tazione* (taster menu) for €7.50, and a good choice of
wines from Campania to take away.

€ Pane & Vino
Via Porto 24 (081 991046). **Open** *Apr-Oct*
11.30am-3pm, 6pm-2am daily. *Nov-Mar* 11.30am-
3pm, 7pm-midnight daily. **Credit** MC, V.
The *pane* (bread) served here, in what is primarily
a wine shop, is extraordinarily good, as are the
cheeses, cold meats and the few hot dishes that
change daily. Wash it all down with something from
the fine range of *vino*, which can be ordered by the
glass or bottle at little more than off-the-shelf prices.

€ Ristorante Pizzeria Pirozzi
Via Seminario 51 (081 983217). **Open** *Apr-Oct*
12.30-4.30pm, 7pm-2am daily. *Nov-Mar* 12.30-
3.30pm, 6.30pm-midnight Tue-Sun. **Average**
Pizzeria €15. *Restaurant* €30. **Credit** AmEx,
DC, MC, V.
Although the pasta and fish dishes are good, especially the *linguine all'astice* (lobster with flat pasta),
locals flock here for Fabio's pizzas (you can watch
him prepare a margherita on YouTube). Fried appe-
tisers such as *crochette* (fried mashed potatoes)
stuffed with cheese and ham also go down well. If
you don't have time for a sit-down meal, grab a
quick bite from the counter near the entrance.

Where to stay

Hotel Hermitage & Park Terme
*Via Leonardo Mazzella 80 (081 984242/www.
hermitageischia.it).* Closed Dec-Mar. **Rates**
€80-€130 double. **Credit** MC, V.
A short stroll from the port, the Hermitage is a
slightly old-fashioned but clean and comfortable
option, set amid fabulous gardens. There are two
pools and a spa with thermal waters and, like many
places on the island, the hotel offers half-board
accommodation. Wi-Fi is laid on in the lounge, but
so are the hotel's entertainment evenings, which
might make online concentration difficult.

Miramare e Castello
*Via Pontano 5 (081 991333/www.miramare
ecastello.com).* Closed late Oct-mid Apr. **Rates**
€280 double. **Credit** AmEx, DC, MC, V.
As its name suggests, this hotel faces the sea (it's literally on the beach), and is eyeball to eyeball with
the Castello. Rooms are tastefully furnished in
shades of blue; needless to say, rates rise for a sea
view or balcony. The spa centre offers weekly pampering packages from €410.

★ Il Monastero
*Castello Aragonese 3 (081 992435/www.albergo
ilmonastero.it).* Closed Nov-Mar. **Rates** €120-
€140 double. **Credit** AmEx, DC, MC, V.
Located inside the Castello Aragonese, Il Monastero
has one of the finest views in the world – and compared to much of the accommodation on Ischia, it's
ridiculously cheap. Most of the 22 rooms have sea
views, and there's a lovely patio where breakfast
and dinner (by reservation only) are served.
▶ *There's no spa pampering here, but guests are
eligible for discounts at the Negombo, see left.*

★ Il Moresco
*Via Emanuele Gianturco 16 (081 981355/www.
ilmoresco.it).* Closed late Oct-mid Apr. **Rates**
€230-€350 double. **Credit** AmEx, DC, MC, V.
The elegant Moresco (part of a group that includes
the Grand Hotel Excelsior across the road) lives up
to its name with low, Moorish-style arches and
wrought ironwork. The gardens are delightful and
it's close to the sea, with a thermal pool in a rocky
cave nearby. Staff are charming and informative.

La Villarosa
*Via Giacinto Gigante 5 (081 991316/www.la
villarosa.it).* Closed Nov-Mar. **Rates** €170-€240
double. **Credit** AmEx, DC, MC, V.
Immersed in a jungly garden close to the centre of
town, this is a homely place with comfortable nooks,
antiques in hidden corners, and a fourth-floor dining room with a fine view over the town. There are
guest chalets dotted among the greenery, as well as
all the usual spa treatments.

The north coast
CASAMICCIOLA TERME

Ischia's second port, Casamicciola, added *terme*
(thermal spring) to its name in 1956. As far back
as the first century AD, however, Pliny the
Elder wrote about the town's Gurgitello spring,
where water bubbles out of the earth at 27°C
(80°F). Centuries later, Casamicciola came up
with the idea of combining luxury hotels and
thermal treatments for medical conditions.

By 1883, when the town was razed by an
earthquake that killed 2,300 people, a stopover

at Casamicciola was an essential part of any young gentleman's grand tour of Europe. Although a decrease in demand for spa cures has driven many centres out of business, there's still plenty of scope here for soaking, sweating and inhaling the waters from the natural wells and springs bubbling from verdant Monte Tabor above the town. The emphasis is on serious cures rather than beauty pampering (*see p226* **Nature's cure?**).

Despite its ancient roots, most of what you see in Casamicciola today was built after the 1883 earthquake. The seafront is crowded with bars, and the desolate shell of the once-glorious **Pio Monte della Misericordia** spa dominates the central stretch; a market (open 6am-3pm Mon & Fri) sells tacky clothes and fresh produce behind the spa's remains.

One block back from the congested coast road, there's a warren of narrow streets and gaily painted houses. East of the Pio Monte, roads striking inland lead to Corso Vittorio Emanuele, which winds uphill. Via Cretaio (left at the T-junction) heads steadily up towards Monte Rotaro (be prepared for a serious hike, or take a taxi). Two kilometres along on the left, there's a green metal bar across a track that leads into a volcanic crater. Thick with myrtle and oak trees and criss-crossed by footpaths, it looks like a sylvan glade. The idyll conceals a surprise, though: if you stumble across anything looking like a rabbit hole, you can put your hand inside to feel the volcanic steam the ground exhales.

Corso Vittorio Emanuele continues to Piazza dei Bagni. Casamicciola's main *gurgitello* spring, below the **Terme Belliazzi** (*see p220*), has pools built by the Romans. Further uphill, Via Paradisiello leads to the huge red *municipio* (town hall) that dominates the town. The view from the square in front is stunning. The town council has also taken over Villa Bellavista, where the **Museo Civico** (*see below*) contains old photos and maps. Still further up is the church of **Sacro Cuore**, dating from 1898.

ꜰʀᴇᴇ Museo Civico Villa Bellavista

Via Principessa Margherita 64, Casamicciola Terme (081 507 2535/www.comunecasamicciola. it/museo). **Open** *June, July, Sept* 9am-1pm Mon, Wed, Fri; 9am-1pm, 3-6pm Tue, Thur; 6-10pm Sun. *Aug* 9am-1pm Mon, Wed, Fri; 6-10pm Sun. *Oct-May* 9am-1pm Mon-Fri. *Guided tours* June-Sept 6-10pm Sun, by request. **Admission** free.

LACCO AMENO

Piazza Santa Restituta and the candy-pink and white 19th-century church of the same name are the heart of this seaside town, built on the remains of one of Italy's first Greek settlements.

The body of Tunisian virgin martyr Restituta arrived on nearby San Montano beach in the fourth century, borne, it was said, by lilies; this miracle is depicted in the church's artworks.

Below, in the **Area Archeologica di Santa Restituta**, are the remains of a fourth-century Christian basilica, a late-antique Roman necropolis and ovens for ceramic production from the Hellenistic period (the third to second centuries BC).

Uphill from the piazza, the 18th-century **Villa Arbusto** houses the **Museo Archeologico di Pithecusae**, named in honour of Ischia's ancient Greek moniker and home to beautifully arranged artefacts. One of its prize possessions is 'Nestor's Cup', inscribed with probably the oldest transcription of a Homeric verse in existence: it dates from around 740BC and was used in a burial ceremony. Part of the villa is dedicated to the life of film producer and publishing magnate Angelo Rizzoli, who once lived here, while its gardens host summer concerts and art installations.

Lacco Ameno's best known landmark, though, is the *fungo* (mushroom) that sits in the water off the seafront promenade. Ten metres (33 feet) tall, the chunk of volcanic rock is thought to have been catapulted here thousands of years ago by a rumbling Monte Epomeo.

Heading west out of town, the **Baia di San Montano** has one of the island's best beaches; follow signs to the Negombo (*see p220* **Taking the plunge**) to reach the long, sandy crescent. There's a public area, a section for guests at the Hotel della Baia (*see right*), and another stretch for people who have paid for a session at the spa.

Area Archeologica di Santa Restituta

Piazza Santa Restituta, Lacco Ameno (081 992442). **Open** 9.30am-12.30pm, 4.30-6pm Mon-Sat. **Admission** €3. **No credit cards.**

★ Museo Archeologico di Pithecusae

Villa Arbusto, Corso Angelo Rizzoli 210, Lacco Ameno (081 900356/www.pithecusae.it). **Open** *Apr-Oct* 9.30am-12.30pm, 4-8pm Tue-Sun. *Nov-Mar* 9.30am-12.30pm, 4.30-6pm Tue-Sun. **Admission** €5. **No credit cards.**

Where to stay & eat

You'll need to arrange your own transport to reach the best restaurant in Casamicciola, which is located in the hills around five kilometres out of town. At **Il Focolare** (Via Cretajo al Crocifisso, 081 902944, www.trattoria ilfocolare.it, closed Wed from Oct-Apr, lunch Mon-Fri, average €35), the D'Ambra family uses mountain produce such as rabbit, snails, chestnuts and herbs to create wonderfully earthy, flavoursome dishes.

Mezzatorre.

Lacco Ameno's seaside restaurants are rather more hit and miss, and sandwiches are often a visitor's best bet. Luckily, Ischia's traditional sandwich, the hearty *zingara* (ham, cheese, tomato, lettuce and mayo on a toasted roll) is served in most places.

The new **Hotel Marina 10** (Piazza Marina 10, 081 900516, www.marina10.it, closed Jan, €85-€110 double) is just off Casamicciola's main thoroughfare. Its 20 modern rooms have the option of garden or sea views.

Lacco Ameno's **Albergo della Regina Isabella** (Piazza San Restituta 1, 081 994322, www.reginaisabella.it, closed Jan-Mar, €310-€450 double) is a grand hotel built in the 1950s by Angelo Rizzoli. It has a pool overlooking the beach, with a glorious spa treatment centre. **Villa Angelica** (Via IV Novembre 28, 081 994524, www.villaangelica.it, closed Nov-Mar, €85 double) is a beautiful, palm-filled hotel with a thermal pool and massage treatments.

Off the road between Lacco and Forio, the **Hotel della Baia** (Via San Montano, 081 995453, www.negombo.it, closed Nov-Mar, €160 double) is quiet, comfortable, and set on one of Ischia's loveliest beaches. Further up the road, down a secluded lane, the stately but charming **Mezzatorre** (Via Mezzatorre 23, 081 986111, www.mezzatorre.it, closed mid Oct-mid Apr, €280-€700 double) has an excellent spa, lovely views from the guestrooms, and stone steps leading down to the sea. Visitors in search of luxurious seclusion can book a suite in a separate building, with a canopied bed and private outdoor patio and sunken whirlpool.

Forio & the west coast
FORIO & AROUND

The largest town on Ischia, with around 20,000 inhabitants, Forio has some of the island's best restaurants and some of its worst traffic jams. In times past its problems were more serious; its exposed position left it prey to attacks by Saracen pirates, so 12 watchtowers were built along the coast. One of them, the late 15th century **Il Torrione**, still dominates the town centre with its craggy crenellations. It's open occasionally for small exhibitions.

There are more than 20 churches in and around Forio, most of which were heavily

---

INSIDE TRACK SPA DIY

If you don't get a chance to visit one of the island's spas (*see p220*), stock up on beauty products at **Ischia Thermae** (17 Via Monsignor Schioppa, Forio, 081 997745, www.ischiathermae.com). Volcanic mud and spring water are among the key ingredients.

La Mortella.

reworked during the 18th century, and none of which observes regular opening hours. The decoration of many of the town's churches and chapels was entrusted to local mannerists Cesare Calise and Alfonso di Spigna.

Standing apart from the town on its headland (where Forio's youth congregate in the evening), the stark, white **Santuario della Madonna del Soccorso** wouldn't look out of place in Greece. It's a mixture of architectural styles (Byzantine, Moorish and Mediterranean), with pretty majolica Stations of the Cross around its steps. Inside, sailors who credited the Madonna with saving them from shipwreck have filled the church's walls with ship-shaped votive offerings in her honour. The adjacent square has breathtaking views over the coast.

In Corso Umberto, a church has stood on the site of **Santa Maria di Loreto** since the 14th century; in Piazza del Municipio, much of the **convento di San Francesco** is now occupied by council offices, but the church can still be visited. In the 17th century, alms were dispensed in nearby **Santa Maria della Grazie** (also known as Visitapovere); in the piazza of the same name, **San Vito** is Forio's parish church.

Just north of Forio, along the road to Lacco Ameno, a sign points left to **La Mortella** (*see right; photos left*), a garden designed by renowned British landscapist Russell Page. Having arrived on the island at the end of the 1940s in search of peace and inspiration, composer Sir William Walton and his young Argentine wife Susana set about turning a wild plot of land (described by their friend Laurence Olivier as nothing but a quarry) into one of Italy's most opulent gardens. It's a beautiful spot, where New Zealand tree ferns unfurl with a prehistoric languor alongside heavily scented Amazon waterlilies.

The William Walton Trust, which maintains the garden, also provides accommodation and coaching for young musicians, and organises weekend classical music concerts from April to June, and in September and October. To get there, take a bus from Lacco Ameno to Forio, or vice versa, and ask the driver to set you down at La Mortella, or take the Forio minibus to the door.

A few kilometres further down the lane, through unspoilt Ischian countryside and past a breathtaking belvedere, is Luchino Visconti's villa, **La Colombaia** (Via Francesco Calise 130). The villa was converted into a film foundation and cultural centre, with regular exhibitions and events, but is currently closed and has no immediate plans to reopen.

Forio also has a sailing school that offers courses for all levels and ages. Lessons at **Scuola Vela Ischia** (Hotel Villa Carolina, Via Marina 50/55, 081 997119, www.scuolavela

ischia.it, closed Nov-Easter) last four hours, and courses range from five days to two weeks (from €250 per person).

★ La Mortella

Via Francesco Calise 35, Forio (081 986220/ www.lamortella.org). **Open** *Apr-mid Nov* 9am-7pm Tue, Thur, Sat, Sun. **Concerts** *Apr-June, Sept, Oct* Sat, Sun; arrive at least 30mins early to be sure of a seat, consult website for performance schedule. **Admission** *Gardens* €12. *Concerts* €20. **No credit cards**.

Monte Epomeo & the south-west

MONTE EPOMEO & BEYOND

Looming over Forio to the east, **Monte Epomeo**, Ischia's highest point at 787 metres (2,582 feet), can be ascended by walking up Via Monterone or Via Bocca to one of the poorly-marked paths that lead up through the glorious Falanga forest and on to the summit.

If Forio's town beaches don't appeal to you, try **spiaggia di Citara** to the south, which has another long stretch of sand – although much of it is monopolised by the fabulous **Giardini Poseidon** (*see p220* **Taking the plunge**).

Sorgeto, another beach treat, can be reached from the nearby village of Panza, although it's easy to miss the flaking, half-hidden signs directing you to the beach. A series of hairpin bends and some long flights of stairs lead down to the rocky cove. In the eastern corner, a thermal spring gushes up between the rocks and into the sea; at about 32ºC (90ºF), it's hot enough to cook an egg. Alternatively, there's normal cold water with hot rock-pool soaking.

Where to stay & eat

Cheap beds can be found at the pretty **Il Vitigno** (Via Bocca 31, 081 998307, www. agriturismoilvitigno.it, closed Dec-Mar, €50-€60 double). The farm's restaurant serves delicious meals made from home-grown produce at its communal tables (average €15); non-residents are welcome, but must book ahead.

Well south of town, perched on a spectacular peninsula jutting out into the sea between Sorgeto beach and Sant'Angelo, the **Hotel Punta Chiarito** (Via Sorgeto 51, 081 908102, www.puntachiarito.it, closed Nov-Dec, €95-€120 double) is another attractive option. Rooms are pleasant, and there's a beautifully landscaped garden with a thermal pool; some bedrooms have kitchens, and the restaurant serves good traditional fare.

Although decent hotels may be in short supply in Forio, the same cannot be said of restaurants. Beneath the Soccorso church, **Umberto a Mare** (Via Soccorso 2, 081 997171, www.umbertoamare.it, closed for lunch & Jan-Mar, average €65) has just ten tables, and cuisine that relies on the daily fisherman's catch: a variety of fresh pastas followed by *al profumo di mare* (the freshest of fish), and desserts that might include apple pie with cream and chocolate. If you can't bear to leave, the hotel has ten bright, cheery rooms (€130-€200 double).

Off the coast road heading south, **Il Melograno** (Via Giovanni Mazzella 110, 081 998450, www.ilmelogranoischia.it, closed Jan-mid Mar, Mon from Sept-Dec & Tue from Oct-Dec, average €70) offers a daily-changing menu, based on market-bought ingredients: excellent raw seafood antipasti, *orecchiette* pasta with clams, mussels, broccoli and chilli, and a wonderful *zuppa di pesce*. The fish is fresh off the boat, and the outside patio is charming. Miles up a tortuous road leading to Monte Epomeo, **Da Peppina di Renato** (Via Bocca, 42, 081 998312, www.trattoriada peppina.it, closed mid Nov-mid Mar, average €40) has great pizza and fantastic meat dishes with seasonal veg. It's closed for lunch for most of the year, bar selected summer Sundays.

Pietratorcia (Via Provinciale Panza 267, 081 907277, www.pietratocia.it, closed mid Nov-Mar, lunch from mid June-mid Sept) is one of Ischia's leading wine producers. Taste the grape on a sunny terrace, where *assaggi* of three different wines and a big plate of cheese and cold meats cost €13; the chef will cook full meals on summer evenings, but only if you order in advance. Visits to the wine cellars can be arranged from April to October.

Nature's cure?

Murky waters and miraculous mud.

Ibsen, Garibaldi, Hans Christian Andersen – they've all taken the waters in Ischia, where the bubbling veins beneath the island's crust made it a spa centre as far back as the the eighth century BC. Greek colonists believed that the hot waters could cure mind and spirit, and were convinced that the sulphurous broth had supernatural powers. Later, pragmatic Romans built their public baths atop the island's hot springs. But the most recent invaders have been tourists, lured by the combination of luxury hotels and spa treatments.

Still, behind even the most opulent spa is the hope that the Greeks might have been right, and the waters really can work wonders. Ischia's waters are the most radioactive in Europe, which might explain why Marie Curie came to study them. Rising from a deep reservoir, they mix with seawater and ground-water before gushing up in hot springs and fumaroles around the island. The hottest springs are at Monte Tabor, above Casamicciola – an area that has been at the heart of Ischia's spa industry for centuries.

Spa treatments here are a serious business. The water, mud and clay from the four main spa towns (Ischia, Forio, Lacco Ameno and Casamicciola – as well as Maronti beach) have different chemical properties, so visitors looking for a cure should find out which waters are said to heal or alleviate their particular ills.

Advocates claim the waters will help a host of ailments, from rheumatism and arthritis to respiratory and gynaecological problems.

Ischia's more traditional, cure-oriented spas are not about pampering, de-stressing or beauty treatments. The water itself is a rather murky green hue, and, by law, treatments are limited to six days a week (normally mornings only) with a doctor present. Many hotels have rather gloomy on-site spa centres, albeit ones with fabulous, naturally-heated thermal water pools outside.

Happily, more hedonistic alternatives are nudging their way into the local spa culture. Five-star hotels like **Il Moresco** (*see p221*) and **Hotel Mezzatorre** (*see p223*) offer posh spa treatments and thermal baths at soaring prices. But the best places at which to indulge in less medicinal therapies are the resorts set amid the tropical gardens between Lacco Ameno and Citara beach. Luxurious treatments abound in upmarket spa resorts like the **Negombo** and **Poseidon** (for both, *see p220* **Taking the plunge**), where you can wallow in mud, get wrapped up in seaweed, stew in heated caves, have yourself hosed down with pressure jets, or just idle in the thermal pools thinking about how you're reducing your cellulite, while checking out (from behind designer sunglasses) the latest swimwear fashions worn by the other guests.

Sant'Angelo.

The south

SANT'ANGELO & MARONTI

Reaching the pretty former fishing village of **Sant'Angelo** can be a traffic nightmare (regular, and crowded, bus services run from Porto and Forio), but lots of Italians think it's worthwhile. Indeed, this may be the one place on the island where Italians outnumber German tourists. They lounge around in the dockside cafés, or stroll insouciantly along the isthmus joining the jumble of white and blue houses to the *scoglio* (rock). A community of Benedictine monks once lived on the rocky promontory, sowing fields of wheat and barley and planting orchards and vineyards. Today, a ruined watchtower keeps lookout – built in the 15th century, and restored by the Bourbons in 1741.

From the village, a clifftop footpath hugs the south coast, above the **spiaggia dei Maronti**. Once a two-kilometre stretch of unbroken sand, Maronti has been eaten away by the sea and storms. Of what remains, the eastern end is best for family fun, and can be reached by bus from Barano. To access the western end, where steam slips out of holes between rocks, take the path leading east out of Sant'Angelo. For the tranquil, deserted coves stranded between the two ends, hire a boat-taxi from Sant'Angelo.

Between Sant'Angelo and Maronti, signs point up a steep valley to the extraordinary **Cava Scura** (*see p220* **Taking the plunge**), a natural hot spring.

THE SOUTHERN VILLAGES

From Sant'Angelo, the SS270 road meanders inland, winding a tortuous route among the leafy, craggy hills to **Serrara, Fontana, Barano d'Ischia**, and then back to Ischia Porto. Alhough architecturally uninspiring, the southern villages offer superb views over the sea and up to Monte Epomeo. In Fontana, don't be deterred by a steep road marked *strada militare* and *vietato l'ingresso* (no entry). It is, in fact, a perfectly legitimate route up to the path for the summit of **Epomeo**; vehicles can be driven as far as the bar-restaurant before the military zone begins, marked with a metal bar across the road.

The path to the left of the bar leads up to an eyrie-like rock formation at the top (the walk will take about 40 minutes), with a truly breathtaking 360-degree view over the island. Below is the hermitage and little chapel of **San Nicola di Bari**, hewn out of the rock in the 15th century and occupied until World War II. It opens erratically, in the mornings only; the key is kept by the local priest in Fontana.

From Barano, a narrow road plunges down through delightful lush countryside to Testaccio and on towards the eastern end of the spiaggia dei Maronti.

Shortly before the SS270 enters Ischia town, a road to the left leads to **Campagnano**, where the church of **San Domenico** has striking 19th-century majolica decoration on its façade; the view from the village down to the Castello Aragonese is glorious.

AROUND NAPLES

Where to stay, eat & drink

In Sant'Angelo, the **Park Hotel Miramare**
(Via Maddalena 29, 081 999219, www.hotel
miramare.it, closed Nov-Mar, €130-€207 double)
is the flagship of a group that also comprises
the **Casa Apollon** next door (same phone
number, €192 double). Guests receive discounts
at the Parco Termale Aphrodite (*see p220*
Taking the plunge). The **Hotel Celestino**
(Via Chiaia 20, 081 999213, www.hotel
celestino.it, closed Nov-Mar, €120-€220 double)
is a reliable option in the village centre.

The finely-situated **Neptunus** (Via Chiaia di
Rose 1, 081 999702, closed Jan-mid Mar, average
€30) perches on a cliff overlooking Sant'Angelo,
cooking up fresh seafood and the occasional
land-sourced speciality such as *coniglio
all'ischitana* (rabbit cooked in tomato sauce)
if you ring in advance.

In the port, **La Tavernetta del Pirata**
(Via Sant'Angelo 77, 081 999251, closed Jan,
Wed in Oct, Nov & Apr, average €20) is
Sant'Angelo's hippest bar, and a good place
to sink an *aperitivo* or snack on seafood; it's
open until midnight. When you can't face any
more seafood, **Da Pasquale** (Via Sant'Angelo
79, 081 904208, www.dapasquale.it, closed
Nov-Feb, Tue in Mar-May, Oct, average €15)
will fill you up with good, cheap pizza and beer.

RESOURCES

Hospital
Ospedale Anna Rizzoli *Via Fundera, Lacco
Ameno (081 507 9111).*

Internet
Turboplay *Via Vittoria Colonna 123, Ischia
Porto (081 981589).*

Police
Carabinieri *Via Casciaro 20, Ischia Porto
(081 991065/emergencies 112).*
Polizia *Via delle Terme (081 507 4711/
emergencies 113)*

Post office
*Via Luigi Mazzella 46, Ischia Ponte
(081 992180).*
*Via de Luca Antonio 42, Ischia Porto
(081 507 4611).*

Tourist information
**Azienda di Cura Soggiorno e Turismo delle
Isole di Ischia e Procida** *Via Antonio Sogliuzzo
72 (081 507 4211/www.infoischiaprocida.it).*
Open 9am-2pm, 3-8pm Mon-Sat.
Ischia's tourist office also has a branch by the Ischia
Porto hydrofoil dock in piazzale Trieste. Published
opening times are not always observed.

GETTING AROUND
By boat

Capitan Morgan (081 985080, www.capitan
morgan.it) organises trips around the island
(tickets €15), and day trips to Procida (€14),
Capri (€25) and the Amalfi Coast (€31).
Ischiabarche (081 984854, www.ischia
market.it/ischiabarche) can arrange day charters
around Ischia (€250-€650) and further afield.

By bus

Sepsa (081 991 808) runs a highly efficient, if
crowded, bus service. The main routes are the
circolare sinistra, which circles the island
anticlockwise, stopping at Ischia Porto,
Casamicciola, Lacco Ameno, Forio, Serrara,
Fontana, Barano, returning to Ischia Porto; and
the *circolare destra*, which covers the same route
clockwise. The services run every 30 minutes,
with buses every 15 minutes during rush hours.
There are also services from Ischia Porto to
Sant'Angelo (every 15mins), Giardini Poseidon at
Citara (every 30mins) and Spiaggia dei Maronti
via Testaccio (every 20mins).

In addition, minibus services operate within
Ischia Porto and Ponte, and in Forio. Buy tickets
before boarding; get them (along with bus maps
and timetables) at the terminus in Ischia Porto,
or at any *tabacchi* or newsstand. Tickets cost
€1.20 (single trip), €1.50 if bought on board, €4
(24hr), €6 (48hr), €15 (weekly) €22 (fortnightly)
and €36 (monthly).

GETTING THERE
By boat

Several boat companies, including **Caremar**
(892 123, 081 017 1998, www.caremar.it),
AliLauro (081 497 2238, www.alilauro.it) and
Medmar/Traghetti Pozzuoli (081 333 4411,
www.medmargroup.it) run hydrofoil and car
ferry services between Ischia (from Porto and
Casamicciola) and the mainland (from Naples
Beverello, Naples Mergellina and Pozzuoli),
plus less frequent ones between Ischia Porto
or Casamicciola and Capri, Sorrento, Procida,
Ponza and Ventotene.

The trip from Naples Beverello to Ischia takes
95 minutes by ferry, and costs around €9 for
passengers (extra for vehicles), depending on
the company. It takes 45 minutes if you take the
hydrofoil (around €15). Caremar is the cheapest
and most crowded service.

Some companies accept internet bookings, but
not credit cards. There may be a service charge
for ordering advance hydrofoil tickets, but it's
worth it on summer Sundays.

Procida

A small but exquisite island idyll.

A mere half-hour's boat ride from the mainland lies the smallest island in the Gulf of Naples. Yet despite covering barely four square kilometres, Procida is the most densely inhabited island in the Med. Happily, it never loses its ability to charm – even when the summer crowds invade and its population doubles.

The local economy once revolved around lemon groves and the sea, but today it's tourism that fills the coffers: smart cafés line the harbours, yachts tie up at the gleaming Marina Grande, and daytrippers pack the sandy beaches. On the downside, holiday homes have sprouted in the old orchards, lemons rot unpicked, and in August the whole place is heaving. But there's always space to stroll through lemon groves, savour a freshly made *granita di limone* or watch the day's catch being unloaded from the boats.

INTRODUCING THE ISLAND

In the Middle Ages, frequent Saracen attacks forced the villagers to flee to the highest point of the island, the **Terra Murata**. The distinctive local architecture, with its steep staircases, arches and loggias, dates from this period.

Procida really began to develop in the 16th century, despite repeated pirate attacks. (In 1544, according to local legend, Barbarossa the barbarian fled the island after a miraculous vision of St Michael in the Terra Murata – but not before indulging in a little rape and pillage.) Medieval Terra Murata was fortified after 1520, but the defence mentality was already fading. Prosperous families from the mainland built summer homes here, shipbuilders constructed family palazzi, and the Marina Grande became the centre of the fishing industry.

Procida was a favourite haunt of the Bourbon kings; in 1744 they bought the **Castello d'Avalos** and turned the island into a royal hunting reserve. As you approach Procida by ferry, the view is dominated by the Castello (an Italian Alcatraz until 1986), surrounded by faded, tumbledown fishermen's houses.

Ferries dock in the **Marina Grande** (*see p230*) among the fishing boats moored in front of modern cafés and restaurants. The fish stalls open in the afternoon, selling the day's catch: prawns, red mullet and squid, as well as *misto di paranza* (small fish and seafood).

Towards the eastern end of the Marina Grande, by the late 18th-century church of **Santa Maria della Pietà** (Via Roma, open 8.30am-noon, 5-8pm daily), the steep Via Vittorio Emanuele leads off to the right up into the centre of the island. Some 100 metres (350 feet) further on the left, Via Principe Umberto, with its old houses, leads to **Piazza dei Martiri**. Savour the view of the castle and the Terra Murata above, with the enchanting fishing village of Corricella below.

The road continues steeply past the forlorn, abandoned Castello d'Avalos. Built in the mid 16th century, the castle belonged to the D'Avalos family until it was bought by the Bourbon kings in the mid 18th century.

From here it's not far to the **Porta di Mezzomo** (1563), which leads into the medieval Terra Murata walled village. There are breathtaking views over Naples and Capri – especially from the hilltop Via Borgo, where the **Abbazia di San Michele Arcangelo** (*see p230*) is built on the edge of the sheer rock. Procida's fascinating Good Friday *processione dei misteri* starts here. In what was once a procession of flagellants, a life-size wooden sculpture of the dead Christ, dating from 1754, is carried under a black veil by fishermen from the Abbazia to Marina Grande. It is followed by the other *misteri* (handmade wooden models of religious scenes), carried by the Turchini fraternity, in white habits and turquoise capes, and by children in medieval costume. Close by, the ruins of 16th-century **Santa Margherita Nuova** stand on the Punta dei Monaci.

From Piazza dei Martiri, the sleepy little harbour at **Corricella** is reached via the Scalinata Scura steps. On the descent, you'll pass tiny houses massed on the rock (some being renovated into chic homes for weekenders). The bay, exposed to African winds, has its own mild microclimate, and bananas grow here.

From the western end of Corricella, steps head up to Via Scotti, where 18th-century buildings have vaulted entrances leading to gardens, lemon groves and terraces overlooking the sea. Pick up Via Vittorio Emanuele again to go to the southernmost part of the island.

From Piazza Olmo, Via Pizzaco leads to **Pizzaco**, where a lovely nature walk rounds a crumbling promontory with fantastic views across to Corricella and Terra Murata. One of the island's nicest beaches, **La Chiaia**, is reached from the piazza via about 180 steps. Flagging spirits can be revived at the excellent trattoria **La Conchiglia** (*see p231*).

Via Giovanni da Procida leads from Piazza Olmo to **Chiaiolella**, Procida's main resort – a small marina, enclosed by two promontories. On the western side of the main island, the kilometre of sand stretching from Chiaiolella to Ciriaccio is Procida's most fashionable (and crowded) beach, the **Lido**. At the southern tip of the Lido, a lane leads to a bridge connecting the island to the nature reserve of Vivara (*see right*).

The north-east of Procida, between the lighthouse on Punta di Pioppeto and Punta Serra, takes you off the beaten track (even in high season), with lanes meandering through lemon groves and fine sea views. From Piazza Olmo, Via Flavio Gioia leads to a belvedere with an outstanding view over Chiaiolella, Vivara and Ischia. A short path hugs the promontory of Punta Serra, overlooking the sea.

Via Flavio Gioia heads to the old cemetery; below is **Pozzo Vecchio** beach, made famous by Michael Radford's charming film, *Il Postino*. There's a café here in summer. The road (at this point, Via Cesare Battisti) passes a restored 16th-century tower and hamlet, before rambling

on past isolated farmhouses and woodlands to the lighthouse; from here, Via Faro leads back to the main road.

Off Procida's south-western tip and reached by a footbridge is the tiny island nature reserve of **Vivara**, inhabited even before Procida: traces of Neolithic remains have been found here. Once a hunting reserve, this is one of the most beautiful and unspoilt nature reserves in all of Italy. Over 150 species of birds live or migrate through here, and it's home to a rare species of rat that walks on its hind legs. Here, too, are the ruins of a hamlet beside the coast and, at the centre of the island, an abandoned manor house with a loggia and an old olive press in the cellar. Vivara is closed to the general public to protect its delicate ecosystem; needless to say, locals have been known to climb through the fence.

The opening of the tourist port in the **Marina Grande** makes Procida ideal for yacht charters. **Blue Dream** (Via Vittorio Emanuele 14, 081 896 0579, www.bluedream charter.com) offers day trips, fishing and diving days, as well as a boat B&B in the Marina Grande. **Ippocampo** (Marina Chiaiolella, 081 810 1437, www.ippocampo.biz) runs day trips (€100) in typical *gozzi* (fishing boats).

Sailitalia Procida/Bluebone (Via Roma 10, 081 896 9962, www.sailitalia.it) is another option, with over 20 years' experience. Unusually, you can plan one-way trips such as Procida to Palermo at no extra cost. Skippers and crew are available on some boats, and prices range from a low-season week for four at €1,300 to a high-season crewed week at €8,000.

FREE Abbazia di San Michele Arcangelo

*Via Terra Murata 89 (081 896 7612/www.
abbaziasanmichele.it).* **Open** *Apr-Oct* 10am-1pm, 3-6pm Mon-Sat. Closed Sun & during religious functions. *Nov-Mar* by reservation only.
Admission *Church* free. *Museum, library & catacombs* €3. **No credit cards**.
Dating from the 11th century, but remodelled in the 17th-19th centuries, the abbey has a painting (1699) by Luca Giordano of Archangel Michael on its coffered ceiling. Inside is an 8,000-strong religious manuscript library, a museum containing religious thanksgiving pictures from shipwrecked sailors, an 18th-century Nativity scene, and a maze of catacombs leading to a secret chapel.

★ FREE Santissima Annunziata or Madonna della Libera

Via SS Annunziata. **Open** 8.30am-noon, 5-8pm daily. **Admission** free.
Inside is a fascinating collection of devotional *ex votos*, painted by grateful sailors saved from storms at sea. The November Festa del Vino is organised by the church committee in the surrounding lanes.

INSIDE TRACK INTO THE BLUE

Procida is a great area for diving, so get your flippers out and see the island through a pair of goggles. The **Procida Diving Centre** (Via Marina Chiaiolella, Lido di Procida, 081 896 8385, www.vacanze aprocida.it) is open year round (weekends only in winter), offering courses, equipment hire and trips with expert instructors.

Corricella.

AROUND NAPLES

Where to eat & drink

In recent years, the choice and quality of restaurants on Procida have improved, but prices have risen to match. In August and on summer weekends, it's best to book ahead.

Sample the local catch opposite the ferry port at **La Medusa** (Via Roma 116, 081 896 7481, closed Tue from Oct-Apr, average €28), with a spanking-fresh *zuppa di pesce* and delicious *pasta con alici e peperoncini verdi*.

For more inventive fish and vegetable dishes, try **Fammivento** (Via Roma 39, 081 896 9020, closed Mon & Jan, average €25), facing the yacht harbour. Among the dishes is *pasta alla genovese di polipo*; pasta in a fragrant, slow-cooked octopus sauce.

By the church of Santa Maria della Pieta, **Bar Roma** (Via Roma 164, 081 896 7460, closed Tue from Oct-Apr) has great cakes. Quaff cocktails at **Bar del Cavaliere** (Via Roma 42, 081 810 1074, closed Mon from Dec-Mar); wait for the boat or just hang out at friendly **Bar Grottino** (Via Roma 121, 081 896 7787, closed Wed from Oct to Apr), which has good snacks and home-made ice cream.

Corricella's **Caracalè** (Via Marina Corricella 62, 081 896 9192, closed Tue & Nov-Dec, Feb, average €35) adds a modern twist to the classics; try fresh *tuna tartare in cannoli croccanti* or *parmigiana di pesce spatola* (silver scabbard fish), with home-made lemon soufflé for afters.

For a romantic meal, hop from Corricella to **La Conchiglia** (including pick-up from your boat) on La Chiaia beach (no car access, steps from Via Pizzaco 10, Piazza Olmo, 081 896 7602, by reservation only Nov-Feb, average €40) for abundant fresh pasta and excellent seafood straight off the family boat; book ahead.

Local ingredients and fresh fish inspire the menu in **Lo Scarabeo** (Via Salette 10, 081 896 9918, closed lunch, Mon & weekdays mid Oct-Easter, average €30); sample homemade aubergine-stuffed ravioli under the lemon trees.

For home cooking on the beach, lunch at low-key **Grotte Blu** (Via Roma 153, 081 896 0345, average €15), tucked behind the ticket offices at Marina Grande. The Procida-style rabbit is delicious, and the takeaway snacks include a roll with mozzarella and *parmigiana di melanzane* and the famous *spaghetti omelette*.

Where to stay

Hotel accommodation is scarce, despite the island's popularity, so book well ahead for peak season. Increasingly, visitors are opting for self-catering deals – ideal for families, budget travellers or those simply craving a bit of privacy.

Graziella Travel (Via Roma 117, 081 896 9594, www.isoladiprocida.it) can arrange accommodation in fishermen's cottages, villas and holiday flats, as well as organising bike hire, boat trips and yacht charters; **EPT Casavacanza** (Via Principe Umberto 1, 081 896 9067, www.casavacanza.net) is another good resource for finding a holiday flat. **Procidatour** (Via Roma 109, 081 896 8089, www.procidatour.it) offers a selection of rooms and apartments. There are also half a dozen camping sites on the island; ask the tourist office (*see right*) for details.

Overlooking Corricella and under the Terra Murata is the romantic **La Casa sul Mare** (Salita Castello 13, 081 896 8799, www.lacasa sulmare.it, closed Jan-Feb, €90-€168 double), housed in an 18th-century palazzo with sunny, air-conditioned rooms and terraces with bay views. There are transfers to La Chiaia beach.

The charming rooms looking out on to the vineyard and gardens of **La Vigna** (Via Principessa Margherita 46, 081 896 0469, www.albergolavigna.it, closed Jan, €90-€200 double), five minutes' walk from Piazza dei Martiri, offer a haven of tranquility from the high season crowds. A tiny wellness centre offers massage and wine-therapy treatments.

In the centre of the island, near La Chiaia, **Casa Giovanni da Procida** (Via Giovanni da Procida 3, 081 896 0358, www.casagiovanni daprocida.it, €70-€110 double) is a 17th-century farmhouse that has been converted into a stylish B&B. Rooms are air-conditioned and split-level, and there's a garden.

The quiet, pastel-coloured **Solcalante** (Via Serra 1, 081 810 1856, www.solcalante.it, €50-€130 double), located midway between Pozzo Vecchio and the bay of Ciraccio, has rooms with private terraces opening on to a garden with panoramic views.

Newly-opened **Hotel Celeste** (Via Rivoli 6, 081 896 7488, www.hotelceleste.it, €50-€130 double) is a bright and breezy establishment, set in a lemon grove a short walk away from Chiaiolella beach.

La Rosa dei Venti (Via Vincenzo Rinaldi 32, 081 896 8385, www.vacanzeaprocida.it) offers beautifully fitted apartments year-round, with a two-bed flat costing from €50 to €80 per night. It's set on the island's north coast, amid citrus trees and vines, and has a private rocky beach. The friendly owners also run the local diving school (*see p230* **Inside Track**) and organise sailing excursions, food events and grape-picking.

Set in lush gardens, the tranquil **Tirreno Residence** (Via Faro 34, 081 896 8341, www. tirrenoresidence.it) also offers apartments (€65 for a two-bed). With free Wi-Fi and foreign phone calls (no mobiles) and a free shuttle service to the beaches and centre, it's great value for money.

RESOURCES

Hospital
Via Alcide de Gasperi 203 (081 810 0510).

Police
Via Libertà 70bis (081 896 7160).

Post office
Via Libertà 72 (081 896 0711).

Tourist information
Azienda di Cura Soggiorno e Turismo delle Isole di Ischia e Procida *Via Antonio Sogliuzzo 72 (081 507 4211/www.infoischiaprocida.it).* **Open** 9am-2pm, 3-8pm Mon-Sat.
The tourist office is on the island of Ischia, but the website also covers Procida.
Pro Loco di Procida *Via Vittorio Emanuele 173 (081 896 9628/www.prolocoprocida.it).* **Open** *Apr-Sept* 9am-1pm, 3-8pm daily. *Oct-Mar* 9am-1pm, 3-7pm daily.

GETTING AROUND

Walking, cycling and buses are all good ways to get around; in summer there are heavy restrictions on private cars and scooters.

By bus
Buses run to all parts of the island. Line 1 departs every 20 minutes from the Marina Grande to the Marina di Chiaiolella, operating for most of the night in July and August. Tickets are €0.80 (buy in advance from *tabacchi* or pay a €0.30 surcharge). The three other lines run every 40 minutes.

By car/scooter
Autoricambi Sprint (Via Roma 28, 081 896 9435) hires out 50cc scooters from €25; **General Rental** (Via Roma 135, 081 810 1132) offers 50cc scooters and city cars.

By taxi
Taxis can be hired from the Marina di Chiaiolella or Marina Grande (081 896 8785); a tour around the island costs roughly €40. Taxis can also be booked on 338 899 9912/368 755 5360.

GETTING THERE

From Naples Beverello/Porto di Massa
Caremar (081 896 7280, www.caremar.it) runs ferries from Naples Porto di Massa (1hr; €8.50) and hydrofoils from Naples Beverello (35mins; €11.60). **SNAV** (081 896 9975, www.snav.it) runs hydrofoils between Naples Beverello and Procida (35mins; €13) and between Procida and Ischia (20mins; €6). During the summer, SNAV also runs hydrofoils from Mergellina and Ischia. A midnight ferry from Naples' Porto di Massa is operated by Medmar (081 333 4411).

From Pozzuoli
Caremar (081 526 2711) runs ferries (35mins; €6.60). **Procida Lines 2000** (081 896 0328) runs car ferries (35mins; rates vary according to size of vehicle); **Procidamar** (081 497 2222) runs a passenger boat service (Apr-Oct).

Pompeii & Vesuvius

Ashes to ashes.

With its wealth of ancient Roman sites and lovely 18th-century villas, set against the backdrop of a quiescent volcano, this place is unique.

The sight of Vesuvius towering over the bay, with the Sorrentine peninsula to the south and Naples to the north, has always held visitors spellbound. At ground level, though, the contrasts are stark. Ugly agglomerations bear all the hallmarks of 20th-century urban blight, with high unemployment, apocalyptic traffic and graffiti-daubed public spaces.

Yet the urban context of the *comuni vesuviani* (the towns around Vesuvius) serves to heighten the dramatic effect: sumptuous Roman villas in quiet countryside overlook demolition-ripe 1950s tower blocks, while lava fields from the 1944 eruption lie wild and deserted, just a few miles from the remains of ruined streets and houses buried in a much bigger blow two millennia before.

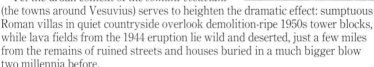

INTRODUCING THE AREA

The Etruscans, Greeks, Oscans and Romans have all occupied the lower slopes of Vesuvius, building various settlements, from towns such as **Pompeii** (*see p239*) and **Herculaneum** (*see p234*) to secluded villas such as Oplontis (*see p239*) and Stabiae (*see p244*).

In the 18th century, the Bourbon monarchs built a royal palace, the **Reggia** (*see p234*), in Portici. Wealthy noblemen soon followed suit, building lavish villas between Portici and Torre del Greco in an area that became known as the **Miglio d'Oro** (Golden Mile).

DIGGING DEEP

Using excavation techniques that would make modern archaeologists shudder, the Bourbons carted off statues and frescoes to be exhibited in the Reggia palace. Many works of art were damaged, and others were smuggled out to private collections around the world. The sites still bear the scars of these cavalier excavations, with tunnels bored through ancient villa walls in an attempt to reach the treasures within. Describing a visit to Herculaneum in the 18th century, poet Thomas Gray told his mother how 'the passage they have made with all their turnings and windings is now more than a mile long'.

Armed with large injections of European Union funds and private sponsorship deals, the normally cash-strapped Italian cultural heritage ministry has been busy capitalising on the area's immense archaeological resources. Grand plans to divert some of the tourist traffic (1.5 million paying visitors pass through Pompeii each year) to lesser-known sites such as Stabiae are afoot; several key services at archaeological sites have been privatised, and new buildings have been opened in Pompeii (albeit mainly to compensate for those closed for restoration).

Some things, though, are here to stay. Ancient Herculaneum is buried beneath the modern town of Ercolano and will never be brought to light. Stray dogs still roam the streets of Pompeii, and the old-style tour guides at the entrance have been compared to minicab drivers outside London clubs, offering a low-quality service at inflated prices. In the streets of the modern *comuni vesuviani,* environmental quality is poor. In the second century AD, the Roman satirist Juvenal complained of 'the swearing of drovers on narrow, winding streets'; today's visitors are plagued by noisy scooters, tearing round like chainsaws on wheels.

The five key archaeological sites (Pompeii, Herculaneum, Oplontis, Stabiae and Boscoreale) can be visited on the Campania Artecard circuit (*see p194*). Alternatively, a combined ticket, which costs €27 and is valid for three days, is available at all sites except Stabiae, where entrance is free (it doesn't have the visitor flow to warrant ticketing facilities). Unlike the smaller sites, Pompeii and Herculaneum now have snack bar facilities.

PORTICI

Portici has the dubious distinction of being the most densely populated town in Europe – though the other *comuni vesuviani* can't be far behind. Left in ruins after Vesuvius erupted in 1631, it was little more than a wasteland when Charles III, Naples' first Bourbon king, gave orders for a palace to be built here. The palace and its grounds, now surrounded by concrete on all sides, give you an idea of what the whole area looked like 200 years ago. The town was the site of over 30 villas along the Miglio d'Oro, and the terminus for Italy's first railway line; the old station now houses the excellent **Museo Ferroviario di Pietrarsa**, *see below*.

★ Museo Ferroviario di Pietrarsa

Via Pietrarsa, Portici (081 472003). **Open** 8.30am-1.30pm Mon-Fri; by appointment only Sat, Sun. **Admission** €5. **No credit cards**.

The first railway on the Italian peninsula was a modest 7.4-km stretch between Naples and Portici, opened with much fanfare by Naples' King Ferdinando II in 1839. The following year, a railway factory and workshops were installed in an area close to Portici called Pietrarsa ('burnt stone' – apt enough, given its proximity to Vesuvius). The factories remained operational until 1975.

The biggest – and arguably the best – railway museum in Europe, the Museo Ferroviario di Pietrarsa is a joy, even for non-train buffs. The buildings housing original workshops and lathes have been minimally and tastefully restored. Pavilion A has a wondrous display of steam locomotives, including a faithful reconstruction of the royal train used for the inaugural trip on the Portici railway in 1839. Across the gardens, Pavilion C showcases the full gamut of 20th-century rolling stock, and an immaculately preserved royal carriage built in 1928. Raised walkways around the carriage allow a good view of the plush upholstery and gilded ceilings. The museum's central courtyard has been made into a Mediterranean garden, with an open-air theatre used for summer concerts.

Detailed information about the museum, in English, is available from the reception area. To find the museum, take the Portici exit from the A3 motorway and head down to the coast road (SS145), turning right towards Naples; the easily missed Museo Ferroviario sign is on the seaward side of the main road in the area called Croce del Lagno. Alternatively, take a train from Naples' Stazione Centrale to Pietrarsa-San Giorgio a Cremano.

★ Reggia di Portici & Orto Botanico

Via Università 100 (081 775 4850/www. ortobotanicoportici.unina.it). **Open** *Sept-July* Reggia 8am-7pm Mon-Fri, by appointment only. Orto 8am-12.30pm Mon-Fri, by appointment only. **Admission** €4; €2 reductions. **No credit cards**.

Designed by Antonio Medrano, the Reggia di Portici is the greatest of all the Vesuvian villas. Ferdinando Fuga worked on it, as did Luigi Vanvitelli. The vast façade looks out across what was once its own private terraced gardens, cascading down towards the seashore. The lower of the Reggia's two buildings is separated from the upper wing (which looks out towards Vesuvius) by a square. Charles and his son Ferdinando had the spoils from digs at Pompeii and Herculaneum brought here, creating a royal antiquarium of incomparable richness; most of the spoils are now held at the Museo Archeologico Nazionale (*see p70*). Since 1873, the Reggia has been home to the Naples University Faculty of Agriculture: to visit, just wander in. On the Vesuvius side of the main road is the *orto botanico* (botanical garden), an impressive collection of over 500 species of native and exotic plants, bordered by the holm oak wood where the royals used to hunt.

▶ *For more on architects Medrano, Fuga and Vanvitelli, see p43.*

ERCOLANO & HERCULANEUM

Although it rivals Portici for urban squalor and traffic noise, Ercolano also has some sumptuous 18th-century villas and a spectacular ancient site. You could drive through the postwar construction catastrophe and never notice the splendour, but as you hurry through Ercolano, erase in your mind's eye everything built since 1945. You're left with some fishermen's huts near the shore, a once-smart late 19th-century main street and assorted *ville* – now crumbling, dilapidated affairs, set in overgrown gardens behind locked, rusting gates.

Because the Reggia di Portici was home to the Bourbon court for several months each year, court hangers-on from all over the Kingdom of the Two Sicilies – anxious to be on hand when honours or cash rewards were distributed – summoned the leading architects of the day to build luxury homes nearby. Soon, the stretch of coast between Naples and Torre del Greco became known as the Miglio d'Oro (Golden Mile).

With the absorption of Naples into the United Kingdom of Italy in 1860, the frivolous, worldly *ville* of the Miglio d'Oro became obsolete; the villas' owners sold them to nouveau riche Neapolitan property speculators, or simply left them to decay. Many were eventually divided up into flats, while others, such as the spectacular **Villa Favorita** (*see p238*), were boarded up and abandoned for generations.

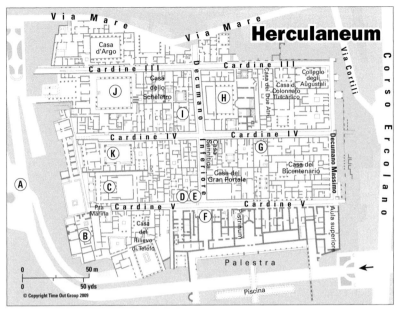

Herculaneum

HERCULANEUM KEY

A Original Shoreline
B Terme Suburbane
C Casa dei Cervi
D Taberna di Priapo
E Thermopolia
F Plaestra
G Casa di Nettuno e Anfitrite
H Terme del Foro
I Casa del Tramezzo di Legno
J Casa dell'Albergo
K Casa dell'Atrio a Mosaico

A handful have been salvaged by the Ente per le Ville Vesuviane (Board of Vesuvian Villas), based in the **Villa Campolieto** (*see p236*). Many of the properties are open to the public and, though the Villa Favorita may have missed out on the Ente's benevolence, its lower park and annexe, the Palazzina del Mosaico, have been restored. The Ente has also given a new lease of life to the **Villa Ruggiero** (*see p238*).

Herculaneum (Scavi di Ercolano)

Corso Resina (081 732 4311/www.pompeii sites.org). **Open** *Apr-Oct* 8.30am-7.30pm daily (ticket office closes 6pm). *Nov-Mar* 8.30am-5pm daily (ticket office closes 3.30pm). **Admission** €11. **No credit cards.**

Bold letters in the text refer to map, above. It was described by the ancients as being *inter duos fluvios infra Vesuvium* ('between two rivers below Vesuvius'), but over the years the topography around Herculaneum has changed beyond all recognition. The rivers have disappeared, the shoreline has moved a kilometre to the west, and the part of Herculaneum that has not been excavated lies some 25m (80ft) below the modern town of Ercolano. Descending from Ercolano, emerging from the newly built tunnels leading into the site and strolling through the ancient town is an extraordinary experience – like entering a time capsule.

The town was probably founded by Greek settlers in the fourth century BC, though most of what can be seen today dates back no further than the second century BC. The town had a grid layout similar to that of its neighbour, Neapolis; at the time of its destruction in AD 79, it had around 5,000 inhabitants. Buried in an airtight layer of solidified volcanic mud (unlike Pompeii, where the volcanic ash took longer to settle and become compressed), organic remains found at Herculaneum have yielded all sorts of insights into everyday life, from diet to clothing and furniture.

Pedestrian access to the site from Corso Resina (just keep heading straight down from Circumvesuviana station on Via IV Novembre) is via an impressive ramp with fine overviews of the Roman town. At the main ticket office halfway down, you should be able to pick up a free site map and a small booklet on Herculaeum in English. At the base of the ramp, site facilities include a book-shop and an audioguide kiosk. From here, you can either follow the footbridge directly across into the site, or take the tunnel leading down to the original shoreline [**A**], the best place from which to admire the towering volcanic deposits. It was near here that 250 skeletons were discovered in the 1980s. They are believed to be the remains of inhabitants over-whelmed by the surge cloud from Vesuvius as they hoped, in vain, to be rescued by sea. Most of the best preserved houses (many with upper storeys still intact) are on either side of Cardo IV and Cardo V, perpendicular to the two *decumani* (main roads).

Near the seaward end of Cardo V, an altar and a statue base stand outside the *terme suburbane* (suburban baths) [**B**]; the statue, dedicated to local dignitary Nonius Balbus, is in Naples' Museo Archeologico Nazionale (*see p70*).

In Insula IV, the Casa dei Cervi (House of the Stags) [**C**] was a villa with a prime seafront location and gazebo. It is named after the two sculptures of deer attacked by hunting dogs found in the garden; the ones here now are replicas. Excavated in the early 20th century, Casa dei Cervi suffered less and preserved more of its upper storeys than the houses in Insula II on the north-western side of the site, excavated 100 years before. Nearby are two shops [**D & E**], identifiable by their broad fronts, which accommodated folding wooden screens to separate the shop from the street. The first [**D**] is the Taberna di Priapo (Priapus's Tavern), complete with waiting room, a rather tired-looking fresco and private inner chambers. On the street corner, with large ceramic jars set into marble counters, is one of the town's *thermopolia* [**E**]; these were the fast-food outlets of the ancient world, and good places in which to pick up garum, a fish-based sauce and popular aphrodisiac.

Where Cardo V meets the lower *decumanus* (one of two main roads), two columns mark the entrance to the large *palaestra* (Insula Orientalis) [**F**], where ball games and wrestling matches would have been staged. Two sides of its rectangular peristyle are still largely buried under volcanic deposits. Within this leisure complex were two *piscinae* (swimming pools or fishponds): one at the centre of the peristyle, tun-nelled out of the rock, which now has a replica of the original bronze hydra fountain; and the other with amphorae for fish farming set into its sides.

The houses in Herculaneum are virtually all named after archaeological finds or architectural peculiarities. The Casa di Nettuno e Anfitrite (House of Neptune and Amphitrite, Insula V) [**G**] on Cardo IV is no exception, taking its name from the beauti-fully preserved mosaic adorning the wall of the secluded *nymphaeum* at the back of the house. It tells the tale of Neptune and Amphitrite: he saw her dancing with the Nereids on the island of Naxos, and spirited her away for marriage.

Opposite are the Terme del Foro (Forum Baths, Insula VI) [**H**], with separate sections for men and women. The women's baths have the more attractive

and better preserved mosaic flooring; the male sec-tion is larger and contains an exercise area and a round *frigidarium*, in addition to the mandatory *apodyterium* (changing room), *tepidarium* and *cali-darium* also found in the female section next door. Note the *apodyteria*, with partitioned shelves for depositing togas and belongings, and the low *podia* to use as seating space while queuing.

Unusually, the Casa del Tramezzo di Legno (House of the Wooden Partition, Insula III) [**J**] has two atria. This suggests that there were originally two houses here, joined together in the first century AD when one of the emerging class of *mercatores* (traders) perhaps bought out the patrician owner. Note the carbonised wooden screen beyond the mar-ble *impluvium,* separating the atrium from the *tablinum,* where the *patronus,* or master of the house, conducted business with his clients.

Further down Cardo IV is the Casa dell'Albergo (House of the Inn, Insula III) [**K**]. One of the largest buildings in Herculaneum, it was undergoing restoration from previous earthquake damage when it was overwhelmed by the eruption in AD 79. Note the small private baths just to the right of the main entrance, with wall decorations in second Pompeiian style. Beyond the atrium is an impres-sive peristyle enclosing a sunken garden. The trunk of a pear tree was found here, suggesting that the garden may have been an orchard. Pear trees have been replanted here in an attempt to recreate the original vegetation.

Outside the main site, just across the road from the bookshop and cafeteria, is the Villa dei Papiri. It's a luxury villa, measuring 250m (870 ft) from end to end, where a total of 87 sculptures – Roman copies of Greek originals – and over 1,000 charred but leg-ible papyrus rolls were unearthed. Most of the papyri are the product of a lesser-known Epicurean poet and scholar called Philodemos, and not, as had been hoped, lost works of Aristotle. The wonderful statues are now in the Museo Archeologico Nazionale in Naples (*see p70*) and the Villa is cur-rently closed for restoration.

Only part of Herculaneum is open at any given time, and a great deal of the site is screened off by unsightly red plastic fencing. A list of the buildings open to the public is posted at the site ticket office.

★ Villa Campolieto

Corso Resina 283, Ercolano (081 732 2134/ *www.villevesuviane.net).* **Open** *Office* 9am-2pm Mon-Fri. *Villa* 9am-1pm Tue-Sun. **Admission** €3 for all villas. **No credit cards.**
Designed by Luigi and Carlo Vanvitelli, the Villa Campolieto was built between 1760 and 1775. The circular portico – where a summer concert season is held – has a fantastic, sweeping view over Ercolano and down to the sea. On the first floor, a few rooms have been restored to their original grandeur and are open to the public; even more are on view during the Villa's frequent and popular

AROUND NAPLES

Herculaneum. *See p234.*

AROUND NAPLES

Villa Favorita Park.

exhibitions. For information and a list of the *ville* in the area, call in at the office on the ground floor, where staff are happy to help.

FREE Villa Favorita Park

Via Gabriele d'Annunzio 36 (081 732 2134).
Open 9am-1pm Tue-Sun. **Admission** free.
No credit cards.

Dotted with gracious pavilions and teahouses, the Villa Favorita's lower park sweeps down towards the sea and a jetty – all that remains of a Bourbon construction that was the nearest thing Italy had to Brighton Pier. On the seaward side of the park is the restored Palazzina del Mosaico, now used for conferences. Meanwhile, the teahouse on the right is the perfect venue for atmospheric summer concerts and opera performances.

▶ *For details of forthcoming events, check online at www.villevesuviane.net.*

Villa Ruggiero

Via Alessandro Rossi 40, Ercolano (081 732 2134). **Open** 9am-1pm Tue-Sun. **Admission** €3 for all villas. **No credit cards.**

The Villa Ruggiero, set slightly back from the main road, was built in the mid 18th century for the baronial Petti family. Note that only the elegant court-yard is on show.

TORRE DEL GRECO

Today displaying much of the urban blight that is common to all the *comuni vesuviani*, in the past Torre del Greco has experienced 'build-'em-high' postwar development and Vesuvius's eruptions. In the heart of the volcano's red alert area, its 110,000 inhabitants – known as *corallini* – blithely press on with business as usual; the manufacture of coral and cameos (hence *corallini*) is a major source of income, along with floriculture.

Coral is highly prized in the East Asian market, so the factories are often visited by tour groups. Skilled artists and trainees can be seen at work at the privately owned **APA Coral & Cameo Factory**, conveniently close to the Torre del Greco motorway exit.

The **Museo del Corallo** has fine 18th-century pieces from the Trapanese school, and attractive cameos on malleable lavic stone.

FREE APA Coral & Cameo Factory

Via Cavallo 6 (081 881 1155/www.giovanniapa. com). **Open** 8.30am-6.30pm daily. **Admission** free. **Credit** AmEx, DC, MC, V.

Negotiate your way in between the tour groups and the quality of the artistry may persuade you to buy.

FREE Museo del Corallo

Piazza Luigi Palomba 6 (081 881 1360).
Open by appointment. **Admission** free.
The museum is on the first floor of the Istituto
Statale d'Arte technical college; a member of staff
can show you round the locked museum, when not
pressed by school duties.

Where to stay & eat

The **Hotel Marad** (Via Benedetto Croce 20,
081 849 2168, www.hotelmarad.it, €140 double),
lodged between the major archaeological sites
and Vesuvius, works fine if you're driving. This
quiet, comfortable hotel includes a good quality
restaurant (average €25) and a swimming pool
tucked round the back.

TORRE ANNUNZIATA & OPLONTIS

Once a thriving town where Neapolitans spent
their summers lazing on black volcanic beaches,
Torre Annunziata lost its allure as a resort long
ago. Instead, it provides plenty of material for
pages of the *cronaca nera* (crime news) in the
local papers. The wondrous archaeological site
of **Oplontis**, though, is its saving grace.

★ Oplontis

*Via Sepolcri 1 (081 862 1755/www.pompeiisites.
org).* **Open** *Apr-Oct* 8.30am-7.30pm daily (ticket
office closes 6pm). *Nov-Mar* 8.30am-5.30pm daily
(ticket office closes 4pm). **Admission** €5.50 (also
valid for Antiquarium di Boscoreale). **No credit
cards.**
On the basis of an inscription on an amphora, this
villa is thought to have belonged to Nero's second
wife, Sabina Poppaea. The prosaically named Villa
A certainly has some of the finest examples of the
second Pompeiian style of wall painting. Whether
or not Poppaea really lived here and indulged in her
asses' milk baths within its finely frescoed walls, she
would have preferred to stay with her husband,
Marcus Otho, rather than take up with Nero, who
arranged for Otho to be posted as governor of the
far-flung province of Lusitania (central Portugal).
Poppaea eventually became imperial wife number
two in AD 62 before – if Tacitus is to be believed –
she was kicked to death by Nero while pregnant
three years later.

This delightful, under visited villa amply merits
a ramble. As you get your ticket or show your
Artecard (*see p194*), you'll be given a helpful site
map and a booklet describing each major room or
living space. The west wing is right up against the
main road; more lies below it, unexplored. West of
the reconstructed main atrium (room 1), the walls of
the *triclinium* (room 6) contain stunning illusionist
motifs. The *calidarium* in the adjoining baths complex (room 3) has a delicate miniature landscape

scene surmounted by a peacock in a niche at the far
end; the adjacent *tepidarium* (room 4) shows off
Roman baths and heating systems: the floor is raised
by *suspensurae* (brick pilasters), enabling warm air
to pass beneath.

Off the portico on the southern side of the site is
an *oecus* or living room (room 8) with spectacular
still life frescoes in the second Pompeiian style; the
cubicula (bedrooms) nearby have frescoes in the
finer, less brash third style. As you leave the warren of *cubicula*, the spaces become more grandiose,
culminating with a large *piscina* (swimming pool)
fringed, in Roman times, by oleander and lemon
trees. The atmosphere of relaxation and contempla-
tion lingers, making this a pleasant antidote to what
the poet Horace would have called the *profanum vul-
gus* (vulgar rabble) down the road in Pompeii.

The site is very close to the Circumvesuviana railway station of Torre Annunziata. Turn left outside
the station, right at the first junction and then
straight across at the traffic lights. The site is 100m
(330ft) down the road on your left. As this is a
depressed area, avoid visits in the early afternoon
when the streets are deserted. By car, take the motorway exit at Torre Annunziata Nord and follow the
brown signposts for 'Scavi di Oplontis'; bear in mind
there is no attended parking at the site.

POMPEI & POMPEII

To many Italians, Pompei (the town, as opposed
to Pompeii, the architectural site) is a place of
pilgrimage. People flock here from all over the
south to pay their respects to the Madonna in
the large, early 20th-century *santuario* on the
main square, Piazza Bartolo Longo, praying for
the kind of miracle that healed a girl suffering
from epilepsy in 1876. Others bring their new
cars to have them blessed and to secure divine
protection; given local driving standards and
roads, this seems a wise precaution.

The sheer volume of religious and cultural
tourism caught modern Pompei by surprise.
Having long reaped the benefits of mass tourism
and given little in return, the town now has some
nice surprises in store: once-seedy lodgings have
given way to well-appointed hotels, and eating
out is no longer hit and miss, especially if you
leave the archaeological site for the centre.

INSIDE TRACK
CROWD CONTROL

Oplontis (*see left*) is less well known
than Pompeii or Herculaneum, and for
this reason it's generally easier to access
and much quieter. Since expectations tend
to be lower, it's often a more satisfying
excavation site to visit, too.

AROUND NAPLES

About three kilometres to the north is the **Antiquarium di Boscoreale**, opened in the 1990s as a permanent exhibition on Pompeii and its environment some 2,000 years ago. Reconstructions show idyllic scenes of wildlife along the River Sarno, now, regrettably, one of the most polluted waterways in Italy.

★ Antiquarium di Boscoreale

Villa Regina, Via Settetermini 15 (081 536 8796/ www.pompeiisites.org). **Open** *Apr-Oct* 8.30am-7.30pm daily (ticket office closes 6pm). *Nov-Mar* 8.30am-5pm daily (ticket office closes 3.30pm). **Admission** €5.50 (also valid for Oplontis). **No credit cards.**

Set incongruously in the middle of a 1960s housing development – indeed, that's how the villa here was originally discovered – the Antiquarium documents daily life, the environment and technology in Roman times. Disparate finds ranging from fishing tackle to ceramic cages for rearing dormice (a favourite Roman delicacy) are displayed alongside life-size photos of original mosaics and frescoes from other sites and museums. In the grounds of the museum is Villa Regina, an ancient farmstead with storage capacity for 10,000 litres (2,200 gallons) of wine. The villa's vineyard has been replanted along ancient rows. The Porta Marina tourist office at Pompeii (*see p247*) will direct you here, though it's best approached via the Circumvesuviana station of Boscoreale, where a skeletal bus service is provided.

★ Scavi di Pompeii

Porta Marina, Piazza Anfiteatro, Piazza Esedra (081 857 5347/www.pompeiisites.org). **Open** *Apr-Oct* 8.30am-7.30pm daily (ticket office closes 6pm). *Nov-Mar* 8.30am-5pm daily (ticket office closes 3.30pm). **Admission** €11. *Audioguide* €6.50; €10 for 2. **No credit cards.**

Bold letters in the text refer to map, see right.

Unlike Rome, where ancient monuments have suffered millennia of weathering, re-use and pillaging, Pompeii had the good fortune (for posterity at any rate) of being overwhelmed by the AD 79 eruption of Vesuvius. The ancient street plan is intact, the town still has its full complement of civic buildings, the houses still have their frescoed walls, and – thanks to painstaking work by generations of archaeologists and vulcanologists – we have a fairly clear picture of what life was like here 2,000 years

---

POMPEII KEY

A   Porta Marina
B   Basilica
C   Forum
D   Tempio di Giove
E   Marcellum
F   Terme del Foro
G   Casa del Fauno
H   Lupanare
I   Porta Ercolano
J   Villa dei Misteri
K   Terme Stabiane
L   Teatro Grande
M   Odeion
N   Casa dei Casti Amanti
O   Palaestra
P   Anfiteatro

---

ago. The picture is still being completed: emergency digs during roadworks on the Naples–Salerno motorway have revealed the full extent of a frescoed leisure complex close to the Sarno river.

Unfortunately, the same attention is not lavished on visitor facilities. The site has only one restaurant-cum-cafeteria of dubious quality, and the maps – if you can get one from the information booth – are not up to date (you may have to backtrack where streets have been blocked off). The registered guides still ply visitors with doses of substandard English and misleading information (while also operating a closed shop to exclude a talented new generation of bilingual archaeologists). To cap it all, wildcat strikes by site guards can mean that entry to Pompeii is impossible. (In this eventuality, get on the first Naples-bound Circumvesuviana train and get off at Torre Annunziata to visit Oplontis, *see p239*, leaving Pompeii till later.)

Allow at least three hours for visiting Pompeii; it will take longer if you intend to see the amphitheatre and the Villa dei Misteri, a good 25 minutes' hike apart. The audioguides offer two-, four- or six-hour itineraries – times that are probably underestimates if you choose to listen to the optional in-depth information supplied. From 10am until 1pm, the *terme suburbane* (suburban baths) near the Porta Marina are open. The Casa del Menandro (House of Menander) near the theatre can be visited at weekends from 2pm to 5pm, and the Casa degli Amorini Dorati (House of the Gilded Cupids) is open from 9am to 6pm daily in summer, closing at 4pm in winter. There is a free internet booking service (www.arethusa.net) for access to these buildings, and reservations must be made at least one day prior to the visit. Despite Pompeii's international appeal, the website is in Italian only: click on '*Prenotazioni*' to start the booking procedure for each house. When choosing time slots, allow 30 minutes to view the site and another 30 to reach the next one comfortably.

**INSIDE TRACK
SUMMER SCORCHER**

There is very little shade at Pompeii, and the sun can be merciless in August. If you can, visit on an overcast day: if not, take precautions against the sun and carry plenty of drinking water.

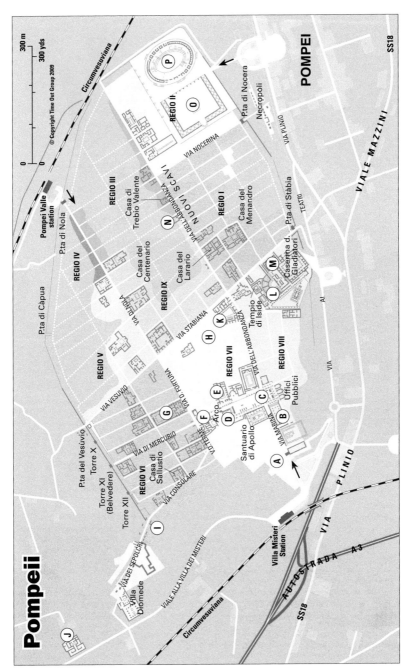

Pompeii

AROUND NAPLES

POMPEI

AROUND NAPLES

Pompeii.

Ask for a site map and free information booklet from the information booth at Porta Marina or Piazza Amfiteatro. Afternoon visits to the site pay dividends, as the crowds start to thin out. The Circumvesuviana railway station Pompei Scavi-Villa dei Misteri is opposite the main Porta Marina entrance to the site; just inside, the forum is a good place at which to get your bearings.

The Porta Marina [**A**], with its separate entrances for pedestrians (on the left) and light vehicles (on the right), is near the original harbour, hence the name. (The shoreline is now much further away than in antiquity, when a canal is thought to have provided access from the sea to the town.) This gate provided the quickest way of getting to that hub of Roman life, the forum – though as the route was also the steepest, most vehicles would proba-bly have taken one of the other seven gates leading into town.

On the right is the basilica [**B**], Pompeii's law court and stock exchange. These rectangular build-ings ending in semicircular apses were the model for early Christian churches.

The forum [**C**] is a rectangular area with a colon-nade surmounted by a loggia running along three sides. Plinths at the southern end indicate that a row of large statues once stood here. At the northern end are the remains of the second-century BC Tempio di Giove (Temple of Jupiter) [**D**] with the cone of Vesuvius behind. As Jupiter was head of the Roman pantheon, it was standard practice to dedicate a tem-ple to him (together with Juno and Minerva) at the centre of town. The temple had already suffered severe damage in an earthquake before AD 79.

The elegant, three-columned portico on the east-ern side of the forum marks the entrance to the *macellum* [**E**], a covered meat and fish market built in early imperial times.

The *terme del foro* (forum baths) [**F**] are small as Roman baths go, but retain much of the original stucco decoration. Within the *calidarium* is a well-preserved marble *labrum* (fountain) with an inscrip-tion in bronze letters around the rim, recording the names of the officials (C Melissaeus Aper and M Staius Rufus) who installed it in AD 3-4, as well as its cost (5,420 sesterces). Except for a short period in early Imperial times, sexes were segregated in all Roman baths; women would have had the morning shift and men the afternoon.

Close to the baths on Via della Fortuna is the Casa del Fauno (House of the Faun) [**G**], named after the small bronze statue in the middle of the marble *impluvium* (the original is in the Museo Archeologico Nazionale; *see p70*). One of the largest and most sophisticated houses in Pompeii, its front section is arranged around two atria; behind is a peristyle with a portico of Ionic columns. Found in the *exedra* (dis-cussion hall) at the far end of the first peristyle, flanked by two *triclinia*, was a million-tessera mosaic (also in the Museo Archeologico Nazionale). It is thought to depict the Battle of Issus in 330 BC,

fought between Alexander the Great and the Persian emperor Darius III. Artists from the Ravenna School of Mosaics are currently involved in a long-term pro-ject to reproduce this remarkable mosaic in situ.

Outside the city walls, through the attractive Porta Ercolano [**I**] leading towards Herculaneum and Neapolis, the Villa dei Misteri (Villa of Mysteries) [**J**] has frescoes in the *triclinium* depict-ing – experts believe – a young woman's initiation into the cult of Dionysus. There are ten scenes of vivid intensity, thought to have been copied by a local artist from a Hellenistic original of the fourth- or third-century BC. The villa was a working farm for much of its existence; the wine-making area is still visible at the northern end.

Stroll down the main street (Via dell'Abbondanza) from the forum towards the amphitheatre and the town takes on a different feel. The shops here can be identified by their broad entrances for easy access from the street. Private houses had *fauces* (narrow passages) – security was a problem in ancient Pompeii, and inhabitants went to great lengths to protect themselves and their property.

The Terme Stabiane (Stabian Baths) [**K**] are a much larger complex than the forum baths, with the exercise area in the middle surrounded by a male and female sections. The stuccoed vault in the men's *apodyterium* (changing room), with its images of nymphs and cupids, is particularly well preserved.

There are also two cases containing gruesome plaster casts of Pompeii inhabitants; a graphic reminder of the last-minute agonies suffered by those who failed to escape in time. The technique of pump-ing liquid cement into the voids left when the victims' bodies decayed was pioneered by Giuseppe Fiorelli in the 1860s. If these have merely whetted your appetite, head over to the Orto dei Fuggiaschi (Garden of the Fugitives) near the amphitheatre, where whole families were overwhelmed and re-emerged as casts two millennia later.

Reopened after extensive restoration work, the Lupanare [**H**] is believed to have been the ancient city's only purpose-built brothel (*lupa* is latin for she-wolf). The explicit wall paintings within have long attracted visitors – for millenia, in fact.

To the south is the theatre complex. The Teatro Grande [**L**] seats about 5,000 and – like so many

AROUND NAPLES

theatres in the ancient world – enjoyed a stunning backdrop, in this case the Sarno river plain in the foreground and the heights of the Mons Lactarius (Monti Lattari) behind. This second-century BC theatre underwent much restoration in antiquity, unlike the adjoining smaller Odeion or Theatrum Tectum [**M**]. The semicircular *cavea* (seating area) was truncated at both ends to facilitate the building of a permanent roof, which would have offered welcome shade to Pompeii's concert-goers.

North of Via dell'Abbondanza, excavations continue around the Casa dei Casti Amanti (House of the Chaste Lovers) [**N**]. The house has been reopened after painstaking restoration work on two frescoes that were chiselled from the walls in 2003. The house has yielded important evidence about life immediately prior to the eruption. Earthquake damage from AD 62 had been repaired, and the inhabitants were trying to patch up cracks from recent tremors, perhaps days before the AD 79 eruption; the rooms were being replastered and painted by teams of craftsmen at the moment Vesuvius erupted. In the rapid getaway, tools were downed and plaster abandoned. The donkeys – turning the grindstone and milling wheat in the adjoining bakery – were left to their fiery fate.

West of the large *palaestra* [**O**] – the rectangular porticoed exercise area dating from the Augustan period – are recently planted vineyards that use grape varieties and training systems thought to have been employed in ancient times. Though the thick, scented nose of ancient Roman wine (drunk diluted) would probably not have appealed to modern palates, thanks to the technologically perfected processes used by the Mastroberardino winery, Villa dei Misteri 2002 was snapped up at dizzying prices.

By Roman standards, the *anfiteatro* (amphitheatre) [**P**] was small, seating about 20,000. Entertainment would probably have been limited to gladiatorial combat, with occasional *venationes* (contests with wild animals) or *naumachiae* (mock sea battles). Though gladiators had a fairly short life expectancy – it was considered an occupation for slaves and social outcasts – records do exist of the odd volunteer signing on for combat. The amphitheatre preserves a fair amount of its seating area, divided into three sections, with a series of *vomitoria* (entrances) near the top.

Where to stay & eat

Conveniently close to the amphitheatre entrance of the Pompeii archaeological zone, the four-star **Hotel Forum** (Via Roma 99, 081 850 1170, www.hotelforum.it, €100 double) is thankfully set back from the main road.

Il Principe (Piazza Bartolo Longo 1, 081 850 5566, www.ilprincipe.com, closed Mon & 3wks Jan, average €40) is one of Campania's finest restaurants, serving ancient recipes gleaned from classical authors. If you make it to dessert,

try the exquisite *cassata Oplontis*, with honey and goat's milk ricotta. For reputedly the best pizza in town, head for the **Ristorante Carlo Alberto**, just opposite Il Principe (Via Carlo Alberto 15, 081 863 3231, average €20).

CASTELLAMMARE DI STABIA & STABIAE

Famed for its spa, shipyards and *biscottifici* (biscuit factories), Castellammare has not only been bypassed by the coast road, but has also suffered gradual industrial decline over the past 30 years. Although the shipyards are once again humming with activity, the transport infrastructure and pedestrian access will have to be massively improved before ancient Stabiae's archaeological heritage can be fully exploited. Castellammare is served by rail, along with hydrofoil and ferry services to Capri; there's also a *funivia* cable car up Monte Faito.

Funivia & Monte Faito
Stazione Circumvesuviana, Castellammare di Stabia (081 879 3097/772 2444/www. vesuviana.it). **Open** *Mid June-Aug* 7.25am-7.15pm daily. *Apr-mid June, Sept, Oct* 7.25am-4.25pm daily. Closed Nov-Mar. **Tickets** €4.65 one way; €6.71 return (€7.23 Sun & daily July, Aug). **No credit cards**.

With its pleasant walks and shady beech woods, Monte Faito provides an escape from the heat in the steamy summer months. An eight-minute ride on the *funivia* from the Circumvesuviana station Castellammare di Stabia whisks you up the mountain, with nerve-tingling vistas over the Bay of Naples. Robins retreat here in summer from the coast, and the distinctive calls of nuthatches can be heard as they flit from tree to tree. Plants tend to flower much later here than down on the coast; for late spring orchids, look in the clearings and in the more exposed areas below the cable car station.

The upper *funivia* station is the start of hiking trails across to Positano: allow four to six hours; take good maps and water and be prepared for plenty of ups and downs. There are also low-key circular routes through the beech forest. The path from the *funivia* to the chapel of San Michele, about three kilometres away, climbs 170m (595ft); you'll be rewarded with splendid views of Vesuvius and the Sarno valley.

FREE Stabiae (Scavi di Castellammare)
Via Passeggiata Archeologica (081 871 4541). **Open** *Apr-Oct* 8.30am-7.30pm daily (last admission 6pm). *Nov-Mar* 8.30am-5pm daily (last admission 3.30pm). **Admission** free.
'Ash was already falling, hotter and thicker as the ships drew near, followed by bits of pumice and blackened stones, charred and cracked by flames: then suddenly they were in shallow water, and the

Monte Faito.

and it was only in the 1950s that the site began to recover from centuries of neglect – although the 1980 earthquake set the work back.

Two villa complexes can be visited: Villa Arianna and Villa San Marco. Both are set just off the Passeggiata Archeologica, the road that skirts around the south-eastern side of Castellammare. For these sites you really need a car, and a skilled navigator to pick out the faded signs pointing to the villas. The ground plans are complex, because of additions and extensions carried out in antiquity, and partly because they were designed to fit the lie of the land. Named after a fresco depicting King Minos's daughter Ariadne, who helped Theseus out of the labyrinth after he killed the Minotaur, Villa Arianna is the oldest structure on the hill. Dating from the first century BC, it was renovated and extended in the first century AD.

Although the frescoed decorations are less spectacular in Villa San Marco, it would have made a pleasant summer retreat for a wealthy Roman magnate. The location was ideal: far away from the imperial intrigues on the other side of the Bay of Naples in Baiae, yet reasonably close to main thoroughfares linking large urban centres like Pompeii and Nuceria (now Nocera). With its 30m (98ft) *natatio* (swimming pool) flanked by rows of plane trees and enclosed on three sides by a peristyle, this was a place for enjoying *otium* (relaxation) to the full.

Where to stay

A welcome addition to the accommodation scene is Crowne Plaza's **Hotel Stabiae** (SS 145 Sorrentina, Km 11, Località Pozzano, Castellammare di Stabia, 081 872 2477, www.ichotelsgroup.com, €120-€240 double). A spectacular conversion of an old cement factory, it has wonderful views of Vesuvius and the Bay of Naples, luxury accommodation and excellent facilities.

Set in verdant gardens, within walking distance of the Stabian villas, the **Grand Hotel La Medusa** (Via Passeggiata Archeologica 5, 081 872 3383, www.lamedusahotel.com, €120-€265 double) is a recently renovated fin de siècle villa, providing the perfect antidote to the hustle down in the *comuni vesuviani*.

VESUVIUS

Before Pompeii and Herculaneum were overwhelmed on 24 August AD 79, Vesuvius was a very different mountain. Possibly as high as 2,000 metres (6,600 feet), it was thickly vegetated; few people suspected they were living close to a major geological hazard.

Today's residents – about 700,000 live in the 13 *comuni vesuviani* around the base and on the lower slopes of the 1,281-metre (4,203-foot) volcano – opt to be as blissfully unconcerned

shore was blocked by debris from the mountain. For a moment my uncle wondered whether to turn back, but when the helmsman advised this he refused, telling him that Fortune stood by the courageous, and they must make for Pomponianus at Stabiae.'

So reads Pliny the Younger's account of his uncle's ill-fated attempt to rescue Pomponianus, a friend living five kilometres south of Pompeii at Stabiae – modern-day Castellammare di Stabia. Pliny wouldn't recognise today's coastline, which extends much further out to sea than it did in AD 79. Nowadays, too, decidedly unlovely postwar urban development rises where his uncle would have encountered shallow water, and the seaside settlement where Pomponianus may have lived is perched on the bluff of a hill called Varano, almost a kilometre inland.

The archaeological site of Stabiae was partially explored and plundered by the Bourbons 200 years ago: some Roman wall paintings left behind were deliberately defaced to enhance the value of artworks removed to adorn the king's palaces. It fell into further disrepair as resources were siphoned off to unearth Pompeii in the 18th and 19th centuries, by this threat as their counterparts 2,000 years ago. They're not about to abandon the fertile volcanic soil: the slopes produce wine (Lacryma Christi, which has shaken off its downmarket reputation thanks to some state-of-the-art wineries), and the area's small *pomodorini* tomatoes (delightful on pasta) earn tidy profits for local farmers. Besides, there are few visible reminders of the danger. Vesuvius does not spew lava like Etna, or eject ash like Stromboli. It lost its *pennacchio,* or plume of smoke, in 1944, and the lava fields created by previous eruptions are gradually being colonised by vegetation, giving the volcano a deceptively benign appearance.

The authorities have abandoned the idea of mass resettlement, and the main focus now is on swift evacuation in the event of an eruption. Given the numbers of people involved and the current road network, early warning of any eruption is critical.

That's where the **Osservatorio Vesuviano** steps in. The institute, which has monitored Vesuvius' activity since 1841, has warned that the volcano could erupt any time between 20 and 200 years from now. The longer it lies dormant (the last eruption was in 1944), the greater the risk.

When the volcano does blow, scientists believe it will not be ash fallout or lava flow that pose the greatest danger to the locals and the landscape, but a surge cloud of the kind that rolled down the mountain in AD 79 at an estimated 65 to 80 kilometres per hour and produced the ultimate open-air *calidarium.*

Reaching a temperature of 400°C, it caused the widespread devastation still evident today.

Vesuvius is now a national park and a UNESCO Biosphere Reserve. But of the 400,000 visitors who trek up to the rim of its cone and peer down into the depths of the crater 200 metres (700 feet) below, few currently stay to enjoy the wilder side of the volcano. The park authority (www.parconazionaledelvesuvio.it) has begun to mark out footpaths; one of the best goes from the town of San Sebastiano al Vesuvio up to the Bourbon observatory. Much of the park, though, is fenced off for security reasons: forest fires (often started deliberately to free up land for building projects) have wrought considerable damage in recent years, and access to certain areas is now only granted for scientific purposes.

Vesuvius is at its best in the early summer, in particular in May or June, when the upper slopes are awash with colour (look out for the leggy Mount Etna broom and red valerian) and nightingales, whitethroats and blue rock thrushes are marking out their territory with prolific song. Start your visit first thing in the morning, and avoid windy days, when conditions on the exposed rim can be harsh.

By far the best approach is from the Circumvesuviana train station in Ercolano. Just outside the station to the left is the Vesuvio Express office (*see right*), which organises an efficient collective taxi service up to the car park. For €10 per person, a minibus ferries you as far up as vehicles can go, allows about 80-90 minutes for the ascent and descent, then

Vesuvius.

completes the return trip – which means a visit could take as little as three hours out of your day.

Once at the car park at Quota 1,000 (1,000 metres above sea level), the standard half-hour route to the cone zigzags along a well-kept path up the mountain's western flank. Although the inside of the crater itself is off limits, there's a good view of steaming fumaroles and stratified pyroclastic deposits on the other side of the crater rim. Fight your acrophobia and peer down into the crater; enterprising plants have moved in, joining several bird species.

Also on the road up the western slope of the volcano, the **Museo dell'Osservatorio Vesuviano** offers a broad overview of the geology of the volcano and the threats it poses, as well as some Heath-Robinson seismographs from the 19th century. It's housed in the old Bourbon observatory, a distinctive Pompeiian-red building that has survived the ravages of at least seven eruptions.

★ Cratere del Vesuvio

(081 771 0939/www.parconazionaledel vesuvio.it/grancono). **Open** 9am-2hrs before sunset daily. **Admission** (including guide) €6.50. **No credit cards.**
Trips to the volcano's crater are suspended during bad weather, or when fog descends.

FREE Museo dell'Osservatorio Vesuviano

Via Osservatorio (081 610 8483/www.ov.ingv.it). **Open** 9am-2pm Mon-Fri by reservation only; 10am-2pm Sat, Sun. Closed Aug. **Admission** free. **No credit cards.**
Look for signs to the Osservatorio at 600m (2,000ft) above sea level, just behind the Eremo Hotel.

TOURIST INFORMATION

Azienda Autonoma di Cura, Soggiorno e Turismo *Via Sacra 1, Pompei (081 850 7255/ www.pompeiturismo.it).* **Open** *Apr-Sept* 8am-7pm Mon-Fri; 8am-2pm Sat. *Nov-Mar* 8am-3.30pm Mon-Fri; 8am-2pm Sat.
Ufficio di Informazione e di Accoglienza Turistica *Via IV Novembre 82, Ercolano (081 788 1243).* **Open** *Apr-Oct* 8am-2.30pm Mon-Sat. *Nov-Mar* 8am-2pm Mon-Fri.
The Ercolano office can also provide information on neighbouring Portici.
Ufficio di Informazione e di Accoglienza Turistica *At the Porta Marina entrance to the archaeological site, by the main ticket office (081 857 5347/www.pompeiisites.org).* **Open** *Apr-Oct* 8.30am-6pm daily. *Nov-Mar* 8.30am-3.30pm daily.
The tourist offices at Pompeii also offer information on Torre del Greco, Torre Annunziata and Castellammare di Stabia.

GETTING THERE

By bus

Run by **ANM** (www.anm.it), buses 157 from Piazza Municipio or 255 from Piazza Carlo III go to Ercolano, and Circumvesuviana runs frequent services from Porto Immacolatella in Naples to Pompei. But given the traffic hell and route complexities, the train is a far better bet.

Vesuvio Express (081 739 3666, www. vesuvioexpress.it) runs a minibus to the car park on Vesuvius from the Ercolano Circumvesuviana station (9am-close of Vesuvius, €10 return). Alternatively, a local **Trasporti Vesuvian** bus (081 963 4420, 081 963 4418) starts from Piazza Anfiteatro in Pompei, stops at Piazza Esedra near the motorway toll booth and at Ercolano train station, then winds its way to the top (€8.60 return from Pompei). Check return times, and say if you need to stop at the Museo dell'Osservatorio.

By car

Most sites are fairly close to the A3 Naples–Salerno motorway. For Herculaneum, take the Ercolano exit and follow the signs to Scavi di Ercolano. For Oplontis, exit at Torre Annunziata Sud, turning right when you hit the first main road. Follow signs to Scavi di Oplontis. For Pompeii, if travelling from Naples take the Pompei Ovest exit from the A3 motorway (Pompeii is beside this exit). From Salerno, take the first Pompei exit.

For Vesuvius, from Torre del Greco or Ercolano, follow signs to Parco Nazionale del Vesuvio.

For Boscoreale, exit at Pompei Ovest and follow signs to the Antiquarium (or ask for directions from the helpful information office at Porta Marina in Pompeii, *see left*.

For Stabiae, take the Castellammare di Stabia exit from the A3 and follow the signs to Sorrento (not Castellammare). Take the first exit (Gragnano) from the Sorrento road; the Passeggiata Archeologica starts at the junction (opposite) where the exit road meets the main Gragnano–Castellammare road.

At Herculaneum and Pompeii you'll have to pay to park; Stabiae and Boscoreale have free parking.

By train

The major sites are served by the **Circumvesuviana** railway (081 772 2444, www.vesuviana.it). If you're travelling from Naples to Pompeii, take the Naples–Sorrento line and get off at Pompei Scavi–Villa dei Misteri. The other Pompei station lies on a different line and is closer to the amphitheatre entrance.

Boscoreale (Boscoreale station) requires a considerable amount of legwork and is very poorly signposted; for Stabiae (Via Nocera station, Castellammare), you need to take bus 1 Rosso from near the station.

AROUND NAPLES

Time Out

timeout.com/travel
Get the local experience

Dream deli counter at Franchi, in the Prati district, **Rome**

© Gian Luca Maggi

Sorrento & Around

Be seduced by the siren city.

Sorrento is enshrined in myth as the land of the sirens; it was here that Odysseus was enchanted by the mermaids' beguiling song. The city became a magnet for the grand tourists of the 18th and 19th centuries, and although these days it is sometimes considered slightly passé, it remains understandably popular. A fine base for visiting the area, it has kept its looks, and makes for a welcome escape from chaotic Naples.

As if to underscore Sorrento's view of itself as 'classic Italy', in 2009 the city handed its Golden Key to Italy's most famous silver screen siren, Sophia Loren. The film star became an honorary citizen, in recognition of the three films she made here – including the sun-drenched romantic comedy *Scandal in Sorrento* in 1955.

INTRODUCING THE AREA

Viewed from Naples, with Vesuvius brooding to the left, the Sorrentine Peninsula seems to resemble an outstretched arm and finger pointed at Capri, lying in the bay like a Modigliani head. The Monte Lattari and foothills, which back Sorrento's cliff-top coastline, are home to lush citrus orchards and olive groves, with tiny towns and villages nestling in their midst. Well-kept paths zigzag discreetly across the peninsula, offering mesmerising views, quite different from those around the corner on the celebrated Amalfi Coast. It has been said that the Sorrento and Amalfi coasts were made by two separate gods: one sweet-tempered, the other irate. Sorrento's is Arcadia; Amalfi's the abyss.

Pretty tiled cupolas and multicoloured pontoons vie for your attention, as do brilliant geraniums and wisteria, the bluest of seas, the greenest of hills, the yellowest of limoncellos and the pinkest of sunburned flesh. In a truly democratic tourist mix, the socks-and-sandals brigade shuffles alongside sauntering local sophisticates, beer-and-tattoo Brits, daytripping Neapolitans and chichi wedding parties.

As is often the case in the Bay of Naples, it's not an easy matter to go for a swim here (*see p260* **Call of the waves**). If it's a watery holiday you're after, opt for a hotel with its own swimming pool, or be prepared to walk or to pay to use a lido.

The area around Sorrento has been inhabited since prehistoric times, as the remains displayed in museums in **Vico Equense** (*see p259*) and **Piano di Sorrento** (*see p258*) show. Etruscans who moved in from the north in the sixth century BC found Greek settlers already in residence, and an uneasy and often violent co-existence ensued until the decline of Etruscan influence in the fifth century BC. When the Romans routed the Greeks, the remaining Etruscans and the local Samnite tribes in the late fourth century BC, they made the peninsula a sought-after holiday destination, building luxury villas along the coast from Castellammare di Stabia out to **Punta della Campanella** (*see p262*).

As the Roman Empire in the west wavered and finally fell, the Goths stampeded along the peninsula, razing small towns as they went. Sorrento, on the other hand, passed formally into the control of Rome's Eastern Empire, ruled from Byzantium (Constantinople). Harried by Lombards, who had established their southern Italian headquarters in nearby Benevento, as well as by power-hungry Amalfi on the other side of the peninsula, and later by marauding Saracen pirates from north Africa, the Sorrentines fought long and hard to keep their independence. However, the Normans (who arrived in the 12th century) were too powerful for them. The towns of the peninsula were soon absorbed into the southern Italian kingdom, their fate inextricably linked to that of Naples.

Piazza Tasso.

SORRENTO

Sorrento became particularly popular with the British between 1943-45, when it was used as a convalescence centre for soldiers; word spread, and it has remained a haven ever since. Still, it's easy enough to leave the package tourist crowd behind, and the town is still very Italian.

The grid plan of the streets stretching west from Piazza Tasso is almost all that's left of Greek and Roman Surrentum; the Normans destroyed much of the Roman fortifications. Most of what remains lies inside the 15th-century walls, and is reached from the traffic-clogged Via degli Aranci ring road. Part of the old city walls are incorporated into the **Parco Ibsen** restaurant (*see p253*).

As late as the 16th century these defences were crucial for the town (and the whole peninsula), subject as they were to attacks by Saracen pirates from across the Mediterranean. On 13 June 1558, the North African marauders sacked Sorrento; a chain of lookout towers, many of which still stand today, was subsequently built along the coast.

The final stretch of the Vallone dei Mulini (valley of the watermills) was another natural border of the city, running from Piazza Tasso to Marina Piccola. The ruined mill on **Piazza delle Mure Vecchie** remained in use until the early 1900s. A more complete picture of how the city once looked can be seen at the **Museo Correale di Terranova** (*see p252*),

where 18th- and 19th-century paintings depict rustic scenes, crumbling town gates and wild, unspoilt coasts.

While Sorrentine youths tend to congregate in the soulless Piazza Lauro, their elders gather in **Piazza Tasso**. Bar tables cluster on the pavement, and the evening *struscio* (stroll) begins and ends here; the surrounding streets of the Centro Storico are closed to traffic between 8pm and midnight daily. Sorrento's most famous literary luminary, Torquato Tasso (1544-95), author of the epic poem *Gerusalemme Liberata* (Jerusalem Delivered) and pastroral drama *Aminta*, lends his name to the town's busiest square; naturally enough, his statue looks over it.

A balcony on the northern side of the square offers views of the dark ravine that leads to **Marina Piccola**, the port from which ferries and hydrofoils depart for Capri and Naples. Stairs lead down from the piazza towards the dock, which is also served by local buses.

Leading out of the south-western corner is the narrow Via Pietà. At no.24, the early 15th-century **Palazzo Correale** has an impressive door and arched upper windows; head into the florist's shop in the courtyard to admire its 18th-century majolica-tiled wall. The windows of the 13th-century **Palazzo Veniero** at no.14 are framed with Byzantine designs in pretty coloured stone.

Via Pietà emerges on to Corso Italia by the Romanesque **Duomo** (*see p252*). The vast cathedral is surrounded by a bishop's palace, now occupied by church offices. From here, Via Sersale leads to the remains of the Roman southern town gate, and a stretch of 15th-century wall. Corso Italia heads on, lined by smart shops, past the small park and art gallery Villa Fiorentino (no.53) and the relatively quiet Piazza Veniero, before curving round the cliff towards Capo (*see p261*).

Turn right down Via Tasso to reach the narrow, souvenir shop-packed **Via San Cesareo**. Here you can pick up examples of

INSIDE TRACK
LOVELY LIMONE

Lemons, lemon flower (*zagara*) honey and limoncello, a potent lemon liqueur, are emblems of this area. With its cooling, wonderfully intense flavour, limoncello is made from lemon peel – so organic lemons are a must.

the marquetry (*intarsio*) for which Sorrento was famous in the 18th century, as well as bottles of the omnipresent limoncello.

One block to the east, where Via Cesareo intersects with Via Giuliani, the arched **Sedile Dominova**, with its fading frescoes, was a 15th-century open-air meeting place. Here the aristocracy discussed local policy; their coats of arms can be seen around the walls. In an ironic twist of fate, the Sedile is now the front porch of a working men's club; pensioners gather there to play cards and chew the fat.

Parallel to Via Cesareo, Via Santa Maria delle Grazie changes name several times as it runs west towards the **Museo Bottega della Tarsia Lignea** (*see p252*), set in the carefully restored 18th-century Palazzo Pomarici Santomasi. Its private collection of *intarsio*, which sits alongside paintings and photographs of old Sorrento, is extensive and beautiful. The ground floor, meanwhile, is dedicated to modern interpretations of the craft.

Several blocks to the north-east, Via Veneto gives on to the **Villa Comunale**, a small but leafy park overlooking the Bay of Naples to Vesuvius, with steps down to the lidos (*see p260* **Call of the waves**) and a pleasant bar at which to soak up the view. Further along Via Veneto is the church of **San Francesco**; beside

its entrance, a small, 14th-century cloister with pretty ogival arches and a garden hosts art exhibitions, music recitals and civil weddings.

Nearby Piazza Sant'Antonino is named after Sorrento's patron saint, whose tomb can be admired in the atmospheric 18th-century crypt of the **Basilica di Sant'Antonino** (open 9am-noon, 5-7pm daily). Though heavy with Baroque features, the basilica stands on the site of an earlier church. An 11th-century door is surrounded by Roman remains, and there's an impressive Nativity scene inside, as well as ex-votos from shipwrecked sailors and two whalebones; Sant'Antonino, the protector of those at sea, supposedly saved a child swallowed by a whale.

Via Marina Grande and narrow, craftshop-lined Via Sopra le Mura lead down to the confusingly named **Marina Grande** (it's smaller than the Marina Piccola). This was once the heart of the fishing village of Sorrento; however, the natural deep-water harbour of the Marina Piccola made a more suitable dock for ferries, and the focus shifted. Today, it's run-down but charming; paint peels from tall, multicoloured houses, stray dogs sleep under seafront benches, kids play football in front of the tiny church of **Sant'Anna** (worth checking out for the glass cabinets of ex-votos) and

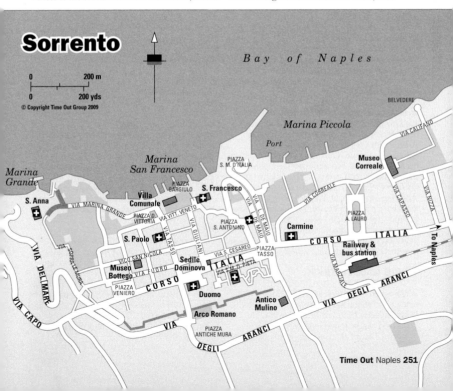

fishermen mend their nets. In fact, it probably looks pretty much as it did when Sophia Loren was here in the 1950s filming *Scandal in Sorrento*. Despite some efforts to tart the area up a bit, it remains, unlike much of Sorrento, amiably down at heel. Its dark, volcanic sand beach is popular with locals, but there are better spots elsewhere (*see p260* **Call of the waves**).

FREE Duomo (Santi Filippo e Giacomo)

Corso Italia (081 878 2248). **Open** *Apr-Oct* 7.30am-12.30pm, 4.30-9.30pm daily. *Nov-Mar* 7.30am-12.30pm, 4.30-8pm daily. **Admission** free.

The Romanesque cathedral that once occupied this site was largely rebuilt in the 15th century. Despite the Duomo's Gothic appearance, its brick-red facade is fairly modern, although the door with the Aragonese coat of arms on the right dates from the late 15th century. The three-aisled interior has 16th- and 17th-century paintings in its chapels and on the ceiling. The bishop's throne (1573) is a jigsaw of ancient marble fragments; the choir stalls are adorned with fine examples of local *intarsio* work.

Museo Bottega della Tarsia Lignea

Via San Nicola 28 (081 877 1942/www. alessandrofiorentinocollection.it). **Open** *Apr-Oct* 10am-1pm, 3-6.30pm daily. *Nov-Mar* 10am-1pm, 3-6.30pm Mon-Sat. **Admission** €8. **Credit** AmEx, DC, MC, V.

In the mid 18th century, Sorrento became famous for its *intarsio*, avidly collected by the Neapolitan royal family and by grand tourists. In addition to its excellent collection of intricately inlaid objects in natural and stained woods, the museum seeks to revive the tradition, and its shop sells contemporary interpretations of marquetry furniture.

★ Museo Correale di Terranova

Via Correale 50 (081 878 1846/www.museo correale.com). **Open** 9am-2pm Mon, Wed-Sun. **Admission** €6. **No credit cards.**

Alfredo and Pompeo Correale, the last male heirs to the title of Count of Terranova, left their grand 18th-century family villa and collection of local art and artefacts to the town in the 1920s, and this museum was opened to hold it all. The archaeological section, with finds from around town, is on the ground floor; upstairs are views of 18th- and 19th-century Sorrento, as well as local furniture, porcelain, time-pieces and clothing. Beyond the camellia garden lies a lookout point with a beautiful view across the bay.

Where to eat & drink

While much of the food served in Sorrento tends to be unremarkable, standards are rising. Locals usually head for the hills to eat, but good food can be found in the centre – often at a price, though there are less costly options.

Recently refurbished **Il Fauno** (Piazza Tasso 13-15, 081 878 1135, www.faunobar.it) is open year round, all day until 1.30am (midnight low season) – though the price for good people-watching is decidedly brisk service. Meanwhile, pizza-lovers head to late-opening **Da Franco** (Corso Italia 265, 081 877 2066), opposite the Giardini di Cataldo; delicious, ridiculously cheap pizzas make up for the plastic cups, paper plates and snappy service.

For people in search of ye olde English style, there are plenty of rather uninspiring pubs; the other-worldly **Circolo dei Forestieri** or 'Foreigners' Club' (Via Luigi di Maio 35, 081 877 3263, closed Apr, May) beside the tourist information office, also draws expats with its wonderful view and handful of lunch options. For fine dining, head to Gennaro Esposito's wonderful **Torre del Saracino** (*see p261*).

Bagni Delfino

Via Marina Grande 216 (081 878 2038/www. ristorantebagnidelfino.com). **Open** noon-3.30pm, 6.30-10.30pm daily. Closed Nov-Mar. **Average** €40-€50. **Credit** MC, V.

The decor of this family-run restaurant is suitably nautical, considering its location: most of the restaurant juts right over the water. It serves simple, good quality fare, and you can't go wrong if you follow the delicious, free bruschetta and tomatoes with a dish of *spaghetti alle vongole* or grilled catch of the day and a carafe of house wine. Smaller appetites might opt for cheese omelette, risotto or gnocchi.
► *Too busy here? Stroll along the marina to the slightly cheaper Di Leva; see below.*

★ Il Buco

Il Rampa Marina Piccola 5 (081 878 2354/www. ilbucoristorante.it). **Open** noon-3pm, 7.30-11pm Mon, Tue, Thur-Sun. Closed Jan. **Average** €75. **Credit** AmEx, MC, V.

Rather unpromisingly, the name of this place means 'the hole' – but that simply refers to its setting in the cellars of an old convent off Piazza Sant'Antonino. In summer, the outdoor tables are a lovely spot at which to sample the mostly fish-based, nouvelle Italian menu (the beautifully-presented portions may look small, but are filling). Service is swift and courteous, and the wine list has some affordable options.

Di Leva

Via Marina Grande 31 (081 878 3826/ www.ristorantedileva.com). **Open** noon-3pm, 7.30-10.30pm daily. Closed Nov-Feb. **Average** €30. **Credit** AmEx, MC, V.

Set by the water's edge in the Marina Grande, this simple trattoria serves up fresh fish, pasta and drinks. Prices are reasonable, service friendly and food strictly no-frills. There are photos of Sophia Loren visiting in 2005 to celebrate 50 years since the filming of *Scandal in Sorrento*.

Duomo.

park just beyond Sorrento's *antiche mura* (old wall), which boasts a childrens' play area as well as a stage for theatrical and musical events. There's a 'lounge bar' for aperitivi and snacks, and a smart restaurant for heartier meals, with an elegant terrace.

★ Photo Food & Drinks

Via Correale 19 (081 877 3686/www.photo sorrento.com). **Open** 6.30pm-2am Tue-Sun. Closed Feb-Mar. **Average** €40. **Credit** AmEx, MC, V.

With its modish red, black and white palette, this lounge-style bar and restaurant is a popular address, particularly at weekends. The friendly atmosphere, scrumptious nibbles provided gratis with drinks, groovy seating and lovely garden attract a predominantly local crowd; photos and projections abound, and there's good music too.

Ristorante La Favorita 'O Parrucchiano' dal 1868

Corso Italia 71 (081 878 1321/www. parrucchiano.it). **Open** noon-3.30pm, 7-10pm Mon, Tue, Thur-Sun. **Average** €35. **Credit** MC, V.

This vast glasshouse restaurant, in business since 1868 and boasting a romantic lemon and orange garden, is an oasis of calm – albeit a rather touristy one – just off the main street. Prices are a little steep (and the frites looked like oven chips on our last visit), but portions are generous and the service is spritely.

Syrenuse

Piazza Tasso (081 807 5582). **Open** 7.30am-midnight daily. **Average** €35. **Credit** AmEx, MC, V.

In a prime location on Piazza Tasso, Syrenuse has had a bit of a makeover, and looks all the better for it. As well as the main menu's pizzas, pastas and salads, the bar has an extensive cocktail menu and offers decent bar nibbles with all drinks. It's great for watching the package tourists drift by as you plot your afternoon's sightseeing.

€ Zi'Ntonio

Via Luigi de Maio 11 (081 878 1623/www. zintonio.it). **Open** noon-3pm, 6.30pm-midnight daily. **Average** €20. **Credit** AmEx, MC, V.

In a tile-lined, wood-beamed dining room, this friendly family trattoria serves good wood-fired pizza and fish dishes (such as spaghetti with clams), and inventive salads (cuttlefish with walnuts and courgette flowers, say). Its sister outpost at Marina Grande overlooks the sea.

Shopping

Corso Italia is packed with clothes shops: the cheaper stores are east of Piazza Tasso, whereas the more upmarket boutiques (MaxMara, Emporio Armani, Furla) are to the west.

Donna Sofia

Via Talagnano 5 (081 877 3532/www.ristorante donnasofia.com). **Open** *May-Oct* noon-11.30pm daily. *Nov-Apr* noon-11.30pm Tue-Sun. **Average** €40. **Credit** AmEx, MC, V.

Book a table here and you'll be picked up (and dropped off again) at your hotel and, once seated, offered a glass of prosecco while you mull over the long list of specials. Choices might include antipasti (courgette flowers, own-made salami), pastas, fish specials and meat dishes. The restaurant starts to get lively at around 9pm.

La Fenice

Via degli Aranci 11 (081 878 1652). **Open** noon-2.45pm, 7-11.30pm Tue-Sun. Closed 2wks Feb. **Average** €30. **Credit** AmEx, MC, V.

Close to Sorrento's main drag, Corso Italia, La Fenice is a good stop for pizzas, pastas and fresh fish. The welcome is warm, the service efficient and the food freshly prepared (check out the fish display before entering). It's popular with locals, so expect things to liven up as the lights go down.

Parco Ibsen

Piazza Antiche Mura (081 878 4294/www.ibsen sorrento.com). **Open** *Bar* 10am-11pm Tue-Sun. *Restaurant* noon-3pm, 7-11pm Tue-Sun. **Average** €30. **Credit** AmEx, DC, MC, V.

Just off the permanently traffic-laden Via degli Aranci, Parco Ibsen is a good find. It's set in a lovely

AROUND NAPLES

Walk Sorrento's heady heights

Amid such rugged terrain, intrepid walkers reap rich rewards.

Trek up and down between Marina Piccola and the centre a couple of times, and you may well decide that walking in the Sorrento area is really not your thing. If steep slopes don't stress you out, however, you'll find that the beautiful and seemingly inaccessible hills around Sorrento afford glorious views and hikes. Often invisible from the road, footpaths criss-cross the area from **Castellammare di Stabia** (*see p244*) to **Salerno** (*see p292*) and Punta della Campanella.

Most paths are colour-coded and, in general, easy to follow. Some tracks are maintained by the Club Alpino Italiano (CAI) mountaineering association, which marks routes with red and white paint flashes on rocks, walls, lamp posts and whatever comes to hand. Paths vary dramatically in difficulty: the further you go from habitation, the less well defined they become; once in a while, you may end up having to cut across someone's vineyard or olive grove.

HALF-DAY WALKS & EASY STROLLS

Sorrento is a starting point for several laid-back, pleasant walks. For one, take the Via Capo west out of Sorrento as far as Capo di Sorrento (or get the bus a few stops), then turn right down to the Roman **Villa di Pollio Felice** and continue on across the wooden bridge as far as the **Bagni della Regina Giovanna** (*see p261*), where you can stop for a swim. Another walk begins by the Sorrento Palace Hotel, where you take the Via Crucis steps (marked out with the Stations of the Cross). The path continues as far as **Sant'Agata** and then on to the **Deserto monastery** (for both, *see p272*). The views from Sant'Agata are stunning, spanning the Bay of Naples and Gulf of Salerno (hence the town's full name, Sant'Agata sui Due Golfi). Either walk can be done in a morning.

If you have the legs for it, carry on from Sant'Agata to the **Marina di Crapolla**, on a path that winds steeply down the hillside to a tiny pebble beach. Aside from the path, the beach is only accessible from the sea, so you're likely to have it all to yourself. The 12th-century church of San Pietro is just behind you, and some Roman walls remain on the beach itself.

People who are good with heights but are not fans of uphill hikes can take the regular Circumvesuviana train to Castellammare and get the *funivia* cable car up to the top of **Monte Faito** (operates Apr-Oct). It's worth the trip for the cable car experience alone; the ride can be followed by a pleasant, level stroll around the peak of the mountain (after Vesuvius, the second highest in the area).

DAY-LONG WALKS

If you have an entire day to spare, embark on a dramatic coast-to-coast walk. The first goes from **Puolo** to **Crapolla**, stopping for a break in Sant'Agata just over halfway. The climb is long and fairly relentless, although the views make it well worthwhile.

Slightly shorter is the walk from **Marina della Lobra** to **Marina del Cantone**. It's no less strenuous, but most of the ascent is in the first hour, leaving you with a long, gradual descent across the spectacular Positano side of the peninsula. Neither walk is recommended for people with bad knees.

More serious walkers will want to try the **Alta Via dei Monti Lattari**, which stretches from **Colli di Fontanelle** above Positano down to **Punta della Campanella**. Said to be a former shepherd's path down from the hills into Sorrento, it's marked by a red and white line. It takes at least a day to walk the length of the path, and it's best to break your journey with a stopover in Massa or Sant'Agata.

The area's other long path is the **Sentiero degli Dei** (Pathway of the Gods). Considerable confusion abounds as to its exact starting and ending point, somewhere between Ravello and Sorrento; the official view is that it leads from Bomerano to Nocella. Meandering as it does along the pinnacle of the mountains – with a sheer descent on either side at times – it's easy to see how the path got its name. This is definitely not one for the fainthearted.

PUNTA DELLA CAMPANELLA

Many of the best walks in the area are near, or end at, the **Punta della Campanella** national park (or 'marine reserve', as it is formally known). It opened in 2000 with the aim of protecting the date shell mollusc (*dattero del mare*) from being harvested out of existence. The park has flourished, despite strong opposition from property developers and powerboat owners. Its name comes from the bell (*campanella*) here that was rung to warn residents when marauding pirates were sighted.

The best entry points to the park are in the towns of Termini or Nerano. From **Termini**, a long, gentle, two- to three-hour walk winds its way down to Punta della Campanella. You're only five kilometres from Capri, and the enchanting island seems close enough to touch. A Greek temple once stood on the tip of the peninsula, although the ruins you can see today are of a second-century Roman villa and the 14th-century bell tower. From **Nerano**, head south to Punta Penna and Punta di Montalto, with its Napoleonic lookout tower. There is a tiny beach at Capitello on the **Baia di Jeranto** (*see p262*) – possibly the most spectacular swimming spot in the area.

More information on the park is available from **Ente Parco Punta della Campanella** (Viale Filangieri 40, Massa Lubrense, 081 808 9877, www.puntacampanella.org; office open June-Sept 9am-1pm, 3.30-7pm Mon-Sat, 9am-1pm Sun; Oct-May 9am-1pm, 3.30-7.30pm Mon, Wed, Fri, 9am-1pm Tue, Thur).

NEED TO KNOW

Some of the painted colours on the signposts have been removed, become contradictory due to changing paths, or simply faded. Don't be embarrassed to ask fellow walkers for directions – most will be happy to help.

In spring or autumn, watch out for sudden, heavy rain showers. Some of the ravine-like paths can become blocked up with leaves and debris, and stone paths can become slippery. In summer, many of the paths have little or no shade for long stretches. Wear a hat, bring suncream and carry plenty of drinking water.

Be aware, too, that Italian farmers sometimes leave large, aggressive dogs to roam freely around what they perceive to be their land. Although they may bark, they rarely bite.

The best places for information on walks are the tourist information offices in **Sorrento** and **Massa Lubrense** (*see p258 and p263*), though the website www.giovis.com is also useful. The local branch of the **World Wide Fund for Nature** (Via Santa Maria Pietà, Sorrento, 081 807 2533, www.wwfpenisolasorrentina.org) can also provide information.

AROUND NAPLES

Monte Faito.

Pretty craftshops line tiny Via Sopra le Mura, while Via Cesareo and its continuation Via Fuoro are the obvious places for souvenirs – particularly limoncello. If you want to see the stuff being made, visit **Limonoro** (Via San Cesareo 51-53, 081 878 5348, www.limonoro.it) or head downtown to **I Giardini di Cataldo** (Corso Italia 267, 081 878 1888, www.igiardini dicataldo.it), where you can wander the old lemon grove before sampling delicious, refreshing granita and limoncello.

For local produce, drop into **Terranova** (Piazza Tasso 16, 081 878 1263, www.fattoria terranova.it). **Gelateria Valestra** (Piazza Angelina Lauro 45, 081 878 5784, closed Thur from Nov-Mar) sells home-made ice-cream and artisan cheeses.

For marquetry souvenirs, try the workshop of **Salvatore Gargiulo** (Via Fuoro 33, 081 878 2420, www.gargiuloinlaid.it, closed Sun am from Nov-Mar).

Arts & entertainment

Sorrento's largely tourist-centred economy rules out a truly vibrant cultural scene, and most of the city's night-time entertainment consists of strolling up and down the traffic-liberated centre, or relaxing in bars and watching others do the work. In summer, lots of temporary venues open up – keep your ear to the ground.

At the **Fauno Notte** *tarantella* club (Piazza Tasso 1, 081 878 1021, www.faunonotte.it, open 9pm, €25), you can catch a cheery – if cheesy – 'Naples by numbers' show that involves music, dance and song and, covers key historical events.

Artis Domus

Via San Nicola 56 (081 877 2073/www.artis domus.com). **Open** *Restaurant* 9pm-midnight daily. *Disco* 9pm-4am Sat. Closed June-Aug. **Admission** €15-€20. **Credit** MC, V.
A small stone doorway leads into the garden of a sumptuous villa. The tanned Versace-wearers of Sorrento congregate here on a Saturday night, when there's live music or a disco, as well as a buffet. Infuriatingly, it closes in high season.

Sorrento Festival

Chiostro della Chiesa di San Francesco (081 807 4033/www.sorrentourism.it). **Concerts** *July-Sept* 9pm. **Tickets** €15-€20. **No credit cards.**
This highly respected summer season of classical concerts gives Ravello (*see p288*) a run for its money. Concerts start at 9pm, and take place in Villa Fondi (Piano di Sorrento), Villa Angelina (Massa Lubrense), Basilica del Lauro (Meta di Sorrento) or the Chiostro di San Francesco (Sorrento). Tickets are on sale at the tourist office on Via Luigi di Maio (*see p258*).

Sorrento.

Teatro Tasso

Piazza Sant'Antonino 25 (081 807 5525/www. teatrotasso.it). **Open** *Box office* 9.30am-1pm, 4-9pm daily. **Shows** *Mid Apr-Oct* 9.30pm daily. **Tickets** €25. **Credit** AmEx, DC, MC, V.
Teatro Tasso's programme leans heavily towards the kind of *folkloristico* musical variety shows that require no knowledge of Italian culture. Watch out for the season of summer shows entitled 'Sorrento Musical'. Cheesier than mozzarella.

Where to stay

The best of Sorrento's hotels are genuinely splendid, and if your bank account is up the strain, you can have a classic grand tourist experience. Henrik Ibsen spent six months at the **Hotel Imperial Tramontano** (Via Vittorio Veneto 1, 081 878 2588, www.hotel tramontano.it, closed Feb, €170-€272 double), where he wrote *Ghosts*. Byron also stayed here, and GB de Curtis penned his famous 'Torna a Surriento' on the terrace overlooking the bay of Naples. For less flush visitors, mid-range hotels can disappoint. We list the better central choices, and a few budget options. Further out, Sant'Agnello is a quieter alternative – and boasts one of the area's top hotels.

Campsites include the **Nube d'Argento** (Via Capo 21, 081 878 1344, www.nubed argento.com, closed Jan-Feb, €8-€10 per person, €5-€10 tent site), which has a decent pool and restaurant. It also offers apartments at the adjoining **La Neffola** (Via Capo 21, 081 878 1344, www.neffolaresidence.com, closed Jan-Feb,

€60 apartment). The town's youth hostel, **Ostello delle Sirene**, is on Via degli Aranci (no.160, 081 807 2925, www.hostel.it, closed 3wks Nov, €18-€20 dorm bed, €55-€70 double).

★ Antiche Mura

Via Fuorimura 7, Piazza Tasso (081 807 3523/ www.antichemura.com). **Rates** €100-€180 double. **Credit** AmEx, MC, V.

This relative newcomer is one of the more reasonably priced options in pricey Sorrento. The Antiche Mura is, as its name suggests, conveniently sited close to the old walls of the town. Rooms are clean, comfortable and simply furnished, and staff are charming and exceedingly helpful. Decent breakfasts with a staggering array of pastries and cakes can be served in the lovely art nouveau-style breakfast room overlooking the terrace, or by the pool.

Bellevue Syrene

Piazza Vittoria 5 (081 878 1024/www.bellevue.it). **Rates** €270-€350 double. **Credit** AmEx, MC, V.

Built on a cliff edge on the site of a second-century BC villa, the Bellevue has been a hotel since 1820, hosting royalty, writers and countless celebrities. Elegant yet modish, it has benefited from a recent makeover by local interior designer Marco de Luca; antiques, frescoes and vaulting are set off by stylish pastel tones. Rooms with sea view are at a premium, but you'll be happy to pay up when you wake to a pure blue sea and Mount Vesuvius. The garden rooms are also lovely, and there are fabulous views from the restaurants. A flight of steps (or a handy lift) will whizz you down to the beach, and there's a pool and a beauty centre.

▶ *Designer Marco de Luca is also the man behind La Minervetta, see p257.*

Casa Astarita

Corso Italia 67 (081 877 4906/www.casastarita. com). **Rates** €70-€110 double. **Credit** AmEx, MC, V.

Occupying part of a 19th-century palace, the Astartita sisters' charming B&B has seven individually decorated rooms; ask for a room at the front, as one at the back is notoriously noisy. There's also a lovely communal breakfast and sitting room, with a library and a majolica-tiled fireplace. The atmosphere is relaxed – help yourself to home-made cakes and limoncello. Its central location on busy Corso Italia, just along from La Favorita (*see p253*), makes this a very popular pad.

Grand Hotel Aminta

Via Nastro Verde, 23 (081 878 1821/www. aminta.it). **Rates** €190-€229 double. **Credit** AmEx, MC, V.

Taking its name from Tasso's pastoral drama *Aminta*, the Grand Hotel is set a few kilometres from Sorrento's centre, and offers quietly elegant accommodation. Common areas retain their 1960s styling, with tiled floors and a curving central staircase, and rooms are light and airy, with wonderful views out to sea or of fertile hillsides. Pleasing details include an iron and free satellite TV in the rooms, and a free courtesy bus into town.

Grand Hotel Excelsior Vittoria

Piazza Tasso 34 (081 877 7111/www.exvitt.it). **Rates** €240-€550 double. **Credit** AmEx, DC, MC, V.

In the hands of the Fiorentino family since 1834, the grandest of Sorrento's grand hotels has seen numerous royals and celebrities pass through its lobby over the years. The most famous tenor of all time, Neapolitan Enrico Caruso, stayed here the week before his death in 1921. Set in five acres of orange and lemon groves, it oozes peace and tranquillity in spite of its central location. Spacious, individually decorated bedrooms are dotted with period furniture (the most incredible is the Aurora, with its frescoed ceilings and 19th-century antiques) and have delightful terraces overlooking the sea or the lush gardens. There are several restaurants, as well as a holistic centre and the wonderful park to explore. Look out for offers and weekend packages.

Hotel Mignon Meuble

Via Sersale 9 (081 807 3824/www.sorrentohotel mignon.com). **Rates** €70-€100 double. **Credit** AmEx, DC, MC, V.

This charming little family-run hotel is set just off Corso Italia, not far from the Duomo. The rooms are clean and old-fashioned, with tiled floors; some have a garden terrace. All rooms have air-conditioning, and street-facing rooms are soundproofed.

★ La Minervetta

Via Capo 25 (081 877 4455/www.laminervetta. com). **Rates** €150-€400 double. **Credit** AmEx, MC, V.

Ten minutes' walk from the town centre, this chic boutique hotel feels miles away in terms of peace and quiet. Twelve bright, individually designed rooms have huge picture windows – some with a terrace, others with a balcony – from which to survey the Bay of Naples and Marina Grande. There's a lovely sun terrace and a beautiful lounge, filled with an eclectic collection of shells, paintings, ceramics, books and magazines. A cold-water pool overlooks the harbour, and there are steps all the way down to the Marina Grande. The enormous breakfasts (fresh fruit salads, cheese and tomato omelettes) are the stuff of legend, and staff couldn't be more helpful.

★ Parco dei Principi

Via Rota 1, Sant'Agnello (081 878 4644/www. grandhotelparcodeiprincipi.net). **Rates** €130-€250 double. **Credit** AmEx, DC, MC, V.

Just beyond Sorrento's town centre, this hip hotel has a distinctly nautical feel. It was designed – building, furniture, fittings and all – in shades of blue and

white by architect Giò Ponti in 1962, and staying here is rather like being on the set of a stylish '60s Italian film. The modernist floor tiles are arranged in a different design in every room. There's also a seawater pool, sauna, private beach and lush botanical garden. A free shuttle service takes you to the Piazza Antiche Mura, where the local bus stops.
▶ *For more of Ponti's bold signature style, check into the Royal Continental in Naples and ask for a room on the Giò Ponti floor; see p108.*

Regina Sorrento Hotel

Via Marina Grande 10 (081 878 2722/www. hotelreginasorrento.it). **Rates** €80-€200 double. **Credit** AmEx, DC, MC, V.

In a quiet area, five minutes from the town square, the Regina is a convenient base for exploring. The en-suite rooms are clean and functional, and most have balconies; the views from the rooftop terrace compensate for its rather bland interior. The hotel has a garden, and you can book private cabins on the beach. You can also use the pool at a nearby hotel, if you pay an extra €8.

Resources

Hospital

Santa Maria della Misericordia *Corso Italia (081 807 2877/533 1225).*

Internet

PC Lab *Via degli Aranci 55 (081 877 3866/877 2812).* **Open** 9.30am-1pm, 3-8.30pm Mon-Sat. Buy an access card at Sorrento Info, Via Tasso 19.

Police

Carabinieri *Via Bartolomeo Capasso 11 (081 878 1010).*
Polizia di Stato *Vico III Rota 14 (081 807 5311).*

Post office

Corso Italia 210 (081 877 0834).

Tourist information

Azienda Autonoma di Cura Soggiorno e Turismo *Via Luigi di Maio 35 (081 807 4033/ www.sorrentotourism.com/www.infosorrento.it).* **Open** *May-Sept* 8.30am-6.30pm daily. *Oct-Apr* 8.45am-4pm Mon-Sat.

Getting around

For getting there, *see p263*. Four red and orange bus lines serve the Sorrento area, and run from 5.30am to midnight. Line A goes from Meta to Capo di Sorrento; line B from the port at Marina Piccola to the centre/ station; line C from the port at Marina Piccola to Sant'Agnello; and line D between Marina Grande and the centre. The terminus is in front

of the Circumvesuviana station, on Piazza Giovanni Battista de Curtis. For information on **UnicoCostiera** tickets, *see p271*.

Car & scooter hire

Avis *Viale Nizza 53 (081 877 3450/878 2459/ www.avisautonoleggio.it).* **Open** *Apr-Oct* 8.30am-1.30pm, 3.30-7.30pm Mon-Fri; 9am-4pm Sat; 8.30am-1pm Sun. *Nov-Mar* 8.30am-1.30pm, 4-7pm Mon-Fri; 8.30am-1pm Sat. **Credit** AmEx, MC, V.
Jolly Servizi & Noleggio *Via degli Aranci 180 (081 877 3450/www.jollyservizi.it).* **Open** *Apr-Oct* 8am-1pm, 4-8pm daily. *Nov-Feb* 9.30am-noon, 4-7pm Mon-Fri. **Credit** AmEx, MC, V.

East from Sorrento

PIANO DI SORRENTO TO SEIANO

Since the building and tourism boom of the 1950s and '60s, what was once a collection of fishing and farming villages, punctuated by the odd stately holiday villa, has become one big urban sprawl – albeit a very pretty one. East of the town is a long, low, whitewashed conurbation of hotels that absorb Sorrento's overflow. Many have pretty gardens and sports facilities that more central hotels don't have the space to offer, but if you want to be in the city centre, check the small print or you may end up out here.

Sant'Agnello's traffic-clogged main street is little more than a funnel into and out of town; more pleasant is the almost-coast road, which cuts past beautiful villas – many of them converted into hotels – and their flower-filled gardens, just a block back from the sea.

Piano di Sorrento still retains the feel of a separate town. On the coast road, set in the 18th-century Villa Fondi, the **Museo Archeologico Georges Vallet** (Via Ripa di Cassano 14, 081 808 7078, closed Mon) offers free admission and contains archaeological finds from the Sorrentine Peninsula: artefacts from necropolises, arrowheads and pre-Roman pottery. In summer, concerts and romantic soirées are held here. A tortuous track leads down to the little harbour, **Marina di Cassano**, whose beach is encroached upon by boats from one of the peninsula's few remaining economically significant fishing fleets.

Meta di Sorrento boasts the area's longest stretch of sand, the **spiaggia di Alimuri**. It's named after a Saracen pirate captain called Ali, who came ashore in the mid 1500s and died (*muri*) there in fierce fighting with the locals. Until a century ago, Meta's marina moored one of Italy's largest shipping fleets, but is now another bustling modern suburb, with hotels

Marina di Equa.

and cafés on sunny *piazze*. In a square on the main road, the **Madonna del Lauro** basilica (open 7am-noon, 4-7pm daily), with its low, tiled dome and neoclassical facade, was rebuilt in the 18th century, but is believed to stand on the site of a temple to Minerva.

After Meta, there is a slight lull in the urban sprawl before the village of **Seiano**, where the 16th-century chapel of **Santa Maria delle Grazie** (closed to the public) has a medieval fresco over its front door. You'll also see the 18th-century church of **San Marco** (opening times vary according to Mass), which has the highest dome on the peninsula.

VICO EQUENSE

Coast road and railway line then cross the breathtaking viaduct over the Murrano river to **Vico Equense**. Less touristy than Sorrento, Vico is a lovely place in which to escape the crowds and mix with the locals.

Then known as Aequana, the town was founded by the Romans, who found its steep, sunny slopes perfect for cultivating grapes – before the Goths razed it in the fifth century. (The area's wine production has since moved uphill to **Gragnano**, where a tasty, slightly fizzy red is still produced today.) The town of Vico Equense was resurrected in the 13th century by King Charles II of Anjou.

Castello Giusso, which now houses privately owned apartments, looms over the town. Its fanciful crenellations are a 19th-century addition to the original medieval building of 1284; the Renaissance section above was added in the mid 16th century. To the south, in Via Puntamare, the church of the **Santissima Annunziata** (open 9-10.30am Mon-Sat; 9am-12.30pm Sun) overlooks a dramatic drop to the sea, making it an essential photo opportunity. The Annunziata was Vico's cathedral until the bishopric was abolished in 1799, when the incumbent, Michel Natale, was hanged for his over-enthusiastic support of the Parthenopean Republic (*see p26*). His portrait is missing from the collection of medallions of former bishops in the sacristy; instead, there's a painting of an angel with a finger raised to its lips, inviting onlookers to draw a veil of silence over Natale's unwise allegiance. Gothic arches from the original 14th-century church are in the side aisles.

Along Viale Rimembranza, the Baroque church of **San Ciro** (open 8.30am-noon, 4.30-7.30pm daily) has a pretty tiled dome. Nearby, in Via San Ciro, the **Museo Mineralogico Campano** (no.2, 081 801 5668, www.museo mineralogicocampano.it, closed Mon, admission €2) has a tremendous collection of minerals, with an especially impressive selection from Vesuvius. Inside the town hall, artefacts from a local necropolis (seventh- to fifth-century BC) are displayed in the **Antiquarium Aequano** (Palazzo Municipale, Corso Filangieri 98, 081 801 9111, open by appointment).

Below the town centre to the east, **Marina di Vico** (where the Metro del Mare service stops) has a short pebbly beach with a handful of restaurants. To the west, the harbour at pretty **Marina di Equa** allows access to long stretches of sun-worshipping space at Pezzolo (where ruins of a first-century AD villa are visible) and Vescovado to the east, and Calcare to the west; the imposing ruin at the far end of Calcare beach was part of a centuries-old lime quarry that closed down in the late 19th century. Marina di Equa itself has a Saracen watchtower and lots of bars, and is home to

---

INSIDE TRACK SIGN-SPOTTING

Finding **Marina di Equa** can be terribly tricky: head out of Vico on the SS145, and keep your eyes peeled for a small sign marked 'Marina di Equa', just beyond the far end of the railway viaduct – blink and you'll miss it.

AROUND NAPLES

Call of the waves

In the land of the sirens, the glinting waves still exert an irresistible appeal.

Villa Communale.

Sorrento is siren country. Once upon a time, a white temple dedicated to the mythical creatures stood high on the cliff tops at Punta della Campanella, known as Sirenusium. The sirens of old were not half-maid, half-fish, but half-bird. One sang, one played the flute and the third a lyre; the sweetness of their music turned men into emotional shipwrecks, making them forget the outside world and die of hunger. Outsmarted by Ulysses – he was bound to his ship's mast, while his men's ears were blocked with wax – the Sirens threw themselves from the cliffs in despair and turned into rocks, the three Li Galli islands. Myths aside, the three nautical miles at the mouth of Capri have always been deeply treacherous, as cross-currents create whirlpools along the rocky coastline.

The sea around Sorrento remains very tempting – though you're more likely to encounter bathing belles or strutting youths than sirens. Swimming here is from colourful, stilted pontoons, jutting out from the base of the cliff, which levy a charge for the privilege.

The **Villa Communale**, originally a monks' vegetable garden, is one of the few stretches of coast open to the public; the rest is privately owned. Since the beach here, the **Spiaggia di San Francesco**, was so tiny, pontoons were built. Beach huts, parasols and loungers create a vibrant

mass of colour against the enticing blue of the sea. To get there, walk down from Villa Communale on a steep, winding path cut into the cliff, or take the lift from the corner of the park. The fare includes access to one of the lidos. Various lidos compete for your cash; they're not cheap, so plan on making a day of it. Average price for entry, a sunlounger and umbrella is €20, and entry without hiring a lounger is forbidden in peak season.

Some lidos have both beach and pontoon; you enter the sea via ladders. The pick of the bunch are: **Marameo** (lido), **Leonelli** (beach and lido) and **Peter's** (beach and lido). Marameo (also a nightclub, www.marameobeach.com) has towels, chic white loungers and four-poster beds. Furthest away on the right, Peter's is cheaper and also cosier. The miniscule free 'beach' is packed with noisy locals playing football and frisbee amid the towels laid end to end.

Another possibility is the beach at **Marina Grande**. Popular with locals, it's mostly free – and the lidos here are cheaper than at San Francesco. **Da Renato** is a friendly option, offering loungers as well as boat hire and trips at reasonable rates. If you fancy a walk before your swim, climb up to Capo, then down to **Bagni della Regina Giovanna** (*see p261*), where there's clean water and good snorkelling.

Further round, **Marina di Puolo** is even nicer. East of Sorrento, try the **spiaggia Alimuri** (*see p258*), **Pezzolo**, **Vescovado** and **Calcare** (*see p259*), **Scrajo Terme** (near Vico Equense) or **Marina di Lobra** (*see p262*).

Divers also find this coastline irresistible – particularly the **Marine Park of Punta della Campanella** (*see pp254-255*). In 1974, Sicilian Enzo Majorca (played by Jean Reno in the film *The Big Blue*) won the world freediving contest round the bay at **Vervece**, a rocky islet opposite Marina di Lobra. Enzo defied the sirens, holding his breath, blocking his ears and diving to 87 metres (285ft). Every September a Mass is held here: divers come in pilgrimage to visit a Madonna, the protector of divers, 15 metres (49ft) underwater. A crown of laurel is laid at her feet, and stones have been placed here by divers from all over the world.

one of the finest restaurants in the area, the wonderful **Torre del Saracino** (*see p261*).

Head inland and uphill from Vico Equense to the *casali* (hamlets): **Moiano** is a starting point for walks in the **Monte Faito** area and across to Positano; **Massaquano** is home to the haunting, Giotto-style 14th-century frescoes of the chapel of **Santa Lucia**.

Where to eat & drink

Vico Equense is home of 'pizza by the metro', thanks to the endeavours of **Gigino Pizza al Metro** (Via Nicotera 15, 081 879 8426, closed evenings, average €15). It's a great barn of a place, open lunchtimes only and popular with busloads of tourists and large Neapolitan families. Stretch-pizzas of all imaginable varieties are served here; order slices of a length to match your appetite. The town is also home to the friendly **Gelateria Latteria Gabriele** (Corso Umberto I 5, 081 879 8744, closed Tue), with its 1960s decor. Try the unusual alpine strawberries and mulberry *granita*, or one of the trademark *rustiche* (savoury rolls). A superb range of local cheeses and *salumi* is also available. In central Vico, **Al Buco** (Via Roma 26, 081 801 6255, closed Mon, average €15) is the ideal trattoria: good pasta, and delicious home-made bread and desserts.

In Marina di Equa, the **Torre del Saracino** (Via Torretta 9, 081 802 8555, www.torredel saracino.com, closed Mon & Jan, Feb, average €60) more than deserves its two Michelin stars. Chef Gennaro Esposito creates some of the best food on this (or any) coast: mouthwatering seafood antipasti, home-made pasta and the freshest of seafood – octopus, squid, shrimp, anchovy – cooked to perfection. A Saracen watchtower guards the romantic patio where dinner is served.

Where to stay

Down a sharp drop off the coast road just east of Vico Equense, the recently refurbished **Hotel Capo La Gala** (Via Luigi Serio 8, 081 801 5757, www.capolagala.com, closed Nov-Mar, €150-€215 double) is a stylish, romantic option with an excellent restaurant; take the Circumvesuviana train to Scrajo Terme (Apr-Sept). The balconies of its 18 tastefully-decorated rooms overhang the wave-battered rocks below, while the swimming pool is filled with mineral-rich water from the nearby Scrajo spring.

Perched above Vico in Santa Maria del Castello, off Via Bosco, the **Agriturismo La Ginestra** (Via Tessa 2, 081 802 3211, www. laginestra.org, €90 half-board, €110 full-board) has simple, bright rooms in a pink farmhouse,

with spectacular views and delicious organic home-cooking (non-residents are welcome to eat here if they book).

Resources

Tourist information
Azienda Autonoma di Cura Soggiorno e Turismo *Via San Ciro 16, Vico Equense (081 879 8826/www.vicoturismo.it).* **Open** *Apr-Sept* 9am-2pm, 3-8pm Mon-Sat. *Oct-Mar* 9am-2pm, 3-5pm Mon-Sat.

West from Sorrento
CAPO & AROUND

Heading west from Sorrento is a delight for the senses. Take the **Citysightseeing Sorrento** bus, which runs a hop-on, hop-off service around the Sorrentine Peninsula (eight daily, departs Piazza Lauro every hr, www.city sightseeing.it, €15).

The developers have yet to reach this area, in part due to the inaccessibility of its roads and the dramatic lie of the land.Towns are hemmed in by lemon and olive groves, and the air in spring and summer is full of the pungent perfumes of wild garlic, myrtle and broom, tumbling down to the sea.

The first stop out of Sorrento is the small village of **Capo di Sorrento**, overlooking Marina Grande, where Maxim Gorky's stay at the **Villa Il Sorito** in the 1920s and '30s is commemorated by a plaque on the front wall. A little further on, a high-walled path leads off the coast road to the right (north). Edged by romantic fields of lemon trees and asphodels, it leads to what is known locally as the **Bagni della Regina Giovanna** (baths of Queen Joan). The medieval queen is said to have bathed here in what was once a sumptuous Roman villa, possibly built by Pollio Felice. The ruins that dot the headland, surrounding a deep seawater inlet, are much easier to interpret after a visit to the **Museo Archeologico Georges Vallet** in Piano di Sorrento (*see p258*), where there's a scale model of the villa. The outcrops of brick are a good place on which to sit and contemplate the sweep of the coast to Sorrento.

Beyond Capo, a pretty road drops down to the tiny **Marina di Puolo**, where there's a sandy beach; note that it's a long walk down from the car park. More citrus orchards and olive groves (nets to collect the falling fruit are stretched out between the trees from October to December, then rolled up and left between the trees in multicoloured swathes) line the winding stretch of coast road from here to the lively town of Massa Lubrense and beyond.

AROUND NAPLES

AROUND NAPLES

MASSA LUBRENSE & BEYOND

Massa comes from the Lombard word for settlement, *mansa*, although the area was already known in ancient times. *Lubrense* is derived from the Latin word *delubrum* (temple); temples to Hercules and Minerva existed in the vicinity. The village has 23 outlying hamlets in its verdant sprawl, along with numerous churches and convents; a famous walk that leaves the centre on the nearest Saturday to April 25 visits them all. A haunting Easter procession, starting in Vico Equense, also terminates here.

There's a great view across to Capri from the belvedere in **Largo Vescovado**. On the other side of the square stands the former cathedral of **Santa Maria delle Grazie** (open 7am-noon, 4.30-8pm daily). It dates from the early 16th century, although it was reworked in 1769. The chapel of Sant'Erasmo, to the left of the main altar, is believed to stand above a temple to Hercules. Directly opposite the church, a road leads down to the attractive hamlet of **Marina di Lobra** (take a scenic shortcut down the first downward flight of steps right from the road; you may, however, want to hitch a lift or wait for the infrequent bus on the way back up).

Halfway down the road, the church of **Santa Maria di Lobra** (open 6.30-8am, 5-8pm daily) has a pretty yellow-and-green tiled dome, a 'miraculous' 16th-century *Madonna and Child* over the altar, and a cool, homely cloister with a tiled well-head. There was a temple here, too, probably dedicated to Minerva. The whole place has a charming, lived-in feel. Simple rooms are available in the adjoining monastery: the **Piccolo Paradiso Hotel** (*see right*) handles the bookings.

From Massa's main square, a road north-west (soon swinging south) heads to the tiny villages of **Santa Maria** and **Annunziata**, home to a rarely opened church and the ruins of the 14th-century **Castello di Massa**. A well-marked walking trail runs from Massa to Annunziata. It's worth taking it, not only for the walk itself but also to see the **Villa Rossi**, where Joaquim Murat holed up after the Battle of Capri and signed the capitulation that put an ignominious end to French rule in Naples.

The coast road out of Massa swings past the church and cemetery of **San Liberatore**. It's a final resting place of incredible beauty on the edge of a cliff, with Capri – once part of the mainland – tantalisingly close on the other side of the bay. The little whitewashed chapel dates from 1420, although it has been heavily restored.

In ancient times, the coast road continued as far as the temple to Minerva on **Punta della Campanella**. Nowadays it curves inland a couple of kilometres short of the point, heading to the small town of **Termini**.

A nondescript place with a marvelous view, Termini is the starting point for walks around Punta della Campanella, down to the Amalfi Coast and along the crests of the peninsula. The lane that heads south opposite the church leads to the chapel of **San Costanzo**; the walk takes around 40 minutes. The chapel is a stark white construction, rarely open; the view down towards the very tip of the peninsula at Punta della Campanella and the Baia di Jeranto immediately to the north is awe-inspiring.

From the same point, another path (grey and green stripes; 90 minutes) follows the headland out to the Saracen watchtower on Punta della Campanella; there are the remains of a Roman villa. The path for **Punta Penna**, with access to Jeranto Bay, begins in Nerano.

Where to stay & eat

Accommodation in and around Massa Lubrense was pretty low-key until the arrival of the spectacular **Relais Blu** (Via Rocanto 60, 081 878 9552, www.relaisblu.com, closed mid Nov-mid Mar, €200-€260 double), with 11 luxurious, beautifully designed rooms, all with sea views. There's a pool and an excellent restaurant, which also offers cookery courses. The four-star **Hotel Delfino** (Via Nastro d'Oro, 081 878 9261, www.hoteldelfino.com, €80-€200 double) is another good bet, also offfering a pool and a first-class restaurant.

Family-run **Hotel La Primavera** (Via IV Novembre 3, 081 878 9125, www.hotella primavera.com, closed mid Jan-mid Feb, €60-€100 double) has clean and simple rooms, most of which have balconies. The restaurant serves excellent seafood (average €30).

If you fancy a stay in a Saracen watchtower turned *agriturismo*, book in at the **Torre Cangiani** (Località Vigliano, 081 533 9849, www.torrecangiani.com, €70 double), where farmer Aldo and his wife Matilde will take care of you.

Massa's premier restaurant is the **Antico Francischiello da Peppino** (Via Partenope 27, 081 533 9780, www.francischiello.com, closed Wed Nov-Mar, average €50), serving good, fresh, traditional seafood and wonderful local cheeses. Rooms with a view are available at the adjoining hotel (€90-€100 double).

In Marina di Lobra, the **Piccolo Paradiso** (Piazza Madonna della Lobra 5, 081 808 9540, www.piccolo-paradiso.com, closed mid Nov-Feb, €88-€134 double) is a more upmarket option, with a swimming pool and scuba diving arranged on request. It also handles the very simple monks' cells for rent at the monastery opposite (€28 per person B&B).

Resources

Tourist information
Proloco *Viale Filangieri 11, Massa Lubrense (081 533 9021/www.massalubrense.it).* **Open** *Apr-Oct* 9am-1.30pm Mon, Wed; 9am-1.30pm, 4-9pm Tue, Thur-Sun. *Nov-Mar* 9am-1.30pm Mon-Thur; 9am-1.30pm, 4-9pm Fri-Sun.

GETTING THERE

From Naples airport
Autolinee Curreri Service (081 801 5420, www.curreriviaggi.it) runs six coaches in each direction daily between Capodichino Airport and Sorrento, stopping at Vico Equense, Piano, Meta and Sant'Agnello; tickets cost €6.

By bus
UnicoCostiera (www.unicocampania.it) runs a coastal bus service with routes from Sorrento across the peninsula to the Amalfi Coast and Salerno. Services are frequent in high season, running every 30 minutes until 8pm, then hourly – the last is at 10pm. For tickets, *see p271*.
  The Sorrento–Meta di Sorrento–Positano–Amalfi route is served by hourly services from around 6.35am to 8.05pm, leaving from outside the train station, but smaller inland towns aren't so well connected. Hourly services run from around 6am to 11pm on the Sorrento–Massa Lubrense–Sant' Agata sui Due Golfi route, but only a few go on to Nerano, Marina di Cantone and Marina di Lobra. Check timetables at tourist offices and bus stops.

By car
Take the A3 motorway to Castellammare di Stabia, then follow the SS145 south-east around the peninsula; it's tortuous and slow, but it's the only way. Take the SS142 to pass through Vico Equense, Piano and Meta, or stay on the SS145 as it swings inland towards Sant'Agata sui Due Golfi. An unnumbered road forks east along the peninsula through Massa to Termini, before rejoining the SS145 at Sant'Agata. Inland roads vary greatly in quality; all have hair-raising bends (sound your horn). The roads get horribly traffic-filled at weekends and in peak season.

By hydrofoil/ferry
Alilauro (081 497 2238) and **Linee Marittime Partenopee** (081 704 1911, www.consorziolmp. it) run hydrofoil services between Naples' port (Molo Beverello) and Sorrento. Services run all year, weather permitting (€9 single; 30mins). From May-mid Oct, **Metro del Mare** (199 446644, www.metrodelmare.com) operates fast ferry connections from Molo Beverello or Mergellina to Sorrento, with useful stops in between (€4.50 single; 45-105mins). A boat service to Capri is also available, through **Caremar** (081 892123, www.caremar.it) and **Linee Marittime Partenopee** (*see above*).

By train
Sorrento is the terminus of the **Circumvesuviana** railway (081 772 2444, www.vesuviana.it), which can be picked up from Naples' train station on Piazza Garibaldi; services run every 30 minutes in both directions and take 75 minutes. The train also stops at Vico Equense, Meta, Piano and Sant'Agnello. The last of the Sorrento–Naples trains leaves at 10.25pm; if you miss it there's a bus at 12.15am. A Naples–Sorrento ticket costs €3.30 and is valid for 180 minutes on any form of public transport between the two towns.

AROUND NAPLES

Marina di Lobra.

The Amalfi Coast

The classiest curves in the world.

It has been nicknamed 'the road of a thousand bends', and Amalfi's weaving and winding coast road hugs the cliff as tightly as any lover. John Steinbeck described it as 'carefully designed to be a little narrower than two cars side by side' in a piece he wrote for *Harper's Bazaar* in 1953, admitting that 'in the back seat, my wife and I lay clutched in each other's arms, weeping hysterically'. Back then, Positano (the title of Steinbeck's feature) wasn't much more than a rarely visited hilltop village.

These days, the area's immense popularity means that traffic generally proceeds at a painfully slow pace. Passengers are more likely to experience awe and wonder than Steinbeck's terror: it's no overstatement to say that the Costiera Amalfitana is one of the most beautiful and dramatic stretches of coastline in the world.

AROUND NAPLES

INTRODUCING THE AREA

The views, the gorgeous azure sea and the plethora of Michelin-starred restaurants don't come cheap, and staying here for any length of time could consume a serious amount of cash. But there are also plenty of simple B&Bs, excellent *trattorie* and good public transport links. Thanks to its rock-solid topography, this strip of coast will never be entirely conquered by money. Unlike St Tropez and other swanky Mediterranean ports of call, Amalfi's harbour has scant space for yachts; moreover, there's precious little flat land on which to land a helicopter, and little in the way of real estate.

New construction projects are hampered by the demanding landscape; that said, there is still a certain amount of building by stealth, whereby a small shed is slowly transformed into a multi-level villa, *senza* planning permission, over years or even decades.

But back to that narrow coast road, which loops back and forth, up and down, in a gasp-inducing sequence of hairpin bends. It's said there are more than 1,000 curves, making it a popular filming location for car ads. Ironically, when you're on it, you'll find it impossible to fully appreciate the ravishing scenery. You'll have your eyes firmly on the bends ahead, and on the cars, bikes, cyclists and three-wheeled vans blithely passing by. In spite of Steinbeck's fears, though, fatal accidents are

almost unheard of. The bends are so frequent and traffic so heavy, there's rarely a chance to build up speed; more likely, judging from the state of locally-owned cars, is a scratch or a dent in your car's bodywork, caused by a carelessly manoeuvring vehicle.

The bus could be a better bet. As a passenger, you'll have all the time in the world to savour the superb views of sharp rocks, Saracen towers, twinkling sea and, somewhere in between, bougainvillea, olive trees and terraced gardens that tumble down to the pastel-painted houses below – many equipped with edge-of-the-world swimming pools. Make sure you get a seat on the seaward side, then sit back and enjoy the ride.

After the land, there's the sea. The locals' seafaring passion and close relationship with the land are genuine sentiments, not merely folklore to be dished up for tourists, and there's a real pride in the region's eventful past. The diminutive city of Amalfi was once a major maritime power, so important that its crest sits alongside those of Venice, Genoa and Pisa on the Italian naval flag. It's often said that the compass was invented here (a dubious claim), and that the first set of maritime laws was passed here (a matter of record). Such naval ingenuity was born of the necessity to regulate Amalfi's bustling commerce and to combat the Pisans and hordes of Saracen pirates drawn to its wealthy shores.

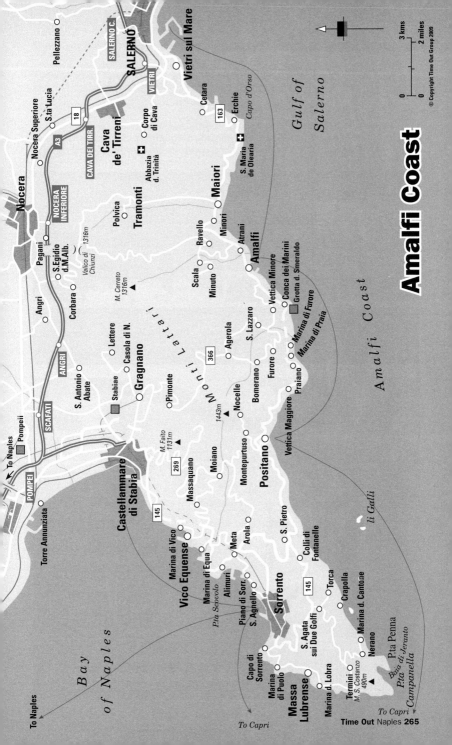

Amalfi Coast

The only practical way to mount an invasion of the imposing cliffs was from the sea – and even today, hopping from town to town on a boat is often more convenient than getting around by bus or car. Even better (though arduous) is to walk. A well-signposted network of paths extends along the whole coast, from short village-to-village strolls to a spectacular long-distance footpath, the Alta Via dei Lattari, that follows the ridge dividing the Amalfi Coast from the Bay of Naples. Walking between two points – the short hop from Ravello to Minori or Atrani, say – is often quicker than taking the bus. The footpath numbers in the text refer to the official CAI (Club Alpino Italiano) numbers, and should be written on markers along the way. The CAI's excellent Monti Lattari map and walking guide can be found in bookshops and *tabacchi* all over the Amalfi Coast.

POSITANO

Positano is not so much a town as a cliff face covered with a jumble of pastel-coloured houses. Unlike Amalfi, it had no long, narrow river valley to expand along and shelter in; life here is vertical and exposed. Perhaps that explains why the town has little history on show: more vulnerable to pirate raids and without the watermills that made Amalfi an industrial power, it kept things low-key and rebuildable. In the 12th and 13th centuries, Positano's merchant fleet rivalled Amalfi's, but thereafter the town declined, coming under the control of a succession of Neapolitan overlords.

In the 19th century, three quarters of the population emigrated to the United States; even today, it's said that Columbus Avenue in New York has more *positanesi* than Positano.

When John Steinbeck came here in 1953 to write his article for *Harper's Bazaar*, Positano was a secret closely guarded by a coterie of Italian writers and painters. But its *dolce vita* star rose rapidly; in the mid '60s, Positano was briefly more fashionable than Capri. Traces of this high tide are visible in the hotels' decor, old seaside postcards and, above all, in the town's very unfashionable 'fashion' shops.

The dramatic topography that made life in Positano so difficult is still seriously photogenic, with stacks of colourful houses clinging to the steep terrain; Positano's near-vertical layout means that almost every house has a clear view over the top of the one in front. But with the views come hefty bills. Like Capri, Positano has deliberately priced itself out of the package tour market: more than two-thirds of its 30 hotels are three star or above, and in high season it's near impossible to find a double room for under €150 a night, unless you've booked weeks or even months in advance.

In high summer, the charmingly narrow streets and alleys can seem endlessly filled with red-faced crowds being squeezed along, sweating with the effort of the climb. Restful it isn't, and with the nakedly money-hungry and surly demeanour of staff in the more touristy shops and restaurants, and the dearth of real attractions other than wonderful views, Positano can soon feel like a trap.

Directions here are either up or down, unless you're in a car – in which case they're round and round for hours. The SS163 coast road hugs the contours in the upper part of town, where it goes by the name of Via Marconi. From the town hall to the west, one-way Viale Pasitea winds down in a series of curves to Piazza dei Mulini, then changes its name to Via Cristoforo Colombo and climbs again to rejoin the coast road on the eastern edge of town. These are the only roads open to traffic; in summer, the lower one is permanently clogged with cars hunting for parking spaces. A strong pair of legs will get you around the centre of town faster than a set of wheels – though if you can't face the climb, there's a regular circular bus service.

From Piazza dei Mulini, narrow, shop-lined Via dei Mulini runs down to the beach past the parish church of **Santa Maria Assunta** (open 8am-noon, 3.30-7pm daily), with brightly-hued majolica dome; there's a 13th-century burnished gold Madonna and Child above the main altar.

The small beach, **Marina Grande**, is a neat patch of fine grey pebbles with colourful fishing boats pulled up in serried ranks. To the right looking seawards is the quay for the Metro del Mare services (*see p304*) to Capri, Amalfi, Salerno and Naples; to the left is a private section of beach. Above the quay, steps lead up to a path that winds around the side of the cliff, past the **Lo Guarracino** restaurant (*see p269*) to the smaller, rockier, but very popular beach of Fornillo, in a bay guarded by two ancient watchtowers. Above Positano lie the perched villages of **Montepertuso** (literally 'lost in the mountain') and **Nocella**. Until a few years ago, the road (and bus) up from Positano ended at Montepertuso. The inhabitants of Nocella either took the mule track from here, or walked straight up the 1,700 steps from Positano. Road access seems not to have spoiled Nocella, whose scattered, rustic houses have breathtaking views.

AROUND NAPLES

INSIDE TRACK FIGHTING FIT

On 15 August, Positano celebrates the **Feast of the Assumption** with a re-enactment of the town's famous victory against the Saracens, which took place in 1558. Expect lots of dressing up.

AROUND NAPLES

Positano.

A new bus route (check the timetables down in Piazza dei Mulini) also means that one of the Amalfi Coast's great hikes is that bit more accessible. The Sentieri degli Dei, or Pathway of the Gods (*see p254* **Sorrento's heady heights**), winds up the side of a sheer cliff to the narrow pass of Colle di Serra, from which there's an easy descent to Bomerano and Agerola (with buses to Amalfi). The spectacular hike isn't particularly difficult, although some walking experience, a good head for heights and plenty of water and sunblock are essential. Allow three hours for the climb to Colle di Serra.

Where to eat

Positano has a lot more restaurants these days, though you'll find it hard to eat on a budget. For drinks and snacks to eat in or take away, central **La Zagara** (*see below*) is a cheap and cheerful option. Down on the beach, **Bar Covo** (Via Regina Giovanna 5, 089 875400, www.covo deisaraceni.it) is also good for ice-cream, cakes and drinks, though its seafront setting is reflected in its prices.

Just outside Positano, past the San Pietro (*see p270*), is **La Taverna del Leone** (Via Laurito 43, 089 875474, closed Tue from Oct-May, average €40), where decent pizzas, pastas and seafood are available at below-average prices.

★ La Cambusa

Piazza Vespucci 4 (089 875432/www.lacambusa positano.com). **Open** *Mar-Nov* noon-4pm, 6.30pm-midnight daily. **Average** €50. **Credit** AmEx, DC, MC, V.
Established in 1970, La Cambusa (meaning 'galley') is a Positano stalwart. It serves good seafood, prepared in every way imaginable – fish soups, tartares, carpaccios, salads and pasta dishes – and offers a prime people-watching view of the beach from its handful of balcony tables.

Donna Rosa

Via Montepertuso 97/99 (089 811806). **Open** *Easter-Oct* 11am-2pm, 6-10pm Mon, Wed-Sun. *Nov, Dec* 11am-2pm, 6-10pm Mon, Thur-Sun. Closed Jan-Mar. **Average** €50. **Credit** AmEx, DC, MC, V.
Perched in the village of Montepertuso, this once-simple trattoria with views over the main village square is now an elegant, romantic restaurant. Smart *positanesi* often drive up here of an evening; the food is better than just about anywhere down on the coast. The pasta that goes into *primi* such as *tagliatelle verdi ai frutti di mare* (green pasta with seafood) is home-made, and main courses and desserts (hot chocolate soufflé) are equally good. Lunchtimes are generally quiet, but if you're planning to eat here on a summer's evening, book at least a day ahead.

Lo Guarracino

Via Positanesi d'America 12 (089 875794/ www.loguarracino.net). **Open** *Easter-Oct* noon-3pm, 6.30-midnight daily. Closed Nov-Mar. **Average** €35. **Credit** AmEx, DC, MC, V.
In a prime position on the footpath that leads around the cliff to Fornillo beach is a long, scenic veranda with splendid views, where you can tuck into basic classics such as *linguine alla puttanesca* (pasta with olives, capers and tomatoes), grilled fish and pizza. The decor is basic and service can be erratic, but on summer evenings it's always packed – call ahead.

Max

Via dei Mulini 22 (089 875056/www.ristorante max.it). **Open** *Mar-Oct* noon-2.30pm, 7-10.30pm daily. Closed Nov-Feb. **Average** €55. **Credit** AmEx, MC, V.
Escape the madding crowds following the trail down to the beach by taking a sidestep down to Max. It's a stylish restaurant, bar and art gallery, serving excellent dishes such as *paccheri con pesce spada* (pasta with swordfish, capers and olives). The wine cellar offers several good wines by the glass, and the outdoor terrace is lovely for warmer days.

Bars & nightlife

Piano bar and café **La Zagara** (Via dei Mulini 10, 089 875964, www.lazagara.com, closed Wed & Nov-mid Mar) has a scenic patio with lemon trees coming up through its red floor and an inner *salotto* with a fireplace for chilly days. The cakes, pastries and fruit sorbets are delicious, and cocktails start at €6; as well as music, there may be a bit of dancing. It's also an internet point.

There are plenty of bars down on the beach. At the eastern end of the main beach, the late-opening **Music on the Rocks** club is located in La Terrazza restaurant (Grotta dell'Incanto 51, 089 875874, 335 422856, www.musiconthe rocks.it, closed Nov-Mar). Here, you'll be treated to smooth piano-bar music or a disco tune or two.

Far and away the most famous club on the Amalfi Coast (not that there's much competition) is the **Africana**, just west of Marina di Praia between Positano and Amalfi (089 874042, closed Oct-May). Housed in its very own rocky cove, the Africana has a glass dance floor inside a grotto, so you can watch the sea crashing below as you dance. A recent refurbishment has brought a new oyster and champagne bar; in the cove below, fishermen hunt for *totani* (baby octopus), undisturbed by the driving beat. An access road leads down between the 21- and 22-kilometre road markers on the main road; otherwise, walk from Marina di Praia. When the club is open, buses run from Positano, along with boats from Salerno, Maiori, Minori, Amalfi and Positano.

Where to stay

★ La Fenice
Via Marconi 8 (089 875513). **Rates** €140
double. **No credit cards.**
A sort of low-budget San Pietro (*see below*), this
charming B&B sprawls up a series of verdant terraces on either side of the main coast road, on the
Amalfi side of town. There are seven rooms in the
main villa (three with terraces), with a further eight
rooms built into the side of the cliff below. A pretty
swimming pool and jacuzzi is open in summer, and
a path descends to a small, semi-private beach. It's
not at all bad for the price, though you'll need to
bring cash to cope with the no credit cards policy.
Between April and October, a three-night minimum
stay is required. Parking is €16 per day extra.

Hotel Bougainville
*Via Cristoforo Colombo 25 (089 875047/www.
bougainville.it).* **Rates** €80-€170 double. **Credit**
AmEx, DC, MC, V.
In a town with limited budget options, Hotel
Bougainville is a welcome addition to the scene. It's
centrally located and family-run, with ever-helpful
staff. Spacious rooms have sea views and balconies,
and are equipped with Wi-Fi and air conditioning.

Maria Luisa
*Via Fornillo 42 (089 875023/www.pensione
marialuisa.com).* Closed Oct-Mar. **Rates** €70-€80
double. **No credit cards.**
This is the cheapest hotel in town, so don't expect
any frills. A simple *pensione* with bright, sea-facing
rooms, it's set on the lane leading down to Fornillo
beach. The panoramic balcony rooms are well worth
the small extra outlay.

Palazzo Murat
*Via dei Mulini 23 (089 875177/www.palazzo
murat.it).* Closed Nov-Mar. **Rates** €280-€425
double. **Credit** AmEx, DC, MC, V.
This characterful 18th-century palazzo, in the centre of the old town, once belonged to Joachim Murat,
king of Naples and Napoleon's brother-in-law. Try
to reserve a room in the old wing, which extends
around two sides of a palm- and bougainvillea-filled
courtyard where classical concerts take place in late
summer. The rooms are furnished with antiques,
and have tiny decorative iron balconies overlooking
the courtyard. In the modern wing, rooms are more
modern in style but significantly cheaper; some have
balconies with sea views. In summer, breakfast is
served under the arches of the entrance patio, and
free boat trips are available. All in all, it's a perfect
refuge for latter-day followers of the grand tour.

Poseidon
*Viale Pasitea 148 (089 811111/www.hotel
poseidonpositano.it).* Closed Nov-Mar. **Rates**
€240-€310 double. **Credit** AmEx, DC, MC, V.

INSIDE TRACK
NO HALF MEASURES

Room 8 1/2 at the über-luxurious **San
Pietro** hotel (*see below*) was so numbered
after film star Marcello Mastroianni spent
a summer here with Catherine Deneuve.
The 'half' refers to Fellini's masterpiece,
8 1/2, in which Mastroianni starred.

The most health-and-fitness-oriented of the town's
hotels, with its own independently run beauty centre, the Poseidon is set in pretty gardens just off
Viale Pasitea. The rooms have panoramic balconies
where breakfast is served, and the restaurant opens
out on to a large terrace with a heated pool. There's
also a gym, a sauna and a hydromassage room. The
rates are competitive for a Positano four-star; parking will set you back an extra €21 per day.

★ San Pietro
Via Laurito 2 (089 875455/www.ilsanpietro.it).
Closed Nov-Mar. **Rates** €420-€760 double.
Credit AmEx, DC, MC, V.
Carlo Cinque built his spectacular villa into the side
of a rocky promontory just east of Positano. Over
the years, more rooms were added – and the idea of
turning this remarkable feat of engineering into a
hotel took shape. Classed as a five-star 'L' (one better than five-star) hotel, it remains one of the most
exclusive in Italy. From the road, the only evidence
of its presence is a discreet sign and a tiny chapel
surrounded by parked cars; a lift descends to the
lobby, which opens on to a hibiscus-strewn terrace.
Its 62 rooms – decorated with Mediterranean
tiles and friezes, and each with a jacuzzi and private balcony – spill down the hillside on 20 rock-
hewn terraces, connected by a warren of stairways.
A second lift goes down through the cliff to the private beach, bar and what must be one of the world's
most dramatically placed tennis courts. The hotel
is still run by Cinque's family, and service is wonderfully attentive. A complimentary shuttle bus
runs round the clock and free boat excursions are
available; the hotel also hosts cookery classes.

Le Sirenuse
*Via Cristoforo Colombo 30 (089 875066/www.
sirenuse.it).* Closed Nov-Mar. **Rates** €280-€840
double. **Credit** AmEx, DC, MC, V.
Everything about the former private villa of the
Marchesi Sersale is tastefully and thoughtfully done,
from its aristocratic Pompeian red façade to the
majolica-covered panoramic terrace, with its pocket-
sized swimming pool and oyster and champagne
bar. The antique-filled rooms exude a lived-in elegance; all bar the standard rooms have sea views
and balconies. The restaurant, La Sponda is one of
the few hotel restaurants in Positano impressive

enough to attract diners from outside. The hotel has a fleet of boats in which guests can explore the coast, and there's a well-equipped gym.

★ Villa Franca
Viale Pasitea 318 (089 875655/www.villafranca hotel.it). Closed Nov-Mar. **Rates** €180-€380 double. **Credit** AmEx, DC, MC, V.
Set above the sea at the point where Viale Pasitea comes closest to the cliff edge, Villa Franca is an elegant, family-run hotel with bright Mediterranean decor and a profusion of plants and flowers. The 28 pretty rooms have cream bedspreads and curtains, frescoed details and panoramic balconies. The hotel also has one of the nicest rooftop swimming pools in Positano, with a magnificent view over the coast as well as a fitness centre. If you can't face the walk down or up, there's a free minibus service.

Resources

Hospital
Croce Rossa Italiana *Viale Pasitea (089 811912)*. **Open** 24hrs daily.

Internet
Pupetto Café *Spiaggia Fornillo (089 875087/ www.pupettocafe.com)*.

Post office
Via Guglielmo Marconi 318, Località Chiesa Nuova (089 875142).

Tourist information
Azienda Autonoma di Soggiorno e Turismo
Via del Saracino 4 (089 875067/www.azienda turismopositano.it). **Open** *June-Sept* 8am-7pm Mon-Sat. *Oct-May* 8.30am-2pm Mon-Sat.

Getting around

By boat
From a booth on the quay to the right of Positano's main beach, **Gennaro & Salvatore** (089 811 613, www.gennaroesalvatore.it) runs boat trips to Capri, the Grotta dello Smeraldo (*see p276*) and the Li Galli islets, inclusive of meals; the company also organises night fishing trips on request. The **Lucibello** brothers (089 875032, www.lucibello.it) run similar excursions; they also hire out boats, canoes and pedalos.

By bus
A local bus service departs from Piazza dei Mulini, taking an anticlockwise circuit of Via Colombo, Via Marconi and Viale Pasitea every 15minutes between 8am and 10pm (winter) or midnight (summer). A less frequent service serves the villages of Montepertuso and Nocella. For details of services in Positano, contact **Flavio Gioia** (089 813077, www.flaviogioia.com).

A **UnicoCostiera** ticket will save you money and a lot of travel headaches. It's an integrated ticket that can be used on all public transport on the Amalfi Coast – SITA and EAV buses and Circumvesuviana trains – from Agerola to Vietri sul Mare (including Amalfi, Minori, Maiori, Positano, Ravello, Salerno and Sorrento). Tickets are sold at SITA and Circumvesuviana ticket offices and cost €2 for 45 minutes, €3 for 90 minutes, €6 for 24 hours and €15 for three days.

Getting there

By boat
Hydrofoils run between Salerno, Amalfi, Positano and Capri one to four times a day, depending on the time of year. Amalfi–Positano shuttle services are more frequent.
Between June and September, there's a direct hydrofoil link to Naples' Mergellina dock, run by **Consorzio Linee Marittime** (081 704191, www.consorziolmp.it). Alternatively, you can take the **Metro del Mare** (*see p304*) fast ferry service from Naples Beverello to Positano, Amalfi, Salerno and beyod (mid Apr-mid Oct). Tickets cost from €4.50 to €17.50.
While it's nice to arrive at your destination by sea, the boats have smeary windows and no open air viewing opportunities; what's worse, the crew may play horrific synth pop over the PA system. It's possible with both services to hop from Positano to Naples via Capri.

By bus & train
SITA (089 873589, www.sitabus.it) runs one morning bus service between Naples and Positano from Monday to Saturday, returning in the early evening. Otherwise, take the Circumvesuviana railway from Naples and change at Meta, just before Sorrento, for the Sorrento–Positano–Amalfi bus.
Buses to Amalfi and Sorrento from Positano stop at the top of Via Colombo and at the top of Viale Pasitea, outside the Bar Internazionale. Bus tickets can be bought from the Bar Internazionale (Via Marconi 164) or at the Bar-Tabacchi Collina (Via Colombo 3-5).
To get here from Naples airport, catch the **Curreri** (081 801 5420, www.curreriviaggi.it) bus to Sorrento (six daily) and change for SITA services (*see above*).

By car
Take the A3 motorway to Castellammare di Stabia, and follow signs to Sorrento. At Meta, 4km east of Sorrento, take the SS163; alternatively, take the slower but more scenic SS145 Nastro Azzurro route across the peninsula from the western edge of Sorrento, passing through Sant'Agata dei Due Golfi. From Salerno, take the SS163, which runs the length of the Amalfi Coast.

WEST OF POSITANO

For many visitors, Positano is the western limit of the Amalfi experience. The rocky, spectacular coastline further west has few hotels or historical sites; administratively part of the province of Naples, it has only a sprinkling of tiny villages, most of them well back from the shoreline, which until relatively recently were only accessible by boat. Even today, the road descends to the sea in only one place, the **Marina del Cantone**, where you'll find a pebbly beach and a couple of restaurants.

It's this remoteness that makes the coast between Punta della Campanella (*see p262*) and Positano worth exploring; this is what the entire Amalfi Coast must have looked like before it was invaded by mass tourism in the 1950s. The lack of roads is the walker's gain: there are some beautiful paths down to hidden coves and wild headlands, and the western section of the **Alta Via dei Lattari** – for serious walkers only – traverses the coast (*see also p254* **Sorrento's heady heights**). Perhaps unexpectedly, this stretch also boasts some of the best restaurants along the coast.

Set in a dip on the ridge dividing Sorrento from the sheer southern coast, **Sant'Agata sui Due Golfi** (Saint Agatha on the Two Gulfs) was a favourite summer resort for well-off Neapolitan families in the 18th and 19th centuries. It doesn't look like much today, with cars vying with agricultural equipment for parking places outside the 17th-century church of **Santa Maria delle Grazie** (open 8am-1pm, 5-7pm daily), which has a monumental, multicoloured inlaid marble altar. But there are two very good reasons for a stopover. One is the Michelin-starred **Don Alfonso 1890** (*see below*); the other is the convent of Il Deserto, situated a kilometre north-west of the town along a (badly) signposted road.

A forbidding bunker built by the Carmelite order in 1679 and now occupied by a closed order of Benedictine nuns, **Il Deserto** (081 878 0199, open by prior arrangement only) has a roof terrace with a view across the peninsula that defies description. You'll need to call ahead; entrance is free, but you can leave a small contribution towards the convent's upkeep.

From Sant'Agata, Via Torricella leads south-east to **Torca**, a tiny village with terrific views over the coast. On the headland to the west are the remains of a 12th-century abbey; on the beach stands a ruined Roman villa. The islet of Isca, just offshore, was owned by the famous Neapolitan playwright Eduardo de Filippo.

The road from Sant'Agata heading west to **Termini**, the jumping-off point for **Punta della Campanella** (*see p262*), is viewless.

Beyond the hamlet of Caso, a side road on the left winds down to the pretty village of Nerano and the seaside resort of **Marina del Cantone**, which has one of the longest beaches on the southern side of the peninsula. This is not necessarily a blessing, as Cantone seems to have expanded into a resort without passing through the limbo of planning permission. Nonetheless, it's still small scale and has a certain low-key charm.

A lovely way to see the coast at close hand is to hire an outboard motor boat from the **Nautica O' Masticiello** hut (081 808 1443, www.masticiello.com, closed Nov-Apr) in the main square. For €70 you'll get three hours – enough to get as far as Positano and still have time to explore coves and inlets along the way. Cantone also has an excellent diving centre offering courses and guided dives, **Diving Nettuno** (Via Vespucci 39, 081 808 1051, www.divingsorrento.com, closed Nov-mid Mar), and the resort makes a good springboard for the breathtaking natural beauty of the **Baia di Jeranto** to the west.

This untouched sandy bay can be reached either by boat (shop around on Cantone beach) or via a marked footpath (no.39) from the church in Nerano. East of Cantone, **Torca** is a three-hour walk away, along a stunning – and strenuous – cliff-hugging section of the Alta Via dei Lattari long-distance footpath. For more on walking in this area, *see p254* **Sorrento's heady heights**.

East of Sant'Agata, the Nastro Azzurro road leads, in 14 spectacular kilometres, to **Positano**. Off the coast are three small islands; once known as Le Sirenuse, they now have the more prosaic name of **Li Galli** – the cockerels. In 1925, the villa on the largest of the islands was bought by dancer and choreographer Léonide Massine; Stravinsky and Picasso were among his guests. Over the pass of **San Pietro**, where the road across from Sorrento joins the Nastro Azzurro, the Amalfi Coast proper comes into view.

Where to stay & eat

Sant'Agata sui Due Golfi might be a bit of a one-horse town, but the horse is a stallion. Alfonso Iaccarino's two Michelin-starred destination restaurant, **Don Alfonso 1890** (Corso Sant'Agata 11, 081 878 0026, www.don alfonso.com, closed Mon & Tue from Apr-mid June, Mon from mid June-Sept, lunch & Mon from mid June-Oct, all Nov-Mar, average €150) is the finest in all Campania. Alfonso's wife Livia and son Mario work front of house, while Alfonso and son Ernesto create the food, based on produce from the family's organic farm at Punta Campanella. Typical dishes include

Roadside stall near **San Pietro**.

pea soup and smoked baby squid filled with local cheese, or grouper flavoured with vanilla, ginger croquettes and an anchovy sabayon. Heavenly desserts complete the picture. You can sleep it all off in one of the suites (€280-€650, closed Nov-Mar), recently refurbished by Sorrentine designer Marco de Luca and beautifully appointed with antique furniture. Breakfasts are out of this world, and there's a pool, tours of the vast wine cellar, trips to the farm and a cookery school to keep guests occupied.

In Marina del Cantone, the **Taverna del Capitano** (Piazza delle Sirene 10/11, 081 808 1028, www.tavernadelcapitano.it, closed early Jan-early Mar, all Mon & Tue lunch from Oct-May, average €65) is an elegant restaurant, housed in a nondescript white building on the seafront. It's presided over by young chef Alfonso Caputo, whose ability to do succulent things with seafood and local garden produce has earned the restaurant two Michelin stars. Upstairs are 15 bright, airy rooms (€160 double).

Cantone's other hot culinary contender, with one Michelin star, is **Quattro Passi** (Via Vespucci 13N, 081 808 2800, www.ristorante quattropassi.com, closed dinner Tue, all Wed & Nov-Mar, average €90), which lies a little way back up the approach road. Set in extensive grounds, it's a stylish place with the heart of a family restaurant and a real vocation for fine food. Starters could be monkfish ravioli or risotto with shrimp and broom flowers, followed by freshly caught red mullet or *pezzogna* (sea bream) parcels with curly lettuce and pine nuts. The cellar – dug into the *tufa* stone – is a cave of oenological wonders. There are also six simple double rooms (€150) and three suites (€180), which look out on to terraces of olive trees.

A boat shuttle service, or an easy, 20-minute cliffside walk (past a ruined watchtower that you can clamber inside), takes you to the pretty little cove of **Recommone** to the east. Quieter and less touristy than Marina del Cantone, it boasts a friendly restaurant, **La Conca del Sogno** (Via San Marciano 9, 081 808 1036, www.concadelsogno.it, closed Nov-Easter, average €45), which does excellent things with fish, tomatoes and mozzarella. The wines are good, too; finish with a glass of *finochietto* (wild fennel liqueur). Accommodation is available.

Resources

See p271.

Getting there

See p271.

Vettica Maggiore.

FROM POSITANO TO AMALFI

Until the mid 19th century, most of the settlements along the Amalfi Coast were accessible only by sea or by tortuous mountain tracks from the other side of the Sorrentine peninsula. Then, in 1853, Ferdinando II of Naples inaugurated the Strada Amalfitana, the dynamite-blasted coastal road connecting Positano with Vietri and Salerno. Originally built to accommodate horse-drawn traffic, the narrow road is now used by lorries, buses, tourist coaches and swarms of private cars; it's hardly surprising that the going can be agonisingly slow, especially in summer.

East out of Positano, the road winds around steep gullies towards **Vettica Maggiore** and **Praiano**, which merge into one another on either side of the Capo Sottile promontory. Neither place has much of a centre, and both are often lumped together as Praiano. Vettica has a small beach and one of the coast's more worthwhile churches, **San Gennaro** (currently *in restauro*, with erratic opening hours), its dome and bell tower clad with colourful tiles. The square outside the church affords good views back along the coast to Positano and beyond. There's also a diving centre, **Centro Sub Costiera Amalfitana** (Via Marina di Praia, 089 822148, www.centrosub.it).

Praiano proper, on the eastern side of the promontory, is a low-key alternative to Positano. It has a charming seaward extension to the east, tiny **Marina di Praia**, a fishing cove consisting of a scrap of beach pinched between two high rock walls. There's just enough room for a few boats, a handful of houses and a couple of bar-restaurants.

A path around the cliff to the right leads to the retro-groovy **Africana** club (*see p269*). The jagged coastline between here and Conca dei Marini is the wildest stretch of the Costiera – nowhere more so than at the **Vallone di Furore**, a deep gully two kilometres beyond Marina di Praia. Such an unrepentantly steep river valley is called an *orrido*, or 'horrid'; its seaward opening is the nearest Italy comes to a fjord. From the viaduct over the valley – from which the Mediterranean Cup high-diving championship takes place every July, and where it is virtually impossible to park at any time – a steep footpath descends to **Marina di Furore**. It's an even tighter squeeze than Marina di Praia, with a few rock-hewn fishermen's huts and a scattering of boats on the narrow beach.

The marina's buildings were recently restored with funds from the Campania regional authority, and include a bar-restaurant (*see p276*), a herbarium, a cinema archive, a cultural centre dedicated to Italy's 'painted villages', and a museum of paper-making inside an old paper mill at the head of the beach. They're grouped under the rather grand name of the **Ecomuseo**. There are no set opening hours; for more information, call 089 830781 or visit www.il fiordodifurore.com.

Also in the Marina di Furore, a few metres above sea level, stands a little stone fishing hut that made it into the movies. It's where Oscar-winning Italian actress Anna Magnani lived for the few days in 1948 that it took to shoot Roberto Rossellini's *L'Amore*, or rather, the first of its two parts – *Il Miracolo*. Magnani played a goatherd who confuses her seducer with St Joseph and believes her unborn child is Christ himself. One critic described Magnani's acting style as 'demented virtuosity'; in life, too, she had a famously hot temper. When she discovered that Rossellini, her lover at the time of making *L'Amore*, had taken up with Ingrid Bergman, her rage knew no bounds. And yet the pair remained friends – and when Magnani died in 1973, she was provisionally laid to rest in the Rossellini family mausoleum. *L'Amore* is neither Rossellini's nor Magnani's best work. Still, there's something about this old fishing hut; ask at bar-restaurant Al Monazeno (*see p276*) for it to be opened up, and see for yourself.

Back on the coast road, just before Conca dei Marini, is the big tourist pull of this stretch: the **Grotta dello Smeraldo** (*see p276*). From the car park on the road above, a lift descends into the cave, where visitors are decanted into box-like rowing boats. Alternatively, various operators offer boat trips from Positano and Amalfi. Every self-respecting Mediterranean tourist destination needs its Blue (or in this case Emerald) Grotto; this one was discovered in 1932, ending Capri's 100-year grotto monopoly. Cave buffs will tell you that it is but a pale imitation of that island's Blue Grotto (*see p202*), but the translucent blue-green light that filters into the cave from an underwater crevice is pretty enough, and a lot cheaper than its rival. The boatmen, who cajole their passengers into seeing Mussolini's profile in the shadow of a stalagmite, are another attraction.

Beyond the headland of **Capo di Conca**, the bay of Amalfi appears at last in all its glory. The sprawl of houses on the hillside to the left is **Conca dei Marini**, which once had a merchant fleet to rival those of its more muscular neighbours, Positano and Amalfi.

The upper part of the town is accessible from the Agerola road, which forks off sharply to the left just past the random collection of houses that call themselves (confusingly) **Vettica Minore**, a couple of kilometres before Amalfi. If you've had enough of the glitz and crowds of the Costiera, this road offers a worthwhile detour – though it's not a short one, and unless you want to press on to Naples, the only way back is the way you came. It begins by heading west, passing the long, barrel-vaulted profile of the **Convento di Santa Rosa**. This was formerly a house of Augustine nuns, famous as the inventors of the *torta di Santa Rosa* – a concoction of flaky pastry, blancmange and dried fruit traditionally eaten on 30 August, Santa Rosa's feast day. Nowadays the abandoned convent is used as an evocative backdrop for the classical concerts of the **Festival di Ravello** (*see p288*).

Rising gently up through the contour lines, the road continues around the upper part of the Vallone del Furore to **Furore** itself, a rugged village that – like so many around these parts – lacks a centre. It does, however, boast some unexpected murals and modern sculptures, and also produces the Amalfi coast's best wine. For a taster, head for the **Gran Furor-Divina Costiera** winery (Via Giovambattista Lama 14, 089 830348, www.granfuror.it, open by appointment), which also goes under the name of its owner, Marisa Cuomo. From precarious vineyards on steep slopes come the grapes that go into the six wines produced here. Furore also does a small trade in prickly pears (*fichi d'india*) and tiny cherry tomatoes (*pomodorini a piennolo*).

Beyond Furore, the road snakes up to the ridge in a series of cramped bends before spilling out into the upland plain of **Agerola**, a collection of agricultural settlements, cut off by rugged terrain from the Costiera below and the Vesuvian plain beyond. Although the coast sells itself as a fertile Garden of Eden, it is Agerola that produces most of the fruit, vegetables, cheese and meat that end up in swanky Amalfi restaurants; the local mozzarella is especially famous. Its small-scale textile workshops also act as sweatshops for Positano's glamorous boutiques. The only visitors that Agerola usually sees are elderly Neapolitans, who come here for the summer cool, and the occasional walker – the Alta Via dei Monti Lattari passes along the ridge that closes the plain to the north (*see p254* **Sorrento's heady heights**).

Grotta dello Smeraldo

1km west of Conca dei Marini on the main coast road (information from APT Amalfi 089 871107/www.amalfitouristoffice.it). **Open** 9am-4pm daily. **Admission** €5. **No credit cards.** If you're not driving, take one of the boats that run to the grotto from Amalfi and Positano.

Where to stay & eat

In Praiano, the whitewashed **Casa Angelina** (Via Gennaro Capriglione, 089 813 1333, www.casaangelina.com, closed Nov-Mar,

€200-€230 double) has a cool, contemporary feel. Whiter than white rooms feature balconies with spectacular sea views to Positano, and common areas are splashed with bright, modern artworks and designer furniture. The hotel also has a gourmet restaurant, two pools, a spa, a cigar bar and its own beach and boat.

On Praiano's main drag, you'll find the **Tramonto d'Oro** (Via Gennaro Capriglione 119, 089 874955, www.tramontodoro.it, closed Nov-Feb, €110-€290 double). It's a friendly, family-run hotel with clean rooms, decent fare and a rooftop pool overlooking the sea and the San Gennaro church. Hidden off a quiet lane below the coast road in Praiano, the **Hotel Le Sirene** (Via San Nicola 10, 089 874013, www. lesirene.com, closed Nov-mid Mar, €90-€100 double) is a simple, pretty hotel with a stone-flagged courtyard (complete with ping-pong table) and views over olive trees and kitchen gardens to the sea. The rooftop terrace is a bonus, as are the friendly owners.

On the main road out of town towards Amalfi, the **Hotel Continental** and **Villaggio Turistico La Tranquillità** (Via Roma 21, 089 874084, www.continental.praiano.it, closed Nov-Mar) is a multipurpose option that's popular with budget travellers. As well as providing scenic camping pitches under the olives for those with canvas (a pitch for two is €40), it also has more conventional rooms (€70-€90), as well as a series of bungalows immersed in greenery on a terrace above the sea, accessible via a rock-hewn staircase.

Back in Praiano's main street, opposite the Tramonto d'Oro hotel (*see above*), the scenic **La Brace** (Via Gennaro Capriglione 146, 089 874226, closed Wed mid Dec-mid Mar & all Nov, average €40) serves simple, good value seafood dishes such as salt-crusted seabass or spaghetti with clams, and Neapolitan pizzas, cooked in a wood-fired oven.

Taking the steps down to the beach from San Gennaro square, you'll find **La Gavitella** (089 813 1319, www.ristorantelagavitella.it, closed Nov-Mar, average €45). The terrace overlooking the sea is lovely for an aperitif, before you tuck into fresh fish and pasta. **Il Pirata** (Via Terramare, 089 874377, closed Nov-Easter, average €30) also enjoys amazing views and specialises in seafood.

In Marina di Praia, **Alfonso a Mare** (089 874091, www.alfonsoamare.it, closed Nov-Mar, average €40) has a huge, covered terrace on the beach and does simple but competent seafood.

Marina di Furore's tiny bar-restaurant **Al Monazeno** (Via Anna Magnani, 089 813004, www.monazeno-fiordo-furore.com, closed Nov-Easter, average €35) is one of the more unusual places in which to have lunch or dinner on the Costiera. Set at the foot of a cliff, overlooking an inlet, it serves snacks and a few more substantial dishes in the classic Amalfi tradition. On the road above, towards Positano, **La Locanda del Fiordo** (Via Trasita 9/13, 089 874813, www.lalocandadelfiordo.it, €70-€120 double) is a stylish B&B with an entrance at road level and rooms (each named after an Italian screen diva) on two rock-hewn terraces below, where steps descend to the sea.

In Vettica, **Vettica House** (Via Maestra dei Villaggi 92, 089 871492, www.hostel scalinatella.com/vetticahouse.htm, closed Nov-Mar, €70-€90 double) offers some of the best budget accommodation on the Costiera. Run by the family that owns **A' Scalinatella** in Atrani (*see p282*), it's a cluster of simple, whitewashed rooms carved into the rock above a fragrant lemon orchard. Be warned: it's a stiff climb up 270 steps (the equivalent of 12 storeys) from the nearest bus stop on the Furore/Agerola road, about 200 metres before the Convento di Santa Rosa; phone ahead for precise instructions on how to get here, and the owner may come to meet you on his scooter. The climb is torturous, but the view from the top repays the effort.

In Furore, the best place in which to stay is the seriously classy five-star **Furore Inn Resort** (Via dell'Amore, 089 830 4711, www. furoreinn.it, closed Dec-Feb, €260-€360 double), sprawling over the hillside and almost a small village in its own right. Its rooms are airy and welcoming, with swish bathrooms, colourful tiled floors and old film posters – particularly of Rossellini films, as the Italian director used Furore as one of his locations. There are three pools (small, large and infinity), a spa, tennis courts and two restaurants, the gourmet Italian Touch and the everyday (but still swish) Volpe Pescatrice, named after the fishing fox of local lore. Be sure to order the delicious *pane saraceno*, rock-hard 'Saracen bread' that is dipped in water before eating. Staff are charming and cheerful, and there are popular cookery and wine-tasting courses.

For sustenance, a good bet is the **Hostaria da Bacco** (Via Giovambattista Lama 9, 089 830360, www.baccofurore.it, closed Fri from Oct-Feb & 3wks Nov, average €30), run by the energetic mayor of this airy sprawl of a village. It draws customers up from the coast with its refined homecooking, using plenty of local produce and seafood in signature creations such as *ferrazzuoli alla Nannarella*, spiral pasta with swordfish, capers and pine nuts – a dish dedicated to actress Anna Magnani, who briefly owned a house down in the Marina. Succulent Agerola cheeses are available, and one of the more unusual local harvests can be sampled in the form of *cicale di Furore* – little almond and prickly pear cakes. The ambience is rustic, the

local wine extremely drinkable, and there's a huge selection of grappas and other spirits with which to finish the meal on a high note. If you can't face the cliff-hugging drive back, there are 18 simple rooms (€80-€100 double).

Resources

See also p282 and p271.

Internet
M&G Service *Via Gennaro Capriglione 27, Praiano (089 874420/www.divinecoast.it).*

Getting there

The villages can all be reached by bus or car from **Positano** (*see p267*) or from Amalfi (*see below*).

AMALFI & ATRANI

Fringed by lemon trees, **Amalfi** is a pretty tourist resort that spills over on to the coast and lines both sides of the steep and fertile Valle dei Mulini. Between the ninth and the 12th centuries, this was a glorious maritime republic – precursor to, and later rival of, Pisa and Genoa. In its prime, Amalfi had 70,000 inhabitants, and many more lived abroad in merchant colonies scattered around the Mediterranean from Tunis to Beirut.

On land, Amalfi's dominion extended over the whole of the Sorrentine peninsula and beyond; at sea, it had few rivals, and its navy protected the republic's independence and won battles for allies such as the Lombards and the Duchy of Naples. The republic survived at least nominally from 839 until the devastating Pisan raids of 1135 and 1137. Then, gradually, a Venetian-style system of government was adopted, led by a doge elected by a council

---

INSIDE TRACK
PUT PEN TO PAPER

The Amalfi Coast has been famous for its paper since the 13th century. The landscape was perfect for paper-making: steep hillsides meant fast streams, and a reliable supply of power to the water mills that drove the machines. Hand-made paper, with deckled (ragged) edges and beautiful watermarks, is still produced locally – and a leather-bound notebook or sheaf of loose sheets makes a lovely souvenir. For more on paper-making, and to buy some paper, visit the **Museo della Carta**, *see p280*).

---

consisting of the menfolk of the town's most important families. Amalfi coined its own money and made its own laws; its maritime code, the Tavole Amalfitane, was recognised across the Mediterranean until well into the 16th century.

Mercantile prosperity continued even after the end of the republic; in the early 14th century, Boccaccio wrote that Amalfi was full of little cities, gardens and fountains, and rich men. But an earthquake in 1343 destroyed most of the old town, and Amalfi didn't really recover until the 19th century, when its spectacular setting and illustrious past began to attract literary and artistic travellers from northern Europe. The **regata storica delle Antiche Repubbliche Marinare** – a ceremonial boat race between Amalfi, Pisa, Genoa and Venice – is a reminder of the town's golden age, held on the first Sunday in June.

Amalfi's narrow, high-sided streets and alleyways mean it's always shady, even in the blazing sunshine. A map can be had from the tourist office, but it's just as rewarding to strike out up steps and side alleys to see what you find – it's amazing how quickly you can lose the crowds.

On its coast side, the pretty, cream-coloured town makes a weak effort at bustling, as the port, bus terminus, bars and restaurants jostle for space on the tiny waterfront. To the east, the grey shingle beach is crowded in summer, although better bathing spots are tucked away in a series of coves and beaches (marked 'Spiagge') to the west, served by a circular ferry service from the main quay.

Dominating the hillside to the west are the collonaded halls of the **Capuchin convent**. Founded in 1212, it was a hotel until 2004, but is now in limbo. Along Corso delle Repubbliche Marinare to the east are the post office and the tourist office; just around the corner, in a palm-shaded piazza, stands the Municipio, or town hall, which houses the small **Museo Civico** (see p280). The sweep of the bay ends in a medieval watchtower that houses the **Luna Convento** restaurant (see p281); the hotel itself occupies a former Franciscan convent on the other side of the road.

From the sea-facing Piazza Flavio Gioia – dominated by a statue of Flavio himself (a man who not only didn't invent the compass, as the plaque at his feet claims, but may never even have existed), the Porta Marinara gate leads into the centre of town. Before you go under it, have a look at what remains of Amalfi's shipyard, the **Arsenale della Repubblica**, beneath an arch to the left of the gate. This was the engine room of the republic, where huge galleys with over 100 oars were built by teams of shipwrights.

The town's central Piazza is dominated by the colourful **Duomo** (see p280). A masterpiece of the Arab-Norman style, it's reached – like everything in this region – by a steep staircase. The lively façade is a doubtful reconstruction of the early 13th-century original; most of it was added after part of the church collapsed in 1861. The pretty, free-standing campanile, from 1276, is the real thing, having been tampered with very little in the course of the centuries. Underneath a lofty porch, the central bronze doors of the Duomo were cast some time before 1066 by a Syrian master and carried back by a local shipping magnate's fleet. The inscription explains that they were donated to the republic by Pantaleone di Mauro Comite, head of the Amalfitan colony in Constantinople.

With its bars and cafés, the piazza in front of the Duomo is a good place in which to rest, refuel and contemplate the nubile nymph splashing in the central fountain. To the north, Via Genova and Via Capuano lead up through an increasingly quiet residential part of town, where the sound of fast-flowing water can be heard everywhere, even at the height of summer. This deep valley – the Valle dei Mulini – was the site of some of Europe's first paper-making factories, powered by a series of watermills; one, at Palazzo Pagliara, has been turned into the **Museo della Carta** (see p280).

The wild upper part of the Valle dei Mulini (take the road that skirts the eastern side of the valley) is well worth exploring. In its alpine upper reaches, the valley becomes the Vallone delle Ferriere, named after the ironworks (ferro means iron) that – like the papermills downstream – drew their power from the fast-moving water of the torrent.

Signposted path no.25 follows the valley floor beneath high rock walls, past a riot of botany to the entrance of the **WWF Riserva Naturale**, which occupies the high part of the valley. From here, a scenic footpath takes a circuit of the valley head, ending up in the village of Pontone, on the ridge between Amalfi and Atrani. A shorter but equally steep path heads up a mere thousand or so steps from Amalfi to the village and castle of **Pogerola**, with a splendid view over the water.

In the days of the republic, **Atrani** – less than a kilometre east of Amalfi along the coast, and accessible on foot via the confusing web of staircases that straggle across the hill – was an upmarket residential quarter. It was razed by the Pisans in 1187, and today feels, if anything, more workaday than its neighbour. It has a busy fishing port and some good examples of local architecture, with a maze of arches, long pedestrian tunnels, staircases and barrel-vaulted houses on different levels. Space is

Amalfi.

so tight here that the main coast road sweeps right across the centre on a viaduct whose arches separate the port from the main square, Piazza Umberto I.

The little church of **San Salvatore de' Bireto**, perched at the top of a flight of steps on the opposite side of the piazza, was where the investiture of Amalfi's doges took place; its name derives from the *berretto,* or ducal cap. The church has been *in restauro* for years; its bronze doors – a gift, in 1087, from the same Amalfitan merchant in Constantinople who commissioned the doors of Amalfi's Duomo – can now be seen in the parish church of **Santa Maria Maddalena** (open Sunday mornings for Mass), which rises high above the road to the east. The dome is a classically colourful example of local style; inside, the original Romanesque was swept aside in a Baroque makeover, but there are some marvellous wooden statues of roasting sinners on the wall to the right of the main door.

High above the town to the west, the 13th-century church of **Santa Maria del Bando** (open Sept only; ask at the town hall on Via dei Dogi) perches on a narrow ledge halfway up a vertical cliff below the **Torre dello Zirro**, a medieval watchtower that locals believe is haunted.

★ FREE Duomo di Amalfi (Cattedrale di Sant'Andrea)

Piazza del Duomo (089 871324). **Open** *Oct-June* 9am-6.45pm daily. *July-Sept* 9am-7.45pm daily. **Admission** *Cathedral* free. *Chiostro del Paradiso* €2.50. **No credit cards.**

The cathedral's interior, recently restored to reduce some of its Baroque excess, is nonetheless a bit of a disappointment in comparison with the clean, Romanesque simplicity of its close cousin in Ravello (*see p289*). Remnants of the original church furniture include the two *amboni* (pulpits) flanking the main altar, some ancient columns, and a beautiful mother-of-pearl cross – another piece of Crusader loot.

Don't miss the delightful Chiostro del Paradiso, entered (for a small fee) through a door at the left end of the porch in front of the Duomo. Built in 1266 as a burial ground for the members of Amalfi's aristocracy, this cloister, with its Moorish-style arches and central garden, is a reminder of the cosmopolitan spirit of the glory days of the maritime republic.

A door leads from the cloister into the Cappella del Crocefisso, the only part of the church to have survived more or less intact from the 12th century. Glass cases hold treasures belonging to the diocese, including a lovely 15th-century marble bas-relief known as La Madonna della Neve, and a bejewelled mitre made for the Anjou court of Naples in 1297.

From the chapel, with its faded 14th-century frescos, stairs lead down to the crypt dedicated to St Andrew, whose mortal remains were stolen

from Constantinople in 1206. The sarcophagus that contains the saintly remains oozes a 'miraculous' fluid that the locals call manna (it's actually a plant extract).

FREE Museo Civico

Piazza del Municipio 6 (089 873 6211). **Open** *Oct-Apr* 8.30am-1pm Mon, Wed, Fri; 8.30am-1pm. 3.30-5.30pm Tue, Thur. *May-Sept* 8.30am-1pm Mon, Wed, Fri; 8.30am-1pm, 4.30-6.30pm Tue, Thur. **Admission** free.

In the town hall, in a room rather grandly referred to as the Museo Civico, you can peer at a late manuscript draft of the Tavole Amalfitane, Amalfi's code of maritime law, and other historical relics.

Museo della Carta

Palazzo Pagliara, Via delle Cartiere 23 (089 830 4561/www.museodellacarta.it). **Open** *Mar-Oct* 10am-6.30pm daily. *Nov-Feb* 10am-4pm Tue-Sun. **Admission** €4 (inc guided tour in English). **No credit cards.**

Photographs and displays illustrate the history and techniques of Amalfi's ancient paper-making industry. Downstairs, the original vats and machinery are preserved.

Where to eat

★ La Caravella

Via Matteo Camera 12 (089 871 029/www. ristorantelacaravella.it). **Open** noon-2pm, 7.30-10.30pm Mon, Wed-Sun. Closed mid Nov-Dec. **Average** €65. **Credit** AmEx, MC, V.

La Caravella opened back in 1959, and in 2009 celebrated its fiftieth anniversary as one of Amalfi's finest restaurants. The two-room restaurant has no view, but does have a lovely collection of Vietri ceramics, excellent seafood, attentive service and an extensive wine list. If you can't decide between the lemon leaves stuffed with fish and grilled with fennel sauce or *pesce del Golfo in crosta di sale* (local fish in a salt crust), try the tasting menu. If it was good enough for Jackie Kennedy…

Da Gemma

Via Fra' Gerardo Sasso 10 (089 871 345/www. trattoriadagemma.com). **Open** 12.30-2.30pm, 7.30-

---

INSIDE TRACK
WATER, WATER EVERYWHERE

As you walk around **Atrani**, keep an eye out for the full bottles of water that stand on the thresholds of the village houses. Ostensibly there to keep cats from urinating on the tiles and plants, they have a more ancient pedigree as wards against malignant spirits.

10.30pm Mon, Tue, Thur-Sun. Closed mid Jan-mid Feb. **Average** €50. **Credit** AmEx, DC, MC, V.
The setting of this popular restaurant is hard to beat: set one storey above the bustle of the main street, the balcony terrace affords views across to Piazza del Duomo. Chef Mario Grimaldi is continuing a tradition of good local cooking that was begun here by his mother, Gemma. The menu looks mostly to the sea, but also includes a few dishes sourced from the hinterland, such as *fettuccine alla genovese* (fettuccine in a beef and onion sauce). Lovers of *zuppa di pesce* (fish soup) will find Gemma's version is hard to beat. The home-made desserts include *melanzane in salsa di cioccolato* (aubergines in chocolate), a local speciality that harks back to Amalfi's days of trade with the Middle East. Book ahead in summer.

€ Da Maria

Via Lorenzo d'Amalfi 14 (089 871880). **Open** noon-3.30pm, 7pm-midnight Tue-Sun. Closed Nov. **Average** €30. **Credit** AmEx, DC, MC, V.
There are plenty of cheap *trattorie* and pizzerie in Amalfi. This one, just up from the piazza on the main street, is a notch above the average, with affable service and reliable homecooking. Don't be put off by the menu in four languages; even for simple starters such as *frutti di mare* (mixed seafood), the standards are generally high. Seafood pasta dishes are tasty and filling, and the pizzas, cooked in a wood oven, are the authentic Neapolitan variety.

★ Maccus

Largo Santa Maria Maggiore 1-3 (089 873 6385/www.maccusamalfi.it). **Open** noon-2.30pm, 7-10.30pm Tue-Sun. Closed Jan, Feb. **Average** €45. **Credit** MC, V.
It's worth exploring the quiet side streets that run parallel to Amalfi's tourist-ridden main drag. Not only do they reveal a lesser-known, more vernacular side of the town, they also harbour some unexpected surprises – such as this lovely little restaurant, a stone's throw north of the Duomo. The courtyard dining area is usually packed, and most of the voices are Italian. The food is simple – mostly pasta and fish – but very nicely done, and big on quality local ingredients. Don't miss the *polpino* (octopus) salad.

Bars & nightlife

Opposite the Duomo in Amalfi, the **Bar Francese** (Piazza del Duomo 20, 089 871 049, closed Jan-Feb) is a good place at which to sit and muse on the passing of empires over a cappuccino and a copy of the *Duchess of Malfi*. The only disco of note in town is **RoccoCo'** (Via delle Cartiere 98, 089 873080, closed Mon-Thur, Sun in Nov-Mar), a rather cheesy place with occasional guest DJs, some way up the valley. Otherwise, jump on a boat to **Africana** (*see p269*).
In Atrani, **Bar Risacca** (Piazza Umberto I 16, 089 872866, www.risacca.com, closed Mon) is the locals' favourite lounging spot; have breakfast here before heading under the arches to the beach, try the bruschetta at lunchtime, or enjoy the evening cool over a campari soda. In high season, it's open until 3am daily.

Shopping

Food is the big draw in Amalfi – especially anything to do with lemons. In Piazza del Duomo, **Pasticceria Andrea Pansa 1830** (no.40, 089 871065, www.pasticceriapansa.it, closed Jan) uses the local fruit in any number of inventive ways: candied lemon rind, *frolla* (a ricotta-filled pastry dome) and sticky *delizia al limone* cakes are especially good. Almond lovers will also appreciate the delicate *paste di mandorla*. The same owners also run the lovely **Cioccolateria** (Piazza Municipio 12, 089 873291, www.andreapansa.it, closed Sun from Oct-May, Jan). For more intoxicating treats, head for the tiny corner outlet of **Antichi Sapori d'Amalfi** (Piazza del Duomo 39, 089 872062, closed Mon pm & all day Tue from Nov-Mar), by the cathedral steps, which makes its own limoncello and fruit liqueurs (a rarity in this neck of the woods).
Paper is the other traditional industry; the best place at which to view and buy some of the high-quality paper still made hereabouts is **La Scuderia del Duca** (Largo Cesareo Console 8, 089 872976, www.carta-amalfi.it, closed Sun from Oct-May). It's a cave of wonders with a good selection of books on Amalfi and the surrounding area; some are in English.

Where to stay

★ Floridiana

Via Brancia 1 (089 873 6373/www.hotel floridiana.it). **Rates** €100-€160 double. **Credit** AmEx, MC, V.
The town's best three-star, the Floridiana is conveniently close to the Duomo and the sea. The converted 12th-century residence boasts a wonderful frescoed salon where breakfast is served, and its rooms are spacious, clean and simply furnished. Some have a private balcony, and several suites have a jacuzzi. The staff are friendly and knowledgeable, and the hotel offers a free tour of Amalfi. Garage facilities are included in the price.

Luna Convento

Via Pantaleone Comite 33 (089 871002/www. lunahotel.it). **Rates** €190-€250 double. **Credit** AmEx, DC, MC, V.
Five minutes from the centre of Amalfi, this tastefully converted former 13th-century monastery

AROUND NAPLES

Atrani. *See p278.*

boasts whitewashed walls, vaulted ceilings and a delightful Byzantine cloister, where breakfast is served in summer. Previous guests included Wagner, Ibsen, Mussolini and Tennessee Williams. The pool is carved out of the rocks beneath the Saracen tower opposite, which houses the restaurant. Rooms – some with sea views – are bright and comfortable, and the desk staff are helpful. Half-board is usually obligatory. Parking costs €20 extra per day.

★ € Residenza del Duca
Via Mastalo II Duca 3 (089 873 6365/www. residencedelduca.it). **Rates** €40-€140 double. **Credit** AmEx, MC, V.
Located in an old palazzo, this lovely hotel is an unbelievably good budget option. The rooms take their names from famous dukes of the republic and are handsomely furnished; many have sea views. Check online for some excellent bargains for two- to three-day stays.

Santa Caterina
SS Amalfitana 9 (089 871012/www.hotelsanta caterina.it). **Rates** €240-€405 double. **Credit** AmEx, DC, MC, V.
A kilometre west of central Amalfi, the clifftop Santa Caterina enjoys breathtaking, uninterrupted views of the coast. Expect light and spacious rooms with hand-painted majolica floors, marble bathrooms and terraces with sea views. The hotel is surrounded by its own flower-filled terraced park, verdant with lemon trees and bougainvillea, where two self-contained suites hide (the Romeo and Juliet is the most spectacular). From the spacious hall, a lift takes guests down to the private beach, pool and one of two on-site restaurants; there's also a fitness centre and a host of beauty treatments, including the signature 'lemon massage'.

€ A' Scalinatella
Piazza Umberto I 5/6, Atrani (089 871492/ www.hostelscalinatella.com). **Rates** €21-€25 dorm; €70-€90 double. **No credit cards**.
The charming, laid-back village of Atrani has no hotel as such. It does, however, have this budget operation, with a couple of hostel-style dormitories in a house off the main street, and a scattering of double rooms and mini apartments all over the village. From April to September, breakfast is served at the Scalinatella bar in the main square, which is also where new arrivals should check in (before 2pm if possible). Open all year, A' Scalinatella acts as a meeting point for backpackers and independent travellers otherwise poorly served on the Amalfi Coast.

Resources

Police
Via Casamare (089 871022).

Post Office
Corso delle Repubbliche Marinare 33 (089 830 4811).

Tourist information
Azienda Autonoma di Soggiorno e Turismo
Corso delle Repubbliche Marinare 27 (089 871107/www.amalfitouristoffice.it). **Open** *May-Oct* 9am-1pm, 3-8pm Mon-Sat; 9am-noon Sun. *Nov-Apr* 9am-1pm, 3-6pm Mon-Fri; 9am-1pm Sat.

Getting around

By boat
The main quay by the bus terminus is the
hopping-off point for regular boats to the
western beaches (marked *spiagge*), which leave
at least every hour 9am-5pm daily from June
to September (€3 return).

By bus
Amalfi's bus terminus is in Piazza Flavio
Gioia on the waterfront. Local services run
to Ravello, Scala and Pogerola. Tickets can be
purchased at the SITA outlet in Largo Scoppetta,
next to the bus terminus. For information on
UnicoCostiera tickets, *see p271*.

Getting there

From Naples airport
Take the Curreri bus to Sorrento (there
are six daily) and change for the SITA
bus to Amalfi.

By boat
It is possible (Apr-Oct) to hop to Amalfi
from Naples via Capri, but unless you want
to spend some time on the island, it's cheaper
and quicker to get the regular boat from Salerno.
Travelmar (089 872950) run ferries (Apr-Oct
only) from Piazza della Concordia and the Molo
Manfredi quay in Salerno to Amalfi and Positano.
Cooperativa Sant'Andrea (089 873190,
www.coopsantandrea.com) goes between
Amalfi, Salerno, Positano, Minori and Maiori.
For **Metro del Mare** services, *see p304*.

By bus
Throughout the day, SITA buses make the
cliff-road journey between Amalfi and Salerno,
with hairpin bends aplenty. For Naples, there
are three main options: via Positano (one daily),
via Agerola (15 daily) or via Vietri (four daily).
Or take the Circumvesuviana train from Naples
and change at Meta for the Sorrento–Amalfi
bus. For times and information, go to www.sita
bus.it. Note that Sunday services on all these
lines are infrequent.

By car
From Naples, leave the A3 motorway at the
Angri exit, just past Pompeii, and follow signs
through the urban blight to the Valico di Chiunzi
pass and Ravello. Equally scenic, but a good deal
longer, is the SS366 route, which crosses over
from Castellammare di Stabia via Gragnano,
Agerola and Furore, to emerge on the coast road
2km west of Amalfi. From Salerno, take the
SS136 road, running along the Amalfi Coast.

By train
There is no Amalfi Coast line; the nearest
station is Vietri, at the eastern limit of the
Costiera, served by only a few very slow trains.
It's better to go to Salerno station (40mins from
Naples) and continue either by boat or SITA bus.

EAST OF ATRANI

This stretch of coast is often seen as little
more than the traffic jam between Amalfi
and Salerno, but if you have time to explore
it, you'll find it has its charms.

Minori, three kilometres east of Atrani (or a pleasant hour's hike from Ravello down an ancient staircase) is by no means picturesque in the Positano sense, but it's a pleasant enough place that justifies a stopover. If you're heading east, this is also one of the few Amalfi Coast towns to have a relatively flat centre, nestled between high valley walls.

In the middle of a warren of houses, the **Villa Romana** (*see p285*) is the only archaeological site on the Costiera that's open to visitors. Excavations began in 1951, but were held up by a catastrophic flood in 1954 that consumed not only the villa but much of Minori and neighbouring Maiori. The property, arranged around a large *viridarium* (courtyard garden), must have belonged to a rich nobleman; it's generously proportioned, and traces of first-century frescos remain on the walls of many of the rooms. Upstairs, an antiquarium contains relics found here and at two other nearby sites.

Above Bar de Riso (*see p285*) lies the **Basilica**. Built around 700 BC on the site of Roman remains, the church venerates the patron saint of Minori, St Trofimena, whose feast day is celebrated on 13 July by a flotilla of boats.

Just around the next headland, **Maiori** nestles in a floodplain that has been a continual source of danger to its inhabitants – but has also given them the space to expand. In the 11th century, the town was girded with walls and used as a shipbuilding centre for the Amalfi Republic. Today, it's the Costiera's only truly nondescript tourist resort, packed with modern hotels that sprang up after the 1954 flood. In its favour, it does have the coast's longest beach, a historic gem of a hotel, the **Casa Raffaele Conforti** (*see p285*), and the fabulous **Torre Normanna** restaurant (*see p285*).

From Maiori, a side road ascends the Valle di Tramonti to the 665 metres (2,327 feet) high Valico di Chiunzi pass. Also accessible from Ravello, it affords amazing views across the construction-plagued Sarno plain to the menacing bulk of Vesuvius. Like Agerola (*see p276*), **Tramonti** itself is not a single village, but a series of communities scattered over a fertile upland plain. It's known for its farm produce, cheese and honey, along with the baskets woven from branches of the chestnut trees that grow here. A cold north wind that Amalfi mariners called the *tramontana* howls out of the mountains that encircle the plain; the word has now become the standard Italian term for a biting northerly.

The coast road east of Maiori negotiates the rocky **Monte dell'Avvocata**, providing spectacular views along the coast. A short distance beyond the 39-kilometre road marker, a path on the left leads up to the rock-hewn chapel of **Santa Maria de Olearia** (open by appointment, 089 877452). Also known as the Catacombe di Badia, the chapel is one of the more unusual holy sites on the coast, and well worth a visit if you can find a place wide enough to leave the car, or persuade the bus driver to set you down. Two hermits were the first to occupy this site in 973; their shrine became a Benedictine abbey, squeezed between the towering rocks, which still has some atmospheric, faded 11th-century frescos.

Beyond the little fishing cove of **Erchie**, with a pretty beach watched over by a Saracen tower (look for the access road on the eastern side of the valley, after the main road has rejoined the shore), the coast road winds along to **Cetara**. It's a fishing village with the now familiar Amalfi Coast shape: long and thin. Historically, this was the eastern limit of the Amalfi Republic, and the place still has a salty, frontier town feel to it. Of all the settlements along the coast, this is the one with the most active fishing fleet; it roams the whole Mediterranean in search of shoals, with the help of two spotter planes.

With its small beach – overlooked by a medieval watchtower – and the honest, unprettified houses that line its single street, Cetara is a good place in which to stop for some sense of what life must have been like here before the tourists poured in. Its two excellent restaurants (*see right*) are another incentive.

East of Cetara, the road sticks close to the sea, passing below what is left of the massive hotel at Punta Fuenti. For years, this illegally built blot on the landscape was at the centre of a struggle between environmental pressure groups and local politicians, who feared a domino effect (and the end of lucrative back-handers) if it were shown that what went up could indeed come down. Finally, in 2000, the bulldozers moved in.

Further east, on the site of the Etruscan town called Marcina, **Vietri sul Mare** is the capital of southern Italy's handcrafted ceramics industry. Although pottery has been made here since Roman times, the locals had lost their touch by the early 20th century. German ceramicists moved into the area and got the industry going again, and today the town is heaving with shops selling the ubiquitous breakables. In Raito, the town adjacent to Vietri, the **Museo Provinciale della Ceramica** (Torretta Belvedere di Villa Guariglia, 089 211835, closed Mon, admission free) traces the history of the local ceramic industry in detail. It's housed in the beautiful Villa Guaraglia, where summer jazz and classical music concerts are also held (www.concertivillaguariglia.it).

INSIDE TRACK
A TASTE OF THE SEA

Forget limoncello: the best souvenir from these parts is a small pot of salted anchovies, or an even smaller pot of pungent *colatura di alici* – a close relative of the salty Roman sauce known as garum, which was made from fermented fish. The **Sapori Cetaresi** (*see below*) in Cetara sells both delicacies.

There are pretty examples of local majolica tiles on the dome of the 18th-century church of **San Giovanni Battista** (open 7.30-10.30am, 5.30-8pm daily). The exterior has been *in restauro* since April 2009, but look inside for the ceramic Stations of the Cross and the brightly coloured statue of Christ. The beach at **Marina di Vietri**, with its seaside bars and gelaterie, is a popular summer attraction.

FREE **Villa Romana & Antiquarium**
Via Capodipiazza 28, Minori (089 852 893).
Open 9am-1hr before sunset daily.
Admission free.

Shopping

If you'd like to invest in some local goodies, visit Minori's **Fes** (Via Roma 24, 089 854 1532, www.fesceramiche.com) for modern ceramic creations, and Maiori's **Sandali Tipici** (Lungomare Amendola 38, no phone, www.sandalitipici.com) for local sandals. Cetara's **Sapori Cetaresi** (Corso Garibaldi 44, 089 262010, www.delfinobattistasrl.it, closed Mon) stocks small jars of *colatura di alici* (anchovy sauce) and earthenware pots of salted anchovies. Housed in a beautiful Gaudi-esque building, Vietri's **Solimene Ceramiche** (Via Madonna degli Angeli 7, no phone) is the place in which to pick up handpainted ceramics with naive animal designs.

Where to eat, drink & stay

In Minori, the best place in which to stay is the **Agriturismo Villa Maria** (Via Annunziata, 089 877197, www.agriturismovilla maria.it, €45-€70 double). It's halfway up a mountain (call Maria's husband Vincenzo to pick you up from outside Bar de Riso), so the views over Minori are fabulous, and the only sound you'll hear is that of a braying donkey or twittering birds. The rooms are clean and simple, and each has its own little terrace to relax on. Maria cooks up a storm using produce from the terraces that fan out down the mountain. If you can't get a room, at least try to come for lunch or dinner.

For years, another reason for stopping off in Minori was to visit the Proto Brothers' superb restaurant, L'Arsenale. Sadly for the town, it was simply too successful, and moved to bigger premises in Maiori (*see below*). In its stead, **Il Pontile** (Via San Giovanni a Mare 25, 089 877110, www.osteriailpontile.it, closed Jan & Thur from Oct-Apr, average €35) opened in June 2008, and is doing its best to keep locals happy with excellent fish and pasta. The lovely tiles are from nearby **Fes** (*see left*).

Minori also boasts the famous **Bar de Riso** (Piazza Cantilena 1, 089 853618, www.deriso.it, closed Wed Oct-May), which sits between the main square and the busy Lungomare. Run by the De Riso family since 1908, the bar serves confectionery created by Salvatore, whose cakes (*sfogliatelle, babà*) and home-made ice-cream are renowned (Sal has written books on the subject). Grab a seat outside and enjoy your cakes with an excellent coffee or *granita di caffè*.

It's not obvious from the cement-lined waterfront, but Maiori also has a historic centre, though floods and other catastrophes have pared it back. Just off pedestrianised Corso della Regina stands a glorious remnant of a more elegant past: the **Casa Raffaele Conforti** (Via Casa Mannini 10, 089 853547, www.casaraffaeleconforti.it, closed Oct-Mar, €95-€190 double). This small, nine-room hotel occupies the second floor of a 19th-century townhouse. Lovely frescoed ceilings, antique furniture and large gilded mirrors set the tone.

The Proto Brothers' latest venture, **Torre Normanna** (Via Diego Taiani 4, 089 851418, www.torrenormanna.net, closed Jan & Thur from Oct-Mar, average €50) offers some of the best food in the region. Set in a Norman tower (the largest and oldest on the Amalfi Coast), it has views over the entire coast. The four brothers serve up simple but expertly executed fare such as pasta with lobster. Choosing local wines ensures that a superb meal is half as expensive as you'd expect.

In Cetara, the **Acqua Pazza** (Corso Garibaldi 38, 089 261606, www.acquapazza.it, closed Feb, Mar & Mon in Sept-May, average €65) is one of those restaurants fans like to keep quiet about. Not that the place is a snooty temple of haute cuisine – far from it: it's the freshness of the seafood, the bravura of the chef at combining them in tasty but simple ways, the friendliness of owner and frontman Gennaro Castiello, and the honest prices that keep the clientele loyal. The never-ending *antipasti* are delicious (some dishes, based on raw tuna, are close to sushi) and a meal in themselves. The local speciality goes into the *linguine con colatura di alici* (anchovy sauce), and the home-made desserts are marvellous. Book well ahead and don't show up too early for dinner: tables in this relaxed establishment aren't generally set until well after 8pm.

Back in the main square, **San Pietro** (Piazzetta San Francesco 2, 089 261091, closed Tue & all Jan, Feb, average €45) is Cetara's other cut-price gourmet seafood temple. The *antipasti misti caldi* are well worth having; dishes such as *farro* (spelt or emmer wheat) with *colatura di alici* and courgettes with clams and prawns follow in a seemingly endless succession. Leave room for excellent pasta dishes such as *tubatoni con pescatrice* (pasta with anglerfish) and make the heroic effort to swallow at least one *secondo* – perhaps the *neonati* (whitebait) in garlic and parsley broth. Finish up with a delicious home-made dessert and mandarin liqueur. It's a little more formal than Acqua Pazza, but all done to an equally high standard; the *piazzetta* is a lovely place to sit on of a summer's evening.

For lovers of luxury, the five-star option is Vietri sul Mare's stylish new **Hotel Raito** (Via Nuova Raito 9, 089 763411, www.hotelraito.it, €275-€319 double). Set a few kilometres outside the bustling town centre, and a ten-minute journey from Salerno, the hotel's appealing extras include a lovely pool overlooking the bay, an excellent restaurant (Il Golfo), a wellness centre and friendly, extremely professional staff. There's a shuttle bus into town, and a 15-minute stroll down a nearby flight of steps takes you to the beach, via a couple of charming churches. Guests with big wallets can take advantage of helicopter and boat facilities. The boutique-style **Relais Paradiso** (www.ragostahotels.com) is due to open in summer 2009; check online for updates.

For an excellent and reasonably-priced lunch or dinner, Vietri's newly opened **Evù** (Via Diego Taiani 1, 089 310237, www.evuevu.com, closed Sun from Oct-Apr, average €25) is a stylish option specialising in pasta and fish dishes. Arrive early for lunch, as it soon fills up.

Down on the beach, the **Il Risorgimento** bar and restaurant (Viale dei Pini, 089 210176) hosts music and club nights.

For more accommodation options, see also **Salerno** (*see p292*), which lies at the furthest end of the Amalfi Coast but only four kilometres from Vietri Sul Mare. It also has the advantage of decent rail and ferry links.

Resources

Tourist information
Associazione Autonoma di Soggiorno e Turismo *Corso Regina 73, Maiori (089 877452/www.aziendaturismo-maiori.it).*

Open *Oct-Mar* 9am-1pm, 3-5pm Mon-Fri. *Apr-Sept* 9am-1pm, 4-7pm Mon-Sat; 9am-1pm Sun.
Circolo Turistico ACLI *Piazza Matteotti, Vietri sul Mare (089 211285/www.comune.vietri-sul-mare.sa.it).* **Open** *Oct-Apr* 10am-1pm, 5-8pm Mon-Fri; 10am-1pm Sat. *May-Sept* 10am-1pm, 5-9pm Mon-Fri; 10am-1pm Sat.

Getting there

By boat
Cooperativa Sant'Andrea (089 873190, www.coopsantandrea.com) runs frequent Salerno–Amalfi–Maiori–Minori–Positano ferry services from Apr-Oct. **Metro del Mare** (www.metrodelmare.com) also runs a service along the coast; for more, *see p304*.

By bus
The regular Amalfi–Salerno SITA bus (half-hourly in rush hour, hourly thereafter) stops in all the localities mentioned above, and more besides.

By car
Take the Vietri exit from the A3 motorway; from here, the SS163 coast road winds its way west.

By train
The station at Vietri sul Mare is served by only a very few very slow trains. Most of the time, it's quicker to go straight to Salerno station (40mins from Naples) and continue by SITA bus.

RAVELLO

Ravello is the aristocrat of the Amalfi Coast. Down below are the chattering sunburned masses, the traffic jams, the long queues for ice-cream. Up here, high above the sea, all is shade, gardens and serenity. Even in high season, when coach parties hit Ravello and troop dutifully around, it's easy to find peace: turn a corner in the old town or visit the lovely gardens in the early evening, and you'll be alone once again.

Overshadowed through most of its early history by its more muscular neighbour, Amalfi, Ravello grew rich on trade. But although Ravello's golden age was almost as florid as Amalfi's – in the 13th century it counted as many as 36,000 inhabitants – its fall from grace was even more dramatic.

With the end of its mercantile empire, Amalfi took to trades such as fishing, paper-making and iron foundries. But in Ravello, the decline from the boom to its present population of around 2,500 was so swift that parts of the town look like a medieval Pompeii, frozen in the 14th century. Traces of the town's heyday are everywhere: in its delightful, treasure-packed Duomo; in the doorways of its palazzi,

Ravello.

with their ancient columns; in the Sicilian-Moorish exoticism of Villa Rufolo's cloisters.

Ravello's romantic ambience of decayed nobility has always attracted writers, artists and musicians, among them Wagner, Liszt, Virginia Woolf and the Bloomsbury group, and DH Lawrence, who wrote parts of *Lady Chatterley's Lover* here. Graham Greene stayed in Ravello while writing *The Third Man*, and Gore Vidal resided here in his sumptuous private villa, La Rondinaia, for many years. The town's musical past is celebrated in a summer classical festival (*see below*).

Staying overnight is the best way to tune in to Ravello's quiet, contemplative atmosphere, best enjoyed in the early morning or at sunset. If you can avoid it, don't drive here: the main non-residents' car park beneath Piazza del Duomo is expensive, even with a 50 per cent reduction for guests of any of the town's hotels, and other spaces are hard to come by. It's better to take the bus from Amalfi; alternatively, Ravello is a long walk up quiet footpaths from Amalfi, Atrani or Minori.

From Atrani, the Ravello road winds up the Valle del Dragone and, doubling back on itself just before a long tunnel, enters the town at **Santa Maria a Gradillo** (open 9am-1pm, 3-6pm daily; if closed ask at the Duomo). The church is a pretty 12th-century Romanesque structure, whose bell tower is a good example of the Arab-Sicilian style, and whose charming interior has been stripped of distracting ornament. The lanes that skirt the church on the right and left both end up in Piazza del Duomo, the civic heart of Ravello, and the **Duomo** (*see p289*), with its imposing bronze doors, intricate high pulpit and light-flooded interior. Its crypt contains the **Museo del Duomo**, a better-than-average collection of late imperial and medieval architectural and sculptural fragments.

Ravello's other must-sees are its famous villas. Both are historical assemblages – the work of expatriate Britons who came, saw, and did a bit of gardening. **Villa Rufolo** (*see p289*), entered via the 14th-century tower to the right of the Duomo, is named after its original 13th-century owners, the Rufolo family, who amassed a fortune acting as bankers for, among others, Charles of Anjou; they're mentioned in Boccaccio's *Decameron*. It was bought by a Scotsman in the mid-19th century and rescued from its semi-derelict state. Romantically restored, its lovely gardens inspired Wagner's *Parsifal*.

In Wagner's honour, a world-class series of classical concerts is held here in the summer, along with the occasional ballet. Though collected under the umbrella of the famous **Festival di Ravello** (*see p195*), these performances, by prestigious Italian and international musicians and orchestras, are not so much a concentrated festival as a long season of open-air concerts, predominantly of chamber music, running from March until the beginning of November. There are also various associated sub-festivals during the year, including the **Concerti di Musica Sinfonica** (symphonic concerts) in July and September's **Settimane Internazionali di Musica da Camera** (Chamber Music Week). The gardens of Villa Rufolo are the main venue, but concerts are also given in the Convento di Santa Rosa in Conca dei Marini (*see p276*) and the bay of Marina di Praia (*see p275*).

The talk of the town, though, is a controversial new auditorium, designed by fêted Brazilian architect Oscar Niemeyer. Detractors protested that bringing more visitors to the area would exacerbate traffic and parking problems, but plans were eventually approved and the curved, white auditorium is due to open in September 2009.

The town's other garden estate, the enchanting **Villa Cimbrone** (*see p289*), is a fair walk from the centre along Via San Francesco, which climbs up past the reworked Gothic church and monastery of the same name, and Via Santa Chiara, which does the same. It's one of the highlights of the Amalfi Coast, and well worth the trek.

Back in Piazza del Duomo, the stepped lane by the side of the tourist office leads up to Via dell'Episcopio; veering to the left, this becomes Via San Giovanni del Toro, site of Ravello's most upmarket hotels, and where the **Belvedere Principessa di Piemonte** provides a great view over the coast to the east. Further along on the left, opposite the fabulous **Hotel Caruso** (*see p290*), the church of **San Giovanni del Toro** conserves much of its original 12th-century appearance. Its mosaic-encrusted pulpit, built for the local Bovio family, rivals those in the Duomo, with another Jonah-swallowing whale and deep blue-green plates of Arab workmanship embedded in the centre of mosaic circles. In a niche in the sacristy is a rare 12th-century stucco statue of Santa Caterina, with traces of the original paintwork. The church is currently *in restauro*, and opening hours are erratic.

After exploring the **Convento Frati Minori Conventuali** on Via San Francesco (089 857146, open 8am-7pm Mon-Sat, 9.30am-7pm Sun), pop into the cloister next door, which often hosts art exhibitions.

If even the slow pace in Ravello is proving too fast, head up to **Scala**, a village perched on the opposite side of the Dragone valley. Older than either Amalfi or Ravello, and once almost as prosperous, Scala is now the sort of place where the arrival of the grocery van is a major event. It has a fine **Duomo** dedicated to San Lorenzo (open 8am-noon, 5-7pm daily), with a 12th-century portal and an interior that conceals a few gems beneath its Baroque facelift. The wooden crucifix over the main altar dates from 1260; to the left is the Gothic tomb of the Coppola family. Note among the figures on the canopy above the tomb that of the rabbi who – according to an apocryphal gospel – had his hands lopped off when he gave the Virgin Mary's coffin a shove.

Scala is the starting point for various walks. The most ambitious (no.51) takes two hours to complete, heading via the peak of Il Castello to Casa Santa Maria dei Monti, with a magnificent view over the Sorrentine peninsula. An easier option is to continue past the Duomo to the hamlet of **Minuto** (whose apt name translates as 'tiny') – served by six buses a day from Amalfi and Ravello – where the road ends just above the pretty 12th-century **Chiesa dell'Annunziata** (open Sun morning for Mass; otherwise knock on the first door on your left down the steps from the road and ask the custodian for the key). Inside are ten ancient granite columns and some very fine Byzantine frescos in the crypt. In the square in front of the church is a drinking fountain; behind this, a stepped path descends to Amalfi via the little medieval village of Pontone; allow around 40 minutes.

Duomo di Ravello & Museo del Duomo

Piazza del Duomo (089 858311/089 857160/ www.chiesaravello.com). **Open** *Church* 8am-noon, 5.30-7pm daily. *Museum* 9am-6pm daily. **Admission** €2. **No credit cards**.
Also known as the Cattedrale di San Pantaleone, the Duomo was founded in 1086; little remains of its original façade, which was reworked in the 16th century. Far more interesting are its central bronze doors, divided into 54 bas-relief panels that tell the stories of the saints and the Passion. Barisano da Trani, who designed them in 1179, was undoubtedly influenced by the Oriental Greek style of the earlier doors at Amalfi and Atrani.

The interior was given a Baroque reworking in 1786: in the early 1980s, the courageous decision was taken to rip it all down and restore the church to something close to its late 13th century appearance. Halfway down the central aisle, two exquisite pulpits are set face to face, as if for a preachers' duel. The *pergamo* (high pulpit) was commissioned by a scion of the local Rufolo family in 1272; six lions support the spiral columns holding up the pulpit, richly decorated with mosaics depicting birds and beasts. The simple *ambone* (low pulpit) opposite was donated by Costantino Rogadeo, the second bishop of Ravello, in 1130. Its mosaics of Jonah being swallowed by the whale (on the right) and

regurgitated (on the left, with a little wave for his fans) are symbols of the Resurrection.

To the left of the main altar is the chapel of San Pantaleone, Ravello's patron saint. It contains a phial of his blood, which is said to liquefy on 27 July each year and stay liquid until mid September.

Down in the crypt is the Museo del Duomo, whose assorted ancient remains include first- and second-century rose marble urns, fragments of the original 12th-century floor, and a delicate marble bust of Sichelgaita della Marra – wife of Nicola Rufolo, who paid for the *pergamo* upstairs.

★ Villa Cimbrone

Via Santa Chiara 26 (089 857459/www. villacimbrone.com). **Open** 9am-30mins before sunset daily. **Admission** €6. **No credit cards**.
Though records of a villa on this site date back to the 11th century, the current building is mostly the work of Lord Grimthorpe (the designer of London's Big Ben), who bought it in 1904. In its heyday in the '20s, it hosted most of the Bloomsbury group; later, Greta Garbo and conductor Leopold Stokowski used it as their love nest.

To see inside the actual villa, you'll need to check in to the Hotel Villa Cimbrone (*see p290*), but the wonderful gardens can be admired by all. Roses, camellias and exotic plants line the lawns and walks, which are less formal than those of Villa Rufolo. There is a pretty faux-Moorish tearoom and – one of the high points of the visit – a scenic viewpoint, the Terrace of Infinity, lined with classical busts. The view, which stretches along the coast for miles, is considered to be the finest on the Amalfi Coast.

Villa Rufolo

Piazza del Duomo (information from tourist office 089 857096). **Open** 9am-8pm daily (closes 5pm on concert days). **Admission** €5. **No credit cards**.
By the time Scotsman Francis Reid bought it in 1851, the Rufolo family's villa and its surrounding garden were little more than tangled ruins. The house was reborn as an eclectic melange, although certain parts – notably the charming, double-tiered Moorish cloister – were not tampered with too much. But it's really the gardens that draw people here, with their geometric flowerbeds amid Romantic ruins. When Wagner saw them in 1880, he knew he'd found the magic garden of Klingsor, the setting for the second act of *Parsifal*.
▶ *For more on the Ravello Festival, celebrating Wagner's musical legacy, see p195.*

Where to eat

Villa Amore (*see p291*) serves hearty fare, specialising in pastas and stuffed pancakes. If the weather is fine, a table on the terrace offers fine views over the Amalfi Coast.

AROUND NAPLES

Cumpà Cosimo

Via Roma 46 (089 857156). **Open** 12.30-3pm, 7.30-11pm daily. **Average** €30. **Credit** AmEx, DC, MC, V.

The decor and dishes are those of a simple trattoria, but the prices are in the restaurant league. The food is good, though: five types of home-made pasta, and excellent meat-based *secondi* such as *salsiccia al finocchietto in mantello di provola* (fennel-flavoured sausage covered in cheese). The ambience is unassuming but friendly, the wine perfectly drinkable.

€ Figli di Papà

Via della Marra 7-9 (089 858302/www. ristorantefiglidipapa.it). **Open** Apr-Sept noon-3.30pm, 7-11pm daily. *Oct-Mar* noon-3.30pm, 7-10pm Mon-Wed, Fri-Sun. **Average** €25. **Credit** AmEx, DC, MC, V.

Housed in a 12th-century palazzo, restored to keep the original vaults and arches intact, this place aims to produce creative cuisine that goes beyond the standard local seafood experience. The food is pretty good, especially for the price, but the staff could do with breaking into a smile from time to time.

▶ *The owners also operate a B&B, the Palazzo della Marra; see below.*

★ Rossellinis

Palazzo Sasso, Via San Giovanni del Toro 28 (089 818181/www.palazzosasso.com). **Open** 7.30-10.30pm daily. Closed Nov-Feb. **Average** €80. **Credit** AmEx, DC, MC, V.

Thanks to chef Pino Lavarra, previously of Raymond Blanc's Manoir aux Quat'Saisons, this hotel restaurant is a destination in its own right. The dining room is rather formal, with its heavy drapes and striped regency chairs, but the seasonally changing menu is beautifully executed and has earned Lavarra two Michelin stars. Dishes are a mix of Neapolitan favourites, Rossellinis classics and Lavarra's new creations, and a 75-page wine list (with six pages devoted to the Campania region) is overseen by an award-winning sommelier. After an exciting amuse-bouche, the pasta course might comprise squid ravioli filled with crab and courgettes, served with ricotta dumplings. *Secondi* are evenly divided between fish and meat, desserts are suitably theatrical, and the service is exemplary; in short, this is perfect celebration dining.

Shopping

Limoncello opportunities abound, but two good sources are **I Giardini di Ravello** (Via Civita 14, 089 872264, closed Sun), which also makes its own extra virgin olive oil, and **Ravello Gusti & Delizie** (Via Roma 28-30, 089 85771, closed all Wed & Thur pm from Jan-Mar) – a tiny shop that also has a selection of wine and deli treats.

Ceramics are the best bet for serious shoppers, although don't expect rock-bottom prices. Giorgio Filocamo's **Museo del Corallo** (Piazza Duomo 9, 089 857461, www.commmune. ravello.sa.it) not only sells jewellery fashioned from coral and shells, but also houses a wonderful family collection of coral dating from Roman times up to the last century.

Where to stay

In addition to the establishments listed below, clean rooms overlooking the square are available at the **Palazzo della Marra** B&B (www.palazzodellamarra.com, €80 double).

Hotel Caruso

Piazza San Giovanni del Toro 2 (089 858801/ www.hotelcaruso.com). Closed Nov-Mar. **Rates** €868-€1,078 double. **Credit** AmEx, MC, V.

Perched on a clifftop high above the sea, this 11th-century palazzo is one of the most talked-about hotels in Italy. Its guestbook postively bulges with celebrity signatures, from Humphrey Bogart and Truman Capote to Jackie Kennedy. Pampered guests spend cocktail hour on the terrace, taking in the panoramic views through Norman arches, or admiring the hotel's 18th-century frescos. The glamour factor is off the scale, with a heated infinity pool, opulent suites, and impossibly chic piano bar and sublime views. The alfresco Belvedere restaurant serves top-notch food.

Hotel Rufolo

Via San Francesco 1 (089 857133/www.hotel rufolo.it). Closed Jan-Feb. **Rates** €250-€330 double. **Credit** AmEx, DC, MC, V.

Undergoing refurbishment at the time of writing (due for completion in summer 2009), the centrally located Rufolo enjoys stunning views down the coast from its garden terrace, and from most guestrooms. The new pool also has a view of the sea; a leisurely length of backstroke will allow you to admire the remains of the Villa Rufolo (*see p289*) next door. The hotel has a restaurant and a spa, and is one of the few hotels in Ravello to have its own parking spaces. DH Lawrence began writing *Lady Chatterley's Lover* here in 1926.

Hotel Villa Cimbrone

Via Santa Chiara 26 (089 857459/www.villa cimbrone.com). Closed mid Nov-Mar. **Rates** €330-€660 double. **Credit** AmEx, MC, V.

A stay in the historic main building of Ravello's famous garden gives you the chance to stroll around in peace after the paying visitors have left. Many of the villa's rooms (all recently refurbished) are museum pieces in their own right, with frescos and antique furniture. Vietri sul Mare tiles add local character, and the library, with its huge stone fireplace, is simply wonderful. Until a few years ago, the villa had few modern conveniences, but now there's air-conditioning, satellite TV and internet access throughout. The lack of car access still makes it difficult to reach, but there are few more romantic hideaways on the Amalfi Coast.

Palazzo Sasso
Via San Giovanni del Toro 28 (089 818181/ www.palazzosasso.com). Closed Oct-Mar. **Rates** €264-€650 double. **Credit** AmEx, DC, MC, V.
This 12th-century palazzo, with its sandy pink façade, is a stylish mix of Empire-style furniture and modern artwork. Its 43 air-conditioned rooms are luxuriously appointed (some with jacuzzis) and have sweeping views over the valley and the coast; some overlook Oscar Niemeyer's new auditorium (*see p288*). There's also a terrace pool and a spa, and a couple of rooftop jacuzzis; one of the suites also has its own terrace and pool. The staff are consummate professionals, and quick to offer help and advice. The breakfasts are superb.
▶ *The hotel is also home to the acclaimed Rossellinis restaurant; see left).*

Palumbo
Via San Giovanni del Toro 16 (089 857244/ www.hotelpalumbo.it). **Rates** €380-€600 double. **Credit** AmEx, DC, MC, V.
Almost next door to the Sasso (*see above*), the Palumbo has been run by the Vuilleumier family since 1875, and is set in the 12th-century Palazzo Gonfalone. The interior blends ancient marble columns and a traditional tiled floor with a profusion of plants and antique furniture; each of the 18 rooms and three suites is individually decorated. The inner courtyard has Moorish pointed arches, and in summer, breakfast and meals are served on the delightful garden terrace. The hotel also makes its own wine, bottled under the Episcopio label.
▶ *The annexe across the road is cheaper (€200 per person, half-board, for two guests sharing a double room), but has a lot less atmosphere.*

★ Villa Amore
Via dei Fusco 5 (089 857135/www.villaamore.it). **Rates** €56 single; €80-€100 double. **Credit** DC, MC, V.
On a quiet, stepped lane close to the Villa Cimbrone lies one of Ravello's best budget options. There are 12 clean and simple rooms; if you snaffle the one with its own garden and views along the coast, consider yourself a winner. Staff are friendly, and there is a decent restaurant with fabulous views. If you come with a car, some free parking spaces can be found at the bottom of Via dei Fusco on Via della Repubblica – though it's a steep climb to the hotel.

Villa Maria
Via Santa Chiara 2 (089 857255/www.villa maria.it). **Rates** €195-€240 double. **Credit** AmEx, DC, MC, V.
This converted villa has a lovely shady garden, with tables and chairs arranged to make the most of the view across the spectacular Dragone valley and the coast. Most of the 23 rooms are light and spacious, and all are simply furnished; room three is a huge suite with a terrace and panoramic views. In summer,

meals with ingredients sourced from the Villa's organic garden are served in the garden. Friendly owner Vincenzo Palumbo also runs the nearby Hotel Giordano (Via Santissima Trinità 14), which is a modern and less atmospheric (but cheaper) option. Guests staying at the Villa Maria can use the Giordano's free parking spaces, and its heated swimming pool.

Villa San Michele
SS163, Castiglione di Ravello, Via Carusiello 2 (089 872237/www.hotel-villasanmichele.it). **Rates** €100-€170 double. **Credit** AmEx, DC, MC, V.
For visitors wanting to combine time in Ravello with easy access to the beach, without maxing out the credit cards, the San Michele is a good option. Located just below the turn-off for Ravello on the main coast road, the hotel is a pretty white villa with blue shutters, set amid terraced gardens ablaze with hibiscus and bougainvillea. The rooms are pretty and light-filled, and all face the sea. Steps descend from the garden to a stone diving platform, deckchairs and beach umbrellas.

Resources

Police
Carabinieri, Via Roma 1 (089 857150).

Post office
Via Roma 50 (081 837 5829).

Tourist information
Azienda Autonoma di Soggiorno e Turismo
Via Roma 18/bis (089 857096/www.ravello time.it). **Open** 9am-1pm, 2-6pm Mon-Sat; 9am-3pm Sun.

Getting around

By bus
A SITA bus runs at least hourly (less frequently on Sundays) from Piazza Flavio Gioia in Amalfi to Ravello between 7am and 10pm (25mins). In Ravello, the bus sets down and turns around just before a short road tunnel; walk through this to Villa Rufolo and Piazza del Duomo. The bus then stops (and turns around) in front of the church of Santa Maria a Gradillo, and continues to Scala, on the other side of the valley, before making the return journey to Amalfi (some services stop at Scala before Ravello). Six buses a day continue beyond Scala to San Pietro and Minuto.
For information on **UnicoCostiera** tickets, *see p271.*

Getting there

Ravello is best approached from Amalfi by bus (*see above* **Getting around**), but if you're driving, follow the signs leading off the coast road.

Further Afield

The way to antiquity.

Geography and history have conspired to give each of Naples' neighbouring provinces a very different feel. Salerno and its surrounding area is a scenic mix of landscapes and cultures, epitomised by the Greco-Roman site of Paestum.

Benevento, the 'city of witches', also has a rich history and assorted ancient remains – including the imposing Arco de Traiano. In a landscape that is dominated by huge expanses of rolling farmland, the local economy remains heavily reliant on agriculture.

Lying north of Naples, the province of Caserta stretches from flat coastal plains high up into the craggy Apennines. It proved an ideal hunting ground for the Bourbon king Carlo III, who built a magnificent palace here, set in elegant formal gardens and well-tended parkland.

SALERNO

The crescent-shaped Gulf of Salerno stretches from Punta della Campanella to Punta Licosa, its northern and southern edges laced with rocky cliffs and beautiful coves, its central part low and flat. **Salerno** lies at the northern end of this plain.

Archaeological evidence shows that the area was settled by Etruscans as early as the sixth century BC. Its official history begins, however, in 194 BC, when the Romans founded a colony called Salernum. Fought over and occupied down the centuries by Goths and Byzantines, it came firmly under the thumb of the Germanic Lombards in 646. Despite internal power struggles and constant harrying by the Saracens, the city flourished. It was the Lombard prince Arechi, local lore relates, who founded the city's illustrious medical school.

But it took the Normans, who conquered Salerno in 1076, to fulfil the city's potential. It became the first capital of what was to become the Kingdom of Southern Italy (Palermo succeeded it in 1127); its Norman court was famous, and its medical school drew patients and students from all over the world.

After centuries of fluctuating fortunes, Salerno became an increasingly insignificant backwater as Naples' star rose under the Angevins and Aragonese. Only after Italian Unification in 1870, as Naples declined, did Salerno start to regain some of its lost vitality.

In World War II, on 8 September 1943, Allied troops landed just south of the city, forcing the Germans to withdraw north; for a five-month period in 1944, Salerno was the seat of the Italian government.

Today, it's a buzzing industrial city with an important port. A new 'maritime terminal', designed by world-famous architect Zaha Hadid, will cement its status. Scheduled for completion in mid 2010, it will also house a café and shops.

The seafront area, badly bombed during World War II, is decidedly postwar functional. The medieval heart of the old town, however, has recently undergone extensive – and controversial – restoration, much of it at the hands of Catalan Oriol Bohigas, the architect responsible for Barcelona's makeover.

Dominating the old centre, Salerno's **Duomo** was begun by the Norman conqueror Robert de Hauteville (known as Guiscard, 'the Crafty') in 1077, in thanks for his victory over the Lombards. The cathedral was heavily restored after an 18th-century earthquake, although subsequent facelifts have revealed large sections of the glorious Romanesque original.

At the base of the imposing gateway leading into the Duomo are a sculpted lion and a lioness feeding her cub, symbols of the power and charity of the Church. The church itself has a porticoed courtyard with columns taken from ancient buildings and a granite basin at its centre, and a spectacular 12th-century bell tower.

AROUND NAPLES

Inside, through enormous bronze doors cast in Constantinople in 1099, the Latin cross-plan church has three naves. The central nave houses two carved and inlaid pulpits: the one on the right features matching paschal (Easter) candlesticks and dates from the early 13th century; the left-hand pulpit, meanwhile, is late 12th century.

The 16th-century wooden choir stalls are preceded by sections of a 12th-century mosaic encrusted iconostasis (screen). Beside the stalls, in the left aisle, a statue of Margaret of Durres, mother of Naples' Angevin king Ladislas, dates from 1435. In the transept and choir are sections of the Duomo's original, spectacular Byzantine-inspired floor. In the cavernous Baroque crypt, columns wind to form interlacing curves; below the main altar lie the remains of St Matthew.

East of the Duomo, Via San Michele leads to the **Museo Archeologico Provinciale**. Housed in the former abbey of San Benedetto (one of 36 religious institutions in the city), the museum's collection testifies to the extensive Etruscan influence in the area, as well as displaying an interesting chance find – a first-century bronze head of Apollo, fished from the Gulf of Salerno in 1930.

Bustling with boutiques and lined with medieval buildings, Via dei Mercanti is the old town's picturesque main thoroughfare. The **Museo della Scuola Medica Salernitana** is housed in the deconsecrated church of San Gregorio, and illustrates the activities of Salerno's renowned medical school. Manuscripts, documents and illustrations are organised in eight sections, each dedicated to a branch of medieval medical knowledge, and chart the school's activities during its heyday in the 11th to 13th centuries and beyond.

Rising above the centre on Colle Bonadies, the **Castello di Arechi** (bus 19 runs uphill infrequently from Piazza XIV Maggio) was once part of a great Lombard defence system, with walls extending from the castle down to the sea. It's worth a look just for the spectacular

view; the castle itself has been extensively restored, and is used as a scenic venue for summer concerts. Opposite the café is a museum displaying ceramics and other artefacts found here. At the time of writing, the network of ancient footpaths linking the castle with the town was impassable in places, although plans have been drawn up to improve access from the town.

FREE Castello di Arechi
Via Croce (089 2854 533/www.ilcastellodi arechi.it). **Open** 9.30am-1.30pm, 3.30pm-1hr before sunset Tue-Sun. **Admission** free. **No credit cards**.

FREE Duomo (Cattedrale di San Matteo)
Piazza Alfano 1 (089 231387/www.cattedrale disalerno.it). **Open** 9.30am-12.30pm, 4-8pm Mon-Fri; 4-8pm Sat, Sun. **Admission** free. **No credit cards**.

FREE Museo Archeologico Provinciale
Via San Benedetto 28 (089 231135/089 225578). **Open** 9am-7pm Tue-Sun. **Admission** free.

★ Museo della Scuola Medica Salernitana
Via dei Mercanti 72 (089 257 3111/089 257 3256). **Open** phone for details. **Admission** phone for details. **No credit cards**.

Where to stay & eat

Hotel Olimpico (Litoranea di Pontecagnano, 089 203004, www.hotelolimpico.it, €70-€130 double) is a four-star hotel with a pool, a short stroll from the sea. It can provide transport from the station, and has good online offers.

Situated right on the beach, the **Grand Hotel Salerno** (Lungomare Clemente Tafuri, 089 704 2028, www.grandhotelsalerno.it, €120 double) is within walking distance of the old town. **Plaza Hotel** (Piazza Vittorio Veneto 42,

Castello di Arechi.

The **Duomo**.

089 224477, www.plazasalerno.it, €105 double)
is a comfortable option opposite the train
station. The town's youth hostel, **Albergo
della Gioventù**, occupies appealing 17th-
century premises near the cathedral (Via Canali,
089 234776, www.ostellodisalerno.it, €39.50
double, €15 dorm bed).

For good seafood, try **Portovecchio** (Molo
Manfredi 38, 089 255222, closed all Mon, Sun
dinner, 2wks Dec, average €35). In the old town,
the **Pizzeria Vicolo della Neve** (Vicolo della
Neve 24, 089 225705, closed lunch & all Wed,
average €30) serves great pizzas and delicious
pasta and beans, as well as its famous *cianfotta*
(a dish made with potatoes, peppers, courgettes,
bacon and tomatoes).

Resources

Hospital
Ospedale San Giovanni *Via San Leonardo
(089 671111).*

Police
Piazza Amendola 8 (089 613111).

Post office
Via Flacco Orazio 26 (089 630 7711).

Tourist information
Ente Provinciali per il Turismo (EPT) *Piazza
Vittorio Veneto 1 (089 231432/toll-free 800
213289/www.turismoinsalerno.it).* **Open** *May-
Sept 9am-2pm, 3-8pm daily. Oct-Apr 9am-2pm,
3-8pm Mon-Sat.*

Getting around

CSTP (089 487286, toll-free 800 016659,
www.cstp.it) operates bus services around
Salerno and surrounding areas. For information
on the Campania Artecard, *see p194.*

Getting there

By bus
SITA (089 386 6711, www.sitabus.it) runs
regular bus services from Piazza Municipio
in Naples.

By car
Salerno is 55km (34 miles) south of Naples on
the A3 motorway.

By train & metro
There are regular services from Naples-Stazione
Centrale on the Naples–Reggio Calabria line.

PAESTUM

The flat, straight coast road out of Salerno skirts wide, sandy beaches where locals flock in summer. There are pine and eucalyptus trees, and fields full of artichokes or strawberries, depending on the season. River buffalo, whose milk is used to produce mozzarella cheese, graze on land that was once a malarial swamp around the mouth of the River Sele. It was on this fertile plain that the Allies battled against the Germans for 20 days in September 1943, eventually forcing them to withdraw north.

Paestrum is recognised as one of the most important sites in Italy, with some exceptional examples of classic Greek architecture from the Magna Grecia period. Its ancient territory starts on the southern bank of the River Sele. The **Santuario di Hera Argiva** (accessible from the coast road and the SS18) was built by the Greeks around 600 BC, at the same time as the city of Poseidonia-Paestum. It was a temple to Hera, goddess of women and marriage. Although the site consists of little more than temple foundations, there's a state-of-the-art learning centre, the **Museo Narrante del Santuario di Hera Argiva** (see p296). It gives useful insights into the cult of Hera, and displays replicas of original finds now housed in the **Museo Archeologico Nazionale** (see p296). The Museo Narrante occupies an imaginatively converted farmhouse on land adjacent to the temple site.

Paestum itself – ten kilometres south of the Santuario – is best known for its three standing Greek temples, though there are traces of continued occupation throughout ancient times, including extensive Roman building works down to the second century AD.

It is thought that the town – originally named Poseidonia – was founded in the early sixth century BC by Greeks from Sybaris, a Greek colony on Italy's south-eastern coast. Like almost all the settlements in Greece and Magna Graecia (southern Italy), the colony had the basic trappings of the Greek *polis*: places of worship, a civic centre (the *agora*), an assembly area for all male citizens (*ekklesiasterion*) and an area for exercise and games (*gymnasion*). In about 400 BC, the city appears to have been overrun by a local tribe, the Lucanians; they unwisely backed Pyrrhus, king of Epirus, in his struggle against the Romans, and were eventually trounced.

In 273 BC Poseidonia became a Roman colony, and the signs of Greek civic life were gradually removed. The *ekklesiasterion* was filled in and replaced by the Roman *comitium* (assembly area) to the south, a forum replaced the Greek *agora* and the temples, though left standing (the pious Romans would never have dismantled them), were probably rededicated to other divinities. The name of the town was modified to a more Roman pronunciation, ending up as Paestum. This overlapping of civilisations can make Paestum a confusing site to visit.

To see it at its best, tour Paestum first thing in the morning or late in the afternoon, after the tour buses have left. Even better, take an atmospheric evening stroll along the pedestrianised road, outside the site but within easy view of the floodlit temples. There are evening tours on Thursdays, Fridays and Saturdays, in Italian: book ahead (082 872 1113, www.infopestum.it, €14).

For standard daytime visits, pass through the impressive ancient city walls – almost five kilometres long and from five metres (16.5 feet) to 15 metres (49 feet) high – and keep to the main road (SS18), which offers easy access to the site and the museum.

At the northern end of the site lies what was previously called the **Temple of Ceres**; in fact, as archaeologists subsequently discovered from the votive offerings, it was dedicated to the goddess Athena. This Athenaion, built in around 500 BC, was a Doric temple with some Ionic features: there was an inner colonnade with Ionic capitals, two of which are now on display in the site museum. The temple was used as a burial site in the early Christian era, then converted into a church in medieval times.

From the Athenaion, a well-preserved Roman road leads south through the site, passing the curious, half-buried sixth-century shrine (*heroon*) to Poseidon in which archaeologists unearthed some finely worked bronze vases (*hydria*), now given pride of place in the museum. Although most of the Greek area was built over in Roman times, the *ekklesiasterion* is the one part of the Greek *agora* that remains recognisable; most of the limestone seating has been lost. A little further south, past Roman residential areas, the Roman civic area begins; nearby are the partially rebuilt arches of the amphitheatre.

Begun during the first century BC, the amphitheatre was enlarged in early imperial times when an outer colonnade was added (only stubs of brick pillars are left). With an estimated capacity of 2,000, the amphitheatre is pint-sized compared to those in Pompeii (see p244), Capua and Pozzuoli (see p89), and is unlikely to have offered the full bloodthirsty gamut of Roman entertainment. Much of it – including the Porta Libitinensis, through which the hapless losers were hauled out – lies under the main road that was hacked through the site in the 18th century.

Close by stand the remnants of other civic buildings from Roman times, all of which were within easy reach of the Roman forum, the hub

AROUND NAPLES

of urban life from the third century BC onwards. The centrepiece of the *campus*, the ancient sports and leisure centre, is the third-century BC *piscina* or swimming pool. It evokes the memorable diving scene in the frescoed Tomb of the Diver on display in Paestum's museum, although the tomb predates the *piscina* by around 200 years. The purpose of the sunken network of limestone pillars remains a mystery to this day.

The architectural jewel of the site, around 100 metres south of the Roman forum, is the remarkably preserved (if misnamed) **Temple of Neptune**. Dedicated perhaps to Poseidon or – according to a recent theory – Apollo, the temple was built in the mid fifth century BC, when the Greek colony was enjoying a period of prosperity.

Like the other temples in Paestum, it was built with local limestone rather than marble. The columns were originally faced with white stucco to imitate marble, and mask the defects of the stone. Together with the sixth-century basilica – more accurately called the **Temple of Hera** – to the south, it rises out of the Paestum plain like a mirage, and continues to throw even the world-weariest of visitors into raptures.

The **Museo Archeologico Nazionale** has some excellent displays of Greek sculptures from the Santuario di Hera Argiva, interesting finds from local necropolises, an extensive collection of frescoed tombs and a Roman section on the top floor. Several information panels give basic information in English.

★ Museo Archeologico Nazionale
Via Magna Grecia 917 (0828 811023). **Open** *Site* 8.45am-4.30pm daily. *Museum* 8.30am-7.15pm daily. Closed 1st & 3rd Mon of mth. **Admission** *Site* €4. *Museum* €4. *Combined ticket* €6.50. **No credit cards**.

▥▥▥▥ Museo Narrante del Santuario di Hera Argiva
Masseria Procuriali, Via Barizzo Foce Sele 29, Capaccio (0828 861440). **Open** *Apr-Oct* 8.30am-3.45pm Tue-Sun. *Nov-Mar* 8.30am-2.45pm Tue-Sat. **Admission** free.

INSIDE TRACK
CULTURAL RICHES

In summer, the **Paestum Festival** (082 881 1016, www.infopestum.it) brings atmospheric concerts, plays and dance to sites around the town's magnificent temples. Expect anything from opera and theatre to tango.

Where to stay & eat

About two kilometres north of Paestum on the road to Capaccio Scalo, the **Azienda Agrituristica Seliano** (Via Seliano, 0828 723634, www.agriturismoseliano.it, closed Nov-Feb, €75-€120 double) occupies two remodelled 19th-century farmhouses and offers riding, a pool and cooking lessons.

In Paestum's archaeological zone, you can stay at the peaceful **Hotel Villa Rita** (Zona Archeologica, Via Nettuno 9, 0828 811081, www.hotelvillarita.it, closed Nov-mid Mar, €80-€90 double), run by a friendly owner, or the lovely **Il Granaio dei Casabella** (Zona Archeologica, Via Tavernelle 84, 0828 721014, closed Dec-Feb, €100-€120 double), set in a restored farm.

Just outside Paestum is the wonderfully stylish, family-run **Il Cannito** (Via Cannito, Capaccio, 0828 196 2277, www.ilcannito.com., €187-€330 double). There are four serene, understated rooms, a restaurant serving good regional food, and a sunny terrace and pool.

Amid a welter of restaurants serving tourist fare, **Nonna Sceppa** (Via Laura 45, Paestum, 0828 851064, www.nonnasceppa.com, closed Thur & Oct, average €40) stands out a mile, thanks to its excellent seafood and good pizzas.

Ristorante Nettuno (Zona Archeologica, Via Nettuno 9, 0828 811 028, www.ristorante nettuno.com, average €30-€40) is an excellent establishment serving reasonably priced, high quality food in stylish surroundings. Note that it's only open in the evening by prior reservation. Beside the museum on Via Magna Grecia, the perfectly decent **Ristorante Museo** (0828 811135, closed dinner, all Mon & Nov-Mar, average €25) serves great mozzarella salads.

Resources

Tourist information
Azienda Automa Soggiorno e Turismo (AAST) *Via Magna Grecia 887 (0828 811016/ www.infopaestum.it).* **Open** 9am-1pm, 1.30-5.30pm daily. Occasionally Aug until 10.30pm.

Getting there

By bus
CSTP (089 487286, toll-free 800 016659, www.cstp.it) runs hourly services to Paestum from the railway station square in Salerno.

By car
The SS18 follows the coast south of Salerno. If you're coming direct from Naples, take the Battipaglia exit off the Salerno–Reggio–Calabria motorway.

Paestum

By train

There are frequent services to Paestum on the Naples–Salerno–Reggio–Calabria line. Paestum town's main station is Capaccio Scalo; from here, infrequent buses run to the ruins. A few trains stop at the smaller Paestum station, which is a ten-minute walk from the archaeological site.

BENEVENTO

Despite appearances – unattractive, late 20th-century development straddles the hillsides and valleys – relics of Benevento's long and distinguished history remain.

In early Roman times, the area known as Maloentum was occupied by the Oscan-speaking Samnites, a fearsome hill tribe. But by the beginning of the fourth century BC, the Samnites were out on a limb, and a peace treaty with Rome was finally concluded in 290 BC. Renamed Beneventum, the settlement where Benevento now stands became a Roman colony in 268 BC. It reaped considerable rewards from its strategic position on the Appian Way, and from its later status as a *municipium* – formally subject to Rome, but governed by its own laws.

In the turbulent centuries that followed the fall of the Roman Empire, Benevento emerged as a Lombard capital whose influence extended throughout southern Italy. Caught in a tug of war between the Normans and the Papacy in the 11th century, it remained a papal stronghold for two centuries before it was sacked (twice) by the Swabian Friedrich II.

Its subsequent history was marked by a lengthy period of papal dominion until 1799, when it was occupied by French troops who indulged in their usual pastime of purloining local artworks and treasures. It also suffered extensive damage during World War II, when an estimated 65 per cent of the town was effectively reduced to rubble.

Today, its plush shop windows and shiny new cars show that Benevento has resisted the urban blight often found in other towns in Campania. Landmarks are well kept, traffic is heavy but fairly well disciplined, and the surrounding countryside is generally well tended and conserved.

The major sights sites are clustered on either side of the main shopping thoroughfare, Corso Garibaldi. Evidence of Benevento's early Roman heritage can be seen at the **Museo del Sannio**, tucked behind the church of Santa Sofia. The museum's galleries are filled with Roman sculptures and fine marble sarcophagi, and the covered courtyard contains finds from the first-century Temple of Isis – one of several Egyptian deities worshipped in the area. Statues of Thoth, Horus and Anubis may seem out of place in an Italian hill town, but eastern cults enjoyed considerable popularity at home as Rome's empire expanded and assimilated new religions. With the arrival of the Lombards in the sixth century, all traces of pagan worship were eliminated: the magic powers of Isis were demonised, perhaps giving rise to the area's reputation for witchcraft. The witches still lend their name to the Benevento liqueur *Strega*, as well as to Italy's most prestigious literary prize.

The museum extends into the delightful 11th-century cloister of the church of **Santa Sofia**, which has elaborately sculpted column capitals that are reminiscent – in style and quality – of medieval masterpieces such as Monreale in Sicily. The church was founded by the Lombard duke Arechi II in 762 AD. Despite 12th-century restoration work, the innovative original plan – an inner hexagon of columns, surrounded by a decagon of pillars – has survived intact. In two of the three apses behind the altar, traces of an eighth-century fresco cycle depict locally-born St Zacharias on the left and a New Testament scene on the right.

Benevento's real jewel, though, is the **Arco di Traiano**, a triumphal arch erected in 114 to celebrate the achievements of the Roman emperor Trajan. Described as 'optimo' in the inscription surmounting the arch, Trajan restored a measure of peace and prosperity to the Empire with his military campaigns in Germany and the Danube area. In spite of its location – the busy inner-city ring road passes to one side of it – the arch's sculpted friezes depicting the emperor performing various civic duties have weathered the millennia remarkably well. Floodlit at night, this is one of Campania's finest monuments.

At the western end of the town is the Teatro Romano, probably built during the reign of Commodus at the end of the second century. Although much of the arcaded superstructure has been lost, parts of the theatre have been extensively restored. With the distant backdrop of the Taburno mountain range, the theatre is an atmospheric venue for summer concerts and plays – contact the local tourist office (*see right*) for information.

ARCOS is the first modern art museum in Sannio. Opened in 2005, the space is dedicated to temporary exhibitions; there is also a bookshop, library and café on site.

ARCOS Contemporary Art Museum
Corso Garibaldi (0824 312465/0824 312506/ www.museoarcos.it). **Open** 9.30am-1.30pm, 4.30-8.30pm Tue-Fri; 10am-2pm, 4.30-9.30pm Sat, Sun. **Admission** €4. **No credit cards.**

★ Museo del Sannio
Piazza Santa Sofia (0824 21818). **Open** 9am-7pm Tue-Sun. **Admission** €4. **No credit cards.**

FREE Santa Sofia
Piazza Santa Sofia (0824 21206). **Open** 8am-noon, 5-7pm daily. **Admission** free.

Teatro Romano
Piazza Caio Ponzio Telesino (0824 47213). **Open** 9am-1hr before sunset daily. **Admission** €2. **No credit cards.**

Where to stay & eat

The obvious choice is the well-appointed **Hotel President** (Via Giovan Battista Perasso 1, 0824 316716, www.hotelpresidentbenevento.it, €115 double), which is conveniently close to the museum. For budget accommodation, there are two historic farmsteads six kilometres north-east of Benevento on the road to Pietrelcina: **Agriturismo Le Camerelle** (Contrada Camerelle, 333 269 9187, www.lecamerelle.it, closed Jan-Mar, €50 double) and **Agriturismo**

La Francesca (Contrada La Francesca, 082 477 6134, www.agriturismolafrancesca.it, €50 double), both owned by the Barricelli family. La Francesca also has a thriving restaurant (average €25-€30), serving up local produce in a nicely restored 17th-century farmhouse.

Resources

Hospital
Ospedale Fatebenefratelli *Viale Principe di Napoli 16 (0824 771111).*

Police
Via de Caro (0824 373111).

Post office
Viale Principe di Napoli 62 (0824 326911).

Tourist information
Ente Provinciale per il Turismo (EPT) *Via Nicola Sala 31 (0824 319938/319911/www. eptbenevento.it).* **Open** 8am-2pm, 2.50-6pm Mon-Fri; 9am-noon Sat.

Getting there

By car
From Naples, take the A1 motorway to Caserta Sud, then the traffic-laden SS7 to Benevento; or take the relatively stress-free, but less direct, A16 Naples–Bari motorway to the Benevento exit.

By train & metro
The **Metro Campania Nord Est** (800 127157, 081 7345268, www.metrocampanianordest.it) runs services between Naples and Benevento.

Trains also run to the main railway station from Napoli Centrale, and from Rome (www.trenitalia. com). Benevento station is a good half-hour's walk from the major sites, though bus 1 runs frequently between the station and the centre.

CASERTA

The Romans called it *Campania Felix* ('happy land') thanks to its fertile soil and privileged position. Nonetheless, Caserta, set 20 kilometres (12 miles) north of Naples, remained something of a quiet backwater until the first Bourbon king, Carlo III, selected it as a peaceful residence where he could indulge his passion for hunting while avoiding Naples' twin dangers of Vesuvius and marauding Saracens.

Inspired by the opulence of the Palace of Versailles, he commissioned leading Neapolitan architect Luigi Vanvitelli (*see p45*) to build the **Reggia** (*see p301* **Profile**), one of Italy's largest palaces. The royal project sparked a Baroque property boom, as hopefuls flocked to cash in on the town's new status.

Begun by Vanvitelli in 1752 and finished by his son Carlo in 1774, the Reggia itself is perhaps the finest example of the Neapolitan Baroque. Although construction work set off at a great pace under the enthusiastic Carlo III (1731-59), it almost ground to a halt in 1759 when he returned to his native Spain to assume the crown there. It wasn't until the 1770s that Carlo's son Ferdinand I (1759-1825) began pushing for the work to be completed.

Within the palace complex is the **Museo dell'Opera**, which contains documents and plans tracing the history of its construction.

Also designed by Luigi Vanvitelli, and modified by his son Carlo, the 120-hectare (296-acre) gardens – **Il Parco** – surrounding the royal palace are a vast expanse of manicured green, traversed by spectacular fountains and pools. Some 700 metres (765 yards) from the palace exit stands the **Fontana di Margherita**, followed by a series of long ponds, at the head of which is the **Fontana dei Delfini** (dolphin fountain). The **Fontana di Eolo** (Aeolus, god of the winds) has six tiered waterfalls; it should have been adorned with 54 statues, but only 29 were completed.

At its far end lies the **Fontana di Ceres** (goddess of fertility). The final fountain, composed of 12 mini waterfalls, has statues of Venus and Adonis. Beyond, the **Grande Cascata** crashes down over greenery from a height of 78 metres (255 feet), flanked by statues of Diana and of Actaeon, who was turned into a stag for daring to observe the bathing goddess.

The stairs on either side of the waterfall lead to the grotto, where water brought from the surrounding hills by the **Acquedotto Carolino** arrives to feed the garden's fountains. Stretching for 40 kilometres (25 miles) and passing through five mountains and over three bridges, the aqueduct was an amazing feat of hydraulic engineering, masterminded by Vanvitelli. There is also an English garden created by William Hamilton, where the first cycad in Europe was planted.

In the 19th century, Caserta became an important military base. The key encounter of Italian Unification – when Giuseppe Garibaldi met King Vittorio Emanuele II and agreed to hand over his southern Italian conquests to the crown – took place at nearby Teano in 1860. Although the economy of the town is primarily agricultural and its industry operates at little more than craft level, modern Caserta is comfortably off by southern Italian standards, and is a lively backdrop to the stately Reggia.

Not far from Caserta is the little town of **San Leucio**, where Ferdinando IV installed a silk factory in one of his old hunting lodges. Inspired by philospher Gaetano Filangeri, he

> ### INSIDE TRACK
> ### PERFECTLY PRESERVED
>
> North-east of Caserta is the little jewel of **Sant'Agata dei Goti**, a charming medieval town. Perched on a rocky *tufa* spur, its centre is almost entirely pedestrianised, making it easy to wander around its wealth of ancient churches, historic treasures and authentic local restaurants.

also instigated a utopian social system that included the building of workers' houses, provision of schooling for children and care for the sick. The factory still produces silks that are prized throughout the world; during the summer, a series of events and concerts are held in the courtyard.

Belvedere di San Leucio
3km NE of Caserta, Via Atrio Superiore (0823 301817/www.realbelvedere.it). **Open** *May-Sept* by appointment only Mon, Fri; visits at 9.30am, 10.45am, noon, 3.30pm, 5pm Sat, Sun. *Oct-Apr* by appointment only Mon, Fri; visits at 9.30am, 10.45am, noon, 3pm, 4.30pm Sat, Sun. **Admission** €6. **No credit cards**.

★ Reggia di Caserta (Palazzo Reale)
Via Douhet 2 (Reggia 0823 277111/448084/800 991199/www.reggiadicaserta.org). **Open** *Reggia* 8.30am-7.30pm Mon, Wed-Sun (last entrance at 7pm). *Mostra* 8.30am-6pm Mon, Wed-Sun. *Parco & Giardino Inglese* 8.30am-1hr before sunset Tue-Sun (last entrance 2hrs before sunset). **Admission** *Reggia, Mostra, Parco & Giardino Inglese* €4.20. *Parco & Giardino Inglese* €2. **No credit cards**.

Where to stay & eat

Built in 2000, the four-star **Grand Hotel Vanvitelli** (Viale Carlo III, 0823 217111, www.grandhotelvanvitelli.it, €150 double) is five minutes' drive from the Royal Palace, and offers clean and comfortable rooms in luxurious surroundings. Of the budget options, the **Hotel Baby** (Via Verdi 41, 0823 328311, €55 double) is one of the more acceptable. Just opposite the Reggia, the **Jolly Hotel** (Viale Vittorio Veneto 13, 0823 325222, www.jollyhotelcaserta.it, €90 double) has disabled facilities.

Surprisingly, the self-service café in the **Reggia**, next to the palace gardens, does reasonable food at highly competitive prices (average €15). Of the surrounding towns, Casertavecchia (*see p300*) offers the best chance of finding a good, atmospheric restaurant.

AROUND NAPLES

Getting there

By bus
CTP (800 482644, www.ctpn.it) runs frequent services from Piazza Garibaldi in Naples to Caserta and Capua; buses marked 'per autostrada' take the motorway, and get there faster.

By car
From Naples, take the A1 motorway and exit at Caserta Sud.

By train
There are frequent services from Naples' Stazione Centrale (journey time 30mins). The station in Caserta is a five-minute walk from the Reggia.

The recently-resurrected **Metro Campania Nord Est** (800 127157, 081 734 5268, www.metro campanianordest.it) also runs services between Naples and Caserta.

Resources

Hospital
Azienda Ospedaliera San Sebastiano di Caserta *Via Palasciano (0823 231111/ www.ospedale.caserta.it).*

Internet
Internet Caffè *Viale Lincoln 89 (0823 322146).*

Police
Piazza Vanvitelli 5 (0823 429111).

Post office
Via Roma 14 (0823 325319).

Tourist information
Ente Provinciale per il Turismo (EPT) *c/o Palazzo Reale (0823 321137/www.eptcaserta.it).* **Open** 9am-4.45pm Mon-Fri; 10am-1pm Sat.

AROUND CASERTA

Thought to have been founded in the eighth century, **Casertavecchia** (Old Caserta) is self-consciously picturesque, with medieval alleyways and a ruined castle. It was the seat of the counts of Caserta until the 16th century, when they moved to the plains below. Deserted during the day, the place springs into life as its many *trattorie* open up in the evening.

The 12th-century cathedral of **San Michele Arcangelo** in Piazza del Duomo (the entrance is round the corner; *see p302*) is one of the finest examples of Romanesque architecture in the region. It has a stunning bell tower with Arabic and French influences, and an eight-sided dome. Ancient columns with Corinthian capitals added to compensate for height differences divide the Latin-cross interior into three aisles.

Every September, Casertavecchia is home to the popular **Settembre al Borgo** festival (0823 550 0011, www.settembrealborgo.it), with music, dance, open-air theatre and exhibitions.

These days, **Santa Maria Capua Vetere** is a quiet old town: with its crumbling palazzi, medieval cobbles and new money, it's hard to imagine it was once the apple of the Roman imperial eye, gateway to the south and to the wealth of oriental sea trade.

Inhabited since the ninth century BC, it flourished under the Etruscans, resisted the Greeks, but fell to the Samnites. When the Romans got down to building the Appian Way in 312 BC, it led to old Capua, now Santa Maria Capua Vetere. The city supported Hannibal during the second Punic War (218-210 BC), but Roman rule was heavy-handedly reinstated after his defeat and an attempted uprising.

By that time, its trade and agricultural sectors were flourishing, and the Seplasia forum (today's Piazza Mazzini) was world famous for perfume. In the first century BC, Livy described old Capua as the biggest and richest city in Italy; for Cicero it was 'a second Rome'.

In AD 465 the city was sacked by the Vandals, and in 841 the Saracens arrived to finish the job. The population took to the hills, where modern Capua now stands. The destruction of the old city was completed by the citizens, who pillaged building material from the ruins until as late as the 19th century. Even archaeologists happily plundered the site and sold off their booty to the highest bidder. This may explain why it took until 1995 for the delightful **Museo Antica Capua** (*see p302*) to claw back some of its heritage. Head for the **Museo Provinciale Campano di Capua** (*see p302*) archeological museum to see the most important collection of Matres Matutae in the world. These votive statues of women holding swaddling children pre-date Christianity. The museum also has a good section relating to the Middle Ages.

The **Duomo** (Basilica di Santa Maria Maggiore, open 8am-noon, 5-7pm Mon-Sat; 8am-1pm Sun) stands in Piazza Matteotti. Founded in 432 on the site of first-century catacombs, it was heavily remodelled in the 17th and 18th centuries.

The **Anfiteatro** is on the other side of town. It's thought there was an arena here in Etruscan times, and there was certainly a gladiator school in 73 BC, when Spartacus and 30 other gladiators broke down its doors in a bid for freedom, sparking the two-year Slave Revolt. The gladiators trained 50,000 supporters, and conducted guerrilla warfare from hideouts on Vesuvius. Six thousand of them later adorned crosses along the Appian Way.

Successive emperors expanded the amphitheatre until it was second only to Rome's

Profile Reggia di Caserta

A palace fit for a king.

Set around four courtyards, the Reggia was built on a lavish scale; today, only a fraction of its 1,200 rooms are open to the public. It cost around six million ducats to build, in spite of savings made by using painted terracotta rather than marble for some of the floors.

The **Scala d'Onore**, with 117 steps carved from one stone block, leads up to the royal apartments. Beyond the upper octagonal hall, the **Salone degli Alabardieri** (halberd bearers) has busts of various queens, and the **Salone delle Guardie di Corpo** (bodyguards) depicts scenes from the lives of the Farnese family, dukes of Parma, a title that passed to King Carlo through his mother Elizabetta Farnese. The bust of Ferdinando I on a mantelpiece is attributed to Antonio Canova. The next room – **Sala di Alessandro** – gets its name from the fresco depicting Alexander the Great's marriage to Roxana; monarchs and their families once waved from the porch outside.

To the left lies the **Appartamento Vecchio** suite, with four rooms dedicated to the seasons. *Primavera* (spring) has paintings by Antonio Dominici; *estate* (summer) features works by Fedele Fischetti, walls covered

in San Leucio silk and a Murano glass chandelier. In the *autunno* (autumn) dining room, frescoes show Bacchus and Ariadne.

In the oriental-looking private study of Ferdinando II (1830-59), a private door and narrow passage behind the mirror lead to the king's bedchamber. Since the king died of a contagious disease, its original contents were destroyed. Next door is the queen's dressing room, followed by the **Sala di Ricevimento**, where guests were received.

Beyond two large reading rooms is the **Biblioteca**, home to over 10,000 volumes. The next room contains a nativity scene with 1,200 figures crafted by 18th-century artisans and dressed in clothes made by the queen and her ladies-in-waiting.

To the right of the Sala di Alessandro are the 19th-century **Appartamento Nuovo**. Here, in the **Sala del Trono** (throne room), the king received ambassadors and hosted glittering balls; lit by 14 Bohemian glass and bronze lamps, it has a gilded throne.

Don't miss the private apartment of Joaquin Murat, Naples' king from 1808-16. His opulent bedchamber is decked out in heavy mahogany furniture; note his initials ostentatiously carved into the chairs. Lastly, wander through the Royal Chapel, whose barrel-vaulted ceiling is reminiscent of the one at Versailles.

BIG SCREEN APPEAL

The palace's splendour has made it a hit with directors. It stood in for the palace of Queen Amidala in *Star Wars: The Phantom Menace*, then that of Queen Jamilla in *Attack of the Clones*. In *Mission: Impossible 3*, meanwhile, it starred as the Vatican.

Colosseum in size. It featured heavily in the Empire's bread-and-circuses policy for whipping up political support and hiding social problems. Crowds were issued tickets with gate numbers (there were around 80 entrances), and elevators brought gladiators, animals and scenery into the arena from the underground passages. The outer wall originally consisted of four tiers of arches with Doric half-columns and busts of the gods set in the keystones, but only part of it still stands; the marble facing was stripped and 'recycled' long ago. The on-site **Museo del Gladiatore** displays a wedge of the amphitheatre, reconstructed with the aid of architectural finds, and an incongruous life-size model of a gladiator. There's commentary (in Italian) and sound effects of action in the arena.

Such an important city attracted the full gamut of religions. The ancient Persian cult of Mithras was probably brought to the town by the gladiators, who were often from the east. The religion divided everything into good and evil; its all-male adherents (it was very popular among Roman soldiers) swore to combat evil. Membership was secret, and there was an initiation ceremony, depicted on the walls of the **Mithraeum**; note that some of the novices are blindfolded. The Tauroctonia, which forms the centre panel on the back wall, shows Mithras slaying a bull, the symbol of brute force and vitality. According to the Mithraic creation myth, all life forms sprang from the blood spilt when Mithras killed the bull, the only other living creature on a barren earth. The channel that runs from the altar collected the blood spilt in animal sacrifices.

On the Caserta–Santa Maria Capua Vetere road is one of Campania's best wine and gourmet food shops, **Enoteca la Botte** (Via Nazionale Appia 168-180, 0823 494040, www.enotecalabotte.it, closed Mon).

Anfiteatro
Piazza 1 Ottobre, Santa Maria Capua Vetere (0823 798864). **Open** 9am-1hr before sunset Tue-Sun. **Admission** *with Mithraeum & Museo Antica Capua* €2.50. **No credit cards**.

Mithraeum
Via Morelli, Santa Maria Capua Vetere. **Open** by request 9am-4pm Tue-Sun; ask at the amphitheatre or museum. **Admission** *with Anfiteatro & Museo Antica Capua* €2.50. **No credit cards**.

Museo Antica Capua
Via Roberto d'Angiò 48, Santa Maria Capua Vetere (0823 844206). **Open** 9am-7pm Tue-Sun. **Admission** *with Anfiteatro & Mithraeum* €2.50. **No credit cards**.

Museo Provinciale Campano di Capua
Via Roma 68, Santa Maria Capua Vetere (0823 961402. **Open** 9am-1.30pm Tue-Sun. **Admission** €4. **No credit cards**.

FREE San Michele Arcangelo
Piazza Vescovado, Casertavecchia (0823 371318). **Open** 9am-1pm, 3.30-8pm daily. **Admission** free.

Where to eat

In Casertavecchia, **La Castellana** (Via Torre 4, 0823 371230, closed Thur from Oct-Mar, average €20) has home-made pasta and game.

A ten-minute drive north of the centre, **Leucio** (Via Giardini Reali, San Leucio, 0823 301241, www.ristoranteleucio.it, closed Mon, dinner Sun, average €30) offers outstanding fish, home-made pasta and excellent service.

Resources

Tourist information
See p300 **Caserta**.

Getting there

By bus
See p300 **Caserta**.

By car
For Casertavecchia, take the Caserta Nord exit from the A1 motorway; it lies 2km north-east lof town on a minor road (signposted). For Santa Maria Capua Vetere, leave the A1 motorway at Caserta Nord; SS7 (Via Appia) from Caserta (4.5km/3 miles).

By train
For Santa Maria Capua Vetere, there's an infrequent service from Caserta.

Enoteca la Botte.

Directory

Getting Around	**304**
Resources A-Z	**307**
Travel advice	307
The local climate	312
Further Reference	**313**
Vocabulary	**314**
Glossary	**315**
Index	**316**
Advertisers' Index	**322**

Getting Around

ARRIVING & LEAVING

By air

Aereoporto Internazionale di Napoli (Capodichino) is 7km or 10mins from Stazione Centrale rail station, 20mins from ferry and hydrofoil ports. **Alibus** (800 639525, 081 763 1111, www.anm.it) runs a direct bus from outside arrivals to Stazione Centrale (Piazza Garibaldi) and Piazza Municipio (near the ferry port). Buses leave every 20mins, 6.30am to 11.30pm daily. Return buses leave Piazza Municipio from 6am to 12.12am daily. Tickets are €3.

Local **orange bus** 3S runs from Arrivals to Garibaldi every 25mins. Buy tickets (€1.10) at any *tabacchi* and stamp them on board.

A **taxi** to central Naples should cost around €12.50 (plus 50¢ for each piece of luggage in the boot).

Aereoporto Internazionale di Napoli *081 789 6111/ toll-free from within Italy 848 888 777/www.gesac.it.*

Major airlines
Alitalia *06 2222, www.alitalia.com*
BA *199 712 266, www.ba.com*
EasyJet *848 887 766, www.easyjet.com*

By boat

Timetables for water transport around the Bay of Naples appear daily in *Il Mattino* and on www.campaniatrasporti.it.

Ferries and hydrofoils regularly depart from Naples' port, Molo Beverello (map p332 L/M12), heading to the islands, Sorrento (€11) and the Amalfi Coast (€15), as well as from the smaller port at Mergellina, for the islands.

The major operators are:

Alilauro *081 497 2238, www.alilauro.it*
Caremar *081 551 3882, www.caremar.it*
MedMar *081 333 4411, www.medmargroup.it*
Navigazione Libera del Golfo *081 552 0763, www.navlib.it*
SNAV *081 428 5555, www.snav.it*

Ferry services to Palermo (daily) and Sardinia (once or twice weekly)

are run by **Tirrenia** (now joined with Caremar, *see above*). **SNAV** runs a hydrofoil to Palermo (Apr-Dec daily). **TTT Lines** (800 915 365, 081 580 2744, www.tttlines.it) sails from Molo Beverello to Catania, Sardinia and Tunisia. See also **Metro del Mare**, *below*.

Hydrofoils to Capri, Ischia and Procida, run by SNAV and Alilauro, also leave from **Mergellina** (map p326 C16), a mile away from the main port.

MedMar and Caremar (for both, *see above*) car ferries also leave for Procida and Ischia from **Pozzuoli**, 12km north-west of Naples.

The **Metro del Mare** (199 600 700, www.metrodelmare.com) runs from Molo Beverello to various points in the gulf and along the Amalfi Coast. Tarifs start at €3.50 for a short hop; Napoli Beverello to Positano is €14; to Amalfi €15.

For more on ferries, see the Getting There sections in the Around Naples chapters.

By bus

Most long-distance buses arrive at and depart from Piazza Garibaldi. **Autolinee Ferrari** (aka CLP) runs to cities in Campania, in other parts of Italy and in continental Europe (081 251 4157, www.clpbus.it). **CTP** (800 200 114, 081 700 1111, 081 700 5104, www.ctpn.it) and **SITA** (081 752 7337, 089 386 6711, www.sita bus.it) serve destinations around Naples and Southern Italy, as well as Tuscany and the Veneto.

By rail

Naples' three mainline stations are **Campi Flegrei**, **Mergellina** and the main station, **Stazione Centrale**. For train information and bookings, contact **Trenitalia**. Call the helpline (89 20 21, 06 6847 5475) or visit www.trenitalia.it.

Stazione Centrale
Piazza Garibaldi (89 20 21).
Map *p329 Q7.*
Most FS trains come and go from here, including the Alta Velocità high speed service to Rome, very fast Eurostar and InterCity trains, and slow regional, direct and local trains. Trains also depart from the Piazza Garibaldi station (two levels

below the main station), which is used by some long-distance services as well as the regional metro.

PUBLIC TRANSPORT

The only public transport most visitors take within Naples is the occasional bus and a funicular or two. Most visitors won't have any reason to travel on the Metro, which is designed primarily for suburban commuters. For getting away from Naples, there are narrow-gauge trains to the south-east and the west, or ferries and hydrofoils to all points around the bay. Apart from that, count on walking (or taking a taxi); city buses are not known for their efficiency and comfort.

Fares & tickets

A single ticket, allowing up to three trips on all metropolitan transport – including one trip only on the metro and funiculars – costs €1.10 and is valid for 90mins (081 551 3109. www.unicocampania.it). A 24hr ticket for unlimited travel on all metropolitan public transport costs €3.10 Mon-Fri; the 3-day ticket costs €20 (includes Alibus & buses on Capri and Ischia). Tickets must be bought at a newsstand, *tabacchi* or ticket machine before boarding, then time-stamped in the machine.

Buses

Traffic makes bus travel in Naples a pain: you're often quicker walking. Still, the dedicated bus lane on Corso Umberto can make bus travel to places between San Carlo opera house and the Stazione Centrale viable. The bus can also be an option when travelling to Mergellina and Posillipo (from Santa Lucia or the Riviera di Chiaia). For lost property, *see p309.*

Bus services are run by ANM (800 639 525, 081 763 1111, www.anm.it). There is no central bus station: some buses run from Piazza Garibaldi, others from Via Pisanelli, near Piazza Municipio, others from Piazza Vittoria. Electronic signs at Metro stations and bus stops give waiting times. Before taking a bus, buy tickets at a *tabacchi* or newsstand and stamp them in the machines on board. Enter buses through the front or back door, and exit through the central ones; before your stop, press the red button.

Circular routes

There are seven **R** routes, four of which intersect in the Via Medina/ Piazza del Municipio area; R5 heads north towards Capodichino.

A-to-B routes

C16 Regular service from Mergellina along Corso Vittorio Emanuele to Piazza Mazzini and Via Salvator Rosa.

C18 The only direct bus from Piazza Vittoria along the seafront, through the Fuorigrotta tunnels to the football.

C21 Posh route from Piazza Sannazzaro in Mergellina that runs up the hill to Capo Posillipo along Via Orazio and Via Petrarca.

C27 Important but crowded route from Piazza Amedeo up Via Tasso to Via Manzoni, right along snobs' alley to Capo Posillipo itself.

C28 Runs into the heart of Vomero from Piazza Vittoria, taking in Via dei Mille, Via Tasso and Via Aniello Falcone along the way.

140 The only bus to run up Via Posillipo from Mergellina. Starts at Santa Lucia, opposite Castel dell'Ovo.

201 In its counter-clockwise run, the 201 hits Stazione Centrale, Via Foria, Piazza Cavour, Piazza Dante and Piazza del Municipio.

Circular shuttle route

E1 Departing from Piazza Gesù Nuovo, it skirts most of the Centro Storico. Stops are within easy walking distance of each other; the bus is useful mostly for shoppers.

Metro

Naples' system of underground and overground railways and trams, operated by **Metronapoli** (800 568 866, 081 559 4111, www. metro.na.it), can be the fastest way to get around parts of Greater Naples. For lost property, *see p309*.

Red M signs indicate a metro station. Tickets are sold at any *tabacchi*, and at machines in every station. They cost €1.10 and are valid on any form of transport within the city for 90mins.

The Metro system has been in the throes of expansion for decades, with new lines and stations set to open every year. There will be ten lines in total, most of which will serve suburban commuters. A few lines that are part of the functioning system are of interest to visitors:

Metro Linea 1 runs from Piazza Dante to Piazza Vanvitelli, then into the north-east suburbs (6am-11pm). **Metro Linea 2** runs from Piazza Garibaldi (beneath Stazione Centrale), skirting Centro, to the Mergellina mainline station and the Campi Flegrei (5.30am-10.59pm).

Also now officially part of the system are two older, narrow-gauge overground railways, one heading west and the other snaking in the other direction, round the bay. Both are fairly ramshackle. The **Circumvesuviana** (8000 53939, www.vesuviana.it, tickets not valid on the urban system) leaves from its own terminus in Corso Garibaldi, south of (but accessible from) Stazione Centrale. Trains run south-east to Oplontis, Pompeii, Herculaneum and Sorrento (5.09am-10.42pm). The **Ferrovia Cumana** (800 001616, www.sepsa.it) runs services from Piazza Montesanto to the Campi Flegrei (5.20am-10.30pm).

Funicular

The four funicular railways (Centrale, Chiaia, Mergellina and Montesanto) only take you to the Vomero and back, but kids love them. Long overdue maintenance work on the **Montesanto** and **Chiaia Funiculars** continues, but services are still regular.

Rail

For information and bookings, call 89 20 21 (open all week, 24hrs a day) or visit www.trenitalia.it. For lost property, *see p309*.

There are three mainline **Ferrovie dello Stato-Trenitalia** (FS) stations in Naples. Most FS trains come and go from **Stazione Centrale** (*see left*), from high-speed services to slower local trains. Below the street-level main station are two lower levels: the first has tickets for the **Circumvesuviana** line (*see above*); the second contains Piazza Garibaldi station (*see left*).

Advance rail tickets can be bought at stations (some automatic machines accept credit cards) or from travel agents with the FS logo. If you don't speak Italian, it can be hard to find the right queue: some desks sell intra-Italy (*biglietti interno/senza supplemento*), Eurostar tickets and high-speed supplements (*supplementi rapidi*); some also sell advance bookings (*prenotazioni*); some only do advance bookings. A separate window caters for international trains (*internazionali*). If you're confused, ask at the Stazione Centrale's busy *informazione* office.

Ticket prices are directly related to distance travelled. Slower trains (*diretti, espressi, regionali* and *interregionali*) are much cheaper than in northern Europe, but supplements mean faster trains – **InterCity** (IC), **EuroCity** (EC), and **Eurostar Italia** (ES) – are closer to the European norm.

Booking a seat is obligatory (and included in the ticket price) on ES trains; reservations can be made up to 15mins before departure. Seats on IC and internal EC routes should be booked 24hrs before departure; reservation is compulsory. If your ES, IC or EC train arrives more than 30mins late and you've booked a seat, you can claim a partial refund at the *rimborsi* booth.

You're liable for a €50 fine if you fail to stamp your ticket – and any supplement – in the yellow machines at the head of each platform before boarding. (If you forget, find the inspector as soon as possible after boarding the train.) This does not apply to **Alta Velocità** tickets.

TAXIS

Taxis can be found at signposted ranks; otherwise, call the numbers below. Authorised white taxis have the city's emblem on the front doors and rear licence plate, and a meter. Steer well clear of unauthorised 'taxi' drivers, who may demand exorbitant sums for short journeys.

As you set off, the meter should read €3. There's a €4.50 minimum charge per trip. On Sundays or holidays the minimum charge becomes €5.50; €2.10 10pm-7am; 50¢ per piece of luggage in the boot, and an extra €3.10 to or from the airport. Prices are fixed between Capodichino and Stazione Centrale (€12.50) and Stazione Centrale and Molo Beverello (€16). Each driver must display this list of fares: if you don't see it, ask for the 'elenco di tariffe predeterminate'.

Cab drivers may try to hike fares, so ensure the meter is on. If you suspect you are being ripped off, make a note of the driver's name and number from the photo ID in the cab; do it ostentatiously and the fare is likely to drop to its proper level. For lost property, *see p309*.

Complaints can be lodged with the drivers' co-operative (the phone number is displayed on the outside of the car) or with the **Servizio Programmazione, Promozione e Controllo Servizi di Trasporto Pubblico** (081 1997 9674).

When you phone for a cab, you'll be given a geographic location followed by a number and a time, as in '*Treviso 14, in tre minuti*' ('Treviso 14, in three minutes'). The driver should put the meter on as you get in; a call supplement of 80¢ will be added. Most taxis accept cash only; a few take credit cards. **Consortaxi** (081 552 5252, www. consortaxi.it), **Free Taxi** (081 551 5151) and **Partenope** (081 560 6666, www.radiotaxilapartenope.it) are generally reliable. Some taxi firms run fixed-rate trips outside Naples at reasonable prices: return to Pompeii for €90, say, or one-way to Positano for €120. Many drivers speak English, making the trip a kind of guided tour.

Ischia has three-wheeled 'micro taxis'; many of Capri's taxis are vintage cars; Sorrento has horse-drawn carriages. Each island has its own fare structure, but be prepared to bargain.

DRIVING

EU visitors can drive on their home country's licences; an international licence is advisable for non-EU citizens. When driving, remember:
● The law insists you wear a seat belt and carry a hazard triangle and reflective safety jacket in your car; scooter-riders and motorcyclists must wear helmets.
● Keep your driving licence, insurance documents, vehicle registration and photo ID on you at all times; when stopped by the police, you may be fined if you can't produce them.
● Flashing your lights means that you won't slow down or give way, and want the person in front of you to switch lanes.
● Neapolitans often ignore red lights, so approach junctions with caution. If traffic lights flash amber, give way to the right.
● Maintain your cool and be prepared for anything; watch out for pedestrians and scooters.
● Italians drive on the right.

Reasons not to drive

● Only vehicles with catalytic converters are allowed in the city between 8.30am and 6.30pm Mon, Wed and Fri. There's an Area Azzurra (Blue Zone) in the centre where only residents can circulate between 7.30am and 6.30pm Mon-Fri. Theoretically no vehicles are permited to circulate around Spaccanapoli from 10am-10pm Mon-Thur and 10am-midnight Fri-Sun (this law is rarely kept). On many Sunday mornings all vehicles

are banned. For more details (in Italian only, unfortunately), refer to www.comune.napoli.it.
● In summer, traffic around Sorrento and on the Amalfi Coast is horrific, as tour buses wind their way along narrow coastal roads. Local day-trippers make things even worse at weekends: if you must drive, stick to weekdays. Otherwise, take a boat.
● On the islands, roads are packed in the summer. You can't take cars to Capri; use public transport or walk on Procida. Car rental on Ischia is relatively cheap, but you can't take the car off the island.

Breakdown services

National motoring groups (Britain's AA or RAC and the AAA in the US) have reciprocal arrangements with the **Automobile Club d'Italia** or ACI, which offers a 24hr emergency service (803 116, 081 725 3811, www.napoli.aci.it) and breakdown assistance. For extensive repairs, go to a manufacturer's official dealer. Dealers are listed in the Yellow Pages under *Auto*; specialists are listed under *gommista* (tyre repairs), *carrozzerie* (bodywork/windscreen repairs) and *marmitte* (exhaust repairs). The English Yellow Pages (www.englishyellowpages.it) lists garages where English is spoken.

Car hire

The minimum age for renting an economy car is 21; you must be 25 to rent a larger-cylinder car.

Avis *Airport (081 780 5790/www. avisautonoleggio.it).* **Open** 7.30am-11.30pm daily. **Credit** AmEx, MC, V. **Other locations** Via Piedigrotta 44 (081 761 8354); Via Partenope 13, Chiaia (081 240 0307).
Europcar *Airport (toll free 199 307 030/081 780 5643/www. europcar.it).* **Open** 7.30am-11.30pm daily. **Credit** AmEx, DC, MC, V. **Other locations** Via Santa Lucia 54, Royal Naples (081 764 9838).
Hertz *Airport (081 780 2971/ www.hertz.it).* **Open** 8am-11.30pm daily. **Credit** AmEx, DC, MC, V. **Other locations** Stazione Centrale (081 206 228).
Maggiore *Airport (081 780 3011/ www.maggiore.it).* **Open** 7.30am-11.30pm daily. **Credit** AmEx, DC, MC, V.
Other locations Stazione Centrale (081 287858).
Thrifty *Airport (081 780 5702/ www.thrifty.it).* **Open** 8am-11pm daily. **Credit** AmEx, DC, MC, V.

Parking

Blue lines on the road mean residents park free and visitors pay (€1-€2/hr) at the pay-and-display machines. Elsewhere, spaces are up for grabs – though look out for signs saying *passo carrabile* (access at all times), *sosta vietata* (no parking) and disabled parking (marked off with yellow lines). '*Zona rimozione*' (tow-away area) means 'no parking', and is valid for the length of the street or until the next tow-away sign with a red line through it. If a street or square has no cars parked in it, assume it's a no-parking zone.

Illegal 'parking attendants' operate in many areas, offering to look after your car for €1 or so. The safest solution is to use pay parking; the Yellow Pages has a full list under *autorimesse e parcheggi*.

Via Brin Parking *Via Brin & Via Volta, Port & University (081 763 2855).* Bus 3S, 194, 195, C81, C82, C89, CS. **Open** 24hrs daily. **Rates** €1.30 4hrs, 30¢ successive hr; €21 80hrs; €35.50 150hrs. **Credit** AmEx, DC, MC, V. An 800-car facility between Stazione Centrale and the port (Porto exit from the ring road or motorway). Buses for Molo Beverello leave every 15mins.

CYCLING

Cycling in Naples proper is not to be recommended, except in certain parks (*see p187*), due to the fast and furious traffic; bike theft is also rife.

WALKING

It's perfectly possible to explore Naples on foot – or the areas of visitor interest, at least. For the hillier parts of town, there are the funiculars and a couple of elevators, though walking is never out of the question. For the densest part of the Centro Storico, it's really the only way to get around.

TOURS

CitySightseeing Napoli (081 551 7279, www.napoli.city-sightseeing. it) offers multilingual city tours in open-top double-decker buses. The 'Art Tour' and 'Bay of Naples' tour depart every 45mins from Piazza Municipio. Tickets (valid 24hrs) cost €22 for adults, €11 for under-15s and €66 for families of five. At weekends, there's a 'San Martino' tour from Piazza Municipio every 2 hours. Hop on and off as you like.

DIRECTORY

Resources A-Z

TRAVEL ADVICE

For current information on travel to a specific country – including the latest news on health issues, safety and security, local laws and customs – contact your home country's government department of foreign affairs. Most have websites with useful advice for would-be travellers.

AUSTRALIA
www.smartraveller.gov.au

CANADA
www.voyage.gc.ca

NEW ZEALAND
www.safetravel.govt.nz

REPUBLIC OF IRELAND
foreignaffairs.gov.ie

UK
www.fco.gov.uk/travel

USA
www.travel.state.gov

ADDRESSES

Addresses are written with the number following the street name, as in Via Toledo 23. The number after the word *'int'* (short for *interno*) is the flat or apartment number. *'Scala'* and *'piano'* numbers refer to staircase and floor numbers.

AGE RESTRICTIONS

At bars, beer and wine can be consumed from the age of 16, spirits from 18. You must be over 18 to drive and over 21 to hire a car. Over-14s with a licence can ride a moped or scooter with a 50cc engine.

ATTITUDE & ETIQUETTE

Although you may be offered all forms of Mediterranean hospitality in Naples, it is sometimes courteous (and expected) to refuse.

Churches are best visited in sober attire, but minor lapses from tourists are usually tolerated. Some churches discourage sightseeing on Sundays and during Masses. Don't visit during Mass unless there are empty side aisles.

Southern Italians have a me-first attitude when driving, boarding a bus or approaching a queue. Although queue-jumpers are often given short shrift, hanging back is taken as a sign of stupidity. When it's your turn, assert your rights.

BUSINESS

Conferences

Most major hotels cater for events of all sizes. **GP Relazioni Pubbliche** (Via San Pasquale a Chiaia 55, Chiaia, 081 401201) can help smooth the way for you.

Couriers

DHL *199 199 345/www.dhl.it.*
FedEx *800 123 800/ www.fedex.com.*
UPS *800 877 877/www.ups.com.*

Office services

GIC'90 *Via Monte di Dio 66, Royal (081 764 7427/www.gic90.com).* Translating services.
Giovanna Pistillo *Vico Prota 9 Mercogliano, Avellino (338 760 5324).* Translating services.
Mail Boxes, Etc *Via Cervantes 94, Piazza Municipio (081 580 0256).* Posting, shipping, copying.

Useful organisations

British Chamber of Commerce for Italy *St Peter's English Language Centre, Riviera di Chiaia 124, Chiaia (081 683 468).*

CONSUMER

If you have a problem, your only recourse is the police at the Questura in Via Medina or at the central train station, where you will need to fill out a form with the help of an officer with limited English.

It may be best to not use your credit card in Naples if possible; recent years have seen an epidemic in bank-card cloning.

CUSTOMS

EU citizens do not have to declare goods that have been brought into or out of Italy for personal use, as long as they have arrived from another EU country. Visitors are also allowed to carry up to €12,500 in cash. For all non-EU citizens, the following limits apply:

● 200 cigarettes or 100 small cigars or 50 large cigars or 250g of tobacco
● 1 litre of spirits (over 22% alcohol) or 2 litres of fortified wine (under 22% alcohol)
● 2 litres table wine
● 50cc of perfume

DISABLED TRAVELLERS

Naples' narrow streets are tricky for people who can't flatten themselves against a wall to let cars by, and cobblestones are tough on wheelchair suspension. Where street-to-pavement ramps do exist, they're likely to be blocked by a car.

Old buildings often have narrow corridors, lifts that are too small for wheelchairs, and inaccessible toilets. Things are improving, with lifts, ramps and disabled-adapted toilets being installed in museums, restaurants and stations. The law requires restaurants to have disabled access and toilets. Few have made the alterations yet, but if you call ahead, most will try to help.

Capri is more wheelchair-friendly. There are small electric carts to get luggage and people up and down. The main paths are steep, but at least there are no stairs. Getting up to town from the port will involve help up the steps to the funicular, and buses are not disabled-friendly.

Upmarket hotels in major resorts cater best to special needs; cheaper hotels and *pensioni* can be trickier.

Transport

Hydrofoil and ferry lines (*see p304* **Boats**) have begun to adapt for wheelchairs. Book ahead to ensure the ferry is not an older model.

In Naples, certain city buses (180, C12, C14, C16, C19, C34, C38, R2, R3), marked with a wheelchair symbol,

DIRECTORY

DIRECTORY

have extra-large central doors, access ramps and a space where a wheelchair can be secured. Elsewhere, the situation varies; contact local tourist offices or bus companies for information.

Naples' Stazione Centrale has a *Direzione servizi alla clientela* (customer services office) near platform five. It can provide information for disabled travellers (081 567 2991, 7am-9pm daily), take reservations (min 24hrs prior to departure) and provide wheelchair assistance and access. Passengers must be at the office at least 45mins before the train departs.

Useful organisations

Ortopedia Morelli *Via Costantinopoli 28/29, Toledo (081 444 281).* **Open** 9am-1.30pm, 4-6.30pm Mon-Fri. **No credit cards.** Wheelchair rental for €3.50 (plus VAT) a day. Book ahead.
SuperAbile *800 810 810/www. superabile.it.* **Open** *Phone enquiries* 9am-7pm Mon-Fri; 9am-1pm Sat. Italy-wide information on hotels, restaurants and job opportunities for people with disabilities.
Turismo Accessibile *www.turismoaccessibile.it.* Information on disabled access in hotels, restaurants, museums and more, in and around Naples.

DRUGS

If you are caught in possession of illegal drugs, you will be taken before a magistrate. If you convince the judge they were for personal use, you may be let off with a fine or ordered to leave the country. Anything more than a tiny amount pushes you into the criminal category; couriering or dealing can land you in prison for up to 20 years.

Sniffer dogs are a fixture at most ports of entry into Italy; customs police will take a dim view of visitors entering with even the smallest quantities of narcotics.

ELECTRICITY

Most wiring systems work on 220V. Two-pin adapter plugs are sold at electrical shops or airports.

EMBASSIES & CONSULATES

Many countries have embassies in Rome, but Naples' consulates can provide emergency help. For a full list, check the phone book under *Ambasciati/consolati*.

Canada *Via G Carducci 29, Chiaia (081 401338/after 1pm 081 407825). Metro Piazza Amedeo/bus C24, C25, C27, C28.* **Open** 9am-1pm Mon-Fri. **Map** p327 G13.
UK *Via dei Mille 40, Chiaia (081 423 8911/emergencies 335 710897/www.britain.it). Metro Piazza Amedeo/bus C24, C25, C27, C28.* **Open** 9am-12.30pm, 2-4pm Mon-Fri. **Map** p327 G12.
USA *Piazza della Repubblica, Mergellina (081 583 8111/ www.usembassy.it). Metro Mergellina/bus 140, C12, C18, C19, C24, R3.* **Open** 8am-1pm, 2-5pm Mon-Fri. **Map** p326 D14.

EMERGENCIES

See also **Accident & emergency** (*right*) and **Police** (*see p310*).

Ambulance 118
Carabinieri (national/military police) 112
Car breakdown (Automobile Club d'Italia) 803 116
Fire brigade 115
Polizia di Stato (national police) 113

GAY & LESBIAN

Visiting gays are unlikely to meet hostility from anyone but members of the unpleasant conservative fringe that exists everywhere.

Arcigay Napoli *Vico San Geronimo alle Monache 19, Centro Storico (081 552 8815/www. arcigaynapoli.org). Bus C25, R1.* **Open** 5-11pm Fri, 6.30-9.30pm Sun. Closed Aug.
Information, advice and events for the gay, lesbian, bi, transgender and transexual communities.

HEALTH

All emergencies will be treated free in the *pronto soccorso* (emergency) departments of public hospitals; *see below*.

EU nationals are entitled to medical care if they have a **European Health Insurance Card (EHIC)**. British travellers can apply online at www.dh.gov.uk. Using an EHIC, however, condemns you to dealing with the intricacies of the Italian health bureaucracy; for short-term visitors, it's generally better to take out health cover under private travel insurance.

Non-EU citizens do not qualify for free healthcare, and should take out private medical insurance before leaving home. The British

and US consulates have lists of English-speaking doctors. For women's health, *see below*.

The tap water in Naples and most nearby resorts is safe to drink. In a country area, ask locals whether or not to stick to bottled water.

Accident & emergency

The following Naples hospitals provide 24hr emergency (*pronto soccorso*) services. Details of emergency treatment outside Naples are under Resources in the Around Naples chapters.

Cardarelli *Via Cardarelli 9, Vomero Alto (081 747 1111). Metro Colli Aminei/bus C38, C39, C40, C41, C43, C44, C76, OF, R4.*
Santobono *Via M Fiore 6, Vomero (081 220 5111). Metro Medaglie d'Oro/bus 181, C34, C39, C41, C44, R1.* **Map** p330 E8.

Contraception & abortion

Condoms are sold in supermarkets or over the counter at chemists. The contraceptive pill is available at pharmacies, although a doctor's prescription is required.

Abortion is legal if performed in public hospitals; health or financial hardship criteria must be proven.

Each district has a *Consultorio familiare* (family-planning clinic), which EU citizens with an EHIC (*see left*) are entitled to use. Ask in any chemist's for the nearest.

AIED *Via Cimarosa 186, Vomero (081 578 2142/www.consultorio napoli.it). Funicular Montesanto to Via Morghen, Centrale to piazzetta Fuga or Chiaia to Via Cimarosa/ bus C28, C31, C32, C36, E4, V1.* **Open** 9.30am-12.30pm, 3.30-7pm Mon-Fri; 9.30am-12.30pm Sat. Closed 2wks Aug. **Map** p330 E10. Check-ups, contraception advice and smear tests at a private clinic.

Dentists

In the case of dental emergencies, make for the hospital casualty departments (*see above*). For non-emergency treatment, try these English-speaking dentists.

Dott Francesco Olivieri *Via Carducci 6, Chiaia (081 245 7003).*
Dott Massimo Palmieri *Via Giulio Palermo 80 (081 1935 3550).*

Opticians

See p149.

Pharmacies

Any *farmacia*, marked by a red or green cross, will give informal advice for simple ailments and can make up prescriptions.

Standard opening hours are 8.30am-1pm, 4-8pm Mon-Fri and 8.30am-1pm Sat. Every pharmacy should have a list by the door indicating the nearest pharmacies open outside normal business hours. Some levy a small surcharge when the main shop is shut and only the late-night counter is open.

For pharmacy listings, see p151.

STDs, HIV & AIDS

AIDS Helpline *800 019 254.*
Open 1-6pm Mon-Fri. Information in Italian on tests and prevention.

HELPLINES

Alcoholics Anonymous *347 544 0254/www.naplesaa.8k.com.*
An English-speaking support group meets at the Anglican/Episcopal Christ Church (*see p311*).
Linea Verde Droga e Alcol *800 278 33.* 24-hour drugs helpline. Italian only.

ID

Under Italian law, you are required to carry photo ID at all times. In reality, you will rarely be asked to show it, except when cashing traveller's cheques or checking into a hotel. Some hotels ask to keep your passport until you check out; you are entitled to ask for your ID back at any time, and should do so if that is your only photo ID.

INSURANCE

Travel insurance is always a good idea. If you rent a car, motorcycle or moped, be sure to pay the extra charge for full insurance cover and sign the collision damage waiver. For health insurance, *see left.*

INTERNET

Most hotels offer internet connection, and there are plenty of internet cafés in Naples. Even small towns in the provinces or on the islands will have an internet café or, at worst, a bar with a cranky computer. Check the Resources at the end of each area chapter, or ask in any computer store (listed in the Yellow Pages, under '*Personal computers e informatica*') for the nearest. Naples options include:

Clic Net *Via Toledo 393, Toledo (081 552 9370/www.clicnet.it).* Metro Montesanto/bus CS, E2, R1, R4. **Open** 9.30am-9.30pm Mon-Sat. **Rates** €2/hr. **No credit cards.** **Map** p328 K9.
Dre@mer-club *Via F de Sanctis 16, Centro Storico (081 420 3277).* Metro Dante/bus 24, CS, E1, R1, R4. **Open** 10am-8pm Mon-Fri. **Rates** €1.30/hr. **No credit cards.** **Map** p328 M8.
Internet Bar *Piazza Bellini, Centro Storico (081 295237/www.internet barnapoli.it).* Metro Dante or Museo/ bus 24, C57, CS, E1, R1. **Open** 9.30am-2am Mon-Sat; 5pm-2am Sun. **Rates** €3/hr. **No credit cards.** **Map** p328 L8.

LEFT LUGGAGE

At Naples' airport, the luggage storage office (081 789 6366) is just outside Arrivals. Open 24hrs, it charges a daily rate of €6 per bag.

The luggage storage office at Naples' **Stazione Centrale** (081 567 2181) is open 8am-8pm daily for drop-offs; bags can be collected 7am-11pm. It costs €4 per item for the first 5hrs, then 60¢ per hour. There is no left luggage at Campi Flegrei or Mergellina stations.

In **Capri**, the luggage storage office (081 837 4575) is operated by Caremar ferries at the port in **Marina Grande**. It's open 9am-6pm daily in summer, 9am-5pm in winter, and costs €3 per item.

In **Sorrento**, the tourist office (*see p251*) may watch your bag during opening hours.

LEGAL HELP

For legal advice, first go to your embassy or consulate (*see left*).

LIBRARIES

Biblioteca Nazionale *Palazzo Reale, Piazza del Plebiscito, Royal Naples (081 781 9231/081 781 9387/www.bnnonline.it).* Bus 140, C22, C25, E3, R2, R3. **Open** Sept-July 8.30am-7.30pm Mon-Fri; 8.30am-1.30pm Sat. Aug 8.30am-1.30pm Mon-Sat. **Map** p332 K13.
Collections include the Officina dei Papiri Ercolanesi, with its ancient papyruses, and the JFK American section, a lending library containing mostly American literature.
Biblioteca San Francesco *Via San Francesco 13, Ravello (089 857 727).* **Open** 9am-1pm, 4-6pm Mon, Wed, Fri. Closed Aug.
A vast, eclectic collection of books in many languages.

Istituto Universitario Orientale *Palazzo Giusso, largo San Giovanni Maggiore, Port & University (081 690 9422/www.iuo.it).* Bus CS, E1, R1, R2, R4. **Open** 8.30am-4pm Mon-Thur; 8.30am-2pm Fri.
Closed 3wks Aug. **Map** p328 L9.
A decent English-language section focuses on North American literature; you'll also find books on and in Chinese, Japanese, Arabic, Finnish and other languages.

LOST PROPERTY

If you lose anything valuable, go immediately to the nearest police station (*see p310*) to make a '*denuncia*' (statement).

If you leave anything on city buses or the metro in Naples, go to the *capolinea* (terminus) of the route and ask there. Failing that, phone the helpline (800 639 525 from Naples, 081 763 2177 from outside Italy, 7am-8pm Mon-Sat).

For items left on SITA buses, call 089 405 145 or 089 386 6711, or see www.sitabus.it. The lost property office at Capodichino Airport is open 7am-8.25pm Mon-Sat (until 1.20pm in Aug; 081 789 6237, 081 789 6765).

MEDIA

Magazines

With naked women often on the covers, Italy's 'news' magazines are not always distinguishable from soft porn at newsstands. Despite appearances, *Panorama* and *Espresso* provide a good round-up of the news. For tabloid scandal, try *Gente, Oggi* or the execrable *Novella 2000* and *Cronaca Vera*.

Newspapers

Italy's newspapers are unsnobbish, blending serious news with well-written, often surreal, crime and human-interest pieces, but stories tend to be long and indigestible. Sports coverage in the dailies is extensive; if you're not sated, try sports rags *Corriere dello Sport, La Gazzetta dello Sport* or *Tuttosport*.

Foreign newspapers and mags are available from newsstands, usually the day after publication. You'll find British broadsheets, tabloids and magazines, as well as the *International Herald Tribune*, which includes the four-page 'Italy Daily', at kiosks in the Stazione Centrale, in Piazza Municipio facing the port, and in Via Calabritto off Piazza dei Martiri.

DIRECTORY

DIRECTORY

Corriere della Sera *www.corriere.it*
To the centre of centre-left, this solid, serious but often dull Milan-based daily is good on crime and foreign news. Its Neapolitan insert, 'Corriere del Mezzogiorno', has good local entertainment listings.

Il Mattino *www.ilmattino.it*
Naples' major daily, *Il Mattino* sits firmly on the political fence. National news is thoroughly covered, but there's only superficial coverage of international affairs.

La Repubblica *www.repubblica.it*
This centre-ish, left-ish paper is good on the Mafia and the Vatican, and comes up with the odd major scoop on its business pages. It has a fairly exhaustive Naples section.

Television

Italy has six major networks – three owned by the state broadcaster **RAI** (RAI 1, RAI 2, RAI 3) and three belonging to Prime Minister Silvio Berlusconi (Rete 4, Canale 5, Italia 1). All are uniformly dreadful.

Radio

There are three state-owned stations: **RAI-1** (89.3 and 94.1 FM stereo and 1332 AM), **RAI-2** (91.3 and 96.1 FM stereo and 846 AM) and **RAI-3** (93.3 and 98.1 FM). They play classical and light music.

AFN *www.afneurope.army.mil*
If southern Italy gets too much, the American Forces Network will shoot you to Smalltown, USA. 106.0 FM (Z-FM) has locally produced programmes and news, and music ranging from pop to country. On 107.0 FM (Power Network) there are talk shows and NPR news bulletins.

Radio Capital *www.capital.it*
88.05 and 104.75 FM. Classics and hits from the UK and US, with lots of home-grown goodies thrown in.

Radio Kiss Kiss Napoli
www.kisskissnapoli.it
99.25 and 103.0 FM. Hits from Italy and abroad, and live broadcasts of Naples' football games.

MONEY

The Euro is legal tender in Italy. By law, you must be given a receipt (*scontrino fiscale*) for any transaction. Even if places try to avoid giving you a receipt for tax reasons, it's your right to ask for one.

Banks & ATMs

Most banks are open 8.20am-1.20pm, 2.45-3.45pm Mon-Fri.

Banks are closed on public holidays, and usually close around noon the day before a holiday.

Most banks have cash machines (*bancomat*) that allow you to withdraw money with major cards. In more out-of-the-way places, ATMs may be switched off at night and at weekends. Always be alert when withdrawing money.

Bureaux de change

Exchange offices (*cambio*) are plentiful at the airport, around Stazione Centrale, on the port side of Piazza Municipio, and near major tourist sites. Rates are not usually as good as at the banks, but *cambio* are conveniently located and open later. When changing money, bring a passport or other ID. Rates vary, and you can pay as much as €10 for each transaction. Beware of places with 'no commission' signs: the rate of exchange may be terrible.

Many banks will give cash advances against a credit card, though they may refuse to do so if you don't have a PIN.

Main post offices also have exchange desks. Commission is €2.58 plus 1.5% for cash transactions up to €1,032.91; traveller's cheques are not changed.

San Paolo/Banco di Napoli *Via Toledo 177/178, Toledo (081 792 4567). Bus CS, E2, R1, R4.* **Open** 8.30am-1.25pm, 2.40-4pm Mon-Fri. **Map** p332 K11.

Travelex *Departures 081 780 1825/Arrivals 081 780 9107.* **Open** *Departures* 5.30am-10pm daily. *Arrivals* 8am-11.30pm daily. Travelex charges €9.30 for up to €64, with commission rising with the size of the transaction. Money can be transferred here from any Travelex branch in the world.

Western Union *c/o Espresso Service, Piazza Garibaldi 69, Port & University (081 207 597). Metro Piazza Garibaldi/bus 14, 191, 192, 194, 195, C30, C40, C58, CS, OF, R2/tram 1.* **Open** 9am-7.30pm Mon-Fri; 9am-5pm Sat. Closed 2wks Aug. **Map** p329 P7. Money sent here should arrive within the hour. The sender pays commission.

Lost/stolen credit cards

Phone one of the 24-hour emergency numbers listed below.

American Express *800 864 046.*
Diners Club *800 393 939.*
Mastercard *800 870 866.*
Visa *800 819 014.*

Tax

Sales tax (IVA) in Italy is a flat 20% and is automatically included in the listed price of everything, in hotels, shops and restaurants.

OPENING HOURS

Most shops keep hours of roughly 8.30am-1pm and 4-7pm or 8pm Mon-Sat. Many close on Saturday afternoon and Monday morning. Office hours are usually similar, but only Mon-Fri. Bars generally open from early morning until around midnight, and also open on Sunday for part of the day. *See above* for the more limited hours of banks, and *see below* for post offices.

POLICE

See also p308 **Emergencies**.

Questura Centrale *Via Medina 75 (081 794 1111/emergency 113). Bus R1, R2, R3, R4.* **Map** p332 L11.

POSTAL SERVICES

Most post-boxes are red and have two slots marked '*per la città*' (for the city) and '*tutte le altre destinazioni*' (everywhere else). Some have a blue sticker on the front for *posta prioritaria* (first class) and should be used only for that.

First-class service promises delivery in 24hrs within Italy, three days for EU countries and longer for anywhere else in the world. Use *posta prioritaria* stamps for letters sent outside Italy. A letter of 20g or less to Italy or any EU country is 60¢, or 80¢ to the US.

The costlier *Postacelere* promises two- to three-day delivery abroad, and allows you to track online the progress of your letter or parcel.

Registered mail ('*raccomandata*') starts at €2.80. It may assure delivery, but is no guarantee of speed. Private couriers (*see p307*) are quicker, but more expensive.

Post office *Palazzo Centrale della Posta, Via Monteoliveto, Toledo (081 428 9685/081 542 3110/ www.poste.it). Bus 24, C57, E2, E3, R1, R3, R4.* **Open** *Sept-July* 8am-6.30pm Mon-Fri; 8am-1.30pm Sat. *Aug* 8am-1.30pm Mon-Fri; 8am-12.30pm Sat. **Map** p328 L10.

RELIGION

You can hear the Catholic Mass in English at the church of **Gesù Nuovo** (*see p55*) on Sunday at 5pm.

Anglican/Episcopal *Christ Church, Via San Pasquale a Chiaia 15, Chiaia (081 411 842). Metro Piazza Amedeo/bus 140, C12, C18, C19, C24, C25, C27, C28, R3.* **Services** 10am Sun. **Map** p327 F13. A hub for the English-speaking community.

Baptist *Chiesa Battista, Via Foria 93, Sanità (081 578 4037/081 751 8294). Metro Piazza Cavour/bus 12, 47, 182, C51, C52.* **Services** 7pm Thur, 11am Sun. **Map** p328 N6. There's a bilingual Italian-English service on Sundays.

Jewish *Comunità Ebraica, Via Santa Maria a Cappella Vecchia 31, Chiaia (081 764 3480). Metro Piazza Amedeo/bus 140, C12, C18, C19, C22, C24, C25, C27, C28, R3/tram 1, 4.* **Services** 9.30am Sat. Closed 3wks Aug. **Map** p327 H13.

SAFETY & SECURITY

Street crime is common in Naples. Pickpockets and bag-snatchers on foot and on scooters are active in main tourist areas and the surrounding region. Be especially attentive when boarding buses and boats, and when entering museums. If you're a victim of any crime, go to the nearest police station to make a *'denuncia'* (written statement). *See also p309* **Lost property**.

Always take precautions. Look as if you know what you're doing and where you're going, and don't carry a wallet in your back pocket. Keep some small bills and change to hand rather than pulling out a large wad of cash to pay for something.

If you stop at a pavement café or restaurant, don't leave bags or coats on the ground or draped across a chair. Wear bags and cameras across your chest or on the side away from the street so you're less likely to fall prey to a motorbike-borne thief (*scippatore*). Don't wear expensive jewellery or watches.

Finally, only take registered, marked taxis.

SMOKING

Smoking is theoretically banned in public offices, bars, restaurants, on public transport or in taxis. For the most part, the law is ignored; still, times are changing and smokers may put out their cigarettes if you diplomatically point out the *vietato fumare* (no smoking) sign.

Tabacchi

Tabacchi or *tabaccherie*, identified by signs with a white T on a black or blue background, are the only places where you can legally buy tobacco products. Most *tabacchi* keep shop hours, but those attached to bars are open later. Many have cigarette machines outside for when the shop is closed (9pm-7am).

STUDY

Naples' universities are the **Università Federico II** (www.unina.it), founded in 1224; the modern **Seconda Università di Napoli** (www.unina2.it); and the **Istituto Universitario Orientale** (www. iuo.it).

Language classes

Centro Italiano *Vico Santa Maria dell'Aiuto 17, Centro Storico (081 552 4331/www.centroitaliano.it). Bus 24, C57, CS, E1, E2, E3, R1, R3, R4.* **Open** 9am-4.30pm Mon-Fri. **Map** p328 L10.

TELEPHONES

Dialling & codes

To make an international call from Italy, dial 00 (or '+' from a mobile phone), then the country code, then the area code (for calls to the UK or Ireland, omit the initial zero) and then the individual number.

To call Naples from abroad, dial your country's international access code (or '+' from a mobile phone), then 39 for Italy and 081 for Naples, followed by the individual number.

All Italian phone numbers must be dialled with their area codes, even if you're phoning from within the area. All numbers in Naples and its province begin 081; this includes Pozzuoli, Ischia, Capri, Sorrento and Pompeii. It doesn't include Positano and Amalfi, which are in the Salerno province, area code 089. Numbers in Caserta begin 0823, and Benevento 0824.

Naples phone numbers usually have seven digits; older numbers may have six digits. If you have difficulties, check the directory (*elenco telefonico*) or ring directory enquiries (12; keep silent through the recorded message and you'll eventually get a human being).

All numbers beginning with 800 are toll-free lines. For numbers starting 840 you'll be charged one unit only (just under 7¢ from a private Telecom phone); 848 numbers are the same cost as a local call. Mobile numbers begin with 3. Regardless of where you're calling from, 199 numbers cost two units a minute. These numbers can only be called from within Italy; some only function within one phone district.

Mobile phones

Owners of GSM phones can use them on 900, 1800 and 1900 bands, but reception can be patchy in some areas of Naples and in hill towns. Visit **Centro Tim** (Via Pessina 24, 081 549 8844) for assistance.

Operator services

To make a reverse-charge (collect) call, dial 170 for the international operator. If you're calling from a phone box, you'll need to insert a coin or card, which will be refunded after your call.

Italian directory enquiries *1254.*
International operator *170.*
Telegrams *186.*
Customer care *187.*

Public phones

Most public phones only accept phonecards (*schede telefoniche*); a few also accept credit cards. The minimum charge for a call is 10¢. Phonecards are sold from *tabacchi* (*see left*), newsstands and bars; break off the perforated corner before using the card. Cards can be used on any phone, public or private: dial the number on the card, then punch in the card's PIN. Cards have expiry dates, after which, no matter how much credit you have, they won't work.

TIME

Italy is 1hr ahead of GMT, 6hrs ahead of New York, and 9hrs behind Sydney. The clocks are moved forward 1hr in spring (*ora legale*) and back 1hr (*ora solare*) in autumn.

TIPPING

In Italy, tipping is discretionary, and you are justified in leaving nothing for service that merited nothing. However, a tip – rarely more than 12% – is appreciated everywhere (and expected in more sophisticated eateries). Most locals leave 10¢ or 20¢ on the counter when buying a coffee or a drink at a bar. The price will be much higher if you sit down at a café table and have the same thing – and your tip should be proportionately higher. It's better to tip in cash than by card.

DIRECTORY

DIRECTORY

Restaurants may add a service charge of 10%-15% to your bill. Don't feel obliged to leave anything over this.

Rounding your fare up to the nearest euro will make taxi drivers happy. In resorts, where maids and waiters work seasonally, tips are especially welcome.

TOILETS

There are few public toilets in the city or in the surrounding area, and those you do come across are likely to be closed. The simplest solution is to go to a bar, fast-food joint or department store. There are modern lavatories at or near most of the major tourist sites; the majority have attendants, who may demand a nominal fee.

TOURIST INFORMATION

Tourist information details are also included in the individual chapters of the Around Naples section.

Ente Provinciale del Turismo (EPT) *Piazza dei Martiri 58, Chiaia (081 410 7211/www.eptnapoli. info). Bus 140, C12, C18, C19, C24, C25, C28, R3.* **Open** 9am-2pm Mon-Fri. **Map** p327 H13.
Other locations Stazione Centrale (081 268 779).
Azienda Autonoma di Soggiorno Cura e Turismo di Napoli *Via San Carlo 9, Royal Naples (081 402394/ www.inaples.it). Bus 24, C25, C82, E3, R2, R3.* **Open** 9am-2pm daily. **Map** p332 K12.
Other locations Piazza Gesù Nuovo, Centro Storico (081 552 3328/081 551 2701); Via Marino Turchi 16, Royal Naples (081 240 0911).
Osservatorio Turistico-Culturale *Piazza del Plebiscito, Royal Naples (081 247 1123/www.comune napoli.it). Bus 140, C22, C24, C25, E3, R2, R3.* **Open** 9am-7pm Mon-Fri; 9am-2pm Sat. **Map** p332 K13.

VISAS

Citizens of Australia, Canada, the European Union, New Zealand and the United States do not need visas for stays of up to three months. After that, they must apply for a *permesso di soggiorno (see right).*

WEIGHTS & MEASURE

The decimal system is universally used. Should you buy produce at a market, 100 grams is called *un etto,* roughly equivalent to 1/4 pound.

WHEN TO GO

Climate

Naples sizzles in July and August, and humidity levels can be high. On the islands and coast, sea breezes make the heat more bearable.

Spring and autumn are usually warm and pleasant but with some heavy showers, particularly in March, April and September. March and October can be wonderful times to visit the islands: they're very quiet but you still stand a decent chance of catching some warmth.

From November to February, it's usually crisp with some sun, but with long spells of dreary weather. In winter, there's a dusting of snow on Mount Vesuvius.

Public holidays

On public holidays (*giorni festivi*), public offices, banks and post offices are closed, as are most shops. Naples shuts down entirely on **19 September,** feast of the city's patron saint, San Gennaro.

August is holiday month, and there are interminable queues on roads to resorts. Many businesses, shops and restaurants close.

1 Jan New Year's Day (Capodanno)
6 Jan Epiphany (La Befana)
Easter Monday (Pasquetta)
25 Apr Liberation Day (Festa della Liberazione)
1 May Labour Day (Festa del Lavoro)
2 June Republic Day
15 Aug Feast of the Assumption (Ferragosto)
1 Nov All Saints' Day (Tuttisanti)
8 Dec Feast of the Immaculate Conception (L'Immacolata)
25 Dec Christmas Day (Natale)
26 Dec Boxing Day (Santo Stefano)

WOMEN

The *maschilista* (macho) southern Italian male can be daunting for the female traveller, but he is, as a rule, more bark than bite. Common sense will get you out of most scenarios.

Avoid lodging or lingering in the area around Stazione Centrale/ Piazza Garibaldi; it's bad enough in the day but really horrible at night. On the other hand, you're quite safe in the Centro Storico. The best lodging choice for safety would be around Royal Naples and Chiaia.

At tourist sights, there's a good chance that would-be Romeos will approach women without male companions. Perfect the art of saying 'no'. A joking tone will be much more effective than reacting in an aggressive or upset fashion.

See p308 **Contraception & abortion.**

WORKING

Working in and around Naples can be difficult in practical terms. You need to obtain various documents, including a *codice fiscale* (tax code) and a *permesso di lavoro* (work permit); non-EU citizens coming to Italy to take up a prearranged job should apply for a working visa from the Italian consulate before arriving.

Visitors should theoretically get a *permesso di soggiorno* (permit to stay) after eight working days in Italy; few do. If you plan to move here without working, you must prove to the police that you can support yourself (or are in full-time education) to get a *permesso di soggiorno. A certificato di residenza* (residence certificate) is needed if you want to buy a car or import your belongings without paying customs duties.

Further Reference

BOOKS

The Ancients

Allan Massie
Augustus, Tiberius, Caesar
Popular rewrites of history.
Suetonius *De Vita Caesarum*
(*Lives of the Caesars*)
Ancient muck-raking by a highly
biased Roman historian.
Virgil *Georgics*
Written during his stay in Naples.

Art & history

Harold Acton
The Bourbons of Naples
A lively historical romp that
focuses on the reign of Ferdinando I.
Bruce Cutler *Seeing the
Darkness: Naples, 1943-1945*
The city during World War II.
Electa Guides *Naples*
An architectural guide.
Paul Ginsborg
A History of Contemporary Italy
Fine introduction to postwar Italy.
Michael Grant
*Eros in Pompeii: The Erotic Art
Collection of the Museum of Naples*
An exploration of erotic imagery in
ancient Pompeii.
Jordan Lancaster
In the Shadow of Vesuvius
A cultural history of Naples.
**Mary Lefkovich &
Maureen Fant**
Women's Life in Greece and Rome
Riveting stuff: topics range from
ancient gynaecology to choosing
a wet nurse.
Donatella Mazzoleni
Palaces of Naples
Some 30 estates and palaces.
Frank J Palescandolo (transl)
The Naples of Salvatore di Giacomo
Work by the Neapolitan poet.
Roberto Saviano *Gomorrah*
A powerful first-hand account of
the Camorra and its activities.

Cuisine

Carla Capalbo *The Food and
Wine Guide to Naples and Campania*
An information-packed foodie tome.
Arthur Schwartz *Naples at
Table: Cooking in Campania*
A gastronomic trip to Campania.
Pamela Sheldon Johns
Pizza Napoletana!
A history of pizza, with recipes.

Fiction

Norman Douglas *South Wind*
A celebration of Bacchic goings-on.
Robert Harris *Pompeii*
The cataclysmic events of 79 AD.
Susan Sontag *The Volcano Lover*
A postmodern bodice-ripper that
centres on the Nelson-Hamilton trio.

Travel & biography

Giacomo Casanova di Seingalt
The Story of My Life
The libertine's autobiography
includes 18th-century Naples.
Johann Wolfgang von Goethe
Italian Journey
The poet's 18th-century travel diary.
Shirley Hazzard *Greene on Capri*
Memoirs of a postwar Capri
resident's meetings with the writer.
Dan Hofstadter *Falling Palace:
A Romance of Naples*
An artfully constructed memoir
about the author's love of the city.
Norman Lewis *Naples '44*
Experiences of an intelligence
officer in wartime Naples.
Axel Munthe
The Story of San Michele
The Swedish doctor's life, times and
love affair with Anacapri.
Susana Walton
Behind the Façade
Bloomsbury moves to Ischia.

FILMS

Il Decameron
dir Pier Paolo Pasolini (1970)
Features Neapolitan locations
and dialects.
Fellini Satyricon
dir Federico Fellini (1969)
The maestro's take on the ancient
picaresque fragment by Petronius.
Gomorrah
dir Matteo Garrone (2008)
Film version of Roberto Saviano's
book (*see left*).
Napoli d'altri tempi
dir Amleto Palermi (1938)
Composer renounces fame and
fortune for anonymity in Naples.
Le Mani sulla Città
dir Francesco Rosi (1963)
Political corruption drama that
captures the essence of Naples.
L'Oro di Napoli
dir Vittorio de Sica (1954)
Tales of Neapolitan life, starring
Sophia Loren and Totò.

Polvere di Napoli
dir Antonio Capuano (1998)
Update of *L'Oro di Napoli*.
Il Postino
dir Michael Radford (1994)
Oscar-winning drama.
Le Quattro giornate di Napoli
dir Nanni Loy (1962)
Oscar-nominated war drama.
**Totò, Peppino e la...
malafemmina**
dir Camillo Mastrocinque (1956)
Three brothers and a naughty girl.
Souls of Naples
dir Vincent Monnikendam (2005)
Documentary: Naples, in splendour
and adversity.
Viaggio in Italia
dir Roberto Rossellini (1954)
A couple's relationship, set against
the backdrops of Naples and Capri.

MUSIC

Edoardo Bennato
Non farti cadere le braccia
Still producing hits after 30 years.
Eugenio Bennato *Taranta Power*
Southern Italian folk songs.
Pino Daniele *Terra Mia*
Melodic blues.
**Nuova Compagnia di Canto
Popolare** *Lo guarracino*
Folk outfit.
Luciano Pavarotti
Favourite Neapolitan Songs
All the classics.
Daniele Sepe *Spiritus Mundi*
Eclectic saxophonist.
Spaccanapoli *Lost Souls*
A modern take on *tarantella*.

WEBSITES

Culture, museums & events

www.campaniartecard.it
All about the Aretcard; *see p194*.
www.comune.napoli.it
The Naples City Council's site.
www.culturacampania.rai.it
www.eptnapoli.info
The tourist board's excellent site.
www.icampiflegrei.it
www.museoapertonapoli.com
www.napolisworld.it

Listings

http://napolinews.too.it
www.napoli.com
www.nottambulando.it
www.touchnapoli.com

Vocabulary

Although hotel and restaurant staff in resorts around Naples will have some grasp of English, don't expect anyone in shops or bars to manage any more than prices in anything but Italian. In Naples itself, foreign-language speakers are even thinner on the ground. The exception to this rule is Sorrento, which is practically a British colony.

ITALIAN & NEAPOLITAN

Italian is spelled as it is pronounced, and vice versa. Grammar books will tell you that the stress falls on the penultimate syllable, but this is not a fail-safe rule.

Pronunciation

Vowels
a – as in *ask*
e – like *a* in *a*ge (closed e) or *e* in s*e*ll (open e)
i – like *ea* in *ea*st
o – as in h*o*tel (closed o) or h*o*t (open o)
u – as in b*oo*t

Consonants
c and *g* both go soft in front of *e* and *i* (becoming like *ch* and *g* in *ch*eck and *g*iraffe respectively).
Before a vowel, *h* is silent. An *h* after *c* or *g* makes them hard, no matter what vowel follows.
Doubled consonants, like those in *cappuccino*, are emphasized by lingering on those syllables.
gl – like *lli* in mi*lli*on
gn – like *ny* in ca*ny*on
qu – as in *qu*ick
r – always rolled
s – either as in *s*oap or in ro*s*e
sc – like *sh* in *sh*ame
sch – like *sc* in *sc*out
z – can be *ds* or *tz*

Neapolitan

Neapolitan dialect is something more than an accent but less than a language, spoken habitually between Neapolitans of all ages and classes: even other Italians don't understand a word of it. Neapolitans tend to…

…leave off the ends of words: *buona ser'* (*buona sera*)
…replace some *e* sounds by *ie*: *tiemp'* (*tempo*, time/weather) or

apiert' (in Italian *aperto*, open).
…replace some words beginning *pi* by a very hard *ki* sound: *cchiù* (in Italian *più*, more).
…replace a hard *sc* (like *sk* in English) by a soft, English-style *sh*: *scusate* (excuse me) becomes a drunken-sounding *shcusate*.
…make *a* sounds longer than other Italians: *Napule'* (Neapolitan for Naples) is *Naapule'*.
… turn *v* into *b* and double consonants: *che volete?* (what do you want?) becomes *ca' bbulit'?*
… turn *d* into *r*: *domenica* (Sunday) becomes *rumenica*.

Other hints
Bene (well) becomes *buono* (good). Indefinite articles: *un/uno* (a/an, masculine) become *nu*; *una* (a/an, feminine) becomes *'na*: *nu ggelat'* (*un gelato*, an ice-cream). Definite articles: *il/lo* (the, masculine) become *'o*; *la* (the, feminine) becomes *'a*: *'o ggelat'* (*il gelato*, ice-cream).

ENGLISH/ITALIAN/ NEAPOLITAN

Basics

hello/goodbye (informal) ciao; *uè uè*
hello (informal) salve; *ttà ppost'?*
good morning buon giorno
good evening buona sera
good night buona notte
please per favore, per piacere
thank you grazie; *grazie assje*
you're welcome prego; *nun' fà nient'*
excuse me, sorry mi scusi (formal), scusa (informal)
I'm sorry mi dispiace; *nun l'aggia fatt' a ppost'*
I don't speak Italian (very well) non parlo (molto bene) l'italiano; *non parl' buon' l'italian'*
I don't/didn't understand non capisco/non ho capito; *n'aggio capit'*
how much is (it)? quanto costa?
open aperto; *apièrt'*
closed chiuso
where is? dov'è?; *a ro'sta?*

Transport

bus autobus
coach pullman
train treno
underground railway

metropolitana (metro)
platform binario
ticket/s biglietto/biglietti
a ticket for… un biglietto per…
one way sola andata
return andata e ritorno

Eat, shop, sleep

See also p112 **The menu**.
a reservation una prenotazione
I'd like to book a table for four at eight vorrei prenotare una tavola per quattro persone alle otto
breakfast/lunch/dinner colazione/pranzo/cena
the bill il conto
is service included? è compreso il servizio?
that was poor/good/(really) delicious era mediocre/buono/(davvero) ottimo
I think there's a mistake in this bill credo che il conto sia sbagliato
more/less ancora/di meno
shoe/clothes size numero/taglia
a single/twin/double room una camera singola/doppia/matrimoniale
a room with a (sea) view una camera con vista (sul mare)

Days & nights

Monday lunedì; *lunnerì*
Tuesday martedì; *mart'rì*
Wednesday mercoledì; *miercul'rì*
Thursday giovedì; *gioverì*
Friday venerdì; *viernerì*
Saturday sabato; *sabbat'*
Sunday domenica; *dumenec'* or *rumenica*
today oggi; *ogg'*
tomorrow domani; *diman'*
morning mattina; *matin'*
afternoon pomeriggio
evening sera; *ser'*
night notte; *nott'*
weekend fine settimana, weekend; *fine semman'*

Numbers
0 zero, 1 uno, 2 due, 3 tre, 4 quattro, 5 cinque, 6 sei, 7 sette, 8 otto, 9 nove, 10 dieci, 11 undici, 12 dodici, 13 tredici, 14 quattordici, 15 quindici, 16 sedici, 17 diciassette, 18 diciotto, 19 diciannove, 20 venti, 30 trenta, 40 quaranta, 50 cinquanta, 60 sessanta, 70 settanta, 80 ottanta, 90 novanta, 100 cento, 200 duecento, 1,000 mille.

Glossary

Amphitheatre (ancient) oval open-air theatre
Apse large recess at the high-altar end of a church; adj apsidal
Atrium (ancient) courtyard
Baldacchino canopy supported by columns
Baptistry building – often eight-sided – outside church used for baptisms
Baroque artistic period from the 17th to 18th centuries, in which the decorative element became increasingly florid, culminating in Rococo (qv)
Barrel vault a ceiling with arches shaped like half-barrels
Basilica ancient Roman rectangular public building; rectangular Christian church
Bas-relief carving on a flat or curved surface where the figures stand out from the plane
Byzantine artistic and architectural style drawing on ancient models, developed in the fourth century in the Eastern empire and developed through the Middle Ages
Campanile bell tower
Capital the decorated head of a column (*see below* Orders)
Cardine (ancient) secondary street, usually running north–south
Caryatid supporting pillar carved in the shape of a woman
Castellated (building) decorated with battlements or turrets (*see also* Crenellations)
Cavea semicircular step-like seating area in an amphitheatre (qv) or theatre
Chapter room room in monastery where monks met for discussions
Chiaroscuro painting or drawing technique using no colours, but shades of black, white and grey
Choir area of church, usually behind the high altar, with stalls for people singing sung mass
Coffered (ceiling) with sunken square decorations
Colonnade row of columns supporting an entablature (qv) or arches
Confessio crypt (qv) beneath a raised altar
Crenellations battlements and/or archery holes on top of building or tower
Cupola dome-shaped roof/ceiling
Crypt vault beneath the main floor of a church

Cryptoporticus underground corridor
Decumanus (ancient) main road, usually running east–west
Domus (ancient) Roman city house
Embrasure a recess around the interior of a door or window; a hole in a wall for shooting through
Entablature section above a column or row of columns including the frieze and cornice
Ex-voto an offering given to fulfil a vow; often a small model in silver of the limb/organ/loved one to be cured as a result of prayer
Fresco painting technique in which pigment is applied to wet plaster
Gothic architectural and artistic style of the late Middle Ages using soaring, pointed arches
Greek cross (church) in the shape of a cross with arms of equal length
Hypogeum (ancient) underground room
Impluvium (ancient) cistern in the middle of a courtyard to gather rainwater, funnelled into it by a sloping roof with a hole in the middle
Insula (ancient) city block
Intarsio technique by which patterns or pictures are made in wooden surfaces by inlaying pieces of different-coloured wood
Latin cross (church) in the shape of a cross with one arm longer than the other
Loggia gallery open on one side
Mannerism High Renaissance style of the late 16th century; characterised in painting by elongated, contorted human figures
Marquetry wooden inlay work, also known as intarsio (qv)
Narthex enclosed porch in front of a church
Nave main body of a church; the longest section of a Latin-cross church (qv)
Necropolis (ancient) literally 'city of the dead'; graveyard
Nymphaeum (ancient) grotto with pool and fountain dedicated to the Nymphs, female water deities; name given to ornate fountains with grottos in Renaissance architecture
Ogival (of arches, windows and so on) curving in to a point at the top
Orders classical styles of decoration for columns, the most common being the very simple Doric, the curlicued Ionic and the leafy, frondy Corinthian

Palaestra (ancient) wrestling school
Palazzo large and/or important building (not necessarily a palace)
Parlatorio a convent or monastery's reception room or room for conversation
Pendentives four concave triangular sections on top of piers supporting a dome
Peristyle (ancient) temple or court surrounded by columns
Piazza (or largo) square
Pilaster square column, often with its rear side attached to a wall
Portal imposing door
Portico open space in front of a church or other building, with a roof resting on columns
Presbytery the part of a church containing the high altar
Proscenium (ancient) stage; arch dividing stage from audience
Reggia royal palace
Reliquary receptacle – often highly ornate – for holding and displaying relics of saints
Rococo highly decorative style fashionable in the 18th century
Romanesque architectural style of the early Middle Ages (c500-1200), drawing on Roman and Byzantine influences
Rustication large masonry blocks, often roughly cut, with deep joints, used to face buildings
Sacristy the room in church where vestments are stored
Sarcophagus (ancient) stone or marble coffin
Spandrel near-triangular space between the top of two adjoining arches and the ceiling or architectural feature resting above them
Stucco plaster
Succorpo similar to a crypt (qv), underground space beneath the apse (qv) of a church
Tablinium (ancient) private study
Tessera small piece of stone or glass used to make mosaic
Transept shorter arms of a Latin-cross church (qv)
Triclinium (ancient) dining room
Triumphal arch arch in front of an apse (qv), usually over the high altar
Trompe l'oeil decorative painting effect to make surface appear three-dimensional
Tufa volcanic stone widely used in building

DIRECTORY

Index

Note: page numbers
given in bold indicate
section(s) giving key
information on a topic;
those in italics indicate
photographs.

A

abortion 308
Abbazia di San Michele
   Arcangelo 229, **230**
Accademia delle Belle
   Arti 70
accident & emergency
   308
accommodation
   98-110
   by price: budget 102-
      106, 110; deluxe 99,
      106; expensive 99,
      101, 104-105, 108;
      moderate 99, 101,
      103-104, 106, 109,
      110
   see also p321
      *Accommodation
      index*
Acquario 53, **84**
Acquedotto Carmignano
   48, **50**
Acropolis 93
Acton, John 24, 26
addresses 307
Age of Enlightenment,
   the 24
age restrictions 307
airlines 304
airport 304
Albergo dei Poveri 24,
   43, 68, 72
Alfonso V (the
   Magnanimous) of
   Sicily, King 22
Amalfi 277, *279*
Amalfi Coast, The 194,
   264-291
Amelio, Lucio 163
Anacapri 208
Andràs of Hungary 21
Angelini, Tito 48, 52
Antiche Terme
   Comunali 216
Anfiteatro, Capua 300,
   302

Anfiteatro Flavio 89, **91**
Aniello, Tommaso
   (Masaniello) 23
Anjous, the 21-23
Antiquarium di
   Boscoreale 240
antiques 151
aperitivi 178
Appian Way, the 17
archaeological sites 9,
   239, 244, 295
architecture 41-46,
   234, 298
Archivio di Stato 65
Arco Felice 88
Arco di Trionfo 42
Arcos, Duke of 23
ARCOS Contemporary
   Art Museum 298
Area Archeologica di
   Santa Restituta 222
Arena Flegrea 96
art, classical 37
art deco 45
art galleries 163-167
art nouveau 45
Ascensione 83
Astroni 88-89
ATMs 310
Atrani 277, *282*
attitude & etiquette 307
Augustulus, Romulus 18
Augustus III 23
Avallone, Mario 123
Aversa 19

B

Bacoli 7, 88
Bagnoli 86
Baia 7, 42, 88, 91, **92**
banks 310
Barbarossa, Friedrich 21
baroque architecture 43
Barrà, Didier 82
bars 131
Basilio, Duke 18
Bassolino, Antonio 31,
   163
beaches 9, 87, 201, 218,
   227, 261, 284, 267
Bee, Betty 61
Bellini, Giovanni 78
Belvedere di San Leucio
   299

Benevento **297-298**
Benevento, Perinetto da
   38
Bentinck, Lord William
   26
Berlusconi, Silvio 34
Bernini, Pietro 82
Besozzo, Leonardo da 38
Bianchi, Pietro 45
Bianco and Valente 61
Biblioteca Nazionale 52
boat hire 211
boating 187
boats 304
Boccaccio 63
Bonaparte, Joseph 26
books 313
book shops 141
Borgo degli orefici 67
Bosco di Capodimonte
   159
Botticelli 78
Bourbons, the 24, 28
bowling 187
Brancaccio, Cardinal
   Rinaldo 56
Breughel 78
Bruno, Giordano 56
bureaux de change 310
buses 304
Byzantines, the 18

C

cabaret & musicals 181
**cafés, bars &
   gelaterie** 131-152
   art of coffee-drinking,
      the 134
   Neapolitan cakes &
      pastries 139
   types of coffee 137
   *see also p322
      Cafés, bars &
      gelaterie index*
Calata del Ponticello a
   Marechiaro 86, 87
Calata San Francesco 80
Calcio Napoli 185, 186
Caligula, Emperor 92
Camaino, Tino da 63
Camorra, the 16, 32-33,
   35, 66
Campania artecard 7,
   194

Campi Flegrei 7,
   88-93
   accommodation 110
   restaurants 130
Canova Antonio 48
canzone napoletana 170
Capo Miseno 88, *89*
Capodimonte 6, 76-78
   accommodation 105
   museum 78
Cappella Brancaccio
   (Sant'Angelo a Nilo) 56
Cappella Pontano 59
Cappella Sansevero 55
Capri 42, 194, **196-214**
Capua 17, 18, 19
Capua Vetere 42
car hire 306
Caracciolo Battista 60
Caracciolo Battistello 39
Caracciolo, Admiral
   Francesco 26, 52
Caracciolo Gianni 75
Caravaggio,
   Michelangelo Merisi
   da 36, 38, 58, 60, 63,
   77
   Flagellation, The 77,
   78
Carbonari 27
Carlos II (Carlo V) 23
Carlo III of the Kingdom
   of Sicily, King (Charles
   III of Spain) 24, 292
Carlo V (Carlos II of
   Spain) 23
Carlos, Don (son of
   Felipe V) 24
Carracci, Annibale 78
Caruso, Enrico 72
Casanova, Giacomo 84
Caserta 43, **298-301**
Castel Capuano 42, 58
Castel Nuovo 21, 42, 49,
   50, *50*, 53
Castel dell'Ovo 17, 42,
   48, **52**, 53
Castel Sant'Elmo 21, 79,
   81
Castellammare di Stabia
   42, **244**
Castello Aragonese 215,
   217, 218, **219**, *219*
Castello di Arechi 293,
   293

Castello Aselmeyer 45, 80
Castello di Baia 92
catacombs
Catacombe di San Gennaro 76
Catacombe di San Gaudioso 71, **72**
Catacombe di San Severo 71, **73**
Cattedrale dell'Assunta 217
Cavallini, Pietro 37, 56
Centro Direzionale 46, **95**
Centro Musei Scienze Naturali 65, 157
Centro Storico 6, 54-63
accommodation 101
DJ bars & clubs 173
cafés, bars 132
gay bars & clubs 168
gelaterie 133
pasticcerie 133
restaurants 116
walks 57
Ceramica Artistica Solimene 46
ceramics 148
Certosa-Museo di San Martino 40, 43, 79, **81**
Championnet, General 26
Charles I of Anjou 21
Charles III of Durres 22
Charles VIII, King of France 22
Chiaia beach, La (Procida) 230
Chiaia to Posillipo 7, 83-87
accommodation 108
cafés & bars 136
DJ bars & clubs 177
gays bars & clubs 168
gelaterie 138
nightlife 170
pasticcerie 139
restaurants 126
Chiaiolella 230
children's attractions 142, **157-159**
Pulcinella 158
churches 44
Cimitero delle Fontanelle 71, 73, **75**
Cimitero Monumentale 96
Cimitero Nuovo 96
cinemas 161

Città della Scienza 86, 159
classical music 182
cleaning & repairs 145
Clement VII, Pope 22
Clemente, Francesco 75
climate 312
Cocceio 93
coffee 131, 134, 137
Colantonio, Niccolò Antonio 38
conferences 307
Consalvo di Cordoba, General 22
Conservatorio di Musica 54, 59, 183
consulates 308
contraception 308
Convitto Nazionale 69
Cordoba, Consalvo di 22
Corenzio, Belisario 39
Correggio 78
Corricella 230, *231*
Corso Umberto 64
Croce, Benedetto 54
couriers 307
credit cards (lost/stolen) 310
crime 311
Croce de Lucca 59
Cuma 7, 42, 93
Cumana railway *92*
customs 307
cycling 306

D

dance 182, 184
Dante 60, 92
Decameron 63
decumani 42
decumanus inferior 54
decumanus maior 58
decumanus superior 63
dentists 308
department shops 141
Dikaiarchia 17
disabled travellers 307
diving 230
Domenichino 78
Donatello 55, 56
Dosio, Giovanni Antonio 82
Drengot, Rainulf 19
driving 306
drugs 308
Duomo 39, 42, 57, 58, **59**
Duomo (Cattedrale di San Matteo), Salerno 292, 293, *293*

E

Edenlandia 95, *96*, **157**
electricity 308
electronics & photography 142
embassies 308
emergencies 308
Ercolano 234
Eremo Santissimo 94
Etruscans, the 292, 233

F

Falcone, Giovanni 32
Fanzago, Carlo 86
Fanzago, Cosimo 56, 59, 81, 82
Farnese, Elisabetta 24
fashion 143
fashion accessories & services 145
Federico, uncle of Ferrandino 22
Felipe V 23, 24
Ferdinando I of Naples (Don Ferrante), King 22, 26
Ferdinando I of the Kingdom of the Two Sicilies, King 27
Ferdinando II (Ferrandino), King 22, 27, 28
Ferdinando III ('the Catholic'), King 22
Fermariello, Sergio 61
festivals
beyond Naples 195
film 154, 162
performing arts 184
music 154-156
theatre 154
Filangeri, Prince Gaetano 45
Filippo, Eduardo de 83
film 160-162
cinemas 161
festivals 154, 162
films about Naples 160, 313
Paolo Sorrentino profile 162
fine dining 11, 210, 272, 290
Fontana, Domenico 51
Fontana dell'Immacolatella 52
Fontana di Nettuno 49
food shops 147
football 96, 185, 186, 189

Forcella 65
Forio & the west coast of Ischia 223
foreign exchange 310
Francesco I 27, 28
Francesco II 28
Franks, the 18
French Revolution 26
Friedrich II, King 21
Funicolare Centrale 79
Funicolare di Chiaia 53, 79
Funicolare di Montesanto 79
funicular railways 79, 80, 214, 305
Funivia 244
Fuorigrotta 88, 163

G

Gaiola, La 86, 87
Galleria Umberto I 49, 53
Galleria della Vittorio 50
galleries 163-167
Memmo Grilli, art director 164
Gambrinus café 48, 132
gardens 201, 225, 288-289
Garibaldi, General Giuseppe 28
gay & lesbian 168-169
associations 169
bars & clubs 168
bookshops 169
cinemas 169
cruising 169
events & one-nighters 168
information 308
gelaterie 131
Gemito, Vincenzo 85
Gentileschi, Artemisia 40
Gerolomini 44
Gesù Nuovo 43, 54, **55**, *55*, 62, 70
Gesù Vecchio 65
Gigante, Giacinto 40
Giordano, Luca 38, 55, 58, 59, 60, 61, 81, 83
Giotto 37, 49, 50, 51, 63
Girolamini, Pinacoteca 60
Goethe 25
Goths, the 18
grand tour, the 25, 40, 80
Greeks, the 17, 233
Grifeo 45
Grotta di Cocceio 93
Grotta di Seiano 86, 87

INDEX

INDEX

Guarino, Francesco 85
Guglia dell'Immacolata
    54
Guglia di San Domenico
    54
Guglia di San Gennaro
    43, 58
Guido, Reni 78
Guiscard, Robert 19

H

Habsburgs, the 22, 23
hairdressers & barbers
    149
Hamilton, Lady Emma
    20, *20*
Hamilton, Sir William
    20, 26, 88
Hannibal 17
health 308
health & beauty shops
    149
helplines 309
Herculaneum 24, 25, 42,
    194, **234-244**, *237*
history 16-29
Hohenstaufen of Swabia,
    Heinrich 21
horseracing *see sport*
horseriding *see sport*
hotels *see
    accommodation*

I

ice-cream 131
ID 309
Innocent II, Pope 19
Innocent IV, Pope 21
insurance 309
internet 309
Ischia 194, 215-228
    Forio & the west coast
        223
    Ischia Ponte 216
    Ischia Porto 216, *217*
    Monte Epomeo & the
        south-west 225
    north coast 221
    Sant'Angelo &
        Maronti 227, *227*
    south, the 227
    spas 220, 226

J

Jacques de Bourbon 22
Jervolino, Rosa Russo
    31, 34
jewellery 145

Joan II, Queen 22, 75
John III, Duke 18
Jones, Thomas 40
Joanna of Spain 22
Juana I, Queen 21, 22
Justinian, Emperor 18

K

Kapoor, Anish 75
Karl, Archduke 23
Keats, John 84
Kosuth, Joseph 60
Kounellis, Jannis 60

L

Lacco Ameno 222
Ladislas, King 22
Lago di Averno 92
Lago Fusaro 93
Lago Lucrino 88
Lajos I, King 22
Lanfranco, Giovanni 81
language classes 311
Lauro, Achille Mayor 46
legal advice 309
Lewis, Norman 44
LeWitt, Sol 60
Liberation *27*, 28
Liberty City Fun 158
Liberty style 107
libraries 309
Lombards, the 18
Longobardi, Nino 61
lost property 309
Louis XIV, King 23
Louis XV 23
Lucullus, General 17
luggage storage 309
Lungomare 85

M

Mack, General Karl 26
MADRe *see* Museo
    d'Arte Contemporanea
    Donna Regina Napoli
mafia 32-33
magazines 309
Magic World 159
Maggio dei Monumenti
    50, 110
Malvito, Tommaso 67
Manfred, King 21
Mani sulla Città, Le 46
Mantegna, Andrea78
Manzoni, Pietro
Maradona, Diego 186
Maria Amelia of Saxony
    24

Marie Antoinette 26
Maria Carolina, Queen
    20, 24, 26, 27
Maria Cristina of Savoy
    27
Marina Grande (Procida)
    230
markets 141, 146, 147,
    151
Maria, Francesco de 63
Marie Antoinette 20, 26
Maronti 227
Masaniello (Tommaso
    Aniello) 23
Maschio Angioino *see*
    Castel Nuovo
Massa Lubrense 262
Materdei 60
Mausoleo 86
media 309
menu glossary 315
Mergellina 85
    nightlife 170
    station 85
Merz, Mario 61
metro 46, 60, 305
    art 60
Metro del Mare 93
Miglio d'Oro 45, 233,
    234
Milliscola 159
Miracoli, I 70
Mithraeum 302
mobile phones 310
modernism 46
Molo Beverello 67
money 310
Mont'Oliveto 44
Monte Echia 6, 51
Monte Epomeo 225
Monte Faito 244, *245*
Monte Nuovo 88
Monte di Pietà 55
Monumental May 50, 86
Mortella, La *224,* 225
Moscati, Giuseppe 56
Mostra d'Oltremare 45,
    96
Mura, Francesco de 60
Murat, Joachim 26
museums & galleries
    archaeological: Museo
        Archeologico dei
        Campi Flegrei 93;
        Museo Archeologico
        Nazionale 70; Museo
        Archeologico
        Nazionale, Paestum
        296; Museo
        Archeologico di
        Pithecusae 222;

Museo Archeologic
    Provinciale 293
art: Certosa-Museo di
    San Martino 81;
    Museo d'Arte
    Contemporanea
    Donna Regina
    Napoli 75; Museo di
    Capodimonte 78
ceramics: Museo
    Nazionale della
    Ceramica Duca di
    Martina 79, **82**
miscellaneous: Museo
    Civico Filangieri 55
porcelain: Reale
    Fabbrica delle
    Porcellane 76
railways: Museo
    Ferroviario di
    Pietrarsa 234
religious artefacts:
    Museo del Tesoro 59
Museo Antica Capua
    300, 302
Museo Archeologico dei
    Campi Flegrei 92, **93**
Museo Archeologico di
    Pithecusae 222
Museo Archeologico
    Nazionale 57, 63, **70**,
    70, *70*, 164, 243
Museo Archeologico
    Nazionale, Paestum
    295, 296
Museo Archeologic
    Provinciale 293
Museo d'Arte
    Contemporanea Donna
    Regina Napoli 46, 72,
    75, *75*, 163
Museo di Capodimonte
    76, **78**, 164
Museo Civico Filangieri
    55
Museo Ferroviario di
    Pietrarsa 234
Museo del Mare 217,
    218
Museo Narrante del
    Santuario di Hera
    Argiva 295, 296
Museo Nazionale della
    Ceramica Duca di
    Martina 79, **82**
Museo dell'Opera 61
Museo dell'Osservatorio
    247
Museo Provinciale
    Campano di Capua
    300, 302

Museo del Sannio 298
Museo della Scuola
  Medica Salernitana
  293
Museo del Tesoro 59
Museo station 60
music & nightlife
  170-178
  Alex Colle, DJ 171
  beach clubs 176
  classical 182
  clubs 171
  festivals 154-156, 172,
  184
  Neapolitan song 172,
  183
  Piedigrotta festival
  155
  shops 152

N

Napoli Sotterraneo 58,
  59, 159
Neapolis 17, 42, 54, 58,
  59
Nelson, Admiral Horatio
  20, 26, 84
newspapers 309
Nola, Giovanni da 63
Normans, the 19, 292
Notte Bianca 173
Nunziatella, La 52

O

Oderisio, Roberto di 37
Odoacer, King 18
office services 307
Ontani, Luigi 61
opening hours 309
opera 180, 181
operator services 311
Oplontis 194, **239**
opticians 149
Orto Botanico, Portici
  234
Orto Botanico, La Sanità
  26, 72, **74**, *74*, **75**
Osservatorio
  Astronomico 78
Otto IV of Brunswick 21

P

Paestum 42, 194,
  295-297
palazzi 41
Palazzo delle Arti Napoli
  (PAN) 46, 83, **84**, 163
Palazzo Calabritto 83

Palazzo Carafa di
  Roccella 46
Palazzo Carafa della
  Spina 54
Palazzo Casascalenda 54
Palazzo Cellamare 49
Palazzo Corigliano 54
Palazzo Cuomo 45
Palazzo Donn'Anna 86
Palazzo Filomarino 54
Palazzo Giusso 65
Palazzo Gravina 43
Palazzo Maddaloni 43
Palazzo Malcoviti 217
Palazzo Marigliano 55
Palazzo Partanna 83
Palazzo Penne 64
Palazzo Pignatelli di
  Monteleone 54
Palazzo delle Poste e
  Telegrafi 45, 68
Palazzo Reale 43, 48, 49,
  51, 53, 78
Palazzo Regina
  Margherita 83
Palazzo San Giacomo 49
Palazzo Sanfelice 45, 71
Palazzo Sangro 54
Palazzo Serra di Cassano
  45, **52**
Palazzo dello Spagnuolo
  45, 71
Palazzo del Vescovado
  217
Paleopolis 42
Palizzi, Filippo 40
Pallonetto 52
PAN *see* Palazzo delle
  Arti Napoli
Pandolf IV of Capua,
  Prince 18
Parco Archaeologico di
  Cuma 93
Parco Archeologico e
  Monumentale di Baia
  92, **93**
Parco dei Campi Flegrei
  88
Parco ex-cimitero degli
  Inglesi 96
Parco della Floridiana
  79, **82**, *82*, 159
Parco del Poggio di
  Capodimonte 94
Parco dei Principi 46, 257
Parco dei Quartieri
  Spagnoli 80
Parco Sommersa di Baia
  93
Parco Urbano dei
  Camaldoli 94

Parco Urbano Virgiliano
  86
Parco Vergiliano 85, **86**,
  159
Parco Viviani 80
parking 306
Parmigianino 78
Parthenope 48
Parthenopean Republic
  17, 26, 52
pasticcerie 131-139, 147
Pedro III, King of
  Aragon 21
performing arts 179-
  184
  cabaret & musicals 181
  dance 184
  festivals 183
  Neapolitan song 183
  opera 181
  Pulcinella 184
  tammuriata 179
  theatre 179
Perino & Vele 61
Petrarch 81
pharmacies 149, 309
photo developers 307
Philippe of Anjou 23
Piazza Amedeo 83
Piazza d'Armi 81
Piazza Bellini 42, 59
Piazza Bovio 67
Piazza Cardinale Sisto
  Riario Sforza 55, 58
Piazza Cavour 70
Piazza Dante 43, 60, **69**,
  69
  metro 60, 69
Piazza Garibaldi 64, 65
Piazza del Gesù 55
Piazza dei Martiri,
  Chiaia 83
Piazza dei Martiri
  (Procida) 229
Piazza Matteotti 45
Piazza del Mercato 67
Piazza del Municipio 49,
  53
Piazza del Plebiscito 45,
  48, 49, *49*
Piazza San Domenico 55
Piazza San Gaetano 42
Piazza Trieste e Trento
  48, 49
Piazza Vanvitelli 79
Piedigrotta 85
Pietà dei Turchini 49
Pinacoteca Girolamini 60
Pino, Marco 38
Pio Monte della
  Misericordia 58, **60**

Pisani, Gianni 61
Pisani, Vettor 61
Pistoletto Michelangelo
  60
Pitloo, Antonio 40
pizza 112
Pizzofalcone 17, 52
police 310
Polish Succession, War
  of 24
Pompei 239
Pompeii 17, 24, 25, 42,
  194, **230**, **239**,
  234-244, *242,* 295
  virtual tour 159
Ponte Aragonese 217
Ponti, Giò 107
Ponti Rossi 76
**Port & University,
  The** 6, 64-67
  accommodation 103
  cafés & bars 135
  DJ bars & clubs 174
  live music
  pasticcerie 135
  restaurants 120
Port'Alba arch 69
Porta Capuana 58
Porta del Carmine 67
Porta di Mezzomo 229
Porta Nolana 64, 65
Porta San Gennaro 70
Portici 24, 45, **27**, **234**
Posillipo 86, 87
Positano 267-271, *268*
postal services 310
Pozzo Vecchio 230
Pozzuoli 7, 17, 88, **89**,
  90, 295
Presti, Bonaventura 81
Preti, Mattia 38, 56
Procida 11, 159, 194,
  229-232
public holidays 312
public phones 311
Pulcinella **158**, 184
puppets 157, **158**
Punic War, Second 17
Punta San Pietro 216

Q

Quadreria dei Girolamini
  58, 60
Quartieri Spagnoli 6, 23,
  43, 68
Quarto 88
*Quattro giornate
  napoletane, le* 28, 29
Quattro Giornate station
  61

INDEX

Questura (police station) 68
queuing 307

R

radio 310
Raphael 78
Ravello 42, **286**, *287*
Reale Fabbrica delle Porcellane 76
Reggia di Caserta (Palazzo Reale) 163, 298, 299, **301**
Reggia di Portici 233, **234**
religion 310
René of Anjou 22
René of Provence, Good King 22
Reni, Guido 81
restaurants 111-130
  drinking 128
  local specialities 118
  Mario Avallone 123
  menu glossary 112
  mozzarella 120
  pizza 117
  pizzerie 115-119, 121-122, 124, 126-127, 129-130
  osterie 115, 117, 124, 126, 129
  trattorie 115-116, 118, 120-122, 126, 129-130
  wine 124
  wine bars 113, 117, 126, 130
  see also p322 restaurants & wine bars index
Ribera, Giuseppe 55
Ribera, José de 38, 39, 81, 82
Rione Alto station 61
Rione Terra 89, **90**
Riserva Naturale Cratere degli Astroni 89
Risorgimento 28
Riviera di Chiaia 45, 84
Robert of Anjou 21, 81
Robert Guiscard ('the Crafty') 19
Roger II, King of Sicily 19
Romans, the 16, 233
Rosa, Salvatore 40
Royal Naples & Monte Echia 6, 48-53
  cafés & bars 132
  hotels 99
  pasticcerie 132
  restaurants 114
  walk 53
Ruffo, Cardinal Fabrizio 26

S

safety 311
sailing *see* boating 187
Salerno 18, 19, 42, **292**
Salvator Rosa station 61
Sammartino, Giuseppe 52, 81
Samnites 17
San Carlo, Teatro 24, 43, 51, **180**, *181*, 182
San Domenico Maggiore *37*, 55, 56, *56*
San Ferdinando (church) 48
San Francesco di Paola 45, 48, **51**
San Gaudioso catacombs 71, 72
San Gennaro 42, 58, 62, **76**
San Giacomo degli Spagnoli (church) 49
San Giorgio Maggiore (church) 45, 55, **56**
San Giovanni Batista
San Giovanni a Carbonara (church) 58, **63**, 75
San Giovanni Maggiore (church) 67
San Giovanni a Mare (church) 67
San Giovanni Pappacoda (chapel) 64
San Girolamo 216
San Giuseppe a Chiaia 84
San Gregorio Armeno 58, **60**, 62
San Lorenzo Maggiore (archaeological site) 42, **61**
San Lorenzo Maggiore (church) 42, 57, 58, **61**
San Martino 42, 81
San Michele Arcangelo 302
San Paolo Maggiore (church) 42, 43, 44, 57, 58, **63**
San Pietro ad Aram **65**, 73
San Pietro a Maiella 38, 59, **63**
San Pietro (Ischia) 216
San Pietro Martire 44, 67
San Severo catacombs 71, 73
Sanfelice, Ferdinando 45, 52, 63, 71, 76
Sanfelice, Pietro 81
Sanità, La 6, 71
Sannazzaro, Iacopo 85
Sant'Agrippino 55
Sant'Angelo 227
Sant'Angelo a Morfisa (church) 56
Sant'Angelo a Nilo (church) 55, **56**
Sant'Anna dei Lombardi 43, 68, **69**
Sant'Antonio in Santa Maria delle Grazie 216
Sant'Eligio Maggiore (church) 67
Santa Caterina a Formiello (church) 58
Santa Chiara (tower) 54
Santa Chiara (church & convent) 42, *43*, 44, 45, 54, **56**
Santa Lucia a Mare (church) 52
Santa Margherita Nuova 230
Santa Maria degli Angeli (church) 52
Santa Maria Annunziata (*see* La Nunziatella)
Santa Maria, Portico (church) 84
Santa Maria del Carmine (church) **66**, *66*, 67, 154
Santa Maria della Catena (church) 52
Santa Maria Donnaregina (church) 63
Santa Maria Incoronata 49
Santa Maria Maggiore (church) 59
Santa Maria dei Miracoli 71
Santa Maria del Parto 85
Santa Maria a Piazza 55
Santa Maria della Pietà 229
Santa Maria di Portosalvo 216
Santa Maria del Purgatorio ad Arco (church) 43, 57, 59, 62, **63**, 73
Santa Maria della Sanità 71, 72, *72*, 73
Santa Patrizia 61
Santa Restituta 42, **59**
Santa Sofia 298
Santa Teresa a Chiaia 83
Santa Teresa degli Scalzi (church) 70
Santi Severino e Sossio 65
Santissima Annunziata 43, 44, **65**
Santissima Annunziata or Madonna della Libera, Procida 230
Santissimi Apostoli 63
Santo Spirito 217
Santuario di San Gennaro 90, **91**
Saracens, the 18
Scaturchio 57, 133
Scavi di Castellammare 244
Scavi di Pompeii 240
scooters (Ischia) 218
scuba diving 189
security 311
Serapeo 89, 91
Sergio IV, Duke 18
Sergio VII, Duke 19
Serra, Richard 75
Shelley, Percy & Mary 84
shoe shops 146
shops & services 140-152
  department stores 141
  Neapolitan designers 150
  markets 141, 146, 147
  souvenir shopping 143, 148
  see also specific products
Siza, Alvaro 75
skiing 190
smoking 311
snacks 113
Solfatara 91
Solimena, Francesco 40, 55, 56
Sorrento 42, 194, **249-263**
  walks 254-255
spas 151, 220
Spaccanapoli 42, **54**, 57
Spadaro, Micco 81
Spartacus 17, 29
Spiaggia del Lido (Ischia) 216
Spiaggia del Pescatori (Ischia) 216, *216*

Spirito Santo 68
sport & fitness
  185-190
  archery 185
  boating 187
  bowling 187
  Calcio Napoli 186
  cycling 187
  fishing 187
  football 186
  golf 187
  gyms 188
  horse racing 185
  horse riding 189
  jogging 189
  marathons 188
  scuba diving 189
  shops 152
  skiing 190
  spectator sports 185
  swimming 190
  tennis 190
  yoga 190
springs 88-93
St Severus 56
St Thomas Aquinas 56
Stabiae 194, **244**
Stadio San Paolo 96, 185
Stanislav I 23
Stanzione, Massimo 39
Stazione Marittima 45, 67
Stazione Zoologica (Acquario) 84
Steinbeck, John 264
study 311
suburbs 94-96
Sulla 17
swimming 190

T

T293 163, 166
tabacchi 311
tammuriata 179
Tancred 21
Tangentopoli 31
tangenziale 79
Tanucci, Bernardo 24
tarantella, the 182
tax 310
taxis 305
Teatro Romano 298
Teatro San Carlo 49, 51, 53, 180, **181**
telephones 311
  dialling & codes 311
  mobile phones 311
  operator services 311
  public phones 311
television 310

Tempio di Mercurio 92
Temple of Mercury 92
tennis 190
Tempio di Giove 93
Terra Murata 229
Terrae Motus 163
theatre 179
  tickets 152
Tiberius 196
ticket agents 152, 304
time 311
tipping 311
Titian 78
toilets 312
Toledo, Don Pedro de 22, 58
Tomba del Tuffatore 37
Toro Farnese 85
Torre Annunziata 239
Torre Gavetta 159
Torre del Greco 236
Torre Ranieri 86
tourist bus 306
tourist information 312
tours 306
trains 304, 305
trams 305
transport 304, 307
travel advice 307
travel agents 152
Tremlett, David 61
Trisorio, Pasquale 163

U

unemployment 32
Università di Napoli Federico II 64, 65
Università Orientale 64, 65
Urban VI, Pope 22

V

Vaccaro, Andrea 60
Vaccaro, Domenico Antonio 45
Valenzi, Maurizio Van Wittel, Gasper 40
Vandals, the 18
Vanvitelli, Carlo 65
Vanvitelli, Luigi 43, 44, 45, 69, 85
Vanvitelli station 61
vegetarians 112
Venusti, Marcello 78
Vergini, Le 70
Vesper Wars 21
Vesuvius 17, *19*, 34, 41, 245-247, *246*
Vettica Maggiore *274*

Via Appia *see* Appian Way 17
Via Chiatamone 84
Via Mergellina 85
Via Orazio 85
Via Pignasecca 69
Via Toledo 43, 68
Via Toledo & La Sanità 68-75
  accommodation 104
  cafés & bars 135
  gay bars & clubs 168
  gelaterie 135
  live music 175
  pasticcerie 135
  restaurants 122
Via dei Tribunali 58
Vico Equense 259
Vico Santa Maria a Cappella Vecchia 84
Vietri sul Mare 46, **284**
Villa Campolieto 236
Villa Communale *84,* 85
Villa Favorita 234, 238
Villa Favorita Park 236
Villa Floridiana 45, 82
Villa Malaparte 45, **198**
Villa Nenzi Bozzi 216
Villa Pausilypon 87
Villa Pignatelli 84, 85
Villa Rosebery 86
Villa Ruggiero
Virgil 17, 86, 92
visas 312
Vittorio Emanuele, Prince of Naples 28
Vittorio Emanuele II of Savoy 28
Vivara 230
Volaire, Pierre-Jacques 40
Vomero 46, **79-82**
  accommodation 105
  cafés & bars 136
  gelaterie 136
  pasticcerie 136
  restaurants 124
vocabulary 314

W

walking 306
walks, suggested
  Centro Storico 57
  Royal Naples 53
War of Polish Succesion 24
War of Spanish Succesion 23
Warhol, Andy 78
water & drinking 309

weather 312
websites 313
weights & measure 312
when to go 312
Whiteread, Rachel 75
wine 11, 276
wine bars 113
women 312
work permits 312
working 312
World War II 28
Wright, Joseph 40

Y

yachting 230, 231

ACCOMMODATION INDEX

Agriturismo Il Casolare di Tobia 110
Ausonia 109
Averno 110
Bella Capri Hotel & Hostel 101, *102*
Cappella Vecchia 11 110
Caravaggio Hotel di Napoli 101
Casa della Nonna, La 106
Chiaia B&B 109
Chiaja Hotel de Charme 99, *100, 101*
Convento, Il 104, *105*
Costantinopoli 104 101
Decumani Hotel de Charme 101, *103*
Donnalbina 7 103
Donna Regina B&B 102
Duomo 102
Europeo & Europeo Flowers 103
Excelsior *106*, 108
Grand Hotel Parker's 106, *107*
Grand Hotel Vesuvio 106
Hotel Cimarosa 106
Hotel des Artistes 102
Hotel del Real Orto Botanico 104
Hotel Executive 103
Hotel San Marco 100
Hotel San Francesco al Monte 105
Hotel 241 Correra 104
Hotel Una 103
Hotel Villa Ranieri 104
Mediterraneo 104

Mercure Napoli
  Angioino Centro 100
Miramare 99
MH Design Hotel 100
Neapolis 102
Palazzo Decumani 102
Palazzo Turchini 100
Paradiso 108
Parteno *108*
Pinto-Storey 109, *109*
Relais Posillipo 109
Romeo 99, *99*
Royal Continental 108
Santa Lucia 109
Suite Esedra 103
Toledo104
Villa Bruna B&B 105
Villa Giulia 110
Villa Medici 110
Vulcano Solfatara 110

**RESTAURANTS
INDEX**

Amici Miei 114
Amico Gamberone, L'
  126
Antica Osteria Pisano
  116
Antica Pizzeria del
  Borgo Orefeci 121
Antica Trattoria da
  Carmine 116
Arte della Pizza, L' 124
Barrique 126
Bersagliera, La 115
Berevino 117
Cantina di Donna'Elena

125
Cantina della Sapienza
  117
Cantina di Sica, La 125
Cantinella, La 115
Capo Blu 130
Casolare da Tobia, Il 130
Chiacchierata, La 115
Ciao Pizza 118
Ciro a Santa Brigida 122
Coco Loco 127
Don Salvatore 127
Donnanna 127
Dora 127
Ettore 115
Europeo Mattozzi 121
Faretto, Al 126
Féfé 130
Foccaccia, La 127
Fratelli La Bufala 115
Friggitoria-Pizzeria
  Giuliano 118
Gallo Nero, Il 126
Fratelli La Bufala 115
Garum, Il 122
Hosteria Toledo 122
Locanda del Grifo, La
  118
Mandara 122
Matteo, Di 118
Mattonella, La 115
Mattozzi 129
Mattozzi Giardino di
  Napoli 121
Michele Da 121
Mimi alla Ferrovia 121
Osteria da Tonino
Osteria Donna Teresa

126
Paguro, Il 129
Palazzo Petrucci 119
Pasqualino, Da 127
Piccolo Ristoro, Il 122
Pizzeria Marino 116
Pizzeria Pellone al Vasto
  122
Poeta, Al 126
Poseidone 129
Prua, La 130
Rosiello 130
Sorbillo 119
Sorriso Integrale, Un 121
Stanza del Gusto 119
Taverna dell'Arte 122
Taverna del
  Buongustaio 122
Terrazza, La 116
Timpani e Tempure 124
Trattoria Castel dell'Ovo
  116
Trattoria La
  Campagnola 120
Trattoria San
  Ferdinanado 116
Transatlantico 116
Trianon 122
Umberto 130
Vecchia Cantina, La 124
Vinarium 130

**CAFES, BARS &
GELATERIE INDEX**

Attanasio Sfogliate
  Calde 135
Bar Guida 136

Bellavia 136
Bilancione 138
Caffè Amadeus 136
Caffè del Professore 132
Caffè dell'Epoca 135
Caffettiera, La 137
Caffetteria Colonna 137
Chalet Ciro 137, *137*
Chalet Primavera p138
Chocolate 138
Dolcezze Siciliane 135
Fantasia Gelati 135
FNAC 136
Frigittoria Vomero 136
Gay-Odin 133
Gelateria della Scimmia
  135
Gran Caffè Aragonese
  132
Gran Caffè Cimmino 138
Gran Caffè Gambrinus
  132
Il... Caffè 135
Intramoenia Caffè
  Letterario 133
Mexico *133*, 135
Moccia 139
Otranto 136
Pastisseria Capriccio di
  Salvatore Capparelli
  135
Pintauro 132
Pinterré 138
Remy Gelo 138
Scaturchio 133
Soave Prodotti Freschi
  Del Latte 136
Torteria, La p139

Advertisers' Index

Please refer to the relevant pages for contact details

Introduction

La Fenice   **8**
Italian Breaks   **8**
Hotel Tramonto D'Oro   **10**
Chiaja Hotel De Charme   **10**
La Minerva   **14**
Palazzo Decumani   **14**

Around Naples

Amalfi Coast
Villa San Michele   **266**

Maps

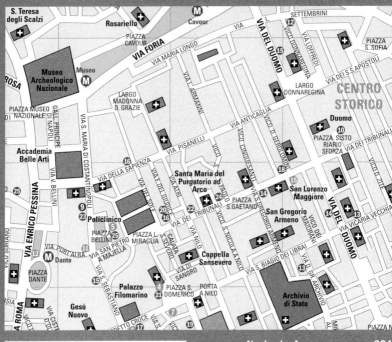

Place of interest	....	
Railway station	....	
Park	....	
Metro station	....	Ⓜ Ⓜ
Metro route	....	
Archaeological site	....	⦙
Area name	....	**VOMERO**
Main road	....	

Naples by Area	**324**
Street Maps	**326**
Street Index	**333**
Naples Metro	**336**

Naples by Area

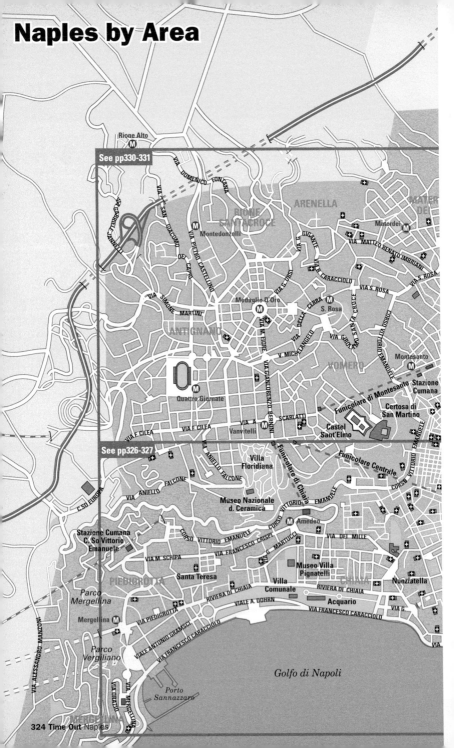

See pp330-331

See pp326-327

Rione Alto

VIA DOMENICO FONTANA

VIA GABRIELE IANNELLI

VIA SAN GIACOMO DEI CAPRI

VIA PIETRO CASTELLINO

ARENELLA

Materdei

VIA MATTEO RENATO IMBRIANI

RIONE SANT'ACROCE

Montedonzelli

VIA B. CARACCIOLO

VIA G. GIGANTE

VIA S. ROSA

VIA S. ROSA

VIA SIMONE MARTINI

Medaglie D'Oro

VIA M. FIORE

VIA DELLA CERRA

S. Rosa

CORSO VITTORIO EMANUELE

ANTIGNANO

VIA SANTA CROCE

VIA CROCE

Montesanto

V. MICHELANGELO

VOMERO

Stazione Cumana

VIA GIANLORENZO BERNINI

Funicolare di Montesanto

Quattro Giornate

SCARLATTI

Certosa di San Martino

Castel Sant'Elmo

VIA F. CILEA

VIA A. Vanvitelli

Funicolare Centrale

VIA F. CILEA

VIA A. ANIELLO FALCONE

Funicolare di Chiaia

Villa Floridiana

CORSO VITTORIO EMANUELE

VIA ANIELLO FALCONE

C. SO EUROPA

Museo Nazionale d. Ceramica

CORSO VITTORIO EMANUELE

VIA DEL MILLE

Stazione Cumana C. So Vittorio Emanuele

Amedeo

VIA M. SCHIPA

VIA FRANCESCO CRISPI

VIA MARTUCCI

Museo Villa Pignatelli

Nunziatella

Santa Teresa

Villa Comunale

RIVIERA DI CHIAIA

CHIAIA

VIA G.

Parco Mergellina

RIVIERA DI CHIAIA

Acquario

Mergellina

VIALE A. DOHRN

VIA FRANCESCO CARACCIOLO

VIA ALESSANDRO MANZONI

VIA PIEDIGROTTA

PIEDIGROTTA

VIALE ANTONIO GRAMSCI

VIA FRANCESCO CARACCIOLO

Parco Vergiliano

VIA ORAZIO

VIA MERGELLINA

Golfo di Napoli

MERGELLINA

Porto Sannazzaro

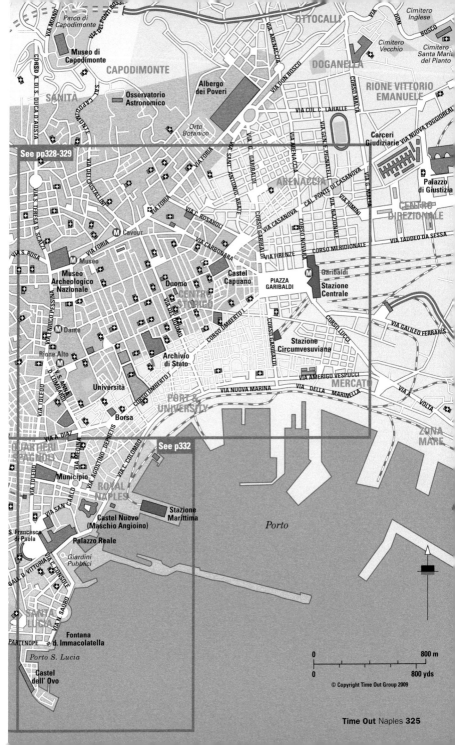

Parco di
Capodimonte

Museo di
Capodimonte

CAPODIMONTE

OTTOCALLI

Cimitero
Inglese

Cimitero
Vecchio

Cimitero
Santa Maria
del Pianto

DOGANELLA

RIONE VITTORIO
EMANUELE

Osservatorio
Astronomico

Albergo
dei Poveri

SANITÀ

Orto
Botanico

Carceri
Giudiziarie

Palazzo
di Giustizia

CENTRO
DIREZIONALE

See pp328-329

ARENACCIA

Cavour

Museo

Museo
Archeologico
Nazionale

Duomo

Castel
Capuano

PIAZZA
GARIBALDI

Garibaldi

Stazione
Centrale

CENTRO
STORICO

Dante

Rione Alto

Archivio
di Stato

Stazione
Circumvesuviana

Università

Borsa

PORT &
UNIVERSITY

VIA NUOVA MARINA

VIA AMERIGO VESPUCCI

VIA DELLA MARINELLA

MERCATO

ZONA
MARE

QUARTIERI
SPAGNOLI

See p332

Municipio

ROYAL
NAPLES

Stazione
Marittima

Porto

Castel Nuovo
(Maschio Angioino)

S. Francesco
di Paola

Palazzo Reale

Giardini
Pubblici

SANTA
LUCIA

PARTENOPE

Fontana
d. Immacolatella

Porto S. Lucia

Castel
dell' Ovo

0		800 m
0		800 yds

© Copyright Time Out Group 2009

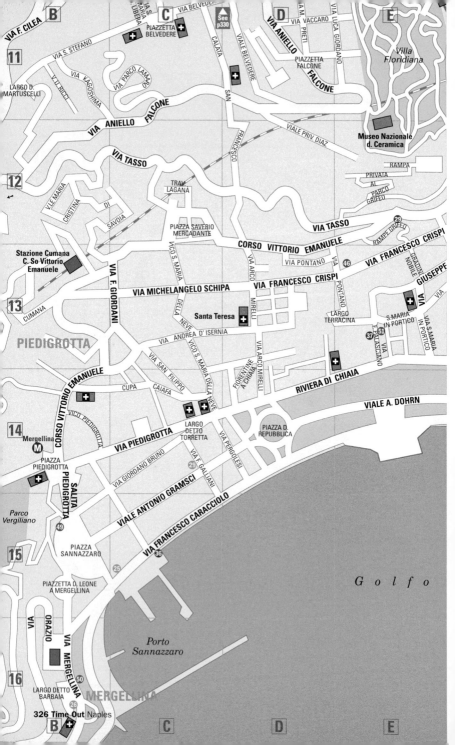

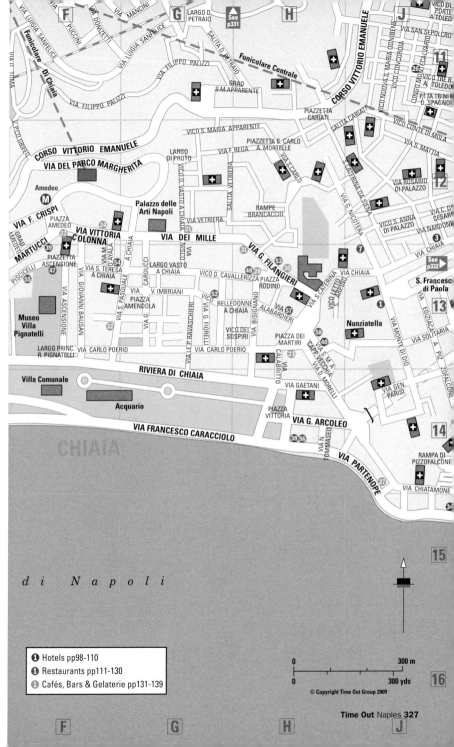

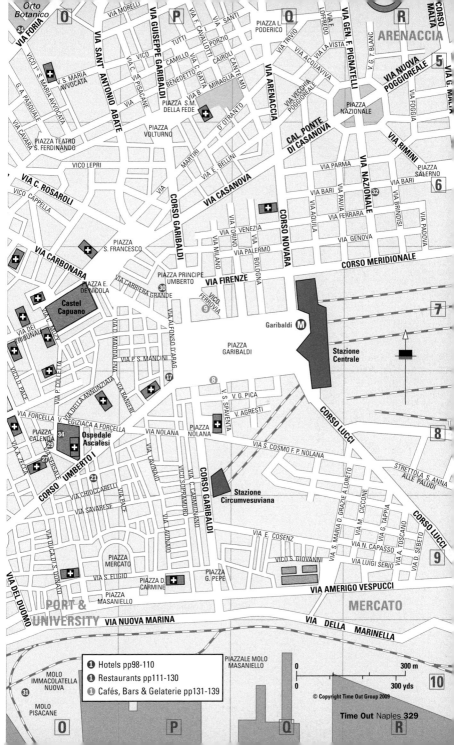

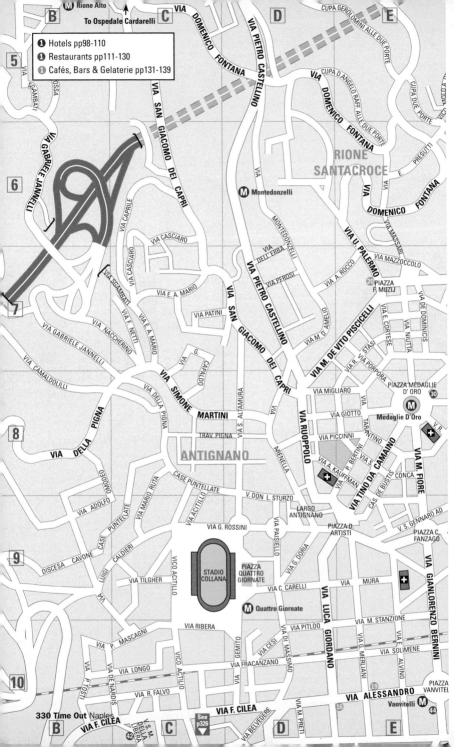

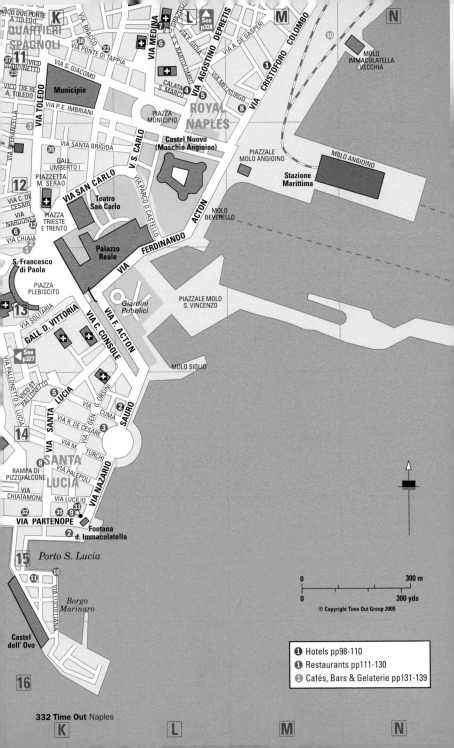

Street Index

A de Gasperi, Via - p332 L11/M11
A Dicostanzo, Via - p328 M10
Acitillo, Via - p330 C9
Acitillo, Vico - p330 C9/C10
Acquaviva, Via - p329 Q5
Acton, Via Gen F - p332 K13/L13
Adolfo Omodeo, Via - p330 B8/B9
Agostino Depretis, Via - p332 L11/M11
Agresti, Via - p329 Q8
Alabardieri, Via - p327 H13
Alessandro Scarlatti, Via - p330 E10, p331 F10
Alfano, Via G B - p328 L5
Alfonso D'Arag., Via - p329 P7
Altamura, Via Saverio - p330 D7/D8/D9
Alvino, Via Enrico - p330 E9/E10
Amedeo, Gradini - p327 F12/F13
Amedeo, Piazza - p327 F12
Amendola, Piazza - p327 G13
Amerigo Vespucci, Via - p329 Q9/R9
Amore, Piazza Nicola - p328 N9
Andrea d'Isernia, Via - p326 C13/D13
Aniello Falcone, Via - p326 B12/C11/C12/D11
Annibale Caccavello, Via - p331 F10/G10
Annunziata, Via della - p329 O8
Anticaglia, Via - p328 M7
Antignano, Largo - p330 D9
Antignano, Via - p331 F8/F9
Antinori, Via - p331 H6/J6
Antonio Gramsci, Viale - p326 B15/C14/C15
Aquila, Via - p329 Q6
Arco Mirelli, Via - p326 D13/D14
Arcoleo, Via G - p327 H14
Arena della Sanità, Via - p328 L6
Arena della Sanità, Vico - p328 K5
Arenaccia, Via - p329 Q5/Q6
Arenella, Salita - p331 F7/F8
Arenella, Via - p330 D8
Armando Diaz, Via - p328 K10/L10
Armanni, Via Luciano - p328 M7
Ascensione, Piazzetta - p327 F13
Ascensione, Via - p327 F13
Atri, Via - p328 L8/M8

Baldacchini, Via - p328 N9
Barbaia, Largo detto - p326 B16
Bari, Via - p329 Q6/R6
Battistello Caracciolo, Via - p331 F7/G7
Belledonne a Chiaia, Vico - p327 G13/H13

Bellini, Piazza - p328 L8
Bellini, Via E - p329 P6/Q6
Bellini, Via V - p328 K8
Belvedere, Piazzetta - p326 C11
Belvedere, Via - p326 C11, p330 D10
Belvedere, Viale - p326 D11
Benedetto Cairoli, Via - p329 P5
Benedetto Croce, Via - p328 L9
Bertini, Via Pacio - p330 E8
Bianchi, Via - p328 K9
Bisignano, Via – p327 H13
Blanc, Via G T - p329 R5
Bologna, Via - p329 Q6/Q7
Bombies, Via - p328 K8
Bonito, Via G - p331 F9/G9
Borghese, Via - p331 G8
Bovio, Piazza G - p328 M10
Bracco, Via - p332 K11
Brancaccio, Rampe - p327 H12
Brindisi, Via - p329 R6

C de Cesare, Via - p327 J12, p332 K12
Cacciottoli, Salita - p331 F9/G8
Cacciottoli, Vico - p331 F9
Caiazzo, Via - p331 F8
Calabritto, Via - p327 H13/H14
Calce, Vico della - p331 J6
Calenda, Piazza - p329 O8
Camaldolilli, Via - p330 B7/B8
Camillo Porzio, Via - p329 P5
Canneto, Piazza - p331 F7/G7
Cantelmo, Via - p329 P5/Q5
Capaldo, Via G - p330 C7/C8
Capasso, Via N - p329 R9
Capecelatro, Via - p331 H6
Capodimonte, Emiciclo - p328 K5
Cappella, Vico - p329 O6
Cappucinelle, Vico - p331 J8
Caprile, Via - p330 C6
Caracciolo Detto Carafa, Via - p331 H5/H6
Carbonara, Via - p329 O6/O7
Carducci, Via G - p327 G13
Carelli, Via C - p330 D9
Cariati, Piazzetta - p327 H11
Cariati, Salita - p327 H12/J11
Carità, Piazza della - p328 K10
Carlo Poerio, Via - p327 F13/G13/H13
Carmignano, Via C - p329 P8/P9
Carmine, Piazza del - p329 P9
Carriera Grande, Via - p329 P7
Casanova, Via - p329 P6/Q6
Casciaro, Via - p330 C6/C7
Case Puntellate - p330 C8
Cattaneo, Via C - p331 F6
Cavallerizza, Vico D - p327 G13/H13

Cavallotti, Via F - p329 P5
Cavara, Via - p328 N5, p329 O5/O6
Cavone, Discesa - p330 B9/C8/C9
Cavour, Piazza - p328 L6/K7
Celebran, Largo o - p331 F8
Celentano, Via B - p328 K6
Cerra, Via della - p331 F8/G7
Cesi, Via - p330 D10
Chiaia, Riviera di - p326 D14/E13/E14, p327 F13/G13/G14/H14
Chiaia, Via - p327 J12/J13, p332 K12
Chiatamone, Via - p327 J14, p332 K14
Chioccarelli, Via - p329 O8/O9
Ciccone, Via M - p329 R8/R9
Cilea, Via F - p330 B10/C10/D10
Cinquesanti, Vico - p328 M7/M8
Cisterna D'Olio, Via - p328 K9
Collenuccio, Via P - p331 H5/J5
Colletta, Via Pietro - p329 O7/O8
Conca, Via S - p330 E8
Concordia, Vico - p327 J11
Confalone, Via - p331 G6/G7
Console, Via Cesario - p332 K13/K14
Conte di Mola, Vico - p327 J11/J12
Cortese, Via E - p330 E7
Cortese, Via G C - p328 M10
Cosenz, Via E - p329 Q9
Covino, Viale - p331 G10
Crispi, Via F - p327 F12
Cristallini, Via dei - p328 L5/L6
Cristoforo Colombo, Via - p328 M10/N10, p332 M11/M12
Croce Rossa, Via - p330 B5
Crocelle, Via - p328 M6
Cuma, Via - p332 K14
Cumana, Via - p326 B13
Cupa Caiafa - P326 C14
Cupa Vecchia, Via - p331 G9/H9

D'Angelo Raff. alle due Porte, Cupa - p330 D5/E5/E6
D'Aquisto, Via S - p331 G6
D'Artisti, Piazza - p330 D9/D9
D'Auria, Via - p331 G9
D'Amelio, Via M - p330 D7
Dante, Piazza - p328 K8
De Bustis, Casale Via - p330 E8/E9
De Curtis, Via A - p328 N5
De Leva, Piazza E - p331 G6
Dell'Erba, Via - p330 D7
Di Gravina, Via G - p331 H6/J5
Diaz, Viale Privato - p326 D12

Discesa della Sanità, Via - p328 K5/K6
Dohrn, Viale Anton - p326 E14
Domenico Fontana, Via - p330 C5/D5/E5/E6
Domenico Martuscelli, Largo - p326 B11
Dominicis, Via de - p330 E7
Don Luigi Sturzo, Via - p330 D8/D9
Donizetti, Via - p327 F11
Donnalbina, Via - p328 L10
Donnaregina, Largo - p328 N7
Donnaregina, Vico - p328 N6/N7
Duca di San Donato, Via - p329 O9
Duca F della Marra, Via - p331 H6
Duomo, Via del - p328 M6/M7/N7/N8, p329 O9/O10

E de Nicola, Piazza - p329 O7
Egiziaca a Forcella, Via - p329 O8
Egiziaca A Piz Zofalcone, Via - p327 J13/J14
Enrico Pessina, Via - p328 K7/K8

Falco, Via de - p331 H5/H6
Falcone, Piazzetta - p326 D11
Falvo, Via R - p330 B10/C10
Fanzago, Piazza C - p330 E9
Ferdinando Acton, Via - p332 K13/L12/L13
Ferdinando Galliani, Via - p326 C14
Ferdinando Palasciano, Via - p326 E13
Ferrara, Via - p329 Q6/R6
Ferrovia, Vico - p329 P7
Filangieri, Via G - p327 H13
Filippo Palizzi, Via - p327 F11/G11
Fiore, Via M - p330 E8/E9
Fiorelli, Via G - p327 G13
Fiorentine A Chiaia, Vico delle - p326 D14
Firenze, Via - p329 P7/Q7
Foggia, Via - p329 R5/R6
Fonseca, Vico - p328 K6
Fontanelle, Calata - p331 J6
Fontanelle, Piazza - p331 H5
Fontanelle, Via D - p331 G5/H5/J5
Forcella, Via - p329 O8
Foria, Via - p328 L7/M6/N5/N6, p329 O5
Formale, Strada del - p328 K10
Forno Vecchio, Via - p328 K9
Fracanzano, Via - p330 C10/D10
Franc. Girardi, Via - p331 J10
Francesco Caracciolo, Via - p326 C15/D14/E14, p327 F14/G14/H14

Francesco Cilea, Via -
p326 B11
Francesco Crispi, Via -
p326 D13/E12/E13
Francesco Giordani, Via -
p326 C13
Francesco Saverio Correra,
Via - p328 K8, p331 J7/J8
Fuga, Piazza F - p331 F10

G Doria, Via G - p330 D9
Gabriele Jannelli, Via -
p330 B6/B7
Gaetani, Via - p327 H14
Gaetano, Piazza S - p328 M8
Galuppi, Corso -
p329 P6/P7/P8/P9
Garibaldi, Piazza -
p329 P7/Q7
Gasparis, Via de -
p328 M5/M6/N5
Gatta, Via C - p329 P5
Gemito, Via - p330 D10
Gen. F Pignatelli, Via -
p329 R5
Gen. G Orsini, Via -
p332 K14
Gen. Parisi, Via - p327 J14
Genova, Via - p329 Q6/R6
Gerolomini alle due Porte,
Cupa - p330 D5/E5
Gerolomini, Vico dei -
p328 M7
Gesù Nuovo, Piazza -
p328 L9
Gesuiti, Viale dei- p331 H6
Giacinto Gigante, Via -
p331 F6/F7
Gianlorenzo Bernini, Via -
p330 E9/E10
Giardinetto, Vico - p332 K11
Gioia, Via F - p332 L11
Giordano Bruno, Via -
p326 B15/C14
Giordano, Via Luca -
p326 D11/E11
Giotto, Via - p330 D8/E8
Giovanni Bausan, Via -
p327 F13
Girolamo Santa Croce, Via -
p331 G8/G9
Giudice, Via F del - p328 L8
Giuseppe Martucci, Via -
p326 E13, p327 F12/F13
Giuseppe Orsi, Via - p331 F7
Grande Archivio, Via D -
p328 N8/N9
Grifeo Gradini Nobile,
Rampe - p326 E12/E13
Guiseppe Garibaldi, Via -
p329 P5

**Imbriani, Via P E -
p332 K11**
Imbriani, Via V - p327 G13
Immacolata, Piazza della -
p331 F8

Kagoshima, Via - p326 B11
Kauffman, Via A -
p330 D8/E8/E9
Kerbaker, Via M -
p331 F9/F10

La Vista, Via - p329 Q5
Laganà, Traversa -
p326 C12
Lammatari, Vico del -
p328 K5
Lavinaio, Via - p329 P8/P9
Leonardo, Piazza - p331 G8
Leone a Mergellina,
Piazzetta de - p326 B15

Lepri, Vico - p329 O6
Liborio, Via - p328 K9/K10
Libroia, Via R - p330 E8,
p331 F8
Ligorio, Via - p331 G10
Loffredi, Via - p328 N6/N7
Loffredo, Via F - p329 Q5
Longo, Via - p330 B10/C10
Luca Giordano, Via -
p330 D9/D10
Lucci, Corso -
p329 Q8/R8/R9
Lucilio, Via - p332 K15
Luculliana, Via -
p332 K15/K16
Luigi Caldieri, Via -
p330 B9/C9
Luigi Serio, Via - p329 R9
Luigia Sanfelice, Via -
p327 F11/G11
Lungo S Raffaele, Vico -
p331 J6/J7

**M d'Ayala, Via -
p327 F12/F13**
M de Vito Piscicelli, Via -
p330 D7/D8/E7
M Preti, Via - p326 D11
Maddalena, Via D - p329 O7
Madonna delle Grazie, Largo
- p328 L7
Maiorani, Vico dei -
p328 M8
Malta, Corso - p329 R5
Malta, Via G - p329 R5
Mancinelli, Via G - p328 K7
Mancini, Via -
p327 F11/G11
Mancini, Via P S - p329 P7
Maria Cristina di Savoia,
Viale - p326 B12
Maria Longo, Via -
p328 L7/M7
Marinella, Via della -
p329 Q9/Q10/R10
Marino e Cotronei, Via -
p331 F5/F6
Mario Ruta, Via -
p330 C8/C9
Mario, Via E A - p330 C7
Martiri D'Otranto, Via -
p329 P5/P6/Q5
Martiri, Piazza dei -
p327 H13
Masaniello, Piazza -
p329 O9/P9
Mascagni, Via P -
p330 B10/C10
Massari, Via - p330 E6/E7
Massimo, Via di - p330 D10
Materdei, Via - p331 J6
Matteo Renato Imbriani, Via
- p331 G6/H6/H7/J7
Mazzella, Via - p331 H5
Mazzini, Piazza - p331 H7
Mazzoccolo, Via - p330 E7
Medaglie D'Oro, Piazza -
p330 E8
Medina, Via - p332 L11
Mercato, Piazza -
p329 O9/P9
Mergellina, Via - p326 B16
Meridionale, Corso -
p329 Q7/R7
Merliani, Via G - p330 E10
Mezzocannone, Via -
p328 M9
Michelangelo, Viale -
p331 F8/F9
Michetti, Via - p331 F10
Migliaro, Via - p330 D8/E8
Milano, Via - p329 P7
Mille, Via dei - p327 G12
Minutoli, Vico - p328 N5

Miracoli, Piazza dei -
p328 M5
Miracoli, Via dei - p328 M6
Miracoli, Vico dei - p328 M5
Miraglia, Piazza L - p328 L8
Miraglia, Via B -
p329 P5/Q5
Miroballo al Pendino, Via -
p328 N9
Moiarello, Salita -
p328 M5/N5
Molo A due Porte, Vico -
p330 E5, p331 F5
Molo Angioino, Piazzale -
p332 M12
Molo Beverello - p332 L12
Molo Immacolatella Vecchia
- p332 M11/N11
Molo Masaniello, Piazzale -
p329 P10/Q10
Molo S Vincenzo, Piazzale -
p332 L13/M13
Molo Siglio - p332 L13
Monte di Dio, Via -
p327 J13/J14
Montecalvario, Vico Lungo -
p327 J11
Montedonzelli, Via -
p330 D5/D6/D7
Monteoliveto, Piazza -
p328 K9
Monteoliveto, Via -
p328 K10/L10
Montesanto, Scala -
p331 H9/J9
Montesanto, Via -
p328 K9, p331 J9
Monti, Salita via -
p331 H8/H9
Monti, Vico dei -
p331 G8/H8
Monticelli, Piazzetta -
p328 L10
Morelli, Via - p329 O5/P5
Morelli, Via D -
p327 H14/J14
Morgantini, Via - p328 K10
Municipio, Piazza -
p332 L11
Mura, Via - p330 E9
Museo Nazionale, Piazza -
p328 K7
Muzij, Piazza F - p330 E7
Muzy, Via C - p329 O7

**Naccherino, Via -
p330 B7/C7**
Nardis, Via de -
p330 B10/C10
Nardones, Via - p327 J12,
p332 K12
Nazario Sauro, Via -
p332 K14/K15/L14
Nazionale, Piazza -
p329 Q5/R5
Nazionale, Via - p329 R6
Netti, Via F - p330 C7
Neve, Vico della - p331 J6
Nicotera, Via G -
p327 H12/J12/J13
Nilo, Porta a - p328 M9
Nilo, Via - p328 M8
Ninni, Via - p328 K9,
p331 J9
Nisco, Via - p327 G13
Niutta, Via - p330 E7
Nocelle, Vico delle -
p331 H7
Nolana, Piazza - p329 P8
Nolana, Via - p329 P8
Nudi, Via dei - p331 J7,
p328 K7
Nunziat. Ai Miracoli -
p328 L5/M5

Nuova Marina, Via -
p329 O10/P9/P10
Nuova Poggioreale, Via -
p329 R5
Nuova S Maria Ognibene,
Vico - p327 J11

Oberdan, Via - p328 K10
Olivella, Piazzetta - p331 J9
Orazio, Via - p326 B15/B16

Pace, Via - p329 O8/P9
Pace, Vico della -
p329 O7/O8
Pacella, Vico - p328 M5
Padova, Via - p329 R6
Pagano, Piazza M - p328 L6
Pagano, Via M -
p328 L6/M6
Paisiello, Via - p330 D9
Paladino, Via G - p328 M9
Palepoli, Via - p332 K14
Palermo, Via - p329 Q6/Q7
Palermo, Via U - p330 E7
Pallonetto S Lucia, Via -
p332 K14
Pallonetto, Vico Storto -
p332 K14
Palmieri, Via L -
p328 M10/N10
Paradiso A Salute, Via -
p331 G6/H6
Parco D Castello, Via -
p332 L12
Parco Grifeo, Rampa Privata
- p326 E12
Parco Grifeo, Via - p327 F12
Parco Lamaro, Via -
p326 C11
Parco Margherita, Via del -
p327 F12/G12
Parma, Via - p329 Q6/R6
Partenope, Via -
p327 H14/J14/J15,
p332 K15
Pasquale G A - p329 O5/O6
Patini, Via - p330 C7
Pavia, Via - p329 Q6
Pedamentina S Martino, Via
- p331 H10
Pellegrino, Via - p331 H6
Pelliccia, Via - p331 H5/H6
Pepe, Piazza G - p329 P9
Pergolesi, Via -
p326 C14/D14
Perosi, Via - p330 D7
Petraio, Largo del -
p327 G11
Petraio, Salita del -
p327 G11/H11
Piazzi, Via G - p328 N5
Pica, Via G - p329 P8/Q8
Piccinni, Via - p330 D8/E8
Piedigrotta, Piazza -
p326 B14
Piedigrotta, Salita -
p326 B14/B15
Piedigrotta, Via - p326 C14
Piedigrotta, Vico - p326 B14
Pietro Castellino, Via -
p330 D5/D6/D7
Pigna, Traversa -
p330 C8/D8
Pigna, Via della -
p330 B8/C8
Pignasecca, Via -
p328 K9/10
Pino, Via del - p328 N5
Pisacane, Via Carlo -
p329 P5
Pisanelli, Via - p328 M7
Piscicelli, Via - p326 E13,
p327 F13
Pitloo, Via - p330 D10

STREET INDEX

Pizzofalcone, Rampa di -
p327 J14, p332 K14
Plebiscito, Piazza -
p332 K13
Poderico, Piazza L - p329 Q5
Pontano, Via - P326 D13
Ponte di Casanova, Calata -
p329 Q6
Ponte di Tappia, Via -
p332 K11/L11
Pontecorvo, Salita -
p328 K8, p331 J7/J8
Pontenuovo, Via -
p328 N5/N6
Porpora, Via - p330 E7/E8
Port'Alba, Via - p328 K8/L8
Porta Massa, Via di -
p328 M10
Porte a Toledo, Vico due -
p332 K11, p327 J11
Porte, Cupa due - p330 E5
Porte, Salita due -
p331 F6/G6
Pratella, Via - p331 F6/G6
Presutti, Via E - p330 E6
Preti, Via M - p330 D10
Principe di Napoli, Gall. -
p328 K7
Principe Umberto, Piazza -
p329 P7
Principessa R Pignatelli,
Largo - p327 F13
Proto, Largo di - p327 G12
Puccini, Via - p327 F11

**Quattro Giornate, Piazza -
p330 D9**
Quercia, Vico della -
p328 K9

**R de Cesare, Via -
p332 K14**
Raffaele Morghen, Via -
p331 F10
Raffaello, Viale -
p331 G8/G9/10/H10
Ranieri, Via - p329 P8
Ravaschieri, Viale P -
p327 G13
Rega, Via F - p327 G12/H12
Repubblica, Piazza della -
p326 D14
Ribera, Via - p330 C10
Rimini, Via - p329 R6
Rocco, Via A - p330 D7/E7
Rodino, Piazza - p327 H13
Roma, Via - p328 K9
Romaniello, Via - p331 G8
Rosario di Palazzo, Via -
p327 J12
Rosaroli, Via Cesare -
p328 N6, p329 O6
Rossini, Via G - p330 C9/D9
Ruoppolo, Via - p330 D8

**S S Apostoli, Via dei -
p328 N7**
S Spaventa, Via - p329 P8
Salerno, Piazza - p329 R6
Salvatore Rosa, Via - p328
K7, p331 G7/H7/J7
Salvatore, Via - p328 K7
San Bartolomeo, Via -
p332 L11
San Biagio dei Librai, Via -
p328 M8/N8
San Carlo A Mortelle,
Piazzetta - p327 H12
San Carlo all'Arena, Porta -
p328 M6/N6
San Carlo, Via - p327 H12,
p332 K12/L12
San Cosmo F P Nolana, Via -
p329 Q8

San Domenico, Piazza -
p328 L9/M9
San Felice, Vico - p328 L5
San Filippo, Via -
p326 C13/14
San Francesco, Calata -
p326 C11/D11/D12
San Francesco, Piazza -
p329 O6/O7/P6/P7
San Gennaro ad Antignano,
Via - p330 E9
San Geronimo, Vico -
p328 M9
San Giacomo dei Capri, Via -
p330 C5/C6/D7/D8
San Giacomo, Via -
p332 K11/L11
San Giovanni Maggiore,
Largo - p328 L9
San Giovanni Maggiore, Via -
p328 M9
San Giovanni, Vico -
p329 Q9
San Gregorio Armeno, Via -
p328 M8
San Mandato, Stada -
p331 H7
San Marco, Calata -
p332 L11
San Maria della Fede, Piazza
- p329 P5
San Maria della Purità, Vico -
p328 K6
San Maria la Nova, Via -
p328 L10
San Martino, Largo -
p331 H10
San Mattia, Via - p327 J12
San Nazzaro, Piazza -
p326 B15
San Nicola a Nilo, Vico -
p328 M8
San Paolo, Vico -
p328 M7/M8
San Pasquale a Chiaia, Via -
p327 F13/G12/G13
San Pietro a Majella, Via -
p328 L8
San Raffaele, Salita -
p331 J6/J7
San Sebastiano, Via -
p328 L8/L9
San Sepolcro, Via -
p327 J11
San Severo a Capodimonte,
Via - p328 K5/L5
San Severo, Calata -
p328 L8/M8
San Teresa degli Scalzi, Via -
p328 K6/K7
Sanfelice, Via G - p328 L10
Sangro, Via di - p328 M8
Sanità, Piazza - p328 K5
Sanità, Via della -
p328 K5/L5, p331 J5
Sant'Anna alle Paludi,
Strettola - p329 R8
Sant'Anna dei Lombardi, Via
- p328 K9
Sant'Anna di Palazzo, Vico -
p327 J12
Sant'Antonio Abate, Via -
p329 O5/O6/P6
Sant'Eligio, Via -
p329 O9/P9
Santa Brigida, Via -
p332 K12/L12
Santa Caterina da Siena, Via
- p327 H12/J12
Santa Caterina, Via -
p327 H13
Santa Chiara, Via - p328 L9
Santa Lucia, Via -
p332 K13/14

Santa Margherita a Fonseca,
Vico - p328 K5/K6
Santa Maria a Capp.
Vecchia, Via - p327 H13
Santa Maria Antesaecula,
Via - p328 L5
Santa Maria Apparente,
Gradini - p327 G11/H11
Santa Maria Apparente, Vico
- p327 G12/H12
Santa Maria Avvocata, Via -
p329 O5
Santa Maria Avvocata, Vico
1° - p329 O5
Santa Maria D Purità, Vico -
p331 J6
Santa Maria del Grazie a
Loreto, Via - p329 Q9/R8
Santa Maria della Libera, Via
- p326 C11
Santa Maria della Neve, Vico
- p326 C13/C14
Santa Maria di
Costantinopoli, Via -
p328 L7/L8
Santa Maria in Portico, Via -
p326 E13
Santa Sofia, Piazza -
p328 N7
Santa Teresa a Chiaia, Via -
p327 F13
Santo Stefano, Via -
p326 B11/C11
Sapienza, Via della -
p328 L7/L8
Savarese, Via - p329 O9/P9
Savarese, Via R - p331 J6
Saverio Mercadante, Piazza -
p326 C12
Schipa, Via Michelangelo -
p326 C13
Scipione Ammirato, Piazza -
p331 H6/J6
Scura, Via P - p328 K9,
p331 J9/J10
Sebeto, Via del - p329 R9
Sedile di Porto, Via -
p328 L10/M10
Serao, Piazzetta M -
p332 K12
Sersale, Via - p329 O8
Settembrini, Via Luigi -
p328 M6/N6
Sgambati, Via -
p330 B5/B7/C7
Simone Martini, Via -
p330 C7/C8/C8
Simonelli, Via G - p328 K10
Sisto Riario Sforza, Piazza -
p328 N7
Sole, Via del - p328 L8
Solimene, Via - p330 E10
Solitaria, Via - p327 J13,
p332 K13
Sopramuro, Vico -
p329 P8/P9
Soriano, Vico - p328 K8
Sospiri, Vico dei - p327 H13
Speranzella, Via - p328 K10,
p332 K11/K12
Stadio Collana -
p330 C9/D9
Stanzione, Via M -
p330 E9/10
Stasi, Via R - p330 E7/E8
Stella, Via della - p328 K6/L6
Suarez, Via - p331 F8
Supportico Lopez - p328 M6

Tappia, Via G - p329 R9
Tarantino, Via - p330 E9
Tarsia, Piazza -
p328 K8, p331 J8
Tarsia, Salita - p331 J8/J9

Tarsia, Via - p328 K9
Tasso, Via -p326 B12/C12/
D12/E12
Teatro S Ferdinando, Piazza -
p329 O6
Telesino, Via A - p331 J5/J6
Tenore, Via - p328 N5
Terracina, Largo -
p326 D13/E13
Tessitore, Vico - p328 M5
Tilgher, Via - p330 C9
Tino da Camaino, Via -
p330 E8/E9
Tito Angelini, Via - p331
G9/G10/H10
Toledo, Via - p328 K9/10,
p332 K11/K12
Toma, Via G - p327 F11
Tommaseo, Via N -
p327 H14
Torino, Via - p329 P6/Q7
Torretta, Largo detto -
p326 C14
Torrione San Martino, Via -
p331 F9
Toscano , Via A.- p329 R9
Tosti, Via P - p330 B10
Toti, Via Enrico - p328 K10
Tre Re a Toledo, Vico -
p327 J11, p332 K11
Tribunali, Via dei - p328
M8/N7/M8, p329 O7
Trieste E Trento, Piazza -
p332 K12
Trinità degli Spagnoli,
Piazzetta - p327 J11
Trinità Maggiore, Calata -
p328 L9
Trivio, Via - p329 Q5
Trone, Vico delle -
p331 G6/H6
Turchi, Via M - p332 K14
Tutti I Santi, Vico - p329 P5

Ugo Ricci, Via - p326 B11
Umberto I, Corso -
p328 M10/N9,
p329 O8/O9/P8
Umberto I, Galleria -
p332 K12

Vaccaro, Via - p326 D11
Vanvitelli, Piazza - p330 E10
Vasto a Chiaia, Largo -
p327 G13
Vasto a Chiaia, Vico D -
p327 G12
Vecchia Poggioreale, Via -
p329 Q5
Venezia, Via - p329 P6/Q6
Ventaglieri, Via - p331 J8/J9
Vergini, Via - p328 M6
Vetriera, Salita - p327 G12
Vetriera, Via - p327 G12
Vicaria Vecchia, Via -
p328 N8
Vicoletto S Arpino, Vico -
p327 H13
Villari, Via A - p328 L6
Vittoria Colonna, Via -
p327 F12
Vittoria, Galleria della -
p332 K13
Vittoria, Piazza - p327 H14
Vittorio Emanuele, Corso -
p326 B13/B14/C12/
D12/D13/E12, p327
F12/G11/G12/H11/J11,
p331 H8/H9
Volturno, Piazza - p329 P6

Zecca, Via A - p329 O8
Zite, Vico delle -
p328 N7/N8

STREET INDEX

Naples Metro

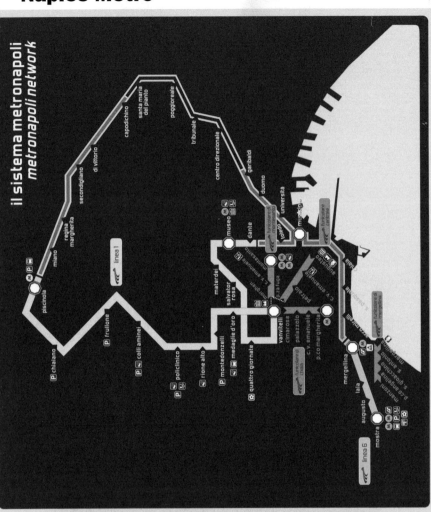